D1591456

CLOVIS: ORIGINS AND ADAPTATIONS

CLOVIS: ORIGINS AND ADAPTATIONS

EDITED BY:
Robson Bonnichsen
Karen L. Turnmire

PEOPLING OF THE AMERICAS PUBLICATIONS
Edited Volume Series

CENTER FOR THE STUDY OF THE FIRST AMERICANS
Oregon State University
Corvallis, Oregon

CLOVIS: ORIGINS AND ADAPTATIONS

C & C Wordsmiths of Blue Hill, Maine, typeset all copy and prepared camera-ready masters for most of the graphics in this book.
Printed in the United States of America by Thompson-Shore, Inc., Dexter, MI.
This book is printed on 100% acid-free paper.

ISBN: 0-912933-08-9

THE CENTER FOR THE STUDY OF THE FIRST AMERICANS

The Center for the Study of the First Americans is an affiliate of the Department of Anthropology at Oregon State University. It was established in July 1981 by a seed grant from Mr. William Bingham's Trust for Charity. The Center's goals are to encourage research about Pleistocene peoples of the Americas, and to make this new knowledge available to both the scientific community and the interested public. Toward this end, the Center staff is developing research, public outreach, and publications programs.

The Center's Peopling of the Americas publication program focuses on the earliest Americans and their environments. This program includes: (1) a monograph series presenting primary data on sites in North and South America which are more than 10,000 years old; (2) a process series presenting new methods and theories for interpreting early remains; (3) an edited volume series presenting topical papers and symposia proceedings; (4) a popular book series making the most significant discoveries and research available to the general public; and (5) a bibliographic series.

In addition, the Center publishes a quarterly newspaper called the *Mammoth Trumpet.* The newspaper is written for both a general and a professional audience. The Center also publishes an annual journal, *Current Research in the Pleistocene.* The journal presents note-length articles about current research in the interdisciplinary field of Quaternary studies as they relate to the field of the Pleistocene peopling of the Americas.

MANUSCRIPT SUBMISSIONS

BOOKS

The Center solicits high-quality original manuscripts in English. For information write to: Robson Bonnichsen, Center for the Study of the First Americans, Department of Anthropology, Oregon State University, Corvallis, OR 97331.

CURRENT RESEARCH IN THE PLEISTOCENE

Researchers wishing to submit summaries in this annual serial should contact editor Jim I. Mead, Department of Geology, Northern Arizona University, Box 666, Flagstaff, AZ 80811 or request Information for Contributors from the Center. The deadline for submissions is January 31 of each calendar year; early submission is suggested.

MAMMOTH TRUMPET

News of discoveries, reports on recent conferences, book reviews and news of current issues are invited.

ADDITIONALLY . . .

Authors are encouraged to submit reprints of published articles or copies of unpublished papers for inclusion in the Center's research library. Exchanges of relevant books and periodicals with other publishers is also encouraged. Please address contributions and correspondence to the Center's library.

PEOPLING OF THE AMERICAS PUBLICATIONS

OTHER TITLES

UNDERSTANDING STONE TOOLS: A COGNITIVE APPROACH
David E. Young and Robson Bonnichsen
ISBN: 0-912933-00-3

ARCHAEOLOGICAL SEDIMENTS IN CONTEXT
Julie K. Stein and William R. Farrand, Editors
ISBN: 0-912933-01-1

ENVIRONMENTS AND EXTINCTIONS:
MAN IN LATE GLACIAL NORTH AMERICA
Jim I. Mead and David J. Meltzer, Editors
ISBN: 0-912933-02-x

NEW EVIDENCE FOR THE PLEISTOCENE PEOPLING OF THE AMERICAS
Contributions in English, Spanish, and Portuguese with extensive English abstracts
Alan L. Bryan, Editor
ISBN: 0-912933-03-8

TAPHONOMY: A Bibliographic Guide to the Literature
Christopher Koch, Compiler
ISBN: 0-912933-05-4

BONE MODIFICATION
Robson Bonnichsen and Marcella H. Sorg, Editors
ISBN: 0-912933-06-2

Contents

Clovis Origins and Adaptations: An Introductory Perspective

DENNIS STANFORD
Smithsonian Institution
Washington, D.C. 20560

INTRODUCTION

Few subjects invoke such heated arguments in New World prehistory as do the origins of Native American populations. Clovis is central to this debate, as many scholars favor the conservative view that Clovis peoples were the original migrants. Other scholars, however, argue that humans entered the New World long before Clovis and, since there are no direct links between Clovis and the northeast Asian Paleolithic, that Clovis is an indigenous development, although some researchers consider the pre-Clovis evidence to be ambiguous. Thus, determining the origins of the Clovis complex is an essential step for resolving questions of the early colonization of the Western Hemisphere. In this volume, the competing hypotheses of New World origins are examined in detail from a number of different perspectives.

This volume consists of papers presented in the *Clovis Origins and Adaptations* symposium at the 1987 INQUA meetings held in Toronto, Canada. Additional contributions by scholars working on Clovis-related topics throughout the Western Hemisphere have been included to balance the presentation. The papers are organized in a north-south sequence, following the traditional ordering of the migration out of Northeast Asia into the American Arctic and southward to the tip of South America.

THE CLOVIS PATTERN

The origin of the North American aborigines has been a controversial topic since the last century (Meltzer 1989). Many early scholars developed a hard-line attitude towards the acceptance of evidence of great antiquity, which continues until the present day. The discovery of extinct bison associated with weapon tips near Folsom, New Mexico, in 1926 produced a new appreciation for the potential time depth of New World populations and led to the establishment of minimal criteria of acceptable evidence (Figgens 1927).

Six years following the Folsom discoveries, distinctive bifacially flaked and fluted weapon tips now known as Clovis points were unearthed with mammoth remains near Dent, Colorado (Figgens 1933). However, the term Clovis comes from a town of that name located near Blackwater Draw, New Mexico, where Clovis points were found stratigraphically below the Folsom horizon (Sellards 1952).

In the years since the initial Clovis discoveries, additional stratified sites have been found, but they are few in number, rendering our understanding of Clovis relatively incomplete. Fluted projectile points occur from the west coast to the east coast of North America and from Alaska to Latin America.

Among the fluted projectile points found throughout

the Americas, there is a wide range of variation. Much of the variation can be explained by idiosyncratic behavior, differences in materials, and artifact rejuvenation, as well as chronological differences. Many fluted points fall significantly outside the expected shape range of Clovis points. These include types such as Batza Tena in the Arctic (Clark, this volume); Peace River fluted from Alberta (Carlson, this volume); Folsom in the Rocky Mountain area and adjacent Great Plains (Bonnichsen et al. 1987); Parkhill, Crowfield, and Debert in the Northeast (Storck, this volume); Cumberland, Dalton, Quad, and Redstone in the Southeast (Dunbar, this volume); and the Latin American fluted fishtail points (Politis, this volume). Compared with the distribution of Clovis, these types are restricted geographically. Folsom is the only fluted-point variant from an unambiguous, dated, stratified context. Because this variant is younger than dated Clovis sites, other variants may also be younger and represent regional developments out of a basal Clovis pattern.

Haynes (1991) has re-evaluated Clovis radiocarbon dates and suggests that the Clovis pattern existed between 11,200 and 10,900 years ago. This shortens the Clovis time span and indicates that it may have been contemporary with other New World cultural patterns dating to the eleventh millennium B.P. (e.g., Nenana [Goebel et al., this volume]; Western Stemmed [Willig, this volume]), rather than ancestral. However, the radiocarbon dates of possible contemporary non-Clovis sites have not been subject to the same critical re-evaluation. Such studies would be enlightening.

The inferred Clovis lithic tool kit from Clovis type sites contains bifacial, fluted projectile points (Figure 1); large bifaces (Figure 2f–h) used for a variety of tasks as well as for projectile-point preforms; blades and blade cores (Figure 3; Figure 4); cutting and scraping tools made on blades (Figure 2a,c; Figure 5a–d) and flakes (Figure 2d,e; Figure 5e); gravers; and a variety of end scrapers (for additional discussion of the Clovis tool kit, see Bonnichsen, this volume). Burins are present but are relatively rare. In addition, bone and ivory tools occur in Clovis assemblages. A large crescent (Figure 2b), typical of Western Stemmed assemblages from the Great Basin (Fagan 1988; Willig 1988), has been recently identified in a Clovis cache from the area of the Wyoming-Idaho border (Frison 1991).

Clovis flint knappers utilized high-quality raw materials for their flaked-stone artifacts. Stone quarry sources would have been relatively untouched during Clovis times; consequently the very best materials would have been available in large quantities. Sources of equally serviceable materials of somewhat lesser quality were at times more accessible. However, Clovis flint knappers generally preferred to use fine-grained raw materials for their formal tools, even if sources were distant. This may reflect respect for the prey animals; special powers attributed to specific stones; or curation of raw materials through time and over large areas, perhaps indicating mobility or trade relationships. These questions need to be addressed in future research.

Large bifaces, blades, and flakes were produced at quarry locations and transported until needed for tool use or manufacture (Bonnichsen et al. 1982). Bifaces could have served as both raw material stock and as functional tools. Bifaces that were manufactured into projectile points may also have served as cutting implements. Points were resharpened until they were no longer useful as weapon tips. They then may have been modified into other tools, such as perforators, scrapers, or burins.

Clovis blades and blade cores have been found at a number of sites, but are apparently more common in the Southeast and southern Plains. Large polyhedral blade cores produced large prismatic and excurvate blades. Blade technology occurs at several localities in New York State (Funk et al. 1969; Ritchie and Funk 1973); at the Williamson site in Virginia (McCary 1951); at the Adams (Sanders 1990) and Ledford sites (Gramly 1990), Kentucky; as well as at several localities in Texas, including the Kincade Rockshelter (Collins et al. 1989). Blade-core tablets (Figure 3a; Figure 4), were first recognized at Pavo Real (49BX52), excavated by the Texas Department of Transportation near San Antonio, Texas (Henderson and Goode n.d.), and at the stratified Aubrey site near Denton, Texas (Ferring 1990).

Microblades or microblade cores are not part of the Clovis technological repertoire. The lack of microblades in Clovis tool assemblages is significant because microblades are pervasive in the late Paleolithic of Northeast Asia and co-occur with bifacial reduction techniques as far back as twenty-five millennia (Derevianko 1989; Drozdov et al. 1990). Microblade traditions are distributed from China through Northeast Asia, the American Arctic, and along the Northwest Coast of North America (Chen 1991). With the possible exception of an early microblade horizon at Bluefish Caves in the northern Yukon (Cinq-Mars 1990), the North American microblade traditions are less than 11,000 years old (Clark, this volume).

Morlan, in this volume, argues that caribou antler was particularly well suited for the manufacture of projectile points slotted for microblade insets. He suggests they were dropped from use in areas where caribou were unavailable. Although this is a possible explanation for the lack of microblades in Clovis assemblages, it should be pointed out that microblades are found inset into other types of osseous materials, particularly those in Northeast Asia. Furthermore, caribou would have been available for Clovis exploitation, especially in the Northeast, but microblades are absent. If microblades were originally part of Clovis technology, alternate explanations for their disappearance are necessary.

The Clovis bone and ivory technologies are not well known, but use of expedient tools and shaping artifacts by bone flaking are part of the technological repertoire. Among the formal tools found at Clovis sites are a shaft wrench (Figure 6d) recovered at Murray Springs, Arizona (Haynes and Hemmings 1968); foreshafts (Figure 6a,b) from Anzick, Montana (Lahren and Bonnichsen 1974), Sheaman, Wyoming (Frison and Stanford 1982), and Ritchie-Roberts, Washington (Mehringer 1989); and a projectile point (Figure 6c) from Blackwater Draw, New Mexico (Hester 1972; Sellards 1952). Blackwater Draw has also produced a possible ivory billet (Boulderian, personal communication 1990), a bone bead, and an awl or punch (Hester 1972). Ivory-working

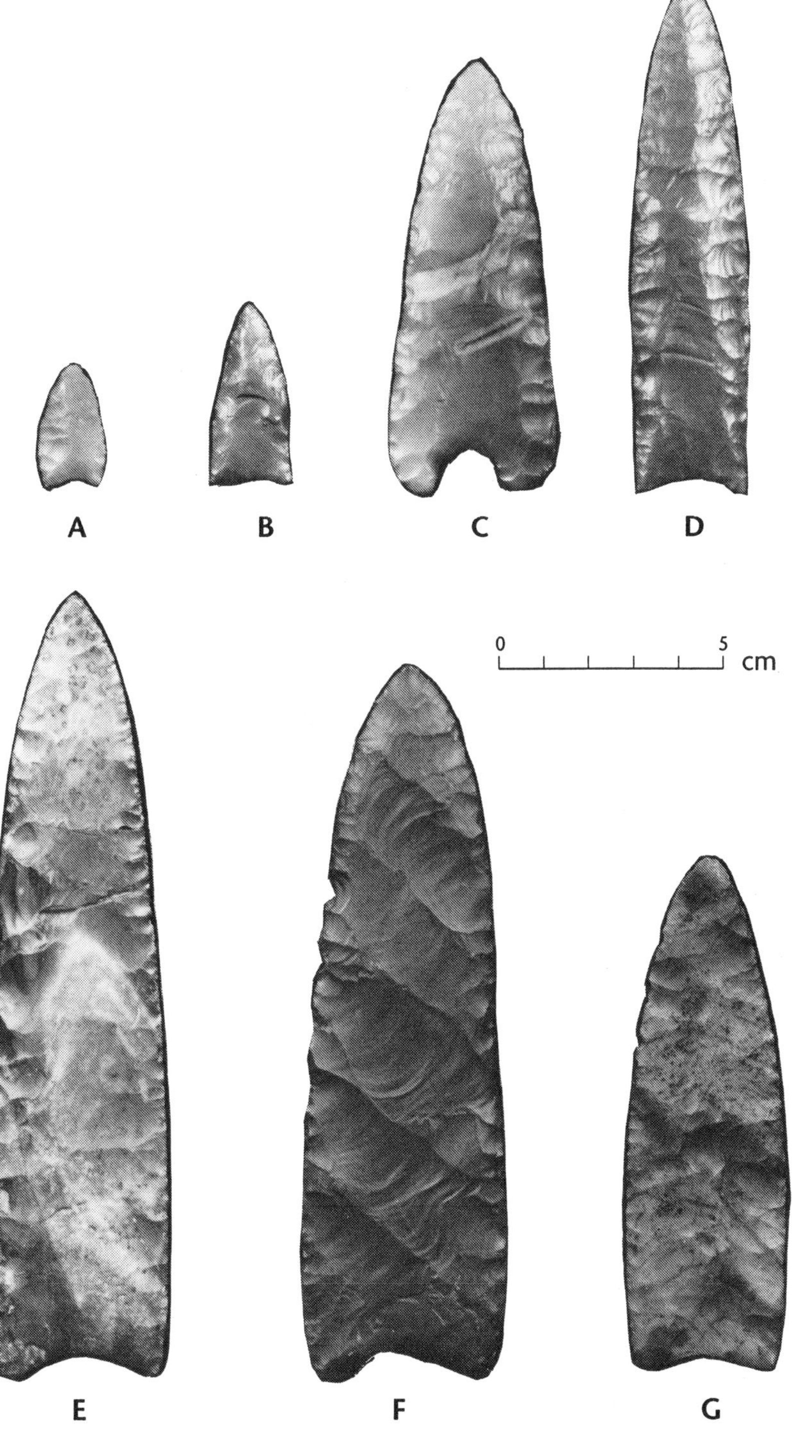

Figure 1. Western Clovis projectile points depicting the range of variation in size and technological attributes: **A, B,** and **D)** Blackwater Draw Locality No. 1; **C)** Colby site; **E)** Drake Cache; **F)** Fenn Cache; **G)** Anzick Cache.

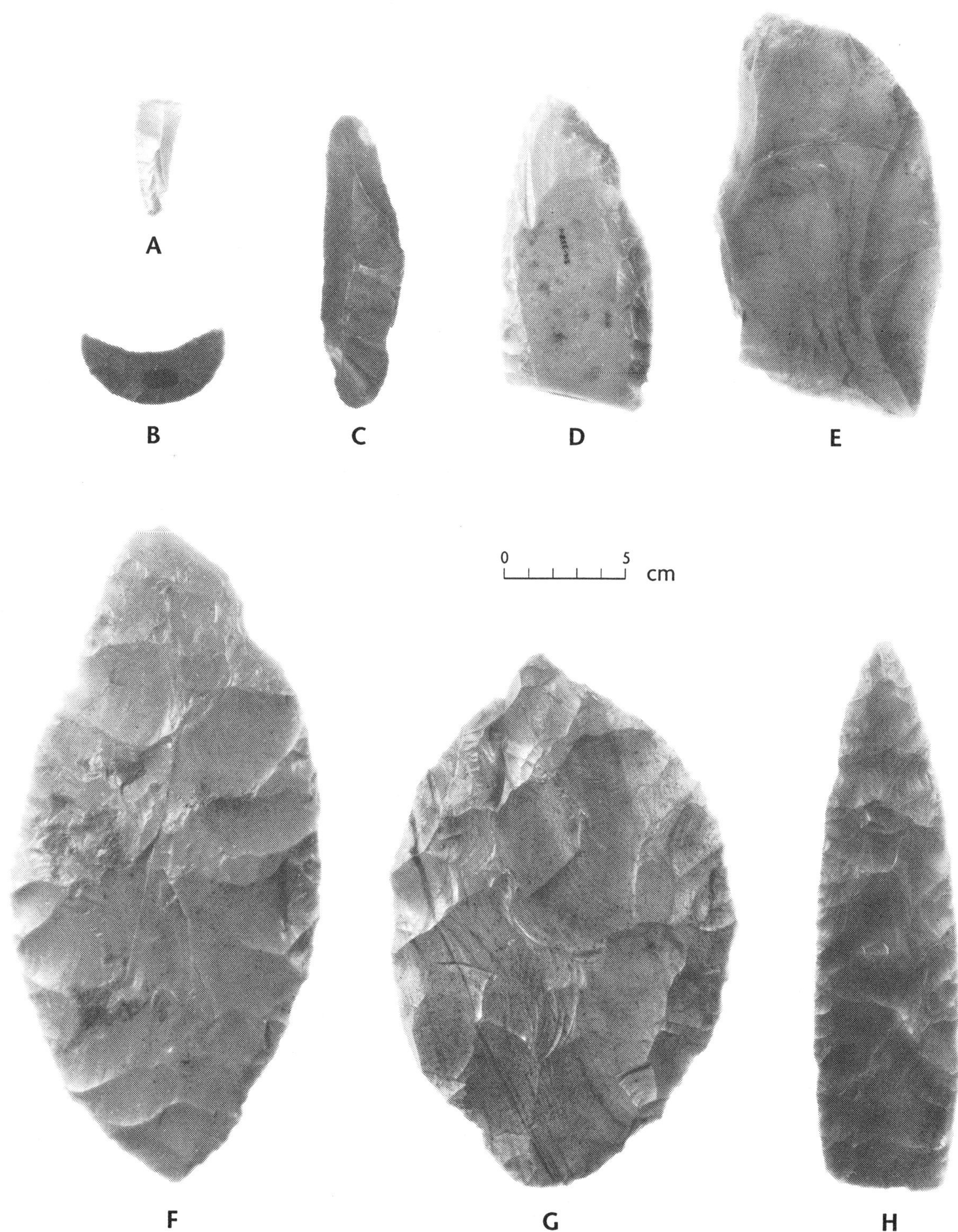

Figure 2. Clovis artifacts: **A)** end scraper, Blackwater Draw Locality No. 1; **B)** crescent, Fenn Cache; **C)** retouched blade, Anzick Cache; **D–E)** retouched flakes, Anzick Cache; **F–H)** large bifaces, Anzick Cache.

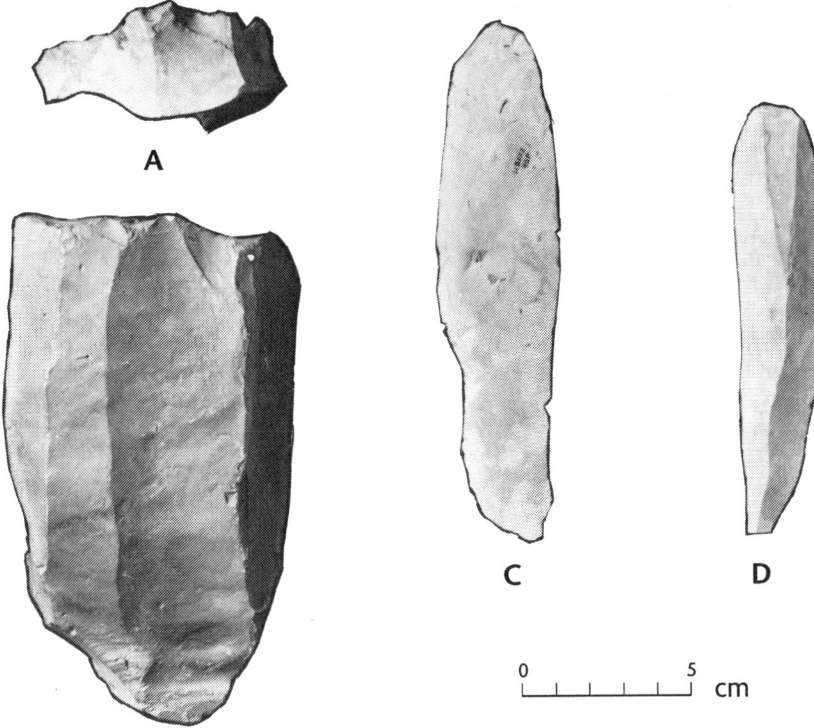

Figure 3. Examples illustrating Clovis blade core technology: **A)** core tablet, Pavo Real (41BX52); **B)** blade core, Adams site; **C–D)** blades, Pavo Real (41BX52).

techniques have been inferred from a culturally modified tusk fragment from Blackwater Draw (Saunders et al. 1990). Ivory and bone artifacts are commonly recovered from submerged sites in Florida, many of which are probably Clovis (Dunbar, this volume).

Caches that contain projectile points, bifaces, and other types of stone tools have been found at the Simon site, Idaho (Butler 1963); the Anzick site, Montana (Lahren and Bonnichsen 1974); the Ritchie-Roberts site, Washington (Mehringer 1989); the Fenn Cache, Idaho (Frison 1991); and the Lamb site (Gramly 1988), New York. Antler, ivory, and bone artifacts that probably served as foreshafts were found at the Anzick and Ritchie-Roberts sites. Red ocher was associated with the Anzick, Ritchie Roberts, Fenn, and Simon caches. At Anzick fragments of human bone were also found, which may indicate that it was a burial site. Human remains did not occur with the other caches. The Drake Cache (Stanford and Jodry 1988) consisted of 13 newly made or resharpened projectile points, a chert hammerstone, and tiny ivory fragments indicative of the former presence of ivory tools, perhaps foreshafts.

Several blade caches have been found which are attributed to Clovis. The Green Cache (Green 1963) consisted of 17 blades found at Blackwater Draw, New Mexico. A second cache of blades was recovered from this site in the spring of 1990 (J. Montgomery, personal communication 1991). The Kevin Davis Blade Cache contained 13 blades found in Navarro County, Texas (Young and Collins 1989).

Clovis settlement and subsistence strategies are beginning to emerge, but much work remains for an adequate definition. Most Clovis sites are associated with water sources, i.e., springs, stream or river terraces, or the shores of lakes and ponds. From the relatively few Clovis campsites excavated, it appears that Clovis groups were small and that their camps were not often occupied for long durations. Large campsites found near quarries may reflect multiple reoccupations over many years. These would include sites such as Thunderbird in Virginia (Gardner 1974); Wells Creek Crater, Tennessee (Dragoo 1973); and the Adams site, Kentucky (Sanders 1990).

When faunal remains are preserved in Clovis sites, mammoth is the most common reoccurring species, leading to the early conclusion that Clovis people were specialized big-game hunters. However, as pointed out by several authors in this volume, new evidence implies that Clovis procurement strategies were aimed at a wider array of plants and animals (Bryan, this volume; Johnson, this volume; McNett 1985). It is likely that Clovis peoples were generalists, exploiting a relatively broad-based economy. This may be responsible, in part, for their apparent success in exploiting diverse ecological systems during a time of rapid climatic change.

ENVIRONMENT

The late Pleistocene was a period of abrupt climatic change that resulted in the extinction of many genera of animals and the reorganization of the remaining biotic communities (Graham and Lundelius 1984). Although it has been suggested that Paleoindians were responsible for the demise of some of these animal taxa (Martin 1984), it is clear that rapid climatic change played an important role in the reorganization of vegetation communities, which contributed to Pleistocene faunal extinctions.

Compilation of climatic data derived from deep-sea and ice cores, simulation models of climatic change, and synthetic overviews of late Pleistocene/early Holocene floral and faunal communities (Graham et al. 1987; Porter 1983; Ruddiman and Wright 1987; Wright 1983) provide a rich data base from which investigators can construct general ecological models and draw inferences about cultural change and adaptation.

Prior to the appearance of the Clovis complex, the great continental and mountain glaciers were rapidly retreating. The melting of these ice masses raised ground-water tables and swelled rivers and streams throughout North America. Large proglacial lakes formed around ice margins. From the Plains westward and from northern Mexico to Canada, pluvial lakes and ponds dotted the countryside. Increased nutrients deposited in the soils by retreating glaciers provided a fertile environment that rapidly reclaimed the denuded landscape (Blundon and Dale 1990). A complex mosaic of open tundra, steppes, grasslands, savannas, woodlands, and forests stretched from sea to sea. On this backdrop, the fauna flourished, and many species that do not co-occur today lived side by side (Graham and Lundelius 1984). The diversity of readily accessible plant and animal resources would have provided an ideal habitat for human colonization.

The complex atmospheric and geophysical changes that transpired during the late Pleistocene created intricate cause-and-effect feedback loops. As the glaciers were reduced, the fresh meltwater not only caused rising sea levels, but decreased ocean salinity and lowered water temperatures. This affected atmospheric circulation patterns, air temperatures, and precipitation patterns, speeding up glacial melt.

By 11,000 years ago the reduction of meltwater runoff from the southern Rockies and Sierra Nevadas caused western water tables to recede (Porter 1988). As the Laurentian ice retreated back to the Great Lakes, meltwater drainage shifted from the Mississippi to the St. Lawrence. Reduction in precipitation resulting from changes in atmospheric circulation variably caused pluvial lakes and ponds to shrink in size, become more saline, and/or hold water only seasonally. Water flow from springs was significantly reduced.

The aridity would have reduced the amount of grasslands, affected their productivity, and diminished their carrying capacity. Humans, as well as other animals, would have concentrated around the available freshwater sources. It was perhaps during this dry period that Clovis first appeared.

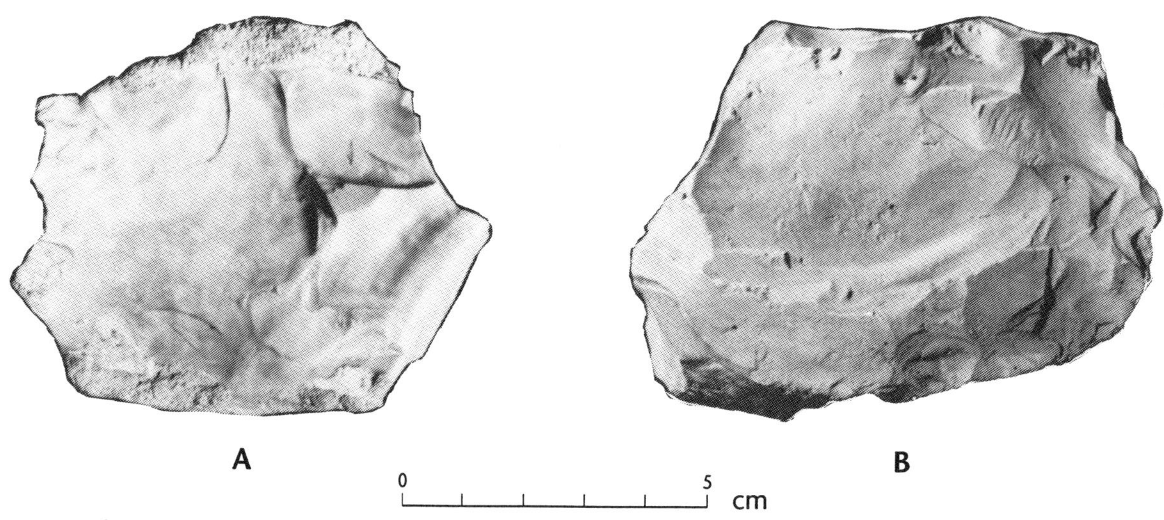

Figure 4. Blade core platforms: **A)** Pavo Real (41BX52); **B)** Adams site.

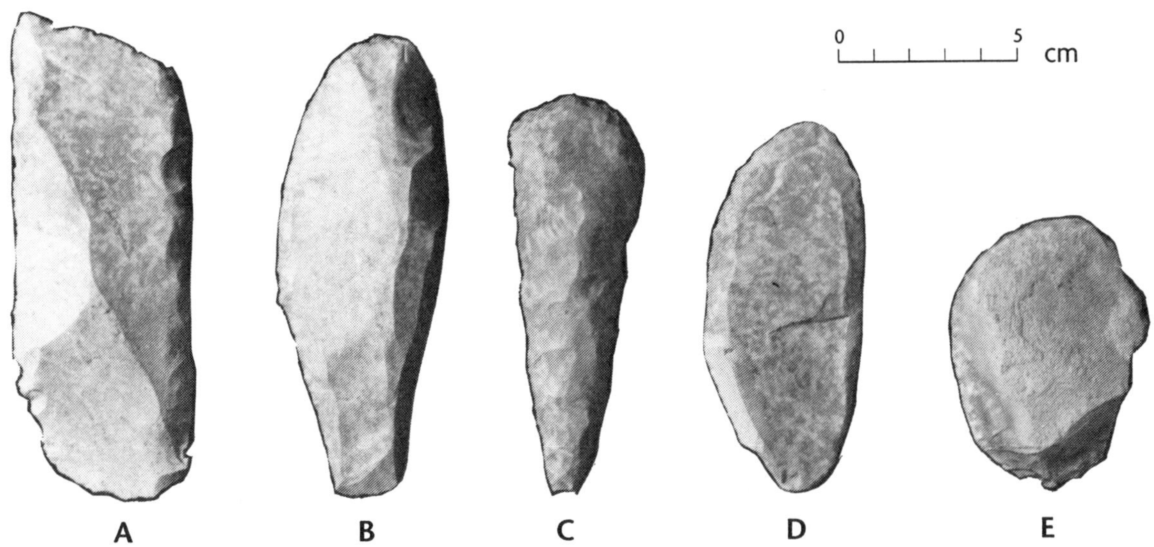

Figure 5. Blade tools: Pavo Real (41BX52).

Water was a critical element in Clovis settlement systems, especially in the West and Southeast, where there is evidence that water sources may have been becoming scarce (Dunbar, this volume; Haynes n.d.). Clovis artifacts are found on lower strand lines of the western pluvial lakes than are artifacts of later ages (Willig 1989, this volume). An analogous situation is reported in southern Colorado (Jodry et al. 1989), and a general drying of springs is indicated at Blackwater Draw and Murray Springs, where wells have been found that were dug by either humans or proboscideans (Haynes n.d.).

CLOVIS ORIGINS

Clovis origins and patterns of adaptation are likely linked to these terminal Pleistocene climatic changes. Bonnichsen et al. (1987) suggest that Clovis developed out of the lanceolate-point pattern as a response to climatic change.

The ancestors of Clovis were likely Early Upper Paleolithic peoples of Siberia who had a technology that produced large polyhedral blade cores and blades, generalized lanceolate bifaces, large scraper planes, a variety of cutting and scraping tools made on blades and flakes, and bone and ivory tools. Similar tool classes are from the early level at Ust-Kova (Drozdov et al. 1990) and Malta (Guerasimov 1935). However, the ancestors of Clovis may have become isolated from other Siberian technologies prior to 25,000 years ago, before microblades became pervasive in Northeast Asia (see Derevianko 1989; Drozdov et al. 1990). The technology of the Paleo-Siberian tradition that led to Clovis was adapted for exploiting the diverse ecosystems of the open steppes, grassland savannas, and tundras.

The flaked mammoth long-bone cores from Old Crow (Bonnichsen 1979; Morlan 1980), which lack stratigraphic context, may be evidence for the early human occupation of eastern Beringia. Even though the famous caribou tibia flesher has been dated to only the last millennium, AMS radiocarbon dating of the bone cores suggests they are between 25,000 and 40,000 years old (Morlan et al. 1990). Morlan points out that these cores did not occur in the fossil record of the Yukon Territory before that time, even though older mammoth fossils are common. Consequently, a new taphonomic process was introduced. Human modification seems a possible candidate.

At the Bluefish Caves, located in the highlands surrounding the Old Crow Basin, Cinq-Mars (1990) found a bone core that has been refitted to a bone flake. These specimens came from Pleistocene deposits, below Paleoarctic tools that are believed to date ca. 14,000 years old. AMS dates of both the core and flake are ca. 24,000 yr B.P. Similarly flaked mammoth bone cores of Clovis age have been found at the Lange-Ferguson Clovis site in South Dakota (Hannus 1989) and at Owl Cave, Idaho (Miller 1989). Flaked mammoth bone has been reported from Blackwater Draw (Hester 1972), as well as at Ust-Kova in Siberia (Drozdov et al. 1990). Bone flaking is another technological link between the Asian Paleolithic and Clovis.

Prior to and during the onset of the early-late Wisconsin glaciation, ca. 24,000 years ago (Richmond 1986:Charts 1A,1B), the MacKenzie Corridor was open

Figure 6. Bone and ivory tools: **A–B)** foreshafts, Anzick Cache; **C)** projectile point, Blackwater Draw Locality No. 1; **D)** shaft wrench, Murray Springs.

for several thousand years. Although environmental conditions may not have been optimal for human survival, it would have been possible to traverse the corridor from Beringia southward. Recent studies indicate that proglacial landscapes revegetate rather rapidly (Blundon and Dale 1990). Lakes and streams would have been available for harvesting fish and migratory waterfowl. Species of mammals would no doubt have also colonized the area.

Hypothetically, as the bands exploiting this area moved further southward, they may eventually have become more isolated from each other. The evidence to support such a scenario is scant for many reasons. The initial colonists were likely few in number and occupied a comparatively small scattering of sites. Most of the archeological record of their passing through the MacKenzie Corridor, as well as evidence of their sites along the eastern ice margin, would have been destroyed by the readvance of the Wisconsin ice.

Evidence for early people exploiting the pluvial lakes and marsh ecosystems in the West would also have been largely obliterated. Campsites would have been situated in nonagrading situations on high ground beyond the marshes or on high strand lines. Unless unique geological conditions caused these sites to be preserved, they would have remained surface features. The waning of these lakes at the end of the Pleistocene and subsequent Holocene refilling may have resulted in later peoples inhabiting the same surface localities, thereby mixing the archeological detritus of multiple generations. Once people were established in the eastern areas of the United States, their campsites would be deeply buried in the terraces of the rapidly agrading river systems with little chance of exposure. The lowest level at Meadowcroft Rockshelter in Pennsylvania may be an exception (Adovasio et al. 1981).

Lanceolate bifaces have been found in sites dated as old or older than Clovis (Bryan, this volume; Carlson 1983). A lanceolate point from Walker Lake, Nevada (McGhee 1889), was associated with proboscidean remains. Two such bifaces from Sandia Cave, New Mexico (Hibben 1941), possibly date between 10,800 and 14,000 years old (Haynes and Agogino 1986). Lanceolate bifaces were found with mammoth remains at Santa Isabel Itzapan, Mexico (Aveleyra 1965; Aveleyra and Maldonado-Koerdell 1953). The deposits that contained these mammoths have been dated elsewhere in the Valley of Mexico between 11,000 and 16,000 years old.

The southward spread of a lanceolate biface pattern has also been documented in South America. Lanceolate weapon tips known as El Jobo points, associated with mastodon remains, have been dated to around 14,000 years old (Bryan et al. 1978). A recent discovery in Venezuela of an El Jobo occupation situated stratigraphically below an occupation level containing fluted fishtail points (T. Dillehay, personal communication 1990) supports the early age of the lanceolate pattern in Latin America. By 13,000 years ago, people making lanceolate bifaces were exploiting the various ecosystems in the neighborhood of Chinchihuapi Creek near Monte Verde, Chile (Dillehay 1989).

Clovis is likely a descendant of this lanceolate pattern. The distinctive fluted projectile point was probably a regional adaptation to exploit the dwindling faunal resources and changing habitats. This transition may have taken place in the southeastern region of the United States. Mason (1962) suggested that the Clovis homeland was in the Southeast because more fluted points and a larger diversity of fluted points exist in this area. Bryan (this volume) has also suggested that Clovis developed in the Southeast.

The most likely candidate for a precursor to the Clovis projectile point in the Southeast is the Suwannee/Simpson point. These points have a distribution that ranges from Florida to central Texas, covering a much larger geographic area than do any of the other southeastern fluted points that are probably descendant from Clovis. Suwannee/Simpson points are currently undated but occurred stratigraphically below Folsom points at Horn Rock Shelter near Waco, Texas (Redder 1985). These weapon tips are similar in outline to Clovis but tend to have slightly expanding bases. They are either weakly fluted or have no flutes at all. The Suwannee/Simpson lithic manufacturing techniques are very close to Clovis. Ivory and bone tools made from horse metapodials have been found in submerged contexts that suggest they may be associated with these types of points (Dunbar, this volume). As far as I know, none of these bone tools have been radiocarbon dated.

It is traditionally thought that Suwannee/Simpson evolved from Clovis (Anderson 1990). As there is no evidence to the contrary, I would suggest that this is not the case and predict that when dated, they may be slightly older than Clovis.

The Miller point from Meadowcroft Rockshelter (Adovasio et al. 1981) is a variant of the lanceolate pattern, but rather than being bipointed or having a convex base, its base tends to be flat to slightly concave. This type of artifact would be a logical intermediate form between the general Siberian lanceolate point and later biface types such as Suwannee/Simpson and Clovis.

Clovis hunters, exploiting the dwindling resources of the open grasslands and parklands, continued expanding north and west. It may well be that they came into contact with their distant cousins when they reached the Great Basin. Perhaps the occurrence of a crescent tool, so typical of the Western Pluvial tradition (Willig 1989), in the Fenn Clovis Cache (Frison 1991) signals cultural interaction between these two groups.

The dry period that may have marked Clovis came to an abrupt end between 10,900 and 10,800 years ago in the Southwest and Plains. Pluvial lakes rose and again watered the countryside. The rangelands improved, and bison populations probably increased dramatically. As in the East, Clovis hunters adapted to new environmental conditions and adjusted their weaponry and settlement patterns accordingly. In the Rocky Mountains and adjacent Plains, Clovis became what we know today as the Folsom culture.

The emergence of the Clovis complex is an interesting anthropological phenomenon. The technology of this period was apparently highly adaptive, allowing for the exploitation of a very large and diverse geographic area during a period of extreme climatic change and biotic reorganization. It was relatively short lived, lasting perhaps only 300 years.

If Clovis peoples were the first migrants to the New World, the founding population must have been extremely large, highly prolific, and/or exceedingly mobile in order to populate the entire North American continent in such a short time. If Clovis was the earliest New World complex, the density and distribution of Clovis artifacts suggest a population explosion of immigrants unparalleled in the history of humankind. Alternatively, Clovis may have developed in North America, perhaps in the Southeast, out of an earlier New World lanceolate-point tradition, which itself had its roots in the northeast Asian Paleolithic core and blade tradition. The papers in this volume examine these issues and present data and hypotheses that further our understanding of Clovis origins and adaptations.

ACKNOWLEDGMENTS

I am most grateful to Robson Bonnichsen, Tom Dillehay, C. Vance Haynes, Jr., and Margaret Jodry for valuable comments, advice, and references, as well as Karen Turnmire and Robson Bonnichsen, editors of this volume, for their expert help and patience. I would like to thank Vic Krantz for his excellent photographs and George Frison, C. V. Haynes Jr., Jerry Henderson, and Thomas Sanders for permission to illustrate various Clovis artifacts.

REFERENCES CITED

Adovasio, J. M., J. D. Gunn, J. Donahue, R. Stuckenrath, and J. Guilday
1981 *Meadowcroft Rockshelter and the Archaeology of the Cross Creek Drainage.* University of Pittsburgh Press, Pittsburgh.

Anderson, D. G.
1990 The Paleoindian Colonization of Eastern North America: A View from the Southeastern United States. In *Early Paleoindian Economies of Eastern North America,* edited by K. B. Tankersley and B. L. Isaac, pp. 163–217. Research in Economic Anthropology, Supplement 5. JAI Press, Greenwich.

Aveleyra A. de Anda, L.
1956 The Second Mammoth and Associated Artifacts at Santa Isabel Ixtapan, Mexico. *American Antiquity* 22:12–28.

Aveleyra A. de Anda, L., and M. Maldonado-Koerdell
1953 Association of Artifacts with Mammoth in the Valley of Mexico. *American Antiquity* 18:332–340.

Bonnichsen, R.
1979 *Pleistocene Bone Technology in the Beringian Refugium.* Archaeological Survey of Canada Paper No. 89. Mercury Series. National Museum of Man, Ottawa.

Bonnichsen, R., E. Lahti, B. Lepper, R. Low, J. McMahon, and J. Oliver
1982 Archaeological Research at the Thoroughfare. In *Archaeological Research at Munsungun Lake: 1981 Preliminary Technical Report of Activities,* edited by R. Bonnichsen. Quaternary Institute, University of Maine, Orono.

Bonnichsen, R., D. Stanford, and J. L. Fastook
1987 Environmental Change and Developmental History of Human Adaptive Patterns; The Paleoindian Case. In *North America and Adjacent Oceans During the Last Deglaciation: The Geology of North America,* vol. K-3, edited by W. F. Ruddiman and H. E. Wright, Jr., pp. 403–424. Geological Society of America, Boulder.

Blundon, D. J., and M. R. Dale
1990 Dinitrogen Fixation (Acetylene Reduction) in Primary Succession Near Mount Robson, British Columbia, Canada. *Arctic and Alpine Research* 22:255–263.

Butler, B. R.
1963 An Early Man Site at Big Camas Prairie, South-central Idaho. *Tebiwa* 6(1):22–33.

Bryan, A. L., R. M. Casamiquela, J. M. Cruxent, R. Gruhn, and C. Ochsenius
1978 An El Jobo Mastodon Kill at Taima-taima, Venezuela. *Science* 200:1275–1277.

Carlson, R. L.
1983 The Far West. In *Early Man in the New World,* edited by R. Shutler, Jr., pp. 73–97. Sage Press, Beverly Hills.

Chen, Chun
1991 Preliminary Comparison of Wedge-Shaped Cores Between North China and North America. In *Ice-Age Archaeology of Asia and the Peopling of the Americas,* edited by R.

Bonnichsen, J. Tomenchuk, and F. Ikawa-Smith. Center for the Study of the First Americans, University of Maine, Orono. Volume in preparation.

Cinq-Mars, J.
1990 La Place des Grottes du Poisson-Bleu dans la Prehistoire Beringienne. *Revista de Arqueologia Americana* 1:9–32. Instituto Panamericana de Geografia e Historia.

Collins, M. D., G. L. Evans, T. N. Campbell, M. C. Winans, and C. E. Mear
1989 Clovis Occupation at Kincaid Shelter, Texas. *Current Research in the Pleistocene* 6:3–5.

Derevianko, A. P.
1989 The late Pleistocene Sites in the Slendia River Basin and Their Significance for Correlation with Upper Paleolithic Assemblages of the Pacific. In *Abstracts of the Circum-Pacific Prehistory Conference,* pp. 36. Seattle.

Dillehay, T. D.
1989 *Monte Verde: A Late Pleistocene Settlement in Chile.* Smithsonian Institution Press, Washington, D.C.

Dragoo, D.
1973 Wells Creek—An Early Man Site in Stewart County, Tennessee. *Archaeology of Eastern North America* 1:1–56.

Drozdov, N. I., V. P. Chekha, S. A. Laukhim, V. G. Koltsova, Ye. V. Akimova, A. V. Yermolayev, V. P. Leontyev, S. A. Vasilyev, A. F. Yamskikh, G. A. Demidenko, Ye. V. Artemyev, N. Vikulov, A. Bokarev, I. V. Foronova, and S. D. Sidoras
1990 *Chronostratigraphy of Paleolithic sites of Central Siberia: The Yensei River Basin.* Institute of History, Philology, and Philosophy, USSR Academy of Sciences, Siberian Branch. Novosibirsk.

Fagan, J. L.
1988 Clovis and Western Pluvial Lakes Tradition Lithic Technologies at the Dietz Site in South-central Oregon. In *Early Human Occupation in Far Western North America: The Clovis-Archaic Interface,* edited by J. A. Willig, C. M. Aikens, and J. Fagan, pp. 389–417. Nevada State Museum Anthropological Papers No. 21. Carson City.

Ferring, C. R.
1990 The 1989 Investigations at the Aubrey Clovis Site, Texas. *Current Research in the Pleistocene* 7:10–12.

Figgens, J. D.
1927 The Antiquity of Man in America. *Natural History* 27:229–239.

Figgens, J. D.
1933 A Further Contribution to the Antiquity of Man in America. *Proceedings of the Colorado Museum of Natural History* 12(2).

Frison, G. C.
1991 *Prehistoric Hunters of the High Plains.* 2nd. edition. Academic Press, New York.

Frison, G. C., and D. J. Stanford
1982 *The Agate Basin Site: A Record of the Paleoindian Occupation of the Northwestern High Plains.* Academic Press, New York.

Funk, R. E., T. P. Weinman, and P. L. Weinman
1969 The Kings Road Site: A Recently Discovered Paleo-Indian Manifestation in Greene County, New York. *New York State Archeological Association Bulletin* 45:1–23.

Gardner, W. H. (editor)
1974 *The Flint Run Paleo-Indian Complex: A Preliminary Report 1971–73 Seasons.* Occasional Publication No. 1. Department of Anthropology, The Catholic University of America, Washington, D.C.

Graham, R. W., and E. Lundelius, Jr.
1984 Coevolutionary Disequilibrium and Pleistocene Extinctions. In *Quaternary Extinctions: A Prehistoric Revolution,* edited by P. S. Martin and R. G. Klein, pp. 223–249. University of Arizona Press, Tucson.

Graham, R. W., H. A. Semken, Jr., and M. A. Graham (editors)
1987 *Late Quaternary Mammalian Biogeography and Environments of the Great Plains and Prairies.* Illinois State Museum Scientific Papers No. 22. Springfield.

Gramly, R. M.
1988 Palaeo-Indian Sites South of Lake Ontario, Western and Central New York State. In *Late Pleistocene and Early Holocene Paleoecology and Archeology of the Eastern Great Lakes Region,* edited by R. S. Laub, N. G. Miller, and D. W. Steadman, pp. 265–293. Bulletin of the Buffalo Society of Natural Sciences No. 33. Buffalo.

1990 *Guide to the Palaeo-Indian Artifacts of North America.* Persimmon Press, Buffalo.

Green, F. E.
1963 The Clovis Blades: An Important Addition to the Llano Complex. *American Antiquity* 29:145–165.

Guerasimov, M. M.
1935 Excavation of the Paleolithic Site in the Village of Malta (Preliminary Report on Excavations in

1928–1932). Reports of State Academy of Historical Sciences. *Kiev History* 118.

Hannus, L. A.
1989 Flaked Mammoth Bone from the Lange/Ferguson Site, White River Badland Area, South Dakota. In *Bone Modification,* edited by R. Bonnichsen and M. H. Sorg, pp. 395–413. Center for the Study of the First Americans, University of Maine, Orono.

Haynes, C. V., Jr.
1991 Contributions of Radiocarbon Dating to the Geochronology of the Peopling of the New World. In *Radiocarbon After Four Decades,* edited by R. E. Tayler, A. Long, and R. Kra. University of Arizona Press, Tucson. In press.
n.d. Archaeological and Paleohydrological Evidence for a Terminal Pleistocene Drought in North America and Its Bearing on Pleistocene Extinction. Ms. submitted to *Quaternary Research.*

Haynes, C. V., Jr., and G. A. Agogino
1986 *Geochronology of Sandia Cave.* Smithsonian Contributions to Anthropology No. 32. Washington, D.C.

Haynes, C. V., Jr., and E. T. Hemmings
1968 Mammoth-bone Shaft Wrench from Murray Springs, Arizona. *Science* 159:186–187.

Henderson, J., and G. Goode
n.d. Pavo Real: An Early Paleoindian Site in South Central Texas. Ms. submitted to *Current Research in the Pleistocene.*

Hester, J. J.
1972 *Blackwater Locality No. 1: A Stratified, Early Man Site in Eastern New Mexico.* Fort Burgwin Research Center, Southern Methodist University, Dallas.

Hibben, F. C.
1941 *Evidences of Early Occupation in Sandia Cave, New Mexico, and Other Sites in the Sandia-Manzano Region.* Smithsonian Miscellaneous Collection Vol. 99, No. 23. Washington, D.C.

Jodry, M. A., D .S. Shafer, D. J. Stanford, and O. K. Davis
1989 Late Quaternary Environments and Human Adaptation in the San Luis Valley, South-Central Colorado. In *Water in the Valley,* edited by E. J. Harmon, pp. 189–209. Colorado Ground-Water Association, Lakewood.

Lahren, L., and R. Bonnichsen
1974 Bone Foreshafts from a Clovis Burial in Southwestern Montana. *Science* 186:147–150.

Martin, P. S.
1984 Prehistoric Overkill: The Global Model. In *Quaternary Extinctions: A Prehistoric Revolution,* edited by P. S. Martin and R. G. Klein, pp. 354–404. University of Arizona Press, Tucson.

Mason, R. I.
1962 The Paleo-Indian Tradition in Eastern North America. *Current Anthropology* 3:227–283.

McCary, B. C.
1951 A Workshop of Early Man in Dinwiddie County, Virginia. *American Antiquity* 17:9–17.

McGee, W. J.
1889 An Obsidian Implement from Pleistocene Deposits in Nevada. *American Anthropologist* 2:301–313.

McNett, C. W., Jr. (editor)
1985 *Shawnee-Minisink: A Stratified Paleoindian-Archaic Site in the Upper Delaware Valley of Pennsylvania.* Academic Press, Orlando.

Mehringer, P. J., Jr.
1989 Of Apples and Archaeology. *Universe* 1(2):2–9.

Meltzer, D.
1989 The Discovery of Deep Time: A History of Views on the Peopling of the Americas. Paper presented at the First World Summit Conference on the Peopling of the Americas, Center for the Study of the First Americans, University of Maine, Orono.

Miller, S. J.
1989 Characteristics of Mammoth Bone Reduction at Owl Cave, the Wasden Site, Idaho. In *Bone Modification,* edited by R. Bonnichsen and M. H. Sorg, pp. 381–395. Center for the Study of the First Americans, University of Maine, Orono.

Morlan, R. E.
1980 *Taphonomy and Archaeology in the Upper Pleistocene of the Northern Yukon Territory: A Glimpse of the Peopling of the New World.* Archaeological Survey of Canada Paper No. 94. Mercury Series. National Museum of Man, Ottawa.

Morlan, R. E., D. E. Nelson, T. A. Brown, J. S. Vogel, and J. R. Southon
1990 Accelerator Mass Spectrometry Dates on Bones from Old Crow Basin, Northern Yukon Territory. *Canadian Journal of Archaeology* 14:75–105.

Porter, S. C. (editor)
1983 *The Late Pleistocene.* Late Quaternary Environments of the United States, vol. 1, H. E. Wright, Jr., general editor. University of Minnesota Press, Minneapolis.

Porter, S. C.
1988 Landscapes of the Last Ice Age in North America. In *Americans Before Columbus: Ice-Age*

Origins, edited by R. C. Carlisle, pp. 1–24. Ethnology Monographs No. 12. Department of Anthropology, University of Pittsburgh, Pittsburgh.

Redder, A. J.
1985 Horn Shelter Number 2: The South End A Preliminary Report. *Central Texas Archeologist* 10:37–66.

Richmond, G. M.
1986 Stratigraphy and Correlation of Glacial Deposits of the Rocky Mountains, the Colorado Plateau and the Ranges of the Great Basin. In *Quaternary Glaciation of the Northern Hemisphere*, edited by V. Sibrava, D. Q. Bowen, and G. M. Richmond. *Quaternary Science Reviews* 5:99–127.

Ritchie, W. A., and R. E. Funk
1973 *Aboriginal Settlement Patterns in the Northeast.* New York State Museum and Science Service Memoir No. 20. Albany.

Ruddiman, W. F., and H. E. Wright, Jr. (editors)
1987 *North America and Adjacent Oceans During the Last Deglaciation: The Geology of North America*, vol. K-3. The Geological Society of America, Boulder.

Sanders, T. N.
1990 *Adams: The Manufacturing of Flaked Stone Tools at a Paleoindian Site in Western Kentucky.* Persimmon Press, Buffalo.

Saunders, J. R., C. V. Haynes, Jr., D. J. Stanford, and G. A. Agogino
1990 A Mammoth-Ivory Semifabricate from Blackwater Locality No. 1, New Mexico. *American Antiquity* 55:112–120.

Sellards, E. H.
1952 *Early Man in America.* University of Texas Press, Austin.

Stanford, D. J., and M. A. Jodry
1988 The Drake Clovis Cache. *Current Research in the Pleistocene* 5:21–22.

Willig, J. A.
1989 Paleo-Archaic Adaptations and Lakeside Settlement Patterns in the Northern Alkali Basin, Oregon. In *Early Human Occupation in Far Western North America: The Clovis-Archaic Interface*, edited by J. A. Willig, C. M. Aikens, and J. L. Fagan, pp. 417–482. Nevada State Museum Anthropological Papers No. 21. Carson City.

Wright, H. E., Jr. (editor)
1983 *The Holocene.* Late Quaternary Environments of the United States, vol. 2, H. E. Wright, Jr., general editor. University of Minnesota Press, Minneapolis.

Young, B., and M. B. Collins
1989 A Cache of Blades with Clovis Affinities from Northeastern Texas. *Current Research in the Pleistocene* 6:26–29.

The Fluted-Point Tradition in the Americas—One of Several Adaptations to Late Pleistocene American Environments

ALAN L. BRYAN
Department of Anthropology
University of Alberta
Edmonton, AB, Canada T6G 2H4

A historical analysis of the quest for Clovis origins illustrates how a reasonable archaeological hypothesis evolved into a model that purports to explain the earliest peopling of the Americas. The "Clovis first" model became a myth when undemonstrated guesses rather than actual research results became accepted as proper means for explaining away contrary data. An alternative model of initial entry along the North Pacific Coast in early Wisconsinan times is able to explain late Pleistocene data from South America as well as North America. The Clovis complex is only one of a variety of adaptations to the diverse late Pleistocene and early Holocene environments of the New World—a relatively late development of a specialized hunting economy and technology necessary for survival on the High Plains.

The popular conception that the earliest Americans were specialized big-game hunters who bravely faced up to and slew mammoths and other huge beasts will die hard because it allows such spectacular and convincing depiction by writers and artists. Although for this and other reasons it may take many years to replace the venerable hypothesis that the earliest Americans (generally identified as Clovis mammoth hunters) were specialized megamammal hunters and not general foragers, I am pleased to see that many scholars (e.g., C. V. Haynes 1987b; Johnson, this volume; Lepper and Meltzer, this volume; Meltzer and Smith 1986) working on the "Clovis Problem" are beginning more carefully to examine data that question long-held assumptions concerning the basic economy and technology that sustained early Americans, and that in turn have sustained this model as the often repeated framework for visualizing the initial peopling of the New World (cf. Bryan 1977).

But this widely accepted model can be seen as a modern archaeological myth, because the empirical basis supporting the hypothesis has been artificially restricted to the readily recognized classic Paleoindian data base that has been well established for the High Plains of North America. If data from elsewhere do not fit the model, then it is assumed there must be something wrong with the contrary data. Although this is a classic circular argument, the model seems to fit the limited data base so well that there has been tremendous resistance to revising the accepted model or even to examining alternative models.

Identification as a myth of the generally accepted model that specialized big-game hunters were the first Americans can be found in Binford's (1981:31–32) useful discussion of how archaeological myths develop. Historically, the model originated from the fact that clear stratigraphic associations of fluted points with extinct Pleistocene fauna were repeatedly discovered on the southern and central High Plains, beginning with verification of the Folsom discovery in 1926. (It is a historical accident that the first verified association of artifacts with extinct fauna was in New Mexico and not in Mexico, Colombia, Venezuela, Brazil, or Chile.) At first, Folsom bison hunters were assumed to be the earliest immigrants to America, but the reported discovery in 1936 of Sandia points stratigraphically beneath Folsom points in Sandia Cave shifted thinking to Sandia as the earliest (Sellards 1952:149). However, repeated discoveries starting in the 1930s of Clovis points associated with mammoth remains, plus recognition that Folsom evidently had developed from Clovis, led to establishment of Clovis as a prime contender for the earliest American culture. The reported evidence from Sandia Cave was disputed (cf. Haynes and Agogino 1986) and the Tule Springs claim for even greater antiquity was shown to be wrong (Haynes 1967), but the evidence for association of Clovis points with mammoths remained unchallenged. The disrepute of Sandia and Tule Springs in the 1960s became the critical factor which led many archaeologists to conclude that the simplest and most plausible interpretation of the North American evidence was that Clovis really was the earliest. More recently, when specimens from several other reputedly early sites (e.g., the Old Crow caribou tibia scraper, the Taber child, and Del Mar man) were shown by laboratory reanalyses not to be early, the possibility that Clovis was first became a generally unstated premise in the minds of most North American archaeologists.

Although nearly all synthesizers of early American prehistory include in their model the theoretical possibility that there was an earlier occupation by people with a less specialized economy and technology, most then immediately state that the earliest incontrovertible evidence for early human occupation remains the Clovis mammoth-kill sites on the Great Plains. Operating with the premise that Clovis is the earliest demonstrated evidence, a series of assumptions based on the evidence from the Great Plains have been extrapolated to fit evidence found elsewhere in North America because fluted points, the diagnostic hallmark of the Llano complex, have been found in most nonglaciated parts of the continent. Gradually a body of inferences and assumptions, all based on an inadequately evaluated premise (cf. Binford 1981:32), became accepted as justification for sustaining the myth as the simplest and seemingly most reasonable model for the peopling of North America. Also, it was easy for North American archaeologists lacking first-hand familiarity with the body of primary data from many parts of the southern continent to extend the model to South America, where fluted "fishtail" points are in fact rare and limited in distribution to the northwestern corner of the continent. I intend to show that evidence from the southern continent, which must have been peopled by descendants of North Americans, constitutes the strongest demonstration that the generally accepted model is mythical that Clovis or an immediate proto-Clovis predecessor represents the earliest Americans.

Due largely to the efforts of C. Vance Haynes (e.g., 1964, 1980, 1982), who has pursued with great persistence the perplexing question of the origins of Clovis, everyone has been convinced that Clovis is the earliest successful adaptation to the New World that so far has been demonstrated. Clovis is the only easily recognized archaeological entity that has been found with extinct taxa in similar geological contexts at three sites (Clovis, Dent, Domebo) on the Great Plains, which have yielded radiocarbon dates between 11,500 and about 11,000 years ago (Haynes 1964, 1970; Haynes et al. 1984). Interestingly, however, Clovis sites in Wyoming (Frison and Todd 1986) and Arizona (Lehner and Murray Springs), as well as the Clovis-like Debert, Vail, Whipple, and Shawnee-Minisink sites in the eastern woodlands have yielded dates between 10,500 and 11,000 yr B.P., a range of time contemporary with Folsom (Haynes et al. 1984). More than a dozen North American fluted-point sites have now been dated between 11,500 and 10,500 yr B.P. Until recently, Haynes (e.g., 1980, 1982) has looked for Clovis origins in the Old World, in the process revitalizing the old logical hypothesis that the earliest Americans must have been adapted to the extreme cold conditions of interior Arctic Beringia and therefore must have had a specialized hunting technology like the people of Upper Paleolithic Europe or the Eskimos, who much later colonized High Arctic Canada and Greenland.

It should be made clear that the question of Clovis origins, which is addressed by this symposium, is not the same as the question of who were the original Americans. Unfortunately, however, these two discrete questions have become compounded into one by many authors because of the fact that Clovis is a repeatedly replicated cultural entity and because of constant reiteration of the hypothesis that the origins of Clovis were in Beringia or even farther west in Eurasia.

Recently, however, Haynes made it clear in his discussion of the papers delivered in Ottawa that he no

Figure 1. Sites mentioned in North America. **1)** Clovis (also Lubbock Lake and Folsom); **2)** Fort St. John (Charlie Lake Cave); **3)** Los Tapiales; **4)** Sandia Cave; **5)** Trail Creek Caves; **6)** Tule Springs; **7)** Smith Creek Cave; **8)** Del Mar; **9)** Bluefish Caves (and Old Crow).

longer believes that the immediate origins of Clovis are to be found in Beringia. Rather, he now ascribes to the alternative hypothesis, first suggested by Krieger (1954) and long supported by myself (Bryan 1969) and others, that fluted points moved north through Alberta to Alaska. On this question Haynes and I are now in essential agreement, and our position clearly separates the question of the origin of Clovis, which has always been Haynes' primary concern, from the question of the origin of the first Americans, which has always been my primary concern. It now seems clear to Haynes (cf. 1987a), as well as to myself, that Clovis originated somewhere in southern North America and not in the Arctic. (Later in this paper I will give reasons for reaching the conclusion that Clovis did not originate in Beringia.) If this is true, then there must be earlier cultural manifestations in southern North America that gave rise to Clovis. As discussed later, my own hunch is that the technological origins of the fluted-point tradition will eventually be found in the Southeast.

Someday the question of Clovis origins will be resolved, but meanwhile archaeologists should not ignore evidence that indicates there were parallel developments of other bifacially flaked-stone projectile-point traditions elsewhere in the Americas. Even in North America, good evidence is accruing that there was a contemporary development west of the Rocky Mountains of bifacial projectile points (a stemmed-point [technological] tradition), which evidently began somewhat earlier and persisted longer in the area than the techno-

logical tradition of making fluted points (Bryan 1980, 1988). The stemmed-point tradition was developed by late Pleistocene foragers who adapted themselves to the rich and diverse environments of many pluvial lakes and rivers, as well as the productive ecosystems of the adjacent mountains. This cultural tradition has generally been referred to as the Western Pluvial Lakes tradition, first defined by Bedwell (1973). People who made Clovis points also penetrated the Intermontane West to take advantage of these productive environments, but so far the radiocarbon-dated evidence does not support the generally accepted model that Clovis people introduced the first bifacial projectile points to the area. Rather, two alternative hypotheses should be considered: (1) that fluted points are relatively later west of the continental divide than the earliest stemmed points; and (2) that the fluted-point tradition persisted much longer west of the Rockies, long after it had been replaced on the High Plains by the stemmed-point tradition (Bryan 1988).

This paper has little to do with Clovis origins because the only Clovis site I ever excavated is the one I found in Guatemala, the southernmost dated (10,700 yr B.P.) Clovis site (Gruhn and Bryan 1977). As the dates on fluted points from Central and South America indicate that fluted points spread south from North America, archaeologists dealing with North American Clovis sites are better able to discuss Clovis origins.

My primary concern continues to be the question of the origin of all early Americans and the subsequent development of local and regional cultural adaptations in all parts of the Americas during late Pleistocene and early Holocene times. My experience excavating many sites in North, Central, and South America has led me to realize that Clovis is just one of several regional developments that were made by general foragers as they adapted to highly variable and rapidly changing late Pleistocene environments. Because Clovis fluted points are archaeologically exceptionally visible, and discovery of new Clovis localities always engenders a great deal of excitement while less spectacular artifact assemblages tend to be ignored, the search for Clovis origins has overshadowed the more important and much more complex question of the origin of the first Americans. Therefore, I see my contribution to this symposium to be an attempt to present an alternative to the hypothesis that Clovis hunters were the first Americans. I will argue that new discoveries in South America provide even more compelling reasons for abandoning the "Clovis first" myth, but first I think it is important to analyze just how this once useful hypothesis evolved into a myth that has served to shut out consideration of alternative hypotheses.

On the face of it, the premises and assumptions supporting the hypothesis seem reasonable enough. The primary assumption, of course, is that the first Americans came from northeast Asia via Beringia. There can be little doubt that this fundamental assumption is correct, but the secondary assumptions logically derived from the basic assumption are all open to question because the possibility is usually ignored of an initial entry along the coast rather than through interior Beringia. If an interior entry is assumed, there can be little question that the people must have been big-game hunters with tailored skin clothing adapted to extreme cold continental climatic conditions, and that they had a specialized technology (including diagnostic flaked-stone artifacts). Quite logically, then, these Clovis or proto-Clovis hunters expanded through the Ice-Free Corridor, adapted themselves to hunting mammoth and bison on the High Plains, and then rapidly expanded their hunting territories in all directions throughout the Americas. On the other hand, an entry along the relatively warm North Pacific Coast may not have required a specialized flaked-stone technology to adapt to this more productive ecosystem.

What started out as a reasonable working hypothesis has been repeated so often, with many embellishments, that archaeologists not cognizant of the available relevant archaeological evidence from all parts of the Americas have accepted the hypothesis with all its derived premises and assumptions as being logically so compelling that it must be true. And if the hypothesis is true, then there must be something wrong with all the claims for "pre-Clovis" or even contemporary non-Clovis cultural manifestations anywhere in the Americas. Operating with the conviction that Clovis really is the earliest American cultural manifestation, skeptics have been able to convince themselves (even without visiting the sites or examining the artifacts in question), as well as others less familiar with the relevant primary archaeological data, that somehow all these claims must be wrong and therefore can be ignored. Bolstered by the fact that several claims for earlier sites have been disproven, by extrapolation all other claims have been placed in limbo with counterclaims by skeptics that the artifacts might be naturefacts, that any real artifacts might be intrusive from a later occupation, that radiocarbon samples might be contaminated, or that the claimant is untrained or untrustworthy. Such arguments have swayed the majority of professional North American archaeologists, who are now convinced that big-game hunters making fluted points must have been the earliest Americans.

Meanwhile, many South American archaeologists have reached different conclusions based on their own quite different materials, which do not include Clovis points but do include many sites dated earlier than Clovis in widely separated parts of the continent (cf. Ardila, this volume; Bryan, 1986; Gruhn, this volume). Several North Americans (including C. V. Haynes 1987b) have suggested that people might somehow have traversed the oceans to South America, but the possibility of an Atlantic crossing is refuted by the fact that all biological affinities of Amerindians are with Asia (cf.

Greenberg et al. 1986; Laughlin and Harper 1988). The possibility of a successful trans-Pacific voyage during the Pleistocene is equally remote. The archaeology of Oceania indicates that although people made it by simple watercraft to Australia and New Guinea by about 50,000 years ago (White and O'Connell 1982), advanced watercraft (the outrigger canoe) were necessary to traverse the open Pacific Ocean (Bellwood 1978) and the process of peopling the far islands of the open Pacific did not start until the fifth millennium B.P. As pointed out forcefully by Griffin (1979), early Amerindians must have come via Beringia. Therefore, the only reasonable conclusion is that the ancestors of all native South Americans must have traversed North America from Northeast Asia. Thus there must be earlier sites in North America than the earliest known sites in South America. As there are several known adaptations to local environments in widely dispersed parts of South America by 13,000 years ago (cf. Bryan 1973, 1986), logically there should also be discrete adaptations to the diverse environments of North America by that time. Clovis remains the best known of these final Pleistocene adaptations in North America, but other cultural manifestations characterized by less diagnostic artifacts remain to be defined as soon as North American archaeologists recognize that the "Clovis first" myth is no longer able to explain a rapidly increasing body of evidence, especially from South America, which is directly relevant to the complex questions of who the first Americans were and how they adapted to the many diverse ecosystems they encountered as they gradually spread through the Western Hemisphere.

Although many archaeologists, after reviewing all the evidence for early sites throughout the Americas, have logically concluded that people may have been in North America for 20,000 or even 40,000 years, most open-minded scholars have been forced to admit that skeptics have always been able to cast doubt on any "pre-Clovis" claim (e.g., Wormington 1983). Although most skeptics cover themselves by stating that it is theoretically possible or even probable that people entered North America before the end of the Pleistocene, they nevertheless feel compelled by their basic *a priori* assumptions to find something wrong with all the so-called "pre-Clovis" claims. While scrutinizing all reports on "pre-Clovis" and equally early non-Clovis sites for some imperfection, they have accepted the fluted-point site reports without comparable criticism. The obvious reason for this double standard is because the skeptics are operating with the conviction that Clovis or perhaps something immediately pre-Clovis really is the earliest. Therefore, continued maintenance of the model requires that any report of a non-Clovis site evidently earlier than or even of equal antiquity to Clovis must somehow be wrong.

In order to cast doubt on any "pre-Clovis" report, skeptics operating with the conviction that Clovis constitutes the only demonstrated evidence for Pleistocene humans in the Americas and therefore must be the earliest apply what they claim is the scientific method of multiple working hypotheses by raising any imaginable question about the validity of the reported radiocarbon dates, the reported stratigraphy, or the report that artifacts and/or human-made features were recovered in proper contexts. In order to put a cloud over any reported "pre-Clovis" site, skeptics, most of whom have never visited the sites in question, suggest remote possibilities that might conceivably be true, such as that an object that looks like an artifact might have been flaked during a flood or an earthquake, or is the product of a waterfall; that the radiocarbon samples might have been contaminated by coal or ground water containing ancient carbonates; that people might have collected old wood to use in their fires; or that the artifacts might have been intruded from later deposits. Although all these "alternative hypotheses" might conceivably be true, in fact, the skeptics present no actual evidence to support their claim that they are true. Nevertheless, the skeptics insist that as long as at least one alternative hypothesis has been presented, then the original report must be considered as "equivocal." A reader usually interprets this statement to mean that the original report is probably in error and therefore should be dismissed.

In fact, this procedure constitutes misuse of the valuable method of multiple working hypotheses (Chamberlin 1965), which is to consider all alternative possibilities based on the actual field evidence and then choose the most reasonable possibility that most sufficiently fits the observed facts. But the method of multiple working hypotheses, when misapplied by injecting speculations that have no basis in fact because they were not observed in the field, can easily accomplish its goal of persuading other scholars that the reported data are suspect without the skeptic's ever visiting the site or having presented any actual new data. Furthermore, the statement by any skeptic of something that might have happened (although it left no evidence) is then often subsequently cited as if it were a fact by other skeptics, who often ignore relevant data to the contrary presented in the original descriptive site report or in subsequent reports in which the alternative possibilities were tested by further field work and rejected because no field evidence for the alternative possibility could be found. Thus the Clovis myth is further defended by the perpetual presentation of erroneous statements and by the omission of relevant data reported from the sites (see Gruhn [1988b], who shows how reported data from Taima-taima have been subjected to this procedure). Binford (1981:247) has forcefully criticized such unscholarly procedures as an easy logical short cut for replacing reported factual data with undemonstrated guesses rather than presenting new data based upon actual research.

I contend that this unproductive method must be

abandoned, as it is capable of forcing the disregarding of any reported data that do not fit a favored model; thus anomalies that conflict with the particular model are put aside, the weaknesses of the accepted model are not recognized, and no progress or change in conceptualization is allowed. In no way should this proposal be construed to imply that suggested alternative hypotheses should not be tested, only that the tests must be done by actual field (or laboratory) research. Many times, skeptics doubtful of the originally reported evidence (Bryan 1973) have been invited to re-excavate Taima-taima, but so far no North American archaeologists have visited the site during or after our 1976 excavations, which are fully published (Bryan et al. 1978; Gruhn and Bryan 1984; Ochsenius and Gruhn 1979). It seems obvious that the reason for the continued neglect of the evidence from this repeatedly dated 13,000-year-old site in Venezuela is because that dated evidence does not fit the "Clovis first" model. My presentation hopefully will make it clear that what is wrong is the generally accepted "Clovis is earliest" model, not what appear to be contrary data. We must consider alternative models which are able reasonably to explain properly reported data in all parts of the Western Hemisphere, not just in south-central North America. Such an explanatory model will be outlined at the end of this paper.

Critics often conclude that disproof of previously accepted claims (e.g., Tule Springs, Del Mar man, or the Old Crow hide scraper) mortally weakens the case for all "pre-Clovis" claims. It is to be expected that during the normal course of scientific advancement some of the reported data on early sites will be proven wrong by proper scientific methods of analysis in the field and the laboratory. Certainly there will be more examples of disproof of claims like Tule Springs, but there can be no acceptable shortcut to the process of proper scientific disproof of each claim by actual field and laboratory research.

The set of assumptions extrapolated from the inference that Clovis points were associated with the earliest Americans because they were consistently found at some dozen sites (Haynes 1970) with mammoth remains on the High Plains and in nearby environmentally similar areas, include the notions: (1) that fluted points, no matter where collected, can be used as horizon markers to identify the earliest projectile-point style in general use; and (2) that their widespread distribution throughout North America indicates the equally widespread presence of an economy based on specialized megamammal hunting, despite the fact that actual bones of large extinct mammals have been found associated with fluted points only at about a dozen sites on the Great Plains and adjacent environmentally similar areas. These assumptions formed the basis for defining a Paleoindian period in North America that preceded all other periods, and the derived concept of a universal economic stage characterized by big-game hunting, which was extrapolated throughout the Americas. It was further assumed: (3) that the Clovis mammoth hunters were members of a single cultural group that was directly or indirectly descended from northern Eurasian mammoth hunters (e.g., C. V. Haynes 1982, 1987a); and (4) that these predatory hunters must have had a specialized cold-adapted Upper Paleolithic (Haynes 1964, 1970) or advanced Middle Paleolithic level of technology (Müller-Beck 1967), in order to have traversed Siberia, crossed the Bering land bridge before it was inundated, and advanced southward through the inhospitable Ice-Free Corridor soon after it last appeared at the end of the Pleistocene. In the end, a universal stage of economic organization had been defined from distribution in limited parts of the Americas of a highly diagnostic bit of technology (fluted points), rather than from properly interpreted archaeological contexts reported from all parts of the Americas.

Fagan (1987) has produced the ultimate statement of the mythical model in a popular book that does not require proper academic citations for statements that purport to be factual. As an example of how maintenance of the myth has superseded the requirement for verifiable fact, Fagan (1987:177) states what he evidently believes to be a widely known fact—that there are "dozens" of sites demonstrating the association of Clovis points with extinct fauna. Associations of Clovis (or Folsom) points with extinct megafauna are in fact rare (Frison 1978:85; Haynes 1970), as well as being relatively restricted in geographical distribution (Wyoming, South Dakota, Colorado, Missouri, Oklahoma, Texas, New Mexico, plus the southeastern corners of Idaho and Arizona). Other skeptics (e.g., Dincauze 1984; Owen 1984; Stanford 1982; Waters 1985; West 1983), who criticize dozens of reports of so-called "pre-Clovis" sites, conveniently forget that very few Clovis sites have been excavated with extinct fauna, and so far only two of these have been described in published monographic reports (Frison and Todd 1986; Leonhardy 1966), although the Lehner site article (Haury et al. 1959) is complete enough to be a monograph. The Clovis type-site report (Hester 1972) is a compilation of short reports. The only Clovis point at Lubbock Lake was found out of context (Johnson 1988). So far, no one has published a critical analysis of the Clovis reports using the same criteria skeptics apply to discredit the much more numerous sites that do not fit the "Clovis first" model. Although there is no space here, such a critical analysis would reveal many problems, including lack of primary stratigraphic association between artifacts and material dated, arbitrary deselection of unfavorable dates, and ascriptive association by artifact typology to produce a "Clovis complex" at eroded sites. In the end, many, if not most, of the fluted-point sites would not meet the rigid "scientific" standards demanded by Dincauze (1984) and others for acceptance of early sites.

Not until Paul Martin transformed the "Clovis is

earliest" idea, which had been evolving for half a century, into a properly falsifiable hypothesis that also purported to explain the extinction of dozens of genera of late Pleistocene mammals, did archaeologists begin to see serious weaknesses in the model. Martin (1973) hypothesized that specialized predatory megamammal hunters rapidly advanced across eastern Beringia about 13,000 years ago and struggled through the frigid Ice-Free Corridor to arrive in Edmonton about 12,000 years ago. As they rapidly exterminated local herds of mammoths, horses, camels, and giant bison, these hunters spread out over North America and charged down the Central American funnel, pushing ever onward in their frantic pursuit of meat to arrive at the Straits of Magellan, where they wiped out the local horse population about 11,000 years ago. Mosimann and Martin (1975) demonstrated with a statistical model that this phenomenally rapid migration across many diverse environmental regions was theoretically possible, but some archaeologists realized that the scenario simply did not fit archaeological reality. However, other archaeologists, including several who had never previously been involved in the complex "early human problem," have ended up supporting the "Clovis first" model. With this unexpected but welcome support from several skeptics, Martin (1987) has boldly expressed his conviction that if we wait long enough all "pre-Clovis" sites will be shown to be wrong, and Clovis big-game hunters will continue to be the uncontested earliest Americans.

In fact the archaeological evidence does not support the conventional "Clovis first" model. Dates available for the few fluted points found in Alaska and the area of the Ice-Free Corridor are not early enough to be pre-Clovis or Clovis in age. Outside of the Great Plains and adjacent environmentally similar areas, there are no sites with primary association of Clovis points and remains of extinct megafauna, although this may be due mainly to lack of bone preservation in forested environments. No Clovis (and few similar non-waisted fluted) points have been found south of Panama (Bryan 1989). And south of the glaciated area of North America, in Central America and South America, a great many earlier radiocarbon-dated occupation sites feature lithic industries technologically unrelated to Clovis. I'll now review these facts.

First of all, no true fluted points have been found in Siberia, a fact which suggests that the land bridge may already have been submerged by the time Alaskan fluted points were being used. This situation is no problem if it is assumed that the technological predecessor of fluted points was a simple lanceolate or willow leaf-shaped form (e.g., MacNeish 1976), which is present in Siberian Late Paleolithic contexts dated 18,000 or more years ago (e.g., Mochanov 1978). Another problem is that Alaskan fluted points have never been found in contexts dated older than 11,400 years (Alexander 1987), whereas Martin's model suggests that they should be more than 12,000 years old in eastern Beringia. In fact, as Don Clark suggests (in this volume), it is more likely that fluted points spread northward from the northern Great Plains, where they are much more common than in Alaska. This hypothesis is supported by the recent discovery of a squat triangular fluted point in a 10,500-year-old context near Fort St. John, British Columbia, located in the Ice-Free Corridor (Fladmark et al. 1988). It should be noted that true Clovis points have never been found north of extreme southern Alberta, where they are very rare.

Although many archaeologists feel that these and other problems relegate Martin's "blitzkrieg" model to an unlikely if not actually disproven category, a variation of the model is nevertheless being maintained. As the vast majority of fluted points have been found east of the Rocky Mountains and south of the Laurentide ice sheet, the hypothesis first presented by Mason (1962) still seems tenable: that the fluted-point tradition was innovated somewhere east of the Rockies. But even Mason (1981) assumed that the technological antecedents of the fluted-point tradition should be discovered somewhere in eastern Beringia, perhaps in a context several thousand years older than Martin's model suggests. An extensive search for earlier contexts has been made in the interior valleys of the Yukon and Alaska, but with disappointing results, partly because of severe disturbance of archaeological contexts by frozen ground conditions. Also, large portions of this region remain inaccessible except by expensive helicopters. Nevertheless, some relevant finds have been reported.

Although strong suggestive evidence still exists for earlier human presence in the Old Crow Basin (Morlan 1986, 1987), the fact that both flaked-stone artifacts and undisturbed archaeological contexts are lacking means that these data are not relevant to the quest for Clovis technological origins. In Alaska lanceolate and triangular projectile points are present slightly before 11,000 yr B.P., in contexts with and without microblades (Alexander 1987; C. V. Haynes 1982, 1987a; Hoffecker 1985; Morlan 1987:see Table 2 for compilation of dates; Morlan and Cinq-Mars 1982; Powers and Hamilton 1978). Bluefish Caves, northern Yukon, have yielded the earliest dated stratigraphic contexts in eastern Beringia. Although original archaeological contexts have been disturbed by cryoturbation, a loess stratum containing butchered mammoth and horse bones as well as a mammoth-bone core and flake has been dated between 12,000 and 25,000 yr B.P., spanning the time that most archaeologists would expect proto-Clovis remains to occur in the area (Morlan 1987).

No bifacial projectile points have been recovered from Bluefish Caves, however. Other than burins, the only technologically diagnostic artifacts are microblades and a microblade core found a meter from the mammoth bones from a zone dateable between 10,000 and 15,000 yr B.P. (J. Cinq-Mars and R. Morlan, personal communications 1987, 1990). Cinq-Mars and Morlan operate with the reasonable hypothesis that the microblades were mounted as lateral barbs into grooved antler or bone projectile points, like those in the Trail Creek Caves on the Seward Peninsula (Larsen 1968) and at various Late Paleolithic sites in Siberia. They also hypothesize that the microblade technology at the Bluefish and Trail Creek Caves is closely related to and possibly stems from the Dyuktai complex, well dated between 18,000 and 12,000 yr B.P. in Dyuktai Cave and possibly earlier at other sites on the Aldan River (Mochanov 1978).

In fact, the distinctive technology for removing microblades from wedge-shaped and other specialized cores is the only diagnostic flaking technique that is clearly traceable by more or less continuous distribution in space and time from Northeast Asia (Japan, North China, and eastern Siberia) into northwestern America (e.g., Aikens and Dumond 1986). The technological tradition has been found in contexts dated about 10,000 yr B.P. in central and southeastern Alaska, and soon thereafter on the north coast of British Columbia, but it seems to have petered out in the arid Columbia Basin after 6500 yr B.P. and on the southern British Columbian coast about 1500 yr B.P. (Carlson 1983:91). The technological tradition of removing microblades from specialized cores also persisted for many millennia in interior Alaska, where it eventually became incorporated into the Northwest Microblade tradition, which is apparently proto-Athabaskan, and the Arctic Small Tool tradition, which is probably proto-Eskimo. Both of these cultural traditions spread eastward into northern Canada long after the continental glaciers had melted.

But significantly, the microblade/specialized-core tradition is not part of the Clovis complex. C. V. Haynes (1970, 1982, 1987a) recognized this fact, but hypothesized that two cultural groups occupied the interior of eastern Beringia at the same time, and that one of these groups, the Clovis (or proto-Clovis) people, never used microblades in Beringia or elsewhere. C. V. Haynes (1987a) hypothesized that the ancestors of Clovis were European Upper Paleolithic mammoth hunters who mixed with Mongoloids genetically when they moved through Siberia but did not accept the microblade technological tradition from them. He hypothesized that these people used lanceolate points but not microblades in Alaska prior to 11,500 yr B.P. and soon thereafter innovated the concept of fluting in the Ice-Free Corridor or on the northern Plains. Certainly the easily procured caribou must always have been a major game animal for any hunters occupying eastern Beringia as well as the Laurentide ice margins. Probably the almost continuous temporal and spatial distribution of the distinctive microblade/specialized-core tradition in Northeast Asia, northwestern North America, and ultimately across northern Canada to Greenland was for many millennia (starting in "pre-Clovis" times) an integral part of caribou-hunting technology. In contrast is the absence of microblades made on specialized cores in northeastern fluted-point sites, where Clovis hunters evidently hunted caribou from southern Ontario to Nova Scotia and New England (Spiess 1984). It seems unlikely to me that Clovis caribou hunters would resist accepting a demonstrably successful ancient technology for hunting caribou as they moved from central Siberia across Beringia and into north-central and northeastern North America. Rather, it seems more likely that if the predecessors of Clovis were in eastern Beringia sometime prior to 12,000 yr B.P., then their immediate descendants, who evidently continued to hunt caribou along the margins of the Laurentide glaciers, should still have been fabricating microblades, which persisted for so many more millennia among caribou hunters across the North American Arctic and Subarctic. I suggest that the significant temporal and spatial distribution of the distinctive microblade/specialized-core tradition renders improbable the hypothesis that Clovis or even proto-Clovis came from interior eastern Beringia; and puts into reasonable light an alternative model, which also would explain why the search for the immediate technological antecedents of the Clovis complex in Beringia or Northeast Asia has been so disappointing.

My alternative hypothesis is that the fluted-point tradition developed indigenously in the southeastern quarter of North America from technological antecedents that may have included unifacially retouched projectile points made on flakes or macroblades, or a transference from bone or antler projectile points. I hypothesize that bifacial projectile points evolved rapidly in the Southeast analogous to the way that bifacial Solutrean points developed from unifacial antecedents in southwestern France (Bordes 1960; Smith 1964) long after the ancient tradition of making bifaces (handaxes) had disappeared from southwestern Europe. After a prolonged search farther east for the origins of Solutrean, archaeologists working in France eventually realized that these distinctive points had evolved right in southwestern France, where they are most numerous. A major difference between the two areas is that Solutrean points died out without spreading very far, while basally fluted points became accepted as an effective part of hunting technology by many groups throughout much of North and Central America. Clovis points proved to be effective for hunting mammoth and giant bison on the High Plains, but they were replaced there by other more efficient point styles soon after 11,000 yr B.P. (Frison 1978). Also, the fact should not be overlooked that specialized hunting of herd mammals, particularly bison, continued to be the only viable way to make a living on the High Plains until the advent of the steel plow and the barbed wire fence (cf. Bryan 1977). The High Plains, and much later the High Arctic, were unusually restrictive North American ecosystems (containing a relatively limited number of edible species of plants and animals) in which a highly specialized technology had to be developed as an integral part of the only prehistoric economic adaptation (specialized hunting) that could maintain occupation of the area without starvation.

I hypothesize that, as subsequently occurred in the High Arctic, this kind of specialized hunting adaptation was a relatively late development. As Mason (1962, 1981) suggested, the spatial and temporal distribution of fluted points south of the continental glaciers indicates an origin for Clovis somewhere in the United States east of the Great Plains. I predict that the association of proto-Clovis with Pleistocene taxa will be demonstrated in the area from Florida to Texas after relevant archaeological contexts have been securely dated (see Dunbar, this volume). From the Gulf Coast, some proto-Clovis foragers moved (perhaps seasonally) north to the thinly forested zone south of the Laurentide glacier to take advantage of the predictable seasonal caribou migrations; while other Clovis hunters seasonally occupied the Great Plains, where eastern foragers had learned to predict where bison could be hunted seasonally and also to take advantage of mammoths congregated at water holes because they were suffering greatly from the abrupt change in climate at the end of the Pleistocene (cf. G. Haynes 1987).

Elsewhere, in ecosystems containing a greater diversity of edible species of plants and animals, people, including fluted-point makers, continued their much more viable general-foraging way of life. These general foragers continued to hunt isolated large mammals in forested or desert regions whenever the opportunity arose. In many of these areas (e.g., the Great Basin, California, eastern woodlands), fluted-point forms continued to be used by general foragers much longer than on the Great Plains, where the necessarily specialized bison hunters were constantly experimenting with more effective hunting techniques, including innovation of ever more efficient projectile-point forms (Bryan 1980, 1988; cf. Musil 1988).

By the mid-1970s I had realized that the radiocarbon dates of between 10,000 and 12,000 yr B.P. from Smith Creek Cave in the central Great Basin meant that willow leaf-shaped and/or stemmed points designed for insertion into socketed hafts and used for hunting mountain sheep (as well as bison and camel) had been employed by foragers adapted to the Great Basin at the same time as Clovis hunters were pursuing mammoths on the Great Plains (Bryan 1979). Thompson (1985) placed the reported data from Smith Creek Cave under a cloud after presenting his explanation of why there was a discrepancy between the radiocarbon dates (12,000–10,000 yr B.P.) on the archaeological materials recovered from cultural contexts and similar dates (13,000–10,500 yr B.P.) on macrofossils from nearby packrat nests, in that the packrat nests contain bristlecone pine remains (Thompson and Mead 1982:Table 1) while bristlecone remains were excavated only from a stratum underlying the Mount Moriah occupation zone. Thompson claims that my radiocarbon dates earlier than 11,000 years from the Mount Moriah occupation zone must be too early, while all his dates are correct. I have shown (Bryan 1988) that careful perusal of my original report, including the main profile, should have revealed to Thompson that the more likely explanation for the discrepancy is because his relatively recent packrats had collected bristlecone and other early plant remains (used by Thompson to obtain dates and to reconstruct past environments) for nest building that were recycled by recent ground squirrels burrowing into stratigraphically older deposits. To resolve the controversy as to which interpretation explains the discrepancy, all dates from Smith Creek Cave should be confirmed. Thompson should confirm his dates by obtaining dates only on fecal pellets deposited by the nest builders, as the wood rats should have eaten mainly fresh plant remains collected from their contemporary living environment and only rarely, if ever, ancient plant macrofossils.

To confirm the range of the three dates (12,150, 11,680, and 10,700 yr B.P.) on wood and charcoal from the 1- to 12-cm-thick stratum of wood ash and silt deposited in a restricted area during periodic reoccupations of the cave by sheep hunters, I obtained accelerator dates on hair samples—10,840 ± 250 yr B.P. (RIDDL-795) on bovid and 12,060 ± 450 yr B.P. (RIDDL-797) on camelid—directly associated with stemmed point bases and other artifacts, in the main Mount Moriah occupation layer. I also recently obtained a date of 10,420 ± 100 yr B.P. (TO-1173) on a segment of double ply S-twist *Apocynum* cordage. All these dates on different materials confirm the range of original dates obtained on charcoal and wood. Evidently, Mount Moriah foragers first occupied Smith Creek Cave about 12,000 yr B.P., before Clovis hunters first occupied the High Plains, and kept returning to the cave until about 10,000 years ago.

I long refrained from presenting my hypothesis of an indigenous development of at least two distinctive projectile-point traditions in North America because there was no clear temporal and spatial break in distribution of bifacial projectile points between North America and Siberia. It remained possible, as many authors had hypothesized, for leaf-shaped or narrow lanceolate points from Siberia to have spread down the western cordilleras and stimulated the development of the stemmed-point tradition as well as other projectile-point forms. I thought that possibly the apparent lack of willow leaf-shaped points in the earliest eastern Beringian sites might be rectified by further work, but to my knowledge willow leaf-shaped points still have not been found there in contexts dated earlier than about 7300 years ago, while lanceolate point styles are no earlier than about 11,800 years ago.

The main problem with trying to demonstrate migration by deriving vaguely similar bifacial projectile-point forms or any other technological trait (e.g., macroblades, burins, end scrapers) known to be early in North America from somewhere in Europe or eastern Asia (e.g., C. V. Haynes 1987a; West 1983) is that it is essential to demonstrate that there was more or less continuous geographical distribution of the technology, as well as an appropriate temporal sequence showing movement from west to east. Such a continuous distribution of a diagnostic technological tradition has been shown only for microblades made on specialized cores. In the case of North American willow leaf-shaped points, the distribution in space and time indicates that willow leaf-shaped points followed fluted points north to Alaska (cf. Bryan 1980). A better case can be made that narrow lanceolate points from early contexts in Alaska (e.g., Alexander 1987; Hoffecker 1985) are somehow related to stemmed points from Kamchatka in one direction and stemmed points from the Intermontane West in the other direction, as Dikov (1988) has hypothesized. At this time, however, I think that the intervening distances are too great, and that the 11,000-year-old lanceolate points in central Alaska were part of a separate local indigenous development of a hunting adaptation before fluted points had diffused northward.

I believe that the evidence for a prolonged technological break between eastern Beringia and subglacial North America is now conclusive enough to be able to present the working hypothesis that the stemmed-point tradition (which includes willow leaf-shaped points because they all have a similar constricted base intended for insertion into a socketed haft) were developed independently by 12,000 years ago south of the continental glaciers in the Intermontane West, while the fluted-point tradition evolved east of the Rockies at about the same time (Bryan 1988). Determining which developed first is not as important as determining what ecological and economic factors stimulated these technological innovations.

The hypothesis of separate origins of fluted and stemmed points implies a model of multilinear evolution of separate (technological) traditions that culminated in several indigenous developments of bifacial projectile points in different parts of North America (cf. Bryan 1977, 1978). Also fitting such a model is the hypothesis of Aikens and Dumond (1986:164) that parallel adaptations to comparable environments by people with a common heritage in Japan and western North America led to convergent development of willow leaf-shaped points in the two areas about 14,000 yr B.P. From an even broader geographical perspective, I have hypothesized that similar convergent developments of bifacial projectile points occurred in several geographically separated late Pleistocene ecosystems in Northeast Asia and the Americas between about 18,000 and 11,000 yr B.P. (Bryan 1990). Of these convergent developments, Clovis was the most spectacular and the fluted-point tradition the most widespread. Because of their spectacular beauty, Clovis fluted points have garnered a disproportionate share of attention by archaeologists as well as the general public.

While pursuing the problem of the original peopling of the Americas in the region of the Ice-Free Corridor (Alberta), I realized that the story of the association of bifacial projectile points and extinct mammals in North America could never be fully comprehended without taking into consideration similar associations in South America, simply because the ancestral South Americans must have come from North America. I therefore decided that in order to comprehend the complex problem of the peopling of North America it was essential to visit all reported early sites in Central and South America. This goal was accomplished during the sabbatical year of 1969/70. I first considered the feasibility of my alternative hypothesis for Clovis origins in 1970 after visiting South American sites, including Taima-taima, El Inga, Tagua Tagua, and Fell's Cave. Available evidence I saw in South America led me to hypothesize in 1973 that at least two distinctive bifacial projectile-point traditions had developed indigenously at opposite ends of the southern continent (Bryan 1973) as effective means for hunting large mammals—El Jobo points for hunting mastodons 13,000 years ago and the Magellanic "fishtail" points for hunting horses and camelids 11,000 years ago in Patagonia, a very similar environment to the North American High Plains.

In order to extend the model of a "universal" specialized big-game hunting (Paleoindian) horizon (or developmental stage) into South America, fishtail points, whether or not fluted, have usually been assumed to belong to or be derived from the fluted-point tradition, which is thought to represent incursion into the continent of specialized big-game hunters. Lynch (1978:469; 1983:103) believes that Clovis hunters were the first South Americans, and he cannot accept that people in South America could have independently invented bifacial projectile points at about the same time that North American Paleoindians were using bifacial points (Lynch 1983:103). Schobinger (1988:204–212) accepts the abundant evidence that there were earlier general foragers but believes that these foragers adopted a big-game hunting economy and technology from new North American immigrants. Lynch's hypothesis that fluted points are found throughout the Andes and in southern South America is based on the collection from El Inga and three examples from Fell's Cave (Bird 1969:Figure 2–1,2). As pointed out by Politis (in this volume), the pseudo-fluting of fishtail points from southern South America is due either to basal thinning or utilizing the facet on the original flake blank. Rouse (1976) first recognized that the 9000-year-old radiocarbon date at El Inga implied that the Magellanic fishtail-point form (dated at 11,000 yr B.P. in Fell's Cave) had spread northward from Patagonia. I hypothesize that the presence of fluted fish-

Figure 2. Sites mentioned in South America. **1)** El Inga; **2)** Los Toldos; **3)** Pikimachay; **4)** Pachamachay; **5)** Taima-taima; **6)** Tagua Tagua; **7)** Tibitó (and El Abra); **8)** Fell's Cave and Las Buitreras; **9)** Monte Verde.

tail points at El Inga, as well as at several undated localities in northwestern South America and Central America, can best be explained as a melding of the southward-diffusing technique of fluting onto the northward-diffusing fishtail-point form, rather than as an independent development of the distinctive technological tradition of fluting in South America (cf. Mayer-Oakes 1986) when it is absent elsewhere in the world. The rare bifacial projectile points known from the critical Panamanian funnel are either Clovis-like or fishtail-fluted forms, but, importantly, willow leaf-shaped points have never been reported from Panama (Bryan 1986, 1989). If willow leaf-shaped points are absent in Panama, the hypothesis is strengthened that the distinctive thick, willow leaf-shaped El Jobo points developed quite independently by 13,000 yr B.P. in northern Venezuela, without stimulus from farther north.

Subsequent excavations at Taima-taima in 1976 confirmed the site as the only known definite mastodon kill site in South America and substantiated my earlier conclusion (Bryan 1973) that the killing had occurred about 13,000 years ago, more than a millennium before mammoths were dispatched by Clovis points on the Great Plains (Bryan et al. 1978; Gruhn and Bryan 1984; Ochsenius and Gruhn 1979). Also relevant is the fact that bifacial projectile points have not been found with the Abriense industry, which was used by general foragers on the Sabana de Bogotá and is radiocarbon dated at several sites between 12,500 and 5000 yr B.P. (Ardila, this volume). The absence of El Jobo points in early highland Colombian sites, even at Tibitó, where people processed remains of mastodons and horses but mainly deer 11,740 ± 110 years ago (Correal 1981, 1986), means that, unlike Clovis, El Jobo points had a very restricted temporal and geographic distribution but, like Clovis, as yet no demonstrated technological predecessors (Bryan 1987). Rouse and Cruxent's (1963) hypothesized technological sequence from thick bifaces to refined bifaces to El Jobo points may well be correct, but the hypothesis remains to be demonstrated stratigraphically.

Several other sites in the Andean region have yielded artifacts in association with extinct fauna. These include Pikimachay Cave, where subtriangular ground-bone points and simple unifacial stone artifacts were found with sloth and horse bones in a context dated 14,150 ± 180 yr B.P. Earlier cultural contexts are possible, but more difficult to demonstrate (MacNeish et al. 1981). Simple flake artifacts were recovered with horse and mastodon at Tagua Tagua in central Chile from a layer dated 11,380 ± 320 yr B.P. (Montané 1968). Farther south in the subantarctic rain forest, mastodon bones first attracted attention to the Monte Verde locality, but subsequent excavation of this unique wet site has indicated that the bones had simply been collected for use. The site was a small settlement where most artifacts, including rectangular structures, were made of wood, although two large stone bifaces were recovered in addition to grooved bolas stones and simple flake tools. This occupation, dated about 13,000 yr B.P., is in a stratum above an earlier occupation level containing simple flake tools and hammerstones associated with charcoal dated to 33,000 yr B.P. (Collins and Dillehay 1986; Dillehay 1986, 1989; Dillehay and Collins 1987). Despite the presence of extinct animal remains, none of these Andean sites has produced actual evidence that the occupants were specialized big-game hunters. Rather, these early Andean people appear to have been general foragers who occasionally took advantage of locally available large mammals in addition to smaller mammals.

On the 4,000-m-high *puna* of Junin in central Peru, Rick (1980) found evidence for a specialized adaptation to hunting vicuña herds supplemented by some plant-food collecting that persisted into ceramic times. Rick (1980:65–67) indicated his earliest date of 11,800 yr B.P. was "probably correct," but he has been reluctant to conclude that Pachamachay had a "pre-Clovis" occupation. Although no extinct fauna have been identified at the cave of Pachamachay, clearly the most effective adaptation to this barren area containing limited edible species was to learn to coexist with herds of a small camelid that could be hunted locally throughout the year with bifacially flaked points. Point types in this area began as squat triangular forms but soon evolved into distinctive leaf-shaped points with lateral spurs. This leaf-shaped point tradition persisted with minor stylistic changes for many millennia, with little evidence for external contact.

In southern Patagonia evidence suggests that a similar economic adaptation emphasizing intensive hunting of herd animals was being developed before the local innovation of bifacial projectile points. The main difference is that extinct equids and camelids, as well as guanacos, were found in a layer dated 12,600 yr B.P. at Los Toldos Cave 3 with unifacially retouched artifacts, including subtriangular points (Cardich 1978:298–299; Cardich et al. 1973). Farther south in Buitreras Cave, a similar unifacial stone industry was recovered from an undated context with evidence that the people trapped ground sloths in the cave (Borrero 1986; Caviglia et al. 1986; Mengoni 1986). Evidently, early Patagonians were utilizing whatever game animals were locally available even before they developed more effective bifacial projectile points. By about 11,000 years ago the occupants of Los Toldos Cave 3 had innovated triangular bifacial projectile points and knives, in addition to well-shaped side and end scrapers. Camelids, both extinct and modern, as well as equids and rheas were evidently hunted (Cardich 1978). Farther south, in Fell's Cave, by 11,000 yr B.P. people hunted horses, guanacos, rheas, and probably sloths with Magellanic fishtail points (Bird 1969).

I hypothesize from these data that it was only at the end of the Pleistocene that people were able to occupy permanently the interior of southern Patagonia and the high *puna* (as well as the High Plains of North America) because the limited number of species of edible plants and animals meant that the foragers who tentatively ventured into these harsh grassland environments first had to develop an economic adaptation to hunting herd animals in order to survive. In other less restrictive ecosystems near other productive environments, including the Sabana de Bogotá and the Chilean subantarctic rain forest, a successful general-foraging economy, which did not require the innovation of bifacial projectile points, could be maintained. In other words, there is little evidence in South America to support the model of a "universal" Paleoindian big-game hunting stage. Rather, general foragers developed viable economic adaptations to local ecosystems, and only a few of those adaptations included specialized flaked-stone technologies as parts of adaptations to hunting herd animals. In most areas, particularly in the forested lowlands, people continued into ceramic times to utilize an ancient simple flaked-stone technology, which could easily be adapted to utilize a wide variety of available plants and animals.

With all these data in mind, let us consider what might have happened to American archaeological thinking and modeling if the history of research had transpired differently. Let us suppose that there had been just as many archaeologists working in South America as in North America throughout this century. Then let us suppose that Tibitó, not Folsom, had yielded the first definite association of artifacts with extinct fauna excavated in the Americas, and that subsequently several other sites in the Andean region confirmed the evidence that these early people evidently had been general foragers who hunted many species, including some now extinct. Eventually, radiocarbon dates would have confirmed that the association of artifacts with extinct fauna meant that people occupied the Sabana de Bogotá in late Pleistocene times. Also, the advent of radiocarbon dating would have shown that some sites, like Pachamachay, were occupied just as early as Tibitó, even though no evidence was found for extinct species, perhaps because none occupied the area at that time. The people living in Pachamachay learned to adapt to a harsh environment by managing local herds of vicuña. Radiocarbon dates would show that bifacially flaked-stone projectile points appeared earliest in northwestern Venezuela, where people in an arid environment evidently took advantage of mastodons congregated around water holes, while people in southern Patagonia learned to trap sloths in caves and to predict where herds of horses and guanacos and flocks of rheas might be intercepted. In northwestern Venezuela, the specialized El Jobo points evidently dropped out of use after the mastodons had been killed off, but the survival of vicuñas on the *punas,* and guanacos and rheas in Patagonia assured the survival of bifacial projectile points after the ground sloths, horses, and extinct species of camelids were gone.

After the advent of radiocarbon dating, Brazilian archaeologists would have been able to incorporate their data on a wide variety of unspecialized lithic industries into the emerging picture of the late Pleistocene occupation of South America. Many sites exist in Brazil in which simple amorphous or unifacial flaked-stone industries used by general foragers are only occasionally associated with extinct fauna, but nevertheless date to the Pleistocene (see Gruhn, this volume).

After digesting all these data, South American archaeologists would have developed a model that the original South American colonists were general foragers who had adapted themselves to all major environmental regions of the continent before the end of the Pleistocene. These early foragers hunted locally available animals, but they specialized in hunting congregations of mammals of various sizes whenever they realized they could easily improve or stabilize their standard of living, as in northwestern Venezuela and on the high *puna;* or they were forced to specialize in hunting certain species of animals that ran in herds or flocks in order to survive in a harsh environment like interior Patagonia. One hypothesis stemming from the emerging model would be that the number and diversity of specialized adaptations to particular ecological niches throughout South America imply that there must have been a considerable amount of time since general foragers first entered the continent.

Looking northward for origins, South American archaeologists aware of all their data would not have been searching for evidence of specialized hunting economies but rather for earlier evidence of general foragers in North America. They would readily recognize that the specialized bison-hunting economy which persisted on the Great Plains for nearly a dozen millennia was simply an essential adaptation by general foragers to a harsh environment that supported relatively few species of edible plants and animals, an adaptation like that made to the restrictive environment of interior southern Patagonia or the high *puna.*

Because they would be sure there must be earlier sites in North America containing simple flaked-stone industries, South American archaeologists would be surprised, if not dismayed, that North American archaeologists were looking back to Siberia for Clovis origins without seriously considering as relevant the evidence for diverse adaptations to different ecosystems in South America. South American archaeologists would also be amazed that North American archaeologists had been consistently claiming that there must be something wrong with all the reported sites (cf. Schobinger 1988:431), which indicate that general foragers using simple flaked-stone industries had occupied much of North America before specialized big-game hunting appeared on the Great Plains about 11,500 years ago. The South American archaeologists would then try to convince their North American colleagues that there really should be earlier sites in North America containing simple flaked-stone technologies in order to provide ancestral traditions for the similar repeatedly confirmed early South American data (Schobinger 1988:88–90). Only by working together with a hemisphere-wide perspective would all American archaeologists be able to give full consideration to the available evidence for an original general-foraging economy and an associated unspecialized flaked-stone technology in Pleistocene contexts in North America as well as South America. After reaching this conclusion, they would turn their attention to western North America and northeastern Asia to find the ultimate source of the unsophisticated basic flaked-stone technology employed by the earliest Americans.

Once it was realized that a specialized big-game hunting economy developed only in those areas of North America having naturally limiting ecosystems, it could be more readily seen that the route pursued by the original foragers would not likely have been through the interior of Beringia and down the Ice-Free Corridor with its extremely limiting environmental conditions characterized by treeless tundra, frozen lakes, and high winds (Schweger and Mandryk 1986). Rather, much more likely, specialized hunters expanded their territory northward into the Ice-Free Corridor later, at the end of the Pleistocene, in pursuit of caribou and bison herds after the mammoths had become extinct on the Plains.

This view leaves the southern shore of Beringia and the Northwest Coast as the most reasonable route of initial entry into America. Fladmark's (1978, 1979) persuasive arguments for an early adaptation to the Northwest Coast can be extended to the rich maritime resources of the southern shores of Beringia (Laughlin and Harper 1988:25–27) relative to the ecologically restrictive interior steppe tundra. The problem, of course, is that it is unlikely that archaeologists will be able to find this evidence for early foraging either in the Bering Sea region or on the outer continental shelf beyond the reach of the Cordilleran glaciers because most of the formerly occupiable areas now lie beneath the postglacial rise in sea level. A concerted effort should be made to look for areas of tectonic uplift that may preserve the evidence on the Northwest Coast, although a much easier approach would be to look south of the glaciated regions where people should have expanded their foraging territories up the rivers.

Although archaeological evidence for the earliest occupation of the Northwest Coast will probably never be recovered, it is known that between about 27,000 and 13,000 yr B.P., the coasts of southern Alaska and British Columbia were heavily glaciated, leaving only a few refugia. Although it is possible that previously well-adapted occupants survived in some refugia, it is unlikely that migrants would have expanded their territory into such difficult ecosystems. It is more likely that northeast Asian coastal-adapted people gradually expanded their foraging territory along the southern shores of Beringia and advanced down the unglaciated outer coast of northwestern North America during the early mid-Wisconsinan, when environmental conditions were very similar to those of the present day (cf. Gruhn 1989). Initial movement through southern Alaska prior to 50,000 yr B.P. would allow ample time for littoral-adapted foragers to continue expanding their territories along the Pacific Coast into South America before 40,000 years ago, thus making reasonable the reported occupations of southern Chile and northeastern Brazil before 30,000 years ago.

In a review of language diversification in different areas of the Americas, Gruhn (1988a) has hypothesized that some of these early littoral-adapted foragers expanded from the Pacific Coast through Central America to the Caribbean, and then spread northward around the Gulf of Mexico before their descendants penetrated the remainder of the eastern woodlands. If this model is correct, the best places to look for early North American sites should be in Oregon, California, and western Mexico, while the earliest sites east of the continental divide should be near the Gulf Coast of Mexico and in southern Texas. This model would predict that the High Plains should have been one of the last regions of the Americas to have been occupied, because it is far from any coast; and sufficient time would have been required for indigenous development of a specialized hunting economy and technology. Based on South American evidence, this model also would predict that unspecialized flake and core tools, many with unifacially retouched high-angled edges designed for working wood, should be recognized in North American Pleistocene contexts.

Gruhn (1988a) has reviewed some of the archaeological evidence that is already available to support the coastal-entry model. This model makes sense of highly diverse "pre-Clovis" and early non-Clovis sites reportedly found throughout the Americas, sites which the defenders of the "Clovis first" model are forced to explain away. It is time to recognize that the "Clovis first" model is an archaeological myth, and move on to consider alternative models that will help to explain the actual field and laboratory data and thereby allow progress in our conceptualization of the complex story of early human economic adaptations and cultural developments within the New World.

ACKNOWLEDGMENTS

I would like to thank Mark Druss, Ruth Gruhn, Ray LeBlanc, Charles Schweger, and Marie Wormington, as well as two unidentified referees, for their constructive criticisms of drafts of this paper. I accepted most but not all of their suggestions, and accept full responsibility for the final version.

REFERENCES CITED

Aikens, C. M., and D. E. Dumond
1986 Convergence and Common Heritage; Some Parallels in the Archaeology of Japan and Western North America. In *Windows on the Japanese Past: Studies in Archaeology and Prehistory*, edited by R. J. Pearson, pp. 163–178. Center for Japanese Studies, University of Michigan, Ann Arbor.

Alexander, H. L.
1987 *Putu: A Fluted Point Site in Alaska.* Simon Fraser University Publication No. 17. Archaeology Press, Simon Fraser University, Burnaby.

Bedwell, S. F.
1973 *Fort Rock Basin, Prehistory and Environment.* University of Oregon Books, Eugene.

Bellwood, P. S.
1978 *Man's Conquest of the Pacific.* Collins, Auckland.

Binford, L. R.
1981 *Bones: Ancient Men and Modern Myths.* Academic Press, New York.

Bird, J. B.
1969 A Comparison of South Chilean and Ecuadorian "Fishtail" Projectile Points. *The Kroeber Anthropological Society Papers* 40:52–71. Berkeley.

Bordes, F. H.
1960 Evolution in the Paleolithic Cultures. In *Evolution After Darwin, Volume 2, The Evolution of Man,* edited by S. Tax, pp. 99–110. University of Chicago Press, Chicago.

Borrero, L. A.
1986 Cazadores de *Mylodon* en la Patagonia Austral. In *New Evidence for the Pleistocene Peopling of the America,* edited by A. L. Bryan, pp. 281–294. Center for the Study of Early Man, University of Maine, Orono.

Bryan, A. L.
1969 Early man in America and the Late Pleistocene Chronology of Western Canada and Alaska. *Current Anthropology* 10:339–365.

1973 Paleoenvironments and Cultural Diversity in Late Pleistocene South America. *Quaternary Research* 3:237–256.

1977 Developmental Stages and Technological Traditions. In *Amerinds and their Paleoenvironments in Northeastern North America,* edited by W. S. Newman and B. Salwen, pp. 355–368. Annals of the New York Academy of Sciences 288.

1978 An Overview of Paleo-American Prehistory from a Circum-Pacific Perspective. In *Early Man in America from a Circum-Pacific Perspective,* edited by A. L. Bryan, pp. 306–327. Occasional Papers No. 1. Department of Anthropology, University of Alberta, Edmonton.

1979 Smith Creek Cave. In *The Archaeology of Smith Creek Canyon, Eastern Nevada,* edited by D. R. Tuohy and D. L. Rendall, pp. 162–251. Nevada State Museum Anthropological Papers No. 17. Carson City.

1980 The Stemmed Point Tradition: An Early Technological Tradition in Western North America. In *Anthropological Papers in Memory of Earl H. Swanson, Jr.,* edited by L. B. Harten, C. N. Warren, and D. R. Tuohy, pp. 77–107. Special Publication of the Idaho State Museum of Natural History, Pocatello.

1986 Paleoamerican Prehistory as seen from South America. In *New Evidence for the Pleistocene Peopling of the Americas,* edited by A. L. Bryan, pp. 1–14. Center for the Study of Early Man, University of Maine, Orono.

1987 The First Americans: Points of Order. *Natural History* 6/87:6–11.

1988 The Relationship of the Stemmed Point and Fluted Point Traditions in the Great Basin. In *Early Human Occupation in Far Western North America: The Clovis-Archaic Interface,* edited by J. A. Willig, C. M. Aikens and J. L. Fagan, pp. 53–74. Nevada State Museum Anthropological Papers No. 21. Carson City.

1989 The Central American Filter Funnel: Earliest American Adaptation to Tropical Forests. Paper presented at the Circum-Pacific Prehistory Conference, Seattle, to be published in, *Routes into the New World,* edited by R. E. Ackerman. Washington State University Press, Pullman.

1990 The Pattern of Late Pleistocene Cultural Diversity in Asia and the Americas. In *Chronostratigraphy of the Paleolithic in North, Central, East Asia and America,* pp. 3–8. Institute of History, Philogy, and Philosophy, Siberian Branch, USSR Academy of Sciences, Novosibirsk.

Bryan, A. L. (editor)
1986 *New Evidence for the Pleistocene Peopling of the Americas.* Center for the Study of Early Man, University of Maine, Orono.

Bryan, A. L., R. M. Casamiquela, J. M. Cruxent, R. Gruhn, and C. Ochsenius
1978 An El Jobo Mastodon Kill at Taima-taima, Venezuela. *Science* 200:1275–1277.

Cardich, A.
1978 Recent Excavations at Lauricocha (Central Andes) and Los Toldos (Patagonia). In *Early Man in America from a Circum-Pacific Perspective,* edited by A. L. Bryan, pp. 296–300. Occasional Papers No. 1. Department of Anthropology, University of Alberta, Edmonton.

Cardich, A., L. A. Cardich, y A. Hajduk
1973 Secuencia Arqueológica y Cronológica Radiocarbónica de la Cueva 3 de Los Toldos (Santa Cruz). *Relaciones de la Sociedad Argentina de Antropología* VII:85–123. Buenos Aires.

Carlson, R. L.
1983 The Far West. In *Early Man in the New World,* edited by R. Shutler, Jr., pp. 73–96. Sage Publications, Beverly Hills.

Caviglia, S. E., H. D. Yacobacchio, y L. A. Borrero
1986 Las Buitreras: Convivencia del Hombre con Fauna Extinta en Patagonia Meridional. In *New Evidence for the Pleistocene Peopling of the Ameri-*

cas, edited by A. L. Bryan, pp. 295–317. Center for the Study of Early Man, University of Maine, Orono.

Chamberlin, T. C.
1965 The Method of Multiple Working Hypotheses. *Science* 148:754–759.

Collins, M. B., and T. D. Dillehay
1986 The Implications of the Lithic Assemblage from Monte Verde for Early Man studies. In *New Evidence for the Pleistocene Peopling of the Americas,* edited by A. L. Bryan, pp. 339–355. Center for the Study of Early Man, University of Maine, Orono.

Correal Urrego, G.
1981 *Evidencias Culturales y Megafauna Pleistocénica en Colombia.* Banco de la Republica, Bogotá.

1986 Apuntes Sobre el Medio Ambiente Pleistocénico y el Hombre Prehistórico en Colombia. In *New Evidence for the Pleistocene Peopling of the Americas,* edited by A. L. Bryan, pp. 115–131. Center for the Study of Early Man, University of Maine, Orono.

Dikov, N. N.
1988 On the Road to America. The First Americans. *Natural History* 1/88:10–14.

Dillehay, T. D.
1986 The Cultural Relationships of Monte Verde: A Late Pleistocene Settlement Site in the Subantarctic Forest of South Central Chile. In *New Evidence for the Pleistocene Peopling of the Americas,* edited by A. L. Bryan, pp. 319–337. Center for the Study of Early Man, University of Maine, Orono.

Dillehay, T. D., and M. Collins
1987 Early Cultural Evidence from Monte Verde in Chile. *Nature* 332:150–152.

Dincauze, D.
1984 An Archaeo-logical Evaluation of the Case for Pre-Clovis Occupations. *Advances in World Archaeology* 3:275–323.

Fagan, B. M.
1987 *The Great Journey: The Peopling of Ancient America.* Thames and Hudson, London.

Fladmark, K. R.
1978 The Feasibility of the Northwest Coast as a Migration Route for Early Man. In *Early Man in America from a Circum-Pacific Perspective,* edited by A. L. Bryan, pp. 119–128. Occasional Papers No. 1. Department of Anthropology, University of Alberta, Edmonton.

1979 Routes: Alternate Migration Corridors for Early Man in North America. *American Antiquity* 44:55–69.

Fladmark, K. R., J. C. Driver, and D. Alexander
1988 The Paleoindian Component at Charlie Lake Cave (Hb Rf 39). *American Antiquity* 53:371–384.

Frison, G. C.
1978 *Prehistoric Hunters of the High Plains.* Academic Press, New York.

Frison, G. C., and L. C. Todd
1986 *The Colby Mammoth Site.* University of New Mexico Press, Albuquerque.

Greenberg, J. H., C. G. Turner II, and S. L. Zegura
1986 The Settlement of the Americas. A Comparison of the Linguistic, Dental and Genetic Evidence. *Current Anthropology* 27:477–497.

Griffin, J. B.
1979 The Origin and Dispersion of American Indians in North America. In *The First Americans: Origins, Affinities and Adaptations,* edited by W. S. Laughlin and S. T. Wolf. Gustav Fischer, New York.

Gruhn, R.
1988a Linguistic Evidence in Support of the Coastal Route of Earliest Entry into the New World. *Man* 23:77–100.

1988b Review of *The Great Journey* by Brian Fagan. *Mammoth Trumpet* 4(2):4–5.

1989 The Pacific Coastal Route of Initial Entry: An Overview. Paper presented at the First World Summit Conference on the Peopling of the Americas, Center for the Study of the First Americans. University of Maine, Orono.

Gruhn, R., and A. L. Bryan
1977 Los Tapiales: A Paleo-Indian Campsite in the Guatemalan Highlands. *Proceedings of the American Philosophical Society* 121:235–273.

1984 The Record of Pleistocene Megafaunal Extinction at Taima-taima, Northern Venezuela. In *Quaternary Extinctions; A Prehistoric Revolution,* edited by P. S. Martin and R. G. Klein, pp. 1128–1137. University of Arizona Press, Tucson.

Haury, E. W., E. B. Sayles, and W. W. Wasley
1959 The Lehner Mammoth Site, Southeastern Arizona. *American Antiquity* 25:2–30.

Haynes, C. V., Jr.
1964 Fluted Projectile Points: Their Age and Dispersion. *Science* 145:1408–1413.

1967 *Geology of the Tule Springs Area,* edited by H. M. Wormington and D. Ellis, pp. 15–104. Nevada

State Museum Anthropological Papers No. 13. Carson City.

1970 Geochronology of Man-Mammoth Sites and Their Bearing on the Origin of the Llano Complex. In *Pleistocene and Recent Environments of the Central Great Plains,* edited by W. Dort, Jr. and J. K. Jones, Jr., pp. 72–92. University of Kansas Press, Lawrence.

1980 The Clovis Culture. *Canadian Journal of Anthropology* 1:115–121.

1982 Were Clovis Progenitors in Beringia? In *The Paleoecology of Beringia,* edited by D. M. Hopkins, J. V. Matthews, Jr., C. E. Schwager, and S. B. Young, pp. 383–398. Academic Press, New York.

1987a Clovis origins update. *Kiva* 52:83–93.

1987b Discussant. Discussion presented at the Clovis Origins Symposium, XII INQUA Congress, Ottawa.

Haynes, C. V., Jr., and G. Agogino

1986 *Geochronology of Sandia Cave.* Smithsonian Contributions to Anthropology No. 32. Washington, D.C.

Haynes, C. V., Jr., D. J. Donahue, A. J. T. Jull, and T. H. Zabel

1984 Application of Accelerator Dating to Fluted Point Paleoindian Sites. *Archaeology of Eastern North America* 12:184–191.

Haynes, G.

1987 Where Elephants Die. *Natural History* 6/87:28–33.

Hester, J. J.

1972 *Blackwater Locality No. 1: A Stratified, Early Man Site in Eastern New Mexico.* Fort Burgwin Research Center, Southern Methodist University, Dallas.

Hoffecker, J. F.

1985 The Moose Creek Site. *National Geographic Society Research Reports* 19:33–49.

Johnson, E.

1988 *Lubbock Lake: Late Quaternary Studies on the Southern High Plains.* Texas A & M University Press, College Station.

Krieger, A. D.

1954 A Comment on "Fluted Point Relationships" by John Witthoft. *American Antiquity* 19:273–275.

Larsen, H.

1968 Trail Creek. *Acta Arctica,* Fasc. XV. Copenhagen.

Laughlin, W. S., and A. B. Harper

1988 Peopling of the continents: Australia and America. In *Biological Aspects of Human Migration,* edited by C. G. Mascie-Taylor and G. W. Lasker, pp. 14–40. Cambridge University Press, Cambridge.

Leonhardy, F. C.

1966 *Domebo: A Paleo-Indian Mammoth Kill in the Prairie-Plains.* Contributions of the Museum of the Great Plains, No. 1. Lawton.

Lynch, T. F.

1978 The South American Paleo-Indians. In *Ancient Native Americans,* edited by J. D. Jennings, pp. 455–489. W. H. Freeman and Company, San Francisco.

1983 The South American Paleo-Indians. In *Ancient Native Americans,* edited by J. D. Jennings, second edition. W. H. Freeman and Company, San Francisco.

MacNeish, R. S.

1976 Early Man in the New World. *American Scientist* 63:316–327.

MacNeish, R. S., A. Garcia Cook, L. G. Lumbreras, R. K. Vierra, and A. Nelken-Turner

1981 *Prehistory of the Ayacucho Basin, Peru, vol. II, Excavation and Chronology.* University of Michigan Press, Ann Arbor.

Martin, P. S.

1973 The Discovery of America. *Science* 179:969–974.

1987 Clovisia the Beautiful! *Natural History* 10/87:10–13.

Mason, R. J.

1962 The Paleo-Indian Tradition in Eastern North America. *Current Anthropology* 5:227–278.

1981 *Great Lakes Archaeology.* Academic Press, New York.

Mayer-Oakes, W. J.

1986 El Inga, A Paleoindian Site in the Sierra of Northern Ecuador. *Transactions of the American Philosophical Society* 76:1–235.

Meltzer, D. J., and B. D. Smith

1986 Paleoindian and Early Archaic Subsistence Strategies in Eastern North America. In *Foraging, Collecting, and Harvesting: Archaic Period Subsistence and Settlement in the Eastern Woodlands,* edited by S. W. Neusius, pp. 1–30. Occasional Paper No. 6. Center for Archaeological Investigations, Southern Illinois University, Carbondale.

Mengoni Goñalons, G. L.

1986 Patagonian Prehistory: Early Exploitation of Faunal Resources (13,500–8500 B.P.). In *New Evidence for the Pleistocene Peopling of the New*

World, edited by A. L. Bryan, pp. 271–279. Center for the Study of Early Man, University of Maine, Orono.

Mochanov, I. A.
1978 Stratigraphy and Absolute Chronology of the Paleolithic of Northeast Asia According to the Work of 1963–1973. In *Early Man in America from a Circum-Pacific Perspective,* edited by A. L. Bryan, pp. 54–66. Occasional Papers No. 1. Department of Anthropology, University of Alberta, Edmonton.

Montané, J.
1968 Paleo-Indian Remains from Luguna de Tagua-Tagua, Central Chile. *Science* 161:1137–1138.

Morlan, R. E.
1986 Pleistocene Archaeology in the Old Crow Basin: A Critical Reappraisal. In *New Evidence for the Pleistocene Peopling of the Americas,* edited by A. L. Bryan, pp. 27–48. Center for the Study of Early Man, University of Maine, Orono.
1987 The Pleistocene Archaeology of Beringia. In *The Evolution of Human Hunting,* edited by M. H. Nitecki and D. V. Nitecki, pp. 267–307. Plenum Press, New York.

Morlan, R. E., and J. Cinq-Mars
1982 Ancient Beringians: Human Occupation in the Late Pleistocene of Alaska and the Yukon Territory. In *Paleoecology of Beringia,* edited by D. M. Hopkins, J. V. Matthews, Jr., C. E. Schweger, and S. B. Young, pp. 353–381. Academic Press, New York.

Mosimann, J. E., and P. S. Martin
1975 Simulating Overkill by Paleoindians. *American Scientist* 63:304–313.

Müller-Beck, H-J.
1967 On Migration of Hunters Across the Bering Land Bridge in the Upper Pleistocene. In *The Bering Land Bridge,* edited by D. M. Hopkins, pp. 373–408. Stanford University Press, Stanford.

Musil, R. R.
1988 Functional Efficiency and Technological Change: A Hafting Tradition Model for Prehistoric North America. In *Early Human Occupation in Far Western North America: The Clovis-Archaic Interface,* edited by J. A. Willig, C. M. Aikens and J. L. Fagan, pp. 373–387. Nevada State Museum Anthropological Papers No. 21. Carson City.

Ochsenius, C., and R. Gruhn (editors)
1979 (1984) *Taima-taima: A Late Pleistocene Paleo-Indian Kill Site in Northernmost South America. Final Report on the 1976 Excavations.* Programa CIPICS, Monografias Cientifica, Universidad Francisco de Miranda, Coro, Venezuela.

Owen, R.
1984 The Americas: The Case Against Ice-Age Human Population. In *The Origins of Modern Humans,* edited by F. H. Smith and F. Spencer, pp. 517–563. Alan R. Liss, New York.

Powers, R., and T. Hamilton
1978 Dry Creek: A Late Pleistocene Human Occupation in Central Alaska. In *Early Man in America from a Circum-Pacific Perspective,* edited by A. L. Bryan, pp. 72–77. Occasional Papers No. 1, Department of Anthropology, University of Alberta, Edmonton.

Rick, J. W.
1980 *Prehistoric Hunters of the High Andes.* Academic Press, New York.

Rouse, I.
1976 Peopling of the Americas. *Quaternary Research* 6:567–612.

Rouse, I., and J. M. Cruxent
1963 *Venezuelan Archaeology.* Yale University Press, New Haven.

Schobinger, J.
1988 *Prehistoria de Sudamérica: Culturas Precerámicas.* Alianza, Madrid.

Schweger, C. E., and C. Mandryk
1986 The Goldeye Lake Pollen Record: Could Man Survive the Ice-Free Corridor? *Ninth American Quaternary Association Abstracts,* p. 162.

Sellards, E. H.
1952 *Early Man in America.* University of Texas Press, Austin.

Smith, P. E. L.
1964 The Solutrean Culture. *Scientific American* 11:86–94.

Spiess, A. E.
1984 Arctic Garbage and New England Paleo-Indians: The Single Occupation Option. *Archaeology of Eastern North America* 12:280–285.

Stanford, D. J.
1982 A Critical Review of Archaeological Evidence Relating to the Antiquity of Human Occupation of the New World. In *Plains Indian Studies,* edited by D. H. Ubelaker and H. J. Viola, pp. 202–218. Smithsonian Contributions to Anthropology No. 30. Washington, D.C.

Thompson, R. S.
1985 The Age and Environment of the Mount Moriah (Lake Mohave) Occupation at Smith Creek

Cave, Nevada. In *Environments and Extinctions in Late Glacial North America,* edited by J. I. Mead and D. J. Meltzer, pp. 111–119. Center for the Study of Early Man, University of Maine, Orono.

Thompson, R. S., and J. I. Mead
1982 Late Quaternary Environments and Biogeography in the Great Basin. *Quaternary Research* 17:39–55.

Waters, M. R.
1985 Early Man in the New World; An Evaluation of the Radiocarbon Dated Pre-Clovis Sites in the Americas. In *Environments and Extinctions: Man in Late Glacial North America,* edited by J. I. Mead and D. J. Meltzer, pp. 125–143. Center for the Study of Early Man, University of Maine, Orono.

West, F. H.
1983 The Antiquity of Man in America. In *The Late Pleistocene,* edited by S. C. Porter, pp. 364–382. *Late Quaternary Environments of the United States,* vol. 2, H. E. Wright, Jr., general editor. University of Minnesota Press, Minneapolis.

White, J. P., and J. F. O'Connell
1982 *A Prehistory of Australia, New Guinea and Sahul.* Academic Press, New York.

Wormington, H. M.
1983 Early Man in the New World, 1970–1980. In *Early Man in the New World,* edited by R. Shutler, Jr., pp. 191–195. Sage Publications, Beverly Hills.

The Northern (Alaska-Yukon) Fluted Points

DONALD W. CLARK
Archaeological Survey of Canada
Canadian Museum of Civilization
Hull, PQ, Canada J8X 4H2

Fluted points from Alaska and the Yukon are dissimilar to Clovis points. Nevertheless, Paleoindian fluted points comparable to those from the North have been found elsewhere in North America, for instance in Alberta. Northern fluted points are not numerous, but their isolation from the main North American distribution poses theoretical questions of whether the northern points bear any generic relationship to southern fluted points, and, if so, what their distribution means regarding Paleoindian prehistory.

Some prehistorians use the occurrence of fluted points in Alaska to explain the apparently sudden appearance of Clovis in the South. Most, however, believe that these points were spread northward through the Plains and across the Cordillera at the end of the Pleistocene by migrating bands or by technological diffusion. This latter method would require a prior population vector in the northern Cordilleran region.

The age of northern fluted points may be crucial to this discussion. Most of these points are not dated, though some of them come from components variously dated from 3500 to as early as 11,500 yr B.P. Distribution analysis is likely to provide more reliable information on their ages than the few existing, possibly inappropriate radiocarbon dates. Limited data place fluted points only in nonglaciated areas of Alaska and the Yukon or in areas free of glacial ice by ca. 11,500 yr B.P. The plotting of future point finds near former glacial margins and precise dating of terminal Pleistocene glacial limits will be important factors in verifying this preliminary finding.

Fluted points are not numerous in Alaska and the Yukon Territory, but their number has increased from a few specimens known during the 1940s to nearly 50 points today. In this paper I intend to briefly discuss the following aspects of Arctic and Subarctic fluted points.

1. Their definition, because the term "fluted point" as used by archaeologists implies more than morphology.
2. Their distribution, which presently forms an isolated cluster.
3. Their description, though for this the reader is referred primarily to previously published papers.
4. Dating, based on radiocarbon dates and hypothetical or inferential age.
5. The cultural context or association with other artifacts and technological complexes.

6. A hypothetical northern culture history within which fluted points may be interpreted.
7. The significance of northern fluted points within North American prehistory.

We have explored several of these topics in previous publications (Clark 1983, 1984a; Clark and Clark 1975, 1980, 1983), and because the body of literature on fluted points is so large, most early authors have not been cited in the present paper. Nevertheless, the discoveries or contributions of A.L. Bryan, C. Vance Haynes, Jr., Frank Hibben, Robert Humphrey, William Irving, Froelich Rainy, R. S. Solecki, A. Thompson, and others are gratefully acknowledged.

DEFINITION

I will not discuss the basic definition of a fluted point, inasmuch as the reader should be knowledgeable on this subject. However, if channeling of the face were the only criterion of a fluted point, we would have to account for certain eastern Paleoeskimo specimens, for side-notched points that exhibit basal thinning flakes as long as the flutes on Clovis lanceolates, and for other scattered, relatively late points that also show pronounced basal thinning. As used by prehistorians the term "fluted point" clearly implies the Paleoindian period.

In areas where the prehistory is relatively well known, later "fluted" points, customarily not dignified by that term, can usually be distinguished from Paleoindian fluted points. This is seen best when a population of points is examined, whereas attribute analysis sometimes is inconclusive when solitary, fragmentary, aberrant, or unfinished points are considered.

These considerations are especially pertinent to the northern situation, where fluted specimens not only differ from the Clovis norm but generally come from undated contexts that do not have proven Paleoindian links. It is necessary to be aware of the possibility of "look-alikes" or independently developed fluted points in the North, regardless of their age or whether true Paleoindian fluted points with Plains affiliations are also present.

OCCURRENCE AND DISTRIBUTION

Distribution

All verified Paleoindian fluted points occur north of the Alaska Range or in the northern Yukon Territory (Figures 1 and 2). There are also a few equivocal fluted points from the southern Yukon Territory. Within this distribution the majority of points have been found in the Koyukuk River drainage, Alaska, from near Hughes northward to the Brooks Range. Other fluted points occur across the breadth of northern Alaska and into the Yukon, extending up to the Arctic coast. A few specimens have been found farther south in the Tanana River drainage, but most are from north of the Yukon River. A considerable gap exists between this distribution and that of the Canadian northwestern Plains. Recent discovery of a series of "trail marker" sites has substantially reduced this gap at its southern end. These sites include the 1983 Charlie Lake Cave find near Fort St. John, British Columbia (Fladmark 1986; Fladmark et al. 1988), two points recovered farther north towards Fort Nelson in 1986 by Ian Wilson (Wilson 1987) (Figure 2:paired triangles), and an isolated, short basal fragment, apparently also from a fluted point, found in 1986 on the surface squarely in the purported Mackenzie Corridor in the uplands of the southwestern District of

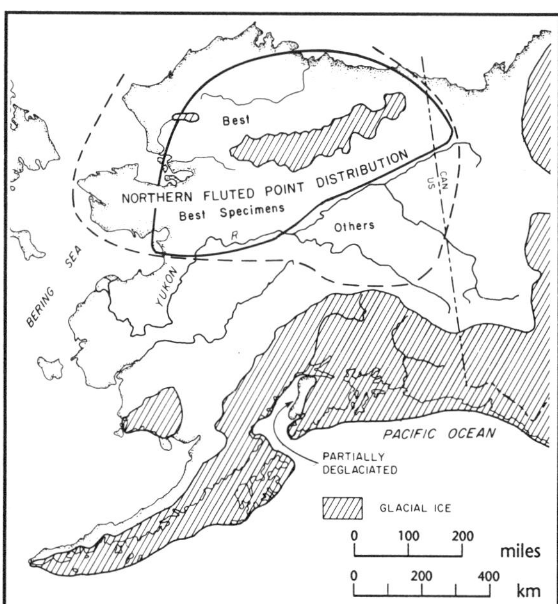

Figure 1. The distribution of northern fluted points in relation to the present landmass and eastern Beringia as it was approximately 12,000 years ago (modified from Clark 1984a).

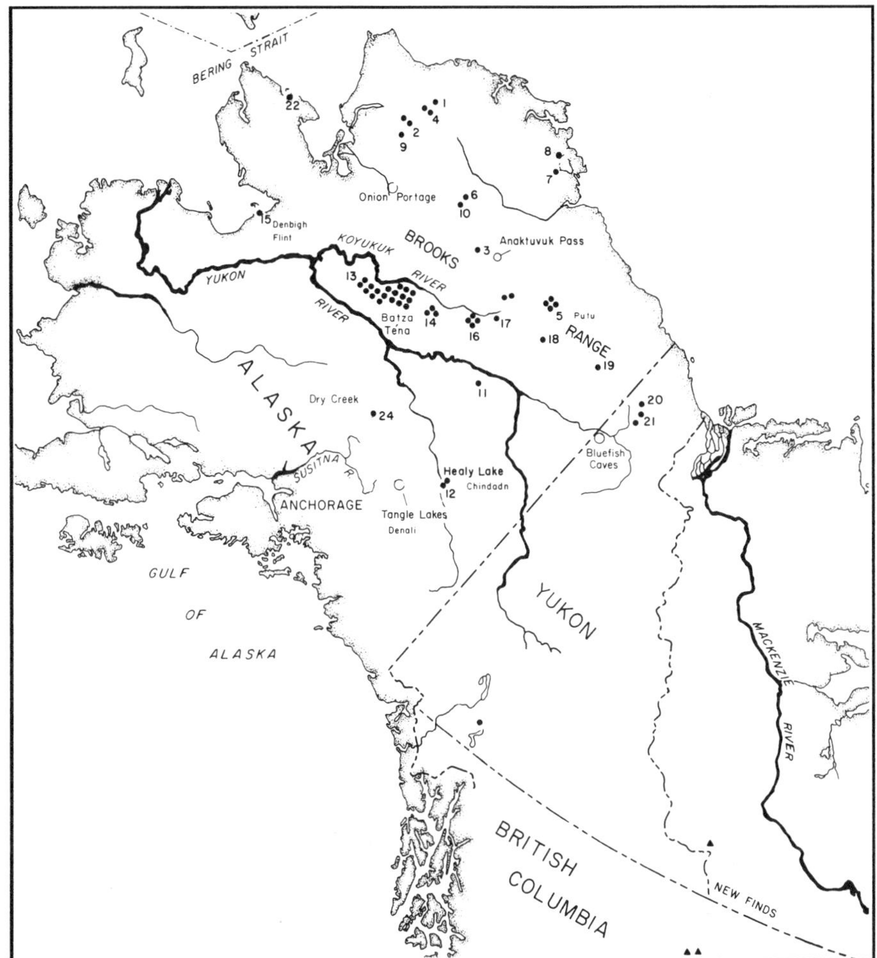

Figure 2. The distribution of northern fluted points. Each dot represents one specimen; the triangles are possible "trailmarker" finds from on and just beyond the northwestern Plains. Numbers are keyed to a list of sites or finds in Clark (1984a).

Mackenzie (C. Hanks, personal communication 1987). We may be on the verge of the moment when it no longer is possible to speak of a discretely separate northern distribution. There should be no such separate distribution if the points north and south are related.

For what may be a slightly later period, Dixon (1986) suggests that points from Jay Creek Ridge, excavated during the Susitna Hydroelectric Project in south-central Alaska, are of Paleoindian derivation and can be linked with the distribution of fluted points. Judging from Dixon's description of concave bases, basal thinning, and grinding at the lower edges, these specimens could be derived from fluted points and are analogous to certain Plano points. This is in accord with their age of slightly more than 7000 yr B.P. and with my interpretation of more or less similar points from other sites in the North, dated or thought to date within the time range of 7000 to 9000 yr B.P. Dixon suggests that the Susitna points demonstrate that descendants of fluted-point Paleoindians had spread from northern Alaska to south-central Alaska by 7000 years ago.

As far as can be demonstrated from present geological information, no fluted points occur on terrain that remained buried by Pleistocene ice after 11,500 years ago. In some cases, however, find spots in the Brooks Range of northern Alaska are not securely dated. The correlation of point distribution with glacial limits possibly offers a feasible mode for dating northern fluted points. Unfortunately, it can be applied only to the lesser number of points found in and adjacent to the Brooks Range, and to certain discoveries from western Canada, since the majority of fluted points have been found in unglaciated Beringia. Moreover, the accuracy or utility of this method is tied to the as yet undetermined duration of northern fluted points. If these points existed throughout the period of rapid deglaciation, much terrain inaccessible to the earliest fluted-point makers could still have been occupied by later fluted-point peoples. Presently the absence of these points on more recently deglaciated terrain supports the validity of the older radiocarbon dates, which I will discuss later.

Occurrence

Most northern fluted points have been found in association with other artifacts rather than as isolated finds. However, most of these sites are very shallow and lack stratigraphy. Many specimens have been collected from poorly vegetated surfaces, though some presently exposed surfaces may have been mantled with soil and humic material in the past. No fluted points have been recovered from any of the old cave sites excavated in Alaska or the Yukon (Trail Creek, Porcupine, Bluefish). Even where specimens have been excavated, there often are interpretive problems involving lack of, or compressed, natural stratigraphy and disturbance through frost action. The most deeply buried context from which a possible fluted point has been recovered is at the Dry Creek site.

DESCRIPTION

Although the fluted points of Alaska and the Yukon (Figure 3) (Clark and Clark 1975:Figures, 1983) differ from classic Clovis specimens, close counterparts to many of the northern points have been found in California, Nevada, Alberta, and British Columbia. This western-style development includes the previously noted Charlie Lake Cave and Pink Mountain, British Columbia, finds; ones from western Alberta, for instance at Sibbald Creek (Gryba 1983); and some Alaskan specimens. Other points from Alaska and the Yukon exhibit more formalized triple fluting (Figure 3d), but could be within the range of variation of a single point population. Some relatively small multiple-fluted points from the midwestern and eastern United States also superficially resemble the northern points. Thus, a northern regional style cannot be determined, particularly when based on only a few superficial comparisons.

These northern points tend to be small compared with classic Clovis specimens. Widths range from 12 to 26.3 mm. Those from the Batza Tena locality (N = 15) average 24.1 mm wide at the base; a larger sample (N = 27), in part scaled from unpublished figures of Girls' Hill (BET-041) (Gal 1977) and other Alaskan specimens, averages only 21.6 mm in basal width. Maximum width is slightly greater, since some specimens are widest near the midpoint. Fluting almost always is multiple; commonly triple, or attempted triple, on both faces with the middle flute having been detached last. Triple fluting has a counterpart in the small lateral flakes or so-called guide flutes of Clovis points. But in the northern points the lateral flutes are not appreciably shorter than the medial flute, though they are partially removed by the medial flute and through flaking directed from the edges. Other common attributes are the U- to V-shaped concave base, often accompanied by carefully prepared basal "ears," and grinding of the edges at the base and adjacent lower sides of the point. Shape, as seen in the few recovered complete points, is quite variable and falls short of the aesthetic ideal of a lanceolate point. Some specimens would not be recognized as fluted points were it not for the fact that they fall within the range of variation of an apparent fluted-point population, which includes some specimens as nicely fluted as good southern examples.

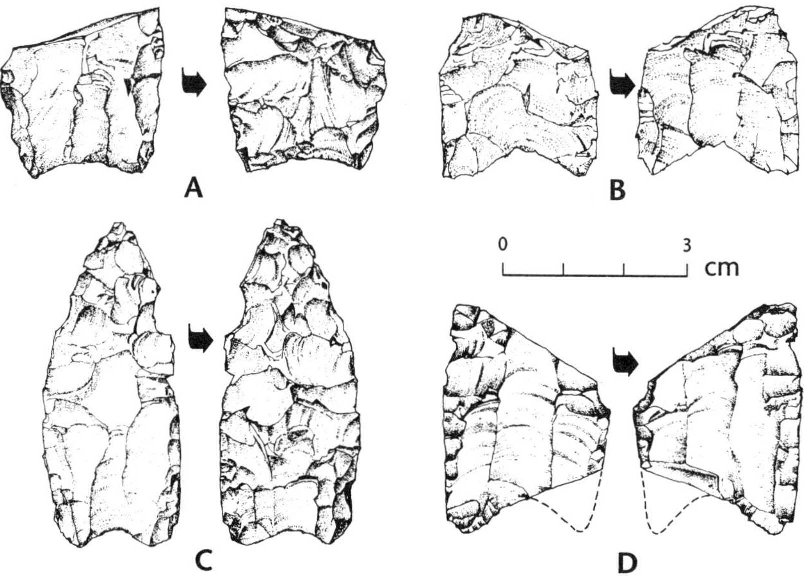

Figure 3. Examples of fluted points from Alaska showing characteristic technological attributes: **A)** Point triple-fluted on one face only; **B)** Unfinished point showing triple thinning flakes on one face and a single broad flake scar on the other face; **C)** Point triple-fluted on one face, slightly thinned on the other face; and **D)** A fine triple-fluted example. All specimens are of obsidian and have suffered natural damage.

DATING

The Dates

There are several radiocarbon dates from sites that could apply to northern fluted points, as well as contributory data that provide age estimates and stop-dates. The interpretation of contributory data, however, is usually based on hypothetical constructs and seldom provides independent dating. The following discussion of proposed dates presents widely varied cultural affiliations and divergent ages, but in this manner it draws attention to problems with the data base and points out differing interpretations.

1. The Iyatayet site at Cape Denbigh produced several dates for the Denbigh Flint complex (dates listed in Giddings 1964). The single fluted point is illustrated by Giddings (1964:Figure 57) and elsewhere; 3800–4000 yr B.P. is a reasonable age consensus. I think the point has been recycled from an older site and possibly reshaped or is an independently developed fluted form, though some persons consider a combined Denbigh-Northern Archaic placement to be the proper context for many or all northern fluted points.

2. Girls' Hill (BET-041) produced a date of 4440 ± 190 yr B.P. for an abundant microblade industry (Gal 1977, personal communications). Other younger dates from this site are reported in Davis (1976:Table 1). Point sketches are in Gal (1977). I suggest that unrecognized, mixed site components are present and that the dates do not apply to the several fluted points recovered from this site. However, Gal (1977) and West (1982) suggest that the fluted form is late, independently developed, and that the date is appropriate for these and other northern specimens.

3. Dog Creek, northern Yukon (site and associations unpublished), yielded a well-fluted specimen, published in Morlan and Cinq-Mars (1982) and in Clark and Clark (1983). Unpublished dates are about the same range as Girls' Hill and Iyatayet. Investigator J. Cinq-Mars states that the dates cannot possibly be shown to bear any relationship to the fluted point (personal communication 1977).

4. The Putu complex of the Putu site, located on the north side of the Brooks Range (Alexander 1987), produced radiocarbon dates of 5700 ± 190, 6090 ± 430, 8454 ± 130, and 11,470 ± 500 yr B.P. (Alexander 1987; Gal 1982). Alexander (1987:36) states that the 6090 and 8454 yr B.P. dates apply to soil overlying the cultural deposit. Although the 8454 yr B.P. date has often been cited as a plausible age for the Putu fluted points, I concur with Alexander that this is a questionable date. Alexander considers the older date of 11,470 yr B.P., which is on charcoal from a hearth feature, to be the more appropriate one. The points are well made. A form of small blade core is associated, but, in my opinion, the assemblage does not appear to belong in the American Paleoarctic tradition.

5. The Mesa site occurs on the north side of the Brooks Range and has been dated to 7620 ± 95 yr B.P. It was reported and the specimens illustrated by Kunz (1982). The site produced at least one fluted point, as well as many unfluted round- to straight-based lanceolates, but few other implements and no microblades or evident American Paleoarctic artifacts were recovered. I interpret the straight- to slightly concave-based examples from this site as later than, and derived from, fluted points. As such, the date is acceptable. However, the more numerous round-based points may be unrelated to fluted points.

6. Healy Lake Village site, Tanana Valley, yielded various dates of ca. 9000 to 11,000 yr B.P. for the lower or Chindadn component (Cook and McKennan 1970; McKennan and Cook 1970). A basally thinned, short lanceolate point comes from the base of the site (Chindadn component). Two concave-based fragments were found in Levels 5 or 6, which comprise either the top of the lower component or a succeeding transition to which a 9000-year radiocarbon date (GX-1340) may apply. The shortest fragment may be fluted but is too incomplete for certain identification. Specimens from the site are largely unpublished. Smithsonian dates SI-737 and SI-739 (Stuckenrath and Mielke 1973) suggest that Chindadn is generally 10,000 years old. Radiocarbon date GX-1341 of 11,090 ± 170 yr B.P. provides an older dating for Level 8 near the base of the deposit, but many persons have expressed reservations regarding this date because it is on bone apatite, which is said to produce erratic results. The dates generally are validated by work elsewhere in the Tanana Valley. Taking into account the range of variation of the northern fluted-point form, I accept the lower specimen as a fluted point, although some investigators (Dixon 1985a) do not. These points can be compared with Plano points with basal thinning. Chindadn has American Paleoarctic elements, but the microblade industry there could be due to mixture with higher levels where microblades are abundant.

7. Dry Creek Component 2, Tanana Valley, is 10,690 ± 250 years old according to the single acceptable date on Component 2. This date is reinforced by an 11,100 yr B.P. date on underlying Component 1, reported by Powers and Hamilton (1978) and Powers et al. (1983). This American Paleoarctic

assemblage contains microblades and a miniature point fluted on one face, among other tools. The point is illustrated in Morlan and Cinq-Mars (1982), where it is erroneously attributed to Dry Creek Component 1; Clark and Clark (1983) repeat this error. Although this point has the basal outline, basal ear, and ground-edge attributes characteristic of fluted points, it is barely acceptable as one because of its small size (width 13 mm) and, as Powers et al. (1983:125) state, "technologically marginal" attributes.

8. Contributory data.
   a. Bifacial points and other bifacial tools have been recovered from several Alaskan sites with dates of 11,000 yr B.P. or greater (Hoffecker et al. 1988; Larsen 1968). None of these tools, excluding the Putu and Healy Lake specimens with uncertain 11,000-year-old dates, are fluted, although some specimens are lanceolate shaped.
   b. Concave-based and poorly fluted points are known from the southern Yukon Territory. Some of these finds are unpublished; however, Clark (1984:Figure 1e) reports an undated specimen found with microblades at a small exposed site at Champagne. In some cases, these points are known to date within the last few millennia (Greer and LeBlanc 1983:32). I do not accept any of these specimens as being of Paleoindian age, although further research may alter this assessment.
   c. Obsidian-hydration measurements have produced the equivalent of a younger and older series of dates on Batza Tena fluted points from the Koyukuk River, Alaska. The younger dates may reflect the effect of heating from forest fires. The thicker hydration measurements support dating to the Paleoindian period, probably within the time range of 9000 to 13,000 years ago. But the method is too imprecise and ambiguous to provide dates that can be used for determining close chronological relationships (Clark 1984b).
   d. Unfluted lanceolate points interpreted as possibly derived from fluted points have been found at several sites in Alaska, some of which are noted above. These points generally date within the range of 7000–8000 yr B.P. but may possibly be as old as 9000 yr B.P.

Discussion of Dating

As can be seen from the foregoing data, the dates support both young and old ages of northern fluted points. However, nearly every date or the specimen to which it may apply can be questioned. Stratigraphically, the point from the thick Dry Creek deposits probably is the most secure. Although its age is based on a single date, this date agrees with ones for related components found elsewhere. However, the Dry Creek point is a seemingly aberrant miniature. Healy Lake also is a good candidate for early dating, but its compressed stratigraphy offers a 2000-year range of dates in the lower component, and the points and fragments from this site are poorly or equivocally fluted. Other sites are beset with similar problems. The proposition that fluted points were made in Alaska about 10,500 years ago, nevertheless, seems to me reasonably acceptable, though not fully proven. Equally acceptable, and preferable for some interpretations, is an age a couple centuries younger, within the error range of Dry Creek II and the Healy Lake radiocarbon dates, that provides a south-to-north time slope between Charlie Lake Cave and Alaska. We have also noted that point distribution vis-à-vis the maximum limits of late Pleistocene glaciers permits an earlier age of about 11,000 or even 11,500 yr B.P. for fluted points, although this does not confirm that the points are that old. Important questions remain concerning the temporal duration of northern fluted points: When did they first appear in the region, when were they last made there, and where, for instance, does a 10,500 yr B.P. date fall within this range? More information is required before these critical questions can be answered. Furthermore, some persons will argue that later dates of 4000 to 5000 yr B.P. are also acceptable. Could late-dating points represent reinvention of the type, or did the fluted style continue for 6000 years?

CULTURAL CONTEXT OR ASSOCIATIONS

Fluted points have been found in association with artifacts of the Denbigh Flint complex (a northwest Alaskan member of the Paleoeskimo Arctic Small Tool tradition), the Northern Archaic tradition, the early American Paleoarctic tradition (characterized by a microblade industry), and in early non-microblade contexts. As is explained in the next section, these industries or traditions span the period from nearly 11,000 years ago (or earlier) to 3400 years ago. Lanceolate points, possibly derived from fluted points, appear in a later phase of an essentially unnamed non-microblade tradition, identified variously as Plano, a "Northern Paleoindian/ Northern Archaic transition" (Dixon 1986), or the northern Cordilleran (Clark 1983). We need not examine here all the possible associations, as this has been done elsewhere (Clark 1984a). Because a possible reinvention of fluting in the Denbigh Flint complex or the Northern Archaic tradition is less critical than the presence of significantly earlier fluted points in the North, attention will focus on the earlier specimens. At one time I doubted that fluted points were actually associated with the early microblade-using American Paleoarctic tradition. Such association does not occur at the fluted-point sites I have investigated, nor is it unequivocal in better-documented excavated Paleoarctic assemblages, with the somewhat uncertain exception of Dry Creek 2 as noted above. There are, however, a large number of fluted points found with microblades at shallow sites and in surface collections, though one may be inclined to see mixed components in these cases.

THE BROADER FRAMEWORK OF SUBARCTIC PREHISTORY

What are the origins of northern fluted points, and how do they relate to the broader questions of New World prehistory and Clovis origins? A Clovis culture as such hardly exists in the North, and fluted points seem to occur there in a multiplicity of contexts. To help understand the contrasting explanations offered for the role of fluted-point makers in northern prehistory, we will first examine the broader framework of prehistory in the western Subarctic.

Old Crow Flats and the Bluefish Caves

We will not draw into this discussion the ca. 30,000-year-old modified bone assemblage from the Old Crow River flats for reasons of the lack of dated lithic assemblages through which to trace connections forward in time, the age of this material, which is too old to be relevant to the fluted-point question, and because of controversies surrounding the identification of bone artifacts. The reader is referred to Morlan and Cinq-Mars (1982) for further information.

Possibly bridging the gap between the Old Crow assemblage and the appearance of northern fluted points are the Bluefish Caves (Cinq-Mars 1979; Morlan and Cinq-Mars 1982). These rockshelters were used briefly and sporadically between approximately 10,000 and 14,000 years ago and evidently had been visited by people several thousand years earlier than this time. The meager lithic assemblage from the shelters can be assigned primarily to the American Paleoarctic tradition, especially on the basis of a wedge-shaped microblade core. Burins, burin spalls, microblades, lithic flakes, and a probable mammoth-bone core and flake are also present.

Early Non-microblade Assemblages

A non-microblade occupation of eastern Beringia and, subsequently, northwestern Canada predates the introduction of microblade technology by the American Paleoarctic tradition (Clark 1983; Hoffecker et al. 1988; see West 1987 for dissenting opinion). Several dates of 11,000 yr B.P. and earlier may apply to non-microblade assemblages. Most of these early assemblages are very small and thus are susceptible to sampling error. This "error" may be in the form of nonrepresentative sampling, as well as unidentified functional differences between activity areas and sites within a single cultural phase. Accordingly, the lack of microblades in the pre-11,000 yr B.P. assemblages has been open to interpretation. However, based on the results obtained in 1986 and succeeding years by W. Roger Powers at the Walker Road site in Alaska, it now is reasonably certain that a valid early non-microblade (and pre-microblade) horizon can be documented. The Walker Road collections include a small pointed biface and tools made on blades or blade-like flakes, but lack fluted points (W. R. Powers, personal communication 1987 and 1988). Elsewhere, lanceolate points have been found in some of the early dated components (Hoffecker et al. 1988). These assemblages from central interior Alaska are termed the Nenana complex. The same component evidently is present in the Chindadn complex (Cook and McKennan 1970; Dixon 1985b). Consequently, I view the Nenana complex as part of a more widespread early occupation of the northern Cordilleran region (Clark 1983; MacNeish 1964).

Arrival of the Asian Microblade Tradition

Present evidence indicates that an Asian-derived microblade and wedge-shaped core technology arrived in Alaska shortly after 11,000 years ago. These tools are documented at 10,700 yr B.P. in Dry Creek 2. Their possible earlier presence at the Bluefish Caves is a unique case that I will not attempt to rationalize here. The small blade industry at the Putu site is not typical of the Paleoarctic tradition, and its date is not necessarily very early, especially if the "error" range is taken into account.

Siberian migrants may have crossed the Bering Strait and the remnants of the Bering land bridge bearing a microblade industry. Otherwise, this technology must have spread by diffusion to the extant pre-microblade population in eastern Beringia, noted above.

Early microblade sites, which sometimes contain larger blades, are commonly grouped into the American Paleoarctic tradition (Anderson 1970; Dumond 1977, 1980), which in all or most of its aspects sometimes also is called the Beringian tradition (West 1981) or the Denali complex (West 1967). Less ancient developments derived largely from the same technological base as the early microblade industry were for several years called the Northwest Microblade tradition (MacNeish 1959a, 1964). Originally defined as Denali by West (1967) from a series of interior Alaskan sites, and later validated as the Paleoarctic form in the Akmak complex of the Onion

Portage site (Anderson 1970), this tradition is best documented today in the Dry Creek 2 assemblage from interior Alaska (Powers et al. 1983). McKennan and Cook (1970) obtained related material from eastern interior Alaska, though their oldest assemblage, Chindadn, may be interpreted as a mixed or transitional component bridging non-microblade and Paleoarctic occupations.

Points have a variable presence in the Paleoarctic tradition. Some lithic projectile points are present, but at Dry Creek most of the round-based points have been identified as functional knives. At the minor Trail Creek Caves component, microblades were inserted into organic hafts for use as points (Larsen 1968). In most areas, the Paleoarctic tradition lasted about 3000 years, until 7500 or 8000 yr B.P., although late phases persisted locally, as in the Southwest Yukon. Early Paleoarctic microblade technology is based on the Siberian Duiktai tradition. Additional forms of microblade cores appeared, either through local development or from contact with the early Holocene Sumnagin culture of eastern Siberia (Anderson 1980). There was also a divergent coastal strain that developed into the earliest maritime cultures of the North Pacific Coast of North America.

Persistence of Non-microblade Technological Complex

The American Paleoarctic tradition, whether introduced by migration or diffused by technology, did not completely supplant its northern antecedents. Non-microblade assemblages persisted east of Alaska, although present evidence for this conclusion is not as firm as it should be. Post-Paleoarctic occupation of about 8000 to 6000 years ago appears to be to be derived primarily from non-microblade antecedents that persisted in the northern Cordilleran region. Many archaeologists, though, see in the same evidence a Plano or terminal Paleoindian migration from the Plains to the vicinity of Bering Strait. The relative and respective roles in northwestern prehistory of peoples from the South, and descendants of the Nenana complex or pre-microblade populations, is an important issue that will be discussed later in this paper.

Archaeologists have yet to find early microblades in the greater part of the Yukon, the Northwest Territories, or the areas of northern Alberta and interior British Columbia where later microblades occur. These lands were deglaciated between 11,000 and 12,000 years ago. I believe that inasmuch as Paleoarctic people were not there, some other people were present. In the far Northwest, Paleoarctic peoples may have pressured the antecedent non-microblade population to move into newly deglaciated lands to the east. There, eventually, they may have met Paleoindians moving up from the South. In reality, the situation is somewhat more complicated. Microblades or cores occasionally are found in undated, apparent Paleoindian sites of the Rocky Mountain foothills region in Alberta and British Columbia. If these finds constitute valid co-occurrences they may indicate that a small, early microblade-using population penetrated that region. Nevertheless, there was no pervasive early Paleoarctic occupation of the midlatitude Rocky Mountain and eastern foothills region.

Evidence of a non-microblade occupation contemporaneous with the Paleoarctic tradition comes from the Engigstciak site of the northern Yukon, located not far inland from the Arctic coast. There, in the 1950s, R.S. MacNeish excavated from deep deposits the "Flint Creek" complex of the Cordilleran tradition (MacNeish 1959b). J. Cinq-Mars of the Archaeological Survey of Canada, in collaboration with E. Nelson, Simon Fraser University, and assisted by the Northern Oil and Gas Action Programme (NOGAP), has obtained radiocarbon dates of approximately 9800 yr B.P. on two Flint Creek-component bones excavated by MacNeish (J. Cinq-Mars, personal communication 1987; Cinq-Mars et al. n.d.). The collection includes lanceolate points, although at the time of this writing, reanalysis had not progressed to the point of determining the temporal range of Flint Creek, which likely includes some material younger than 9800 years. Nor has it been determined exactly how or if the early dates from this site apply to the lanceolate projectile points.

Late Paleoindians Move North

As the Pleistocene drew to a close and the ice sheets melted, the zone of land available for occupation in southern Canada widened. Fluted-point hunters moved into this new territory. In Saskatchewan and some regions farther east, there is a correlation between the distribution of fluted points and glacial recession on the southern shores of large proglacial lakes. This might also be the case in the Birch Hills of northeastern Alberta, where numerous fluted points occur on what was formerly a peninsula extending into glacial Lake Peace (Ball 1989). During part of the late Pleistocene, northwestern Alberta and adjacent interior British Columbia are seen as having an ice-free corridor that extended north and south (Reeves 1981). A northward-extending fluted-point distribution, possibly with both early and late specimens, can therefore be expected within this corridor. Thus far, fluted points generally do not appear to extend north of the Peace River into the corridor region. The recent finds from Pink Mountain (Wilson 1987) and the Northwest Territories are exceptions. It is anticipated that the "First Albertans" project will recover pertinent information from parts of this area (Ball 1988). One dated specimen comes from Charlie Lake Cave, located in British Columbia at approximately the southern edge of the former corridor, in an area geographically connected with the Plains (Fladmark et al.

1988). The age of this find and small associated assemblage is approximately 10,500 yr B.P., or, taking three radiocarbon dates at their one-sigma "error" range, between 10,220 and 10,890 yr B.P. During the millennium or longer before this site was occupied, extensive areas of northern Alberta were deglaciated, followed by essentially the entire Mackenzie River drainage and most of the land to the west (cf. Dyke and Prest 1986a, 1986b). Part of this area may have been ice-free throughout the last stadial of the late Pleistocene (Rutter 1980). Though (in 1987) there is presently little evidence from the northwestern Plains that fluted-point hunters were pressing against ice margins or entering an ice-free corridor, we should wait for the results from current investigations before forming any conclusions concerning early human-ice relationships in that region. Additionally, whether or not deglaciation was so rapid that it threw any orderly northward shift of tundra, forest, and grassland ecozones into chaos may not be a cogent consideration, since fluted-point peoples seen to have been able to adopt a range of lifeways. Nevertheless, ecological conditions may have a bearing on the sustained inhabitability of the region.

By about 10,000 years ago time had run out on fluted points, or fluting as a style. Northward migration or population spread continued on the part of the Plano people, who are thought to be the descendants of fluted-point makers. There is little doubt that Plano people occupied the plains-parkland transition zone, though few of these sites are dated. Plano populations expanded onward into the early boreal forest and eventually northward to the tundra in the Northwest Territories. (Sites on the Barrengrounds may have been closer to the forest, which subsequently shifted southward.) Some archaeologists attribute Plano to a big-game hunting lifeway of the grasslands, and they correlate the northern Plano occupation with early Holocene climatic change and shifts in the distribution of the boreal forest and grasslands. According to the model held by many researchers, Plano hunters turned westward into the Yukon and Alaska during their northern expansion, where they either hunted the herbivores of relict grasslands or adopted new subsistence lifeways. This is a convenient and logical model that accounts for many scattered or undated finds. One hazard, though, is that there are "look-alikes" in the North that are not Plano. A dated 6000- to 8000-year-old Agate Basin Plano complex has been identified in the Keewatin and adjacent areas of the central Canadian Subarctic (Gordon 1981; Wright 1981), but to an overwhelming degree, reported Agate Basin points from northern Canada are look-alikes that are less than 2000 years old. Another problem is that, given the likelihood that styles changed across space, a relatively distant Plano assemblage or point from the North might not match any particular Plano complex or point from the Plains.

For the northwestern interior region of Alaska and adjacent Canada, the hypotheses of a Subarctic Plano migration and an earlier fluted-point Paleoindian migration from the South need to be rationalized. Were there two separate migrations, continuous migration or diffusion, or a single early migration followed by parallel development of Plano-like forms in the North and South? At one time, a northern "backwash" could be proposed to account for the presence of Alaskan fluted points and no elaboration of this hypothesis was required because northern fluted points were so rare. This no longer is the case.

One can foresee that at the end of the Pleistocene people moving northward from the Plains met other groups expanding eastward from the Yukon or northern Cordilleran region. Those moving eastward would have been descendants of previous inhabitants of Beringia, especially, according to my interpretation, the non-microblade people who had persisted from earlier times. This meeting of long-separated peoples may have occurred in the Mackenzie Valley and along the eastern flanks of the Cordillera. There is some diversity of opinion among archaeologists over which early northern assemblages can be attributed to Plano inhabitants and which to a western Subarctic origin. Most assemblages are placed in the Plano group, although it seems to me that this is done mainly out of adherence to the northward migration model or for summary convenience. The best-defined northern Plano unit is the Beverly focus of Agate Basin, found principally in the District of Keewatin (Wright 1981). Less certain as Plano components, at least in my mind (Clark 1983), are the 7000-year-old Acasta Lake complex found at the east end of Great Bear Lake (Noble 1981), 6000- or 8500-year-old lithics from Fisherman Lake in the Southwest District of Mackenzie (Millar 1981), the small 7200-year-old basal component of the Canyon Creek site in the Southwest Yukon (Workman 1974), the 7600-year-old Mesa site in Northwest Alaska (Kunz 1982), and comparable Alaskan sites of similar age.

End of Prehistory: Demise of the Pure Microblade Tradition; Development of Northern Archaic and Mixed Technology

Microblade technology has a complicated history in western North America. Here we focus on the interior northern Alaska-Yukon region central to the fluted-point topic.

Between 7000 and 8000 years ago, northwestern interior non-microblade peoples were again occupying areas of Alaska where the Paleoarctic tradition had formerly prevailed. Some or most of these non-microblade peoples may have descended from the earlier non-microblade inhabitants of the region, while others may have derived from fluted-point or Plano Paleoindian migrants from the South.

Non-microblade people continued to prosper in many regions at the expense of Paleoarctic microblade inhabitants. With the adoption of notched points, notched-cobble implements, and certain other tools, beginning about 6000–6500 years ago, technology phased into the Northern Archaic tradition. That development evidently took place in the northern zone of Alaska and the Yukon. At the same time that the Northern Archaic was developing, a late or derivative Paleoarctic population expanded eastward through the southern Yukon territory (Workman 1978), across northern British Columbia, into the Mackenzie Valley (Millar 1981) and into northern Alberta (LeBlanc and Ives 1986). Details of this expansion are still extremely sketchy.

Later, the Northern Archaic tradition expanded south of the Alaska Range and into the southern Yukon. In much of interior Alaska north of the Alaska Range and immediately east in the central Yukon, there was some form of Northern Archaic-microblade tradition amalgamation or acculturation. This combination also appears in the Mackenzie drainage. Outside of areas with this amalgamated technology, microblade use was terminated. This occurred relatively early at some localities, either because of local technological change or expansion of non-microblade populations, and slightly later elsewhere upon being supplanted by the Northern Archaic. There is no conclusive evidence for continuation of a pure microblade or late Paleoarctic tradition beyond about 5000 years ago. Unmixed microblade collections of more recent age, lacking notched points, come from loci that appear to have been specialized activity areas not representative of whole technological complexes. However, at some localities, occupation by people with a combined Northern Archaic and microblade technology continued until about 1800 years ago or later. Over most of the western Subarctic the Northern Archaic tradition is traced through local variants to the late prehistoric period and is seen as proto-Athapaskan. But it would be unwise to attribute the entire variable Northern Archaic construct to ancestral Athapaskan Indians.

HYPOTHETICAL POSITIONING OF NORTHERN FLUTED-POINT MAKERS

We will examine the ways in which fluted points can be accommodated within the framework of northern prehistory outlined in the preceding section. Three hypotheses are considered: (a) northern origin of Clovis or fluted points; (b) southern origin of fluted points; and (c) independent development. The difference between the southern and northern hypotheses is not only the direction of the subsequent spread of technology. The southern hypothesis simply explains an episode in northern prehistory; the northern hypothesis pertains to the very origins of Clovis and the controversies that are carried in train.

Northern Origins of Clovis

Only one hypothesis can accommodate a northern Clovis origin without conflicting with presently available information. This is that fluted points were developed in the non-microblade culture of Alaska and the Yukon that predated the American Paleoarctic tradition. They then were taken south through a geographic corridor about 11,500 years ago. Evidence supporting this hypothesis is weak and has grown even weaker since this paper was first presented in 1987. Nevertheless, a northern fluted-point origin remains possible, especially considering that most northern fluted-point finds are not satisfactorily dated. Considerable interest centers on current investigations in Alaska of the early pre-11,000-yr B.P. horizon (Hoffecker et al. 1988). Although I had originally believed that these sites would hold the key to Clovis origins within the context of the northern hypothesis, continued excavation, especially at the Walker Road site, has failed to show that fluted points are part of the local inventory of that period. Apparently, it will be necessary to look elsewhere for the development of fluted points and the relationship (if any) between the Nenana complex and Clovis. Separate events in northern Paleoindian prehistory may be indicated by northern fluted points and the Nenana complex respectively.

There is some concern regarding the limiting effects of late Pleistocene glacial conditions along a north-south corridor during the Clovis time range. Current estimates are that by the time under consideration, beginning shortly before 11,400 years ago, a broad ice-free corridor lay open east of the Rocky Mountains and across the northern Yukon Territory (Dyke and Prest 1986: Map Sheet "12 000 years before present," Map Sheet "11 000 years before present").

Southern Origins

More than one hypothesis could accommodate this explanation of northern fluted-point origins. A governing factor is that a prior southern fluted-point source was available. Although one would have existed, within the broadest limits, between 10,000 (or slightly later) and 11,500 years ago, when we consider that the immediate source probably was localized and restricted to northwestern Alberta and adjacent British Columbia, the time window should be narrowed to between about 11,000 and 9800 years ago. The single dated fluted-point component found in this area, Charlie Lake Cave, is approximately 10,500 years old (Fladmark et al. 1988:377). Sibbald Creek, located farther south in the Alberta foothills, produced a date of 9570 ± 320 yr B.P. (GX-8808) (Gryba 1983:122) that approximately dates a point similar to the Charlie Lake Cave specimen. Two principal mechanisms would account for the northward spread of fluted points: style diffusion and migration. Both probably occurred in specific instances, but we look primarily to one or the other to link North and South. Because a southern fluted-point origin means that these points would be younger in the North, it may be pertinent that the multiple fluting and small size that characterize northern specimens tend to be late in the South (C. Vance Haynes, personal communication 1987; Meltzer and Dunnell 1987). Given, though, that much of the North American variation in fluting is poorly dated, I believe it premature to conclude that all small and multiple-fluted points are late.

Selective acceptance of radiocarbon dates presently available from the North and manipulation within their "error" range support the southern-origins hypothesis by providing an apparent time slope. If this conclusion is correct, eventually it should have a broader, acceptably dated basis for its support. We have noted that the weakness of this base is the primary reason for persisting uncertainty.

Diffusion

Diffusion necessitates that there was already a population or vector in place in the northern Cordilleran region. At the outset this could have been the non-microblade inhabitants. From them the fluted-point style may have diffused westward to American Paleoarctic people. This hypothesis fits the northern Yukon and Alaskan situation reasonably well as a plausible explanation, although diffusion would have occurred during a period in which deglaciation was just finishing in parts of the Cordillera, in the southern Yukon, and northern British Columbia. Moreover, there is no evidence of any early northern population west of the Rocky Mountains in the District of Mackenzie. It appears, therefore, that diffusion would have required a substantial initial migration thrust into the Yukon Territory or western Northwest Territories.

Migration

The migration hypothesis moves former midlatitude fluted-point peoples into the North. Presently, the comparative data base for Paleoindians in northern British Columbia and northern Alberta is so scant, and Arctic assemblages so suspect of component mixing, that it is difficult to recognize site or ethnic intrusion. Possibly some assemblages identified with in situ non-microblade people belong, instead, to Paleowesterners recently arrived in the North from the Pacific Northwest states and interior British Columbia. The migration hypothesis also requires that after Paleoindians arrived in the North, they coexisted with the Paleoarctic inhabitants, perhaps in a territorial mosaic. The Paleoindians gave the gift of fluted points to their contemporaries. With this hypothesis, as more information becomes available, we can expect to see evidence of ethnic and technological diversity in the western Subarctic 10,000–10,400 years ago.

Inasmuch as the previously discussed Plano migrations would have occurred only shortly before the development of the Northern Archaic tradition, these migrations are irrelevant to the fluted-point question. I believe that some early Holocene Plano-like points in the Yukon and Alaska are the result of parallelism, possibly sharing with Plano proper a mutual but separate fluted-point ancestry.

Independent Development

Some plain northern lanceolate points could be derived from fluted points. Can that developmental model be turned around so that these unfluted points become the *antecedents* of northern fluted points, which would not be especially old? This concept appears to be supported by some researchers (cf. West 1982). Given a lanceolate format, a sporadic but widespread penchant for basal thinning, and the common practice of grinding lower and basal edges, it would be easy to develop a fluted point from certain lanceolate points. The technological situation in the North would have been ripe for this to occur between 6000 and 8000 years ago. That development, if it did occur, would account for the presence of fluted points in the subsequent Northern Archaic tradition and in sites of mixed microblade and Northern Archaic technology. Through diffusion, the persisting points would then have reached the Denbigh Flint complex. If this were the case, fluted-point finds at earlier sites would have to be explained, as would the lack of fluted points in many important excavated Northern Archaic assemblages. Independent development, however, does not exclude other hypotheses, and once this possibility is acknowledged, a number of permutations and all conceivable degrees of complexity are possible! The other hypotheses alone fail to account for the presence of fluted points in some Northern Archaic and amalgamated Northern Archaic-microblade sites, without dismissing these components as being mixed.

CONCLUSION

Certain data sets support each of the three interpretations of northern fluted points. Moreover, all these interpretations are largely compatible with northern prehistory as it is known today. Considering the interpretations to which each piece of data has been subjected to render it usable or palatable, the question of northern fluted-point origins should remain open and the choice between hypotheses should not be arbitrarily finalized.

During recent decades, new information has been recovered and processed through several hypotheses. The data traps have been reset with greater skill. We wait. Will the trapping season ever close? Today the data base is much richer and the answers, though incomplete, are more fulfilling in historiographic and culture-processual content. I believe that for northern points we are close to resolving the origins questions. The "final answer" is long overdue even though the question no longer carries the excitement and focus of attention it has had during past decades. This lack of resolution nevertheless is a block to the recounting of prehistory. A time should come when we will have the green light to go forward with regional historiography concomitant to an understanding of the integration and transformations that took place between North and South in Clovis times.

REFERENCES CITED

Alexander, H. L.
1987 *Putu: A Fluted Point Site in Alaska.* Simon Fraser University Publication No. 17. Archaeology Press, Simon Fraser University, Burnaby.

Anderson, D. D.
1970 Akmak: An Early Archaeological Assemblage from Onion Portage, Northwest Alaska. *Acta Artica,* Fasc. XVI. Copenhagen.
1980 Continuity and Change in the Prehistoric Record from North Alaska. In *Senri Ethnological Studies No. 4,* edited by Y. Kotani and W. B. Workman, pp. 232–251. National Museum of Ethnography, Osaka.

Ball, B. F., compiler
1988 Alberta, in "1987 Research Reports." *Canadian Archaeological Association Newsletter* 8(1):9–13.

Cinq-Mars, J.
1979 Bluefish Cave I: A Late Pleistocene Eastern Beringian Cave Deposit in the Northern Yukon. *Canadian Journal of Archaeology* 3:1–32.

Cinq-Mars, J., E. Nelson, and R. MacNeish
n.d. Engigstciak Revisited: Early Holocene Dates from the Bison Pit. Ms. in possession of authors.

Clark, D. W.
1983 Is There a Northern Cordilleran Tradition? *Canadian Journal of Archaeology* 7:23–48.
1984a Northern Fluted Points: Paleo-Eskimo, Paleo-Arctic, or Paleo-Indian? *Canadian Journal of Anthropology* 4:65–81.
1984b Some Practical Applications of Obsidian Hydration Dating in the Subarctic. *Arctic* 37:91–109.

Clark, D. W., and A. McF. Clark
1975 Fluted Points from the Batza Tena Obsidian Source of the Koyukuk River Region, Alaska. *Anthropological Papers of the University of Alaska* 17(2):31–38.
1980 Fluted Points at the Batza Tena Obsidian Source, Northwestern Interior Alaska. In *Early Native Americans,* edited by D. Browman, pp. 141–159. Mouton, The Hague.
1983 Paleo-Indians and Fluted Points: Subarctic Alternatives. *Plains Anthropologist* 28:283–291.

Cook, J. P., and R. A. McKennan
1970 The Village Site at Healy Lake, Alaska. Paper presented at the 35th Annual Meeting of the Society for American Archaeology, April 30, May 1–2, 1970, Mexico City.

Davis, L. B.
1977 Preliminary Hydration Rate Determinations and Associated Hydration Alternatives: The Alyeska Archeology Project. In *Pipeline Archeology,* edited by J .P. Cook, pp. 10–65. University of Alaska, Institute of Arctic Biology, Fairbanks.

Dixon, E. J.
1985a Review of *Paleoecology of Beringia,* edited by D. M. Hopkins, J. V. Matthews, Jr., C. E. Schweger, and S. B. Young. *North American Archaeologist* 6:83–94.
1985b Cultural Chronology of Central Interior Alaska. *Arctic Anthropology* 22(1):47–66.
1986 The Northern Paleoindian/Northern Archaic Transition in Alaska. Paper presented at the 13th Annual Meeting of the Alaska Anthropological Association, Anchorage.

Dumond, D. E.
1977 *The Eskimos and Aleuts.* Thames and Hudson, London.
1980 The Archaeology of Alaska and the Peopling of America. *Science* 200:984–991.

Dyke, A. S., and V. K. Prest
1986a *Late Wisconsinan and Holocene Retreat of the Laurentide Ice Sheet.* Geological Survey of Canada, Map 1702A.
1986b *Paleogeography of Northern North America, 18 000–5000 Years Ago.* Geological Survey of Canada, Map 1703A.

Fladmark, K. R.
1986 *British Columbia Prehistory.* Canadian Museum

of Civilization, National Museums of Canada, Ottawa.

Fladmark, K. R., J. C. Driver, and D. Alexander
1988 The Paleoindian Component at Charlie Lake Cave (HbRf 39), British Columbia. *American Antiquity* 53:371–384.

Gal, R.
1977 Paleo-Indians of the Brooks Range: A Tradition of Uncontrolled Comparison. Paper presented at the Society for American Archaeology annual meeting, St. Louis.

1982 Appendix I: An Annotated and Indexed Roster of Archaeological Radiocarbon Dates from Alaska, North of 68 Latitude. *Anthropological Papers of the University of Alaska* 20(1–2):159–180.

Giddings, J. L., Jr.
1964 *The Archeology of Cape Denbigh.* Brown University Press, Providence.

Gordon, B. C.
1981 Man-environment Relationships in Barrenland Prehistory. *Musk-ox* 28:1–19.

Greer, S. C., and R. J. LeBlanc
1983 Yukon Culture History: An Update. *Musk-ox* 33:26–36.

Gryba, E. M.
1983 *Sibbald Creek: 11,000 Years of Human Use of the Alberta Foothills.* Archaeological Survey of Alberta Occasional Paper No. 22. Edmonton.

Hoffecker, J., C. F. Waythomas, and W. R. Powers
1988 Late Glacial Loess Stratigraphy and Archaeology in the Nenana Valley, Central Alaska. *Current Research in the Pleistocene* 5:83–86.

Kunz, M. L.
1982 The Mesa Site: An Early Holocene Hunting Stand in the Iteriak Valley, Northern Alaska. *Arctic Anthropology* 20(1–2):113–122.

Larsen, H.
1968 Trail Creek: Final Report on the Excavation of Two Caves on Seward Peninsula, Alaska. *Acta Artica,* Fasc. XV. Copenhagen.

LeBlanc, R. J., and J. W. Ives
1986 The Bezya Site: A Wedge-shaped Core Assemblage from Northeastern Alberta. *Canadian Journal of Archaeology* 10:59–98.

MacNeish, R. S.
1959a A Speculative Framework of Northern North American Prehistory as of April 1959. *Anthropologica* ns. 1:1–178 & chart.

1959b Men Out of Asia; As Seen from the Northwest Yukon. *Anthropological Papers of the University of Alaska* 7(2):41–70.

1964 *Investigations in the Southwest Yukon: Archaeological Excavations, Comparisons, and Speculations.* Papers of the R. S. Peabody Foundation for Archaeology, Vol. 6(2). Phillips Academy, Andover.

McKennan, R. A., and J. P. Cook
1970 Prehistory of Healy Lake, Alaska. *Proceedings VIIIth Congress of Anthropological and Ethnological Sciences, 1968* 3:182–184. Tokyo.

Meltzer, D. J., and R. C. Dunnell
1987 Fluted Points from the Pacific Northwest. *Current Research in the Pleistocene* 4:64–67.

Millar, J. F. V.
1981 Interaction Between the MacKenzie and Yukon Basins During the Early Holocene. In *Networks of the Past: Regional Interaction in Archaeology,* edited by P. F. Kense and P. G. Duke, pp. 259–295. Archaeological Association of Calgary, Calgary.

Morlan, R. E., and J. Cinq-Mars
1982 Ancient Beringians: Human Occupations in the Late Pleistocene of Alaska and the Yukon Territory. In *Paleoecology of Beringia,* edited by D. M. Hopkins, J. V. Matthews, Jr., C. E. Schweger, and S. B. Young, pp. 353–381. Academic Press, New York.

Noble, W. C.
1981 Prehistory of the Great Slave Lake and Great Bear Lake Region. In *Subarctic,* edited by J. Helm, pp. 97–106. Handbook of North American Indians, vol. 6, W. C. Sturtevant, general editor. Smithsonian Institution, Washington, D.C.

Powers, W. R., and T. D. Hamilton
1978 Dry Creek: A Late Pleistocene Human Occupation in Central Alaska. In *Early Man in America from a Circum-Pacific Perspective,* edited by A. L. Bryan, pp. 72–77. Occasional Papers No. 1. Department of Anthropology, University of Alberta, Edmonton.

Powers, W. R., R. D. Guthrie, and J. F. Hoffecker
1983 *Dry Creek: Archeology and Paleoecology of a Late Pleistocene Alaskan Hunting Camp.* Submitted to the National Park Service, Contract CX-9000-7-0047.

Reeves, B. O. K.
1981 Bergs, Barriers and Beringia: Reflections on the Peopling of the New World. In *Quaternary Coastlines and Marine Archaeology,* edited by P. M. Masters and N. C. Fleming, pp. 389–411. Academic Press, New York.

Rutter, N. W.
1980 Late Pleistocene History of the Western Canadian Ice-free Corridor. *Canadian Journal of Anthropology* 1:1–8.

Stuckenrath, R., and J. Mielke
1973 Smithsonian Radiocarbon Measurements VIII. *Radiocarbon* 15:388–424.

West, F. H.
1967 The Donnelly Ridge Site and the Definition of an Early Core and Blade Complex in Central Alaska. *American Antiquity* 32:360–382.

1981 *The Archaeology of Beringia.* Columbia University Press, New York.

1982 Making Points with Points. *The Quarterly Review of Archaeology* 3(3):6–7.

1987 Migrations and New World Origins: Review of A Comparison of the Linguistic, Dental and Genetic Evidence by Greenberg, Turner and Zegura. *The Quarterly Review of Archaeology* 8(1):11–14.

Wilson, I. R.
1987 The Pink Mountain Paleo-Indian Site. In *Archaeology in Alberta 1986,* edited by M. Mange, pp. 217–219. Archaeological Survey of Alberta Occasional Paper No. 31. Edmonton.

Workman, W. B.
1974 First Dated Traces of Early Holocene Man in the Southwest Yukon Territory, Canada. *Arctic Anthropology* XI Supplement:94–103.

1978 *Prehistory of the Aishihik-Kluane Area, Southwest Yukon Territory.* Archaeological Survey of Canada Paper No. 74. Mercury Series. National Museum of Man, Ottawa.

Wright, J. V.
1981 Prehistory of the Canadian Shield. In *Subarctic,* edited by J. Helm, pp. 86–96. Handbook of North American Indians, vol. 6, W. C. Sturtevant, general editor. Smithsonian Institution, Washington, D.C.

The Nenana Complex of Alaska and Clovis Origins

TED GOEBEL, ROGER POWERS,
AND NANCY BIGELOW
Department of Anthropology
University of Alaska Fairbanks
Fairbanks, AK 99775

Excavations at the Walker Road and Dry Creek sites in central Alaska have produced artifact assemblages dated to approximately 11,300 yr B.P. These cultural remains have been assigned to the Nenana complex, based on similarities in lithic technology and tool kits. Comparative lithic analyses of the Nenana complex and Clovis show that, with the exception of projectile-point styles, these industries are very similar. The significance of these results is discussed, in terms of both Clovis origins and the peopling of the Western Hemisphere.

INTRODUCTION

While no archaeologist has yet confirmed the existence of an Alaskan or Siberian antecedent of the Clovis culture, there is no doubt that the first Paleoindians entered the New World via Beringia. Excavations throughout the past decade at the central Alaskan sites of Dry Creek, Moose Creek, and Walker Road have uncovered evidence for a late Pleistocene hunting culture in central Alaska that was approximately contemporaneous with the Clovis culture (Figure 1). These early cultural remains, now assigned to the Nenana complex, have been found in well-stratified loess deposits at four sites: Walker Road, Dry Creek, Moose Creek, and Owl Ridge (Figures 2 and 3). Each has been C-14 dated to between 11,000 and 12,000 yr B.P., but only at Walker Road and Dry Creek have excavations produced relatively large tool assemblages (Powers and Hoffecker 1989). Technologically, the Nenana complex, as defined by Powers and Hoffecker (1989), consists predominantly of a core and blade industry with unifacially worked end and side scrapers, perforators, wedges, and large planes manufactured on cobbles, as well as bifaces and bifacial projectile points (Goebel 1988).

The purpose of this paper is to report the results of a comparative lithic analysis of two Nenana complex assemblages (Walker Road and Dry Creek Component I), two Clovis assemblages (Blackwater Draw and Murray Springs), and a single Denali complex assemblage (Dry Creek Component II). These assemblages have been analyzed with a Soviet modification of the Bordian typological system formulated by S.V. Markin (1983, 1986) of the Institute of History, Philosophy, and Philogy, Siberian Branch, Academy of Sciences at Novosibirsk, U.S.S.R. With this system we have been able to better describe: (1) primary working techniques (the activities performed in the manufacturing of tool blanks); (2) secondary working techniques (the processes involved in shaping or modifying a blank into a specific tool form); and (3) the tool kits of the assemblages.

Each of the Alaskan sites and respective artifact assemblages is described in detail below. The Blackwater Draw and Murray Springs collections are treated in less detail, since they have been included solely for comparative reasons.

Walker Road[1]

Walker Road is a multicomponent open-air site located in central Alaska, ten miles north of Healy (Figure 2). It is situated in the foothills of the North Alaska Range, along a south-facing bluff created by the incision of the Healy-aged glacial outwash terrace by Cindy and James Creek. At the Walker Road site, the Healy terrace surface is capped by a 1-m-thick deposit of aeolian silts.

Walker Road was discovered in 1980 during a reconnaissance survey conducted by J.F. Hoffecker, then a graduate student at the University of Chicago (Hoffecker 1985a). Hoffecker's initial test pit uncovered several deeply buried lithic artifacts. In 1984, J. F. Hoffecker and W. R. Powers again tested the loess mantle and discovered a circular hearth and more

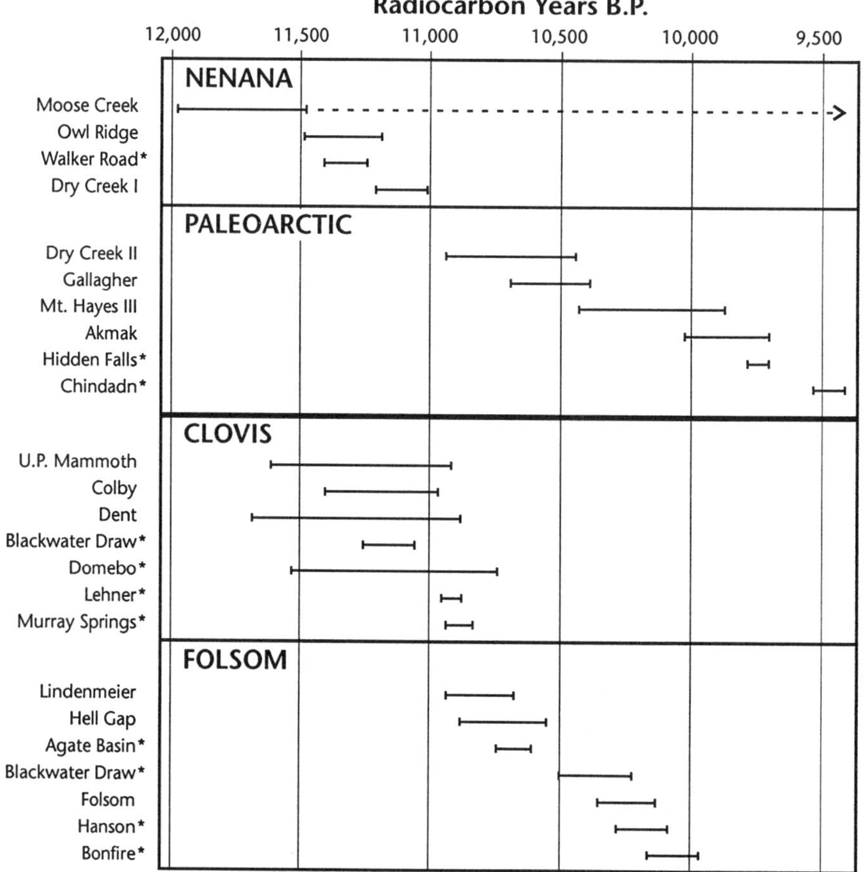

Figure 1. C-14 ages of Nenana, Paleoarctic, Clovis, and Folsom sites. (Clovis and Folsom dates after Haynes 1980, 1982, 1987; Haynes et al. 1984).

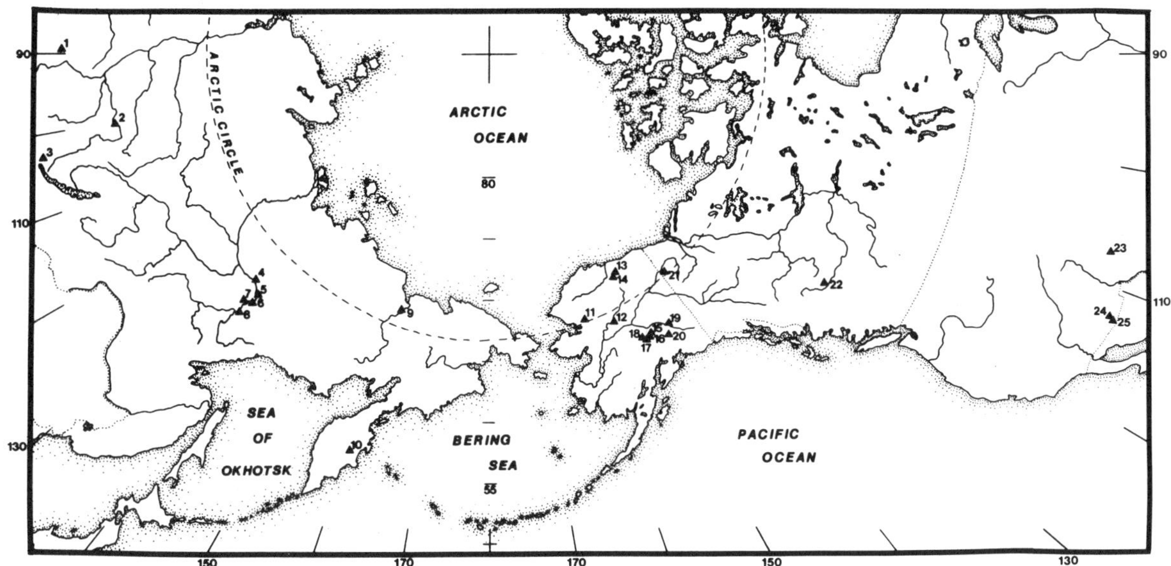

Figure 2. Upper Pleistocene and Early Holocene sites of Northeast Asia and North America mentioned in text: **1)** Malaya Siya; **2)** Ust'-Kova; **3)** Mal'ta; **4)** Ikhine; **5)** Ezhantsy; **6)** Verkne Troitskaya; **7)** Ust'-Mil'; **8)** Diuktai Cave; **9)** Berelëkh; **10)** Ushki Lake; **11)** Akmak; **12)** Batza Tena; **13)** Gallagher; **14)** Putu; **15)** Moose Creek; **16)** Walker Road; **17)** Dry Creek; **18)** Owl Ridge; **19)** Healy Lake; **20)** Mt. Hayes 111; **21)** Bluefish Caves; **22)** Charlie Lake Cave; **23)** Blackwater Draw; **24)** Murray Springs; **25)** Lehner.

lithics. Charcoal from the hearth dated to 11,820 ± 120 yr B.P. (Beta-11,254). Intensive excavations of over 150 m^2 from 1985 to 1988 led to the discovery of two major cluster areas, together containing over 4,500 lithic remains. During the four years of testing and excavation at Walker Road, our major research goal has been to further clarify the terminal Pleistocene archaeological record in central Alaska and its significance for the peopling of the New World.

Geologic Stratigraphy[2]

The late Quaternary stratigraphy at Walker Road can be broadly described as a series of loesses containing varying amounts of aeolian sand, and two major paleosol horizons, each recording a mesic period of vegetative growth and pedogenesis (Figure 3). The Nenana complex artifacts lay at the base of the loess deposit (Loesses 1 and 2) (Figure 3), which is in turn underlain by glacial outwash assigned to the early Wisconsin (?) Healy glaciation (Wahrhaftig 1958). These terminal Pleistocene loesses are weakly oxidized and for the most part unweathered.

Loesses 1 and 2 are overlain by Sand 1, a regional deposit found in the Nenana Valley that registers sharp climatic deterioration and increased wind velocity. Loess 3 stratigraphically overlies Sand 1 and is capped by Loess 4, containing a broad grey-black paleosol complex which displays whitish streaks and lenses (Pedocomplex 1) recording multiple episodes of soil formation. The highly contorted nature of this paleosol may be the result of local earthquake activity or, more likely, the result of solifluction and other cryogenic site deformation processes. A single C-14 date of 8720 ± 250 yr B.P. (AA- 1692) from this stratigraphic unit indicates an early Holocene age.

A second paleosol complex (Pedocomplex 2), dominated by browns and reddish browns, has been identified nearer the top of the stratigraphic section in Loesses 5 and 6 and Sands 2 and 3. Two C-14 dates from the bottom of this paleosol indicate a late Holocene age: 3816 ± 79 yr B.P. (AA 1693), and 4415 ± 95 yr B.P. (GX-12875). The top of the section, furthermore, is dominated by the modern soil (Loess 6 and Sand 4), which displays distinct O, A, and B horizons and also contains a late prehistoric cultural level characterized by several undiagnostic artifacts.

Cultural Remains

The Walker Road site consists of two stratigraphically distinct components. Component II is late Holocene in age and will not be dealt with here. Component I, the Nenana complex occupation of the site, lies within Loesses 1 and 2. Horizontally, this component appears to extend at least 40 m along the bluff and up to 15 m inward from the bluff edge. Initial C-14 dating (through conventional methods on cultural charcoal) of this

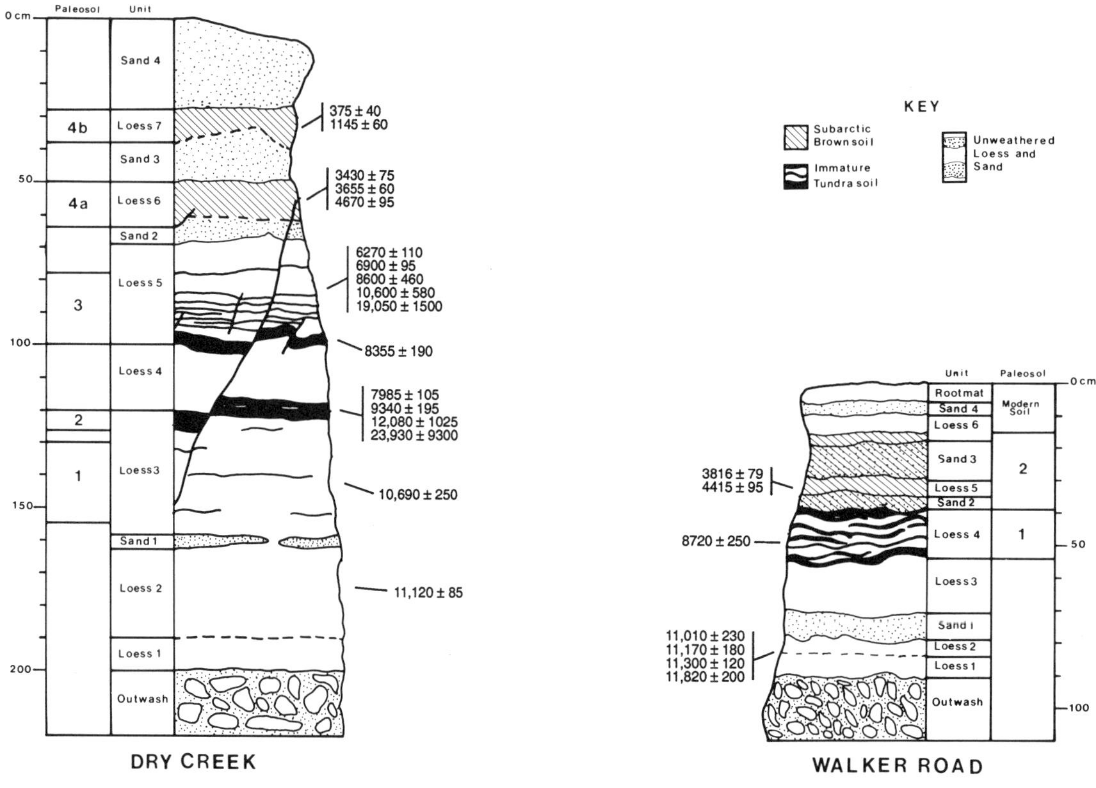

Figure 3. Representative stratigraphic sections from the Dry Creek and Walker Road sites.

component in 1984 indicated an age of 11,820 ± 120 yr B.P. (Beta-11,254); subsequent dating through AMS techniques (on cultural charcoal) have produced three C-14 dates of 11,300 ± 120 yr B.P. (AA-2264); 11,170 ± 180 yr B.P. (AA-1681); and 11,010 ± 230 yr B.P. (AA-1683). The average of these four dates (Figure 1), 11,330 ± 80 yr B.P., has been obtained through the methods described by Long and Rippeteau (1974).

The Walker Road lithic assemblage is characterized by a core and blade industry, with a tool kit including end scrapers, side scrapers, wedges, perforators, bifacial "knives," bifacially worked Chindadn points (Cook 1969), and large cobble tools, some in the form of planes. Significantly, no microblade cores, microblades, or associated microcore debitage have been recovered.

Dry Creek[1]

The Dry Creek site, also located in the Nenana Valley near Healy, Alaska (Figure 2), lies along the south-facing bluff edge of the Healy terrace. The site contains three stratigraphically distinct cultural levels that are contained in aeolian deposits overlying glacial outwash (Figure 3) (Powers 1983a:42; Powers and Hamilton 1978). Dry Creek was discovered by C. E. Holmes in 1973. Subsequent testing and excavations occurred in 1974, 1976, and 1977, exposing 347 m^2 of the terminal Pleistocene living surface (Powers et al. 1983).

Although the Dry Creek geological and cultural stratigraphy is described in detail by Powers (1983a) and Thorson and Hamilton (1977), a brief review will be given here. The Nenana complex occupation lies in Loess 2 at Dry Creek and is terminal Pleistocene in age, as suggested by a single C-14 date (on charcoal) of 11,120 ± 85 yr B.P. (Thorson and Hamilton 1977). Loess 2 is separated from Loess 3 and Paleosols 1 and 2 by Sand 1, which apparently records the same cold snap with accelerated winds as noted at Walker Road. Paleosols 1 and 2 have been characterized as immature tundra soils consisting chiefly of dark organic A horizons (Thorson and Hamilton 1977:161). These paleosols may be tentatively correlated with the McKinley Park interstadial (11,800–10,500 yr B.P.) and are followed by renewed loess deposition (Loess 4), representing the final Pleistocene cold oscillation (10,500–9500 yr B.P.). Powers and Hoffecker (1989) have tentatively correlated this cold period with the McKinley Park IV alpine moraine (Ten Brink and Waythomas 1985:26–27).

The early Holocene "period of maximum summer

warmth" (McCulloch and Hopkins 1966) is exhibited at Dry Creek by a distinctive tundra soil complex (Paleosol 3) consisting of a very complex sequence of well-developed organic horizons alternating with light gray and yellowish-brown horizons (Thorson and Hamilton 1977:161). Cryoturbation and/or tectonic activity have heavily disturbed this stratigraphic unit, causing a highly distorted appearance that has been identified elsewhere in the Nenana Valley, including Walker Road (Powers and Hoffecker 1989). The remaining stratigraphic sequence reflects a continuation of alternating phases of aeolian sand and loess deposition, which has been correlated respectively to episodes of Neoglacial advances and Holocene forest soil formation (Powers and Hoffecker 1989).

Component I

The initial occupation of the Dry Creek site, contained in Loess 2 and C-14 dated to 11,120 ± 85 yr B.P., has been assigned to the Nenana complex based on a tool kit that includes end scrapers, side scrapers, bifacially worked triangular projectile points, bifacial "knives," and large cobble tools (Powers and Hoffecker 1989). A lithic analysis conducted by Powers (1983b) has shown that this Nenana complex occupation displays a primary technology directed towards the production of blades and flakes which served as tool blanks. In addition, no microblades, microblade cores, or microcore debitage were found in association with these materials.

Component II

Dry Creek Component II, C-14 dated to 10,690 ± 250 yr B.P., represents the second major occupation of the Dry Creek site (Powers and Hamilton 1978). The Component II assemblage consists chiefly of subprismatic blade cores, wedge-shaped microblade cores, microblades, burins, side scrapers, large cobble tools, projectile points (several types including Agate Basin/Hell Gap-like), and other bifacial tools. This assemblage exhibits close morphological and metric parallels to other Denali complex sites in central Alaska (Powers and Hoffecker 1989). The Denali complex has been assigned to the Paleoarctic tradition, based on similarities in constituent artifacts and radiocarbon dates (Dumond 1977:40; West 1967, 1981).

Blackwater Draw[1]

The Blackwater Draw artifacts included in this analysis consist exclusively of Clovis-aged cultural material recovered in situ as reported by Hester (1972:183–220). These include the lithic assemblages excavated by teams from the High Plains Ecology Project (Hester 1972:54), Eastern New Mexico University (Hester 1972:56), and the El Llano Archaeological Society (Hester 1972:71; Warnica 1966). Casts of the Clovis blade cache reported by Green (1963) were also included. The 1961–1962 salvage investigations at the Blackwater Draw gravel pit concentrated on the excavation of an early Holocene/late Pleistocene watering hole that revealed the remains of a Paleoindian mammoth kill, as well as an adjoining multicomponent campsite (Hester 1972:178). The Clovis component was found to be stratigraphically distinct from the later Folsom, Portales, and Archaic levels (Evans 1951; Hester 1972:147; Sellards 1952) and has produced a set of three radiocarbon dates averaging 11,170 ± 100 yr B.P. (Figure 1) (Haynes 1987; Haynes et al. 1984). Details on the dating and stratigraphy of the site can be found in Haynes and Agogino (1966) and Haynes (1975).

Murray Springs[1]

Located in the San Pedro Valley, Arizona, the Murray Springs site is surrounded by some of the richest Paleoindian archaeology in the western United States. Within a few miles of this site are the Lehner, Naco, Escapule, Navarette, and Leikem sites, all Clovis localities dated to the terminal Pleistocene, ca. 11,000 yr B.P. (Huckell 1982). Haynes et al. (1984:188) have reported a total of eight radiocarbon dates for the Murray Springs Clovis occupation, the average of which is 10,900 ± 50 yr B.P. (Figure 1). Excavations at Murray Springs from 1966 to 1971 revealed three major Clovis activity areas: a mammoth kill, a bison kill, and an associated campsite, all of which are considered contemporaneous (Haynes 1980:118; Hemmings 1970).

METHODOLOGY

Each artifact (tools and debitage) was examined for the presence of specific attributes that led to its assignment in an artifact type and class. The typology is based on definitions originally designed by Markin (1983, 1986) and slightly modified by the authors to better fit North American assemblages. Definitions of the tool classes are presented below; tool type definitions are provided in Goebel (1990). While some of the conventional tool names used here imply function, our designations are based purely on morphological attributes.

1. *Retouched Flakes.* These are irregularly shaped artifacts that display marginal retouching or utilization. Otherwise, these implements have not been modified.
2. *Retouched Blades.* These are blades with use-wear and/or retouching along one or both margins. Blades are characterized by parallel sides, as well as one or more parallel arrises (dorsal ridges). Length-to-width ratios have not been employed in

this classification, because blade length is often dependent on the height of the core. The use of small cobbles of various cherts, quartzites, and rhyolites collected from local Nenana Valley outwash deposits did not favor the manufacturing of large cores and elongate blades at the Nenana complex sites.

3. *End Scrapers.* These are artifacts that have a transversely (in relation to the axis of the blank) retouched scraping edge, which is generally steep and arched ("end scraper retouch").
4. *Side Scrapers.* Artifacts classified in this group are usually made from flakes and retouched on at least one of the lateral margins of the blank. Lateral margins were usually retouched to form a specifically shaped working edge.
5. *Cobble Tools.* These are all tools manufactured on cobbles or pebbles. Many still exhibit cortical surfaces and occur in the form of unifacial choppers, bifacial chopping tools, hammerstones, and planes.
6. *Perforators.* These tools, also referred to in the literature as awls, gravers, and drills, have a distinctive point or spur, usually formed through one or two converging concave edges.
7. *Wedges.* These tools display bipolar crushing and/or flaking which is often bifacial. (It is possible that wedges, also referred to as *pièces ésquillées*, are not actually tools, but are instead the by-products of a bipolar primary working technique, in which a small cobble is rested on a large anvil stone and then struck from above with a third rock, or hammerstone.)
8. *Notches.* These artifacts display a single marginal notch or concavity.
9. *Bifaces.* This group includes all objects that have been reduced bifacially, excluding projectile points and chopping tools. Asymmetrical bifaces with points have also been included in this group.
10. *Projectile Points.* These are bifacially worked tools that display a pointed end and are usually symmetrical in outline and finely retouched.
11. *Denticulates.* These tools display a series of adjacent notches along the tool margin, creating a flaked, tooth-like working edge.
12. *Pointed Tools.* These are unifacially worked tools, known in the Soviet Union as *ostrokonechniki*, that display a point at the distal end of the tool. They are unlike perforators in that they are usually symmetrical and quite large. The longitudinal cross-sections of these tools also show the formation of a point, unlike convergent side scrapers, which display blunt angles of convergence. Pointed tools are known to Mousterian typologists as Levallois or Mousterian points.
13. *Burins.* These tools are defined as having at least one working edge formed by the removal of an edge at a right angle to the plane of the blank.
14. *Retouched Microblades.* These are microblades displaying marginal retouching and/or use-wear. Microblades can be defined as extremely narrow blades (generally <4 mm in width) struck from prepared prismatic microblade cores.

In an attempt to characterize primary working techniques, tools were also classified according to blank type: blade, flake, or cobble.

Basic statistics of the tool assemblages were prepared through use of the computer program BMDP 2D. These results have been displayed in the form of cumulative frequency graphs. In addition, a cluster analysis was performed through application of the program BMDP 2M, comparing the Clovis and Alaskan sites on the basis of tool class frequencies. The method used was centroid linkage, in which the Chi Square distance is calculated to produce a dendrogram that measures and graphically displays relative distances between the collections.

RESULTS

The results of our analyses of the Walker Road, Dry Creek, Blackwater Draw, and Murray Springs collections are briefly outlined below. These results are preliminary in nature, and much more analysis is currently underway at the University of Alaska Fairbanks. Each assemblage is described separately in some detail. Comparative statistical and cluster analysis results are then presented regarding the similarities and differences between the Clovis sites and their Alaskan temporal counterparts.

Walker Road

The Walker Road assemblage consists of 4,491 lithic remains, 184 (4.1%) of which are considered tools. The majority of the tool classes represented in the Walker Road assemblage include retouched flakes and blades, end scrapers, side scrapers, and cobble tools (Table 1). The majority of raw materials utilized include brown and tan cherts, chalcedony, quartzite, rhyolite, and basalt. Obsidian appears to be the only raw material of a nonlocal source, although no studies have been performed to trace points of origin.

Retouched flakes and blades together make up almost 50% of the entire tool assemblage. The retouched blades consist mainly of unilaterally and bilaterally retouched blades (>5 cm in length), whereas bladelets (<5 cm in length) and blade-like flakes occur in lower numbers. Some of these are illustrated in Figure 4.

End scrapers make up the largest portion of the shaped tools found at Walker Road. In fact, 36 (19.6%) of

Table 1. Tool Types—Walker Road.

	TYPE	NO.	%	% CUM.
1.	**Retouched Flake**			
1.00	Retouched Flake Frag.	21	11.4	11.4
1.01	Retouched Flake	30	16.3	27.7
2.	**Retouched Blade**			
2.00	Retouched Blade Frag.	1	0.5	28.2
2.01	Unilaterally Ret. Blade	13	7.1	35.3
2.02	Bilaterally Ret. Blade	10	5.4	40.7
2.03	Unilaterally Ret. Bladelet	1	0.5	41.2
2.04	Bilaterally Ret. Bladelet	7	3.8	45.0
2.05	Uni. Ret. Blade-like Flake	3	1.6	46.6
2.06	Bi. Ret. Blade-like Flake	2	1.1	47.7
3.	**End Scraper**			
3.00	End Scraper Frag.	5	2.7	50.4
3.01	End Scraper on Blade	16	8.7	59.1
3.02	End Scraper on Flake	6	3.3	62.4
3.03	Pan-shaped End Scraper	5	2.7	65.1
3.04	Steeply Keeled End Scraper	1	0.5	65.6
3.05	Double-end Scraper	1	0.5	66.1
3.06	Circular End Scraper	1	0.5	66.6
3.07	End Scraper/Burin	0	0.0	66.6
3.08	Spurred End Scraper	1	0.5	67.1
4.	**Side Scraper**			
4.00	Side Scraper Frag.	2	1.1	68.2
4.01	Single-straight Side Scraper	2	1.1	69.3
4.02	Double-straight Side Scraper	0	0.0	69.3
4.03	Single-convex Side Scraper	1	0.5	69.8
4.04	Double-convex Side Scraper	3	1.6	71.4
4.05	Straight-convex Side Scraper	0	0.0	71.4
4.06	Single-concave Side Scraper	1	0.5	71.9
4.07	Convergent Scraper	3	1.6	73.5
4.08	Transverse Scraper	2	1.1	74.6
4.09	Angle *(Déjeté)* Scraper	2	1.1	75.7
5.	**Cobble Tool**			
5.00	Cobble Tool Frag.	1	0.5	76.2
5.01	Double Plane	2	1.1	77.3
5.02	Convergent Plane	1	0.5	77.8
5.03	Quadrilateral Plane	0	0.0	77.8
5.04	Transverse Plane	3	1.6	79.4
5.05	Chopper	2	1.1	80.5
5.06	Chopping Tool	1	0.5	81.0
5.07	Hammerstone	1	0.5	81.5
5.08	Anvil Stone	3	1.6	83.1
5.09	Pebble Retoucher	1	0.5	84.6
6.	**Perforator**			
6.00	Perforator Frag.	0	0.0	83.6
6.01	Single Perforator	6	3.3	86.9
6.02	Multiple Perforator	2	1.1	88.0
7.	**Wedge**			
7.00	Wedge Frag.	0	0.0	88.0
7.01	Wedge	7	3.8	91.8
8.	**Notch**			
8.00	Notch Frag.	1	0.5	92.3
8.01	Notch	6	3.3	95.6
9.	**Biface**			
9.00	Biface Frag.	2	1.1	96.7
9.01	Oblong Biface	0	0.0	96.7
9.02	Triangular Biface	0	0.0	96.7
9.03	Spatulate Biface	0	0.0	96.7
9.04	Elliptical Biface	0	0.0	96.7
9.05	Oval Biface	0	0.0	96.7
9.06	Ovate Biface	0	0.0	96.7
9.07	Lanceolate Biface	1	0.5	97.2
9.08	Discoidal Biface	0	0.0	97.2
9.09	Deltoid Biface	0	0.0	97.2
9.10	Misc. Biface	0	0.0	97.2
10.	**Projectile Point**			
10.00	Projectile Point Frag.	0	0.0	97.2
10.01	Chindadn Point	3	1.6	98.8
10.02	Lanceolate Point	0	0.0	98.8
10.03	Triangular Point	0	0.0	98.8
10.04	Bipointed Point	0	0.0	98.8
10.05	Stemmed Point	0	0.0	98.8
10.06	Notched Point	0	0.0	98.8
10.07	Clovis Fluted Point	0	0.0	98.8
11.	**Denticulate**			
11.00	Denticulate Frag.	0	0.0	98.8
11.01	Denticulate	2	1.1	99.9
12.	**Pointed Tool**			
12.00	Pointed Tool Frag.	0	0.0	99.9
12.01	Pointed Tool	0	0.0	99.9
13.	**Burin**			
13.00	Burin Frag.	0	0.0	99.9
13.01	Burin On Snap	0	0.0	99.9
13.02	Dihedral Burin	0	0.0	99.9
13.03	Angle Burin	0	0.0	99.9
13.04	Transverse Burin	0	0.0	99.9
13.05	Burin Spall	0	0.0	99.9
14.	**Retouched Microblade**			
14.00	Ret. Microblade Frag.	0	0.0	99.9
14.01	Uni. Ret. Microblade	0	0.0	99.9
14.02	Bi. Ret. Microblade	0	0.0	99.9
	TOTAL	184	99.9	

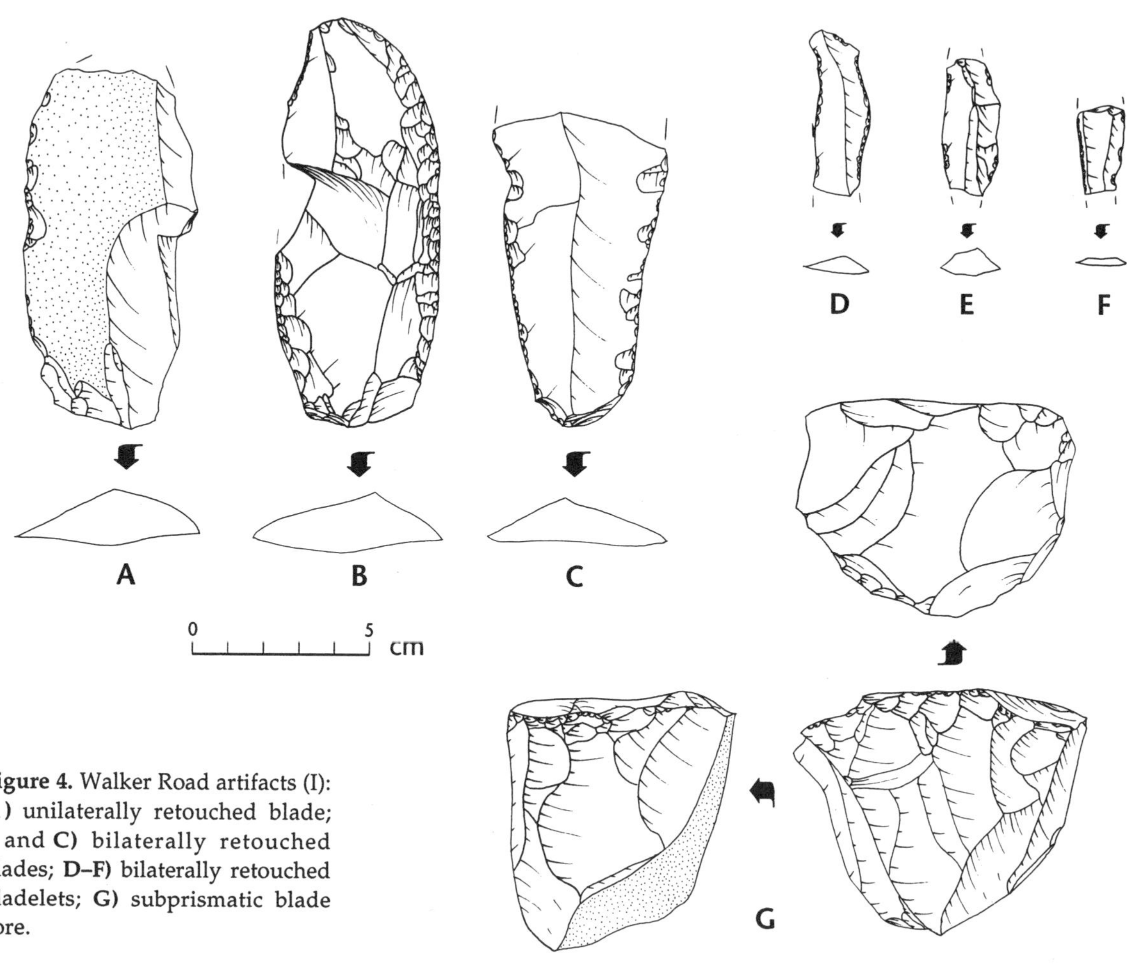

Figure 4. Walker Road artifacts (I): **A)** unilaterally retouched blade; **B** and **C)** bilaterally retouched blades; **D–F)** bilaterally retouched bladelets; **G)** subprismatic blade core.

the Walker Road tools are end scrapers. They occur in a variety of sizes and shapes, as Figures 5 and 6 show, and have been classified into the following seven tool types: end scrapers on blades (16), end scrapers on flakes (6), pan-shaped end scrapers (5), end scraper fragments (5), double-end scrapers (1), circular end scrapers (1), steeply keeled (or carinated) end scrapers (1), and spurred end scrapers (1).

Side scrapers also make up a considerable portion of the Walker Road assemblage. Single-convex and double-convex side scrapers on large flakes occur most frequently (Figure 7a,b). Convergent (Figures 6j and 7c) and transverse scrapers have also been identified, as well as one single-concave scraper and two angle *(déjeté)* scrapers.

Bifaces and projectile points occur in very small numbers. One of the more complete bifacial preforms is lanceolate in shape. The three complete projectile points have been classified as Chindadn points, which are small bifacially worked teardrop-shaped implements (Figure 6k,l,m).

Cobble tools constitute a significant component of the Walker Road tool kit. Six of the 15 cobble tools recovered have been called plano-convex tools, or planes, which display very smooth, sometimes cortical, ventral surfaces and extremely steep flaked dorsal surfaces (Figure 8). The worked margins of these planes display direct percussion flaking, as well as some crushing. These artifacts were apparently heavy-duty tools. Identical tools occur in assemblages of the same age as the Nenana complex in the Angara Region of central Siberia and are thought to have functioned as planes for smoothing and shaping wood surfaces (Medvedev 1969). Other cobble tools found at Walker Road include two choppers, one chopping tool and hammerstone, as well as one pebble retoucher and three anvil stones. The hammerstone and pebble retoucher display crushing and flaking along otherwise cortical surfaces, suggesting their use as implements for directly removing flakes from the margins of other tool blanks.

The wedges (7) *(pièces ésquillées)* exhibit bipolar crushing and flaking, which, like the planes described

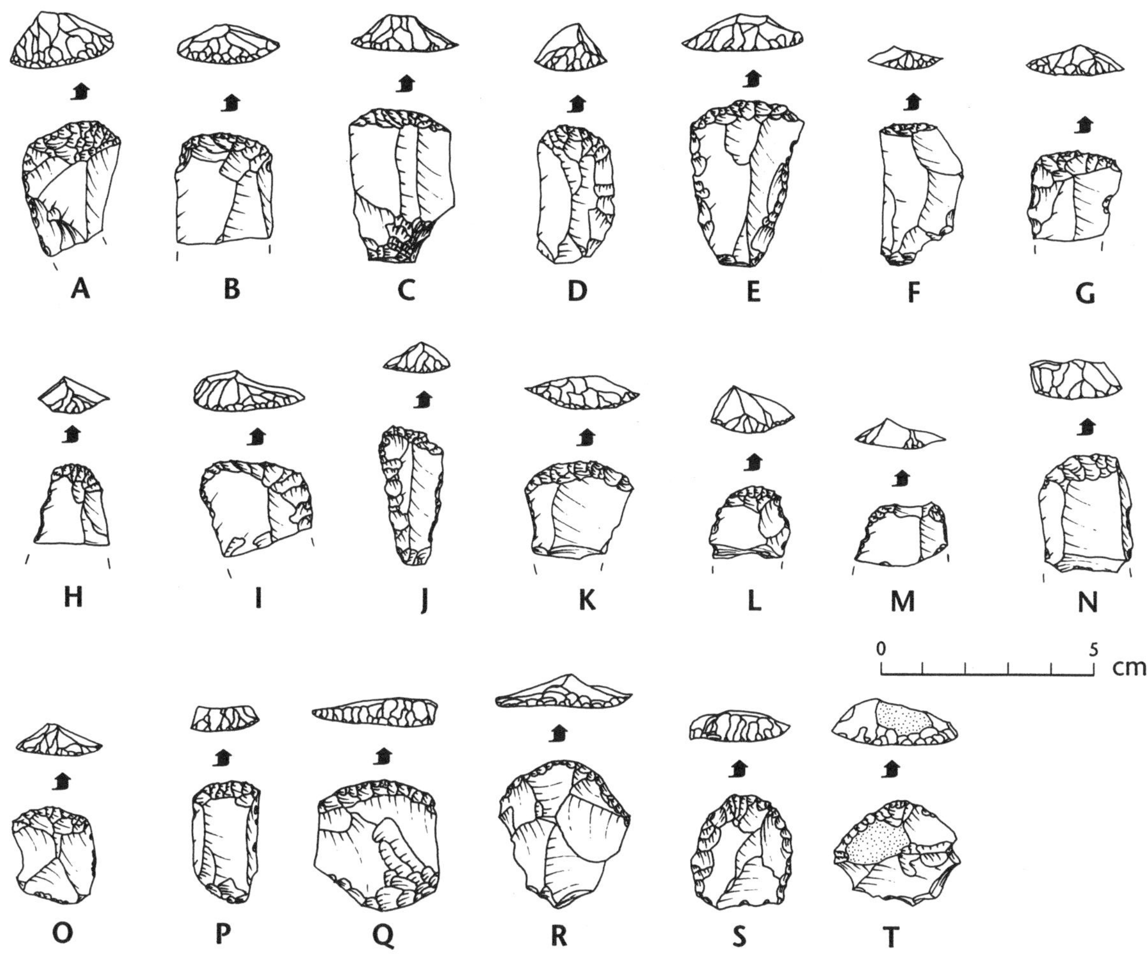

Figure 5. Walker Road artifacts (II): **A–N** and **P)** end scrapers on blades; **O** and **Q–T)** end scrapers on flakes.

above, suggest a considerable amount of wood or bone working (Figure 7h,i).

Eight perforators were recovered from the Walker Road site, two of which are multiple perforators, displaying more than one "graver" tip (Figure 7e). Two single perforators (Figure 7d) are bimarginally retouched and symmetrical in form. The other perforators are unifacial, usually with single hooked or curved spurs (Figure 7f,g).

It is significant to note the absence of both burins and retouched microblades in the Walker Road assemblage, two tool classes commonly found in most Alaskan Paleoarctic sites in great quantities.

In terms of primary working and blank selection, the Walker Road industry reflects both blade and flake technologies. Of 148 identified tool blanks in the assemblage, 58 (39.2%) are blades, 71 (48.0%) are flakes, and 19 (12.8%) are cobbles. Five cores have also been recovered from the site: two small subprismatic blade cores (Figure 4g) and three flake cores.

As suggested above, bifacial technology is only weakly represented at Walker Road. Only three (1.6%) of the Walker Road tools are bifacial. Bimarginal/bipolar (19), alternate (2), reverse (2), and invasive (3) forms are also present.

Dry Creek Component I

The Dry Creek Component I assemblage consists of 4,524 lithic remains, 56 (1.2%) of which are implements. Table 2 shows the relative frequencies of each of the tool types in the Dry Creek Component I assemblage. Of the modified tools, end scrapers, side scrapers, bifaces, projectile points, and cobble tools are the most prominent. By and large the Dry Creek Component I lithic industry contains local raw materials, including cryptocrystalline cherts and coarse-grained quartzites. It is difficult to ascertain whether nonlocal raw materials occur in the assemblage, since no obsidians have been identified and most of the cherts can be found today in the local outwash and flood-plain gravels. It is possible, however,

Table 2. Tool Types—Dry Creek Component I.

	TYPE	NO.	%	% CUM.		TYPE	NO.	%	% CUM.
1.	**Retouched Flake**				7.	**Wedge**			
1.00	Retouched Flake Frag.	5	8.9	8.9	7.00	Wedge Frag.	0	0.0	82.1
1.01	Retouched Flake	1	1.8	10.7	7.01	Wedge Tool	1	1.8	83.9
2.	**Retouched Blade**				8.	**Notch**			
2.00	Retouched Blade Frag.	1	1.8	12.5	8.00	Notch Frag.	0	0.0	83.9
2.01	Unilaterally Ret. Blade	3	5.4	17.9	8.01	Notch	2	3.6	87.5
2.02	Bilaterally Ret. Blade	0	0.0	17.9	9.	**Biface**			
2.03	Unilaterally Ret. Bladelet	3	5.4	23.3	9.00	Biface Frag.	1	1.8	89.3
2.04	Bilaterally Ret. Bladelet	2	3.6	26.9	9.01	Oblong Biface	0	0.0	89.3
2.05	Uni. Ret. Blade-like Flake	0	0.0	26.9	9.02	Triangular Biface	3	5.4	94.7
2.06	Bi. Ret. Blade-like Flake	2	3.6	30.5	9.03	Spatulate Biface	0	0.0	94.7
3.	**End Scraper**				9.04	Elliptical Biface	0	0.0	94.7
3.00	End Scraper Frag.	2	3.6	34.1	9.05	Oval Biface	0	0.0	94.7
3.01	End Scraper on Blade	5	8.9	43.0	9.06	Ovate Biface	0	0.0	94.7
3.02	End Scraper on Flake	3	5.4	48.4	9.07	Lanceolate Biface	0	0.0	94.7
3.03	Pan-shaped End Scraper	0	0.0	48.4	9.08	Discoidal Biface	0	0.0	94.7
3.04	Steeply Keeled End Scraper	2	3.6	52.0	9.09	Deltoid Biface	0	0.0	94.7
3.05	Double-end Scraper	2	3.6	55.6	9.10	Misc. Biface	0	0.0	94.7
3.06	Circular End Scraper	3	5.4	60.6	10.	**Projectile Point**			
3.07	End Scraper/Burin	1	1.8	62.4	10.00	Projectile Point Frag.	2	3.6	98.3
3.08	Spurred End Scraper	0	0.0	62.4	10.01	Chindadn Point	0	0.0	98.3
4.	**Side Scraper**				10.02	Lanceolate Point	0	0.0	98.3
4.00	Side Scraper Frag.	0	0.0	62.4	10.03	Triangular Point	1	1.8	100.1
4.01	Single-straight Side Scraper	1	1.8	64.2	10.04	Bipointed Point	0	0.0	100.1
4.02	Double-straight Side Scraper	0	0.0	64.2	10.05	Stemmed Point	0	0.0	100.1
4.03	Single-convex Side Scraper	0	0.0	64.2	10.06	Notched Point	0	0.0	100.1
4.04	Double-convex Side Scraper	0	0.0	64.2	10.07	Clovis Fluted Point	0	0.0	100.1
4.05	Straight-convex Side Scraper	0	0.0	64.2	11.	**Denticulate**			
4.06	Single-concave Side Scraper	1	1.8	66.0	11.00	Denticulate Frag.	0	0.0	100.1
4.07	Convergent Scraper	1	1.8	67.8	11.01	Denticulate	0	0.0	100.1
4.08	Transverse Scraper	1	1.8	69.6	12.	**Pointed Tool**			
4.09	Angle *(Déjeté)* Scraper	0	0.0	69.6	12.00	Pointed Tool Frag.	0	0.0	100.1
5.	**Cobble Tool**				12.01	Pointed Tool	0	0.0	100.1
5.00	Cobble Tool Frag.	0	0.0	69.6	13.	**Burin**			
5.01	Double Plane	0	0.0	69.6	13.00	Burin Frag.	0	0.0	100.1
5.02	Convergent Plane	0	0.0	69.6	13.01	Burin On Snap	0	0.0	100.1
5.03	Quadrilateral Plane	1	1.8	71.4	13.02	Dihedral Burin	0	0.0	100.1
5.04	Transverse Plane	0	0.0	71.4	13.03	Angle Burin	0	0.0	100.1
5.05	Chopper	4	7.1	78.5	13.04	Transverse Burin	0	0.0	100.1
5.06	Chopping Tool	0	0.0	78.5	13.05	Burin Spall	0	0.0	100.1
5.07	Hammerstone	0	0.0	78.5	14.	**Retouched Microblade**			
5.08	Anvil Stone	0	0.0	78.5	14.00	Ret. Microblade Frag.	0	0.0	100.1
5.09	Pebble Retoucher	0	0.0	78.5	14.01	Uni. Ret. Microblade	0	0.0	100.1
6.	**Perforator**				14.02	Bi. Ret. Microblade	0	0.0	100.1
6.00	Perforator Frag.	0	0.0	78.5		TOTAL	56	100.1	
6.01	Single Perforator	2	3.6	82.1					
6.02	Multiple Perforator	0	0.0	82.1					

that the occurrence of a single artifact manufactured on moss agate with no corresponding debitage is an indication of at least one exotic raw material.

The most important class of tools is the end scrapers, making up 32% of the tool kit. These include end scrapers on blades (5), circular end scrapers (3), steeply keeled (or carinated) end scrapers (2), and double-end scrapers (2) (Figure 9). One has also been burinated, making it the only composite tool in the assemblage.

Three of the four bifaces appear to be projectile-point preforms. Each is triangular in shape (Figure 10b,e) and appears to have been manufactured and broken at the site. It is not clear, however, whether any were actually utilized as tools.

Two of the three projectile points are basal fragments, most likely broken in the haft during use. These two fragments (Figure 9q,r), along with the complete triangular projectile point (Figure 9s), are straight-based and

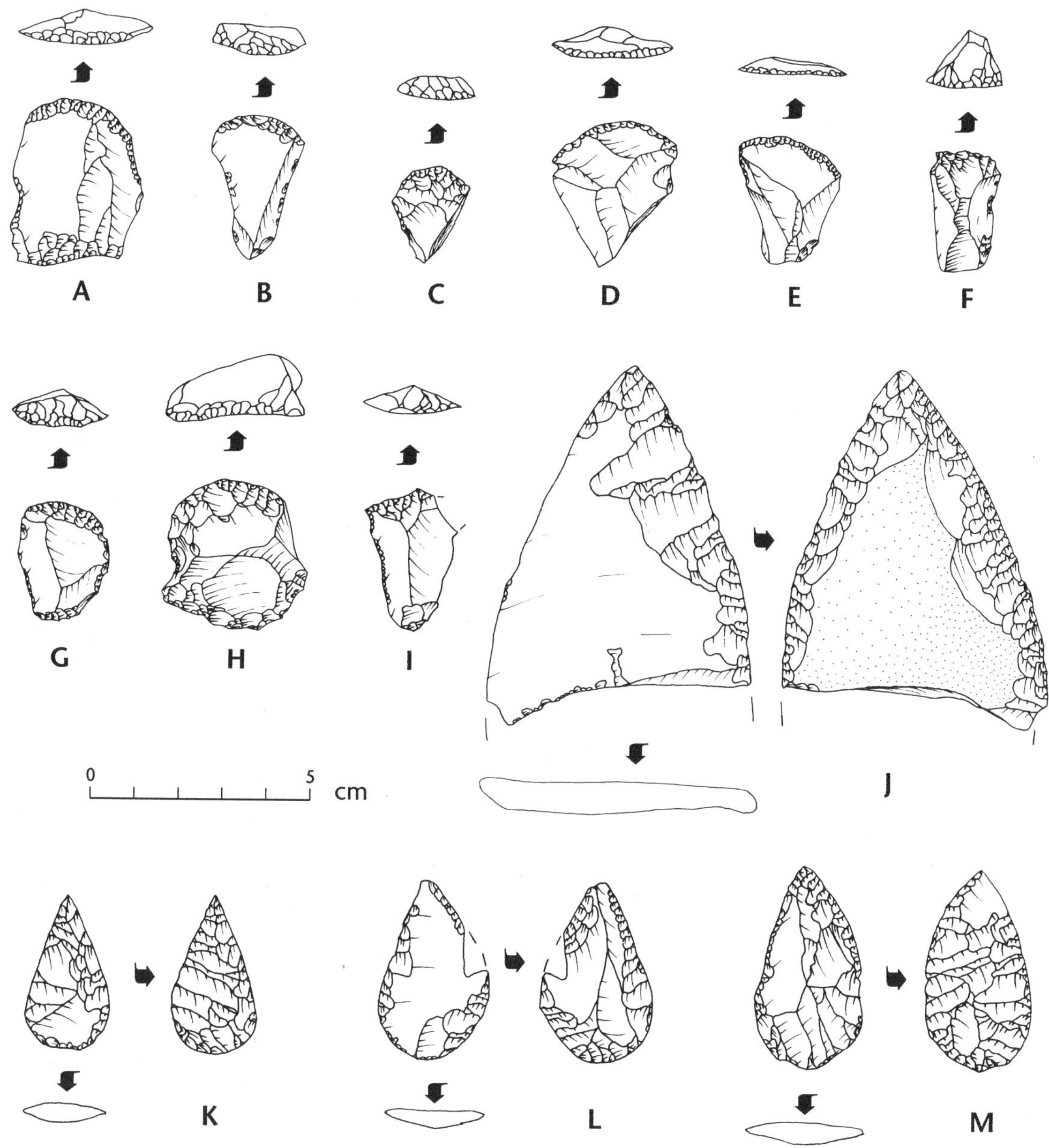

Figure 6. Walker Road artifacts (III): **A)** end scraper on flake; **B–E)** pan-shaped end scrapers; **F)** steeply keeled end scraper; **G)** double-end scraper; **H)** circular end scraper; **I)** spurred end scraper; **J)** convergent scraper; **K–M)** Chindadn projectile points.

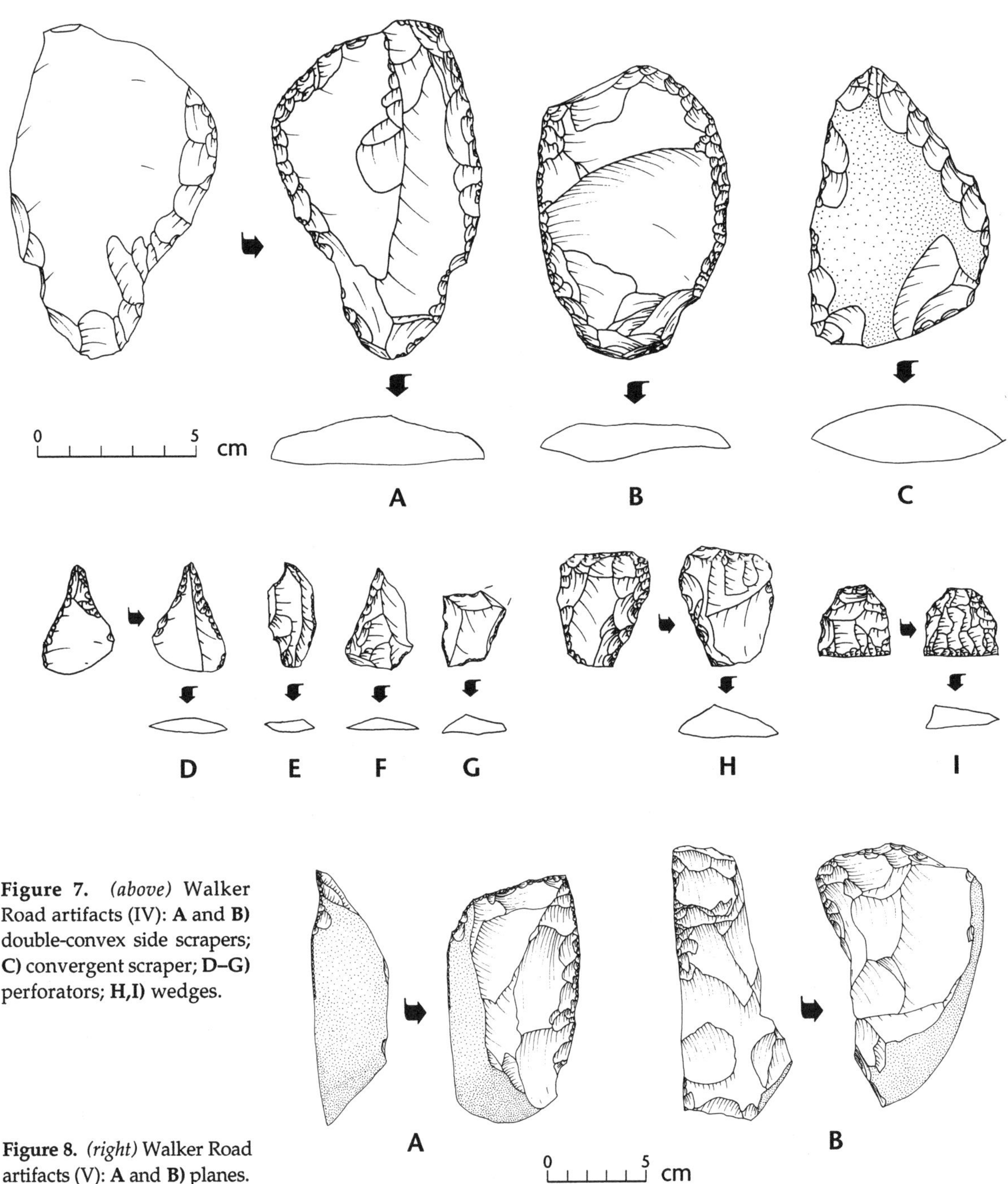

Figure 7. *(above)* Walker Road artifacts (IV): **A and B)** double-convex side scrapers; **C)** convergent scraper; **D–G)** perforators; **H,I)** wedges.

Figure 8. *(right)* Walker Road artifacts (V): **A** and **B)** planes.

basally thinned. The two fragments probably possessed triangular shapes similar to the complete specimen.

Among the cobble tools are four unifacially worked choppers and one plane with four worked edges (Figure 10c). This plane has a flat ventral surface and a highly carinated dorsal surface, very similar in form to those planes described above in the Walker Road assemblage.

The remainder of the Dry Creek Component I assemblage consists of perforators (2) (Figure 9o,p), notches (2) (Figure 10d), and a wedge (Figure 9j). Also, eleven retouched blades were identified (Figure 9k,l), five of them less than 5 cm in length, categorized as retouched bladelets. This lack of elongate blades may attest to the poor raw materials available in the vicinity of the Dry Creek site.

Of 42 identifiable tool blanks, 21 (50%) are blades, suggesting a high propensity toward the manufacture and use of blades and bladelets. Sixteen (38%) of the

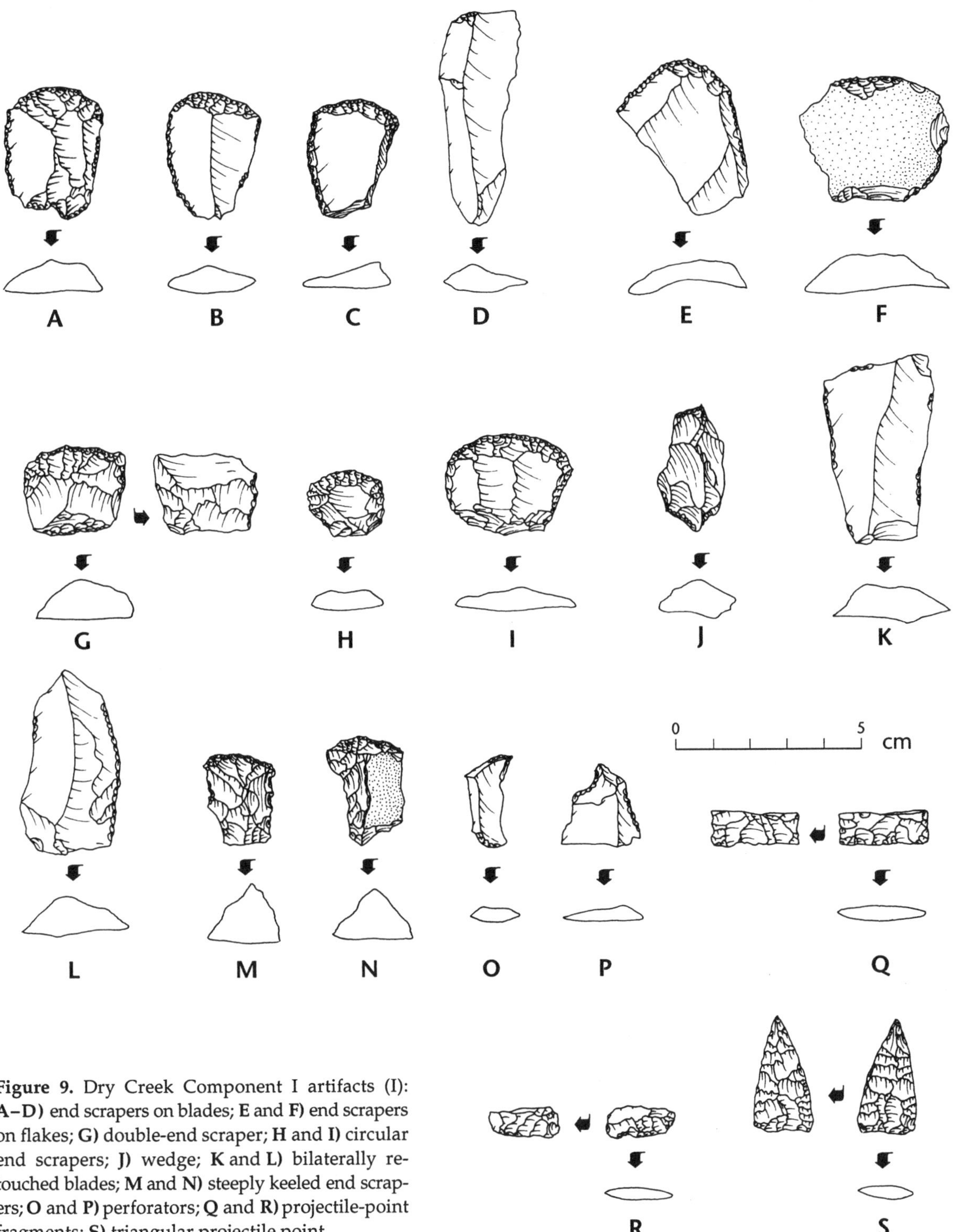

Figure 9. Dry Creek Component I artifacts (I): **A–D)** end scrapers on blades; **E** and **F)** end scrapers on flakes; **G)** double-end scraper; **H** and **I)** circular end scrapers; **J)** wedge; **K** and **L)** bilaterally retouched blades; **M** and **N)** steeply keeled end scrapers; **O** and **P)** perforators; **Q** and **R)** projectile-point fragments; **S)** triangular projectile point.

tools were made on flakes, and five (12%) on cobbles. No complete cores have been identified in this assemblage.

Seven tools (12.5%) are bifacially worked, whereas 43 (77%) are unifacially worked. The bifacial retouching is generally flat and irregular in nature, except on the finished projectile point, which displays fine subparallel flaking. Bimarginal/bipolar (3), alternate (2), and invasive (1) forms also occur.

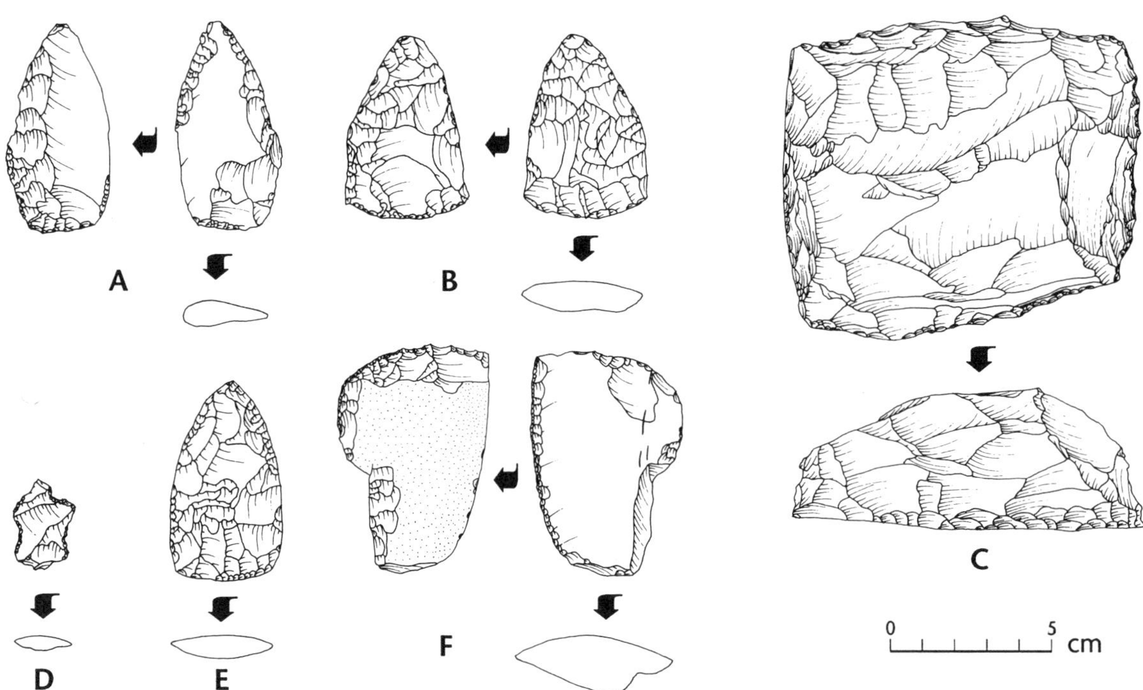

Figure 10. Dry Creek Component I artifacts (II): **A)** bifacially worked tool preform; **B** and **E)** triangular bifaces; **C)** plane; **D)** notch; **F)** convergent scraper.

Dry Creek Component II

The Dry Creek Component II assemblage, assigned by Powers (1983b) to the Denali complex, consists of over 28,000 artifacts, 330 (ca. 1.2%) of which are finished tools. The most prominent of the major tool groups in this assemblage are burins, bifaces, retouched microblades, and side scrapers (Table 3). Of perhaps equal importance are the retouched flakes, which make up 18.2% of the Dry Creek Component II assemblage. This Denali complex assemblage consists of a variety of raw materials, mostly gray chert, chalcedony, quartzite, rhyolite, and diabase. All the Dry Creek Component II raw materials can be found locally, with the exception of obsidian, which is represented at the site by 70 microblades and two core tablets. Obsidian tools include retouched microblades, burins, projectile points, retouched blades, and retouched flakes. Preliminary results of hydration neutron-activation source analyses reported by J. P. Cook suggest that these obsidians have sources at Batza Tena, the Wrangell Mountains, and one other unknown locality (Cook, personal communication).

Eighty-four burins and burin spalls were identified in this assemblage, 25% of the tool kit. Transverse burins and burins on snaps are the major types present, while dihedral turns burins on snaps are the major types present, while dihedral and angle burins occur less frequently (Figure 11a–c). The high frequency (15%) of burin spalls attests to the significant use, resharpening, and reuse of these sharp-edged implements.

A total of 10 projectile points and point fragments have been identified in the Dry Creek Component II assemblage. The single complete specimen is lanceolate in form and displays a concave base (Figure 11p), but is smaller than the other straight-based basal fragments assigned to this class (Figure 11l–o,q).

Similarly, a large number of bifaces were identified in the Dry Creek Component II collection (Figure 12), many of which can be grossly classified as primary bifaces displaying large flake scars, cortex, irregularities in shape and thickness, and, in many cases, elongate and oval outlines. These primary blanks include the majority of biface fragments and miscellaneous biface types, as well as many discoidal, ovate, and oval bifaces. Dry Creek Component II also produced oblong, triangular, spatulate, elliptical, and lanceolate bifaces, which can be classified as secondary bifaces, often displaying elongate shapes and well-formed points and bases. The spatulate bifaces, in particular, could be classified as projectile points, except for their asymmetrical forms (Figure 12c,e).

Retouched microblades are also well represented in the Dry Creek Component II assemblage. Twenty-six (72%) of these display unilateral use-wear, which con-

Table 3. Tool Types—Dry Creek Component II.

	TYPE	NO.	%	% CUM.
1.	**Retouched Flake**			
1.00	Retouched Flake Frag.	22	6.7	6.7
1.01	Retouched Flake	38	11.5	18.2
2.	**Retouched Blade**			
2.00	Retouched Blade Frag.	1	0.3	18.5
2.01	Unilaterally Ret. Blade	2	0.6	19.1
2.02	Bilaterally Ret. Blade	4	1.2	20.3
2.03	Unilaterally Ret. Bladelet	5	1.5	21.8
2.04	Bilaterally Ret. Bladelet	4	1.2	23.0
2.05	Uni. Ret. Blade-like Flake	6	1.8	24.8
2.06	Bi. Ret. Blade-like Flake	2	0.6	25.4
3.	**End Scraper**			
3.00	End Scraper Frag.	0	0.0	25.4
3.01	End Scraper on Blade	1	0.3	25.7
3.02	End Scraper on Flake	0	0.0	25.7
3.03	Pan-shaped End Scraper	0	0.0	25.7
3.04	Steeply Keeled End Scraper	0	0.0	25.7
3.05	Double-end Scraper	0	0.0	25.7
3.06	Circular End Scraper	0	0.0	25.7
3.07	End Scraper/Burin	0	0.0	25.7
3.08	Spurred End Scraper	0	0.0	25.7
4.	**Side Scraper**			
4.00	Side Scraper Frag.	3	0.9	26.6
4.01	Single-straight Side Scraper	1	0.3	26.9
4.02	Double-straight Side Scraper	0	0.0	26.9
4.03	Single-convex Side Scraper	2	0.6	27.5
4.04	Double-convex Side Scraper	8	2.4	29.9
4.05	Straight-convex Side Scraper	0	0.0	29.9
4.06	Single-concave Side Scraper	1	0.3	30.2
4.07	Convergent Scraper	8	2.4	32.6
4.08	Transverse Scraper	3	0.9	33.5
4.09	Angle *(Déjeté)* Scraper	0	0.0	33.5
5.	**Cobble Tool**			
5.00	Cobble Tool Frag.	0	0.0	33.5
5.01	Double Plane	0	0.0	33.5
5.02	Convergent Plane	0	0.0	33.5
5.03	Quadrilateral Plane	0	0.0	33.5
5.04	Transverse Plane	0	0.0	33.5
5.05	Chopper	4	1.2	34.7
5.06	Chopping Tool	10	3.0	37.7
5.07	Hammerstone	4	1.2	38.9
5.08	Anvil Stone	0	0.0	38.9
5.09	Pebble Retoucher	1	0.3	39.2
6.	**Perforator**			
6.00	Perforator Frag.	0	0.0	39.2
6.01	Single Perforator	4	1.2	40.4
6.02	Multiple Perforator	0	0.0	40.4
7.	**Wedge**			
7.00	Wedge Frag.	0	0.0	40.4
7.01	Wedge	0	0.0	40.4
8.	**Notch**			
8.00	Notch Frag.	0	0.0	40.4
8.01	Notch	3	0.9	41.3
9.	**Biface**			
9.00	Biface Frag.	14	4.2	45.5
9.01	Oblong Biface	2	0.6	46.1
9.02	Triangular Biface	1	0.3	46.4
9.03	Spatulate Biface	8	2.4	48.8
9.04	Elliptical Biface	5	1.5	50.3
9.05	Oval Biface	9	2.7	53.0
9.06	Ovate Biface	3	0.9	53.9
9.07	Lanceolate Biface	2	0.6	54.5
9.08	Discoidal Biface	1	0.3	54.8
9.09	Deltoid Biface	1	0.3	55.1
9.10	Misc. Biface	15	4.6	59.7
10.	**Projectile Point**			
10.00	Projectile Point Frag.	9	2.7	62.4
10.01	Chindadn Point	0	0.0	62.4
10.02	Lanceolate Point	1	0.3	62.7
10.03	Triangular Point	0	0.0	62.7
10.04	Bipointed Point	0	0.0	62.7
10.05	Stemmed Point	0	0.0	62.7
10.06	Notched Point	0	0.0	62.7
10.07	Clovis Fluted Point	0	0.0	62.7
11.	**Denticulate**			
11.00	Denticulate Frag.	2	0.6	63.3
11.01	Denticulate	0	0.0	63.3
12.	**Pointed Tool**			
12.00	Pointed Tool Frag.	0	0.0	63.3
12.01	Pointed Tool	0	0.0	63.3
13.	**Burin**			
13.00	Burin Frag.	0	0.0	63.3
13.01	Burin On Snap	12	3.6	66.9
13.02	Dihedral Burin	6	1.8	68.7
13.03	Angle Burin	3	0.9	69.6
13.04	Transverse Burin	14	4.2	73.8
13.05	Burin Spall	49	14.9	88.7
14.	**Retouched Microblade**			
14.00	Ret. Microblade Frag.	0	0.0	88.7
14.01	Uni. Ret. Microblade	26	7.9	96.6
14.02	Bi. Ret. Microblade	10	3.0	99.6
	TOTAL	330	99.6	

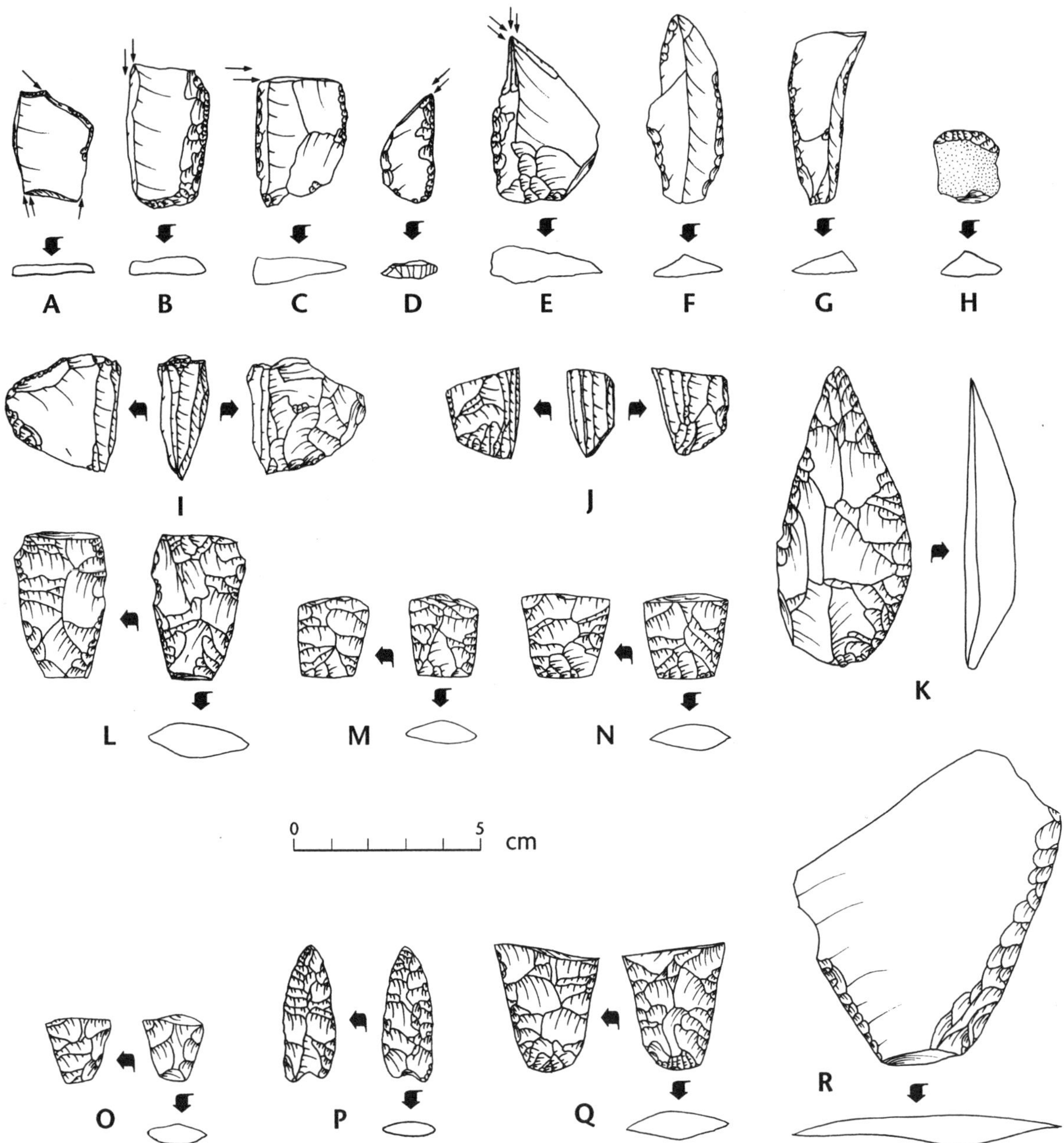

Figure 11. Dry Creek Component II artifacts (I): **A)** burin on a snap; **B)** angle burin; **C** and **D)** transverse burins; **E)** dihedral burin; **F** and **G)** bilaterally retouched bladelets; **H)** end scraper on flake; **I** and **J)** wedge-shaped microblade cores; **K)** convergent scraper; **L–O** and **Q)** projectile point fragments; **P)** lanceolate projectile point; **R)** side scraper.

firms the notion that microblades were inset into antler or bone projectile points as side blades (e.g., Guthrie 1983).

Side scrapers are also a major component of this Denali complex industry (Figure 11k,r), mostly occurring in the form of convergent, double-convex, and single-convex side scrapers.

Retouched blades also occur (Figure 11f,g); however, eight of the 24 (33%) retouched blades are actually blade-like flakes with highly irregular lateral margins. This leaves the actual retouched blade count at 16, only 4.9% of the tool assemblage.

Significantly, this Denali complex assemblage lacks end scrapers, perforators, and wedges. The sole Dry Creek Component II end scraper, shown in Figure 11h, was manufactured on a cortical flake and displays steep marginal retouching along its distal margin.

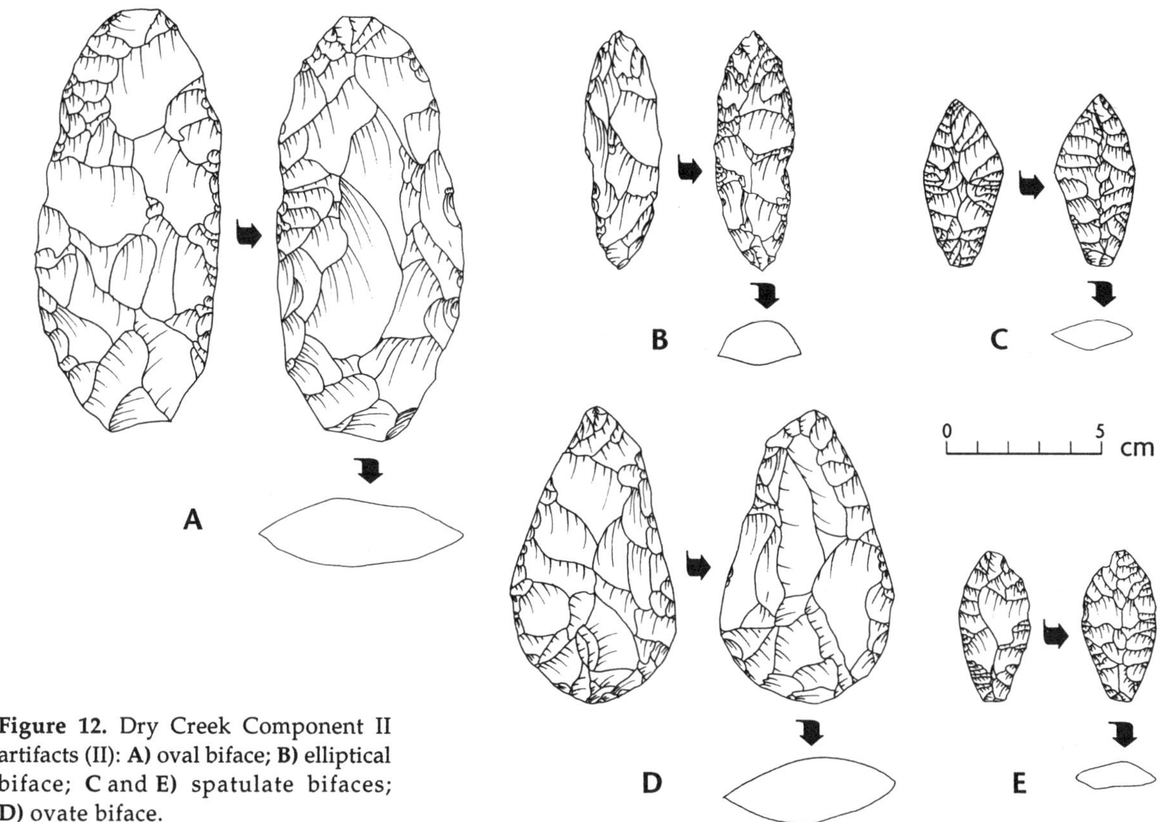

Figure 12. Dry Creek Component II artifacts (II): **A)** oval biface; **B)** elliptical biface; **C** and **E)** spatulate bifaces; **D)** ovate biface.

A total of 200 tool blanks were identified in the Dry Creek Component II collection. Of these, 81 (40.5%) are blades (and microblades), 98 (49%) are flakes, and 21 (10.5%) are cobbles. Of the tools made on blades, 36 are retouched microblades. The remaining 45 "macro" blades make up 23% of the total number of tool blanks identified. Cores from Dry Creek Component II include chiefly wedge-shaped microblade cores (21) (Figure 11i,j) and large subprismatic blade cores (4).

As indicated above, bifacial technology is an important component of this industry. Seventy (21%) tools have been worked bifacially, whereas 222 (68%) are unifacial. Bimarginal (15), alternate (4), reverse (10), and invasive (6) forms are also present.

Blackwater Draw

The Blackwater Draw sample analyzed consists of 211 lithic remains, 127 (60.2%) of which are tools. Among the major tool classes, the most prominent are retouched blades, side scrapers, projectile points, end scrapers, retouched flakes, bifaces, and perforators (Table 4). Raw materials at Blackwater Draw include cherts, chalcedony, quartzite, basalt, and slate. The cherts include Edwards Plateau brown chert, Alibates, and Quitaque, three cryptocrystalline rocks from known sources on the Llano Estacado of West Texas and eastern New Mexico.

Retouched blades make up 40.1% of the tool assemblage (Figure 13a,b,f), including 18 specimens from the Clovis blade cache (Green 1963). When these 18 blades are excluded, the number of retouched blades drops to 33, or 26% of the Blackwater Draw tool assemblage. Blackwater Draw blades display very thick triangular cross-sections, usually with only one arris, and in some cases marginal retouching.

Bifaces and projectile points are dominant features of this assemblage (Figure 13c,e,g–i). Sixteen Clovis fluted points have been identified, and other bifacial pieces occur in a variety of forms, many of which are projectile-point preforms. Another aspect of the bifacial industry at Blackwater Draw includes retouched and utilized flakes, many of which were manufactured on bifacial thinning flakes, rather than on flakes removed from prepared cores.

The remaining classes of the Blackwater Draw industry include end scrapers, side scrapers, perforators, and cobble tools. Of the several varieties of end scraper types, end scrapers on blades and spurred end scrapers are the most notable (Figure 14g). Side scrapers were usually manufactured on large flakes with prominent bulbs of percussion (Figure 14a). The two cobble tools

Table 4. Tool Types—Blackwater Draw.

	TYPE	NO.	%	% CUM.
1.	**Retouched Flake**			
1.00	Retouched Flake Frag.	4	3.1	3.1
1.01	Retouched Flake	7	5.5	8.6
2.	**Retouched Blade**			
2.00	Retouched Blade Frag.	0	0.0	8.6
2.01	Unilaterally Ret. Blade	5	3.9	12.5
2.02	Bilaterally Ret. Blade	36	28.3	40.8
2.03	Unilaterally Ret. Bladelet	3	2.4	43.2
2.04	Bilaterally Ret. Bladelet	2	1.6	44.8
2.05	Uni. Ret. Blade-like Flake	1	0.8	45.6
2.06	Bi. Ret. Blade-like Flake	4	3.1	48.7
3.	**End Scraper**			
3.00	End Scraper Frag.	0	0.0	48.7
3.01	End Scraper on Blade	8	6.3	55.0
3.02	End Scraper on Flake	0	0.0	55.0
3.03	Pan-shaped End Scraper	2	1.6	56.6
3.04	Steeply Keeled End Scraper	0	0.0	56.6
3.05	Double-end Scraper	0	0.0	56.6
3.06	Circular End Scraper	0	0.0	56.6
3.07	End Scraper/Burin	0	0.0	56.6
3.08	Spurred End Scraper	1	0.8	57.4
4.	**Side Scraper**			
4.00	Side Scraper Frag.	1	0.8	58.2
4.01	Single-straight Side Scraper	6	4.7	62.9
4.02	Double-straight Side Scraper	6	4.7	67.6
4.03	Single-convex Side Scraper	0	0.0	67.6
4.04	Double-convex Side Scraper	1	0.8	68.4
4.05	Straight-convex Side Scraper	0	0.0	68.4
4.06	Single-concave Side Scraper	0	0.0	68.4
4.07	Convergent Scraper	3	2.4	70.8
4.08	Transverse Scraper	0	0.0	70.8
4.09	Angle *(Déjeté)* Scraper	2	1.6	72.4
5.	**Cobble Tool**			
5.00	Cobble Tool Frag.	0	0.0	72.4
5.01	Double Plane	0	0.0	72.4
5.02	Convergent Plane	0	0.0	72.4
5.03	Quadrilateral Plane	0	0.0	72.4
5.04	Transverse Plane	0	0.0	72.4
5.05	Chopper	0	0.0	72.4
5.06	Chopping Tool	1	0.8	73.2
5.07	Hammerstone	1	0.8	74.0
5.08	Anvil Stone	0	0.0	74.0
5.09	Pebble Retoucher	0	0.0	74.0
6.	**Perforator**			
6.00	Perforator Frag.	0	0.0	74.0
6.01	Single Perforator	4	3.1	77.1
6.02	Multiple Perforator	3	2.4	79.5

	TYPE	NO.	%	% CUM.
7.	**Wedge**			
7.00	Wedge Frag.	0	0.0	79.5
7.01	Wedge Tool	0	0.0	79.5
8.	**Notch**			
8.00	Notch Frag.	0	0.0	79.5
8.01	Notch	1	0.8	80.3
9.	**Biface**			
9.00	Biface Frag.	3	2.4	82.7
9.01	Oblong Biface	0	0.0	82.7
9.02	Triangular Biface	0	0.0	82.7
9.03	Spatulate Biface	0	0.0	82.7
9.04	Elliptical Biface	1	0.8	83.5
9.05	Oval Biface	0	0.0	83.5
9.06	Ovate Biface	0	0.0	83.5
9.07	Lanceolate Biface	1	0.8	84.3
9.08	Discoidal Biface	1	0.8	85.1
9.09	Deltoid Biface	1	0.8	85.9
9.10	Misc. Biface	1	0.8	86.7
10.	**Projectile Point**			
10.00	Projectile Point Frag.	1	0.8	87.5
10.01	Chindadn Point	0	0.0	87.5
10.02	Lanceolate Point	0	0.0	87.5
10.03	Triangular Point	0	0.0	87.5
10.04	Bipointed Point	0	0.0	87.5
10.05	Stemmed Point	0	0.0	87.5
10.06	Notched Point	0	0.0	87.5
10.07	Clovis Fluted Point	16	12.6	100.1
11.	**Denticulate**			
11.00	Denticulate Frag.	0	0.0	100.1
11.01	Denticulate	0	0.0	100.1
12.	**Pointed Tool**			
12.00	Pointed Tool Frag.	0	0.0	100.1
12.01	Pointed Tool	0	0.0	100.1
13.	**Burin**			
13.00	Burin Frag.	0	0.0	100.1
13.01	Burin On Snap	0	0.0	100.1
13.02	Dihedral Burin	0	0.0	100.1
13.03	Angle Burin	0	0.0	100.1
13.04	Transverse Burin	0	0.0	100.1
13.05	Burin Spall	0	0.0	100.1
14.	**Retouched Microblade**			
14.00	Ret. Microblade Frag.	0	0.0	100.1
14.01	Uni. Ret. Microblade	0	0.0	100.1
14.02	Bi. Ret. Microblade	0	0.0	100.1
	TOTAL	127	100.1	

are large ad hoc implements manufactured on coarse-grained materials, unlike the bifaces and unifaces that were manufactured on cryptocrystalline rocks such as Alibates and Edward's Plateau chert.

Analyses of tool blanks suggest that Blackwater Draw primary working techniques included the production of blades and flakes, as well as the production of bifaces reduced from cobbles. Sixty-two of the 92 identified blanks (67.4%) are blades, 27 (29.3%) are flakes, and 3 (3.3%) are cobbles. Even when the Clovis blade-cache sample is deleted from the analysis, 60% of the remaining tools appear to have been made on blades. Only a single flake core was identified in the Blackwater Draw sample; yet it is clear that the majority of the blades were removed from what appear to be large prismatic blade cores.

Although fluted points and bifacial "knives" are considered to be major components of the Clovis industry, it is interesting to note that of 127 tools analyzed, only 25 (19.7%) are bifacially worked. These include the bifaces and projectile points shown in Figure 13. Unifacial (94), alternate (2), and invasive (5) forms are also present.

Murray Springs

The Murray Springs Clovis assemblage, consisting of 85 implements and over 12,000 pieces of debitage, is very similar to Blackwater Draw. It is dominated by large percentages of projectile points and bifaces, retouched blades and flakes, end scrapers, and side scrapers (Table 5). Raw materials found at Murray Springs include cherts, chalcedony, jasper, obsidian, limestone, and quartzite. Examples of exotic raw materials include a single projectile point with no associated debitage, manufactured on petrified wood from north of the Mogollon

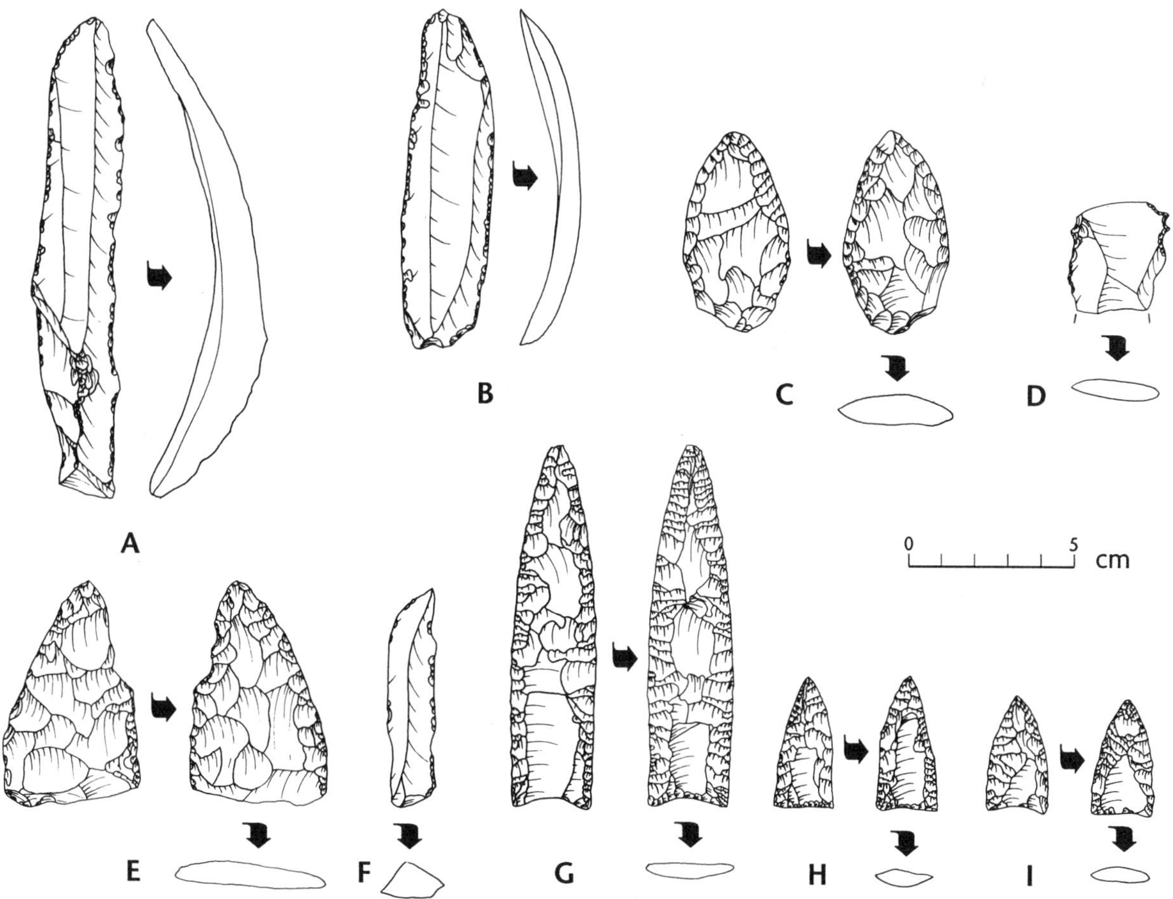

Figure 13. Blackwater Draw artifacts (I): **A)** crested blade, bilaterally retouched; **B)** bilaterally retouched blade; **C)** oval biface; **D)** multiple perforator; **E)** lanceolate biface; **F)** bilaterally retouched blade; **G–I)** Clovis fluted points.

Table 5. Tool Types—Murray Springs.

	TYPE	NO.	%	% CUM.
1.	**Retouched Flake**			
1.00	Retouched Flake Frag.	14	16.5	16.5
1.01	Retouched Flake	8	9.4	25.9
2.	**Retouched Blade**			
2.00	Retouched Blade Frag.	0	0.0	25.9
2.01	Unilaterally Ret. Blade	3	3.5	29.4
2.02	Bilaterally Ret. Blade	8	9.4	38.8
2.03	Unilaterally Ret. Bladelet	0	0.0	38.8
2.04	Bilaterally Ret. Bladelet	1	1.2	40.0
2.05	Uni. Ret. Blade-like Flake	0	0.0	40.0
2.06	Bi. Ret. Blade-like Flake	5	5.9	45.9
3.	**End Scraper**			
3.00	End Scraper Frag.	0	0.0	45.9
3.01	End Scraper on Blade	5	5.9	51.8
3.02	End Scraper on Flake	1	1.2	53.0
3.03	Pan-shaped End Scraper	1	1.2	54.2
3.04	Steeply Keeled End Scraper	0	0.0	54.2
3.05	Double-end Scraper	0	0.0	54.2
3.06	Circular End Scraper	0	0.0	54.2
3.07	End Scraper/Burin	0	0.0	54.2
3.08	Spurred End Scraper	0	0.0	54.2
4.	**Side Scraper**			
4.00	Side Scraper Frag.	1	1.2	55.4
4.01	Single-straight Side Scraper	0	0.0	55.4
4.02	Double-straight Side Scraper	1	1.2	56.6
4.03	Single-convex Side Scraper	0	0.0	56.6
4.04	Double-convex Side Scraper	2	2.4	59.0
4.05	Straight-convex Side Scraper	0	0.0	59.0
4.06	Single-concave Side Scraper	0	0.0	59.0
4.07	Convergent Scraper	1	1.2	60.2
4.08	Transverse Scraper	0	0.0	60.2
4.09	Angle *(Déjeté)* Scraper	0	0.0	60.2
5.	**Cobble Tool**			
5.00	Cobble Tool Frag.	0	0.0	60.2
5.01	Double Plane	0	0.0	60.2
5.02	Convergent Plane	0	0.0	60.2
5.03	Quadrilateral Plane	0	0.0	60.2
5.04	Transverse Plane	0	0.0	60.2
5.05	Chopper	2	2.4	62.6
5.06	Chopping Tool	0	0.0	62.6
5.07	Hammerstone	1	1.2	63.8
5.08	Anvil Stone	0	0.0	63.8
5.09	Pebble Retoucher	0	0.0	63.8
6.	**Perforator**			
6.00	Perforator Frag.	0	0.0	63.8
6.01	Single Perforator	0	0.0	63.8
6.02	Multiple Perforator	1	1.2	65.0
7.	**Wedge**			
7.00	Wedge Frag.	0	0.0	65.0
7.01	Wedge Tool	0	0.0	65.0
8.	**Notch**			
8.00	Notch Frag.	0	0.0	65.0
8.01	Notch	1	1.2	66.2
9.	**Biface**			
9.00	Biface Frag.	7	8.2	74.4
9.01	Oblong Biface	0	0.0	74.4
9.02	Triangular Biface	0	0.0	74.4
9.03	Spatulate Biface	0	0.0	74.4
9.04	Elliptical Biface	1	1.2	75.6
9.05	Oval Biface	0	0.0	75.6
9.06	Ovate Biface	0	0.0	75.6
9.07	Lanceolate Biface	2	2.4	78.0
9.08	Discoidal Biface	0	0.0	78.0
9.09	Deltoid Biface	0	0.0	78.0
9.10	Misc. Biface	0	0.0	78.0
10.	**Projectile Point**			
10.00	Projectile Point Frag.	2	2.4	80.4
10.01	Chindadn Point	0	0.0	80.4
10.02	Lanceolate Point	0	0.0	80.4
10.03	Triangular Point	0	0.0	80.4
10.04	Bipointed Point	0	0.0	80.4
10.05	Stemmed Point	0	0.0	80.4
10.06	Notched Point	0	0.0	80.4
10.07	Clovis Fluted Point	16	18.8	99.2
11.	**Denticulate**			
11.00	Denticulate Frag.	0	0.0	99.2
11.01	Denticulate	0	0.0	99.2
12.	**Pointed Tool**			
12.00	Pointed Tool Frag.	0	0.0	99.2
12.01	Pointed Tool	0	0.0	99.2
13.	**Burin**			
13.00	Burin Frag.	0	0.0	99.2
13.01	Burin On Snap	0	0.0	99.2
13.02	Dihedral Burin	0	0.0	99.2
13.03	Angle Burin	1	1.2	100.4
13.04	Transverse Burin	0	0.0	100.4
13.05	Burin Spall	0	0.0	100.4
14.	**Retouched Microblade**			
14.00	Ret. Microblade Frag.	0	0.0	100.4
14.01	Uni. Ret. Microblade	0	0.0	100.4
14.02	Bi. Ret. Microblade	0	0.0	100.4
	TOTAL	85	100.4	

Rim, approximately 225 km north of the site, as well as obsidian from east-central Arizona near the town of Morenci (Huckell n.d.).

As at Blackwater Draw, retouched blades and flakes make up a considerable portion of the tool kit. Most blades are large, triangular in cross-section, and usually display marginal retouching or only slight traces of use-wear (Figure 15a,b,f). Many of the retouched flakes appear to have been removed from primary and secondary bifaces, rather than prepared flake cores.

The majority of the end scrapers were manufactured on blades (Figure 15e,h,i), although one end scraper manufactured on a flake was identified. Interestingly, all but one of the side scrapers were retouched along both lateral margins, perhaps indicating prolonged use and resharpening (Figure 15c).

Sixteen (18.2%) projectile points (all fluted) were identified, as were ten bifaces and biface fragments, labeled by Huckell (n.d.) as primary and secondary bifaces, or projectile-point preforms.

Cobble tools and burins are only minimally represented. Each ad hoc cobble tool was manufactured on a coarse-grained, locally procured raw material. The single Murray Springs burin, shown in Figure 15g,

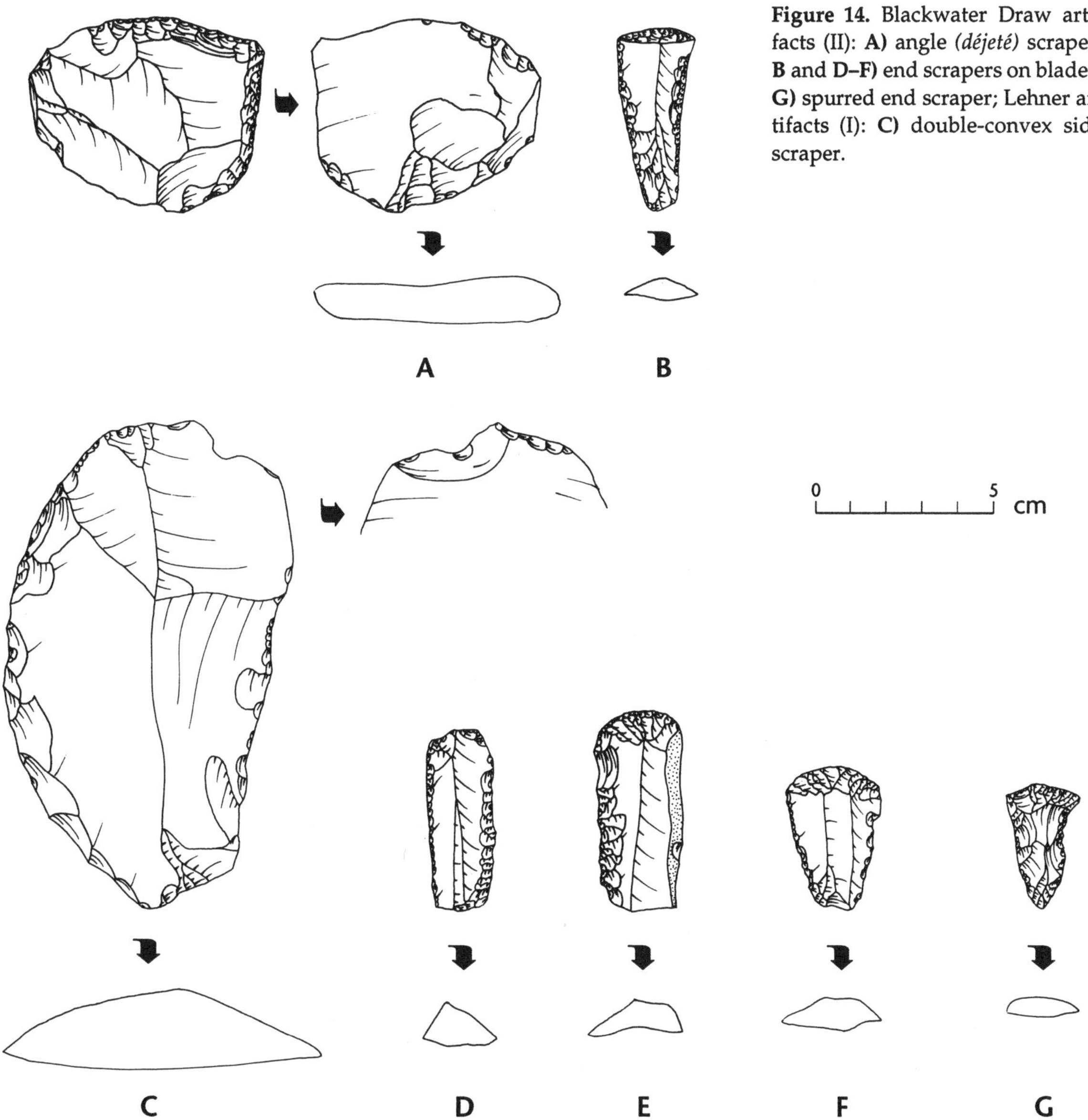

Figure 14. Blackwater Draw artifacts (II): **A)** angle *(déjeté)* scraper; **B** and **D–F)** end scrapers on blades; **G)** spurred end scraper; Lehner artifacts (I): **C)** double-convex side scraper.

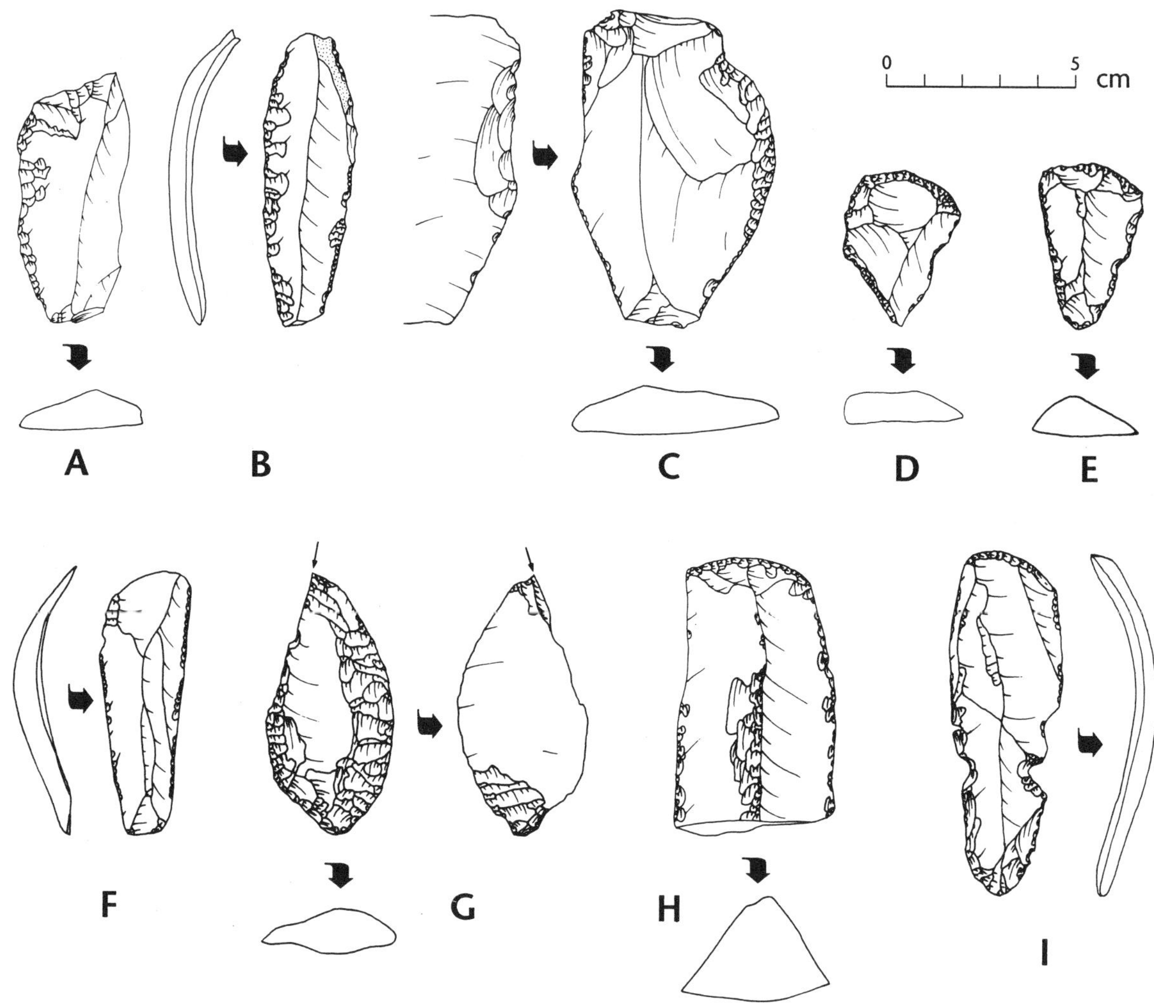

Figure 15. Murray Springs artifacts (I): **A)** unilaterally retouched blade; **B** and **F)** bilaterally retouched blades; **C)** double-convex side scraper; **D)** pan-shaped end scraper; **E, H,** and **I)** end scrapers on blades; **G)** angle burin.

displays several burin facets extending across the ventral surface of the tool; however, these facets may not have been intentional burin blows, but flake scars produced in an attempt to remove the distal curvature of the blank's ventral surface.

An analysis of Murray Springs tool blanks revealed that the majority of tools were manufactured on blades. Of 44 identifiable blanks, 23 (52.3%) are blades, 18 (40.9%) are flakes, and 3 (6.8%) are cobbles. Two blade cores were identified in the Murray Springs assemblage. One is a single-platform monofrontal blade core and the other, although fragmentary, displays a portion of the striking platform as well as several proximal blade facets.

In terms of secondary working, 29 (33%) of the 88 stone tools from Murray Springs are worked bifacially, whereas 50 (56.8%) are unifacial. Alternate (3) and reverse (2) forms are also present.

TYPOLOGICAL COMPARISONS

Quantitative comparisons of the assemblages described above were accomplished through the use of cumulative percentage curves (Figure 16), as well as a cluster analysis (Figure 17). The cumulative percentage graph compares and contrasts each of the assemblages according to relative frequencies of tool types and classes, whereas the cluster analysis utilizes only the relative frequencies of each major tool class to measure distances between each assemblage.

The Nenana industries contrast technically and typologically with the Denali industry. Burins and retouched microblades dominate the Dry Creek Component II tool kit but are not present in the Nenana complex assemblages. Walker Road and Dry Creek Component I tool kits are dominated by end scrapers and retouched blades, two tool forms nearly absent from the Dry Creek Component II assemblage.

On the other hand, the Nenana complex industries do appear very similar to Clovis. Similarities include high numbers of end scrapers and side scrapers, retouched blades and flakes, bifaces, and projectile points, as well as moderate numbers of perforators, wedges, denticulates, and notches. The major differences between the Clovis and Nenana tool kits, however, include the absence of fluted points in the Nenana complex, and the near-absence of large cobble tools and the complete absence of Chindadn points in Clovis.

The cluster analysis shows results similar to the cumulative graph (Figure 17). The Walker Road and Dry Creek Component I industries form Cluster 1, characterized by high frequencies of retouched flakes and blades, end scrapers, and side scrapers, and moderate numbers of bifaces and projectile points. Cluster 2, the Clovis group, is similar to the Nenana group in that both Blackwater Draw and Murray Springs have high numbers of retouched flakes and blades, end scrapers, and side scrapers; however, the Nenana group does not include high frequencies of projectile points. Cluster 3, the Denali group, is most distinct, with high numbers of burins and retouched microblades, two major tool classes not found in Clovis or Nenana tool kits.

DISCUSSION

The Paleoarctic Tradition

The Paleoarctic tradition is represented locally in central Alaska by the Denali complex (Dumond 1980; West 1967, 1981). At Dry Creek Component II, the Denali complex is characterized by a prismatic blade and microblade technology, as well as a secondary technology including unifacial and bifacial techniques. The Dry Creek Component II tool kit includes a number of retouched and/or utilized microblades, burins, and lanceolate projectile points with straight to concave bases and slightly expanding sides, similar in form to Agate Basin and Hell Gap points from the Great Plains (Powers 1983b). The apparent scarcity of end scrapers in Denali complex assemblages may reflect the use of wedge-shaped microcores or burins as composite scraping tools.

As Figure 1 shows, the earliest C-14 date for the Paleoarctic comes from Dry Creek Component II, 10,690 ± 250 yr B.P.; thus it appears to be at least 500 years younger than the Nenana complex occupation of central Alaska.

West (1981) and Powers and Hoffecker (1989) suggest that the Denali complex displays close technological ties with the Late Paleolithic Diuktai culture of

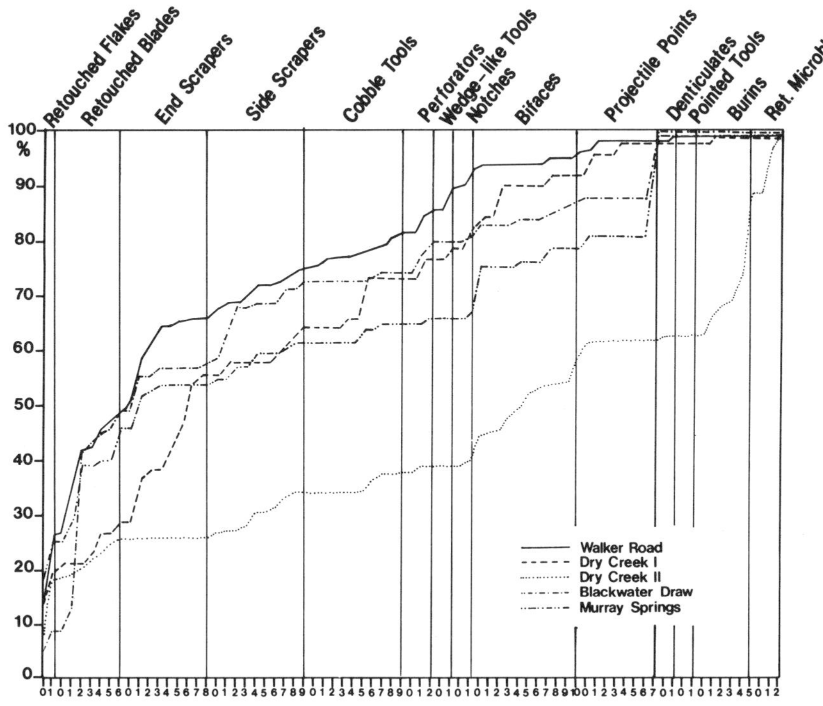

Figure 16. Cumulative percentage graph comparing Walker Road, Dry Creek (Components I and II), Blackwater Draw, and Murray Springs tool types.

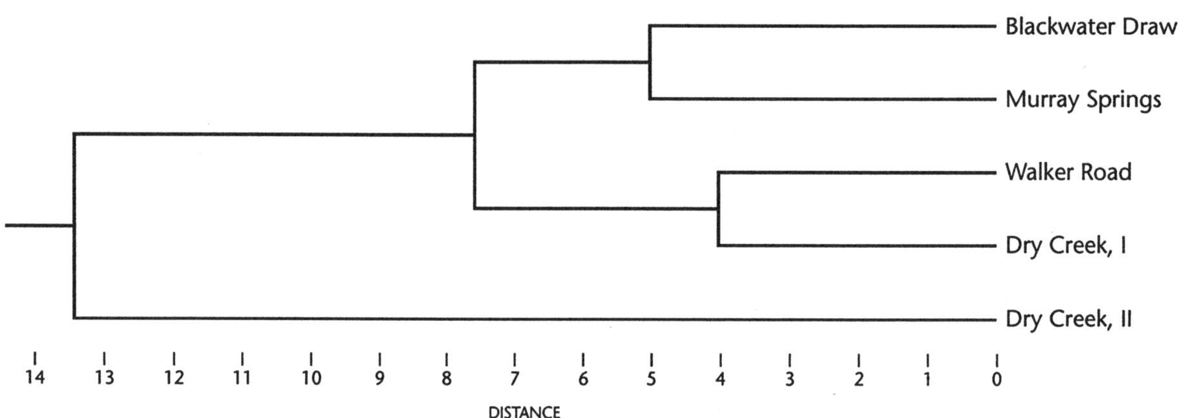

Figure 17. Dendrogram illustrating results of cluster analysis based on major tool types.

Northeast Asia, based on the presence of wedge-shaped cores and microblades, burins, and bifacial projectile points. Possible Denali antecedents can be traced to Ushki, Layer VI (ca. 10,500 yr B.P.), Diuktai Cave (12,000 to 14,000 yr B.P.), and Verkne-Troitskaya (14,000 to 18,000 yr B.P.) (Dikov 1977; Mochanov 1977) (Figure 18). At Ushki, distinctive straight-based lanceolate projectile points have been found that are similar to those from Dry Creek Component II (Dikov 1977).

Artifacts from the Bluefish Caves in the Yukon Territory also exhibit technological affinities with the Paleoarctic tradition, although the lithic assemblage there is small and includes only a few burins, microblades, and a single microcore (Cinq-Mars 1979; Morlan 1987, 1988). C-14 dates range from 12,200 to 24,800 yr B.P., but the direct association of the cultural remains with the dated substances has not been clearly demonstrated. Adovasio et al. (1988) argue that:

> the absence of hearths or definable living floors in any of the Bluefish Caves . . . coupled with the absence of clearly defined stratigraphy and the impossibility of satisfactorily associating the flaked stone artifacts with the radiocarbon dates must render these sites presently unacceptable or unconvincing to many researchers [Adovasio et al. 1988:45].

Therefore, no evidence exists that suggests the human occupation of eastern Beringia prior to the appearance of the Nenana complex in central Alaska between 12,000 and 11,500 yr B.P.

The Clovis Tradition

The results of our analysis demonstrate conclusively that at Blackwater Draw and Murray Springs a major element of the Clovis primary technology was the manufacture of blades, many of which served as tool preforms. Both assemblages display numerous retouched (or utilized) blades, as well as many other tools made on blades. It is clear that most Clovis blades were removed from prismatic blade cores, especially at Murray Springs, where at least one, and possibly two, cores were recovered. The blades found in the Blackwater Draw blade cache clearly exhibit attributes similar to Eurasian Early Upper Paleolithic blades. One blade in particular, shown in Figure 13a, could be classified as a *lame à crête,* or "crested blade," displaying a bifacially flaked ridge along the distal portion of its dorsal surface. Other blades from Blackwater Draw and Murray Springs display core face, or ridge, rejuvenation, a method utilized to rid the core front of irregularities (Figure 15h). Blades and blade cores have been found at other Clovis sites, including Williamson (Haynes 1972) and Anadarko (Hammat 1970), as well as at several newly discovered sites such as 41-BX-52 in Texas (Stanford, personal communication) and the Adams site in Kentucky (Gramly and Funk 1989).

A second major aspect of Clovis primary technology was the production of bifaces and fluted projectile points. Huckell (n.d.) has proposed that bifaces were the mainstay of the Clovis industry in the San Pedro Valley, and this appears to have been the case at Blackwater Draw as well. Bifaces not only served as fully functional implements, but also as light, highly portable flake cores.

The Clovis tool kit consists of fluted points, bifaces, end scrapers, side scrapers, retouched blades and flakes, perforators, and cobble tools. Although wedges were not identified in the Blackwater Draw and Murray Springs assemblages, these tools have been found at a number of early Paleoindian sites, including Shoop, Debert, and Vail (Gramly 1982; Haynes 1982; MacDonald 1968). Burins, although represented at Murray

Springs by a single specimen, are rare (Haynes 1982). The Clovis industry, therefore, has a major Eurasian Early Upper Paleolithic element, which includes the use of blade tools, as well as the use of a number of bone and ivory implements (Haynes 1982:389). Müller-Beck (1966, 1967) attempted to link Clovis to the Eurasian Mousterian tradition, based on common appearances of bifaces, projectile points, and side scrapers; however, these tool forms are not solely *fossiles directeurs* of the Mousterian, but are conservative features of the Siberian and east European Early Upper Paleolithic records as well. Similarly, no Levallois blanks or Mousterian pointed tools have been found in the Blackwater Draw or Murray Springs assemblages, a further indication of the lack of "Mousteroid" elements in Clovis.

The Nenana Complex: Paleoindian or Paleoarctic?

As the results of the cumulative frequency distribution and cluster analysis suggest, the Nenana complex is more closely related to the Clovis tradition than to the Denali complex. The Nenana complex C-14 chronology, lithic technology, and tool kit all exhibit close parallels to Clovis, rather than the later Paleoarctic tradition.

Chronology

The Nenana complex has been consistently dated to the period between 11,000 and 12,000 yr B.P. (Figure 1). The Moose Creek dates of 11,730 ± 250 yr B.P. (GX-6281), 10,640 ± 280 yr B.P. (I-11227), 8940 ± 270 yr B.P. (A-2144), and 8160 ± 260 yr B.P. (A-2168) are on soil organics from a paleosol complex stratigraphically above the cultural remains, and act as upper limiting ages for the artifact-bearing loess horizon (Hoffecker 1985b; Powers and Hoffecker 1989). It should be noted, however, that the Moose Creek Nenana complex occupation lies within the site's basal loess unit, which appears to have been deposited prior to 11,000 yr B.P., based on C-14 dates from Walker Road, Dry Creek, and Owl Ridge. This suggests that the Nenana complex assemblages are

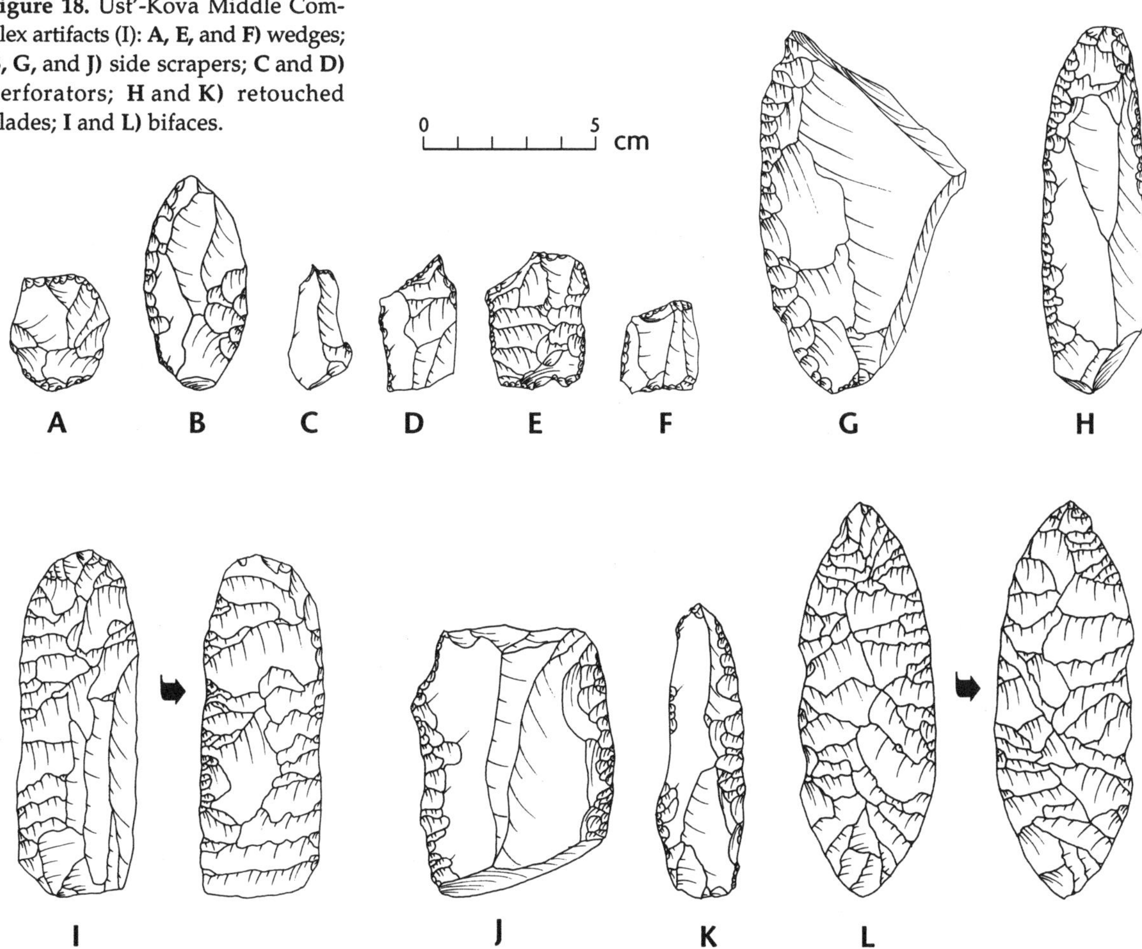

Figure 18. Ust'-Kova Middle Complex artifacts (I): **A, E,** and **F)** wedges; **B, G,** and **J)** side scrapers; **C** and **D)** perforators; **H** and **K)** retouched blades; **I** and **L)** bifaces.

roughly contemporaneous with Clovis and clearly predate the earliest Denali complex assemblages by at least 500 years (Figure 1).

Primary Technology

The Nenana complex displays both core and blade, as well as core and flake technologies. Tool blank and debitage analyses at Walker Road show that both technologies were stressed somewhat equally. The Dry Creek Component I tool kit is dominated by tools made on blades, although no cores were recovered. This trend is also seen in Clovis, where many blades and blade tools were produced, most likely from large prismatic cores. Both Clovis and Nenana industries also display flake technologies, although Clovis flake tools were often removed from bifaces or projectile-point preforms. Another salient feature that both Clovis and Nenana share is the total absence of microblades and microblade cores, a major characteristic of the later Denali complex and Paleoarctic tradition.

Secondary Technology

It is beyond the scope of this paper to discuss all the specific retouching techniques that were used to create tools, although we do note that there is much in common between the Nenana complex and the Clovis tradition (Goebel 1990). Here we will only deal briefly with bifacial points.

Both the Nenana complex and Clovis tradition display bifacial technologies, although no fluted points have been found in association with the Nenana complex materials. Instead, Nenana projectile points come in two distinct forms: (1) small and large triangular-shaped points from Dry Creek and Owl Ridge (Figure 9s), and (2) small teardrop-shaped Chindadn points from Walker Road (Figure 6k–m). Chindadn points have been found at two other central Alaskan sites: the Healy Lake Chindadn type site and the Chugwater site, both located along the Tanana River southeast of Fairbanks (Cook 1969; Lively 1988). At each of these localities, the Chindadn points were found in association with end scrapers and other processing implements.

Fluted points in Alaska (i.e., Batza Tena and Putu) have yet to be found in clear late Pleistocene stratified contexts and appear to be younger in age than the Nenana and Clovis assemblages (Dumond 1980; Haynes 1987; West 1981). It is our opinion that the Alaskan fluted points thus far found are not directly related to the development of Clovis fluted points and are instead late arrivals from the northern Great Plains. We would tentatively suggest that the apparent absence of early fluted points in Alaska and the complete absence of such points in North Asia argues for a point of origin south of the Wisconsin ice sheet.

Tool Typology

Other major tool groups found repeatedly in the Nenana complex assemblages include end scrapers, side scrapers, retouched blades and flakes, cobble tools, perforators, and wedges. Nenana complex end scrapers occur in a variety of forms (Figures 5 and 6), many of which have been identified by Irwin and Wormington (1970) in other western Paleoindian assemblages. One spurred end scraper has been identified in the Walker Road assemblage (Figure 6i), a type often recognized as a Paleoindian *fossile directeur* (Rogers 1986).

Nenana side scrapers also display forms reminiscent of Clovis and other early Paleoindian tool kits, especially the single- and double-convex side scrapers sometimes referred to as "human-ear form" scrapers, manufactured on large flakes. These scraper types have been identified in the Murray Springs, Blackwater Draw, and Lehner collections (Figures 14c and 15c) (Goebel 1989).

Wedges *(pièces ésquillées)* occur in the Walker Road and Dry Creek Component I assemblages, as well as in many eastern Paleoindian assemblages, including Debert and Shoop. Wedges, as well as planes, may indicate some degree of woodworking; however, local pollen cores in central Alaska suggest that only shrub birch *(Betula)* and perhaps spruce *(Picea)* grew in central Alaska during the late Pleistocene (Ager 1975).

Other Nenana complex cobble tools include ad hoc forms such as hammerstones, pebble retouchers, and anvil stones manufactured on local coarse-grained raw materials, a pattern often repeated at many Clovis sites (Huckell n.d.). These cobble tools, however, are not diagnostic forms.

The common occurrence of perforators also lends support to Clovis-Nenana technological ties, as does the apparent lack of Paleoarctic tools such as microblades and burins.

CONCLUSIONS

We conclude here that the central Alaskan Nenana complex, dated to approximately 11,300 yr B.P., reflects many aspects of early Paleoindian technology seen in the continental United States. With the exception of projectile-point forms, Nenana complex tool kits and technology are virtually identical to Clovis industries. Neither the Clovis nor the Nenana industry display wedge-shaped cores, microblades, or transverse burins, three *fossiles directeurs* of the central Alaskan Denali complex. Therefore, the Nenana complex, which predates the central Alaskan microblade industries by at least 500 years, should not be regarded as Paleoarctic.

This suggests to us that the Clovis tradition and the Nenana complex might be local northern and southern remnants of the same initial peopling event, referred to by Turner (1984, 1985, 1986) and Greenberg et al. (1986)

as "Macro-Indian." As the timing of this migration is debatable, at least two contrasting models could explain the close technological ties seen between the Clovis and Nenana industries.

Model 1: A Late Entry

The first model assumes that the similarities between Clovis and Nenana reflect a late entry which occurred about 12,000–13,000 yr B.P., when receding continental ice sheets in North America finally permitted the rapid movement of northern groups carrying bifacial projectile points through the Ice-Free Corridor and into midlatitude North America (Haynes 1987).

Immediate Siberian precursors of the early Paleoindians are as yet unknown, although several northeast Asian industries display tool kits somewhat reminiscent of the Nenana complex. Excavations at Ushki I, Layer VII, C-14 dated to ca. 13,000 yr B.P., have produced bifacially flaked stemmed projectile points and end scrapers, but no wedge-shaped cores or microblades (Dikov 1979:33; Dikov and Titov 1984:79–81). Similarly, at Berelekh, Mochanov (1977:79–81) identified another industry containing two bifacial projectile-point tips, several retouched blades, and a possible microcore preform. Since no wedge-shaped microcore industries predating 11,000 yr B.P. have been found in either eastern or western Beringia, it is possible that a separate tradition with a lithic industry based on bifacial points existed in the Subarctic regions of Kamchatka, Chukotka, Alaska, and the Yukon Territory (Powers and Hoffecker 1989). Already it is apparent that non-microblade industries were in Kamchatka as early as 13,000 yr B.P., and the Nenana Valley by 11,500 yr B.P., where they clearly predate later microblade industries. This Beringian point industry, which includes Ushki, Layer VII, as an earlier phase and the Nenana complex as a later phase, is a likely antecedent to Clovis, based on its age, lithic technology, and geographic extent (Dikov 1979; Haynes 1982:396; Powers and Hoffecker 1989).

Model 2: An Early Entry

The second model assumes that the Clovis tradition and the Nenana complex were remnants of a much earlier peopling event. The widespread occurrence of blades and blade tools in the Clovis and Nenana industries is evidence that such an event occurred no earlier than 35,000 yr B.P., since the transition to the Upper Paleolithic in Siberia appears to have occurred at about that time (Larichev et al. 1988). Bifacial working in the form of knives is added to the Early Upper Paleolithic core/blade technique about 24–25,000 yr B.P. (Vasil'evskii et al. 1988). The absence of a microblade technology in the early Paleoindian industries may be an indication that the founding migration into the Americas took place prior to the miniaturization of the north Asian lithic industries and the widespread adoption of the composite inset technique (wedge-shaped cores, microblades and transverse burins) after ca. 18,000 yr B.P.[3] Hence, this peopling event probably occurred ca. 22,000–25,000 yr B.P., during the early Duvanny Yar interval (Isotope stage 2) but before the closing of the Ice-Free Corridor.

Excavations at the Ust'-Kova site in the northern Angara region of central Siberia have produced an Early Upper Paleolithic industry C-14 dated to 23,920 ± 310 yr B.P. (KRIL-381) (Vasil'evskii et al. 1988) that could potentially be called an early progenitor of the American Paleoindian tradition. The Ust'-Kova middle complex includes prismatic blade cores as well as a number of Upper Paleolithic tool types, including retouched blades, end scrapers, perforators, and wedges; yet no wedge-shaped cores or microblades have been noted (Vasil'evskii et al. 1988) (Figure 18). Furthermore, the Ust'-Kova tool kit includes a considerable amount of bifacial working, mostly in the form of knives and not projectile points. Also included in the tool inventory are several planes similar in form to those found at Walker Road and Dry Creek Component I.

Summary

Thus, although no proven Siberian or Alaskan antecedent to the Clovis culture has yet been found, it seems to us that the early Paleoindians originated from a Siberian ancestral population, which carried a tool kit including retouched blades, bifacial points and knives, end scrapers, side scrapers, perforators, and wedges. Moreover, these first Paleoindians colonized eastern Beringia prior to the development and spread of the central Siberian Late Upper Paleolithic microblade industries after 18,000 yr B.P.

Dating the subsequent peopling of the Americas south of the Laurentide ice sheet is more problemmatic. The early peopling event proposed above lacks indisputable evidence, suggesting that the founding Paleoindian migration through the Ice-Free Corridor did not take place until after 13,000 yr B.P. This period between 14,000 and 11,000 yr B.P. is a critical one for New World prehistory, and only future research will define the genetic relationship of the Nenana complex to the later Denali complex and to the Clovis tradition. For the present, it is a working hypothesis that the Nenana complex industry is Paleoindian in nature, technologically very similar to Clovis stone industries found on the High Plains of the western United States at approximately the same time.

Footnotes

1. The Walker Road collection is currently housed at the Department of Anthropology, University of Alaska

Fairbanks. The Dry Creek collection is curated by the University Museum, University of Alaska Fairbanks. The Blackwater Draw artifacts included in this analysis are in the custody of Mr. James Warnica of Portales, New Mexico, as well as the Department of Anthropology, Eastern New Mexico University. Casts of the artifacts from the University of Pennsylvania Blackwater Draw collection were made available by C. Vance Haynes, Department of Anthropology, University of Arizona. The Murray Springs artifacts analyzed are housed at the Arizona State Museum, University of Arizona.

2. Geoarchaeological analyses of the Walker Road site were conducted by Nancy H. Bigelow. Complete results will be presented in her M.A. Thesis, Department of Anthropology, University of Alaska Fairbanks.

3. The earliest unquestionable occurrence of microcores and microblades in Northeast Asia is at Verkne-Troitskaya, firmly C-14 dated to about 18,000 yr B.P. (Mochanov 1977). Earlier "proto"-Diuktai sites have been claimed, including the Ezhantsy, Ust'-Mil', and Ikhine localities; yet these were found in secondary geologic contexts, and associated C-14 dates are in question. It is possible that the wood samples from each of these sites were naturally introduced into archaeological contexts through site deformation processes and do not in actuality represent the age of the cultural materials (Hopkins 1985; Morlan 1987; Powers 1973; Yi and Clark 1985). An in situ development of the Diuktai tradition reaching back to the Boutellier or Happy interval, therefore, is highly unlikely, although this has been suggested by Mochanov (1977). It is much more probable that the Diuktai tradition saw a more southerly origin, perhaps in the Angara region of southern Siberia or in North China.

AKNOWLEDGMENTS

We are grateful to the various funding sources for this research, including the the National Geographic Society and the University of Alaska Fairbanks (Museum Geist Fund, Vice Chancellor for Research, College of Liberal Arts, and Summer Programs). Special thanks is due to the various institutions that allowed us to view the Clovis artifact collections, including the University of Arizona Museum and Eastern New Mexico University. We are particularly indebted to Mr. James Warnica of Portales, New Mexico, and Dr. C. Vance Haynes, University of Arizona. We also wish to thank Bruce Huckell, Mike Jacobs, and John Montgomery. Invaluable editing services were provided by Carrin Halffman, Dennis Stanford, Vance Haynes, John Hoffecker, and Dave Hopkins. For giving us access to the Ust'-Kova artifacts, we wish to thank N.I. Drozdov, Head of the Laboratory of Archaeology and Paleogeography of Central Siberia, U.S.S.R. Academy of Sciences, Siberian Division, Krasnoyarsk. Finally, we wish to dedicate this paper to all the students from Alaska and elsewhere who have contributed to the extensive field and lab work carried out in the Nenana Valley since 1973.

REFERENCES CITED

Adovasio, J. M., A. T. Boldurian, and R. C. Carlisle
1988 Who are Those Guys?: Some Biased Thoughts on the Initial Peopling of the New World. In *Americans Before Columbus: Ice-Age Origins*, edited by R. C. Carlisle, pp. 45–62. Ethnology Monographs No. 12. Department of Anthropology, University of Pittsburgh., Pittsburgh.

Ager, T. A.
1975 *Late Quaternary Environmental History of the Tanana Valley.* Ohio State University Insitute of Polar Studies Report No. 54. Columbus.

Cinq-Mars, J.
1979 Bluefish Cave I: A Late Pleistocene Eastern Beringian Cave Deposit in the Northern Yukon. *Canadian Journal of Archaeology* 3:1–32.

Cook, J. P.
1969 *The Early Prehistory of Healy Lake.* Unpublished Ph.D. dissertation, Department of Anthropology, University of Wisconsin. Madison.

Dikov, N. N.
1977 *Arkheologicheskie Pamiatniki Kamchatki, Chukotki i Verkhnei Kolymy [Archeological Monuments of Kamchatka, Chukotka, and the Upper Kolyma].* Nauka, Moscow.

1979 *Drevnie Kul'tury Severo-Vostochnoi Azii [Ancient Cultures of Northeast Asia].* Nauka, Moscow.

Dikov, N. N., and E. E. Titov
1984 Problems of the Stratification and Periodization of the Ushki sites. *Arctic Anthropology* 21(2):69–80.

Dumond, D. E.
1977 *The Eskimos and Aleuts.* Thames and Hudson, London.

1980 The Archeology of Alaska and the Peopling of America. *Science* 209:984–991.

Evans, G. L.
1951 Prehistoric Wells in Eastern New Mexico. *American Antiquity* 17:1–8.

Goebel, F. E.
1988 The Nenana Complex and Clovis Origins. Paper presented at the 16th Annual Meeting of the Alaska Anthropological Association, Anchorage.

1989 *The Nenana Complex: Paleoindian or Paleoarctic?* Submitted to the Geist Fund Committee, University of Alaska, Fairbanks.

1990 *Early Paleoindian Technology in Beringia: A Lithic Analysis of the Alaskan Nenana Complex.* Unpublished master's thesis, Department of Anthropology, University of Alaska, Fairbanks.

Gramly, R. N.
1982 *The Vail Site: A Paleo-Indian Encampment in Maine.* Bulletin of the Buffalo Society of Natural Sciences No. 30. Buffalo.

Gramly, R. N., and R. E. Funk
1989 What is Known and Not Known about the Human Occupation of the Northeastern United States until 10,000 B.P. Paper presented at the First World Summit Conference on the Peopling of the Americas, Center for the Study of the First Americans, University of Maine, Orono.

Green, F. E.
1963 The Clovis Blades: An Important Addition to the Llano Complex. *American Antiquity* 29:145–65.

Greenberg, J. H., C. Turner II, and S. L. Zegura
1986 The Settlement of the Americas: A Comparison of the Linguistic, Dental, and Genetic Evidence. *Current Anthropology* 27:477–497.

Guthrie, R. D.
1983 Osseous Projectile Points: Biological Considerations Affecting Raw Material Selection and Design Among Paleolithic and Paleoindian Peoples. In *Animals and Archaeology: Hunters and their Prey,* edited by J. Clutton-Brock and C. Grigson, pp. 273–294. BAR International Series 163, Oxford.

Hammat, H. H.
1970 A Paleo-Indian Butchering Kit. *American Antiquity* 35:141–52.

Haynes, C. V., Jr.
1972 Stratigraphic Investigations at the Williamson Site, Virginia. *The Chesopiean* 10:107–113.

1975 Pleistocene and Recent Stratigraphy. In *Late Pleistocene Environments of the Southern High Plains,* edited by F. Wendorf and J. J. Hester, pp. 57–96. Fort Burgwin Research Center, Southern Methodist University, Dallas.

1980 The Clovis Culture. *Canadian Journal of Anthropology* 1:115–121.

1982 Were Clovis Progenitors in Beringia? In *Paleoecology of Beringia,* edited by D. M. Hopkins, J. V. Matthews, Jr., C. E. Schweger, and S. B. Young, pp. 383–399. Academic Press, New York.

1987 Clovis Origin Update. *Kiva* 52:83–93.

Haynes, C. V., Jr., and G. Agogino
1966 Prehistoric Springs and Geochronology of the Clovis site, New Mexico. *American Antiquity* 31:812–21.

Haynes, C. V., Jr., D. J. Donahue, A. T. Jull, and T. H. Zabel
1984 Application of Accelerator Dating to Fluted Point Paleoindian Sites. *Archaeology of Eastern North America* 12:184–191.

Hemmings, E. T.
1970 *Early Man in San Pedro Valley.* Unpublished Ph.D. dissertation, University of Arizona, Tucson.

Hester, J. J.
1972 *Blackwater Locality No. 1: A Stratified, Early Man Site in Eastern New Mexico.* Fort Burgwin Research Center, Southern Methodist University, Dallas.

Hoffecker, J. F.
1985a Archeological Field Research: 1980. *National Geographic Society Research Reports* 19:48–59.

1985b The Moose Creek Site. *National Geographic Society Research Reports* 19:33–48.

Hopkins, D. M.
1985 Comments on Dolitsky (1985). *Current Anthropology* 26:371–372.

Huckell, B. B.
1982 *The Distribution of Fluted Points in Arizona: A Review and an Update.* Archaeological Series No. 145. Cultural Resource Management Division, Arizona State Museum, University of Arizona, Tucson.

n.d. Clovis Lithic Technology: A View from the Upper San Pedro Valley. Ms. in possession of author.

Irwin, H. T., and H. M. Wormington
1970 Paleo-Indian Tool Types in the Great Plains. *American Antiquity* 35:24–34.

Larichev, V., U. Khol'ushkin, and I. Laricheva
1988 The Upper Paleolithic of Northern Asia: Achievements, Problems, and Perspectives. I. Western Siberia. *Journal of World Prehistory* 2:359–396.

Lively, R.
1988 *Chugwater (FAI-035).* Submitted to U. S. Army Corps of Engineers, Alaska District.

Long, A., and B. Rippeteau
1974 Testing Contemporaneity and Averaging Radiocarbon Dates. *American Antiquity* 39:205–215.

MacDonald, G. F.
1968 *Debert: A Palaeo-Indian Site in Central Nova Scotia.* Anthropology Papers of the National Museum of Canada No. 16. Ottawa.

Markin, S. V.
1983 Paleoliticheskoe Mestonakhozhdenie Shorokhovo na Srednei Tomi [The Paleolithic Locality of Shorokhovo on the Middle Tom]. In *Paleolit Sibiri [The Paleolithic of Siberia],* pp. 93–100. Nauka, Novosibirsk.

1986 *Paleoliticheskie Pamiatniki Basseina Reki Tomi [The Paleolithic Monuments of the Tom River Basin].* Nauka, Novosibirsk.

McCulloch, D. S., and D. M. Hopkins
1966 Evidence for an Early Recent Warm Interval in Northwestern Alaska. *Geologic Society of America Bulletin* 77:1089–1108.

Medvedev, G. I.
1969 Results of the Investigation of the Mesolithic in the Stratified Settlement of Ust'-Belaia 1957–1964. *Arctic Anthropology* 6(1):61–73.

Mochanov, Y. A.
1977 *Drevneishie Etapy Zaseleniia Chelovekom Severo-Vostochnoi Azii [Most Ancient Stages of Human Settlement in Northeast Asia].* Nauka, Novosibirsk.

Morlan, R. E.
1987 The Pleistocene Archaeology of Beringia. In *The Evolution of Human Hunting,* edited by M. H. Nitecki and D. V. Nitecki, pp. 267–307. Plenum Press, New York.

1988 Pre-Clovis People: Early Discoveries of America. In *Americans Before Columbus: Ice-Age Origins,* edited by R. C. Carlisle, pp. 31–44. Ethnology Monographs No. 12. Department of Anthropology, University of Pittsburgh, Pittsburgh.

Müller-Beck, H.
1966 Paleohunters in America: Origins and Diffusion. *Science* 152:1192–1210.

1967 On Migrations of Hunters Across the Bering Land Bridge in the Upper Pleistocene. In *The Bering Land Bridge,* edited by D. M. Hopkins, pp. 373–408. Stanford University Press, Stanford.

Powers, W. R.
1973 Paleolithic Man in Northeast Asia. *Arctic Anthropology* 10:1–106.

1983a The Geology of the Dry Creek Site. In *Dry Creek: Archeology and Paleoecology of a Late Pleistocene Alaskan Hunting Camp,* by W. R. Powers, R. D. Guthrie, and J. F. Hoffecker. Submitted to the National Park Service, Contract No. CX-9000-7-0047.

1983b Lithic Technology of the Dry Creek Site. In *Dry Creek: Archeology and Paleoecology of a Late Pleistocene Alaskan Hunting Camp,* by W. R. Powers, R. D. Guthrie, and J. F. Hoffecker. Submitted to the National Park Service, Contract No. CX-9000-7-0047.

Powers, W. R., R. D. Guthrie, and J. F. Hoffecker
1983 *Dry Creek: Archeology and Paleoecology of a Late Pleistocene Alaskan Hunting Camp.* Submitted to the National Park Service, Contract No. CX-9000-7-0047.

Powers, W. R., and T. D. Hamilton
1978 Dry Creek: A Late Pleistocene Human Occupation in Central Alaska. In *Early Man in America from a Circum-Pacific Perspective,* edited by A. L. Bryan, pp. 72–77. Occasional Papers No. 1. Department of Anthropology, University of Alberta, Edmonton.

Powers, W. R., and J. F. Hoffecker
1989 Late Pleistocene Settlement in the Nenana Valley, Central Alaska. *American Antiquity* 54:263–287.

Rogers, R. A.
1986 Spurred End Scrapers as Diagnostic Paleoindian Artifacts: A Distributional Analysis on Stream Terraces. *American Antiquity* 51:338–341.

Sellards, E. H.
1952 *Early Man in America.* University of Texas Press, Austin.

Ten Brink, N. W., and C. F. Waythomas
1985 Late Wisconsin Glacial Chronology of the North-Central Alaska Range: A Regional Synthesis and its Implications for Early Human Settlement. *National Geographic Society Research Reports* 19:15–32.

Thorson, R. M., and T. D. Hamilton
1977 Geology of the Dry Creek Site: A Stratified Early Man Site in Interior Alaska. *Quaternary Research* 7:149–176.

Turner, C. G. II
1984 Advances in the Dental Search for Native American Origins. *Acta Anthropogenetica* 8:23–62.

1985 The Dental Search for Native American Origins. In *Out of Asia: Peopling the Americas and the Pacific,* edited by R. Kirk and E. Szathmary, pp. 31–78. *Journal of Pacific History,* Canberra.

1986 The First Americans: The Dental Evidence. *National Geographic Research* 2:37–46.

Vasil'evskii, R. S., V. V. Burilov, and N. I. Drozdov
1988 *Arkheologicheskie Pamiatniki Severnozo Priangar'ia [Archeological sites of the Northern Angara Region]*. Nauka, Novosibirsk.

Wahrhaftig, C.
1958 *Quaternary Geology of the Nenana River Valley and Adjacent Parts of the Alaska Range.* U. S. Geological Survey Professional Paper 293-A.

Warnica, J. M.
1966 New Discoveries at the Clovis Site. *American Antiquity* 31:345–357.

West, F. H.
1967 The Donnelly Ridge Site and the Definition of an Early Core and Blade Complex in Central Alaska. *American Antiquity* 23:360–382.

1981 *The Archaeology of Beringia.* Columbia University Press, New York.

Yi, S., and G. Clark
1985 The "Dyuktai Culture" and New World Origins. *Current Anthropology* 26:1–20.

Clovis from the Perspective of the Ice-Free Corridor

ROY L. CARLSON
Department of Archaeology
Simon Fraser University
Burnaby, BC, Canada V5A 1S6

Both the origin and demise of the Clovis fluted point are rooted in the existing technology of the times and efforts to improve cost-effectiveness. Cultural components earlier than 11,500 yr B.P. with blade and biface technology are potentially ancestral Clovis (proto-Clovis), and the logical ancestral point type is the slotted bone or antler point with side-hafted blade segments. Non-Clovis variations in fluting are derived from regional Clovis populations and mark the beginning of the decline of fluting as a hafting technique. The Ice-Free Corridor cannot be ruled out as the probable route of a proto-Clovis population movement from Beringia about 14,000 years ago.

The Ice-Free Corridor is a concept long familiar to New World archaeologists. It is a zone along the eastern flanks of the Canadian Rockies in which ice-free conditions may have existed during part of the late Wisconsin. Its northern portion is in the Mackenzie River Basin and its southern terminus near the 49th Parallel. The archaeological significance of the Corridor is that it is a logical route by which the earliest New World aborigines could have spread south from Beringia to the Plains and beyond. The model of migration via this route presupposes that sometime during glacial retreat the Cordilleran ice sheet to the west and the Laurentide to the east parted, and a Paleo-Moses led his band from the frigid unglaciated environs of Beringia to a land of elephant, horse, and bison south of the 49th Parallel. The most recent statement of this model is that of Haynes (1987). Today, the Alaska Highway traverses part of the Corridor, as it is still the most feasible land route between the Arctic and continental North America. The purpose of this paper is to summarize the archaeological evidence from the part of this corridor in southern Alberta and northeastern British Columbia, and to discuss its bearing on Clovis origins. The nature of the available data preordains an emphasis on the technological and typological aspects of fluted points, and their developmental relationships, rather than on paleoecology, stratigraphy, or the total content of Clovis culture.

Early archaeological research along this route (Bliss 1939; Johnson 1946; Johnson and Raup 1964; MacNeish 1954, 1956, 1960, 1964) produced little data bearing on Paleoindian cultures and none on fluted points. Assemblages near Great Bear Lake (MacNeish

1956:Plate 5), which were initially considered to be Paleoindian, are now thought to be much younger and possibly related to the 2000-year-old Taltheilei Shale tradition (Clark 1981:108). A study (Wormington and Forbis 1965) of projectile points in private collections provided the first information on fluted points in Alberta; one definite Folsom point, several Clovis, and many Plainview were reported, along with numerous Plano and other later unfluted types. Following a survey in Banff National Park in 1969, Christiansen (1971) first described in detail the Clovis points from Lake Minnewanka. Test excavations by McIntyre and Reeves (1975) and Reeves (1976) indicated that no intact deposits remained at that site. McIntyre also excavated a Clovis fluted point, which he considered reused, from middle Holocene silt deposits near Calgary (Wilson 1983). M. Wilson (1983:Figure 83) later mapped the distribution of fluted points in the Corridor and estimated a count of more than 40 fluted points from Alberta. More recently Gryba (1983:122) excavated two fluted points and a Midland point from the lower levels of the Sibbald Creek site, which may be associated with a C-14 date of 9570 ± 320 yr B.P. (generally considered to be too young on several grounds), and has since undertaken a survey of fluted points in private collections. He reports 35 sites in Alberta (Gryba 1985, 1987) containing over 170 points of various types belonging to the fluted-point tradition (Ball 1989:16).

In British Columbia recent research has resulted in the discovery of five sites with fluted points in the Corridor portion of the province. This work began in 1974 when Fladmark (1981) recognized an early type of point with multiple thinning or fluting scars in collections from two sites. In 1983 Fladmark excavated to the base of the deposits in front of Charlie Lake Cave, a deep stratified site on the margin of glacial Lake Peace (Fladmark et al. 1988). A fluted point from the earliest component there is directly associated with C-14 dates ranging from 10,100 ± 210 to 10,770 ± 120 yr B.P. I. Wilson (1986) discovered an additional site with two fluted points near Pink Mountain between the headwaters of the Halfway and the Beaton rivers (tributaries of the Peace) and the Sikinni Chief (which flows into the Liard). The site, at an elevation of 3,750 feet (1,143 m), is above the highest strand line of glacial Lake Peace (Mathews 1980). Fragments of two microblade cores, a Scottsbluff point, and several scrapers and post-Paleoindian points were also found. The site is an unstratified lithic scatter, and no datable material was discovered. Further survey the following year (Wilson and Carlson 1987) resulted in the discovery of five additional sites that probably belong to the period of Paleoindian cultures. Only one of them, the Anderson site on the headwaters of the Halfway River, yielded a fluted point, and it was too fragmentary to classify further. The addition of this site makes a total of at least 40 sites with various types of fluted points in the Corridor area of British Columbia and Alberta.

Typologically, the fluted points (Figure 1) range from Clovis to Folsom to unnamed types described as "basally-thinned triangular," such as those from Charlie Lake Cave and Sibbald Creek (Vickers 1986), and "basally-thinned broad," like those from the Alberta farmlands east of the foothills (Gryba 1987). This same range of types is found to the east in Saskatchewan (Kehoe 1966). It is impossible to give completely exact counts of these types in southern Alberta because of the way they are reported in the literature, but there are at least four which are Clovis (i.e., Carlson 1983:Figure 6.8a,d; Wormington and Forbis 1965:Figure 55), one that is clearly Folsom (Wormington and Forbis 1965:157), and two others that may be Folsom (Vickers 1986:Figure 7). The two point fragments from Pink Mountain (Wilson 1986) have multiple basal thinning scars and exhibit deeply concave bases. At least nine points from Alberta are basally thinned triangular (Vickers 1986:Figure 6), as is the dated one from Charlie Lake Cave in British Columbia. There are nine broad, multiple-fluted points from Alberta (Gryba 1987). There may well be no real distinction between the broad and triangular multiple-fluted/basally thinned types other than that the latter may be intensively reworked examples of the former. I previously referred to these variations as Peace River fluted (Carlson 1983:83), and it is this group that is by far the most common in the Ice-Free Corridor and along its eastern margin. This group is similar to both Arctic fluted points (see Clark, this volume) and to points from the Great Basin called Black Rock Concave Base (Bryan 1980). In my opinion these types or styles should not be considered Clovis, but Clovis derivatives and examples of the demise of fluting.

What is fluting and what is its significance? First and most obviously, it is a specialized and somewhat cumbersome technique of basal thinning intended to facilitate hafting a biface to a shaft to make an effective weapon for hunting. It begins with Clovis and climaxes with Folsom; whereas Clovis is very widespread, Folsom is one of a number of later regional variants. Fluting is specialized and cumbersome in that it requires careful preparation of the blank from which the channel flake is struck, analogous to core preparation techniques for blades, and requires considerable skill and time in execution. Second, its specialized technical nature and limited time span, combined with its appearance as part of the earliest widespread weapons technology in a continuous distribution in the New World, indicate a single historical origin for the technique, which further implies that fluting was originally the custom of a single ethnic group. The earliest known fluted points are found in the Clovis culture (Haynes 1982, 1987; Haynes et al. 1984; Hester 1966), and it must be assumed that fluting was developed in this culture to solve a hafting problem. In theory, fluting represents a more efficient hafting method than whatever preceded it. That fluted points appear in every culture area of the New World from the

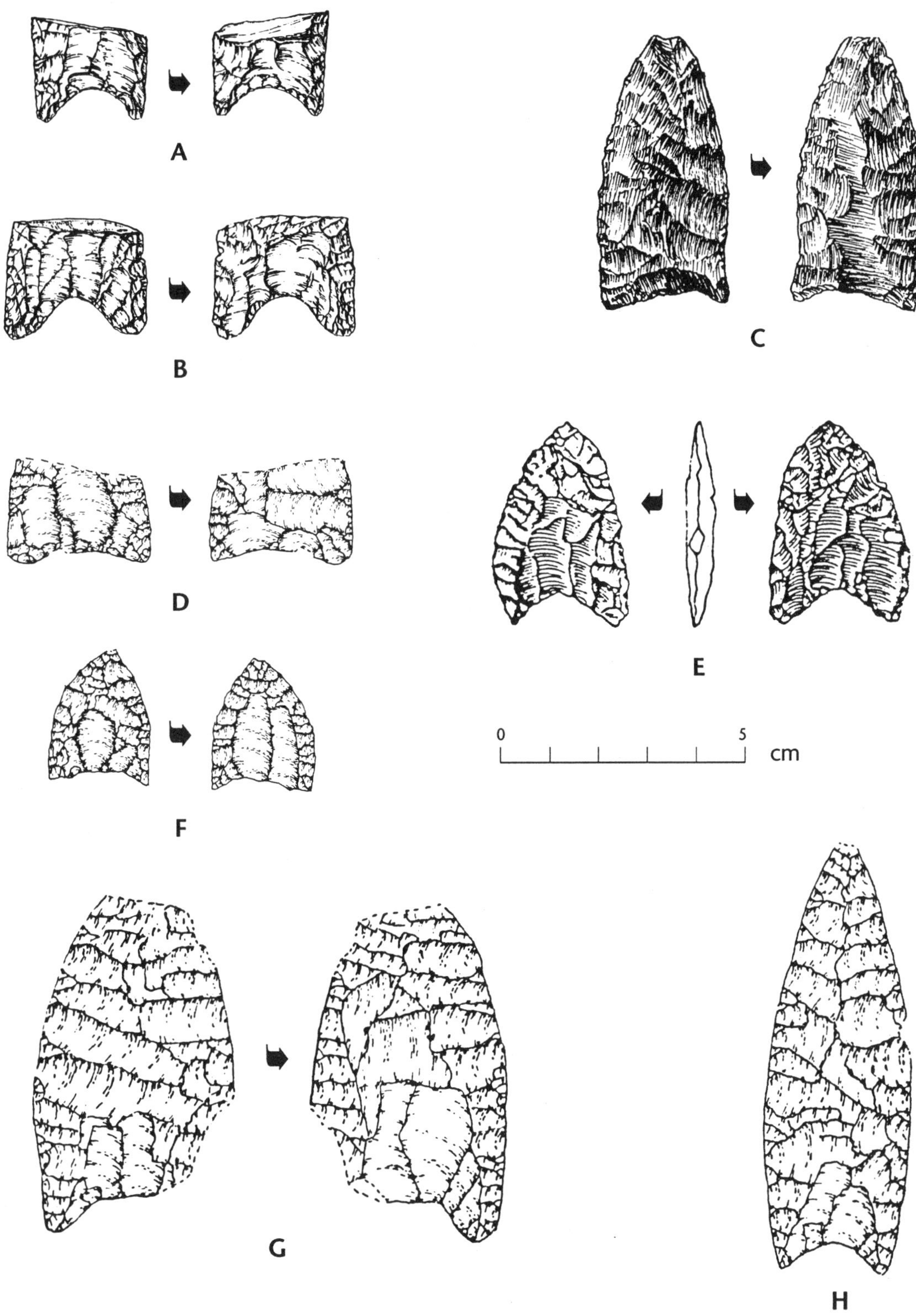

Figure 1. Late types of fluted points from the Corridor and adjacent flatlands. **A** and **B)** Pink Mountain, BC; **C)** Gerret site near Fort St. John, BC; **D** and **F)** Sibbald Creek site, AB; **E)** Charlie Lake Cave, BC; **G)** Bergen, AB; **H)** Penhold, AB *(A and B courtesy of Ian Wilson; C and E courtesy of Knut Fladmark; D and F–H courtesy of Eugene Gryba).*

Arctic to Tierra del Fuego (except for the northwest coast north of the Strait of Juan de Fuca) at or near the bottom of the accepted archaeological sequence suggests that fluting was spread by an original founding population which, in the course of population expansion (Haynes 1964, 1969, 1982; Martin 1973), would have undergone continuous segmentation into separate bands as a result of growth and geographic spread. A multiplication of separate bands with their own knappers plus transmission of technical knowledge from generation to generation, combined with experimentation to produce a more efficient weapon, would have resulted in variations in fluting as geographic expansion and band segmentation took place.

Conceptually there is little difference between preparing a biface for fluting and preparing a core for removal of a particular flake or blade. Channeled by the existing technical knowledge, fluting could have arisen overnight in the mind of a knowledgeable flint knapper working in a technological milieu in which both bifaces and blades from prepared cores were customary products. The key conceptual factors in the inception of fluting would have been the equation of channel flakes with blades and the understanding that flakes of a specialized type, such as blades or channel flakes, can and must be removed only after correct core preparation. Such a conception would also contribute to the perpetuation of fluting as the correct way to prepare a biface for hafting until such time as a better technique evolved. Marriage of bifaces with blade-core preparation techniques could produce a fluted point readily haftable in a split-stick shaft. The benefit of such a projectile head over what preceded it would theoretically be in terms of reduced costs in time or raw materials and increased benefits in haftability and functional efficiency. Following this reasoning, a fluted point should represent a simplification of projectile-point making rather than the opposite, an elaboration from a simpler prototype such as basal thinning, as has frequently been hypothesized. If this model is valid, then what is the prototype for the fluted point?

A logical ancestor of the Clovis fluted point is the bone or antler point in which multiple blade segments were bilaterally side-hafted to form the cutting edges, such as have been found in Upper Paleolithic and Neolithic sites in Siberia. The cost in time and raw material to make such points by preparing a blade core, striking the blades, breaking them and choosing the best segments, preparing and grooving a piece of antler or other organic material, inserting the blade segments and securing them in place, and then inserting and fastening the whole thing in a shaft is considerably more than that required by a knapper experienced in both blade and biface production to flake, flute, and haft a biface. Such points in the collections in Irkutsk and Novosibirsk that I have examined, that have their blade segments still in place, are all Neolithic. However, there are both prismatic stone blades and slotted bone points missing their blades that come from Upper Paleolithic assemblages. That such artifacts were used as projectile points is attested to by the discovery by Abramova and Grechinka of a slotted antler point with blades found penetrating a bison scapula (Chard 1974:Figure 1:18). Bryan (1969) has pointed out that the general development of stone points may be related to the development of the atlatl because it requires a spear with a heavier tip than that available from organic materials. This idea is unlikely since there is a diminution through time in size and weight of atlatl dart tips and, presumably, of shafts in the interests of a more efficient weapon. The only logical instance where a bone point with stone inserts might be more cost-efficient than a fluted point would be if raw material of a size large enough to make a stone biface were not available.

The Clovis fluted point may or may not have been developed before early peoples spread south from Beringia. The detailed analysis of Clovis C-14 dates (Haynes et al. 1984) indicates that proto-Clovis should date in the period just preceding 11,500 years ago. In the Late Paleolithic Diuktai culture of Siberia, the technological milieu includes both prepared blades and cores, and bifacial techniques (Mochanov 1984). This culture encompasses the right time period of at least 15,000 to 12,000 years ago for Clovis origins. Logically, such a Diuktai component should be one in which wedge-shaped microblade cores had not yet appeared, and there are such variants (Mochanov 1984:717) although they are less well known than those with wedge-shaped cores and microblades. Perhaps West (1981:192) is correct in his speculation that ancestral Clovis technology was best represented on the Bering Platform, which is now under water. Because no fluted points are found in Diuktai, it seems reasonable to assume this marriage between bifacial and prepared core techniques, which produced the earliest Clovis fluted points (if this hypothesis is correct), took place somewhere between Siberia and the limits of Clovis distribution in North America.

All the known fluted points in Alaska and the Arctic are Arctic fluted rather than classic Clovis, and are considered to be post-Clovis in age (Clark, this volume). The fluted points from Putu (Alexander 1987) are pressure fluted (Flenniken, personal communication), which is probably an indicator of their lateness in the sequence. The absence of Clovis fluted points in the Arctic cannot be taken to mean either that Clovis progenitors did not come from there or that the earliest fluted points were not developed there. The harsh environment of the late Wisconsin would have kept Arctic populations extremely small in size and difficult, if not impossible, to discover archaeologically. Rapid transit of one or more small groups down the eastern slope of the Rockies during a single season of favorable climatic conditions would be difficult to discover archaeologically. Archaeological survey and testing has still barely touched the southern portion of the Ice-Free Corridor, and if in situ data are to be found, an intensive search is required. The predictable model is that once a group or groups reached the more favorable conditions south of the glaciated regions, they would eventually expand in size to the point of archaeological visibility.

Whitthoft (1952, 1954) seems to have been the first archaeologist to champion the development of fluting from core and blade technology. His frame of reference was the Enterline chert industry, which is now considered to be post-Clovis in age. Haynes (1964) also pointed out the similarity between blade production and multiple fluting on points from the Arctic, with the implication that such points could be ancestral to Clovis. Regardless of the age of these particular examples and the assumption that they are Clovis derivatives, there is no reason not to extend this idea to classic Clovis, since blades from prepared cores have been found in such components (Green 1963; Warnica 1966). If the innovations that brought about the Clovis fluted point were channeled by existing technical knowledge as suggested above, then ancestral Clovis should be a culture with both bifacial technology and a prepared blade and core industry. Are there any cultures closer than Diuktai to the center of Clovis distribution that fit this requirement and occupy the right temporal position?

The answer to the preceding question is "maybe." Five sites or complexes need to be discussed: Putu in the Brooks Range and the Nenana complex in central Alaska; Meadowcroft in Pennsylvania; Wilson Butte Cave in Idaho; Smith Creek Cave in Nevada; and Taima-taima in Venezuela. The Putu site (Alexander 1987) has C-14 dates of 11,470 ± 500 yr B.P. on charcoal from an early hearth, and dates ranging from 8454 ± 130 to 5700 ± 190 yr B.P. on scattered charcoal and soils higher up in the same stratigraphic zone. The lithic assemblage from this zone includes Arctic fluted points, Putu points (lanceolate points with thick bases), a triangular point, prismatic blades, microblades, and other Upper Paleolithic-type tools. There are no wedge-shaped cores. The question of how the C-14 dates and the different types of stone tools relate temporally to each other cannot be answered by the context. If the blades and Putu points belong with the 11,470 ± 500 yr B.P. date, and the Arctic fluted points with the more recent date, then the former are at the temporal boundary between Clovis and proto-Clovis. Dates on the Nenana complex of central Alaska at the Moose Creek site range from 8160 to 11,730 yr B.P., but are all on soil organics, and at least one of the dates has no direct cultural association (Hoffecker 1985). The artifact assemblage includes blade and Putu point fragments, retouched flakes, and small ovate bifaces. Haynes (1987) considers the Nenana complex to be proto-Clovis of non-Diuktai origin. It is obviously the same complex represented in part of the Putu site assemblage. The climatic reconstruction in the Nenana Valley (Hoffecker 1985:43) indicates a cold phase just preceding the time of the Nenana assemblage and an earlier warm phase centered between 12,500 and 14,000 yr B.P. This earlier period seems a more appropriate time for proto-Clovis in Beringia, although it might be argued that Nenana and Putu are later derivatives of that hypothetical culture and little removed from it technologically.

At Meadowcroft Rockshelter in Pennsylvania, the early C-14 dates have now been averaged at 14,500 yr B.P. (Adovasio and Carlisle 1988). This is not an unreasonable date for proto-Clovis, and the lithic assemblage does include a biface and a nondescript blade (Adovasio et al. 1983). (Exactly how averaging the dates contributes to an understanding of the real age of the relevant component at Meadowcroft, or indeed of any component with a wide range of dates, is, however, beyond my comprehension.)

At Wilson Butte Cave, Gruhn (1965) has a single C-14 date of 14,500 ± 500 yr B.P. on an assemblage consisting of a crude biface, a blade, and a flake (Crabtree 1969). Objections have been raised by Haynes (Bryan 1969) that the date is on a sample of rodent bones, which may not accurately date the artifacts, but at face value the small assemblage does fit the proto-Clovis technological requirements outlined above.

At Smith Creek Cave in Nevada, Bryan (1979, this volume) has a series of C-14 dates from about 10,700 to 14,200 yr B.P., which could place the earliest (Mt. Moriah) occupation there earlier than or contemporaneous with Clovis, and a lithic assemblage that includes biface fragments but no blades. However, the point fragments look as if they belong to the stemmed-point tradition (Carlson 1983) of the Basin and Plateau, which most evidence indicates is post-Clovis in time (Carlson 1988). Bryan (this volume) has answered Thompson's criticism of the dates, but that still leaves a dating latitude too wide to insure acceptability of the Mt. Moriah occupation as proto-Clovis on the basis of dating. On the basis of Willig's (this volume) stratigraphic data from the Dietz site in Oregon and all radiocarbon dates from sites in the Columbia-Snake drainage (Ames et al. 1981; Rice 1972), the stemmed-point tradition is post-Clovis in age. In the Great Basin, there is a C-14 date of 13,200 ± 720 yr B.P. at Fort Rock Cave (Bedwell 1973), but the large standard deviation renders it useless for precise dating. There is also a C-14 date of ca. 11,700 yr B.P. at Ca-Cal-S342 on the western slope of the Sierra Nevada in California, which may be associated with a stemmed point (Peak et al. 1986). Part of the problem is that Clovis occupations in the Great Basin and California are all undated, and Clovis there could be older than on the Plains and predate some of these early dates on components of the stemmed-point tradition. Somewhat further afield are sites in Venezuela and Ecuador that are also potential proto-Clovis occupations.

At Taima-taima and Muaco in Venezuela, two

fragments of El Jobo points have been found in association with mastodon remains in contexts with a C-14 chronology placing them between 12,580 and 14,200 years ago (Bryan and Gruhn 1979:53–58). The thick El Jobo point, with its poorly designed base for hafting, is a reasonable candidate typologically for proto-Clovis in that fluting would improve its haftability as an atlatl dart tip by reducing the thickness of the shaft necessary to accommodate the thick butt of the point and thus permit better penetration of the spear.

At El Inga in Ecuador, stemmed (fishtail) fluted points occur as part of a technological complex that does include blades and cores. Although the dating problems there do not preclude the possibility that this assemblage is proto-Clovis, with fluting spreading north as Mayer-Oakes (1984) suggests, the points seem more advanced than Clovis, hence are probably younger. My guess is that the points from Central America that are both fluted and stemmed (Bird and Cooke 1978; Lynch 1983) are transitional in time as well as in type (between fluting and stemming) and are ancestral to the fishtail forms in South America. Fluting, then, would have originated somewhere to the north of Central America.

The demise of fluting is as intriguing as its beginning. As mentioned earlier, the majority of fluted points from the Ice-Free Corridor and all of those from the Arctic appear to be post-Clovis in age and related to the disappearance of fluting as an attribute of hafting technology. The disappearance of fluting was probably the result of the same processes that brought it about. The most persuasive arguments on the demise of fluting are those presented by Musil (1988), who hypothesizes that a fluted biface is a less cost-efficient projectile head than the stemmed or notched forms that succeed fluted points in the archaeological record of the New World. He points out that in terms of increased penetration power, reduced likelihood of shaft damage, and ease of point reuse and resharpening upon breakage, stemming is a much better configuration for hafting than is fluting. That fluting was replaced by stemming over its entire area of distribution in North America is a pretty good indicator that stemming is a more efficient hafting method than fluting (Carlson 1983:83), even though experimentation has not yet demonstrated the specific strengths and weaknesses of the two techniques as postulated by Musil.

The regional variations in fluted points are probably responses to the same factors that led finally to the adoption of stemming as the most common biface modification for hafting during the transition from the Paleoindian to later periods. In cultures such as Clovis, in which hunting played a major role in subsistence and the stone-tipped spear was the principal weapon, it is axiomatic that increased efficiency in making and repairing this weapon would have taken place through time. On the north-central Plains, Frison (this volume) hypothesizes a linear development from Clovis to Goshen to Folsom on the one hand, and from Goshen to Agate Basin on the other. In the Northeast (Storck, this volume), the Gainey, Barnes, and Crowfield types look like experiments with fluting techniques, which can be interpreted as efforts to improve haftability and increase cost efficiency. In the Southeast, Clovis fluted points are of such classic form and so widespread (Dunbar, this volume) that Bryan (this volume) suggests they originated there. Other fluted points in this same region, such as Cumberland, Quad, and Dalton (Mason 1962), appear to mark the decline of fluting, which is rapidly succeeded by stemming and notching. Arctic fluted and Peace River fluted points belong in this same late category. The Midwest (Justice 1987) shows overlapping distributions of Clovis and the derived fluted types common to surrounding regions. In the Great Basin, Clovis is probably succeeded by the thinner Black Rock Concave Base type (Bryan 1980) and by stemmed forms. The concave-based stemmed types (Bedwell 1973:Figure 20; Rice 1972:Figure 8; Riddell and Olsen 1969:Figure 2h,m) of the stemmed-point tradition may eventually turn out to be the transitional types. In the Northwest, fluted points are very rare but typologically cover the range from Clovis (Gerity 1960; Minor 1985; Osborne 1956) to some resembling Folsom, to unnamed derived forms. It is clear that fluted points constitute both an early horizon and a cultural tradition with both ancient and derived forms.

Greenberg (Greenberg et al. 1986) has recently presented his full classification of New World Indian languages in which he recognizes three super-phyla: Na-Dene, which includes Tlingit, Haida, and Athabascan; Eskimo-Aleut, which includes only these two groups; and Amerind, which includes all other Native languages of North and South America and is considered to be the oldest group. Turner (1989) provides correlative groupings based on dental anthropology. The distribution of the fluted-point tradition does correlate rather well with the distribution of Amerind and with the distribution of Turner's most widespread Sinodont subtype. Although we as students were always warned not to correlate race, language, and culture, we were also told of the exception—the Eskimo—who proved the rule. It should be kept in mind that, like the Eskimo, the New World's initial population must have been a thin scatter of bands over a vast area. Under such conditions both linguistic and technological divergence are predictable phenomena, and the variations we see in fluting are best explained in this way. Such variations could arise through experimentation by individual knappers and spread rapidly. If this is the case, C-14 may never be able to provide critical datings, and typology and seriation will have to be used to establish local sequences, as with the Gainey, Barnes, and Crowfield types (Storck, this volume).

The preceding paragraphs concentrate on the rise and fall of fluting. Hypotheses advanced are that proto-

Clovis is a culture with biface and blade technology, of which there are potential examples in Siberia and as far south in the New World as Venezuela; that the producers of fluted points were the ancestors of speakers of the Amerind language super-phylum and constituted a fluted-point tradition that spans North and Central America, with derived forms in South America; and that both the origin and the demise of the distinctive Clovis fluted point were rooted in the existing lithic technology of the times and promoted by continuous efforts to build a better mouse trap.

It should be obvious to most readers that what has been said above is a variation of what has come to be known as the Clovis model of the peopling of the New World, a model that has been developed in several variations, most forcibly by Martin (1973) and Haynes (1964, 1982, 1984, 1987). Bryan (this volume), however, tells us that the Clovis model is dead. Both Bryan's and Bonnichsen's (this volume) papers are related to the alternative to the Clovis model, which holds that the New World was settled much earlier by peoples with a generalized food-collecting subsistence base. Owen (1984) and Dincauze (1984) have recently criticized much of the basis for that model, and Lynch (1990) has provided additional evaluation of the South American data. There is no need to repeat their critiques here, only to state that *if* advocates of an *early* pre-Clovis occupation of the Americas wish to be taken seriously, they will have to adopt a much more critical attitude toward artifact identification, the degree of contextual association between artifacts and relevant non-artifacts, and the problem of varying C-14 dates on single components.

If Taima-taima, Wilson Butte Cave, and Meadowcroft can provisionally be considered proto-Clovis, the Clovis model may be considered altered but certainly not dead. All that needs to be postulated is a forward wedge of proto-Clovis peoples, not an ancient substratum of general foragers who used unmodified river pebbles for tools. It has been demonstrated (Ochsenius and Gruhn 1979) that, within the legitimate bounds of archaeological probabilities, elephant hunters were at Taima-taima 12,000 to 14,000 years ago. Place proto-Clovis with a population of 40 or 50 at Edmonton 13,500 years ago, rather than Martin's (1973) 104 at 11,500 yr B.P., change a fluted-point technology to a biface and blade proto-Clovis technology marking the forward edge of population expansion, and the Clovis model still lives. If the forward edge of population expansion did not include fluted points, then some variations in fluting might be the result of adoption of the technique (Bonnichsen, this volume) by earlier residents, as opposed to the hypothesis that fluting variations largely represent the technique in decline. However, such groups would theoretically already have the antecedent biface and blade technology, and their presence need not predate fluting by any lengthy period of time.

Notes

1. This paper is based on my presentation at INQUA entitled "Filling the Gap" and on my remarks as an invited discussant at this same symposium. I wish to thank four anonymous assessors for their remarks, which have resulted in the expansion of this paper.
2. The 1987 survey in the vicinity of Pink Mountain was supported by funds from the President's Research Grant Committee, Simon Fraser University, and by the B.C. Government Heritage Conservation Branch, Victoria.
3. My reaction to Drozdov's presentation at INQUA was that the bifaces he discussed were interesting but too far removed in time, space, and technology to be directly relevant to the question of Clovis origins.
4. The Levallois technique, which, like blade production, involves specialized core preparation and flake removal, is also an acceptable prototype for fluting. It has not been presented here as such because it is not found in potential proto-Clovis assemblages. The presence of Levalloisoid technology in northwestern North America is post-Clovis and related to cobble-reduction strategies (Carlson 1979:214).

REFERENCES CITED

Adavasio, J. M., J. Donahue, K. Cushman, R. C. Carlisle, R. Stuckenrath, J. D. Gunn, and W. C. Johnson
1983 Evidence from Meadowcroft Rockshelter. In *Early Man in the New World*, edited by R. Shutler, pp. 163–190. Sage Publications, Beverly Hills.

Adovasio, J. M., and R. C. Carlisle
1988 The Meadowcraft Rockshelter. *Science* 239:713–14.

Alexander, H. L.
1987 *Putu: A Fluted Point Site in Alaska.* Simon Fraser University Publication No. 17. Archaeology Press, Simon Fraser University, Burnaby.

Ames, K. M., J. P. Green, and M. Pfoertner
1981 *Hatwai (10NP143): Interim Report.* Archaeological Reports No. 9. Boise State University, Boise.

Ball, B. F.
1989 Current Research: Alberta. *Newsletter of the Canadian Archaeological Association* 9(1).

Bedwell, S. F.
1973 *Fort Rock Basin Prehistory and Environment.* University of Oregon Books, Eugene.

Bird, J. B., and R. G. Cooke
1978 The Occurrence in Panama of Two Types of Paleo-Indian Projectile Points. In *Early Man in America from a Circum-Pacific Perspective,* edited

by A. L. Bryan, pp. 263–272. Occasional Papers No. 1. Department of Anthropology, University of Alberta, Edmonton.

Bliss, W. L.
1939 Early Man in Northwestern Canada. *Science* 89:344–346.

Bryan, A. L.
1969 Early Man in America and the Late Pleistocene Chronology of Western Canada and Alaska. *Current Anthropology* 10:339–365.
1979 Smith Creek Cave. In *The Archaeology of Smith Creek Canyon, Eastern Nevada,* edited by D. R. Tuohy and D. L. Rendall, pp. 162–215. Nevada State Museum Anthropological Papers No. 17. Carson City.
1980 The Stemmed Point Tradition: An Early Technological Tradition in Western North America. In *Anthropological Papers in Memory of Earl H. Swanson, Jr,* edited by L. B. Harten, C. Warren, and D. Tuohy, pp. 77–107. Special Publication of the Idaho State Museum of Natural History, Pocatello.

Bryan, A. L., and R. Gruhn
1979 The Radiocarbon Dates of Taima-Taima. In *Taima-Taima: A Late Pleistocene Paleo-Indian Kill Site in Northernmost South America. Final Report on the 1976 Excavations,* edited by C. Ochsenius and R. Gruhn, pp. 53–58. Programa CIPICS, Monografias Cientifica, Universidad Francisco de Miranda, Coro, Venezuela.

Carlson, R. L.
1979 The Early Period on the Central Coast of British Columbia. *Canadian Journal of Archaeology* 3:211–227.
1983 The Far West. In *Early Man in the New World,* edited by R. Shutler, Jr., pp. 73–96. Sage Publications, Beverly Hills.
1988 The View from the North. In *Early Human Occupation in Western North America: The Clovis Archaic Interface,* edited by J. A. Willig, C. M. Aikens, and J. L. Fagan, pp. 319–324. Nevada State Museum Anthropological Papers No. 21. Carson City.

Chard, C. S.
1974 *Northeast Asia in Prehistory.* University of Wisconsin Press, Madison.

Christensen, O. A.
1971 *Banff Prehistory: Prehistoric Settlement and Subsistence in Banff National Park.* Manuscript Report Series No. 67. National Historic Sites Service, Ottawa.

Clark, D. W.
1981 Prehistory of the Western Subarctic. In *The Subarctic,* edited by J. Helm, pp. 107–129. Handbook of North American Indians, vol. 6, W. C. Sturtevant, general editor. Smithsonian Institution, Washington, D.C.

Crabtree, D. H.
1969 A Technological Description of Artifacts in Assemblage 1, Wilson Butte Cave, Idaho. *Current Anthropology* 10:366–370.

Dincauze, D.
1984 An Archaeo-Logical Evaluation of the Case for Pre-Clovis Occupations. *Advances in World Archaeology* 3:275–323.

Fladmark, K. R.
1981 Paleo-Indian Artifacts from the Peace River District. *BC Studies* 48:124–135. Vancouver.

Fladmark, K. R., J. C. Driver, and D. Alexander
1988 The Paleoindian Component at Charlie Lake Cave (HbRf39). *American Antiquity* 53:371–384.

Gerity, T.
1960 Clovis Points from Oregon. *Screenings* 9(4). Portland.

Green, F. E.
1963 The Clovis Blades: An important addition to the Plano Complex. *American Antiquity* 29:145–165.

Greenberg, J. H., C. G. Turner II, and S. L. Zegura
1986 The Settlement of the Americas: A Comparison of the Linguistic, Dental, and Genetic Evidence. *Current Anthropology* 27:477–479.

Gruhn, R.
1965 Two Early Radiocarbon Dates from the Early Levels of Wilson Butte Cave, South-central Idaho. *Tebiwa* 8:57.

Gryba, E. M.
1983 *Sibbald Creek: 11,000 years of Human Use of the Alberta Foothills.* Archaeological Survey of Alberta Occasional Paper No. 22. Edmonton.
1985 Evidence of the Fluted Point Tradition in Alberta. In *Contributions to Plains Prehistory,* edited by D. V. Burley, pp. 22–38. Archaeological Survey of Alberta Occasional Paper No. 26. Edmonton.
1987 Current Research. *Newsletter, Association of Consulting Archaeologists* 2(3). Calgary.

Haynes, C. V., Jr.
1964 Fluted Points: Their Age and Dispersion. *Science* 145:1408–1413.
1969 The Earliest Americans. *Science* 166:709–715.
1982 Were Clovis Progenitors in Beringia? In *The Paleoecology of Beringia,* edited by D. M. Hopkins, J. V. Mathews, Jr., C. Schweger, and

S. B. Young, pp. 383–398. Academic Press, New York.

1984 Mammoth Hunters of the USA and USSR. In *Beringia in the Cenozoic Era,* edited by V. L. Kontrimavichus, pp. 557–570. Amerind Publishing Company, New Delhi.

1987 Clovis Origins Update. *Kiva* 52:83–93.

Haynes, C. V, Jr., D. J. Donahue, A. J. T. Jull, and T. H. Zabel

1984 Application of Accelerator Dating to Fluted Point Paleoindian sites. *Archaeology of Eastern North America* 12:184–191.

Hester, J. J.

1966 Origins of the Clovis Culture: *XXXVI Congreso International de Americanistas* 1:129–142. Seville.

Hoffecker, J. F.

1985 The Moose Creek Site. *National Geographic Society Research Reports* (1978 projects) 19:33–49.

Johnson, F.

1946 An Archaeological Survey along the Alaska Highway, 1944. *American Antiquity* 11:183–186.

Johnson, F., and H. M. Raup

1964 *Investigations in the Southwest Yukon: Geobotanical and Archaeological Reconnaissance.* Papers of the R. S. Peabody Foundation for Archaeology, Vol. 6(1). Phillips Academy, Andover.

Justice, N. D.

1987 *Stone Age Spear and Arrow Points of the Midcontinental and Eastern United States.* Indiana University Press, Bloomington.

Kehoe, T. F.

1966 The Distributions and Implications of Fluted Points in Saskatchewan. *American Antiquity* 31:530–539.

Lynch, T. F.

1983 The Paleo-Indians. In *Ancient South America* edited by J. D. Jennings, pp. 87–138. W. H. Freeman and Company, San Francisco.

1990 Glacial-Age Man in South America? A Critical Review. *American Antiquity* 55:12–36.

MacNeish, R. S.

1954 The Pointed Mountain site near Fort Liard, Northwest Territories, Canada. *American Antiquity* 19:234–253.

1956 Two Archaeological Sites on Great Bear Lake, Northwest Territories, Canada. *Annual Report of the National Museum of Canada for the Fiscal Year 1953–54.* Department of Northern Affairs and National Resources.

1960 The Callison Site in Light of Archaeological Survey of Southwest Yukon. *National Museum of Canada Bulletin* 162:1–51.

1964 *Investigations in Southwest Yukon: Archaeological Excavations, Comparisons, and Speculations.* Papers of the R. S. Peabody Foundation for Archaeology, Vol. 6(2). Phillips Academy, Andover.

Mason, R. J.

1962 The Paleoindian Tradition in Eastern North America. *Current Anthropology* 5:227–278.

Martin, P. S.

1973 The Discovery of America. *Science* 179:969–974.

Mathews, W. H.

1980 Retreat of the Last Ice Sheets in Northeastern British Columbia and Adjacent Alberta. *Geological Survey of Canada Bulletin* 331.

Mayer-Oakes, W. J.

1984 Fluted Projectile Points: A North American Shibboleth Viewed in South American Perspective. *Archaeology of Eastern North America* 12:231–247.

McIntyre, M., and B. O. K. Reeves

1975 *Archaeological Investigations: Lake Minnewanka Site (EhPu-l).* Submitted to Parks Canada, Calgary.

Minor, R.

1985 Paleo-Indians in Western Oregon: A Description of Two Fluted Projectile Points. *NARN* 19(1):33–40.

Mochanov, Y. A.

1984 Paleolithic Finds in Siberia. In *Beringia in the Cenozoic Era,* edited by V. L. Kontrimavichus, pp. 694–724. Oxonian Press, New Delhi.

Musil, R. R.

1988 Functional Efficiency and Technological Change: A Hafting Tradition Model for Paleo-Indian North America. In *Early Human Occupation in Western North America: The Clovis Archaic Interface,* edited by J. A. Willig, C. M. Aikens, and J. L. Fagan, pp. 373–387. Nevada State Museum Anthropological Papers No. 21. Carson City.

Ochsenius, C., and R. Gruhn (editors)

1979 *Taima-Taima; A Late Pleistocene Paleo-Indian Kill Site in (1984) Northernmost South America. Final Report on the 1976 Excavations.* Programa CIPICS, Monografias Cientifica, Universidad Francisco de Miranda, Coro, Venezuela.

Osborne, D.
1956 Early Lithic in the Pacific Northwest. *Research Studies of the State College of Washington* 24:38–44. Pullman.

Owen, R. C.
1984 The Americas: The Case Against an Ice-Age Population. In *The Origins of Modern Humans: A World Survey of the Fossil Evidence,* edited by F. H. Smith and F. Spencer, pp. 517–563. Alan R. Liss, New York.

Peak, A. S., D. L. True, and D. R. Tuohy
1986 CA-Cal-S342, An Early Holocene Site on the West Slopes of the Sierra Nevada, California. Paper presented at the Great Basin Anthropological Conference, Las Vegas.

Reeves, B. G.
1976 *1975 Archaeological Investigations Lake Minnewanka Site (EhPu-l).* Submitted to Parks Canada, Calgary.

Rice, D. G.
1972 *The Windust Phase in Lower Snake River Region Prehistory.* Report of Investigations No. 50. Washington State University Laboratory of Anthropology, Pullman.

Riddell, F., and W. H. Olsen
1969 An Early Man Site in the San Joaquin Valley, California. *American Antiquity* 34:121–130.

Turner, C. G. II
1989 Teeth and Prehistory in Asia. *Scientific American* 260:88–96.

Vickers, J. R.
1986 *Alberta Plains Prehistory: A Review.* Archaeological Survey of Alberta Occasional Paper No. 27. Edmonton.

Warnica, J. N.
1966 New Discoveries at the Clovis Site. *American Antiquity* 31:345–357.

West, F. H.
1981 *The Archaeology of Beringia.* Columbia University Press, New York.

Wilson, I. R.
1986 *The Pink Mountain Site (HhRr1): Archaeological Assessment and Monitoring of an Early Man Site in Northeastern B.C.* Submitted to the Heritage Conservation Branch, Victoria.

Wilson, I. R., and R. L. Carlson
1987 *Heritage Resource Inventory in the Vicinity of Pink Mountain Northeastern B.C.* Submitted to the Heritage Conservation Branch, Victoria.

Wilson, M.
1983 *Once Upon a River: Archaeology and Geology of the Bow River Valley at Calgary, Alberta, Canada.* Archaeological Survey of Canada Paper No. 114. Mercury Series. National Museum of Man, Ottawa.

Witthoft, J.
1952 A Paleo-Indian Site in Eastern Pennsylvania: An Early Hunting Culture. *Proceedings of the Philadelphia Academy of Natural Sciences* 96:464–495.
1954 A Note on Fluted Point Relationships. *American Antiquity* 19:271–273.

Wormington, H. M., and R. G. Forbis
1965 *An Introduction to the Archaeology of Alberta, Canada.* Denver Museum of Natural History, Denver.

Clovis Technology and Adaptation in Far Western North America: Regional Pattern and Environmental Context

JUDITH A. WILLIG

Department of Anthropology
Washington State University
Pullman, WA 99164-4910

The Clovis tradition represents the earliest culture accepted without controversy in North America. The Llano-Clovis big-game hunting tradition came to be archaeologically indexed by the association of diagnostic Clovis-type fluted points with extinct megafauna at well-dated kill sites in the Southwest and Plains. By 1980 Clovis had achieved pan-continental status, but many questions remain regarding origins, dating, and economy. Besides "fluting," widespread assemblages share broadly similar tool kits and site types, yet striking variations exist in regional point morphology, environmental settings, inferred economy and dating in a cultural horizon once noted for its homogeneity. The significance of variation cannot be assessed until regional assemblages are adequately sampled and dated. Variability may be due to sampling error, but temporal and cultural differences are more likely.

In the Far West, Clovis sites are abundant but not firmly dated. Available data suggest rapid regional development of the western Clovis tradition out of a brief, basal Clovis presence, immediately followed by Western Stemmed, much like Clovis-Folsom-Plano on the Plains. Pre-Clovis assemblages are claimed, but either dates or human workmanship are questioned. Western Clovis sites are found in many environmental settings, but those producing major point concentrations occur along the margins of shallow lake-marsh-stream systems. Associations with megafauna are reported but not confirmed. Paleoenvironmental and settlement-subsistence data suggest a diverse economy keyed to local mesic resources like fish, fowl, plants, and large and small game. Recent evidence suggests the need for regional definitions like "western Clovis," which expand the original scope of Llano-Clovis to accommodate adaptational variants of the specialized big-game strategy postulated for initial Clovis colonizers.

INTRODUCTION: CONTEXT AND DEFINITION OF LLANO-CLOVIS

The Clovis fluted-point tradition represents the earliest widespread cultural complex accepted without controversy in North America. It is radiocarbon dated between 11,630 and 10,620 yr B.P. (Haynes et al. 1984) from kill sites in the Great Plains and Southwest in buried, stratigraphic associations with extinct Pleistocene megafauna (Haynes 1964, 1969, 1971, 1980). Pre-Clovis assemblages have been asserted, but most of these are questioned as to either dates or human workmanship (Dincauze 1984). Sites like Fort Rock Cave (Bedwell 1970), Wilson Butte Cave (Gruhn 1965), and Meadowcroft Rockshelter (Adovasio et al. 1977) have produced dates on cultural assemblages as early as 13,000–14,500 yr B.P., but these are not too far outside the time range of Clovis. Interest in the possibility of an even earlier presence has increased in recent years, but the claims are as yet unsupported by reliable evidence (Dincauze 1984; Jennings 1986; Willig and Aikens 1988). This controversy still rages on and will not be addressed here.

The definition and characterization of "Clovis" culture, technology, and lifeway have been developing and expanding ever since Sellards (1952) first proposed the concept of the "Llano" big-game hunting complex to explain pre-Folsom mammoth kill sites in the southern Plains and Southwest. Based on excavations at Blackwater Draw—the "Clovis" type site near Clovis, New Mexico (Hester et al. 1972; Wormington 1957)—the complex came to be archaeologically indexed by the association of diagnostic Clovis-type fluted points with extinct megafauna, as evidenced at other sites in Arizona like Naco (Haury et al. 1953), Lehner (Haury et al. 1959), and Murray Springs (Haynes 1980).

FORMULATION OF CONTINENTAL CLOVIS

By 1980 fluted points remarkably similar to Clovis had a pan-continental distribution from Alaska and the Canadian Plains, south to central Mexico, Central America, and South America, and from the west-to-east coasts of North America, across a tremendous range of environmental settings. With the exception of minor local differences, the basic Clovis tool kit was said to be the same throughout North America, regardless of striking differences in paleoenvironmental settings and subsistence remains. Similarity in fluted-point forms and tool kits in such widespread assemblages was the basis for expanding the well-dated western Llano-Clovis horizon into a continental Clovis pattern of small groups of highly mobile, wide-ranging foragers and big-game hunters focusing on mammoth, bison, and other now-extinct late Pleistocene game for food, shelter, and clothing (Haynes 1964, 1980).

Evidence to support this pan-continental pattern came from studies of the size, location, and internal composition of kill and quarry sites and a few base camps, as well as from lithic sourcing (Haynes 1980:118, 1982:393). Throughout North America, the few known base camps are far outnumbered by a multitude of single isolated finds (Aikens 1983b; Haynes 1980; Meltzer 1988; Willig et al. 1988). Clovis campsites are generally small and few in number compared with later cultures, have few activity areas and low artifact densities, and are located close to game takes, watering sources, and/or lithic quarries. Lithic sourcing studies indicate that both immediately local and exotic stone as distant as 150–300 km were utilized (Haynes 1980:118, 1982:393; Meltzer 1988; Warnica 1966).

VARIATION IN CLOVIS

Since 1980 research on the fluted-point tradition has greatly intensified—in the North (Clark 1984, this volume), in the South (Lynch 1983), in the East (Brennan 1982; Gramly 1984; Kraft 1983; Meltzer 1988), and in the West (Willig et al. 1988). With this tremendous increase in Paleoindian research comes the realization that there is a great deal of variation in assemblages which are far distant from the "Clovis" type site in New Mexico. There is a growing awareness among researchers of distinct regional variations in point morphology, environmental settings, inferred economic patterns, and dating in a cultural horizon once noted for its homogeneity. The papers in the 1987 INQUA Symposium were filled with references to variation of some degree in all the regions covered (see Bonnichsen, Clark, Frison, Keenlyside, Storck, this volume).

Pan-continental assemblages share broadly similar tool kits and point forms. Low population density is inferred from the presence of widely scattered sites with few base camps. This seems to validate at least one aspect of the Llano-Clovis pattern, i.e., small, highly mobile, wide-ranging groups. But outside of the Southwest and Great Plains, the two most critical "hallmarks" of the Llano-Clovis pattern have been challenged by: (1) a conspicuous lack of megafaunal associations and the presence of settlement-subsistence data that suggest more diverse economies; and (2) interassemblage variations in technology and styles of fluted points—regional variants which are said to be distinct from the diagnostic Clovis-type fluted-point complexes defined from the Southwest and Plains.

EXPLAINING THE VARIATION IN CLOVIS

The full range of this variation in fluted-point complexes and its significance cannot be properly assessed until regional assemblages are firmly dated and adequately sampled. Much of the variability may be due to mere sampling error, although temporal and cultural differences are more likely causes. The papers presented in this volume are a first step towards a synthesis and comparison of each regional data base, so that we can better understand the variation. It may be that we have overextended the scope of the "Llano-Clovis" pattern as it was originally defined in the Southwest, or it may be that the time has come to formulate a series of new, more regional definitions for North America. The evidence from the Far West of North America, which I will review in this paper, seems to suggest a definite need for the latter.

Associations with Extinct Megafauna

The clear association with megafaunal kills—the first index of the Llano-Clovis complex—has yet to be documented outside the Plains and Southwest, although many such claims have been made. In the East evidence for human exploitation of mastodon and mammoth is still extremely scarce, despite an abundance of both fluted-point sites and proboscidean finds (Meltzer 1988:22). Only the Kimmswick site provides an unambiguous association of fluted points with mastodon remains (Graham et al. 1981).

In the West claims have been made for associations of human artifacts with a variety of now-extinct Rancholabrean fauna, including mammoth, horse, camelid, sloth and bison. Reports include China Lake, California (Davis 1978a), the Willamette Valley and Paisley Five Mile Point Cave No. 3 in Oregon (Cressman 1966; Cressman and Laughlin 1941), and Wilson Butte Cave, Idaho (Gruhn 1961). Most of these have been questioned as being either too surficial or indirect to be confirmed (Heizer and Baumhoff 1970; Jennings 1986; Jennings and Norbeck 1955). However, the faunal remains recently recovered from the Old Humboldt site (26Pe670) in Nevada offer intriguing possibilities (see discussion below under Dietetic Diversity). Only at Owl Cave (Wasden site) in eastern Idaho are fluted points found in association with elephant (Butler 1986; Miller and Dort 1978), and these are Folsom points, not Clovis.

Furthermore, the environmental data suggest that it is doubtful that the Far West could ever have supported extensive herds of large terrestrial grazers (Daugherty 1962; Haynes 1988; Meltzer 1988; Simms 1988). There is evidence that such animals were present in small numbers and probably taken opportunistically (Madsen 1982; Madsen et al. 1976), but Simms (1988) points out that their availability would have been shifting and unpredictable through time and across space in the Great Basin. Therefore, a strategy continuously dependent on large game would have been ecologically unlikely. These data suggest that the concept that expansion of Llano-Clovis specialized "big-game" hunting on a continental scale must be seriously questioned.

Clovis Point Morphology

The second hallmark that certifies inclusion into the "Clovis" complex is the presence of the diagnostic Clovis fluted point. This point type is characterized by: (1) long, relatively narrow longitudinal flakes removed from both sides of a biface from a specially prepared basal platform; (2) parallel or slightly convex sides and concave bases; (3) flutes usually extending halfway up the point from base to tip; and (4) lengths ranging from 4 to 12.5 cm, but averaging 7.5 cm (Haynes 1982; Wormington 1957:263). But the presence of variation has always allowed for much latitude in the definition, including: (1) flutes removed from only one side; (2) multiple flutes instead of single channel flakes; (3) flutes extending the full length of the point; (4) points made on blades rather than bifaces; and (5) differences in shape, size, edge grinding, and other attributes (Haynes 1982; Wormington 1957).

Fluted points in North America display a wide range of variability in size and shape, and the width, length, and number of flutes vary from multiple to single fluting to basally thinned. Fluting occurs on concave- and straight-based points, and even on stemmed and shouldered points dating to later time periods. This range in variation, along with distinct regional styles, has been reported for assemblages as far distant as interior Alaska (Clark, this volume), the Maritimes and Great Lakes regions of the Northeast (Keenlyside, this volume; Storck 1984, this volume), the Great Basin of the Far West (see discussion below), Central America (Snarskis 1979; Willey 1966), and South America (Lynch 1983).

Spatial (Cultural) Variation

Does the variation represent distinct regional but contemporary adaptations by groups far distant from the New Mexico type site? During a time of rapid, punctuated environmental change from 11,500–10,000 yr B.P. (Bryson et al. 1970; Mehringer 1986), different Paleoindian groups may have responded quickly by developing their own unique adaptive strategies geared to regional habitats. This would be evidenced by different settlement patterns and subsistence data, and corresponding technologies.

This kind of early regionalization could have developed very quickly with the spread of Clovis folk across North America. It was certainly established by 10,000 yr

B.P., as evidenced by the tremendous increase in cultural and technological diversity and population growth in traditions like Western Stemmed, Folsom-Plano, Dalton, and El Inga Stemmed. There is growing evidence for distinct regional adaptive strategies during Clovis time as well—in the Maritimes and Great Lakes regions in the Northeast (Keenlyside, this volume; Storck 1984, this volume), the forested Southeast (Meltzer 1988), and pluvial lake basins in the Far West (see discussion below). But the contemporaneity of these patterns must be validated by radiocarbon dates in each region, in order to discount the possibility that the differences are temporal.

Observed technological differences might be the result of local, functional, or stylistic variations on the general theme of "fluting"—i.e., a widely recognized hafting technique superimposed over a number of regional, contemporary complexes, each with its own "production code," reduction sequence, and unique regional style (Bonnichsen and Young 1980; Young and Bonnichsen 1984). While this may be difficult to test, it is true that North American archaeology seems to have been under the spell of what could be called the Clovis *"Fluting Supremacy Bias"*—i.e., our overemphasis on this one feature (fluting) has somewhat blinded us to variation. In the absence of secure chronological control, we are left with comparing a series of fluted points that are broadly similar to Clovis, united primarily by the presence of the "flute" as a widely recognized form of basal thinning for hafting.

With the exception of the eared, waisted forms so characteristic of the eastern U.S. (Mason 1962; Meltzer 1988; Willey 1966), most of the observed intraregional differences in fluted-point assemblages fall within the expected range of variation for a single pan-continental Clovis cultural complex. Studies of fluted-point collections from Texas, Colorado, New Mexico, Arizona, California, and Virginia reveal that the morphological variation *within* individual collections is as great as the variation *between* collections (Haynes 1964:1408). Most of this intrasite variation is probably not temporal, since it is clearly visible in the 30 specimens from the Clovis type site itself (Hester et al. 1972:Figures 89 and 90, pp. 98–99; Warnica 1966:Figures 3 and 6, pp. 349–350), which is narrowly conscribed in time between 11,040 ± 240 yr B.P. (A-490) and 11,630 ± 350 yr B.P. (A-491) (Haynes et al. 1984:188).

Temporal Variation

Are the observed variations due to temporal differences—i.e., cultural developmental changes in time along a continuum of evolving technology keyed to more efficient weapon forms and hafting elements (cf. Musil 1988), and changing environmental adaptations keyed to increasingly diversified regional habitats? From this viewpoint, the variation represents a sequence beginning with one colonizing continental Clovis culture and continuing through transitional periods when fluting was modified or only casually continued while the stemmed and Plano point forms of the early Holocene were being developed.

At the Lehner site, the actual range of radiocarbon dates from Clovis levels is 11,470 ± 110 yr B.P. (SMU-308) to 10,620 ± 300 yr B.P. (SMU-347), which clearly overlaps with Folsom (Haynes et al. 1984:188). For the East, Meltzer (1988) and others (Haynes et al. 1984) contend that the fluted presence there actually dates from 10,600 to 10,200 yr B.P., with a gradual time-transgressive movement from the Southeast to the Northeast following deglaciation. This is also within the time range of Folsom and early Plano complexes, not Clovis.

Therefore, the presence of "fluting" alone should not be the basis for automatic temporal inclusion into the well-dated Clovis horizon of the Southwest and Plains. The cultural versus temporal significance of fluting must be determined separately for assemblages in each region. Had Folsom points never been dated or found stratigraphically above Clovis points at sites like Blackwater Draw, New Mexico, we might still be considering Folsom as a contemporary regional variant, rather than a temporally distinct development derived from Clovis.

Sampling Error

Is the observed variation due to differences in sampling size and bias in the record? It is true that our sample of fluted-point complexes in North America is still "woefully inadequate" (Haynes 1980:116). But even within the core area of Clovis, a wide range of variation in the size and degree of fluting occurs in small assemblages like the 8 points at Naco (Haury et al. 1953:Figures 6 and 7, pp. 8–9) and the 13 points from Lehner (Haury et al. 1959:Figure 3, see also Figures 12 and 13, pp. 16–17), as well as in larger assemblages like the 30 specimens from Blackwater Draw (Hester et al. 1972:Figures 89 and 90, pp. 98–99; Warnica 1966:Figures 3 and 6, pp. 349–350). Therefore, it seems unlikely that sampling size errors can explain the variation. It also seems unlikely that errors from sampling bias can explain the rarity of documented associations between fluted points and hunted megafauna outside of the Plains and Southwest. Both fluted-point sites and finds of extinct megafauna are found in abundance across North America, in many different environmental settings. Mere geographic overlap does not demonstrate significant association (Dansie et al. 1988; Haynes 1988; Meltzer 1988).

In sum, current evidence from North America suggests that regional variations in fluted-point assemblages are probably both temporally *and* culturally based. Well-dated Llano-Clovis complexes in the Southwest and Plains display as much variation in size range and degree of fluting *within* sites as they do *between* sites. Yet we now know that the eared, waisted forms more characteristic of the eastern U.S. are younger than Clovis and contemporary with Folsom (Haynes et al. 1984; Meltzer 1988). Similar kinds of variation in fluted-point assemblages of the Far West have an important bearing on these issues.

DISTRIBUTION AND CONTEXT OF WESTERN CLOVIS

The area covered by the Far West, for the purposes of this discussion, includes that region of North America west of the Rocky Mountains to the Pacific Coast, and from southern British Columbia to portions of northern Mexico (*sensu* Carlson 1983). It includes the Great Basin and Plateau of the Intermontane West, Desert West, and Far West described by Daugherty (1962), Jennings (1964), and Aikens (1983b), with the addition of coastal areas in California, Oregon, and Washington (Figure 1). Ecologically, the Far West also includes portions of southern Arizona and New Mexico that fall within the Basin and Range province. However, the southwestern data are well known as part of the "core area" that fostered our conception of Llano-Clovis. Therefore, for the purposes of regional cross-comparison, it will be excluded here.

Archaeologists once believed the Clovis culture had no significant presence in the Far West, but by 1960 fluted points had been reported from many sites throughout California, Oregon, Washington, Idaho, Nevada, and Utah, indicating that the fluted tradition was well established here, as elsewhere on the continent (Aikens 1983b). Some regional summaries are available (Aikens 1983b; Butler 1978; Carlson 1983, 1988; Davis and Shutler 1969; Madsen et al. 1976; Moratto 1984; Tuohy 1968, 1969, 1974, 1985, 1986; Wallace 1978; Willig et al. 1988). The current range of distribution for fluted complexes in the Far West, referred to here as *Western Clovis* (*sensu* Willig and Aikens 1988), now includes western Washington and the Puget lowlands, southern British Columbia and the entire Columbia-Snake River system in the north, as well as California and the entire Basin-Range province of western North America (Figure 1).

Most fluted-point sites in the Far West consist of scattered surface finds of single isolated specimens that lack datable, buried stratigraphic context. Sites generally occur on or near the surface of exposed or deflated late Pleistocene deposits formed in alluvial fans, springs, streams, and lake-marsh shorelines. At major sites, fluted points most often co-occur in multicomponent contexts with a variety of other western diagnostic tools ranging in age from 10,500 to 7500 yr B.P. (Aikens 1978; Davis 1978a; Tuohy 1968, 1974), most of which are assigned to the *Western Stemmed* tradition (*sensu* Willig and Aikens 1988).

In a few cases, fluted points have been recovered from undated, shallow depths (30–40 cm) in fan or stream alluvium, lake beds, or beach terrace deposits, such as Borax Lake, California (Harrington 1948; Meighan and Haynes 1968, 1970), Alkali Lake, Oregon (Willig 1988, 1989), the Simon site cache in Idaho (Butler 1963), and the Old Humboldt site (26Pe670) in Nevada (Rusco and Davis 1987). At the newly discovered Ritchie-Roberts Clovis cache in central Washington, fluted points have been recovered in situ in buried context 70 cm below the surface, along with scrapers, bifaces, and beveled bone shafts (Mehringer 1988a, 1988b, 1989).

Only seven localities in the Far West have produced major concentrations of Clovis-type fluted points (Figure 1 and Table 1): (1) 49 specimens from China Lake, California; (2) 49 points from Tulare Lake, California; (3) 20 specimens from the Borax Lake and Clear Lake area of California; (4) 58 points from the Tonopah Lake and Mud Lake area of Nevada; (5) 21 points from the Sunshine Locality, Nevada; (6) 60 fluted points from the Dietz site in the Alkali Basin, Oregon; and (7) 14 points from the Richey-Roberts Clovis cache in central Washington.

How do far western fluted assemblages compare with typical Clovis sites in the Southwest and Plains in terms of dating, environmental context, technology, and site distribution? Is there evidence for a pan-western Clovis cultural

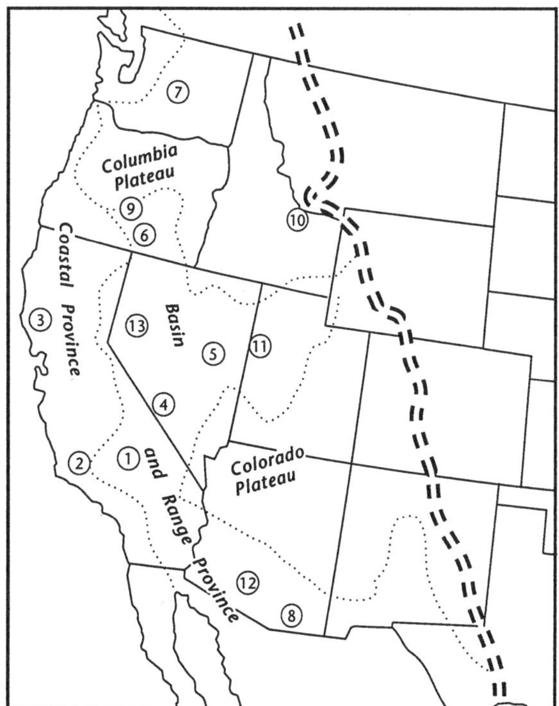

Figure 1. Map of far western North America showing locations of sites discussed in text, which have produced major concentrations of western Clovis points (Table 1) and/or radiocarbon dates of Clovis age (Tables 2A and 2B). (Adapted from Aikens 1983b and Jennings 1964.)

Table 1. Localities in the Far West that Have Produced Major Concentrations of Clovis-Type Fluted Points. (From Willig 1989:10).

SITE/LOCALITY*	NO. FLUTED POINTS	REFERENCES
China Lake California (1)	49	Davis 1967, 1975, 1978a, 1978b
Tulare Lake California (2)	49	Riddell and Olsen 1969 Wallace and Riddell 1988
Borax Lake Clear Lake California (3)	20	Fredrickson 1973, 1974 Fredrickson and White 1988 Harrington 1948 Meighan and Haynes 1968, 1970
Tonopah Lake Mud Lake Nevada (4)	58	Campbell and Campbell 1940 Kelly 1978; Pendleton 1979 Tuohy 1968, 1969, 1988
Sunshine Locality Lake Hubbs Nevada (5)	21	Hutchinson 1988 Tuohy 1988; York 1975, 1976
Dietz Site (35LK1529) Alkali Lake Basin Oregon (6)	60	Fagan 1984a, 1984b, 1986, 1988 Willig 1984, 1985, 1988, 1989
Ritchie-Roberts Cache Washington (7)	14	Mehringer 1988a, 1988b, 1989
Total number points:	271	

*Site location(s) are plotted by number on Figure 1.

and economic pattern that is distinct from the East? A capsule summary of what we *do* know is a sobering first step in developing a definition for a western Clovis pattern. There are distinct limitations in the current western data base, especially in the lack of buried, datable deposits and subsistence remains. Despite this, there is much that can be induced about the western Clovis lifeway from detailed study of technology and environmental context at major sites. Comparative studies of tool kits, typology, reduction sequences, and lithic sourcing, coupled with paleoenvironmental research, can greatly inform us about human settlement and land-use patterns in the past. These are exactly the kinds of data we can gather from far western fluted-point sites.

CHRONOLOGICAL PLACEMENT OF WESTERN CLOVIS

Absolute Dating

With the possible exception of the rediscovery of a fluted point excavated from Danger Cave, Utah (Table 2A), there are no radiocarbon dates for Clovis-type fluted points recovered in reliable, buried contexts in the Far West. Two fluted points were excavated from the "lowest levels" of Danger Cave by Elmer Smith in 1941, but the points disappeared before they could be examined (Jennings 1957:47). Recently, Utah Museum of Natural History staff rediscovered one of the points in an unrelated collection (Holmer 1986:94–95). Jennings cautions that a precise one-to-one correlation of Smith's levels with those of later excavations cannot be guaranteed (1957:47), but six radiocarbon dates from the lowest levels (Level I: Sands 1 and 2) provide an approximate time range of 10,270 ± 650 yr B.P. (M-202) to 11,453 ± 600 yr B.P. (C-609) for the fluted point. At China Lake, California, dates of 12,200 ± 200 yr B.P. (UCLA-1911B) and 13,300 ± 150 yr B.P. (UCLA-1911A) on subsurface tufa layers provide a maximum age for the overlying surface scatters of fluted points (Davis 1978a). The authors caution that the tufa dates may be 500 to 1000 years too old, but a correction factor would place them within the time range of Clovis in the Southwest and Plains.

Other sites in the Far West (Table 2A) have produced dates within the Clovis time range documented at southwestern sites like Lehner and Murray Springs (Table 2B), but they lack the necessary association with Clovis-type fluted points. When graphed together in chronological order (Figure 2), the two sets of data seem to be compatible, with dates ranging between 11,950 and 10,770 yr B.P. A hearth from Cougar Mountain Cave No. 2 in Oregon produced a date of 11,950 ± 350 yr B.P. (Gak-1751) (Bedwell and Cressman 1971:18), and dates on cultural charcoal from the Connley Caves range from 11,200 ± 200 yr B.P. (Gak-2141) to 10,100 ± 400 yr B.P. (Bedwell 1973). Fishbone Cave, Nevada, produced a date of 11,200 ± 250 yr B.P. (L-245) on a fragment of twined juniper bark found in association with a human burial, basketry fragments, and two large chert knives (Adovasio 1986; Orr 1956, 1974). At Tulare Lake, uranium series (230Th) analysis on human skeletal remains from the Witt site produced a date of 11,380 ± 70 yr B.P. (Wallace and Riddell 1988).

At Ventana Cave, the lowest occupation levels in the volcanic debris layer, which produced artifacts of the Ventana complex, are dated to 11,300 ± 1200 yr B.P.(A-203) (Haury and Hayden 1975). No fluted points were recovered, but the deposits include one unfluted concave-based point and a leaf-shaped point in association with bison, horse, sloth, and tapir (Haury 1950). At Jaguar Cave, Idaho, remains of domestic dog and 268 butchered mountain sheep were recovered from deposits dating from 11,580 ± 250 to 10,320 ± 350 yr B.P. (Butler 1986:128; Wright and Miller 1976). However, no stone tools were associated with the sheep remains.

There is an early date of 13,200 ± 720 yr B.P.(Gak-1738) at Fort Rock Cave, Oregon (Bedwell 1970, 1973), but the validity of the association has never been resolved (Aikens 1982:143; Haynes 1971). At Smith Creek Cave, Nevada, Bryan reports five dates on culturally deposited hearth charcoal that range from 9940 ± 160 yr B.P. (Tx-1420) to 11,140 ± 200 yr B.P. (Tx-1637) for the Mt. Moriah Stemmed point occupation floor. Recently, dates on bovid, camelid, and artiodactyl hair samples from the occupation zone produced dates of 10,840 ± 250 yr B.P. (Riddl-795), 12,060 ± 450 yr B.P. (Riddl-797), and 14,220 ± 650 yr B.P. (Riddl-796), respectively (Bryan 1988), but the cultural association of the hair has not been demonstrated and the underlying (sterile) pine needle zone dates to 12,600 ± 170 yr B.P. (A-1565) (Bryan 1979:190, 1980:83).

Relative Dating

Three main prospects for placing far western fluted points in a relative time frame are: (1) typological comparisons with dated Clovis assemblages in the Southwest and Plains, which currently have a range of 11,630 to 10,620 yr B.P. (Haynes et al. 1984); (2) typological comparisons with dated fluted points in the East, which now are said to date from 10,600 to 10,200 yr B.P. (Haynes et al. 1984; Meltzer 1988); and (3) local typological, stratigraphic, and obsidian-hydration studies of western Clovis and Western Stemmed complexes, which often co-occur at sites in the Far West. Western Stemmed complexes are dated within a very broad range between 11,000 and 7500 yr B.P. (Bryan 1980, 1988; Willig and Aikens 1988).

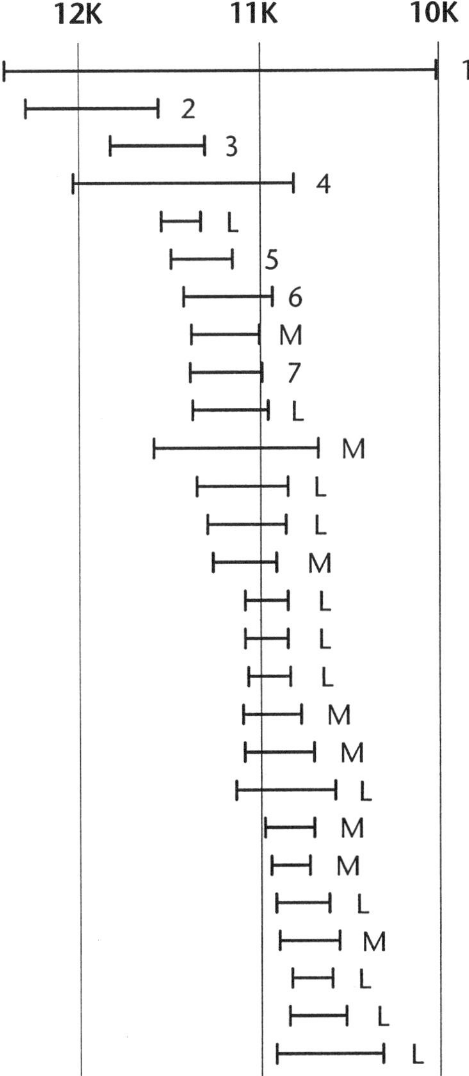

Figure 2. Radiocarbon dates relevant to far western Clovis occupation (Tables 2A and 2B). Graphed in chronological order: **1** = Ventana Cave; **2** = Cougar Mt. Cave #2; **3** = Jaguar Cave; **4** = Danger Cave; **5** = Witt Site; **6** = Fishbone Cave; **7** = Connley Cave #4B; **L** = Lehner Site; **M** = Murray Springs (K = Thousands of Years Ago).

Table 2a. Radiocarbon Dates of Clovis Age in the Far West* (Willig 1989:22).

SITE/LOCATION*	DATE (YR B.P.)[a]	LAB NO.	**	REFERENCES
Cougar Mt. Cave No.2 35LK55/A Oregon (9)	11,950 ± 350	Gak-1751	CH	Bedwell 1970, 1973 Bedwell and Cressman 1971
Jaguar Cave Idaho (10)	11,580 ± 250	n.d.	CH	Butler 1978 Sadek-Kooros 1966 Wright and Miller 1976
Danger Cave 42TO13 Utah (11)	11,453 ± 600 10,270 ± 650	C-609[b] M-202[b]	US CH	Jennings 1957 Jennings 1957
Witt Site CAKin32 California (2)	11,380 ± 70	n.d.	BN	Wallace and Riddell 1988
Ventana Cave Arizona (12)	11,300 ± 1200	A-203	CH	Haury 1950 Haury and Hayden 1975
Fishbone Cave 26Pe3e Nevada (13)	11,200 ± 250	L-245	SS	Orr 1956, 1974 Thompson et al. 1987
Connley Cave #4B 35LK50/4B Oregon (9)	11,200 ± 200	Gak-2141	CH	Bedwell 1970, 1973 Bedwell and Cressman 1971

*Site location(s) are plotted by number on Figure 1.

[a]Dates are listed in general order from oldest to youngest. Note that only in the case of Danger Cave and the Witt site are Clovis points present.

Type of material dated (CH** = charcoal; **SS** = shell; **BN** = bone; **US** = uncharred sheep dung).

[b]Fluted points would be bracketed between these two dates.

TYPOLOGICAL COMPARISONS WITH CLOVIS IN THE PLAINS AND SOUTHWEST

It is important to remember that no one set of eyes has yet looked upon all known fluted points from the Far West. However, published illustrations and technological studies suggest that western Clovis points compare very well with Clovis types from the Southwest and Plains in form, size, presence of edge and basal grinding, channel scratching, breakage patterns, and refinement of pressure flaking (Haynes 1987). There is a wide range of variation in size, and the degree of fluting grades from singly to multiply fluted, to basally thinned. Like other regions, western Clovis assemblages need to be firmly dated and large samples studied before this variation can be properly assessed, but most of the variation could easily fall within the range expected for a contemporary, continental, or pan-western Clovis culture.

The same range in variation visible in the specimens from Blackwater Draw and Arizona sites like Lehner (Figure 3) can also be seen in fluted specimens illustrated from 14 different western sites (Davis and Shutler 1969:Figures 2-5, pp. 164–167). At the Dietz site in the Alkali Lake Basin of Oregon, there is a wide range of sizes among the 60 fluted-point fragments recovered (Figures 4 and 5), which probably reflects functional or individual variation within the Clovis population represented (Fagan 1984b, 1988). The same wide range in size is visible in specimens reported from Borax Lake (Figures 6 and 7) and Tulare Lake in California (Riddell and

Table 2b. Radiocarbon Dates Associated with Southwestern Clovis Sites (Willig 1989:21).

SITE/LOCATION*	DATE (YR B.P.)	LAB NO.	**	REFERENCES
Lehner Site[a]	11,470 ± 110	SMU-308	CH	Haynes et al. 1984
Arizona (8)	11,170 ± 200	SMU-264		
	10,710 ± 90	SMU-340		
	10,700 ± 150	SMU-297		
	10,620 ± 300	SMU-347		
	11,080 ± 230	SMU-196		
	10,950 ± 110	SMU-194		
	10,950 ± 90	SMU-290		
	10,860 ± 280	SMU-164		
	11,080 ± 200	SMU-181		
	10,940 ± 100	A-378		
	10,770 ± 140	SMU-168		
Murray Springs Arizona (8)	11,190 ± 180	SMU-18		
	11,150 ± 450	A-805		
	11,080 ± 180	Tx-1413		
	10,930 ± 170	Tx-1462		
	10,890 ± 180	SMU-27		
	10,840 ± 140	SMU-42		
	10,840 ± 70	SMU-41		
	10,710± 160	Tx-1459	CH	Haynes et al. 1984

*Site location(s) are plotted by number on Figure 1.
[a]Three groups represent three separate features sampled.
Type of material dated (CH** = charcoal).

Olsen 1969:Figures 1 and 2, pp. 121–122) and from the Tonopah and Mud lake areas of Nevada (Campbell and Campbell 1940:8; Pendleton 1979; Tuohy 1968:Figure 3, p. 30, 1969:Figures 6 and 7, pp. 172–173).

Attribute analysis of 12 fluted points from various sites in southern Idaho, including the 5 specimens from the Simon site cache (Butler 1963:Figure 3, p. 29; Butler and Fitzwater 1965), revealed a wide range of morphological and technological variation (Titmus and Woods 1988; Woods and Titmus 1985). There was a definite bimodal distinction in length between the Simon points (over 18.2 cm long) and all others, suggesting their possible functional use as grave goods for a Clovis burial not unlike the Anzick site in Montana (Lahren and Bonnichsen 1974). Along similar lines, the largest and most exquisite fluted points yet reported in North America are the 14 points recovered from the Ritchie-Roberts Clovis cache in central Washington, with lengths ranging from 10 cm up to 23 cm (Mehringer 1988a:500–503, 1988b:Figure 1, 1989).

In a recent study by Carl Phagan, attributes of seven fluted points from Fort Irwin in the Mohave Desert, California, were subjectively compared with Clovis points from the Plains, Midwest, Rocky Mountains, and Great Basin (Warren and Phagan 1988). All seven fell easily within the known range of variation for the Clovis-type fluted point, especially those from the West. In addition to "fluting," western complexes also share the same pan-continental Clovis tool kit, including a variety of core, flake, and blade tools, large heavy scrapers, and bifacial blanks that compare favorably with other assemblages reported from North America (Clark 1984; Haynes 1982, 1987).

TYPOLOGICAL COMPARISONS WITH EASTERN FLUTED POINTS

Far western fluted points do not compare well with the longer eared, more waisted forms reported from eastern North America. In the 1960s Mason (1962) and Willey (1966) noted the presence of two distinct regional styles in North American fluted points, with eared, waisted forms more characteristic in the East, as opposed to the "classic" Clovis-type forms described from the Southwest and Plains. We now know that this East-West variation is temporally based—since most fluted points in the eastern U.S. date from 10,600 to 10,200 yr B.P. (Haynes et al. 1984; Meltzer 1988). Fluted points reported from Mexico, Guatemala, Costa Rica, and Ecuador display clear affinities to the waisted, eared eastern North American forms, suggesting that they are of equal age, or even slightly younger (Lynch 1983; Snarskis 1979; Willey 1966).

RELATIONSHIP OF WESTERN CLOVIS TO WESTERN STEMMED

Clovis-type fluted points in the Far West often co-occur with a variety of shouldered, stemmed, and lanceolate point types of the Western Stemmed tradition. The Western Stemmed tradition is currently dated within a broad range of 11,000–7500 yr B.P., which may overlap western Clovis (Aikens 1983b; Bryan 1980, 1988; Willig and Aikens 1988). This geographic and possible temporal

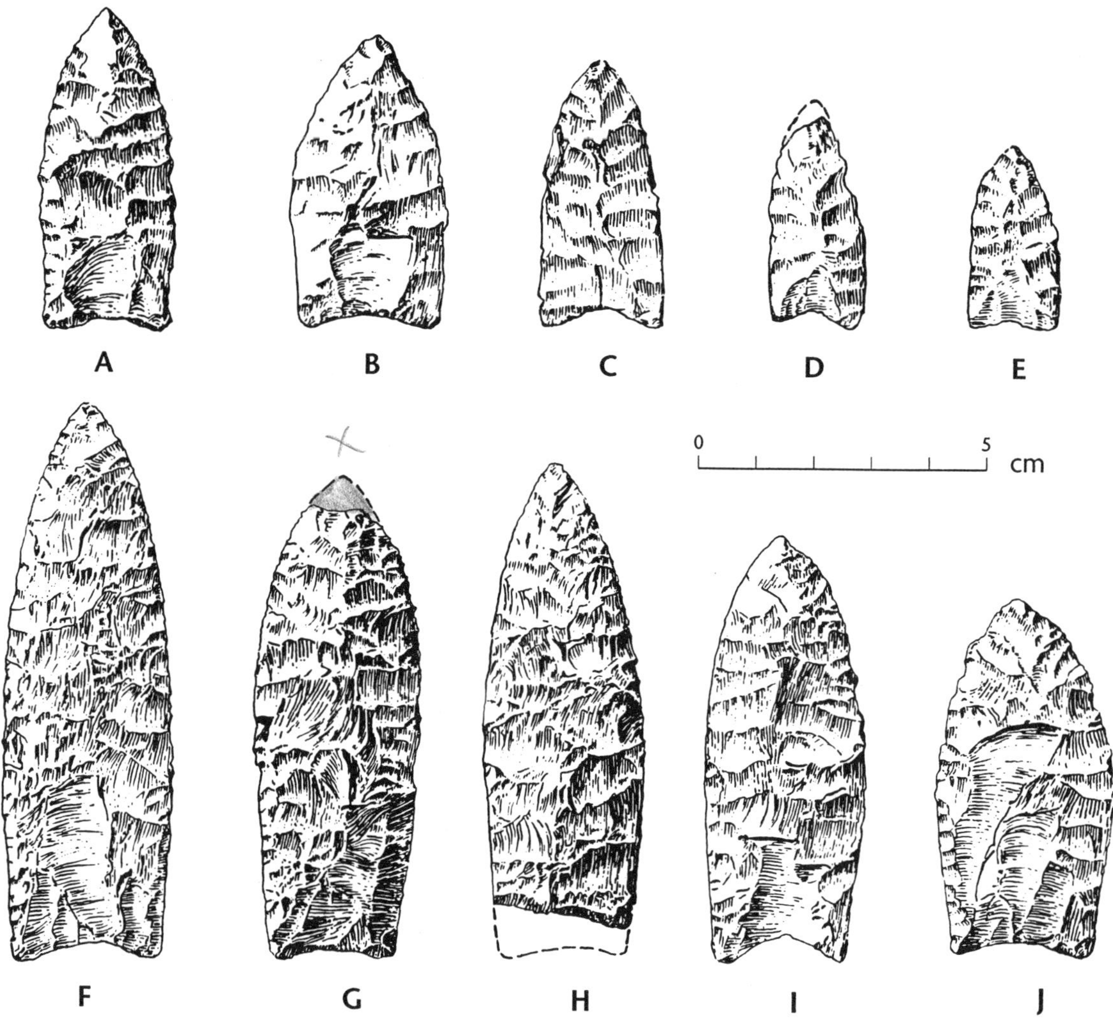

Figure 3. Clovis fluted points recovered from the Lehner site, Arizona, showing typical range of variation in size and morphology of southwestern Clovis points: **A)** #A-12682; **B)** #A-12686; **C)** #A-12681; **D)** #A-12678; **E)** #A-12683; **F)** #A-12685; **G)** #A-12684; **H)** #A-12680; **I)** #A-12677; **J)** #A-12679. (Reprinted from Haury et al. 1959:17.) (Scale conversion based on measurement of 97 mm length given for Specimen #A-12685.)

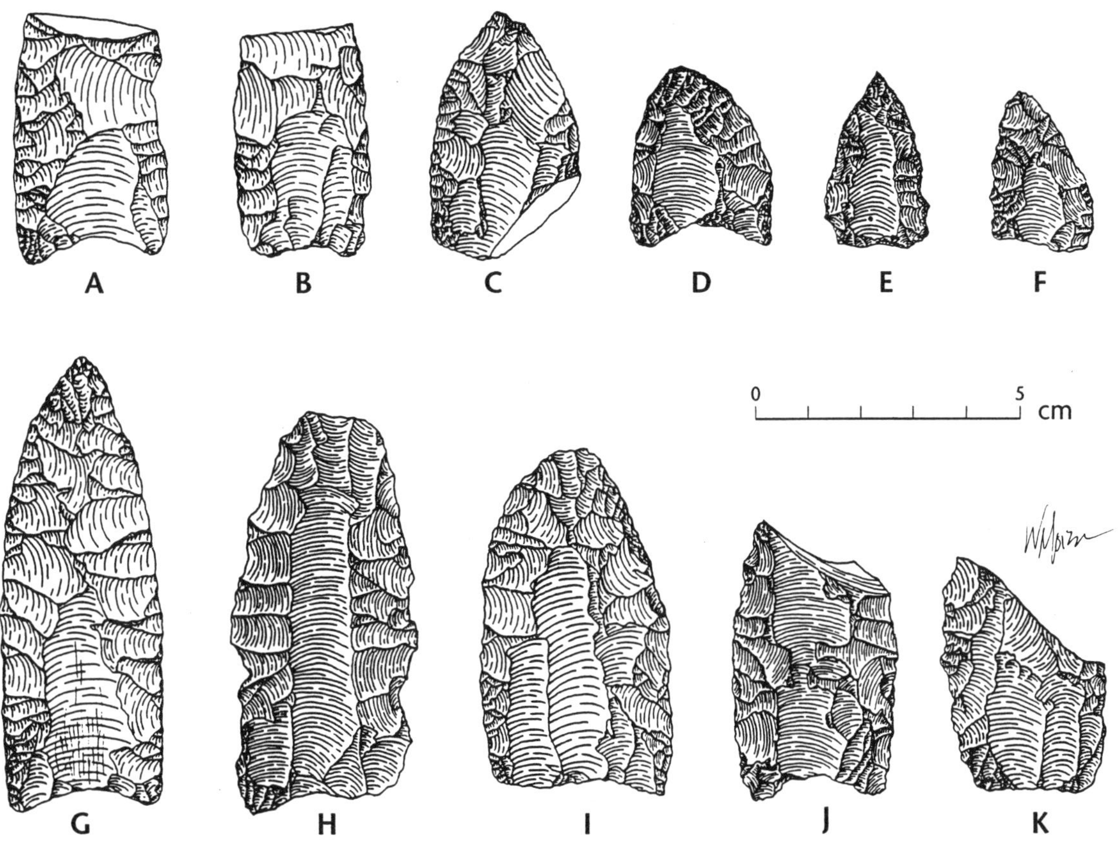

Figure 4. Sample of western Clovis points from the Dietz site, Oregon, showing range of variation in size and morphology: **A)** #553-417; **B)** #553-435; **C)** #553-14; **D)** #553-260; **E)** #553-241; **F)** #553-232; **G)** #553-319; **H)** #553-258; **I)** #553-262; **J)** #553-19; **K)** #553-199. (Drawings by Wyndeth V. Moisan.)

overlap has led scholars to postulate that Western Stemmed complexes are derivatives of western fluted (Aikens 1978, 1983a). This is a situation that is analogous to Folsom points following, and perhaps slightly overlapping, Clovis in the Plains and Southwest (Frison 1978; Haynes et al. 1984).

Some authors still believe that stemmed and fluted complexes are contemporary (Bryan 1980, 1988), but there is yet no accepted evidence for the occurrence of stemmed points in dated, stratigraphic contexts that clearly precede Clovis in the Far West. The co-occurrence of stemmed and fluted points along the same shorelines does not demonstrate they are the same age. As early as 1940, the Campbells noted the horizontal, spatial separation of fluted points from Lake Mohave clusters along the margins of Pleistocene Lakes Owens and Tonopah (Campbell and Campbell 1940; Pendleton 1979:287; Warren and Phagan 1988)—an observation that has recently gained support from geomorphic and stratigraphic research at the Dietz site in Alkali Lake Basin, Oregon (Willig 1984, 1985, 1988, 1989).

The horizontal stratigraphy at the Dietz site (35LK1529), in the northern Alkali Lake Basin of Oregon, suggests that fluted points clearly precede stemmed points because the two assemblages occur on different fossil shorelines that are separable in time. Stemmed points are confined to a narrow zone along two later, higher shorelines at 1,316 and 1,315.4 m elevation, while fluted points have a wider distribution downslope, extending to a lower, earlier shoreline at 1,314.8 m elevation. Geomorphic and stratigraphic evidence clearly separate the shorelines, and therefore the assemblages, in time.

In addition, vertical stratigraphic separation of surficial stemmed-period campsites from buried Clovis-age occupation surfaces may be demonstrable at two localities in the northern Alkali Lake Basin, pending results of radiocarbon dating. At Localities 1 and 2, surficial stemmed-point clusters are separated from buried, flake-bearing units of possible Clovis age by 70–90 cm of sterile deposits. No fluted points have yet been recovered from these buried paleosols, but in-process radiocarbon dates on bone, charcoal, and

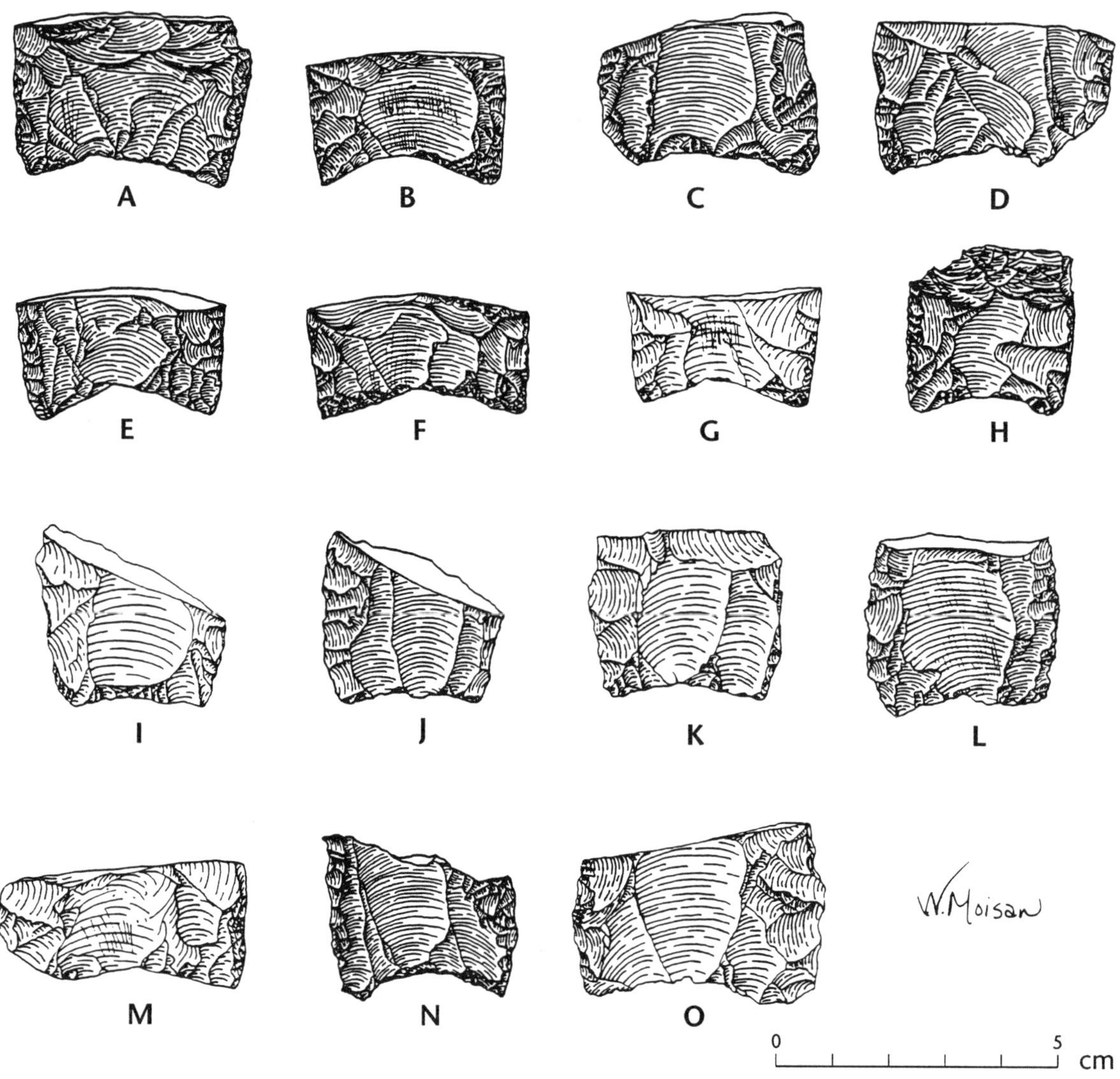

Figure 5. Sample of western Clovis base fragments from the Dietz site, Oregon: **A)** #553-99; **B)** #553-196; **C)** #553-169; **D)** #553-201; **E)** #553-2; **F)** #553-18; **G)** #553-430; **H)** #553-6; **I)** #553-412; **J)** #553-3; **K)** #553-5; **L)** #553-7; **M)** #553-431; **N)** #553-188; **O)** #553-4. (Drawings by Wyndeth V. Moisan.)

shell may prove these deposits to be Clovis in age (Willig 1988, 1989).

Some technological studies in the Far West have reported being able to distinguish fluted from stemmed assemblages based on differences in tool kits, reduction sequences, and flaking techniques. Pendleton (1979) analyzed a series of both fluted and unfluted concave-based points and stemmed points from Lake Tonopah, most of which were collected by the Campbells from single-component clusters (Campbell and Campbell 1940; Pendleton 1979:287). Her analysis revealed marked differences in the reduction sequences, manufacturing techniques, and raw material preferences between fluted concave-based assemblages and stemmed-point assemblages. Fluted points exhibited a higher degree of refinement in every stage of manufacture, with a greater degree of pressure flaking and technological control. Fagan (1984b, 1988) has reached similar conclusions from studies of single-component clusters of fluted and stemmed points at the Dietz site in Oregon. He reports that tool kits, "tool manufacturing techniques and methods of platform preparation for the production of bifaces are strikingly different" for fluted and stemmed-point clusters, suggesting that both temporal and cultural differences exist between the two assemblages (Fagan 1988:389).

These data suggest that western Clovis predates the Western Stemmed point tradition. This temporal precedence must still be demonstrated from securely dated

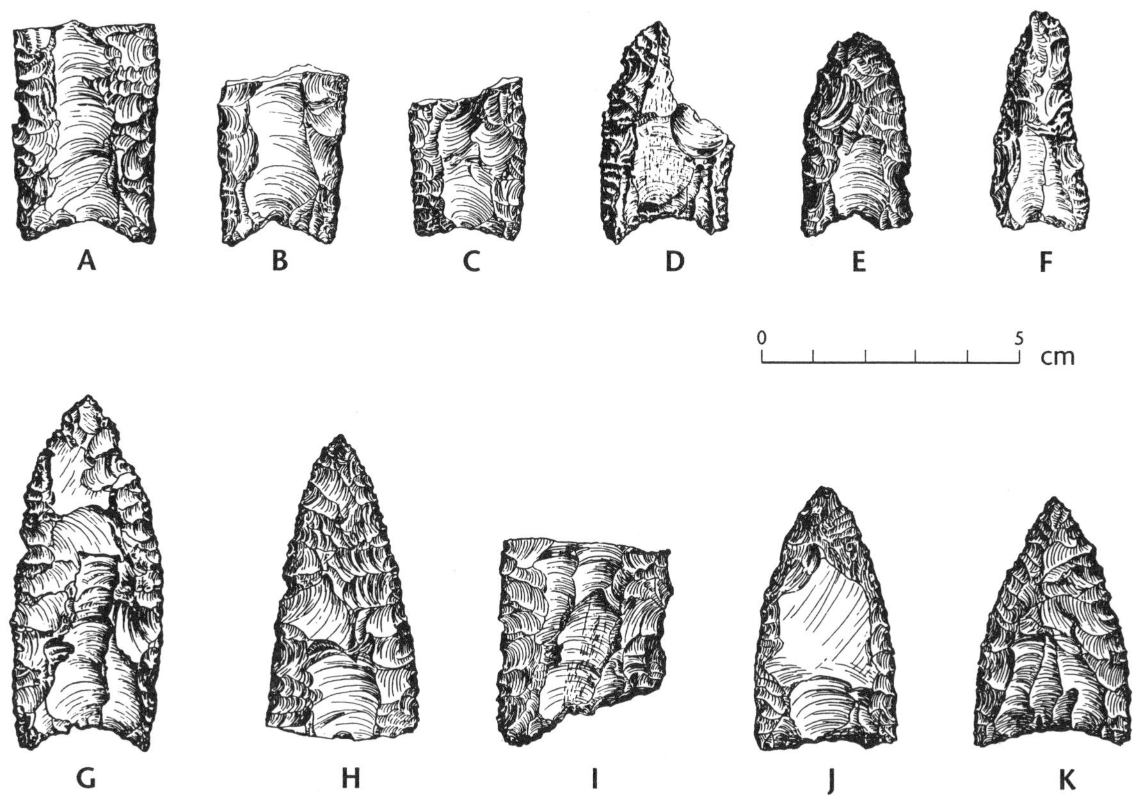

Figure 6. Sample of western Clovis points from the C.C. Post Collection at Borax Lake, California, showing range of variation in size and morphology: **A)** #18-F-1106; **B)** #18-F-1105; **C)** #18-F-5375; **D)** no #; **E)** no #; **F)** no #; **G)** no #; **H)** #18-F-2235; **I)** #18-F-1104; **J)** #18-F-1594; **K)** #18-F-2469. (Reprinted from figures and plates in Harrington 1948:62–74.)

Figure 7. Sample of western Clovis base fragments from the C.C. Post Collection at Borax Lake, California: **A)** 18-F-2796; **B)** 18-F-1600; **C)** no #; **D)** 750-G-54; **E)** 750-G-217; **F)** 750-G-216; **G)** 18-F-1102; **H)** 18-F-2490; **I)** 750-G-431. (Reprinted from figures and plates in Harrington 1948:62–74.)

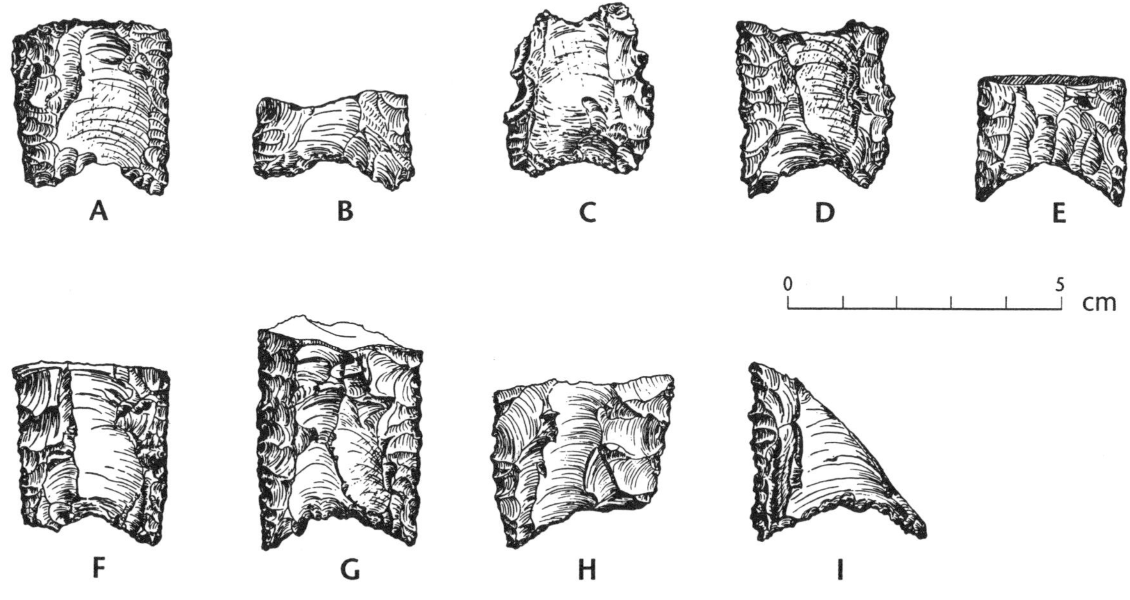

stratigraphy, but ongoing work with lithic sourcing and multiple, source-controlled obsidian hydration holds much potential for refining our chronological control of western Clovis sites (Fredrickson and White 1988; Hughes 1984, 1986). The preference for raw material seems to be high-quality, usually local, cryptocrystalline silicate at Tulare Lake (Riddell and Olsen 1969), China Lake (Davis 1978a), Tonopah Lake (Pendleton 1979), and sites in Idaho (Titmus and Woods 1988). The Dietz site is an exception, being almost entirely dominated by obsidian, both local and distant (Fagan 1984a, 1984b, 1988).

There are other lines of evidence that suggest the historical development of the Western Stemmed tradition from western Clovis. The typology of early western assemblages could be interpreted as a complete temporal continuum of forms—with fluted Clovis grading into fluted and unfluted basally thinned, concave-based, and even stemmed and shouldered styles of later Archaic periods. Pendleton's analysis of 108 fluted and unfluted concave-based points and stemmed points from Lake Tonopah (1979) revealed that the points varied widely in size and ranged in a continuum from typical fluted Clovis forms to unfluted basally thinned forms, with many points falling somewhere in between. Of the 108 points studied, all were basally thinned, while only 38 (35%) were fluted. Similar continua can be deduced from other major fluted-point assemblages in the West.

Of 30 Tulare Lake specimens, 12 are unifacially fluted, 8 are bifacially fluted, and 7 are basally thinned (Riddell and Olsen 1969; Wallace and Riddell 1988). Of the 20 Borax Lake finds, 14 are bifacially fluted and 2 are unifacially fluted (Fredrickson and White 1988; Harrington 1948; Meighan and Haynes 1970). A similar gradational continuum of fluted into stemmed forms seems to be present in the Alkali Lake Basin of Oregon (see Figures in Willig 1989); and in an assemblage described by Butler from Coyote Flat, Oregon (Butler 1970:Figures 3 and 4, pp. 46–47). These may represent "transitional" forms in a gradually developing temporal continuum between fluted and stemmed types, or they may represent various stages of reduction, or reuse and reworking of "relict" tools (Willig 1989).

This continuum of gradual blending from Paleoindian into Archaic point types was pointed out long ago by Aikens (1978) and is well documented from dated sequences in the Plains and Southwest (Frison 1978; Frison and Stanford 1982; Haynes 1964, 1980), where Clovis gives rise to Folsom and Plano forms. In northeastern North America, Storck (1984, this volume) has proposed a similar sequence with the Gainey-Parkhill-Crowfield complexes in the Great Lakes region, based on technological and stylistic comparisons, thermoluminescence dating, and geological associations. Keenlyside (this volume) has reported the gradual blending of styles in the transition between the Paleoindian and Archaic periods in the Maritimes region.

Fluted points in Central and South America often cooccur with both fluted and unfluted versions of stemmed fishtail or Magellan points, which have a time range of 11,000 to 10,000 yr B.P. (Lynch 1983). The fluted-point forms seem to grade into the stemmed forms, with many transitional forms in between (Lynch 1983:Figures 3.5 and 3.6; Snarskis 1979:Figures 2 and 3). Of the 18 fluted points recovered from the Turrialba site in Costa Rica, some resemble western Clovis (Type 2: Figure 2a,c), some resemble the waisted, eared eastern forms (Type 1: Figures 2d,e, and 3b), and one resembles a fluted version of a stemmed fishtail or Magellan point. The shallow deposits are undated, but fluted and stemmed points can be separated on the basis of horizontal stratigraphy because they occur on separate, consecutive river terraces. All the fluted points resembling northern styles were found exclusively on the uppermost terrace, which dates somewhere between 12,000 and 10,000 yr B.P. The single fluted Magellan point was found on the third, or lowest, terrace (Snarskis 1979).

In conclusion, based on the available evidence, it can be postulated that both eastern fluted points and Folsom, dating from 11,000 to 10,000 yr B.P., are local developments derived from a brief ancestral continental Clovis horizon dating from 11,500 to 11,000 yr B.P. From this, it follows that the earliest Western Stemmed complexes, appearing between 11,000 and 10,000 yr B.P., can also be seen as local developments arising from a brief but basal western Clovis presence, which probably dates from about 11,500 to 11,000 yr B.P. (see Figure 2). This would mean that Western Stemmed complexes are contemporary with both Folsom and eastern fluted occupations, and would explain the extreme rarity of Folsom in the Far West and the lack of typological closeness between western Clovis and the eastern fluted points. If Clovis-Stemmed complexes in the West are historically related in the same way as Clovis-Folsom-Plano sequences on the Plains, we should expect to find some evidence of slight temporal overlap in radiocarbon dates and transitional point forms. This overlap is clearly present in the current range of Plains radiocarbon dates and may also be represented by such transitional forms as Goshen on the Plains (Frison 1978, this volume) and Black Rock Concave Base in the West (Carlson 1988; Clewlow 1968). As seen above, western Paleoindian complexes are rich in examples of transitional forms characteristic of historically related continua.

PALEOENVIRONMENTAL CONTEXT AND ECONOMY OF WESTERN CLOVIS

Current archaeological research has been experiencing a focus upon the concept of adaptation—the human response to environmental change (Jennings 1986; Kirch

1980). Kirch has called this an "elegant" concept, capable of integrating the eclectic and "disparate" data so peculiar to the field of archaeology (1980:102). In the absence of dated subsistence remains, the most reliable data for reconstructing prehistoric adaptive strategies are those generated from studies of site distribution and geomorphic context with respect to the paleolandscape and its resource constraints. Studies of paleoenvironmental context, site distribution, and lithic sourcing can greatly inform us about past human settlement and land-use patterns. When supplemented by ecology (Kirch 1980) and hunter-gatherer theory (Binford 1980), this can provide the basis for inferences about western Clovis paleoeconomy and adaptation, thereby providing a fuller characterization of Paleoindian lifeways. The value of this approach is best illustrated by examining the evidence for dietetic diversity, environmental context, and settlement pattern at major western fluted-point sites.

Western Clovis complexes share the same pan-continental pattern—many small scattered sites and only a few large campsites. They are widely distributed across a variety of environmental settings, including coastal, montane, and lowland valley zones. The variety of settings and dispersed site distribution pattern could be interpreted as support for a Clovis lifeway characterized by small, highly mobile, wide-ranging groups focused on the hunting of extinct megafauna. But like the East, the Far West suffers from a lack of megafaunal kill sites, and the specialized "big-game" hunting concept may not apply here.

Dietetic Diversity

Some scholars have argued for a more generalized, broad-spectrum, subsistence strategy during Clovis time (Dent 1985; Gardner 1983; Griffin 1964; Meltzer and Smith 1986). There is evidence in the East for dietetic diversity (Meltzer 1988), with remains of caribou, birds, and fish at Dutchess Quarry Cave (Kopper et al. 1978), giant land tortoise at Little Salt Spring, Florida (Clausen et al. 1979), and grape, hawthorn plum, hackberry, and blackberry at Shawnee-Minisink (Dent 1985). Even the sites on the Plains and Southwest have produced evidence of a variety of small game that would have supplemented the taking of an occasional mammoth, like the charred bear and rabbit bones recovered at Lehner, Arizona (Haynes 1980). The faunal assemblage at Blackwater Draw included deer, wolf, peccary, antelope, turtle, rodents, and birds, in addition to mammoth, bison, horse, and camel, although Haynes (1964) cautions that these could be secondary deposits.

In the West at Fishbone Cave (P3e), Nevada, the remains of fish, marmot, horse, camel, and bird bones were found associated with a human burial wrapped in cedar bark, which dated from 10,900 ± 300 yr B.P. to 11,250 ± 250 yr B.P. (Orr 1956, 1974). At the Old Humboldt site in Nevada (26Pe670) one fluted point and two stemmed points were recovered from shallow alluvium deposits in association with a small, diversified assemblage of mammals, birds, fish, and molluscs that included waterfowl egg, three species of rabbits, bison, 76 clams, and one large Lahonton trout (Dansie 1987; Rusco and Davis 1987).

In the northern Alkali Lake Basin (Willig 1989), noncultural faunal remains and microfossils recovered from shallow lake-shore strata deposited just prior to Clovis and Stemmed-era occupations provide valuable paleoenvironmental clues. These remains include large grazers, fish (tui chub and suckers), marsh-loving gastropods, and possibly frog. More importantly, there is increasing evidence from many western lake basins of a diversified spectrum of game and floral resources associated with shallow lake-marsh habitats between 12,000 and 10,000 yr B.P. (Willig 1989; Willig and Aikens 1988).

Environmental Context and Settlement Pattern

Although it is true that western fluted points are found in a variety of environmental settings, it is a most intriguing fact that, with the exception of the Ritchie-Roberts cache in Washington (Mehringer 1988a), all six western sites with large fluted-point concentrations are situated along the lowest strand lines in pluvial lake basins once occupied by shallow lakes, marshes, and stream-fed deltas during the terminal Pleistocene. This may be a factor of sampling bias, but seems unlikely considering that some fairly large portions of the West have now been systematically surveyed archaeologically.

This unique site distribution and the lack of any definitive kill sites or clear association with extinct fauna have led a number of scholars to postulate a pre-Archaic lake-marsh adaptation in far western North America (Aikens 1978, 1983a; Clewlow 1968; Davis 1978a; Heizer and Baumhoff 1970; Madsen 1982; Rozaire 1963; Wilke et al. 1974; Willig 1984, 1988). Currently, there are no datable subsistence remains from western Clovis sites, so the time depth and degree of cultural dependence on these early lake-marsh resources is yet to be defined. To test this hypothesis, focus should be placed upon the context and distribution of fluted-point sites with respect to their paleoenvironmental settings. There is much we can infer about western Clovis economy and adaptations by studying the geomorphic context and settlement pattern of major lake basin sites with respect to the terminal Pleistocene landscape and the kinds of plant and animal resources that would have been available.

Clovis occupation in the West spans a period of major climatic change involving desiccation of once-extensive pluvial lake systems and a steadily declining megafauna population (Aikens 1983a; Davis 1982; Meltzer and Mead 1983; Mehringer 1977, 1986). Mehringer has eloquently described the cultural and environmental history of the Great Basin as an area characterized by successive human adaptive responses to a continuum of environmental changes involving "sharp, punctuated" climatic events (Mehringer 1986:31). In fact, the only thing that remained constant throughout the postglacial environmental history of the Great Basin was change itself. This variability may have been the most important factor in "shaping cultural or technological adaptations" (Mehringer 1977:148).

In such a situation of punctuated change and fluctuations in lake levels, people and fauna alike would have been attracted to dependable food and water sources for obvious reasons. Fluctuations in the size and stability of these shallow basin lakes and marshes would have greatly affected the paleoeconomy and settlement pattern of local Clovis populations by controlling the abundance and distribution of critical food and water resources (Madsen 1982; Weide 1968, 1974).

The pan-western outline of climatic change begins with terminal Pleistocene desiccation of lakes, rivers, and springs from about 12,600 to 10,600 yr B.P., followed by a general trend in aridity from 10,600 to 7500 yr B.P. But research in recent years has emphasized basin-specific reconstructions and local subregional variation (Aikens 1983a; Jennings 1986; Madsen and O'Connell 1982; Willig 1989). This focus has greatly expanded and refined our knowledge of terminal Pleistocene lake chronologies. It is now clear that, despite an apparent synchrony of changes in lake levels, glacial episodes, and atmospheric circulation patterns, there were marked differences in lake history and conditions in each basin.

The expansions and recessions of lake levels in individual basins varied considerably in the rate and degree of hydrologic changes, in concert with a number of local factors, including: (1) precipitation and evaporation ratios; (2) basin geometry and geologic substrate; (3) size and elevational relief of contributing watersheds; and (4) the balance of surface to subsurface inflow (Benson 1978; Smith and Street-Perrott 1983). The microclimates in each basin would have differentially affected local resources, so careful reconstruction of each basin's microenvironment and lake history within the Clovis time frame has significant bearing upon our interpretations of paleoeconomy and lifeway.

The significance of this kind of basin-specific variation becomes clear with even a cursory look at four of the six basins containing major fluted-point localities: Tulare Lake, California; Alkali Lake, Oregon; and Tonopah and Mud lakes, Nevada. Figure 8 shows the four selected basins side by side at the same scale to illustrate differences in drainage areas (within broken lines). Alkali Lake Basin has a relatively small, low-relief watershed, while Tulare, Tonopah, and Mud lakes are all well watered from high-relief watersheds in adjacent ranges. Hachured areas outline the approximate size of the water body that would have existed during the Clovis occupation, based upon the last maximum high stands in each basin (white area) and the elevational position of major fluted-point sites (stars).

No large-scale systematic archaeological surveys have been conducted along the lower shorelines in these basins except in Alkali Lake Basin (Willig 1988, 1989) and in some areas associated with Kelly's work (Kelly 1978) north of Tonopah. The only apparent commonality between the basins, other than containing major sites along shallow fossil lakes/marshes, is that they share a roughly 20:1 (or greater) ratio of drainage area to lake size (surface) relevant to western Clovis occupation. This suggests that these six basins were probably excellent regional candidates for maintaining reliable food and water resources to support local Clovis groups during the terminal Pleistocene. In the northern sub-basin of Alkali Lake, the watershed that fed the Dietz site lake/marsh is substantially larger than any of the surrounding sub-basins (Willig 1984, 1988, 1989).

Fluted-point sites studied in 1930–1940 at Tonopah Lake, Nevada, (Figure 9a) are located along the northeast shore at 4,810 ft. (1,466 m) elevation, where water was shallowest and where the constantly shifting channels of Peavine Creek produced a rich deltaic marshland area (Campbell and Campbell 1940; Kelly 1978; Pendleton 1979)—a situation identical to that proposed for the Sunshine Locality in northeastern Nevada (Hutchinson 1988; Tuohy 1988; York 1975, 1976). Profile A-A' shows the position of the Tonopah sites at 4,810 ft. (1,466 m) elevation and a well-defined lower strand line at 4,740 ft. (1,445 m) elevation that would have supported a 5- to 10-foot lake level (Figure 9b). At nearby Mud Lake (Figure 10a), fluted points have been found as high as 5,280 ft. (1,609 m) elevation at the Lowengruhn Beach Ridge site (Tuohy 1968) and as far down as 5,200 ft. (1,585 m) elevation or lower (Pendleton 1979). Profile A-A' shows the distribution of sites along a gentle gradient down to a well-defined 5,200 ft. (1,585 m) contour line, which would have held 15 to 20 feet of water (Figure 10b).

At Tulare Lake, California, (Figure 11a) the Witt site is located at 192 ft.(58.5 m) elevation along the southern shore, just north of Dudley Ridge (Riddell and Olsen 1969; Wallace and Riddell 1988). Today, the lake is controlled by canals for agricultural irrigation; but hopefully, some of the low-relief shore features still survive for study. Profile A-A' through the Witt site shows its position with respect to a well-defined shoreline at 185 ft. (56.4 m) elevation, which would have held 5 to 6 feet of water (Figure 11b).

At the Dietz site (35LK1529) in Oregon, extensive site survey, surface collections, mapping and stratigraphic studies of lake-shore sediments, artifact contexts, and

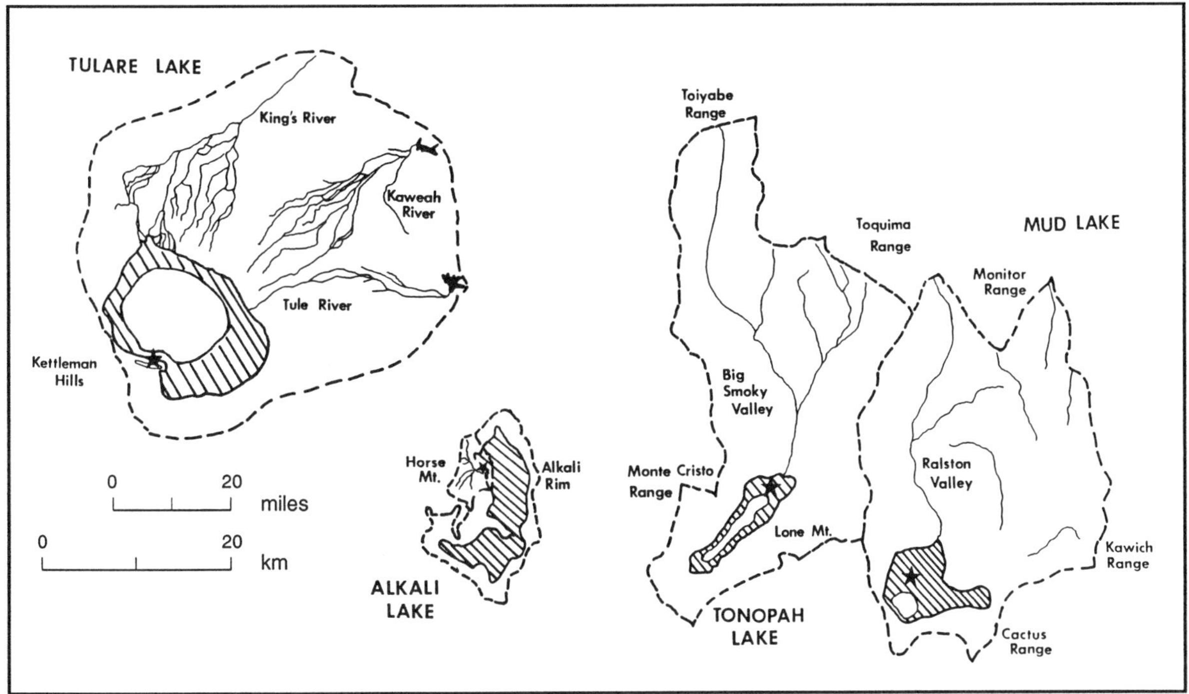

Figure 8. Map of four western lake basins containing major western Clovis sites (stars): Tulare Lake, California; Alkali Lake, Oregon; and Tonopah and Mud lakes, Nevada. Basins are shown side by side at the same scale to illustrate differences and similarities in contributing watersheds (within broken lines) and shallow lake levels (hachured lines) that may have been present during occupation.

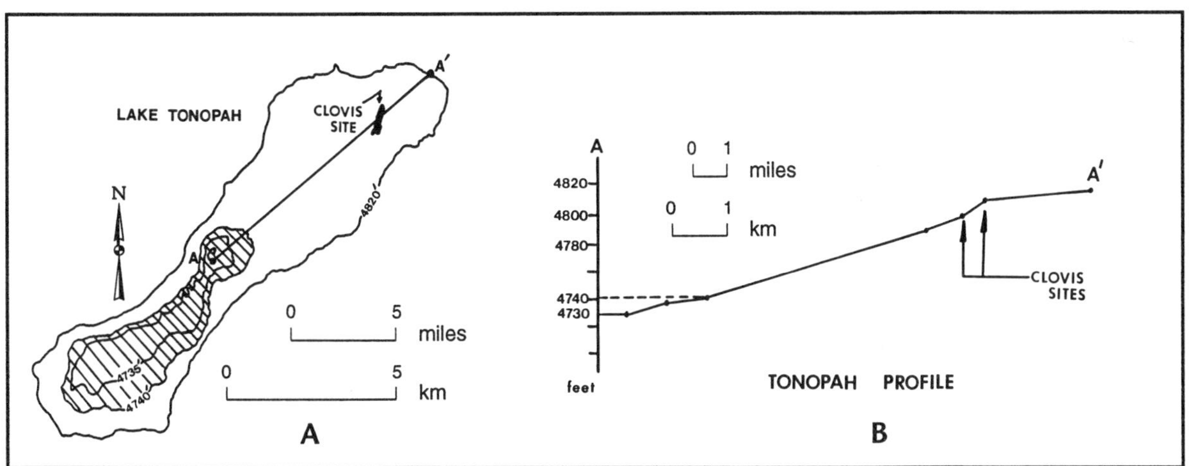

Figure 9a. Map of Tonopah Lake, Nevada, showing topographic position of a major Clovis site with respect to shallow lake levels (hachured).

Figure 9b. Generalized profile (A-A') across Tonopah Lake Basin, Nevada, showing elevational position of a major Clovis site with respect to a shallow lake level at 4,740 ft. (1,445 m) elevation.

site distributions have helped reconstruct early human settlement patterns and lake history in the northern Alkali Basin (Willig 1984, 1985, 1988, 1989). The Dietz site has produced 60 fluted-point fragments (Figures 4 and 5) and 31 stemmed points. These occur, for the most part, in spatially discrete, single-component clusters, which together extend for 1,250 m along low-relief, fossil shorelines (Figure 12). Careful mapping and

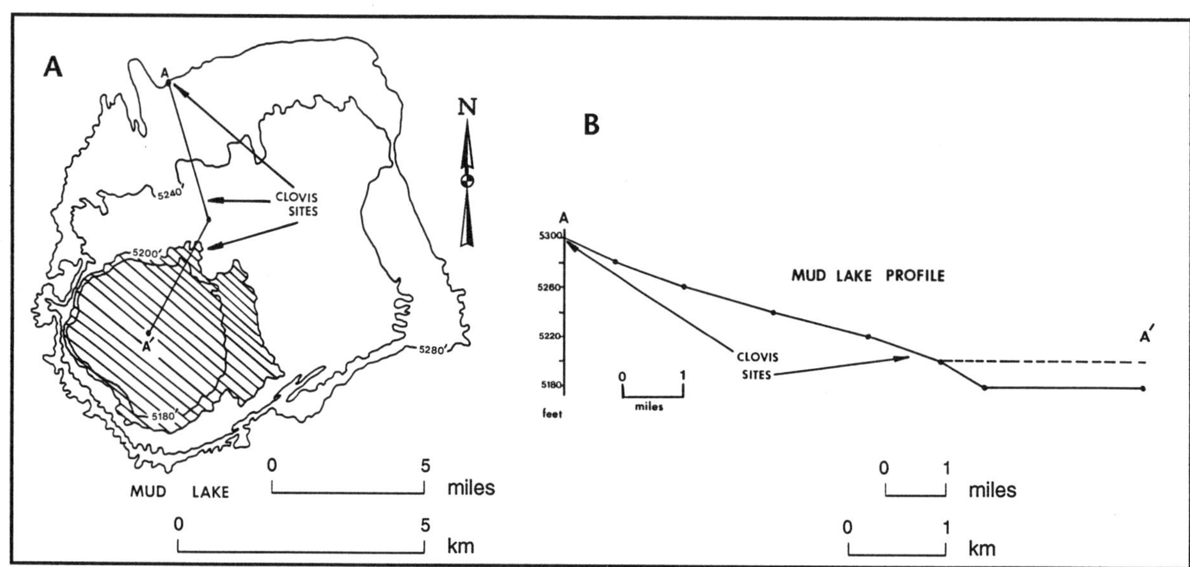

Figure 10a. Map of Mud Lake, Nevada, showing topographic position of major Clovis sites with respect to shallow lake levels (hachured).

Figure 10b. Generalized profile (A-A') across Mud Lake Basin, Nevada, showing elevational range of major Clovis sites with respect to a shallow lake level at or near 5,200 ft. (1,585 m) elevation.

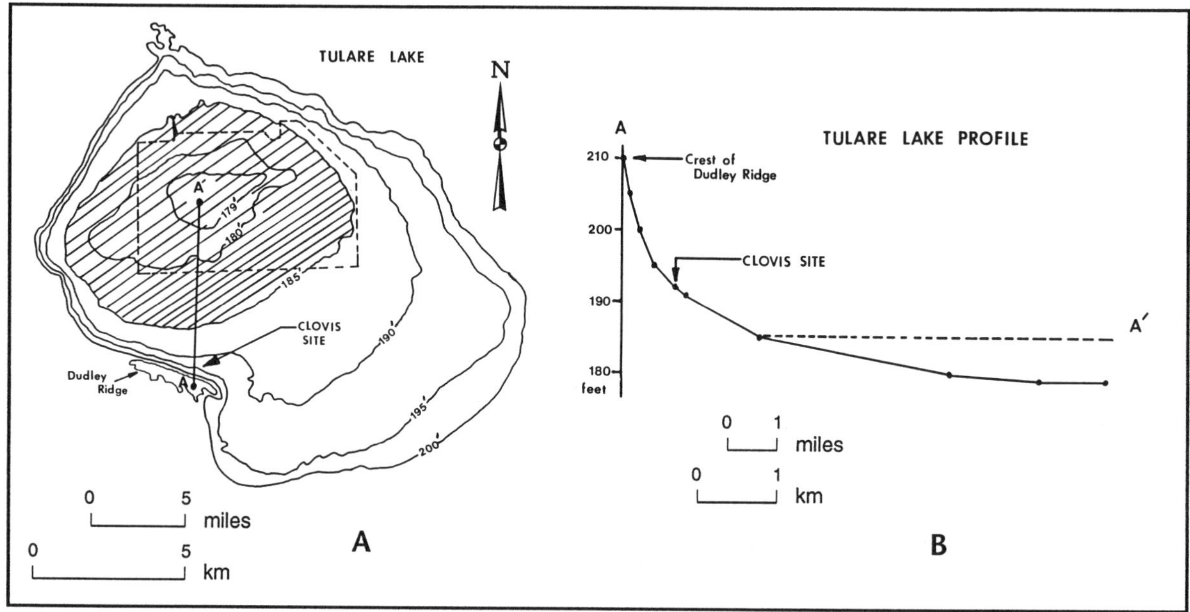

Figure 11a. Map of Tulare Lake, California, showing topographic position of the Witt Clovis site (CAKin32) at the base of Dudley Ridge and the shallow lake level at or near 185 ft. (56.4 m) elevation (hachured) that may have been present during occupation (Riddell and Olsen 1969; Wallace and Riddell 1988).

Figure 11b. Generalized profile (A-A') across Tulare Lake Basin, California, showing elevational position of the Witt Clovis site (CAKin32) with respect to the shallow lake level at or near 185 ft. (56.4 m) elevation that may have been present during occupation (Riddell and Olsen 1969; Wallace and Riddell 1988).

cross-correlation of artifacts, occupation surfaces, and lake levels have demonstrated a clear vertical and horizontal separation of western Clovis from stemmed-era occupation—the strongest case yet reported in the Far West for separating these two assemblages in relative time (Willig 1988, 1989).

The evidence suggests a terminal Pleistocene western Clovis occupation at the Dietz site oriented to the northwestern shore of a small, shallow lake or marsh (30 to 50 cm deep) in the center of the basin (Figure 13). This was followed by a substantial two-stage lake-side settlement of Western Stemmed groups in the early Holocene at 31 sites that line the periphery of two slightly deeper (1.5 to 2 m deep), closely sequent lakes (Figure 14). Marsh fringes spanned the entire northern basin (Willig 1988, 1989).

Systematic programs of archaeological survey and detailed mapping of site distribution and time-diagnostic tools with respect to fossil habitats should be undertaken in *all* the pluvial lake basins in the West containing major fluted-point sites. Special focus should be given to the more subtle, low-relief shore features of the postpluvial period, which are often neglected by scholars of the "full-pluvial persuasion." As each basin's lake history is refined, basin geometry and water levels could be incorporated into predictive models of precipitation-evaporation ratios and hydrologic budgets for different shoreline occupations. Detailed reconstructions of settlement pattern, paleolandscape, and accompanying resources in each basin are our best avenue for establishing a fuller characterization of the western Clovis lifeway.

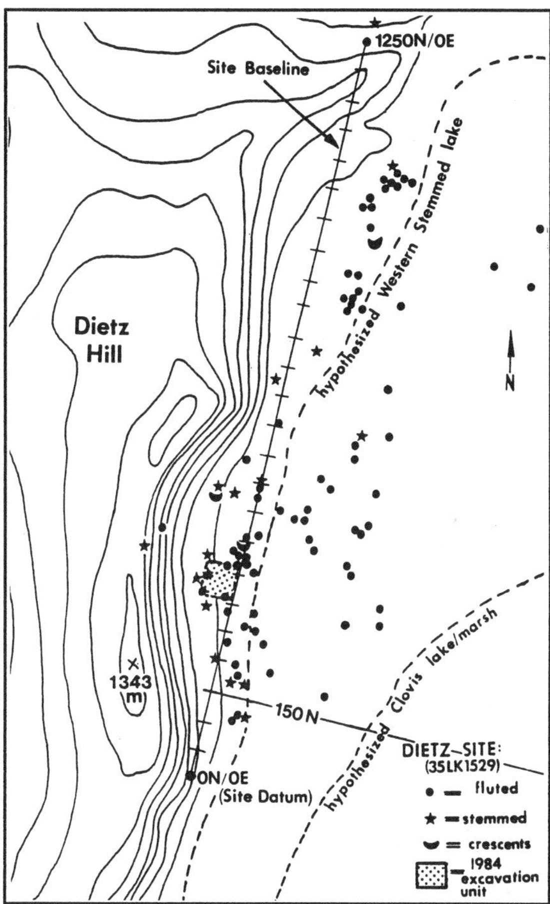

Figure 12. Horizontal distribution of fluted and stemmed projectile points at the Dietz site (35LK1529) in relation to shallow lake levels reconstructed during western Clovis (1,314.8 m) and Western Stemmed (1,316 m) period occupations.

CONCLUSIONS

There is much we still do not know about Clovis in the Far West, but typological and technological studies suggest that western Clovis complexes represent a complete temporal continuum between Clovis fluted and the gradually diversifying forms of the Western Stemmed and Early Archaic complexes. It is hypothesized that the earliest Western Stemmed complexes, appearing about 11,000 to 10,000 yr B.P., are local developments out of a brief but ancestral western Clovis presence. There is some temporal overlap expected in dates, as the two follow closely in time. Horizontal stratigraphy at the Dietz site in the northern Alkali Basin, Oregon, (Willig 1988, 1989) indicates that western Clovis clearly precedes Western Stemmed in time. A similar sequence can be seen with Folsom and eastern fluted points, dating from 11,000 to 10,000 yr B.P., developing out of an earlier pan-continental Clovis presence dating from 11,500 to 11,000 yr B.P.

The typology and intrasite variation of far western fluted-point complexes compare favorably with Llano-Clovis, but the paleoenvironmental context and settlement pattern of major sites in western pluvial lake basins suggest that western Clovis may also represent a regional, cultural-adaptational variant of the specialized big-game hunting tradition implied by "Llano." This lends support to earlier suggestions that the broad-spectrum adaptation of later western Archaic cultures may have its roots in Clovis time (Aikens 1978, 1983a; Daugherty 1962; Heizer and Baumhoff 1970; Jennings and Norbeck 1955). This is in keeping with the paleowestern vs. paleoeastern distinction in subsistence base first made by Wormington (1957:20). Such an early development of Archaic-style broad-spectrum adaptation would be a natural outgrowth of the variability and regional diversity that characterize the environmental history of the Far West over the last 12,000 years.

Other scholars have argued for a more generalized, broad-spectrum, subsistence strategy during Clovis time (Dent 1985; Gardner 1983; Griffin 1964; Meltzer and

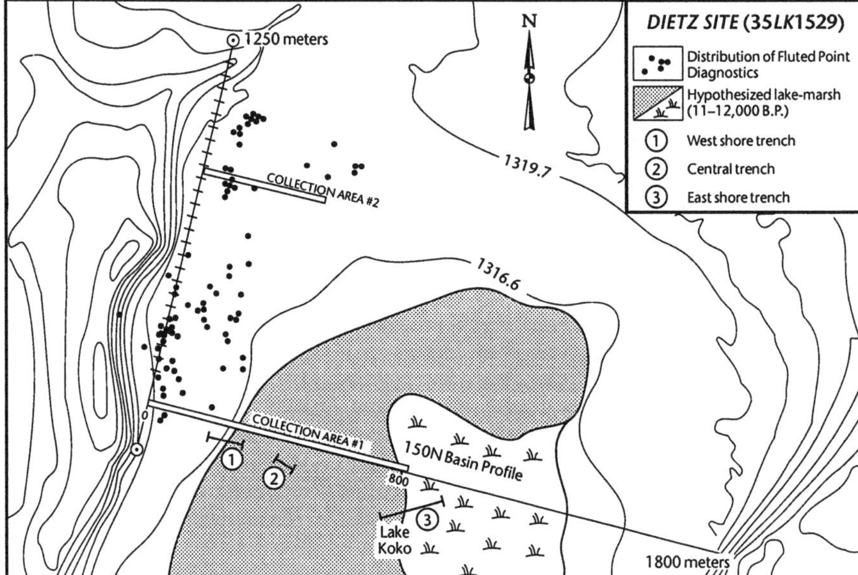

Figure 13. Western Clovis (fluted) point distributions at the Dietz site (35LK1529), in relation to the shallow lake level reconstructed at 1,314.8 m elevation.

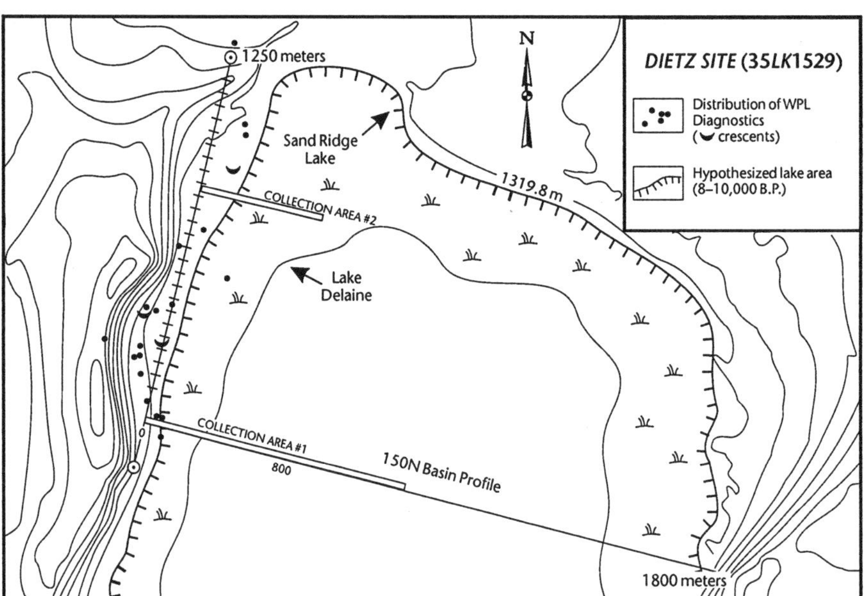

Figure 14. Western Stemmed artifact distributions at the Dietz site (35LK1529) in relation to the shallow lake levels reconstructed at 1,316 m and 1,315.4 m elevation.

Smith 1986). As discussed above, there is evidence in the East for such varied items as caribou, birds, fish, giant land tortoise, grape, hawthorn plum, hackberry, and blackberry in the Clovis-age diet. The evidence from the Far West, Southwest, and Plains also speaks for a diversified menu of deer, bear, wolf, peccary, antelope, turtle, rodents, marmot, birds, fish, and molluscs, which would have supplemented a diet of large terrestrial game.

Some envision Clovis people as wide-ranging, highly mobile generalists with a specialized focus on hunting large terrestrial mammals, but with an opportunistic stance in relation to all other food resources (Kelly and Todd 1988). This strategy would be the most efficient way to accommodate periodic resource stresses caused by late Pleistocene environmental changes, and probably best explains the situation envisioned for the brief period of initial colonization across North America. But in order to ensure continued survival during a time of rapidly increasing aridity and unpredictable, punctuated climatic change, the earliest Clovis folk would have to learn about and adapt very quickly to local and regional "menus" and ecological niches. Human groups already accustomed to flexible foraging practices within a large range would have quickly and naturally gravitated, along with the game they hunted, to places where hydrologic and geomorphic conditions were well suited for maintaining stable, concentrated patches or "sweet spots" of edible foods and fresh water.

In Florida, fluted-point sites distinctly cluster near limestone sinkholes of potable water and in close proximity to major lithic sources (Dunbar, this volume). Paleoindians could have easily "tethered" themselves to these mesic "sweet spots," while still maintaining wide-ranging logistical foraging within the region. If conditions changed for the worse, the search would begin for a new spot. In the pluvial lake basins of the Great Basin and California, and possibly southern Arizona and New Mexico as well, the pivot of this "tether" would have been the biotically rich littoral zones and riparian habitats of shallow lake and marsh systems and the streams that fed them (Willig 1989). In the Plateau region to the northwest, this would have translated into a riverine focus, especially in the cooler, wetter, more ecologically diverse eastern Plateau where the majority of early Holocene sites are concentrated (Ames 1988).

In these well-watered settings where an abundance and diversity of resources could be found in one concentrated area, western Clovis folk could have practiced a more diversified hunting and gathering lifeway keyed to locally available fish, fowl, and vegetal foods, in addition to both large and small game animals drawn to the locality as a favorable watering source. This kind of adaptive strategy would produce a few large, redundantly utilized campsites in key spots, and many small, logistical sites that are less "visible" in the archaeological record (Binford 1980)—the pattern currently reflected in the far western record.

Based on these data, it can be hypothesized that the earliest occupants in North America developed generalized, broad-spectrum adaptive strategies much earlier than was once thought. Initial Clovis colonizers, focusing on large terrestrial game, had to be flexible enough to change quickly, not gradually, in concert with the emerging mosaic of regional environmental resources so characteristic of the Pleistocene-Holocene transition (Willig 1989). In western pluvial lake basins, Clovis folk would have maximized success by retaining a flexible wide-ranging strategy, while "tethered" to mesic micro-environments where a wide range of food and water resources were concentrated and maintained despite increasing aridity. Diversification through time in technology and culture, in concert with environmental change, eventually culminated in the development of fully blown western Archaic adaptations out of this basal "paleo-Archaic" foundation.

ACKNOWLEDGMENTS

I would like to extend my deepest gratitude to Drs. C. Melvin Aikens and Robson Bonnichsen for the invitation to participate in the 1987 INQUA symposium on Clovis research. Without their generosity and encouragement, this publication would not have been possible. Research conducted since 1983 in the northern Alkali Lake Basin and at the Dietz site has involved the support and contributions of a multitude of students, faculty and friends, both amateur and professional, who donated many hours of time in the field and lab. Research has been conducted under a cooperative agreement between the University of Oregon Anthropology Department and the Bureau of Land Management (BLM). Mr. William J. Cannon (Lakeview District Archaeologist) and Dr. Richard C. Hanes (Oregon State Office) have been particularly instrumental in coordinating joint efforts.

Financial support for Alkali Basin research came primarily from National Science Foundation (NSF) Grant BNS84-06447 and NSF Dissertation Improvement Grant BNS87-13659. Other institutions and grants that have provided funds for a variety of analyses include the BLM (Lakeview District and Oregon State Office), the Bowerman Foundation of Eugene, Oregon, the Association of Oregon Archaeologists, and two Archaeological Research Trust Fund Grants administered through the University of Oregon Anthropology Department.

All artifact illustrations are the artistic products of Wyndeth V. Moisan, many of which were completed on location at California State University at Sacramento, where the collections were undergoing obsidian sourcing analyses by Dr. Richard E. Hughes. This documentation would not have been possible without the facilities and hospitality offered by Hughes at Sacramento, and by Dr. David A Fredrickson at Sonoma State University, where the artifacts were photographed. I am most especially indebted to Dr. C. Melvin Aikens for his continuing guidance, encouragement and support over the years.

REFERENCES CITED

Adovasio, J. M.

1986 Prehistoric Basketry. In *Great Basin,* edited by W. L. D'Azevedo, pp. 194–205. Handbook of North American Indians, vol. 11, W. C. Sturtevant, general editor. Smithsonian Institution, Washington, D.C.

Adovasio, J. M., J. D. Gunn, J. Donahue, and R. Stuckenrath

1977 Meadowcroft Rockshelter: A 16,000 Year Chronicle. In *Amerinds and Their Paleoenvironments in Northeastern North America,* edited by W. S. Newman and B. Salwen, pp. 137–159. Annals of the New York Academy of Sciences No. 288.

Aikens, C. M.
1978 Archaeology of the Great Basin. *Annual Review of Anthropology* 7:71–87.
1982 Archaeology of the Northern Great Basin: An Overview. In *Man and Environment in the Great Basin,* edited by D. B Madsen and J. F. O'Connell, pp. 139–155. SAA Papers No. 2. Society for American Archaeology, Washington, D.C.
1983a Environmental Archaeology in the Western United States. In *The Holocene,* edited by H. E. Wright, Jr., pp. 239–251. Late Quaternary Environments of the United States, vol. 2, H. E. Wright, Jr., general editor. University of Minnesota Press, Minneapolis.
1983b The Far West. In *Ancient Native Americans,* edited by J. D. Jennings, pp. 149–202. W. H. Freeman and Company, San Francisco.

Ames, K. M.
1988 Early Holocene Forager Mobility Strategies on the Southern Columbia Plateau. In *Early Human Occupation in Far Western North America: The Clovis-Archaic Interface,* edited by J. A. Willig, C. M. Aikens, and J. L. Fagan, pp. 325–360. Nevada State Museum Anthropological Papers No. 21. Carson City.

Bedwell, S. F.
1970 *Prehistory and Environment of the Pluvial Fort Rock Lake Area of Southcentral Oregon.* Unpublished Ph.D. dissertation, Department of Anthropology, University of Oregon, Eugene.
1973 *Fort Rock Basin Prehistory and Environment.* University of Oregon Books, Eugene.

Bedwell, S. F., and L. S. Cressman
1971 Fort Rock Report: Prehistory and Environment of the Pluvial Fort Rock Lake Area of South-central Oregon. *University of Oregon Anthropological Papers* 1:1–25.

Benson, L. V.
1978 Fluctuation in the Level of Pluvial Lake Lahontan During the Last 40,000 Years. *Quaternary Research* 9:300–318.

Binford, L. R.
1980 Willow Smoke and Dog's Tails: Hunter-gatherer Settlement Systems and Archaeological Site Formation. *American Antiquity* 45:4–20.

Bonnichsen, R., and D. Young
1980 Early Technological Repertoires: Bone to stone. In *The Ice-Free Corridor and Peopling of the New World,* edited by N. W. Rutter and C. E. Schweger pp. 123–128. *Canadian Journal of Anthropology* 1.

Brennan, L. A. (editor)
1982 A Compilation of Fluted Points of Eastern North America by Count and Distribution: An AENA Project. *Archaeology of Eastern North America* 10:27–46.

Bryan, A. L.
1979 Smith Creek Cave. In *The Archaeology of Smith Creek Canyon,* edited by D. R. Tuohy, pp. 164–251. Nevada State Museum Anthropological Papers No. 17. Carson City.
1980 The Stemmed Point Tradition: An Early Technological Tradition in Western North America. In *Anthropological Papers in Honor of Earl H. Swanson, Jr.,* edited by C. N. Warren and D. R. Tuohy, pp. 77–107. Special Publication of the Idaho State Museum of Natural History, Pocatello.
1988 The Relationship of the Stemmed Point and Fluted Point Traditions in the Great Basin. In *Early Human Occupation in Far Western North America: The Clovis-Archaic Interface,* edited by J. A. Willig, C. M. Aikens, and J. L. Fagan, pp. 53–74. Nevada State Museum Anthropological Papers No. 21. Carson City.

Bryson, R. A., D. A. Baerreis, and W. M. Wendland
1970 The Character of Late-glacial and Post-glacial Climatic Change. In *Pleistocene and Recent Environments of the Central Great Plains,* edited by W. Dort, Jr. and J. K. Jones, pp. 53–74. University of Kansas Press, Lawrence.

Butler, B. R.
1963 An Early Man Site at Big Camas Prairie, South-central Idaho. *Tebiwa* 6:22–33.
1970 A Surface Collection from Coyote Flat, Southeastern Oregon. *Tebiwa* 13:34–57.
1978 *A Guide to Understanding Idaho Archaeology: The Upper Snake and Salmon River Country.* 3rd ed. Special Publication of the Idaho Museum of Natural History. Pocatello.
1986 Prehistory of the Snake and Salmon River Area. In *Great Basin,* edited by W. L. D'Azevedo, pp. 127–134. Handbook of North American Indians, vol. 11, edited by W. C. Sturtevant, general editor. Smithsonian Institution, Washington, D.C.

Butler, B. R., and J. R. Fitzwater
1965 A Further Note on the Clovis Site at Big Camas Prairie, South-central Idaho. *Tebiwa* 8:38–40.

Campbell, E. W. C., and W. H. Campbell
1940 A Folsom Complex in the Great Basin. *Masterkey* 14:7–11.

Carlson, R.
1983 The Far West. In *Early Man in the New*

World, edited by R. Shutler, Jr., pp. 73–96. Sage Publications, Beverly Hills.

1988 The View from the North. In *Early Human Occupation in Far Western North America: The Clovis-Archaic Interface*, edited by J. A. Willig, C. M. Aikens, and J. L. Fagan, pp. 319–324. Nevada State Museum Anthropological Papers No. 21. Carson City.

Clark, D. W.
1984 Northern Fluted Points: Paleo-Eskimo, Paleo-Arctic, or Paleo-Indian. *Canadian Journal of Anthropology* 4:65–81.

Clausen, C. J., A. Cohen, C. Emiliana, J. Holman, and J. Stipp
1979 Little Salt Spring, Florida: A Unique Underwater Site. *Science* 203:609–614.

Clewlow, C. W., Jr.
1968 Surface Archaeology of the Black Rock Desert, Nevada. *University of California Archaeological Survey Reports* 73(1):1–94. Berkeley.

Cressman, L. S.
1966 Man in Association with Extinct Fauna in the Great Basin. *American Antiquity* 31:866–867.

Cressman, L. S., and W. S. Laughlin
1941 A Probable Association of Mammoth and Artifacts in the Willamette Valley, Oregon. *American Antiquity* 4:339–344.

Dansie, A. J.
1987 The Rye Patch Archaeofaunas: Change Through Time. In *Studies in Archaeology, Geology and Paleontology at Rye Patch Reservoir, Pershing County, Nevada* edited by M. Rusco and J. Davis, pp. 156–182. Nevada State Museum Anthropological Papers No. 20. Carson City.

Dansie, A. J., J. O. Davis, and T. W. Stafford, Jr.
1988 The Wizards Beach Recession: Farmdalian (25,500 yr B.P.) Vertebrate Fossils Co-occur with Early Holocene Artifacts. In *Early Human Occupation in Far Western North America: The Clovis-Archaic Interface*, edited by J. A. Willig, C. M. Aikens, and J. L. Fagan, pp. 153–200. Nevada State Museum Anthropological Papers No. 21. Carson City.

Daugherty, R. D.
1962 The Intermontane Western Tradition. *American Antiquity* 28:144–150.

Davis, E. L.
1967 Man and Water at Pleistocene Lake Mohave. *American Antiquity* 32:345–353.

1975 The Exposed Archaeology of China Lake, California. *American Antiquity* 40:39–53.

Davis, E. L. (editor)
1978a *The Ancient Californians: Rancholabrean Hunters of the Mohave Lakes Country.* Natural History Museum of Los Angeles County Science Series No. 29. Los Angeles.

Davis, E. L.
1978b Associations of People and a Rancholabrean Fauna at China Lake, California. In *Early Man in America from a Circum-Pacific Perspective*, edited by A. L. Bryan, pp. 183–217. Occasional Papers No. 1. Department of Anthropology, University of Alberta, Edmonton.

Davis, E. L., and R. Shutler, Jr.
1969 Recent Discoveries of Fluted Points in California and Nevada. In *Miscellaneous Papers on Nevada Archaeology*, edited by D. L. Rendall and D. R. Tuohy, pp. 154–169. Nevada State Museum Anthropological Papers No. 14. Carson City.

Davis, J. O.
1982 Bits and Pieces: The Last 35,000 Years in the Lahontan Area. In *Man and Environment in the Great Basin*, edited by D. B. Madsen and J. F. O'Connell, pp. 53–75. SAA Papers No. 2. Society for American Archaeology, Washington, D.C.

Dent, R. J.
1985 Amerinds and Their Environment: Myth, Reality, and the Upper Delaware Valley. In *Shawnee Minisink: A Stratified Paleoindian-Archaic Site in the Upper Delaware Valley of Pennsylvania*, edited by C. W. McNett, Jr., pp. 123–163. Academic Press, Orlando.

Dincauze, D.
1984 An Archaeo-logical Evaluation of the Case for Pre-Clovis Occupations. In *Advances in World Archaeology*, edited by F. Wendorf and A. E. Close, pp. 275–323. Academic Press, Orlando.

Fagan, J. L.
1984a The Dietz Site: A Clovis Base Camp in South-central Oregon. Paper presented at the 49th Annual Meeting of the Society for American Archaeology, Portland.

1984b Northern Great Basin Fluting Technology at the Dietz Site. Paper presented at the 19th Biennial Great Basin Anthropological Conference, Boise.

1986 Western Clovis Occupation in Southcentral Oregon: Archaeological Research at the Dietz Site 1983–1985. *Current Research in the Pleistocene* 3:3–5.

1988 Clovis and Western Pluvial Lakes Tradition Lithic Technologies at the Dietz Site in South-central Oregon. In *Early Human Occupation in Far Western North America: The Clovis-Archaic Interface,* edited by J. A. Willig, C. M. Aikens, and J. L. Fagan, pp. 389–416. Nevada State Museum Anthropological Papers No. 21. Carson City.

Fredrickson, D. A.
1973 *Early Cultures of the North Coast Ranges.* Unpublished Ph.D. dissertation, Department of Anthropology, University of California, Davis.
1974 Cultural Diversity in Early Central California: A View from the North Coast Ranges. *Journal of California Anthropology* 1(1):41–53.

Fredrickson, D. A., and G. G. White
1988 The Clear Lake Basin and Early Complexes in California's North Coast Ranges. In *Early Human Occupation in Far Western North America: The Clovis-Archaic Interface,* edited by J. A. Willig, C. M. Aikens, and J. L. Fagan, pp. 75–86. Nevada State Museum Anthropological Papers No. 21. Carson City.

Frison, G. C.
1978 *Prehistoric Hunters of the High Plains.* Academic Press, New York.

Frison, G. C., and D. J. Stanford
1982 *The Agate Basin Site: A Record of the Paleo-Indian Occupation of the Northwestern High Plains.* Academic Press, New York.

Gardner, W. M.
1983 Stop Me If You've Heard This One Before: The Flint Run Paleoindian Complex Revisited. *Archaeology of Eastern North America* 11:49–64.

Graham, R. W., C. V. Haynes, Jr., D. Johnston, and M. Kay
1981 Kimmswick: A Clovis-Mastodon Association in Eastern Missouri. *Science* 213:1115–1117.

Gramly, R. (editor)
1984 New Experiments Upon the Record of Eastern Paleo-indian Cultures. *Archaeology of Eastern North America* 12.

Griffin, J. B.
1964 The Northeast Woodlands Area. In *Prehistoric Man in the New World,* edited by J. D. Jennings and E. Norbeck, pp. 223–258. University of Chicago Press, Chicago.

Gruhn, R.
1961 *The Archaeology of Wilson Butte Cave, South-central Idaho.* Occasional Papers of the Idaho State College Museum No. 6. Pocatello.
1965 Two Early Radiocarbon Dates from the Lower Levels of Wison Butte Cave, South-central Idaho. *Tebiwa* 8:57.

Harrington, M. R.
1948 *An Ancient Site at Borax Lake, California.* Southwest Museum Papers No. 16. Los Angeles.

Haury, E. W.
1950 *The Stratigraphy and Archaeology of Ventana Cave.* University of Arizona Press, Tucson.

Haury, E. W., E. Antevs, and J. F. Lance
1953 Artifacts with Mammoth Remains, Naco, Arizona: Parts I–III. *American Antiquity* 19:1–24.

Haury, E. W., and J. D. Hayden
1975 Preface 1975. In *The Stratigraphy and Archaeology of Ventana Cave,* pp. v, vi. 2nd ed. University of Arizona Press, Tucson.

Haury, E. W., E. B. Sayles, W. W. Wasley, and E. Antevs
1959 The Lehner Mammoth Site, Southeastern Arizona and Geological Age of the Lehner Mammoth Site. *American Antiquity* 25:2–42.

Haynes, C. V., Jr.
1964 Fluted Projectile Points: Their Age and Dispersion. *Science* 145:1408–1413.
1969 The Earliest Americans. *Science* 166:709–715.
1971 Time, Environment and Early Man. *Arctic Anthropology* 8:3–14.
1980 The Clovis Culture. In *The Ice-Free Corridor and Peopling of the New World,* edited by N. W. Rutter and C. E. Schweger, pp. 115–121. *Canadian Journal of Anthropology* 1.
1982 Were Clovis Progenitors in Beringia? In *Paleoecology of Beringia,* edited by D. B. Hopkins, J. V. Mathews, Jr., C. E. Schweger, and S. B. Young, pp.383–398. Academic Press, New York.
1987 Clovis Origin Update. *The Kiva* 52:83–93.

Haynes, C. V., Jr., D. J. Donahue, A. J. T. Jull, and T. H. Zabel
1984 Application of Accelerator Dating to Fluted Point Paleoindian Sites. *Archaeology of Eastern North America* 12:184–191.

Haynes, G.
1988 Spiral Fractures, Cutmarks and Other Myths about Early Bone Assemblages. In *Early Human Occupation in Far Western North America: The Clovis-Archaic Interface,* edited by J. A. Willig, C. M. Aikens, and J. L. Fagan, pp. 145–151. Nevada State Museum Anthropological Papers No. 21. Carson City.

Heizer, R. F., and M. A. Baumhoff
1970 Big Game Hunters in the Great Basin: A Critical Review of the Evidence. *Contributions of the University of California Archaeological Research Facility* 7:1–12. Berkeley.

Hester, J. J., E. L. Lundelius, Jr., and R. Fryxell
1972 *Blackwater Locality No. 1: A Stratified Early Man Site in Eastern New Mexico.* Fort Burgwin Research Center, Southern Methodist University, Dallas.

Holmer, R. N.
1986 Common Projectile Points of the Intermountain West. In *Anthropology of the Desert West: Essays in Honor of Jesse D. Jennings,* edited by C. J. Condie and D. D. Fowler, pp. 89–115. University of Utah Anthropological Papers No. 110. Salt Lake City.

Hughes, R. E.
1984 Obsidian Sourcing Studies in the Great Basin: Problems and Prospects. In *Obsidian Studies in the Great Basin,* edited by R. E. Hughes, pp. 1–19. *Contributions of the University of California Archaeological Research Facility* No. 45. Berkeley.
1986 *Diachronic Variability in Obsidian Procurement Patterns in Northeastern California and South-central Oregon.* University of California Publications in Anthropology No. 17. Berkeley.

Hutchinson, P. W.
1988 The Prehistoric Dwellers at Lake Hubbs. In *Early Human Occupation in Far Western North America: The Clovis-Archaic Interface,* edited by J. A. Willig, C. M. Aikens, and J. L. Fagan, pp. 303–318. Nevada State Museum Anthropological Papers No. 21. Carson City.

Jennings, J. D.
1957 *Danger Cave.* University of Utah Anthropological Papers No. 27. Salt Lake City.
1964 The Desert West. In *Prehistoric Man in the New World,* edited by J. D. Jennings and E. Norbeck, pp.149–174. University of Chicago Press.
1986 Prehistory: Introduction. In *Great Basin,* edited by W. L. D'Azevedo, pp. 113–119. Handbook of North American Indians, vol. 11, W. C. Sturtevant, general editor. Smithsonian Institution, Washington, D.C.

Jennings, J. D., and E. Norbeck
1955 Great Basin Prehistory: A Review. *American Antiquity* 21:1–11.

Kelly, R. L.
1978 *Paleo-Indian Settlement Patterns at Pleistocene Lake Tonopah, Nevada.* Unpublished B.A. honors thesis, Department of Anthropology, Cornell University, Ithaca, NY.

Kelly, R. L., and L. C. Todd
1988 Coming into the Country: Early Paleoindian Hunting and Mobility. *American Antiquity* 53:231–244.

Kirch, P. V.
1980 The Archaeological Study of Adaptation: Theoretical and Methodological Issues. In *Advances in Archaeological Method and Theory,* vol. 3, edited by M. B. Schiffer, pp. 101–156. Academic Press, New York.

Kopper, J., R. Funk and, L. Dumont
1978 Additional Paleoindian and Archaic Material from the Dutchess Quarry Cave Area, Orange County, New York. *Archaeology of Eastern North America* 8:125–137.

Kraft, H. C. (editor)
1983 Fluted Point Survey. *Archaeology of Eastern North America* 11.

Lahren, L. A., and R. Bonnichsen
1974 Bone Foreshafts from a Clovis Burial in Southwestern Montana. *Science* 186:147–150.

Lynch, T. J.
1983 The Paleo-Indians. In *Ancient South Americans,* edited by J. D. Jennings, pp. 87–137. W. H. Freeman and Company, San Francisco.

Madsen, D. B.
1982 Get it Where the Gettin's Good: A Variable Model of Great Basin Subsistence and Settlement Based on Data from the Eastern Great Basin. In *Man and Environment in the Great Basin,* edited by D. B. Madsen and J. F. O'Connell, pp. 207–226. SAA Papers No. 2. Society for American Archaeology, Washington, D.C.

Madsen, D. B., D. R. Currey, and J .H. Madsen
1976 Man, Mammoth and Lake Fluctuations in Utah. *Antiquities Section Selected Papers* 2:43–58. Utah Division of State History, Salt Lake City.

Madsen, D. B., and J. F. O'Connell (editors)
1982 *Man and Environment in the Great Basin.* SAA Papers No. 2. Society for American Archaeology, Washington, D.C.

Mason, R. J.
1962 The Paleo-Indian Tradition in Eastern North America. *Current Anthropology* 3:227–278.

Mehringer, P. J., Jr.
1977 Great Basin Late Quaternary Environments and Chronology. In *Models and Great Basin Prehistory: A Symposium,* edited by D. D. Fowler, pp. 113–167. University of Nevada Desert Research Institute Publications in the Social Sciences No. 12. Reno.
1986 Prehistoric Environments. In *Great Basin,* edited by W. L. D'Azevedo, pp. 31–50. Handbook of North American Indians, vol. 11, W. C. Sturtevant, general editor. Smithsonian Institution, Washington, D.C.

1988a Weapons Cache of Ancient Americans. *National Geographic* 174:500–503.

1988b The Richey-Roberts Clovis Cache, East Wenatchee, Washington. *Northwest Science* 62(5):271–272.

1989 Of Apples and Archaeology. *Universe* 1(2):2–8. Washington State University, Pullman.

Meighan, C. W., and C. V. Haynes, Jr.

1968 New Studies on the Age of the Borax Lake Site. *Masterkey* 42:4–9.

1970 The Borax Lake Site Revisited. *Science* 167:1213–1221.

Meltzer, D. J.

1988 Late Pleistocene Human Adaptations in Eastern North America. *Journal of World Prehistory* 2:1-52.

Meltzer, D. J., and J. I. Mead

1983 The Timing of Late Pleistocene Mammalian Extinctions in North America. *Quaternary Research* 19:130–135.

Meltzer, D. J., and B. D. Smith

1986 Paleo-indian and Early Archaic Subsistence Strategies in Eastern North America. In *Foraging, Collecting and Harvesting: Archaic Period Subsistence and Settlement in the Eastern Woodlands,* edited by S. Neusius, pp. 1–30. Occasional Paper No. 6. Center for Archaeological Investigations, Southern Illinois University, Carbondale.

Miller, S. J., and W. Dort, Jr.

1978 Early Man at Owl Cave: Current Investigations at the Wasden Site. In *Early Man in America from a Circum-Pacific Perspective,* edited by A. L. Bryan, pp. 129–139. Occasional Papers No. 1. Department of Anthropology, University of Alberta, Edmonton.

Moratto, M. J.

1984 *California Archaeology.* Academic Press, Orlando.

Musil, R. R.

1988 Functional Efficiency and Technological Change: A Hafting Tradition Model for Prehistoric North America. In *Early Human Occupation in Far Western North America: The Clovis-Archaic Interface,* edited by J. A. Willig, C. M. Aikens, and J. L. Fagan, pp. 373–387. Nevada State Museum Anthropological Papers No. 21. Carson City.

Orr, P. C.

1956 *Pleistocene Man in Fishbone Cave, Pershing County, Nevada.* Nevada State Museum Department of Archaeology Bulletin No. 2. Carson City.

1974 Notes on the Archaeology of the Winnemucca Caves, 1952–1958. In *Collected Papers on Aboriginal Basketry,* edited by D. R. Tuohy and D. L. Rendall, pp. 47–59. Nevada State Museum Anthropological Papers No. 16. Carson City.

Pendleton, L. S.

1979 *Lithic Technology in Early Nevada Assemblages.* Unpublished master's thesis, Department of Anthropology, California State University, Long Beach.

Riddell, F. A., and W. H. Olsen

1969 An Early Man Site in the San Joaquin Valley, California. *American Antiquity* 34:121–130.

Rozaire, C. E.

1963 Lake-side Cultural Specializations in the Great Basin. In *The 1962 Great Basin Anthropological Conference,* pp. 72–77. Nevada State Museum Anthropological Papers No. 9. Carson City.

Rusco, M. K., and J. O. Davis

1987 *Studies in Archaeology, Geology and Paleontology at Rye Patch Reservoir, Pershing County, Nevada.* Nevada State Museum Anthropological Papers No. 20. Carson City.

Sadek-Kooros, H.

1966 *Jaguar Cave: An Early Man Site in the Beaverhead Mountains of Idaho.* Unpublished Ph.D. dissertation, Department of Anthropology, Harvard University, Cambridge.

Sellards, E. H.

1952 *Early Man in America.* University of Texas Press, Austin.

Simms, S. R.

1988 Conceptualizing the Paleo-Indian and Archaic in the Great Basin. In *Early Human Occupation in Far Western North America: The Clovis-Archaic Interface,* edited by J. A. Willig, C. M. Aikens, and J. L. Fagan, pp. 41–52. Nevada State Museum Anthropological Papers No. 21. Carson City.

Smith, G. I., and F. A. Street-Perrott

1983 Pluvial Lakes of the Western United States. In *The Late Pleistocene,* edited by S. J. Porter, pp. 190–212. Late Quaternary Environments of the United States, vol. 1, H. E. Wright, Jr., general editor. University of Minnesota Press, Minneapolis.

Snarskis, M. J.

1979 Turrialba: A Paleo-Indian Quarry and Workshop Site in Eastern Costa Rica. *American Antiquity* 44:125–138.

Storck, P. L.
1984 Glacial Lake Algonquin and Early Palaeo-Indian Settlement Patterns in Southcentral Ontario. *Archaeology of Eastern North America* 12:286–298.

Thompson, R. S., E. M. Hattori, and D. R. Tuohy
1987 Paleoenvironmental and Archaeological Implications of Early Holocene and Late Pleistocene Cave Deposits from Winnemucca Lake, Nevada. *Nevada Archaeologist* 6(1):34–38.

Titmus, G. L., and J. C. Woods
1988 The Evidence of Paleo-Indian Occupation in Southern Idaho. Paper presented at the 41st Annual Northwest Anthropological Conference, Tacoma, WA.

Tuohy, D. R.
1968 Some Early Lithic Sites in Central Nevada. In *Early Man in Western North America*, edited by C. Irwin-Williams, pp. 27–38. Eastern New Mexico University Contributions in Anthropology No. 1.

1969 A Brief Note on Additional Fluted Points from Nevada: Appendix. In *Miscellaneous Papers on Nevada Archaeology*, edited by D. L. Rendall and D. R. Tuohy, pp. 154–178. Nevada State Museum Anthropological Papers No. 14. Carson City.

1974 A Comparative Study of Late Paleo-Indian Manifestations in the Western Great Basin. In *A Collection of Papers on Great Basin Archaeology*, edited by R. G. Elston and L. Sabini, pp. 90–116. Nevada Archaeological Survey Research Paper No. 5. Reno.

1985 Notes on the Distribution of Clovis Fluted and Folsom Projectile Points. *Nevada Archaeologist* 5(1):15–18.

1986 Errata and Additional Notes on the Great Basin Distribution of Clovis Fluted and Folsom Points. *Nevada Archaeologist* 5(2):2–7.

1988 Paleoindian and Early Archaic Cultural Complexes from Three Central Nevada Localities. In *Early Human Occupation in Far Western North America: The Clovis-Archaic Interface*, edited by J. A. Willig, C. M. Aikens, and J. L. Fagan, pp. 217–230. Nevada State Museum Anthropological Papers No. 21. Carson City.

Wallace, W. J.
1978 Post-Pleistocene Archaeology, 9,000–2,000 B.C. In *California*, edited by R. F. Heizer, pp. 25–36. Handbook of North American Indians, vol. 8, W. G. Sturtevant, general editor. Smithsonian Institution, Washington, D.C.

Wallace, W. J., and F. A. Riddell
1988 Prehistoric Background of Tulare Lake, California. In *Early Human Occupation in Far Western North America: The Clovis-Archaic Interface*, edited by J. A. Willig, C. M. Aikens, and J. L. Fagan, pp. 87–101. Nevada State Museum Anthropological Papers No. 21. Carson City.

Warnica, J. M.
1966 New Discoveries at the Clovis Site. *American Antiquity* 31:345–357.

Warren, C. N., and C. Phagan
1988 Fluted Points in the Mojave Desert: Their Technology and Cultural Context. In *Early Human Occupation in Far Western North America: The Clovis-Archaic Interface*, edited by J. A. Willig, C. M. Aikens, and J. L. Fagan, pp. 121–130. Nevada State Museum Anthropological Papers No. 21. Carson City.

Weide, M. L.
1968 *Cultural Ecology of Lakeside Adaptation in the Western Great Basin.* Unpublished Ph.D. dissertation, Department of Anthropology, University of California, Los Angeles.

1974 North Warner Subsistence Network: A Prehistoric Band Territory. In *A Collection of Papers on Great Basin Archaeology*, edited by R. G. Elston and L. Sabini, pp. 62–79. Nevada Archaeological Survey Research Paper No. 5. Reno.

Wilke, P. J., T. F. King, and R. L. Bettinger
1974 Ancient Hunters of the Far West? In *A Collection of Papers on Great Basin Archaeology*, edited by R. G. Elston and L. Sabini. pp. 80–90. Nevada Archaeological Survey Research Paper No. 5. Reno.

Willey, G. R.
1966 *An Introduction to American Archaeology, vol. 1: North and Middle America.* Prentice-Hall, Englewood Cliffs, NJ.

Willig, J. A.
1984 Geoarchaeological Research at the Dietz Site and the Question of Clovis Lake/Marsh Adaptation in the Northern Great Basin. *Tebiwa* 21:56–69.

1985 Paleo-Indian Occupation in the Alkali Lake Basin of South-central Oregon: Current Status of Geoarchaeological Research. Paper presented at the 38th Annual Northwest Anthropological Conference, Ellensburg, WA.

1988 Paleo-Archaic Adaptations and Lakeside Settlement Patterns in the Northern Alkali Lake Basin, Oregon. In *Early Human Occupation in Far*

Western North America: The Clovis-Archaic Interface, edited by J. A. Willig, C. M. Aikens, and J. L. Fagan, pp. 417–482. Nevada State Museum Anthropological Papers No. 21. Carson City.

1989 *Paleo-Archaic Broad Spectrum Adaptations at the Pleistocene-Holocene Boundary in Far Western North America*. Unpublished Ph.D. dissertation, Department of Anthropology, University of Oregon, Eugene.

Willig, J. A., and C. M. Aikens
1988 The Clovis-Archaic Interface in Far Western North America. In *Early Human Occupation in Far Western North America: The Clovis-Archaic Interface*, edited by J. A. Willig, C. M. Aikens, and J. L. Fagan, pp. 1–40. Nevada State Museum Anthropological Papers No. 21. Carson City.

Willig, J. A., C. M. Aikens, and J. L. Fagan (editors)
1988 *Early Human Occupation in Far Western North America: The Clovis-Archaic Interface*. Nevada State Museum Anthropological Papers No. 21. Carson City.

Woods, J. C., and G. L. Titmus
1985 A Review of the Simon Site Collection. *Idaho Archaeologist* 8(1):3–8.

Wormington, H. M.
1957 *Ancient Man in North America*. Denver Museum of Natural History Popular Series No. 4. Denver.

Wright, G. A., and S. J. Miller
1976 Prehistoric Hunting of New World Wild Sheep: Implications for the Study of Sheep Domestication. In *Cultural Change and Continuity: Essays in Honor of James Bennett Griffin*, edited by C. E. Cleland, pp. 293–312. Academic Press, New York.

York, R.
1975 A Preliminary Report on Test Excavations and Controlled Surface Collecting in Long Valley, Nevada. *Nevada Archaeological Survey Reporter* 8(1):4–10.

1976 Corrections and Additional Data on "A Preliminary Report on Test Excavations and Controlled Surface Collecting in Long Valley, Nevada." *Nevada Archaeological Survey Reporter* 9(1).

Young, D. E., and R. Bonnichsen
1984 *Understanding Stone Tools: A Cognitive Approach*. Center for the Study of Early Man, University of Maine, Orono.

Fluted Points from the Snake River Plain

GENE L. TITMUS AND JAMES C. WOODS
Herrett Museum
College of Southern Idaho
Twin Falls, ID 83303

Southern Idaho has been recognized as an important region for Paleoindian occupation. Among the most temporally sensitive manifestations of this period are fluted points, which have been recovered from the Snake River Plain and adjacent drainages. Review of the morphology and technology of a collection of fluted points recovered from southern Idaho suggests that while these points fit within the standard definitions of Clovis and Folsom types, some features may not be commonly shared with fluted points from other regions of North America. The implications of this difference are addressed and a hypothesis is offered concerning design characteristics of fluted points from this region.

INTRODUCTION

The Snake River Plain has a documented culture history extending back to the initial peopling of the New World. Among some of the well-known early sites are Wilson Butte Cave (Gruhn 1961), Owl Cave (Miller 1982; Miller and Dort 1978), the Simon site (Butler 1963; Butler and Fitzwater 1965; Woods and Titmus 1985), and Jaguar Cave (Sadek-Kooros 1966).

The most temporally sensitive and generally accepted evidence for an early occupation of the area consists of fluted points reported from this region. Two decades ago, enough fluted points had been recovered from southern Idaho to allow the proposal of a strong cultural affinity between the Snake River Plain and the Great Plains to the east (Swanson 1961, 1962, 1966; Swanson and Bryan 1964). Although additional fluted points have been recently reported (Titmus and Woods 1988), no attempt has been made to re-examine the early interpretations of the Paleoindian period in this region. This paper is a re-examination of the fluted points from the Snake River Plain and a discussion of their technological features that may ultimately allow more specific comparisons with fluted points from other portions of North America.

Although hundreds of fluted points have been recovered from southern Idaho, only 28 of these from 20 sites are discussed in the following review. Specimens were included only if previously reported in the literature or if reliable contextual information was available (Table 1).

TECHNOLOGICAL REVIEW OF SOUTHERN IDAHO FLUTED POINTS

Of 38 fluted points reported in the literature from the study area, 28 were available for examination, including 12 Clovis and 16 Folsom points. (Several of the published specimens belong to private owners and were unavailable for study for a variety of reasons. Several others with published descriptions were not available, but sufficient descriptive information was available to allow inclusion in this review.) The following discussion will briefly address morphological diversity, flaking and fluting technology, basal dulling, and the evidence for thermal alteration and resharpening of this collection of fluted points from the Snake River Plain and adjacent drainages in southern Idaho (Figure 1).

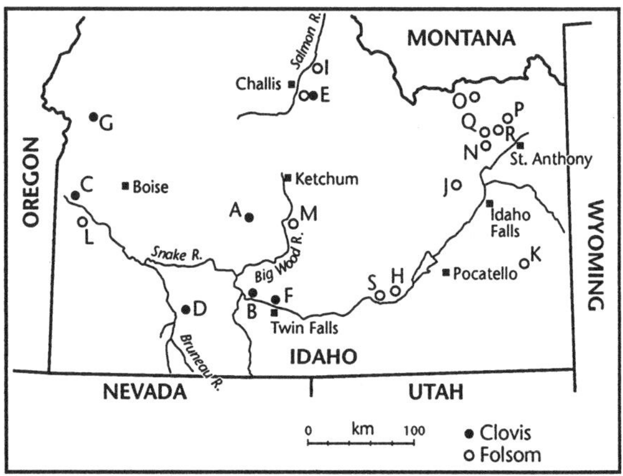

Figure 1. Locations of fluted points in southern Idaho. **A)** Simon; **B)** Crystal Springs; **C)** Alkalai Springs; **D)** West Clover; **E)** Big Flat; **F)** Blue Lakes; **G)** Paddock Valley Reservoir; **H)** Lake Channel; **I)** Ellis; **J)** Wasden (Owl Cave); **K)** Henry; **L)** Reynolds Creek; **M)** Timmerman Hill; **N)** South of Juniper; **O)** Rockchuck Ridge; **P)** NG-2; **Q)** NJ East; **R)** Wright's; **S)** Gifford Hot Springs.

Morphological Diversity

Metric data on the 28 fluted points should be viewed with caution, as many of the study specimens are damaged. For this analysis, dimensions are presented for comparison when that specific dimension is complete. Thus, the following maximum length comparisons include only those specimens with intact proximal and distal ends. Maximum width comparisons are provided only when both the lateral margins are intact, regardless of whether the proximal or distal ends are damaged.

The Clovis materials range in length from 7.8 to 18.2 cm; the Folsom materials range in length from 3.7 to 3.9 cm. Widths range from 3.2 to 3.9 cm on the Clovis points and from 2.3 to 2.4 cm on the Folsom points. Maximum thickness ranges from 0.8 to 1.0 cm for Clovis and from 0.5 to 0.6 cm for Folsom. A very consistent morphological attribute noted is the basal width, which is measured 1 cm from the basal indention (this eliminates basal width variation resulting from rounded barbs). Basal widths range from 3.0 to 3.7 cm on Clovis points and from 2.1 to 2.4 cm on Folsom points.

There appear to be two general groupings of Clovis points, based on the variable of maximum length. Three of the five Simon site projectiles and one from northern Idaho (Figure 2a,b,c,f) suggest that some Clovis specimens are nearly twice the length of the other group (Table 1). The cache-like distribution, presence of ocher, and unusually large size of artifacts at the Simon site have led Bonnichsen (1977) to propose that this may have been a burial locale similar to the Anzick site in Montana (Lahren 1969). Pavesic (1985) provides evidence that the practice of exaggerating the scale of tools, and the use of caches and ocher were employed in burials in the region during later periods. It is important to note that both longer and shorter Clovis fluted points were also recovered from the Anzick site, which has been interpreted as a burial locale (Butler 1963; Lahren 1969). The bimodal distinction in tool length has also prompted the suggestion that two functional categories might be represented, the longer representing lance or knife blades, the shorter representing projectile points (Butler, personal communication 1985). However, the unusually long Clovis specimens from the West all seem to be found in caches. There is no contextual or use-damage evidence to suggest an association with implied hunting situations.

Only two of the 12 Folsom points included in this study are complete, and both specimens are comparatively short. Several fragments (Figure 3g,j,o,s), however, suggest that some Idaho Folsom points were considerably longer. It is possible that some of this diversity in size may be attributed to projectile-point rejuvenation, but it appears that Folsom points, like Clovis points, may have been manufactured in two distinct size groups.

Raw Material Selection

The raw materials preferred by the makers of fluted points in the study area were highly variable. Microcrystalline silicates ranged from moderately fine-grained cherts to extremely fine-grained chalcedonies of many

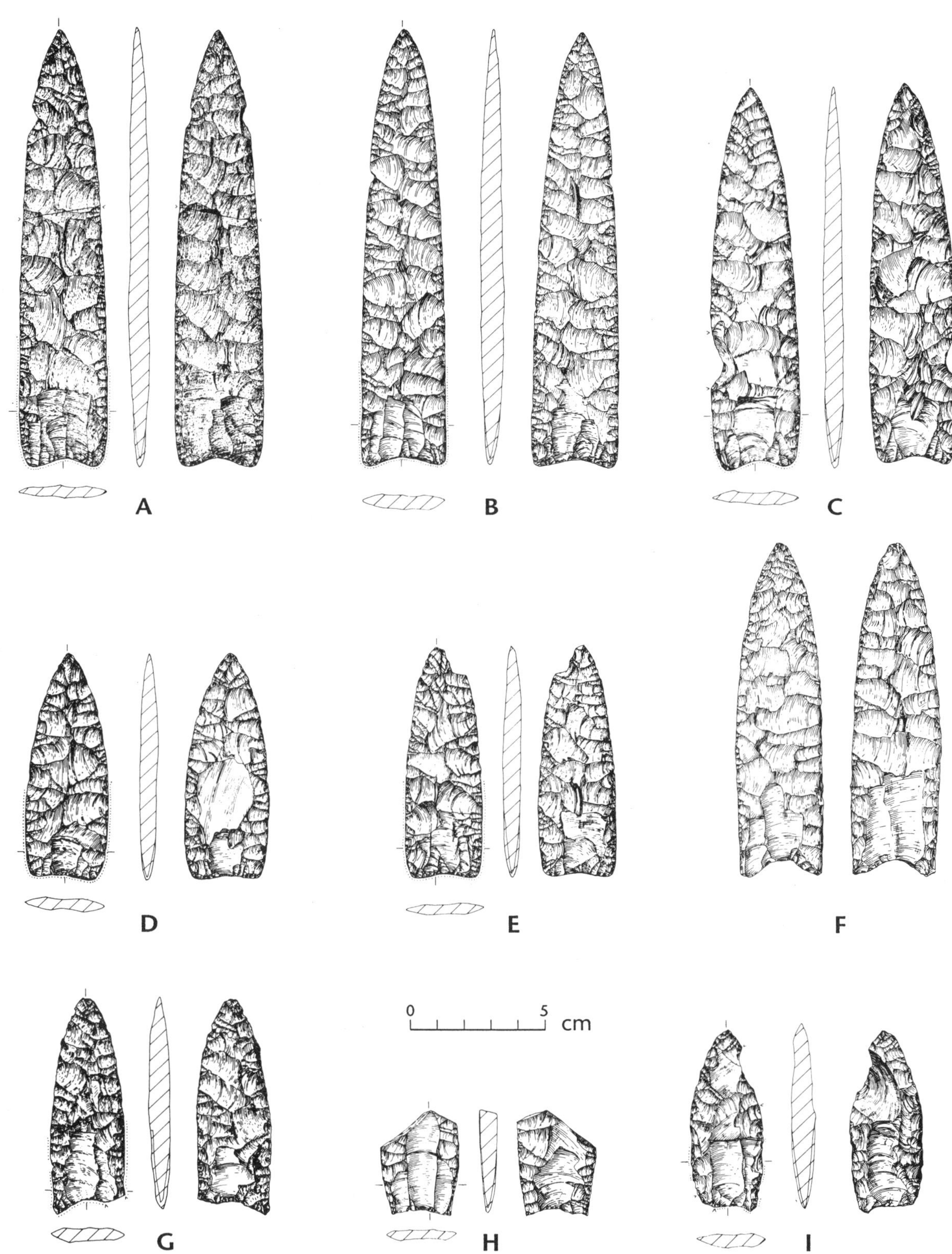

Figure 2. Fluted points from southern Idaho.

Table 1. Contextual and Morphological Data of the Study Collection.

FIGURE	TYPE	REFERENCE	SITE NAME	SITE NUMBER
1a	Clovis	Butler:1963	Simon	10-CM-7
1b	Clovis	Butler:1963	Simon	10-CM-7
1c	Clovis	Butler:1963	Simon	10-CM-7
1d	Clovis	Butler:1963	Simon	10-CM-7
1e	Clovis	Butler:1963	Simon	10-CM-7
1f	Clovis	Potter & Aageson:1974	Nez Perce Co.	no number
1g	Clovis	Murphey:1985	Crystal Springs	10-GG-207
1h	Clovis	Huntley:1985	Alkalai Springs	10-OE-867
1i	Clovis	Peterson:1988	Cascade Res.	10-VY-563
2a	Clovis	Druss & Druss:1986	West Clover	10-OE-3197
2b	Clovis	Titmus & Woods:1988	Big Flat	no number
2c	Clovis	Titmus:1988	Blue Lakes	no number
2d	Folsom	Campbell:1956	Lake Channel	no number
2e	Folsom	Butler:1972	Big Flat	no number
2f	Folsom	Butler:1972	Ellis	no number
2g	Folsom	Miller & Dort:1978	Wasden	10-BV-30
2h	Folsom	Miller & Dort:1978	Wasden	10-BV-30
2i	Folsom	Miller & Dort:1978	Wasden	10-BV-30
2j	Folsom	Butler:1980	Henry	10-CU-34
2k	Folsom	Moe:1982	Reynolds Creek	10-OE-2055
2l	Folsom	Titmus:1985	Timmerman Hill	no number
2m	Folsom	Titmus & Woods:1988	Big Flat	no number
2n	Folsom	Titmus & Woods:1988	South of Juniper	no number
2o	Folsom	Titmus & Woods:1988	Rock Chuck Ridge	no number
2p	Folsom	Titmus & Woods:1988	NG-2	no number
2q	Folsom	Titmus & Woods:1988	NJ East	no number
2r	Folsom	Titmus & Woods:1988	Wrights	no number
2s	Folsom	Titmus & Woods:1988	Gifford Hot Sp.	no number

– Missing value.
All measurements in centimeters.

* A = Maximum length
B = Maximum width
C = Maximum thickness
D = Depth of basal indention
E = Width of base, measured 1 cm up from basal indention
F = Length of obverse channel flake
G = Total width of channel flake scars on obverse face
H = Length of perverse channel flake
I = Total width of channel flake scars on perverse face
J = Length of right lateral edge dulling
K = Length of left lateral edge dulling
L = Basal dulling

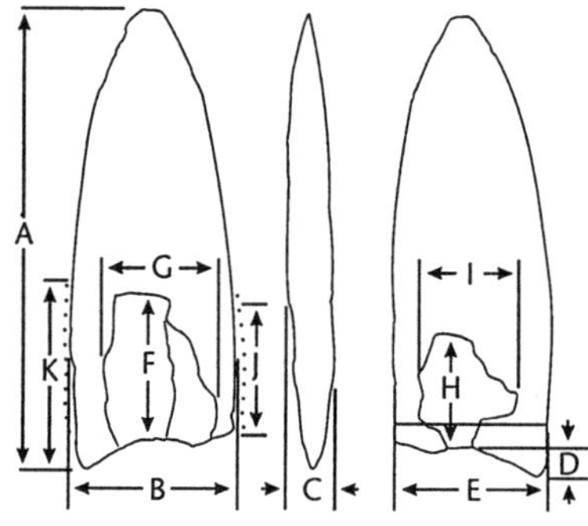

MAP	ATTRIBUTE VARIABLES*												MATERIAL
	A	B	C	D	E	F	G	H	I	J	K	L	
a	18.2	3.9	0.8	0.4	3.7	3.6	2.8	3.3	3.2	4.6	5.4	yes	microcrystalline silicate
a	18.2	3.7	0.9	0.4	3.7	3.0	2.5	2.3	2.2	4.4	4.1	yes	microcrystalline silicate
a	15.9	3.9	0.8	0.4	3.6	3.2	1.9	2.9	2.1	2.1	2.2	yes	microcrystalline silicate
a	9.4	3.6	0.8	0.2	3.4	1.8	1.5	2.1	1.9	4.1	3.7	yes	microcrystalline silicate
a	9.6	3.4	0.8	0.2	3.3	2.8	1.8	3.0	2.0	4.0	4.0	yes	microcrystalline silicate
–	13.2	3.6	0.9	0.6	–	3.4	2.6	3.1	2.8	2.9	2.5	–	microcrystalline silicate
b	9.1	3.2	1.0	0.5	3.0	2.9	2.4	2.3	2.0	3.2	3.0	yes	microcrystalline silicate
c	4.5	3.8	0.8	0.2	2.5	4.1	2.7	1.5	2.2	0.0	0.0	no	microcrystalline silicate
g	7.8	3.3	1.1	–	–	2.8	1.5	3.4	1.8	2.9	1.5	yes	obsidian
d	7.8	3.0	0.9	0.5	2.9	5.3	1.6	5.4	1.7	2.9	2.8	yes	microcrystalline silicate
e	2.5	3.6	0.7	0.4	2.7	1.5	1.7	2.0	2.4	2.4	1.8	yes	microcrystalline silicate
f	1.9	3.3	0.5	0.4	2.9	–	2.2	–	1.7	1.7	1.9	yes	microcrystalline silicate
h	3.9	2.4	0.6	0.2	1.8	3.1	1.3	2.0	1.4	2.1	2.4	yes	microcrystalline silicate
e	2.9	2.4	0.5	–	–	–	1.7	–	0.1	2.4	2.5	no	microcrystalline silicate
i	2.3	2.6	0.5	–	–	–	1.5	–	1.8	1.9	2.1	no	microcrystalline silicate
j	3.6	2.7	0.5	–	–	–	1.5	–	1.3	–	–	–	obsidian
j	4.1	2.6	0.6	–	–	–	1.4	–	0.0	2.0	0.8	no	obsidian
j	2.6	2.8	0.4	–	–	–	1.1	–	1.0	–	–	no	obsidian
k	4.2	2.6	0.6	0.6	2.3	–	1.2	–	1.8	2.8	1.4	no	obsidian
l	2.7	1.7	0.6	–	–	–	0.4	–	1.2	1.4	0.9	–	obsidian
m	3.0	2.3	0.5	0.4	–	–	1.6	–	1.0	2.7	2.4	yes	obsidian
e	2.4	2.6	0.5	–	–	–	1.9	–	1.2	1.3	1.1	no	microcrystalline silicate
n	3.5	2.7	1.4	–	–	–	1.9	–	1.5	–	–	no	obsidian
o	4.5	2.7	0.7	–	–	–	1.5	–	1.7	–	–	no	obsidian
p	2.3	2.6	0.5	–	–	–	1.7	–	1.7	–	–	no	obsidian
q	2.1	2.4	0.5	–	–	–	1.6	–	1.8	–	–	yes	microcrystalline silicate
r	3.7	2.3	0.6	–	1.5	–	1.0	–	1.2	–	–	–	microcrystalline silicate
s	4.4	2.6	1.7	–	2.3	–	2.0	–	1.7	–	–	yes	obsidian

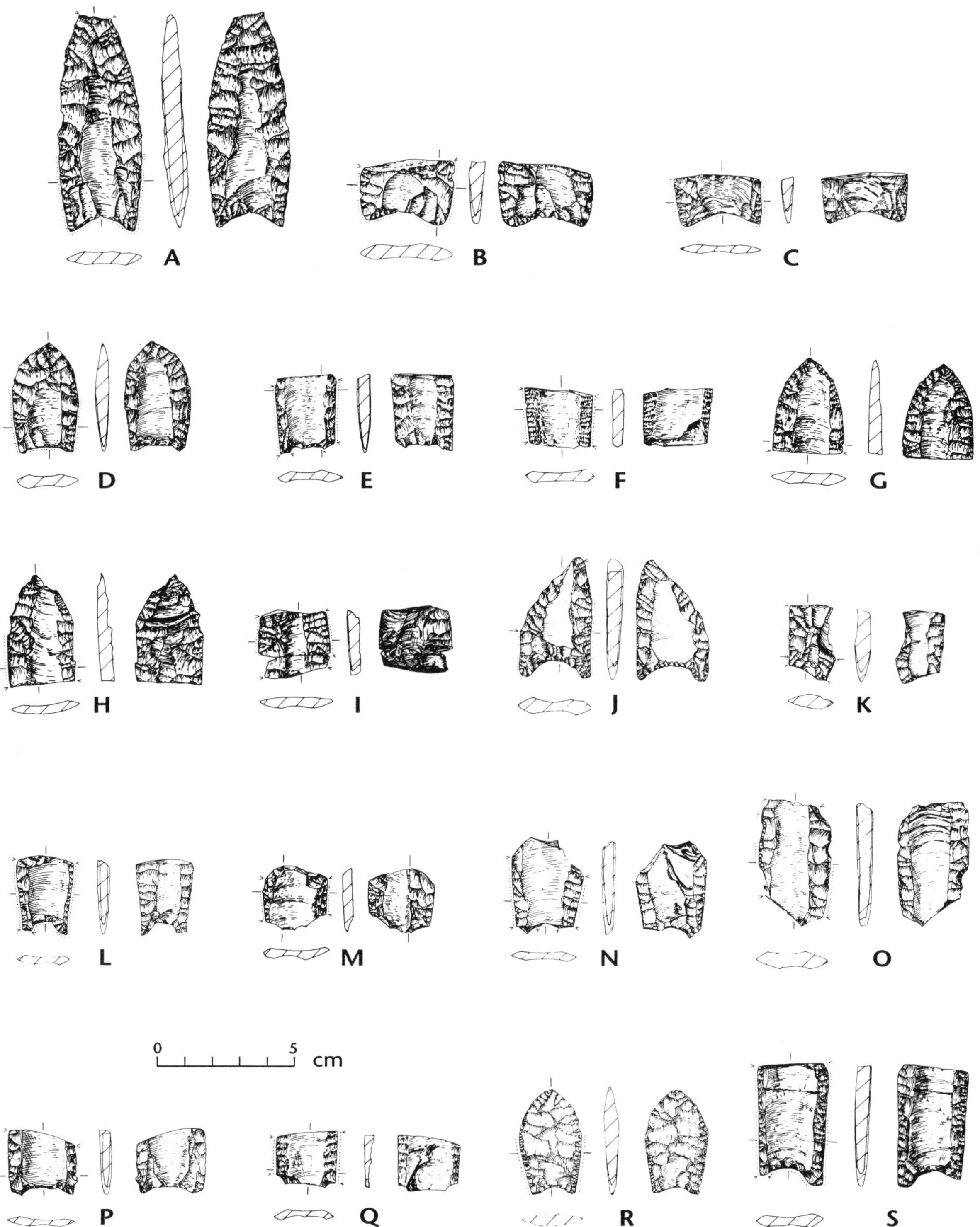

Figure 3. Fluted points from southern Idaho.

colors. Several varieties of obsidian were used, although a systematic sourcing study was not attempted as most specimens are from private collections.

Of the 13 Clovis points, 11 (84.6%) were made of microcrystalline silicates and 2 (15.4%) were made of opaque or translucent obsidian. Of the 20 Folsom points, 12 (60%) were made of obsidian and 8 (40%) were made of microcrystalline silicates. This distribution suggests that the commonly held notion of Paleoindian preference for the tougher silicates should be viewed with some caution. Perhaps the ready access to obsidian in this region (Sappington 1981a, 1981b) influenced the apparent preference for volcanic glass. The variety of raw materials used for fluted points indicates the knappers were obtaining materials from a very broad spectrum of sources. Specific material type may not have been a major consideration.

Pressure-Flaking Technology

The pressure-flaking technology evident on the Idaho Clovis specimens is relatively consistent. Pressure-flake scars are generally oriented collaterally and spaced irregularly, with the exception of the Simon specimens, where flake spacing is fairly consistent. Bulbs of force are usually shallow, and the margins bear the traces of substantial margin straightening as indicated by the presence of numerous shallow, irregular flake scars.

Several specimens retain traces of prepared platforms that were not completely removed by the margin straightening or sharpening sequence. As a result, it can be determined that the pressure-flaking platforms were not set up along the midline of the point. Rather, they were established closer to the face from which the next series of flakes were to be detached (Bonnichsen 1977:200). There is no evidence to suggest that these prepared platforms were abraded, although light buffeting (Young and Bonnichsen 1985:98) was evidently employed. Use of this platform preparation technique can allow the removal of flat, collateral flakes.

The same pressure-flaking technique used on Clovis specimens appears to have been used to produce many of the Folsom points from the Snake River Plain. However, several Idaho Folsom points suggest that an additional pressure-flaking technique was sometimes employed. This second variety involves the careful and systematic removal of narrow collateral flakes (Figure 3f,q,s), which yields a pattern of pressure-flake scars much like those on the classic Lindenmeier specimens (Wormington 1957:31–37). This second variety of pressure flaking requires a straight margin and the creation of a uniformly beveled, lightly abraded platform that must run the full length of the tool margin for consistent removal and spacing of the pressure flakes.

The two variations of pressure flaking were used to produce two Folsom points found in close proximity near Challis (Figure 3e,f). While the general tool morphology of these two specimens is distinctively Folsom, the pressure-flaking technology is quite different, and this difference remains to be adequately explained.

Fluting Technology

The most distinctive attribute of Clovis and Folsom materials is the existence of channel-flake scars on one or both faces. It has now been demonstrated that channel flakes of all configurations can be removed using percussion, indirect percussion, or pressure flaking (Crabtree 1966; Flenniken 1978; Gryba 1988; Irwin 1968). As a result, we feel that it is no longer as important to focus on the technique of fluting, as it is the rationale. The purpose behind the incorporation of this feature into the design of large lanceolate points has been addressed by numerous authors. Recently, Titmus (1987) proposed that fluting was a design element that would make the shaft/projectile juncture more durable, increasing the functional reliability (Bleed 1986) of the complete projectile system.

Although little is known about the techniques used to haft fluted points, approaching this problem by analyzing the basal-area morphology, basal-margin preparation, and hafting experimentation allows for the presentation of a hypothesis concerning the morphology of the proximal ends of Clovis points.

The Clovis specimens in this study collection reveal a wide diversity of channel-flake scar characteristics. Some channel flakes might be better described as attempts at simple basal thinning (Figure 2b). Other specimens bear long, carefully executed channel-flake scars (Figure 2g). Channel-flake morphology on the Idaho fluted points tends to support Bonnichsen's suggestion that tools with wide, flat cross-sections generally yield short channel flakes, whereas tools with pronounced biconvex cross-sections will promote the removal of longer channel flakes.

The removal of negative bulbs adjacent to the channel-flake scars on many specimens (e.g., Figure 3a), as well as multiple channel-flake scars on many of the Clovis specimens, suggests that the purpose of fluting was the provision of a flat, tapering cross-section at the area of contact between the foreshaft and the projectile. When wrapped with sinew or rawhide, this V-shaped juncture would provide equal impact-force distribution on the foreshaft surface area in contact with the fluted surface of the point. The value of this design, besides providing a very firmly attached point, is that it helps prevent any localized areas of stress on the foreshaft, especially in the area where the point base seats against the bottom of the foreshaft groove.

This extremely acute cross-section is very consistent on Clovis points in the study collection. One of the most constant morphological attributes of these points is the cross-section thickness measured at the area adjacent to the termination of margin dulling. This same measurement on Clovis points from Naco, Lehner, and Escapule attests to the consistency of this feature on Clovis from other sites in the West as well (Table 2). The consistent cross-section of Clovis points might allow for easy replacement of points damaged beyond repair, as new points would easily refit in the old foreshaft.

Hafting experiments have shown that when the seat in the foreshaft is prepared to exactly fit the contour of the basal margin of the point and the foreshaft width is slightly less than the point base width, the sides of the basal indention serve to prevent lateral movement of the point base within the haft. With the basal margin of the point firmly in contact with the foreshaft, impact or static loads are more likely to be absorbed without damage to the point/foreshaft juncture.

Basal Margin Dulling

Intentionally dulled basal margins are one of the more salient attributes of fluted points. This dulling is variously called "grinding," "abrading," or "dulling." Most authors suggest this dulling facilitated hafting by preventing cutting of the fiber wrapping by sharp, freshly flaked lateral margins (see Wormington 1957:23; Young and Bonnichsen 1985:119).

Table 2. Clovis Point Cross-section Thicknesses, Measured at Termination of Basal Dulling.

SITE	SPECIMEN	CROSS-SECTION THICKNESS
Naco II	A2FF:9:2	0.70
Naco I	A-10902	0.73
Naco I	A-10903	0.80
Naco I	A-10900	0.75
Naco I	A-10901	0.75
Naco I	A-11-913	0.65
Naco I	A-11-9:2	0.80
Lehner	12680 #7	0.60
Lehner	A-12674 #1	0.65
Lehner	12682 #9	0.70
Lehner	12676 #3	0.70
Lehner	A12677	0.70
Lehner	A12685	0.70
Lehner	A12679	0.70
Lehner	A12686	0.69
Simon	1a	0.70
Simon	1b	0.71
Simon	1c	0.60
Simon	1d	0.70
Simon	1d	0.60
Crystal Spr.	1g	0.70
West Clover	2a	0.64

All measurements in centimeters.

During this review of fluted points from the Snake River Plain, special attention was given to the location and type of margin dulling employed in their manufacture. Dulling occurs on both margins of all but one specimen. The average length of dulling was 3.4 cm (29.5% of maximum length) on complete Clovis points and 2.1 cm (57.8% of maximum length) on complete Folsom points. Dulling also extends across the basal concavity on 10 of the 11 Clovis points with intact bases and 4 of the 8 Folsom points with intact bases (Table 1).

A close examination of dulled basal and lateral margins on the points in the study collection raises two questions concerning the method and rationale for this attribute. First, why are the basal concavities frequently dulled if the purpose of margin dulling is simply to prevent cutting the haft wrapping? The basal margin, which is generally indented, would rest against the bottom of the groove prepared in the foreshaft and would not contact any haft wrapping. Second, experimental studies have shown that a few strokes with a hammerstone or abrader, or a light "buffeting" (Young and Bonnichsen 1985:98) with a billet or hammerstone are all that is necessary to sufficiently dull acute angles and prevent cutting of any soft wrapping. Furthermore, several experiments have shown that sinew or fiber wrapping is quite resilient to damage from a freshly flaked tool margin if lateral movement of the point in the haft is prevented (Woods 1987). With this in mind, it seems odd that the lateral and basal margins of nearly every point in the study collection reveal a dulling process that went well beyond what would be necessary to protect even the softest of wrappings. The lateral and basal margins on every Clovis point and half the Folsom points in this collection are dulled, but neither "abraded" nor "ground" is an accurate term to describe the tool margins.

Visual examination of the margins reveals that they are extremely light-reflective in direct lighting. Low-power microscopy indicates that the nature of the dulling is more accurately defined as a "polish" (see also Frison and Bradley 1980:31). This choice of terminology is derived from numerous use-wear studies where the nature of polish has been defined (Ahler 1979; Del Bene 1979; Del Bene and Shelley 1979; Diamond 1979; Kamminga 1979; Odell 1979).

Although there is much disagreement over the mechanics of polishing, most agree that a polished surface is identifiable by a high luster and smooth surface topography (Del Bene 1979:171). Using this criterion, we can determine that many of the specimens from southern Idaho have polished lateral and basal margins (Figure 4). This can be easily contrasted to specimens whose margins are ground with coarse abrasives (Figure 5). It is possible that there were reasons for polishing tool margins other than the prevention of damage to the haft wrapping.

Polishing may have served to strengthen the projectile at the area where much bending stress was anticipated. In a recent study (Woods 1987), it was shown that the basal portion of a lanceolate form was subject to breakage from many forms of use-stress, especially bending stresses. A polished margin strengthens the projectile in that area by removing irregularities that would otherwise encourage fracture initiation. It is possible that basal concavities were nearly always polished, along with the lateral margins, in an effort to prevent fracture initiation at that area.

Preliminary replication experiments by the authors have shown that a bright polish can be created very easily using ocher as a polishing agent. The ocher can be used in a dry, powdered form or in suspension with saliva or water. Various materials have been used to polish a pre-ground margin, including leather, wood, and flat stone surfaces. If ocher is applied over an abrasive surface, such as a fine-grained quartzite, flint, or chert, and the margin is not pre-ground, abrasion and polish occur simultaneously but material attrition is slowed considerably. The time required to "polish" one tool margin seldom exceeds three minutes.

It is thus possible that ocher may have a functional as well as ritual purpose. It has already been established that ocher is commonly recovered at sites that are interpreted as workshops (Frison and Bradley 1980). Furthermore, low-power microscopic examination reveals that many of the fluted points from the study area retain traces of ocher in surface irregularities.

Although early experiments relied on ocher as a polishing agent, subsequent attempts have revealed that polished margins can be obtained without the use of ocher in approximately the same time as with ocher. Margins must first be abraded using quartizite, obsidian, or a microcrystalline material as the abrader. In most instances, the abrading stone can be made of the same material as the tool being ground.

With most stone-on-stone abrading, the friction at the point of contact results in a fine silica powder which acts as an efficient abrasive. After this preliminary abrading, polish can be obtained by adding a suspension agent such as water or saliva to the silica powder. Polish usually starts about one minute after moisture is added. After three or four additional minutes, the polish is well developed. The abrader stone upon which the margin was contacting shows distinctive wear traces, including grooving and/or polish.

It was noted that obsidian could not be used to polish obsidian. In this instance, dulling would occur, but a reflective surface could not be created. However, obsidian margins can be polished using ocher or an appropriate microcrystalline material.

Some of the specimens from southern Idaho retain evidence that indicates they were probably initially ground with an abrasive agent, then polished in a separate action. On these margins, the grinding appears to extend slightly further along the lateral margins than does the polish. The other fluted points that are "polished" show some variation in the polishing technique. Some were heavily abraded, then polished; some were polished without any prior abrasion. On others, the polish rounds the tool margin, suggesting the use of a yielding polishing pad. A few of the fluted points in this collection have a distinctively flat-polished surface, indicating a hard polishing surface.

Resharpening

Every fluted point examined reveals some degree of damage. Some breakage is attributable to manufacturing error, many specimens were apparently broken during use, and some reveal traces of postdepositional damage. Although 10 of the 28 fluted points are nearly complete, many reveal evidence that implies some amount of rejuvenation. Several fragmentary specimens also share attributes that suggest postdamage rejuvenation. This evidence is briefly addressed in an effort to document the hypothesis that the makers of these fluted points were willing to invest time to salvage a damaged tool, an effort that attests to the value of these items to their users.

The most extensive evidence of rejuvenation is suggested on an obsidian Folsom point from the Wasden site (Figure 3h), which reveals that at one time in the point's use-life it was broken, inverted, and resharpened, with the proximal end becoming the new distal end. The point was then broken again at the new distal end and resharpened while still secured in the haft. It should be noted that an alternative explanation is possible. In some replication experiments, channel flakes have been successfully removed from alternate ends of the preform. Evidence for this procedure is apparent on several of the Lindenmeier specimens (Jeff Flenniken, personal communication 1988). This possibility could eliminate one portion of the use-sequence suggested above. It would not discount the other evidence for resharpening and reuse as noted.

Butler has also noted evidence of reworking a damaged Folsom point (Figure 3j). He suggests that this point was broken, then reused as a graver or narrow scraping bit (Butler 1980:12). An additional Folsom specimen from the study collection reveals that it was resharpened to the extent of almost obliterating the channel-flake scars (Figure 3r). This assumes that channel flakes were removed after final shaping of the original tool form.

Clovis points were also resharpened. Flake-scar patterns as well as attributes evident at the distal termination of the margin dulling suggest that a recently

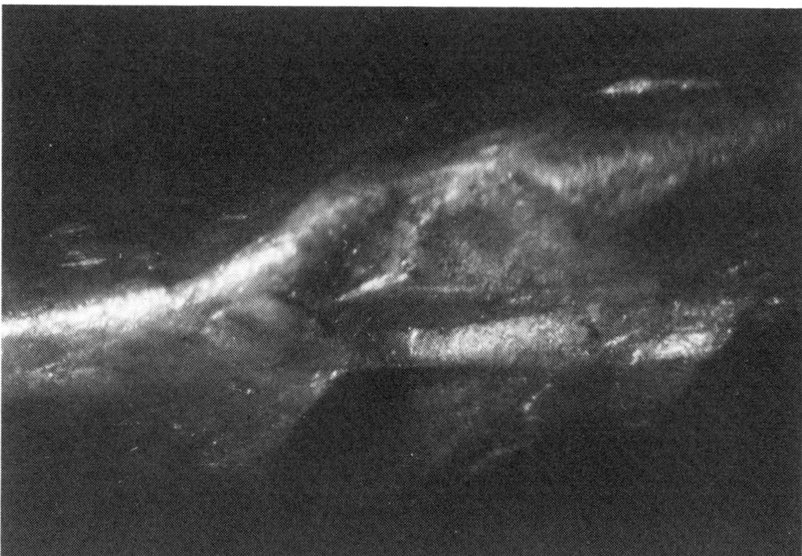

Figure 4. Micrograph (10X) of dulled and polished margin on Clovis point from Ellis, Idaho (Figure 2b).

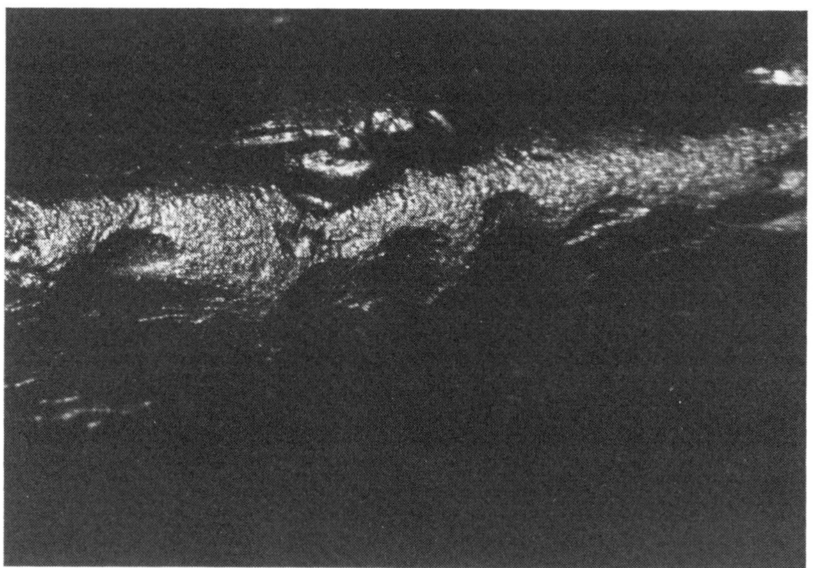

Figure 5. Micrograph (10X) of dulled basal margin on Folsom point from Gifford Hot Springs, Idaho (Figure 2c).

recovered specimen from the Bruneau Desert (Druss and Druss 1986) was apparently resharpened while the point was still secured in the haft (Figure 3a). The evidence for this resharpening includes an abrupt change in the tool outline at the termination of the margin polish, a difference in the proximal and distal flaking patterns, and the presence of pressure flakes that invade the channel-flake scar. Although "invasive" flakes alone do not indicate resharpening, none of the invasive flakes extend onto the channel-flake scar in the area where the wrapping would have prevented access to the tool margins during resharpening.

The resharpening of damaged points while they were still held in the haft suggests that the shaft/projectile juncture was of reliable enough design to allow significant damage to the distal end of the projectile without damage to the adhesion of the two projectile elements. The fact that some points were resharpened at all indicates the relative value of these products to their users and suggests that fluted points were part of a reliable design system (Bleed 1986).

Thermal Alteration

Many of the fluted materials from southern Idaho retain attributes that strongly imply the use of heat treatment. Two bifaces from the Simon site have distinctive potlid fractures and all the Simon specimens have the lustrous surface that is often used as an identifying feature of heat-treated materials. The best documentation of this process, however, is evident on a Clovis point from Crystal Springs, which is made of dark brown chalcedony (Figure 2g). Due to the presence of an associated macroblade of exactly the same material (Murphey 1985), it is quite certain that the projectile was thermally altered. The macroblade retains all the characteristics of an unaltered microcrystalline material, whereas the projectile exhibits a greasy luster that normally indicates thermal alteration (Crabtree and Butler 1964; Purdy 1974).

SUMMARY

This paper briefly reviews the technological diversity of fluted points from the Snake River and adjacent drainages in southern Idaho. Initial comparison reveals that the fluted points assembled for this study possess a wide range of attribute variation. This variation was surprising, considering the relatively small size of the Snake River Plain.

Although it may be premature to use a technological feature like basal-margin treatment to define similarities or differences between fluted points, it is quite interesting to note the wide range of morphological and technological variation evident on fluted points from a relatively restricted geographical area, such as the Snake River Plain of Idaho. Most comparisons of fluted-point materials have involved generalized comparisons of materials from extensive geographical areas. Inter-regional comparisons are not often addressed and remain an important variable in the reconstruction of Clovis and Folsom period culture history.

Considering the consistent design attribute of the basal portion of fluted points, it appears that the juncture between the point and whatever substance served as the foreshaft medium was extremely important. The cross-section morphology and margin dulling all serve to negate fracture initiation from use-related stresses. A polished margin is much stronger than a ground margin, as edge imperfections and striations from grinding are eliminated. An analogy would be the rounded and polished edges of plate glass used as table tops or deep-water submarine glass (Freiman 1988). The consistent V-shaped cross-section created by the basal thinning or fluting process allowed for maximum contact between the point and haft medium and an acute-angle juncture for equal impact-force distribution.

By the nature of its design, the hafting system for fluted points was very durable. This durability would extend the use-life of the system and would also help insure that when it failed, the point would not fracture inside the haft element. Experiments have shown that the preparation of the shaft/foreshaft element with stone tools is difficult and much more time-consuming than manufacture of the point. If point failure occurs within the haft juncture, damage to the shaft or foreshaft is very possible. The careful preparation of the basal portion of fluted points, including carefully engineered contact between the point and foreshaft, the elimination of lateral movement by use of a concave base, and margin dulling and polish all served to make fluted points part of a very durable hunting system.

ACKNOWLEDGMENTS

The authors wish to thank Mrs. Virginia Farmer, Kelly Sampson, Mr. and Mrs. W.D. Simon, and Vard and DiAnn Wright for the opportunity to examine specimens from their collections. We also wish to thank Kelley Murphey, Margaret Wyatt (Boise District BLM), Marion McDaniel (Challis National Forest), Richard Holmer (Idaho Museum of Natural History), and Mike Jacobs (Arizona State Museum) for their assistance in making specimens available for analysis. Dan Meatte (Idaho State University) provided bibliographic assistance, and the Herrett Museum, College of Southern Idaho, provided logistical support.

REFERENCES CITED

Ahler, S. A.

1979 Functional Analysis of Nonobsidian Chipped Stone Artifacts: Terms, Variables, and Quantification. In *Lithic Use-Wear Analysis*, edited by B. Hayden, pp. 301–328. Academic Press, New York.

Bleed, P.

1986 The Optimal Design of Hunting Weapons: Maintainability and Reliability. *American Antiquity* 51:737–747.

Bonnichsen, R.

1977 *Models for Deriving Cultural Information from Stone Tools.* Archaeological Survey of Canada Paper No. 60. Mercury Series. National Museum of Man, Ottawa.

Butler, B. R.

1963 An Early Man Site at Big Camas Prairie, Southcentral Idaho. *Tebiwa* 6:22–34.

1972 Folsom Points from the Upper Salmon River Valley. *Tebiwa* 15:72.

1980 A Folsom Point Multipurpose Tool from the Little Blackfoot River. *Idaho Archaeologist* 3(3):10–13.

Butler, B. R., and J. R. Fitzwater
1965 A Further Note on the Clovis Site at Big Camas Prairie, South-Central Idaho. *Tebiwa* 8:38–40.

Campbell, J. M.
1956 A Folsom Site in Idaho. *Plains Anthropologist* 6:1–2.

Crabtree, D. E.
1966 A Stoneworker's Approach to Analyzing and Replicating the Lindenmeier Folsom. *Tebiwa* 9:3–39.

Crabtree, D. E., and B. R. Butler
1964 Notes on Experiments in Flint Knapping: 1. Heat Treatments of Silica Minerals. *Tebiwa* 7:1–6.

Del Bene, T. A.
1979 Once Upon a Striation: Current Models. In *Lithic Use-Wear Analysis,* edited by B. Hayden, pp. 167–178. Academic Press, New York.

Del Bene, T. A., and P. H. Shelley
1979 Soapstone Modification and Its Effects on Lithic Implements. In *Lithic Use-Wear Analysis,* edited by B. Hayden, pp. 243–258. Academic Press, New York.

Diamond, G.
1979 The Nature of So-Called Polished Surfaces on Stone Artifacts. In *Lithic Use-Wear Analysis,* edited by B. Hayden, pp. 159–166. Academic Press, New York.

Druss, M., and C. Druss
1986 *Summary Report: Cultural Resources Inventory, West Clover Fire Rehab.* Submitted to Bureau of Land Management, Boise District Office.

Flenniken, J. J.
1978 Reevaluation of the Lindenmeier Folsom: A Replication Experiment in Lithic Technology. *American Antiquity* 43:473–480.

Freiman, S. A.
1988 Effects of Chemical Environments on Slow-Crack Growth in Glass and Ceramics. Manuscript in possession of the authors.

Frison, G. C., and B. A. Bradley
1980 *Folsom Tools and Technology at the Hanson Site, Wyoming.* University of New Mexico Press, Albuquerque.

Gryba, E. M.
1988 A Stone Age Pressure Method of Folsom Fluting. *Plains Anthropologist* 33:53–66.

Gruhn, R.
1961 *The Archaeology of Wilson Butte Cave, South-Central Idaho.* Occasional Papers of the Idaho State College Museum No. 6. Pocatello.

Huntley, J. L.
1985 A Clovis Fluted Projectile Point from Southwest Idaho. *Idaho Archaeologist* 8(1):13–14.

Irwin, H. T.
1968 *The Itama: Early Late-Pleistocene Inhabitants of the Plains of the United States and Canada and the American Southwest.* Ph.D. dissertation, Department of Anthropology, Harvard University.

Kamminga, J.
1979 The Nature of Use-Polish and Abrasive Smoothing on Stone Tools. In *Lithic Use-Wear Analysis,* edited by B. Hayden, pp. 143–158. Academic Press, New York.

Lahren, L.
1969 Wilsall Excavations: An Exercise in Frustration. *Proceedings of the Montana Academy of Science* 29:147–150.

Miller, S. J.
1982 The Archaeology and Geology of an Extinct Megafauna/Fluted-Point Association at Owl Cave, the Wasden Site, Idaho: A Preliminary Report. In *Peopling of the New World,* edited by J. E. Ericson, R. E. Taylor, and R. Berger, pp. 81–95. Ballena Press, Los Altos.

Miller, S. J., and W. Dort, Jr.
1978 Early Man at Owl Cave: Current Investigations at the Wasden Site, Eastern Snake River Plain, Idaho. In *Early Man in America from a Circum-Pacific Perspective,* edited by A. L. Bryan, pp. 129–139. Occasional Papers No. 1. Department of Anthropology, University of Alberta, Edmonton.

Moe, J. M.
1982 A Folsom Point from the Owyhee Mountains of Southwestern Idaho. *Idaho Archaeologist* 6(1 & 2):45–46.

Murphey, K.
1985 Early Man at Crystal Springs. Paper presented at the 12th Annual Meeting of the Idaho Archaeological Society, Boise, Idaho.

Odell, G. H.
1979 A New Improved System for the Retrieval of Functional Information from Microscopic Observations of Chipped Stone Tools. In *Lithic*

Use-Wear Analysis, edited by B. Hayden, pp. 329–344. Academic Press, New York.

Pavesic, M. G.
1985 Cache Blades and Turkey-Tails: Piecing Together the Western Idaho Burial Complex. In *Stone Tool Analysis: Essays in Honor of Don E. Crabtree,* edited by M. G. Plew, J. C. Woods, and M. G. Pavesic, pp. 55–89. University of New Mexico Press, Albuquerque.

Peterson, N. H.
1988 A Clovis Point from Long Valley, Idaho. *Idaho Archaeologist* 10(2):41–42.

Potter, S. R., and D. D. Aageson
1974 A Clovis Fluted Point from the Nez Perce Country. *Tebiwa* 17:92–93.

Purdy, B. A.
1974 Investigations Concerning the Thermal Alteration of Silica Minerals: An Archaeological Approach. *Tebiwa* 17:37–66.

Sadek-Kooros, H.
1966 *Jaguar Cave: An Early Man Site in the Beaverhead Mountains of Idaho.* Unpublished Ph.D. dissertation, Department of Anthropology, Harvard University, Cambridge.

Sappington, R. L.
1981a A Progress Report on the Obsidian and Virtophyre Sourcing Project. *Idaho Archaeologist* 4(4):4–17.
1981b Additional Obsidian and Vitrophyre Source Descriptions from Idaho and Adjacent Areas. *Idaho Archaeologist* 5(1):4–7.

Swanson, E. H.
1961 Folsom Man in Idaho. *Idaho Yesterdays* 5(1):26–30.
1962 Early Cultures in Northwestern America. *American Antiquity* 28:151–158.
1966 Cultural Relations Between Two Plains. *Archaeology in Montana* 7(2):1–2.

Swanson, E. H., and A. L. Bryan
1964 *Birch Creek Papers No. 1. An Archaeological Reconnaissance in the Birch Creek Valley of Eastern Idaho.* Occasional Papers of the Idaho State University Museum No. 14. Pocatello.

Titmus, G. L.
1985 The Timmerman Hill Folsom. *Idaho Archaeologist* 8(2):37–38.
1987 Clovis and Folsom in Idaho: Where, How, and Why. Paper presented at the 1987 Idaho Archaeological Society Conference, Boise.
1988 The Blue Lakes Clovis. *Idaho Archaeologist* 10(2):39–40. Boise.

Titmus, G. L., and J. C. Woods
1988 The Evidence for the Paleo-Indian Occupation in Southern Idaho. Paper presented at the 1988 Great Basin Anthropological Conference, Park City.

Woods, J. C.
1987 *Manufacturing and Use Damage on Pressure-Flaked Stone Tools.* Unpublished master's thesis, Department of Sociology, Anthropology, and Social Work, Idaho State University, Pocatello.

Woods, J. C., and G. L. Titmus
1985 A Review of the Simon Clovis Collection. *Idaho Archaeologist* 8(1):3–8.

Wormington, H. M.
1957 *Ancient Man in North America.* Denver Museum of Natural History Popular Series No. 4. Denver.

Young, D. E., and R. Bonnichsen
1985 Cognition, Behavior, and Material Culture. In *Stone Tool Analysis: Essays in Honor of Don E. Crabtree,* edited by M. G. Plew, J. C. Woods, and M. G. Pavesic, pp. 91–131. University of New Mexico Press, Albuquerque.

The Goshen Paleoindian Complex: New Data for Paleoindian Research

GEORGE C. FRISON
Department of Anthropology
University of Wyoming
Laramie, WY 82071

The Goshen Paleoindian cultural complex was first recognized at the Hell Gap site (48G0305) in Goshen County, southeastern Wyoming, in the early 1960s. Interest was short-lived due to a lack of supporting data. However, this changed in 1985 with results of investigations at the Mill Iron site (24CT30) in Carter County, southeastern Montana, which produced in situ evidence of diagnostic projectile points closely similar to those from Hell Gap. Accelerator radiocarbon dates from Mill Iron average over 11,000 years in age.

Goshen, as it appeared at the Hell Gap site, was first thought to be a Clovis variant and later, a separate complex. The evidence is still insufficient to resolve the problem. Two mammoth rib fragments from Mill Iron, one of which is a tool or weapon haft, do not unequivocally establish the presence of mammoth there at that time, but suggest they were there not long before. Goshen is manifest by a well-developed pressure-flaking technology that could have been a direct precursor of Folsom. Many Goshen-type projectile points are also similar to those of the Plainview type common to the southern Plains and have been mistakenly identified as such. A bison bone bed at the Mill Iron site containing parts of at least 30 animals apparently killed in the late fall or early winter suggests that Goshen represents early Paleoindian groups whose subsistence strategies were similar to both Folsom and Agate Basin.

THE GOSHEN PALEOINDIAN COMPLEX: NEW DATA FOR PALEOINDIAN RESEARCH

The Hell Gap site (48G0305) is located in southeastern Wyoming along the valley of an intermittent stream on the eastern side of the Hartville Uplift (Figure 1). The latter is a minor north-south trending landform about 56 by 40 km, with a maximum topographic relief of about 245 m above the surrounding plains. The Spanish Diggings (Dorsey 1900; Saul 1969), which produce an excellent grade of quartzite, are located on the northwestern side of the Hartville Uplift, while the central part of the Uplift produces large quantities of excellent chert. Both resources were utilized extensively and undoubtedly contributed to the apparent popularity of the area in Paleoindian times. Along with this was the protection from the elements and the strategic location afforded by the Hell Gap site with regard to the movements of large animals, particularly bison.

The Hell Gap site was excavated during the late 1950s and early 1960s, and provided a useful chronology of Paleoindian cultural complexes on the northwestern Plains based on stratigraphy, radiocarbon dates, and diagnostic artifacts (Irwin-Williams et al. 1973). The site is in Goshen County, Wyoming, and the oldest component recognized at the site was named Goshen, followed in sequence by the Folsom, Midland, Agate Basin, Hell Gap, Alberta, Cody, and Frederic cultural complexes. Goshen was first described as a variant of Clovis (see Irwin 1968); later (Irwin-Williams et al. 1973) it was interpreted as a separate cultural complex between Clovis and Folsom in time.

There were three main excavation localities at the Hell Gap site, but only Locality 1 (see Irwin Williams et al. 1973:Figure 1) produced material thought to be diagnostic of the Goshen Paleoindian complex. The Hell Gap Paleoindian chronology has been extremely useful for Paleoindian studies for over two decades. Although the assemblages of diagnostic items from the Paleoindian components were limited in size and contained many broken, reworked, incomplete, and unfinished specimens, the Hell Gap site assemblages contained a wealth of evidence of lithic manufacture technology for all of the Paleoindian cultural complexes. Unfortunately, these data remain largely unpublished.

The Goshen concept languished and has been mainly

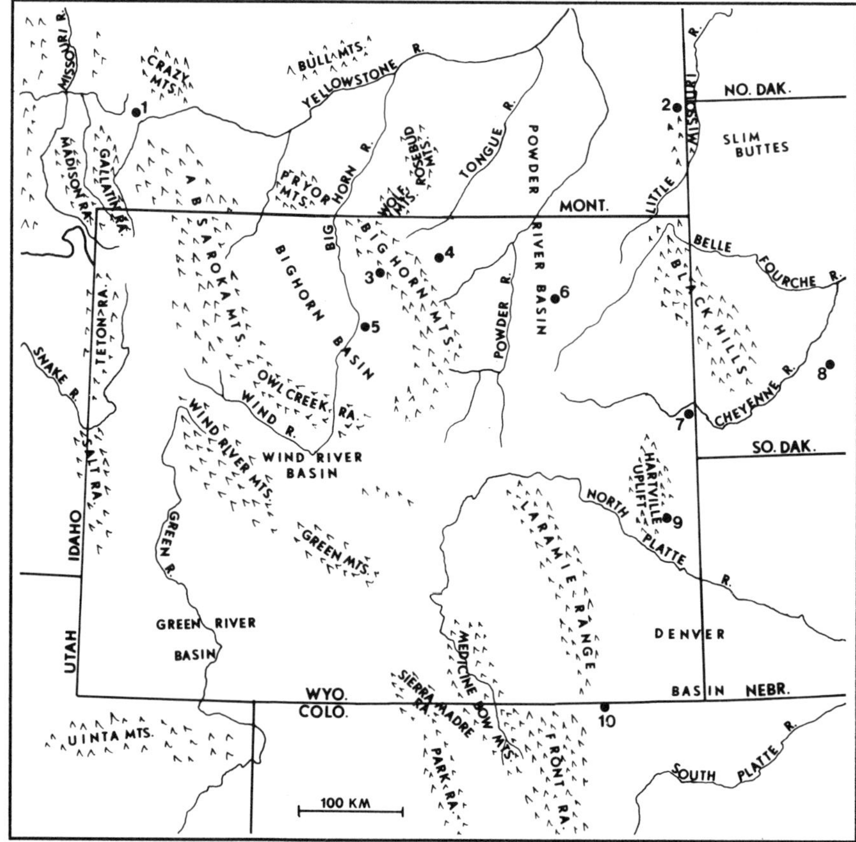

Figure 1. Map of Wyoming and adjacent areas in surrounding states showing archaeological sites containing Clovis, Goshen, and/or Folsom components: **1)** Anzick (24PA506); **2)** Mill Iron (24CT30); **3)** Hanson (48BH329); **4)** Kaufman Cave (48SH301); **5)** Colby (48WA302); **6)** Carter/Kerr-McGee (48CA12); **7)** Agate Basin (48NO201); **8)** Lange-Ferguson (39SH33); **9)** Hell Gap (48GO305); **10)** Lindenmeier (5LR13).

a subject of conjecture since the Hell Gap investigations, primarily because of a lack of further supporting evidence. However, it has been revived since 1985 as the result of the analysis of data recovered from the Mill Iron site (24CT30), located in southeastern Montana (Figure 1).

THE MILL IRON SITE (24CT30)

The Mill Iron site (24CT30) is located in the Humbolt Hills area of Carter County, southeastern Montana, in an area of low ridges and hills that comprise the northernmost extension of the Black Hills (Figure 1). It is in a valley drained by Humbolt Creek, a fourth-order meandering ephemeral stream that flows northwest into Box Elder Creek (Figure 2), which empties into the Little Missouri River. The Goshen cultural level is exposed around the edge of an isolated flat-topped butte approximately 20 m high and 35 m in diameter at the top (Figure 3). The top surface of the butte slopes approximately 4° to the southwest. There is also a narrow extension of the butte in this same direction (Figure 4).

The geology and soils study of the site and the area is still in a preliminary stage (Albanese 1987) and is only briefly summarized here. The tributaries to Humbolt Creek are incised into the Upper Cretaceous Hell Creek Formation (Miller et al. 1977), which is composed of interbedded claystones, lignitic shales, coals, and sandstone lenses. Four step-like Quaternary geomorphic surfaces are recognizable within the valley of Humbolt Creek. The top of the butte containing the Mill Iron site represents the highest and oldest of these surfaces. Other remnants of surfaces of the same age are present within the Humbolt Creek Valley (Figure 3). At one time the butte was connected to a larger and higher landform capped with a resistant sandstone that is located to the northeast. The distance separating the two is about 65 m. The time of the separation of the two landforms is not known, but the presence of a Late Archaic cultural level in a restricted area beneath the present surface on the east side of the butte suggests that the removal of deposits separating the two landforms has occurred within the last 2,000 to 2,500 years.

The Goshen component is buried 1.4 to 2 m beneath most of the top surface of the butte (Figure 5a). An undulating buried erosional surface lies 0.4 to 1.3 m above the preserved portion of the Goshen cultural level. The sediments below this erosional surface are composed of sandy colluvium and ephemeral stream gravels. Shallow first-order ephemeral stream channels within these deposits have removed portions of the cultural level and resulted in some disturbance in other parts. Three soils are present at the Mill Iron site. The upper two lie above the buried erosional surface, and the other lies beneath it. In descending order they consist of A–C, A–C, and A–BK horizons. The BK horizon of the lowest soil is superimposed on the Goshen cultural level and was formed prior to the formation of the overlying erosional surface, since the A horizon of that soil was removed over much of the site area by the erosional event that created the surface.

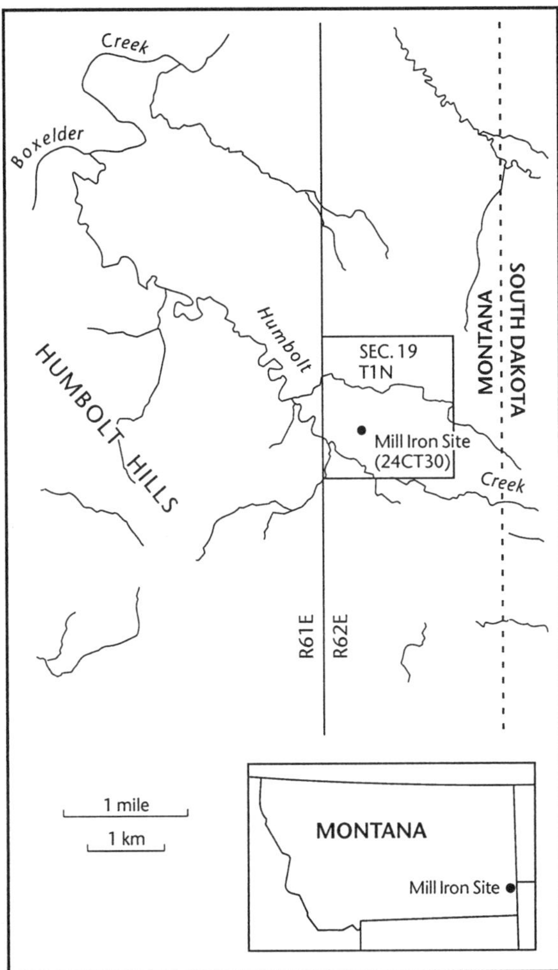

Figure 2. Location map of the Mill Iron site (24CT30).

Test excavations and backhoe trenches revealed an in situ Late Archaic level approximately 0.6 m below the surface of the east part of the butte. The geology is still largely unresolved in this part of the site. The Goshen level is seen in profile at both ends of the backhoe trench (Figure 6), but disappears in the vicinity of the Late Archaic level. On the other hand, the Late Archaic level has not as yet been identified in any of the deposits overlying the Goshen level. There are also marked soil differences here, below the Late Archaic level, that are not present elsewhere. At first the Late Archaic level was believed to be in the fill of an old channel, but this is no longer believed to be the case. Additional study of the deposits underlying the Late Archaic level is needed to resolve the problem.

The Goshen cultural level in the campsite/processing area (Figure 5a) is essentially parallel to the modern surface and is in place, although exposure for some time is indicated by deep weathering cracks and subsequent exfoliation of the top sides of bison bones (Figure 5b), compared with the nearly pristine bottom surfaces of the same bones. Some downslope movement of detached bone fragments, stone flakes, and artifacts has also occurred. This suggests a period or periods of exposure, but little, if any, actual postdepositional movement of the larger bones.

In 1987 a bison bone bed was discovered in the southwest extension of the butte (Figure 4). The southern edge of the bone bed had been undercut by an ephemeral stream, and part of the bone bed had slumped into the channel. Subsequent aggradation covered the channel deposits and slumped bone so that they were not visible on the steep slope of the butte (Figure 7). Stream flow in the buried channel was from northeast to southwest. Evidence of the old stream channel appeared in the wall profile (see Figure 4) connecting the two site areas.

Pollen studies at the site are incomplete, but preliminary indications are that for the past 11,000 years there have been no environmental changes severe enough to cause more than modification in quantity of the grassland plants established there at that time. The vegetation pattern in the Mill Iron site area since before Goshen times has been one of alternating shrub and grassland, with pine and juniper on the nearby hills (Scott-Cummings 1987).

ARCHAEOLOGICAL INVESTIGATIONS AT THE MILL IRON SITE

The presence of the site was realized when both bone and chipped-stone artifacts were observed eroding out of a cultural level exposed in profile on the steep,

Figure 3. The flat-topped butte (1) at the Mill Iron site **A)** looking east, and **B)** looking south. Land surface of the same age as the butte top (2,3).

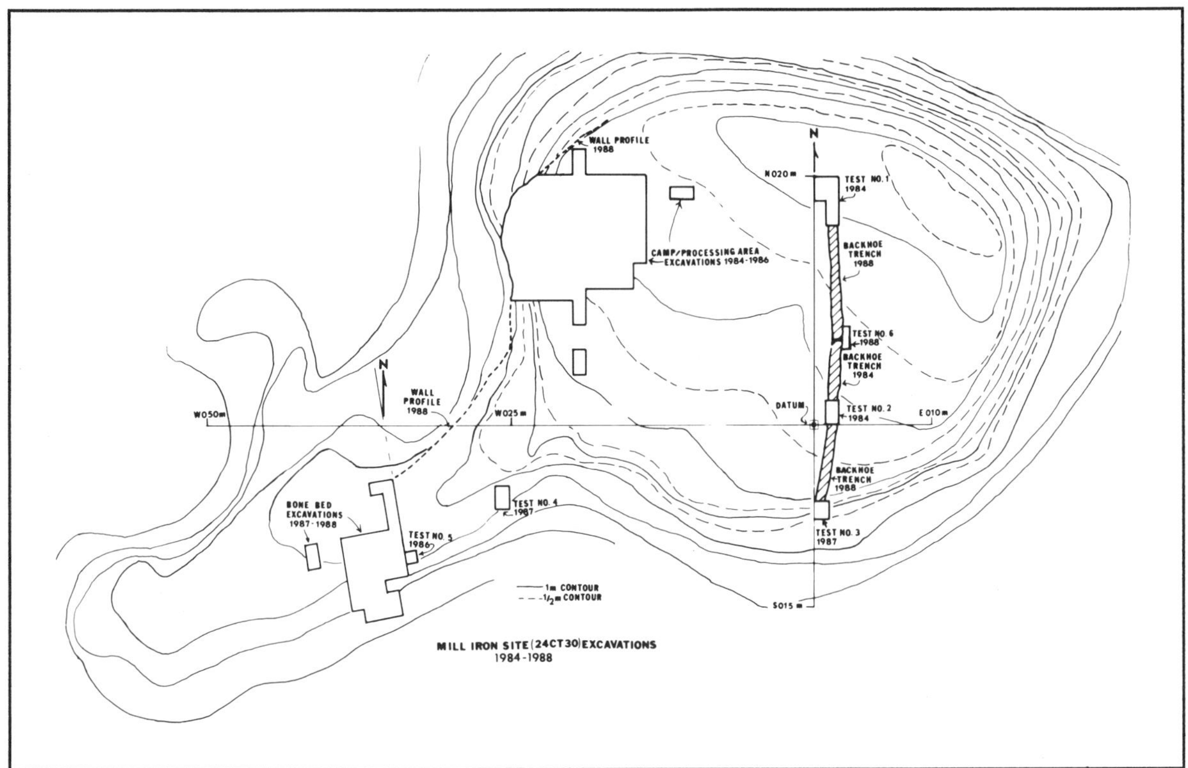

Figure 4. The Mill Iron site excavations from 1984 through 1988.

unvegetated slopes of the butte. Systematic testing of the site was initiated in 1984. Site excavations at Mill Iron from 1984 through 1986 (see Figure 4) were in an area that is arbitrarily designated a camp/meat-processing area. The cultural deposits here were essentially intact except for a period or periods of exposure indicated by the previously mentioned bone weathering. However, there is evidence of an ephemeral stream channel through the cultural level in a 1-by-4-m test trench directly east of the main excavation block (Figure 4).

Nine radiocarbon dates were obtained from the Mill Iron site: five from the camp/processing area and four from the bison bone bed (see Table 1). Numbers 1, 3, and 5 are very close in time and are from charcoal believed to have blown out of a surface hearth of cultural origin. The charcoal was recovered as fragments scattered on what at present is the leeward side of the feature. Two other dates (Numbers 2 and 4) are younger.

A similar situation resulted with the radiocarbon dates from the bison bone bed. Two dates (Numbers 7 and 8) are older and close in time to the older dates from the camp/processing area. Two other dates (Numbers 6 and 9) are younger and close in time to the younger dates from the camp/processing area.

There are several possible explanations: all speculative in nature with no way to present proof that any one is right. The three older dates from the camp/processing area and the two older ones from the bone bed could be correct dates for the site event or events. On the other hand, they could be from logs that were of considerable age when burned. The younger dates may also correctly date the site or they could have resulted from postoccupation burning, an event or events for which there is substantial evidence in the form of burned upper surfaces on both bone and stone materials (see, for example, Figure 12e) in the camp/processing area and on bone in the bone bed.

If the older dates are correct, the age of the Goshen complex would be contemporaneous with Clovis; if the more recent ones are correct, they would compare favorably with the older radiocarbon dates on Folsom. The radiocarbon dating of Goshen can not be resolved from existing data although it is important that this problem be pursued.

Faunal materials recovered to date in the camp/processing area include the partial skeletal remains of at least four bison, demonstrating evidence of butchering and processing. However, since only about 10% of the potential camp/processing area is excavated, and it is not known how much in addition has eroded away; the total number of bison originally present at this part of the site could have been considerably more.

Two mammoth rib fragments were recovered. A conical hole formed in the end of one (Figure 8) was first

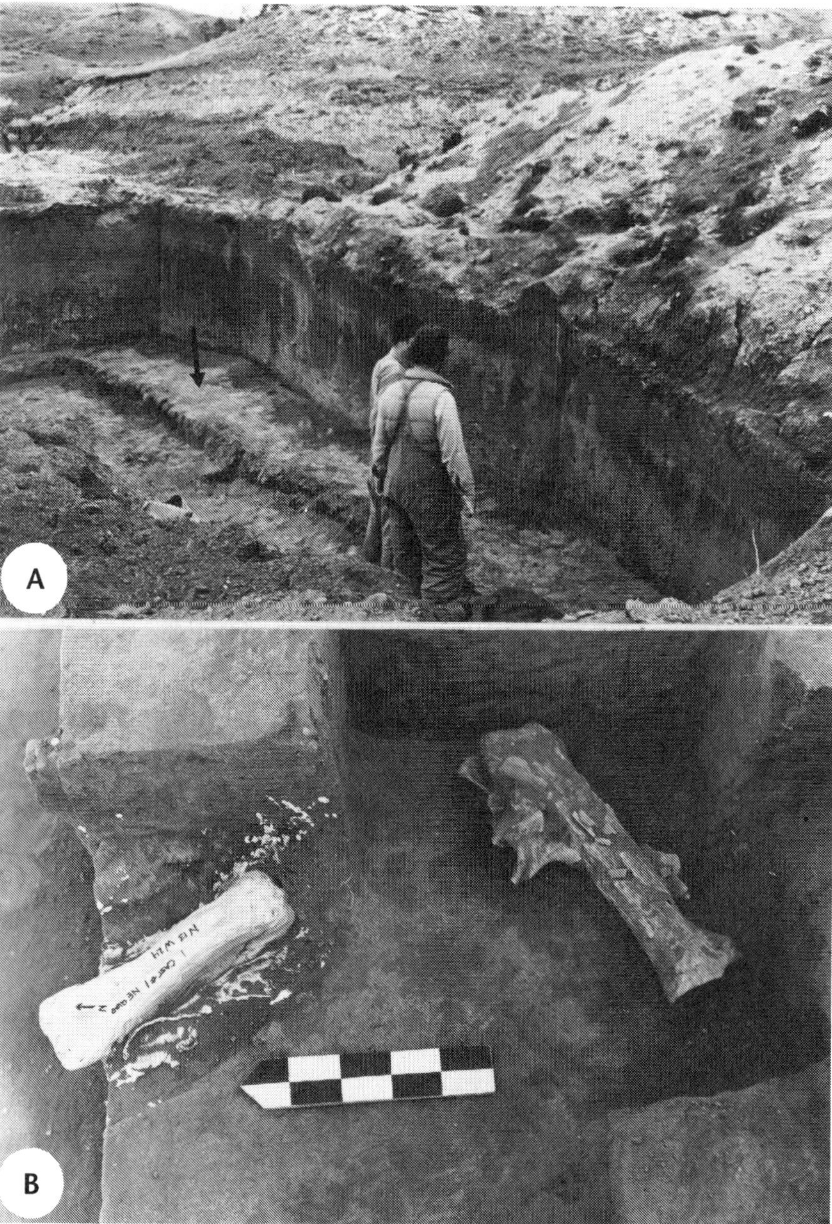

Figure 5. A) Profile (1.8 m in height) extending down to just above a strip of the intact Goshen cultural level (arrow), and **B)** a cast bison metatarsal and exposed radius in the camp/processing area at the Mill Iron site.

thought to have been done to manufacture some sort of tool haft. However, a conical hole does not function well in holding a tool during use, and it is now suggested that the specimen could be the distal end of a main shaft designed to hold a foreshaft as demonstrated (Figure 9). Unlike other bone recovered, the rib exhibits extensive gnawing. A concentration of residue from handling may have attracted rodents.

Projectile points comprise the only reliable diagnostics of the Goshen component, although the range of variation in shape and flaking technology is such that reliable identification of some specimens lacking good context may not be possible. The projectile-point asemblage from the camp/processing area (Figures 10, 11, and 12d,e) demonstrates a highly developed pressure technique of final biface reduction and blade edge retouch highly reminiscent of Folsom. A distinctive basal thinning is present that is easily distinguished from actual fluting as seen in either Clovis or Folsom points. Impact breaks are found on several specimens (Figures 10a, 11a,c,d, and 12d) and refitting of broken sections was possible with two specimens (Figures 10a and 11a). Rejuvenation of broken specimens was also accomplished; at least two (e.g., Figures 11b and 12d)

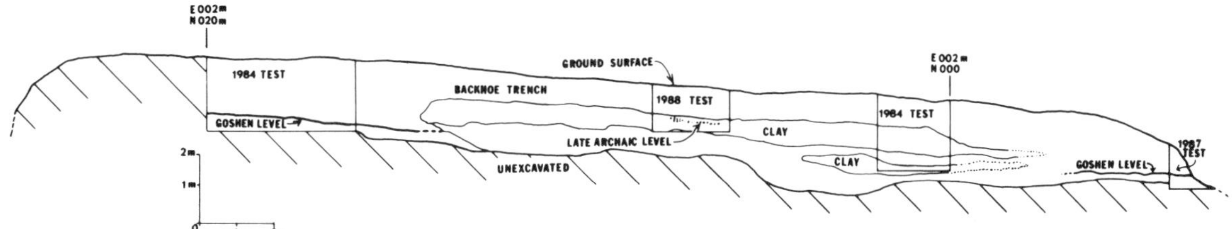

Figure 6. North-south profile at the Mill Iron site demonstrates the relationship between the Late Archaic and Goshen levels at the east part of the butte.

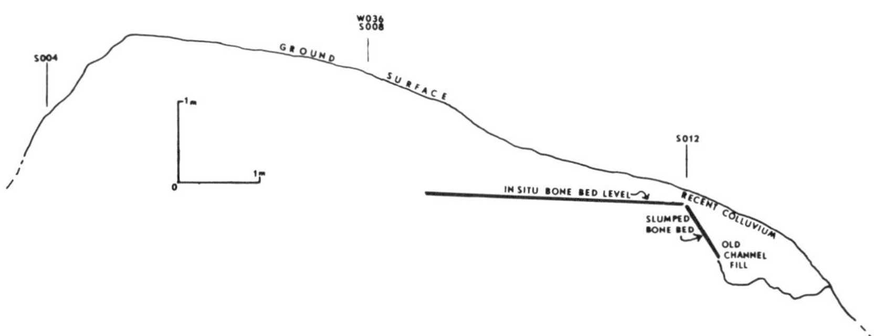

Figure 7. North-south profile at the Mill Iron site demonstrates the relationship between the bone bed and the ephemeral stream channel that undercut its south edge.

Figure 8. Worked and rodent-chewed section of mammoth rib from the camp/processing area at the Mill Iron site.

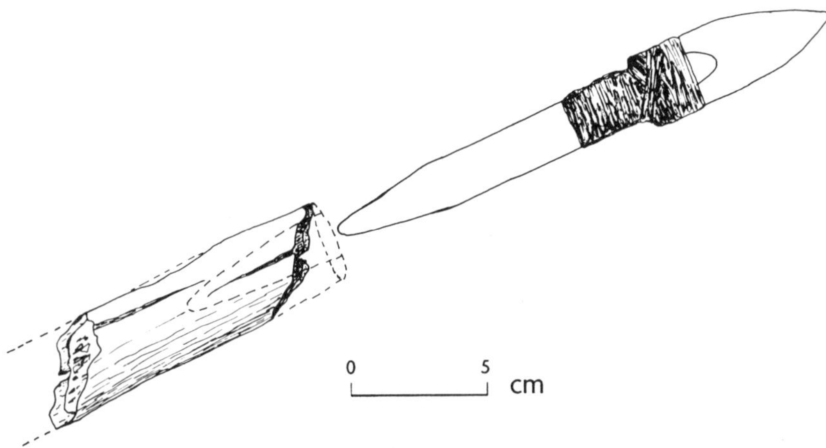

Figure 9. Suggested use of the worked mammoth rib fragment in Figure 8.

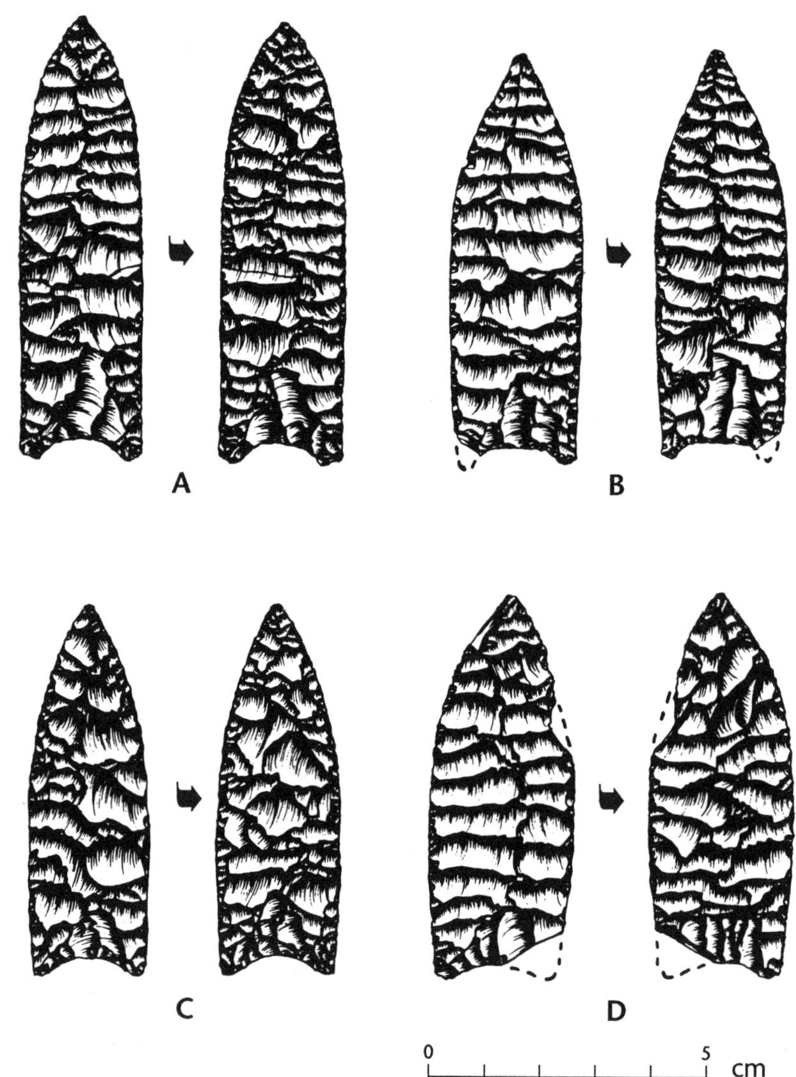

Figure 10. Projectile points from the Mill Iron site camp/processing area.

demonstrate bases formed by reworking snapped-off distal ends. The end of an impact flake scar is present on one (Figure 12d).

Goshen projectile points demonstrate all the necessary prerequisites of lithic technology needed to accomplish the final stage of fluting as manifested in Folsom assemblages. In addition, many flakes modified for tool use and other debitage demonstrate a technological stage of platform isolation, faceting, and grinding that is almost identical to platform preparation on Folsom channel flakes.

Several formal tool types are found in the camp/processing area assemblage. Nine end scrapers vary in size, but all demonstrate convex working edges ranging in width from 11 to 25.7 mm, with edge angles from 48 to 79°. Working edge wear varies from light abrasion to step fracturing. Noticeably lacking are end scrapers with projections or spurs at one or both corners of the working edge. Five specimens have a single notch on a side adjacent to the working edge. A transverse scraper (Figure 13a), a single-pronged graver (Figure 13e), a three-pronged graver (Figure 13c), backed blades (Figure 14a), and backed flakes (Figures 12b, 13b,d, and 14b,c) constitute the bulk of the tool assemblage. These tools demonstrate steep flaking on the backed edge, along with what appears to be dulling that is assumed to have been for protection of the hand during use. One specimen (Figure 13d) is a flat piece of silicified wood that separated along the contact between annual rings and was backed by a deliberate burin spall on one edge. A distal end of a

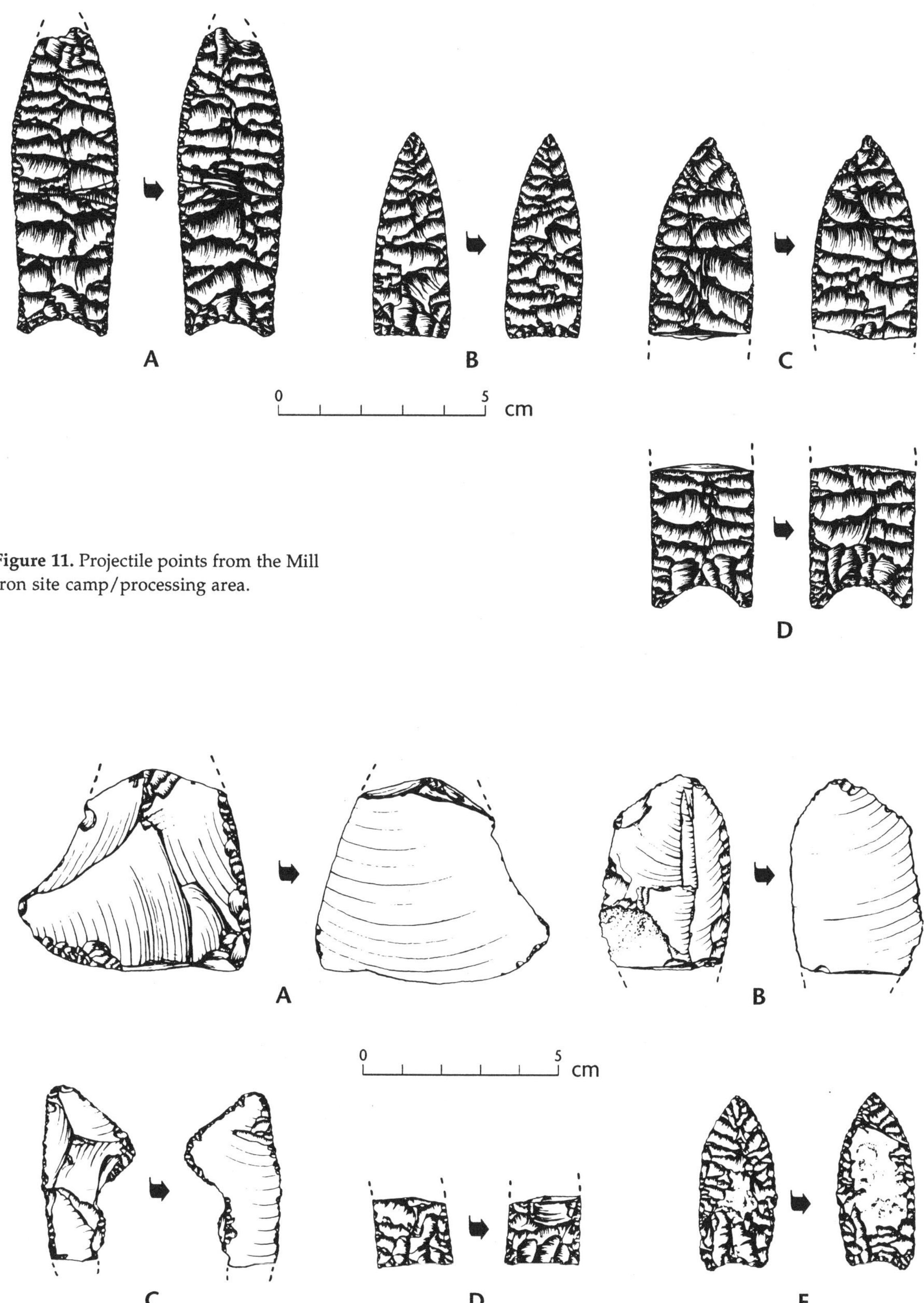

Figure 11. Projectile points from the Mill Iron site camp/processing area.

Figure 12. A–C) Retouched flake tools, and **D,E)** projectile points from the Mill Iron site camp/processing area.

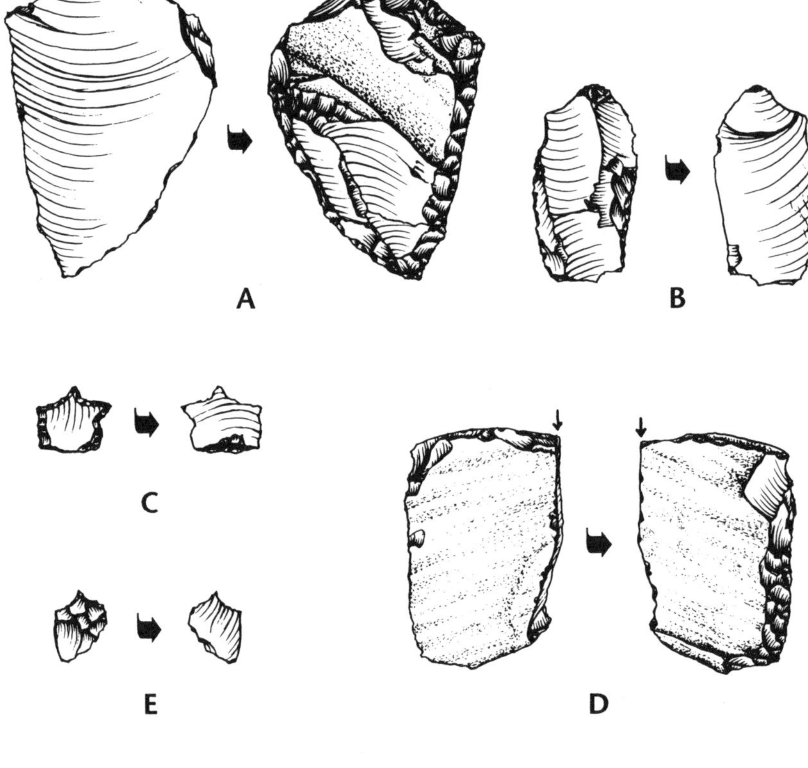

Figure 13. A) Transverse scraper; **B,D)** retouched flakes; **C)** three-pronged graver; and **E)** a single-prong graver from the Mill Iron site camp/processing area.

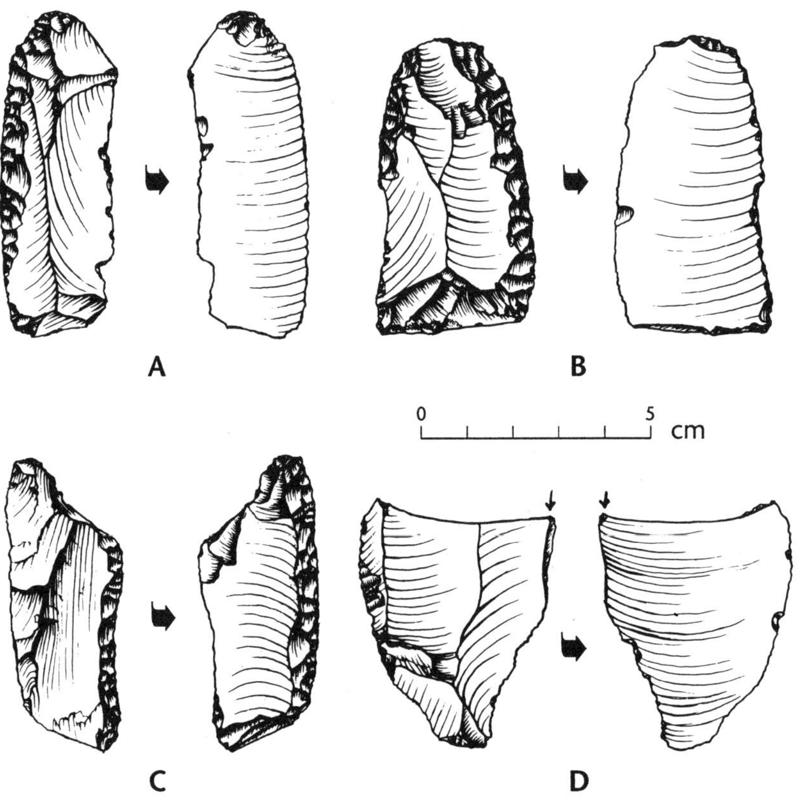

Figure 14. A) Blade tool, and **B–D)** retouched flake tools from the Mill Iron site camp/processing area.

wide, thin flake that was the result of a transverse bend break (Figure 14d) has either an accidental or deliberate burin spall removed from one side, and the resulting working edge is dulled from use. In addition, there are several flakes with either a unilateral (Figure 12a) or a bilateral retouch (Figure 12c) that demonstrate cutting and/or scraping use.

Two *pièces ésquillées* were recovered. One, with a heavily battered poll 15.9 mm thick, was split through the center as the result of a heavy blow, presumably during use. The two broken pieces (Figure 15a,b) were refitted (Figure 15c). The poll end was hit with a blow that removed a flake from it (Figure 15b2d) and simultaneously initiated the split from the opposite end so that two separate striking platforms merged into a single flake scar (Figure 15b2). As the tool split, one of the pieces apparently remained stationary while the other progressed forward and removed flakes from the center outward, as demonstrated on the conjoining faces of the split (Figure 15a2e). This would suggest that the tool was wedged tightly when it split and that one piece was forced to move against the other while both were held together under pressure. Subsequent to the split, one piece (Figure 15b) was utilized further, although it was reversed so that the original distal end became the poll end. Twelve use flakes (Figure 16a,b) were refitted, thus confirming the function of the tool. A distal end that broke during earlier use was also recovered (Figure 16c,d) and a use flake was refitted to it.

The Mill Iron site evidence does not support an argument that the *pièces ésquillées* from Mill Iron reflect a lithic reduction technique of bipolar flaking. Instead, these specimens resulted from use of selected flakes as tools, probably wedges. Certainly the flakes and resulting flake scars that refit to the tool are significantly different in morphology from flakes removed in normal reduction strategies observed in tool or weaponry manufacture. In addition, the raw materials used in manufacture were porcellanite and a relatively poor local material known as Tongue River Silicified Sediment (TRSS). Both materials are relatively soft, but withstand pounding use much better than the more brittle cherts and quartzites.

One large hammer or anvil stone (Figure 17) of TRSS was manufactured at the site, since most of its manufacture flakes were recovered and refitted. Its morphology suggests a tool that was partially buried during use, leaving exposed a protruding sharp edge over which bison long bones were broken. It would have functioned equally well as a hand-held hammerstone. One of the refitted flakes is the other *pièce ésquillée.* Included in the tool assemblage are two other hammerstones of the same TRSS material and another made of a locally obtained banded chert.

The only identifiable feature encountered at the site is a burned area of soil about 60 cm in diameter that is believed to have been a surface hearth. Charcoal fragments were recovered both east and west of the feature—the direction of prevailing winds at the present time. These charcoal fragments provided the three oldest accelerator dates in Table 1.

Stone-flaking materials include silicified wood and

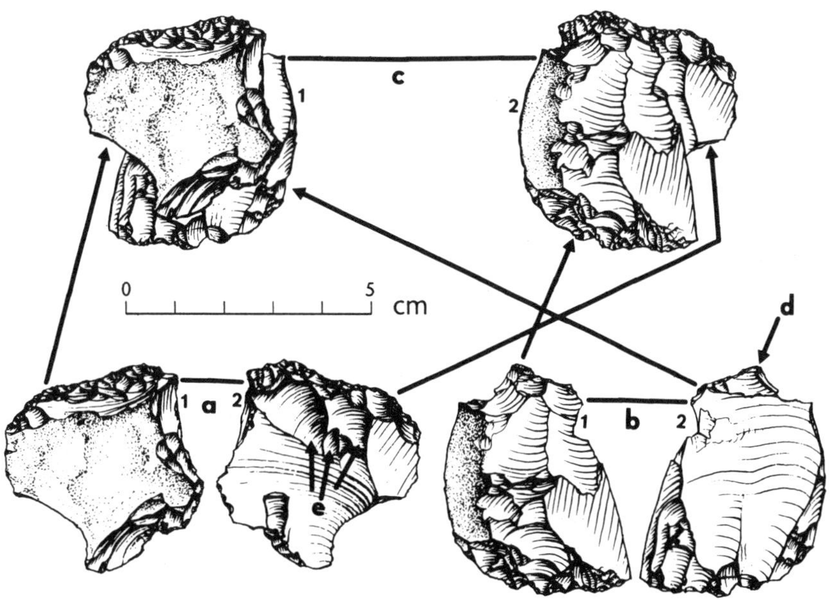

Figure 15. Refitted parts of a *pièce ésquillée* from the Mill Iron site camp/processing area.

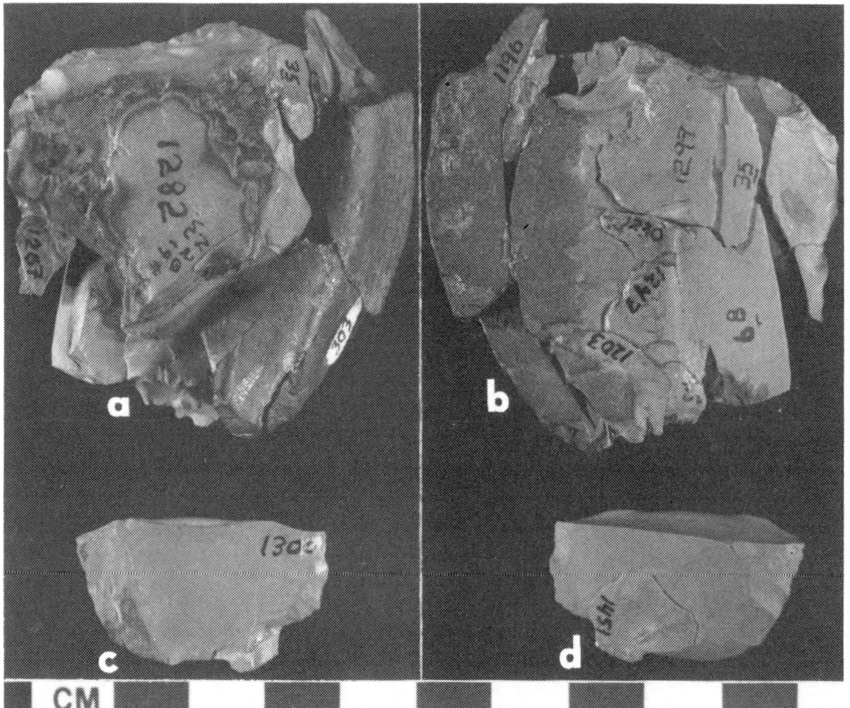

Figure 16. A,B) Use flakes refitted in the *pièce ésquillée* in Figure 15, and **C,D)** the distal end broken earlier from the same tool with one refitted use flake.

Figure 17. Chopper or anvil stone from the Mill Iron site camp/processing area.

TRSS, which are found in the immediate site area; porcellanite, which occurs widely within a few kilometers of the site; and a banded chert, which is presently known to occur only in volcanic ash deposits within a very restricted area locally. Several chert tools and projectile points are of material that most likely came from the Hartville Uplift, 400 km to the south in Wyoming. A small amount of chert and quartzite from unknown sources is also present.

THE MILL IRON SITE BONE BED

The bison bone bed (Figures 4 and 18) has been excavated and the bone curated, but it is in the early stages of analysis. A tentative minimum number of animals from the area investigated (approximately 18 m^2) is 30 bison, calculated on mandibles. Most of the bone was in an extremely deteriorated condition and impregnated with salts; recovery and stabilization required careful treatment to prevent total loss through powdering, crumbling, and exfoliating. This kind of deterioration resembles conditions in the camp/processing area, but is somewhat different in character. On the other hand, as is true of bones found in the camp/processing area, the undersides of bones from the bison bone bed are relatively well preserved. *Bison* is the only genus identified

Table 1. Accelerator Mass Spectrometer Dates from the Mill Iron Site.

NO.	LAB. NO.	DATE
	Camp/Processing Area	
1	Beta-13026	11,340 ± 120 yr B.P.
2	Beta-16178	11,010 ± 140 yr B.P.
3	Beta-16179	11,320 ± 130 yr B.P.
4	Beta-20110	10,760 ± 130 yr B.P.
5	Beta-20111	11,360 ± 130 yr B.P.
	Bison Bone Bed	
6	NZA-623	10,990 ± 170 yr B.P.
7	NZA-624	11,560 ± 920 yr B.P.
8	NZA625	11,570 ± 170 yr B.P.
9	AA-3669	10,770 ± 85 yr B.P.

to date from the bone bed. Tooth eruption on mandibles from animals up to five years of age indicates a time of death restricted to late fall or early winter (Todd and Rapson 1987). However, any detailed and meaningful discussion of the taphonomy or speciation of the remains from either the camp/processing area or the bone bed must await further analysis.

Eight complete projectile points and six fragments were recovered from the bone bed. With one exception (Figure 19c) they resemble quite closely those from the camp/processing area. One (Figure 20d) demonstrates reworking of the distal end; another (Figure 20b) is strongly suggestive of having been reworked from a midsection of a Clovis point; the distal end of what appears to be a flute is clearly visible near the base. This apparent flute could also be the end of an impact fracture, in which case the directions were reversed when the point was reworked and the original distal end became the base.

The single exception mentioned above (Figure 19c) demonstrates an unusual pressure-flaking technology, in which the distal end of the flakes dives toward the longitudinal midline of the projectile point, resulting in a relatively thin cross-section. The distal end is elongated but lacks a sharp point. It lacks also the basal thinning common to the other projectile points; basal thinning would have been difficult, considering the already extreme thinness of the specimen that resulted from the unique flaking technology.

Projectile-point fragments from the bone bed include impact flakes, a base, and several odd pieces. One of the latter was refitted to the base, and two others were refitted to form a midsection. The same raw stone-flaking materials are represented in the bone bed as in the camp/processing area.

Two refitted pieces of a biface tool (Figure 21) demonstrate well-developed percussion-flaked biface reduction, along with a pressure-flaked working edge retouch. There is a strong suggestion that these pieces were part of a large biface that was broken by a deliberate radial fracture to produce separate tools. Slight differences in working edge reduction and use-wear indicate the two pieces were used differently after they were separated. A smaller biface was reduced in size through continued unilateral, percussion, and pressure flake removals during resharpening procedures.

Three thin biface-reduction flakes recovered from the bone bed are similar to the tool shown in Figure 13b in that each has a backed edge and a sharp opposite cutting edge. Their small size would not preclude them from

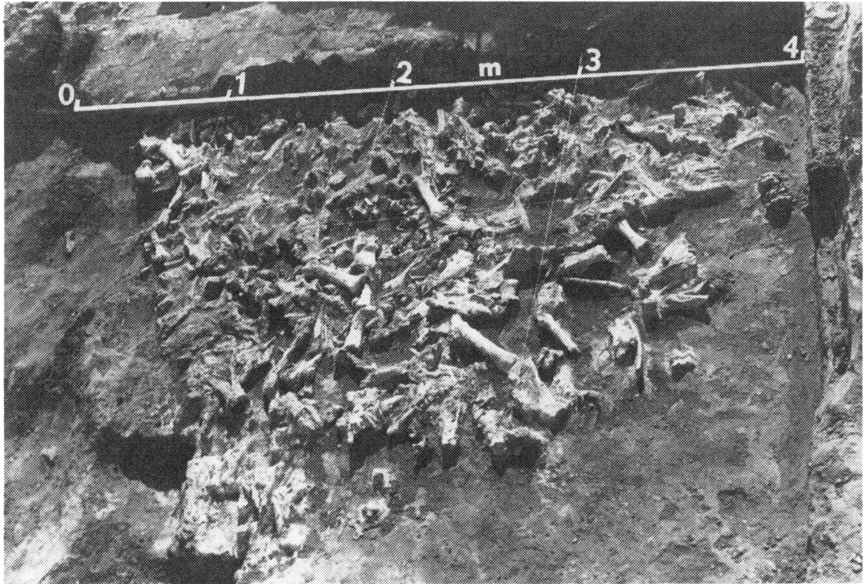

Figure 18. Part of the bison bone bed at the Mill Iron site looking west. Bones that slumped into an old ephemeral stream channel on the left side of the photograph (see Figure 7) are not yet exposed.

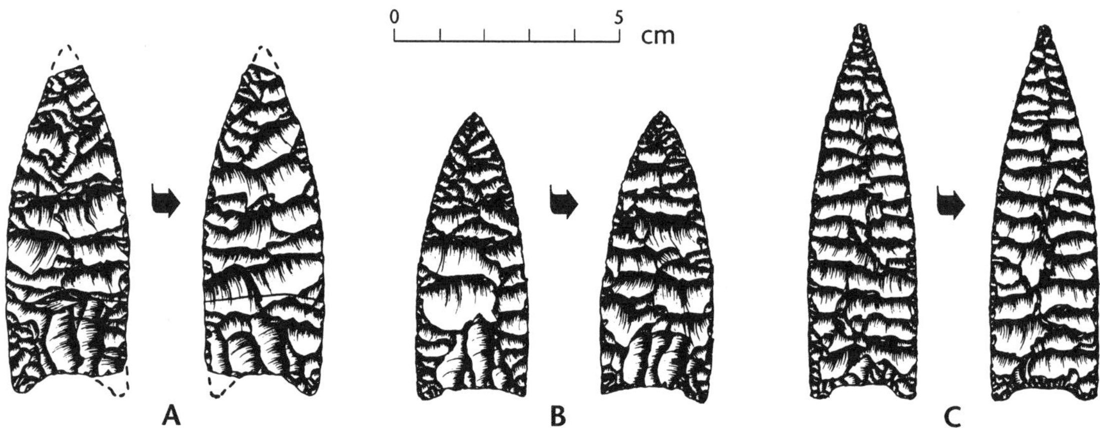

Figure 19. Goshen-type projectile points from **A)** Carter/Kerr-McGee site (48CA12); **B)** Kaufman Cave (48SH301); and **C)** the bone bed at the Mill Iron site.

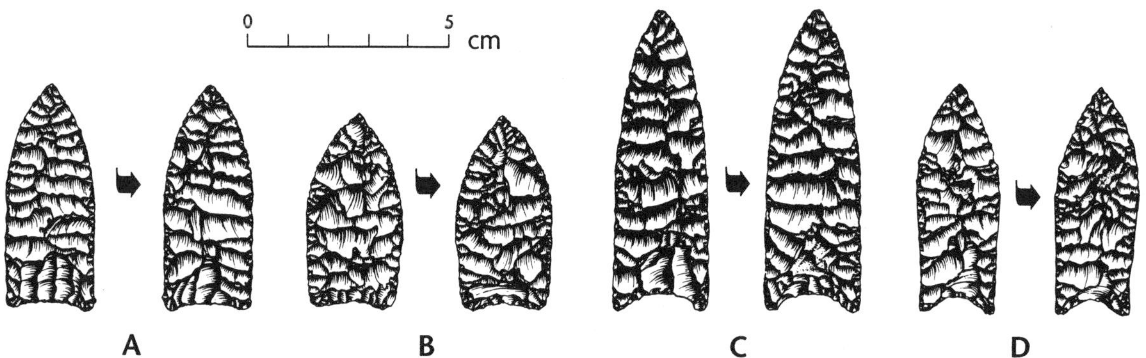

Figure 20. Projectile points from the Mill Iron site.

having been used as cutting tools to remove meat from carcasses. Experimental use of similar flakes confirms that they perform well in this context, analogous to removing the meat from a carcass using a backed razor blade.

IMPLICATIONS OF THE MILL IRON SITE FOR FURTHER PALEOINDIAN STUDIES

Too heavy a dependence on the Mill Iron site data to further define the Goshen cultural complex should probably be avoided at this stage in the investigations. Moreover, in addition to the Hell Gap site data there is other evidence to consider. The Carter/Kerr-McGee site near Gillette, Wyoming, (Frison 1984) is a stratified Paleoindian site in which the bottom in situ component lay stratigraphically below a Folsom level dated at 10,400 ± 600 yr B.P. (RL-917) and was consequently considered to be Clovis. With the new evidence now available on Goshen lithic technology, it appears that the projectile points (e.g., Figure 19a) should be classified as Goshen. The Carter/Kerr-McGee site was a remnant of an animal kill site located near the head of a steep-sided arroyo. Most of the site had been removed by erosion, but the small remnant of the in situ Goshen component contained camel and several other unidentified bone fragments.

Recently, the Powars II site (48PL330), a Paleoindian site located a short distance from the Hell Gap site, was brought to the attention of the writer. The site was actually exposed nearly a century ago on a steep talus slope by a cut for a railroad track. Although only a preliminary investigation has been done to date, the site is apparently a Paleoindian red pigment mine. Besides stone and bone quarrying tools, it has produced a melange of Paleoindian projectile points typologically identifiable as Clovis, Goshen, Folsom, unfluted Folsom

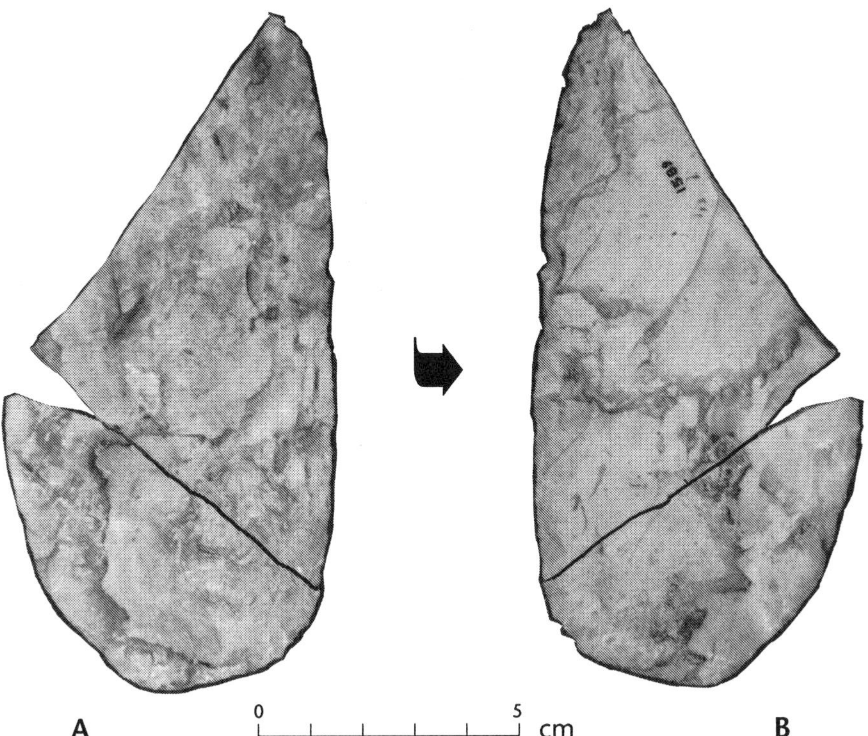

Figure 21. Biface from the Mill Iron site bone bed.

(Midland?), Hell Gap, probably Cody, and Frederick (see Irwin-Williams et al. 1973 for drawings of the diagnostics). However, the greatest number of projectile points (at least 12) are unmistakably Goshen.

The site deposits exposed on the talus slope, apparently spoil dirt from Paleoindian mining efforts, will require extensive investigation before a reliable stratigraphy can be established and the extent of the mining efforts known. However, the results should ultimately reveal more of the local Paleoindian chronology and cultural activities than are presently known. Certainly the presence of projectile points in this quarrying operation is different from the numerous nearby quarries for stone-flaking materials, where only quarrying tools are found. In the writer's opinion, it is not too far afield to suggest that ritual activity was strongly associated with red ocher procurement. Red ocher is a common occurrence in Paleoindian sites, as well as in the burial contexts of all prehistoric cultural periods.

The Bentzen-Kaufmann Cave site near Sheridan, Wyoming, was excavated in 1958 by the Sheridan Chapter of the Wyoming Archaeological Society (Grey 1962, 1963). An unmistakable Goshen projectile point (Figure 19b) was recovered there under a rock fall in association with part of a mammoth scapula. Unfortunately, there is no good description or understanding of the surrounding matrix, and there is no date on this cultural level. In addition to Goshen materials in actual archaeological sites, there are a number of surface finds of Goshen projectile points that have hitherto been misidentified as Plainview and relegated to a post-Folsom period.

This body of data allows alternative ideas and thinking regarding the early Paleoindian period on the northwestern Plains. Although no Clovis material was found at Hell Gap, it may nonetheless be present there, since this is a large area that was only partially investigated. Two projectile points recovered recently from a site about 2 km south of Hell Gap along the same drainage are classic Clovis. Surface finds of similar classic Clovis materials regularly occur in the Hartville Uplift and surrounding areas of southeastern Wyoming, northeastern Colorado, and western Nebraska. These finds raise two possibilities; either Clovis and Goshen were separate in time, or Goshen respresents Clovis groups that developed a highly sophisticated pressure-flaking technology at an early date.

Sites in this general area have yielded what might be interpreted as at least one and possibly two known Clovis variants besides Goshen. The Sheaman site in the Agate Basin locality (Frison and Stanford 1982) produced one projectile point and a cylindrical-shaped ivory point with a tapered base morphologically similar to bone specimens from Clovis contexts at Blackwater Draw in New Mexico (Hester 1972:117) and the Anzick site in Montana (Lahren and Bonnichsen 1974). Upon closer examination, what was interpreted as fluting on the complete Sheaman site projectile point (Frison and Stanford 1982:153) is not too dissimilar from the basal thinning found on Goshen points. The point also demonstrates a good deal of final pressure thinning, more than is ordinarily found on the so-called classic Clovis. The specimen could easily be regarded typologically and technologically as intermediate between Clovis and Goshen. The Sheaman site also produced a large debitage assemblage, from which Bradley (1982:203–208) described one of the few known detailed accounts of Paleoindian lithic reduction technology from actual site data. This description may, in reality, apply to Goshen rather than Clovis, or it may eventually prove to be equally applicable to both.

The Colby Mammoth Kill site, located in north-central Wyoming (Frison and Todd 1986), produced four projectile points that seem to be a morphological variant of Clovis, but demonstrate an unmistakable Clovis projectile-point manufacture technology. Because only bone radiocarbon dates were obtained, the chronological position of the site is open to question, since many bone dates from other sites in the area have been unsatisfactory.

Considering once more the Hell Gap site, the small sample of projectile points from there labeled Goshen are remarkably similar to points from Mill Iron, lower-level Carter-Kerr/McGee, Bentzen-Kaufmann Cave, and the recently discovered Paleoindian pigment mine close to the Hell Gap site. Unfortunately, the one complete Goshen specimen from Hell Gap is missing and close observations could not be made. However, several flakes and flake and blade tools from the Hell Gap Goshen level demonstrate identically the same platform isolation, faceting, and grinding features as the ones from the Mill Iron site.

There are a number of specimens labeled Midland (unfluted Folsom points?) in the Hell Gap site assemblage. Stratigraphically, some of these are difficult to separate from the Folsom specimens. Other Folsom sites, such as Hanson (Frison and Bradley 1980), the Folsom components at Agate Basin (Frison and Stanford 1982), and Lindenmeier (Wilmsen and Roberts 1978), also confirm that not all Folsom projectile points were fluted. It is suggested here that it may have been the unfluted part of the Folsom assemblages that developed into Agate Basin in post-Folsom times.

To pursue another line of thought toward an understanding of a possible Folsom-to-Agate Basin transition, consider that many Folsom projectile-point preforms are relatively long and narrow. The Hell Gap site yielded Agate Basin projectile points in the later production stages, but only one in the final stage. One can start with a large Folsom preform and instead of preparing it for fluting, simply continue a transmedial flaking process to produce the lenticular cross-section diagnostic of the Agate Basin projectile point. Actually, many pre-fluting stages of Folsom preforms are remarkably similar to the penultimate production stages of Agate Basin projectile-point manufacture, as can be observed in the Hell Gap site assemblage. The final production stage produces the Agate Basin projectile-point form, represented by the one Hell Gap site specimen from the Agate Basin component and nearly the entire Agate Basin projectile-point assemblage at the Agate Basin site (see Frison and Stanford 1982).

Agate Basin developed into Hell Gap; in fact, the beginnings of the distinctive shouldering of Hell Gap projectile points can be seen in the relatively large Agate Basin projectile-point assemblage from the Agate Basin site (see, for example, Frison and Stanford 1982:Figure 2.52g). Only a few Hell Gap specimens were recovered at the Hell Gap site, and these were either incomplete, broken in manufacture, or reworked. In order to visually comprehend the variations of Hell Gap projectile points, one needs to go to large assemblages from bison kills, such as those from the Casper (Frison 1974) and Jones-Miller (Stanford 1978) sites.

CONCLUSIONS

The ideas and data in this paper are in a preliminary stage and presented mainly to stimulate further research. In a recent article, Haynes (1987) discusses ideas that might be pursued in reaching an understanding of the origins of Clovis. The Goshen cultural complex and the Mill Iron site assemblage, in particular, are mentioned as evidence that could eventually help to resolve this elusive problem in New World prehistory. However, the implication that the Goshen cultural complex as seen at the Mill Iron site might have been derived from something in North America older than Clovis is not supported by the present Mill Iron site data or by data from other Goshen contexts.

There is a large body of Paleoindian data (e.g., the Hell Gap site materials) that needs to be studied. New research is producing problems whose solution will require reinvestigation of Paleoindian sites such as Agate Basin, Hell Gap, and Lindenmeier. A carefully planned program of research and analysis promises to resolve some of the questions recognized in High Plains Paleoindian studies, as well as pointing out new questions.

Bone beds resulting from Paleoindian animal kills still constitute an area for significant data gathering and analysis. Each bone bed demonstrates great diversity with regard to composition and formation. It is not yet possible to conceptualize the amount and kind of cultural activity involved in bone bed formation. Consider, for example, some of the Paleoindian sites in the central and northwestern Plains, including Olsen-Chubbuck (Wheat 1972); Jones-Miller (Stanford 1978); Hudson-

Meng (Agenbroad 1978); Agate Basin (Folsom), Agate Basin (Agate Basin), Agate Basin (Hell Gap) (Frison and Stanford 1982); Casper (Frison 1974); Frasca (Fulgham and Stanford 1982); Carter/Kerr-McGee (Frison 1984); Jurgens (Wheat 1979); Colby (Frison and Todd 1986); Lange-Ferguson (Hannus 1983); and Horner (Frison and Todd 1987), to mention several that are best known. They share some common elements, but each is unique in terms of the amount and kinds of disarticulation and breakage from butchering and processing, the utilization of meat products, the amount of carnivore damage, the age and sex structure of the animals involved, seasonality of events, and landforms used in procurement. At this point, the Mill Iron site provides still another bison bone bed for study and analysis, and one of the oldest known in North America that resulted from cultural activity. Present indications are that it will be unique among other known Paleoindian cultural bone beds, opening the possibility for new interpretations of their true cultural meanings.

At the present time the data on Goshen are not sufficient to determine whether Henry Irwin was right in identifying Goshen as a Clovis variant, as he did in his dissertation (Irwin 1968), or whether it is a separate cultural complex between Clovis and Folsom (Irwin-Williams et al. 1973). Only further research can resolve the problem. From the evidence to date we do know that the knappers in the Goshen group or groups developed what is basically a Folsom-type, pressure-flaking, projectile-point preform-reduction technology. They experimented successfully with basal thinning and developed the technology of striking-platform preparation necessary to set the stage for the development of fluting as it is known and recognized in Folsom. If the Mill Iron site dates are correct, Goshen groups must have been contemporaneous with late Clovis. If so, they developed a highly sophisticated pressure-flaking technology quite early.

The presence of two mammoth bones at the Mill Iron site does not confirm the presence of mammoths at that time, but does suggest they were around not too long before. The suggestion that the one mammoth rib section was the end of a main shaft (Figure 9) was inspired after observing a similar item made of a whale rib on the distal end of a harpoon shaft designed to socket a foreshaft. This specimen is in an ethnographic collection of Siberian Eskimo artifacts in the Museum of Ethnology in Leningrad, USSR.

The similarity between Goshen and Folsom pressure-flaking technology as expressed in final form in projectile-point manufacture is sufficient to suggest that Goshen is a direct precursor of Folsom. The basal thinning present in Goshen is only a step away from the highly developed fluting that followed in Folsom. Whether fluting developed in response to functional needs or as an art form is open to question. The similarity of Goshen biface reduction, as demonstrated on the two specimens from Mill Iron (Figure 20), the one from the Sheaman site (Frison and Stanford 1982:Figure 2.91a), and on Clovis bifaces from the Anzick site (Bruce Bradley, personal communication), suggests a close relationship between Goshen and Clovis.

Folsom fluting apparently developed suddenly, rapidly spread over a wide area, and just as quickly died out. However, interpretation of the Hell Gap site data suggests a nonfluting technology was maintained during Folsom times that may have been a direct precursor of the Agate Basin projectile point. In fact, many Folsom projectile-point preforms at prefluting stages could easily be used to produce either a Folsom or an Agate Basin projectile point. Hell Gap projectile points developed directly out of the Agate Basin type.

If these observations can be better confirmed, it may very well have been that for approximately 1,500 years of early Paleoindian time there existed a well-developed stone-flaking technology that was expressed differently in both time and space by a number of innovations reflected mainly in projectile-point types representing a number of Paleoindian groups. These kinds of diachronic and synchronic changes in technology closely approximate the situation observed in the archaeological record, where there are many intermediate and indeterminate specimens that are difficult to place in any of the presently recognized discrete Paleoindian projectile-point type categories. This hypothesis is supported by stratigraphy, radiocarbon dates, and the technological study of several single- and multiple-component Paleoindian sites in a relatively restricted geographical area. Careful investigation of new sites is needed, along with the reinvestigation and reinterpretation of the data from sites investigated earlier, particularly the Hell Gap site, in order to meaningfully continue these avenues of Paleoindian research.

The Mill Iron site demonstrates the need to find and recognize deposits of the proper age in order to locate the in situ Paleoindian sites required to provide reliable stratigraphic and cultural data. It also identifies some of the geological processes that are continually depleting the finite and fragile Paleoindian data base and underscores the urgency to protect and judiciously allocate this data base for future research.

ACKNOWLEDGMENTS

Funds for the Mill Iron site investigations were provided by the Montana Bureau of Land Management, the National Geographic Society, and the National Science Foundation. Research facilities were provided by the University of Wyoming and the Office of the Wyoming State Archaeologist. The project would not have been possible without the help and support of the Miles City, Montana, Regional District of the Bureau of Land Management; Burt Williams, Montana State Archaeological Director for the Bureau of Land Management; and

Gerald Clark and Will Hubbell from the Miles City District.

Outside consultants on the project included John Albanese, Galen Burgett, Gerald Clark, Dave Fraley, Richard Earnst, William Eckerle, Russell Greaves, C. Vance Haynes, Eric Ingbar, Ruthann Knudson, Marcel Kornfeld, Lee Kreutzer, Marshall Lambert, Rhoda Lewis, Mark Miller, Jill Onken, Dave Rapson, Richard Reider, Linda Scott-Cummings, Carl Spath, Lawrence Todd, Bill Volk, Danny Walker, Burt Williams, William Woodcock, Sr., and George Zeimens.

Site workers include Kaoru Akoshima, Kyle Baber, Ray Baker, Mary Bloom, Elizabeth Cartwright, Cary Craig, B.J. Earle, June Frison, Sandy Hanson, Howard Haspel, Susan Hughes, Laura Jones, Allan Korell, Mary Lou Larson, William Latady, Dave McKee, John Lund, Glen Miller, Karen Miller, Russell Nelson, Sue Ryan, John Potter, Michael Sheehan, Michael Stafford, Dale Wedel, Linda Ward-Williams, and Jennifer Woodcock.

My sincere apologies to anyone I have overlooked.

REFERENCES CITED

Agenroad, L. D.
1978 *The Hudson-Meng Site: An Alberta Bison Kill in the Nebraska High Plains.* University Press of America, Washington, D.C.

Albanese, J. P.
1987 Geology of the Mill Iron Site (24CT30), Carter County, Montana. Paper presented at the 53rd Annual Meeting of the Society for American Archaeology, Phoenix.

Bradley, B. A.
1982 Flaked Stone Technology and Typology. In *The Agate Basin Site; A Record of the Paleoindian Occupation of the Northwestern Plains,* edited by G. C. Frison and D. J. Stanford, pp. 181–203. Academic Press, New York.

Dorsey, G. A.
1900 An Aboriginal Quartzite Quarry in Eastern Wyoming. *Field Columbian Museum Anthropological Series* 2(4):233–243.

Frison, G. C.
1974 *The Casper Site: A Hell Gap Bison Kill on the High Plains.* Academic Press, New York.
1984 The Carter/Kerr-McGee Paleoindian Site: Cultural Resource Management and Archaeological Research. *American Antiquity* 49:288–314.

Frison, G. C., and B. A. Bradley
1980 *Folsom Tools and Technology at the Hanson Site, Wyoming.* University of New Mexico Press, Albuquerque.

Frison, G. C., and D. J. Stanford
1982 *The Agate Basin Site: A Record of The Paleoindian Occupation Of the Northwestern High Plains.* Academic Press, New York.

Frison, G. C., and L. C. Todd
1986 *The Colby Mammoth Site: Taphonomy and Archaeology of a Clovis Kill in Northern Wyoming.* University of New Mexico Press, Albuquerque.
1987 *The Horner Site: The Type Site of the Cody Cultural Complex.* Academic Press, Orlando.

Fulgham, T., and D. J. Stanford
1982 The Fracsa Site: A Preliminary Report. *Southwestern Lore* 48:1–9.

Grey, D.
1962 The Bentzen-Kaufman Cave Site, 48SH301. *Plains Anthropologist* 7:237–245.
1963 Fossil Mammoth Bone from Kaufman Cave. *Plains Anthropologist* 8:53–54.

Hannus, L. A.
1983 *The Lange/Ferguson Site: An Event of Clovis Mammoth Butchery with the Associated Bone Tool Technology.* Unpublished Ph.D. dissertation, Department of Anthropology, University of Utah.

Haynes, C. V., Jr.
1987 Clovis Origin Update. *Kiva* 52:83–93.

Hester, J.J.
1972 *Blackwater Locality No. 1: A Stratified Early Man Site in Eastern New Mexico.* Fort Burgwin Research Center, Southern Methodist University, Dallas.

Irwin, H. T.
1968 *The Itama: Late Pleistocene Inhabitants of the Plains of the United States and Canada and the American Southwest.* Unpublished Ph.D. dissertation, Harvard University, Cambridge.

Iwrin-Williams, C., H. Irwin, G. Agogino, and C. V. Haynes, Jr.
1973 Hell Gap: Paleo-Indian Occupation on the High Plains. *Plains Anthropologist* 18:40–53.

Lahren, L. A., and R. Bonnichsen
1974 Bone Foreshafts from a Clovis Burial in Southwestern Montana. *Science* 186:147–150.

Miller, M. R., W. M. Bermel, R. N. Bergantino, J. L. Sonderegger, P. M. Norbeck, and S. A. Schmidt
1977 *Compilation of Hydrogeological Data for Southeastern Montana.* Montana Bureau of Mines and Geology, Open File Report HY 77-1.

Saul, J. M.
1969 Study of the Spanish Diggings, Aboriginal Flint

Quarries of Southeastern Wyoming. *National Geographic Society Research Reports, 1964 Projects,* pp. 183–199. Washington, D.C.

Scott-Cummings, L.
1987 *Pollen Analysis of Stratigraphic Deposits at the Mill Iron Site, Southeastern Montana.* Report prepared for the Bureau of Land Management District Office, Miles City, Montana.

Stanford, D. J.
1978 The Jones-Miller Site: An Example of Hell Gap Bison Procurement Strategy. In *Bison Procurement and Utilization: A Symposium,* edited by L. B. Davis and M. Wilson, pp. 90–97. Plains Anthropologist Memoir No. 14.

Todd, L. C., and D. J. Rapson
1987 Bonebed Analysis and Paleoindian Studies: The Mill Iron Site. Paper presented at the 53rd Annual Meeting of the Society for American Archaeology, Phoenix.

Wheat, J. B.
1972 *The Olson-Chubbuck Site: A Paleo-Indian Bison Kill.* Society for American Archaeology Memoir No. 26.

1979 *The Jurgens Site.* Plains Anthropologist Memoir No. 15.

Wilmsen, E. N., and F. H. H. Roberts
1978 *Lindenmeier 1934–1974: Concluding Report on Investigations.* Smithsonian Contributions to Anthropology No. 24. Washington, D.C.

Imperialists Without A State: The Cultural Dynamics of Early Paleoindian Colonization As Seen from the Great Lakes Region

PETER L. STORCK
Department of New World Archaeology
Royal Ontario Museum
Toronto, ON, Canada M5S 2C6

Three fluted-point complexes have been identified in Ontario: Gainey, Parkhill, and Crowfield. These are identified by differences in point typology and lithic technology, tool kit contents, and patterns of raw material use and site distribution. Geological evidence and typological comparisons with dated material elsewhere suggest that the three complexes represent a temporal succession beginning with the initial colonization of the region by Gainey complex peoples, a Clovis-related "culture."

The widely held view that a Clovis or Clovis-related "base culture" was transmitted by a colonizing population has recently been challenged. An alternative hypothesis proposes that the concept of the fluted biface spread by diffusion through existing populations, which then developed distinctive "production codes" in point manufacture by adapting indigenous technologies.

In examining the "diffusion hypothesis," this paper argues that the fluted point had ideational as well as technological significance and that this would have made it less susceptible to diffusion. Furthermore, other data indicate that fluted-point-making peoples everywhere shared the same basic cultural strategies, perceptions, values, and possibly beliefs. This reflects the spread of not one but several ideas. Because of the complexity of diffusion in this instance, it is scientifically more economical to accept as the mechanism of transmission a colonizing population that attempted to maintain a specific cultural identity.

INTRODUCTION

This paper has two objectives: (1) to present a brief overview of our current understanding of early Paleoindian (fluted point) complexes in Ontario; and (2) to summarize evidence which indicates that these complexes, and those throughout North America as a whole, were spread initially by a Clovis or Clovis-related colonizing population and later by descendent populations that attempted to maintain a particular cultural identity.

Early Paleoindian cultures are well represented in the Great Lakes region. This is especially true in southern Ontario, where, within the past 20 years, the discovery and excavation of a number of new sites have substantially increased our understanding of early Paleoindian technology, community/settlement patterns, and band movements.

There is evidence for at least three fluted-point complexes in southern Ontario: Gainey, Parkhill, and Crowfield (Deller 1982; Deller and Ellis 1988; Ellis 1984; Storck 1982). All are identified, in part, by single fluted-point types (Figure 1) that appear to be restricted to particular complexes.

The Gainey complex is identified by the Gainey point type (Figure 1a-c), both of which are named after a site in Michigan (Simons et al. 1983, 1984a, 1984b). The point type is characterized by parallel sides, a shallow base, and, most commonly, by single flute scars, which are often quite short. In southern Ontario, the Gainey complex is represented by eight and possibly as many as eleven sites (Deller and Ellis 1988; Storck 1979, 1988b). For technological and stylistic reasons, the Gainey point type is regarded as the earliest expression of fluted-point technology in the Great Lakes region, analogous, for example, to Clovis in the West and possibly Bull Brook in the East.

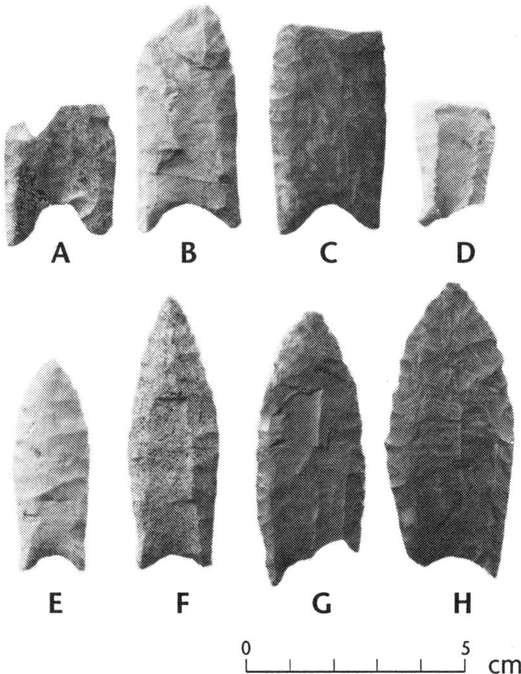

Figure 1. Selected fluted-point types from Ontario: **A–C)** Gainey type; **D–F)** Barnes type; **G** and **H)** Crowfield type.

The Parkhill complex is identified by the Barnes point type (Figure 1d–f) (Deller and Ellis 1982, 1988; Roosa 1977; Storck 1983; Wright and Roosa 1966). This point type is named after the site in Michigan where it was first identified (Wright and Roosa 1966); the complex itself is named after the Parkhill site in southern Ontario (Roosa 1977). The Barnes point type is a medium to small leaf-shaped point with a pronounced "waist" and single or occasionally multiple fluting that was conducted from a well-prepared, centrally located basal platform. For typological reasons the point type is regarded as closely related to Folsom in the West and Cumberland in the Southeast and midcontinent region (see, for example, Deller 1988). In southern Ontario, the Parkhill complex is represented by 11 and possibly as many as 20 sites (Deller and Ellis 1988; Storck 1982), two of which (the Parkhill and Fisher sites) are quite large. The Fisher site, for example, covers an area of approximately 55 acres and contains 19 artifact concentrations, which produced over 30,000 artifacts (Storck 1982, 1983; Storck et al. n.d.). Geological studies indicate that the site is situated adjacent to the former shoreline of a glacial lake, Lake Algonquin, and that one of the lowest-lying artifact concentrations (Area C-East), if occupied contemporaneously with the lake, would have been situated only a few meters from the edge of the lake (Nolin 1981; Nolin and Gwyn n.d.). The strong geological association of the Fisher site and the majority of other sites in the Parkhill complex with Lake Algonquin suggests that the complex may date between approximately 11,500 and 10,400 yr B.P., the geological estimate for the age of the Main stage of the lake (Eschman and Karrow 1985; Karrow et al. 1975) with which the sites are associated.

The Crowfield complex is represented by the Crowfield point type (Figure 1g-h) and is named after a site in southwestern Ontario (Deller and Ellis 1982, 1984, 1988). Crowfield points are very wide and thin and often exhibit multiple flute scars on both faces. In southern Ontario, the Crowfield complex is represented by only a few isolated surface finds and three or possibly four sites, all of which are quite small (Deller and Ellis 1988). Deller and Ellis (1988) infer that this is the youngest complex in the early Paleoindian occupational sequence, in part because the Crowfield point type most closely resembles the unfluted Holcombe point type, which they believe, on typological grounds, postdates 10,400 yr B.P.

In addition to point typology, the Gainey, Parkhill, and Crowfield complexes are also seen as differing in other important respects including: (1) raw material selection; (2) patterns of blank production for tool manufacture; (3) contents of the tool kit; and (4) patterns of site distribution (Deller 1988; Deller and Ells 1988; Ellis and Deller 1988). Geological evidence and typological comparisons with dated material elsewhere suggest that the Gainey complex is the earliest of the three complexes and Crowfield the latest. This and evidence that the three point types are part of a typological continuum suggest that the three complexes represent a temporal succession of related cultures broadly similar, in part, to that which has been documented in western North America on the basis of both stratigraphic and chronometric evidence. The sequence is presumed to begin with the Gainey complex, which is regarded as a Clovis-related occupation. This concept of a Clovis or Clovis-related "parent" culture followed by a succession of historically related cultures is implicit in much of the literature concerning early Paleoindian material in North America. Indeed, the widespread typological uniformities seen in fluted-point assemblages throughout the continent have been interpreted as indicating that they were derived from a single parent culture that was spread by a colonizing population (see, for example, Haynes 1964; Martin 1973; Morlan 1977; Mosimann and Martin 1975).

This notion has recently been questioned. In an attempt to illustrate the application of the cognitive approach in the study of stone tools, Young and Bonnichsen (1984) studied selected fluted points from Montana and Maine and concluded that they were made by different "production codes." They argue that this indicates that the concept of the fluted projectile point may have been spread, not by a single colonizing population, but by cross-cultural diffusion through several indigenous populations, which then produced their own variations using traditional technologies (see also Bonnichsen and Young 1980).

A comprehensive evaluation of this interpretation would have to consider several issues, such as: (1) the quality of the data interpreted as evidence for different "production codes" (for a discussion of questions surrounding the Maine artifacts see Spiess and Wilson 1987); (2) the advantages and limitations of the cognitive and other approaches in the study of material culture; (3) the theory and knowledge of diffusion as an agent of cultural transmission; (4) the strength of the evidence for pre-Clovis occupation(s) in North America; and, finally, (5) the ability of the "diffusion hypothesis" to explain not only differences but similarities among fluted-point assemblages across North America. The remainder of this paper will focus on this last issue: the validity of the diffusion hypothesis for explaining the distribution of the concept of the fluted biface and other widespread elements in early Paleoindian assemblages. I will attempt to show that this hypothesis is inadequate because it is based on only one aspect of material culture—the technology of projectile-point manufacture—and, secondly, because it fails to consider the underlying behavior and beliefs that shaped the material culture and gave it significance. As a result, the "diffusion hypothesis" underestimates the amount of diffusion that would be required to account for similarities in fluted-point assemblages across the continent and, therefore, ignores entirely the question of whether diffusion would have been a feasible agent of cultural transmission in this instance.

Young and Bonnichsen's interpretation raises a number of important questions. First, does the presence of regionally distinct production codes in fluted-point manufacture necessarily imply that the notion of the fluted biface was spread by diffusion? Somewhat related to this is the question of the function and significance of fluting. Although obviously an important part of weapon making, did the process of fluting also involve religious or other beliefs and, if so, would these also necessarily have been transmitted by diffusion? Finally, is there evidence that cultural strategies, perceptions, and values were also shared throughout the area of distribution of fluted-point assemblages? If so, is it likely that these too could have been transmitted by cross-cultural diffusion to a variety of peoples who previously had their own adaptations and beliefs?

The following discussion will be concerned primarily with the technological and cultural significance of the concept of fluting in projectile-point manufacture and with the implications that this may have with respect to the "migration" and "diffusion" hypotheses. The paper will conclude with a brief consideration of the possible underlying cultural significance of other aspects of early Paleoindian material culture and subsistence with respect to these two hypotheses.

THE FLUTED POINT: TECHNOLOGICAL AND IDEATIONAL SIGNIFICANCE

Level of Manufacturing Complexity

Replicative experiments and detailed technological studies of archaeological material have determined that the fluted point, whether Clovis, Folsom, or some other related form, is a very complex tool to make. In his study of the Lindenmeier Folsom, Crabtree (1966) identified a total of 35 factors that had to be considered in replicating a "classic" Folsom point. A large number of these have a direct influence on whether or not the fluting process will be successful and concern the technical requirements of thinning. Crabtree and other experimentalists do not claim to have identified all the steps involved or the exact methods that were used to manufacture the Lindenmeier Folsom. They have, however, documented the technological complexity of the manufacturing process and, therefore, the high level of technical knowledge and skill required of the prehistoric knapper.

Young and Bonnichsen (1984) propose that the fluted biface diffused across North America as a concept, not as a physical entity carried by a colonizing population, and that it was readily accepted because it afforded a dramatically improved method of hafting. They argue that the groups that adopted this concept developed their own distinctive biface/fluting technologies by modifying their pre-existing skills ("production codes") for tool manufacture. However, considering the complexity of biface production for fluting and the fluting process itself and, secondly, the magnitude of the technological discontinuity between Clovis (the earliest known fluted-point manifestation) and the as yet poorly documented pre-Clovis cultures, it is reasonable to ask whether the concept of a fluted biface could, in fact, have been diffused without the transfer of at least some of the skills required to produce that tool form.

In addition to documenting the existence of pre-Clovis populations, advocates of the diffusion hypothesis must demonstrate that the necessary skills pre-existed that would have permitted the concept of the fluted biface to have been adopted without technological assistance. It is necessary to go beyond this, however, and to ask whether the variation in fluted-point manufacture could not be attributed simply to human variation stemming from the same basic cultural pattern, rather than from different cultural traditions, particularly considering the wide geographic area and the substantial period of time over which fluted points were made. It is also necessary to ask whether the fluted point may have had ideational as well as technological and functional significance. Does it reflect the presence of underlying beliefs or values and, if so, would these have added to the complexity of the diffusion process? What also is the cultural context of the fluted projectile point in North American assemblages? Is it the only common element linking these assemblages, or, alternatively, does it appear to be part of an integrated complex of technology/ideas that would also have to be accounted for by diffusion if we accept this as the explanation for the spread of the concept of the fluted biface itself? These questions require a re-examination of ideas regarding the purpose of fluting and the context of the fluted point in early Paleoindian tool assemblages as a whole.

The Purpose of Fluting

It is generally believed that fluting was done in order to thin the spear point for hafting. The thinned point requires a less bulky haft, and the flute scars serve as a "slot" into which the shaft was "seated" to increase friction in the binding and thereby improve lateral stability. Frison and Stanford (1982) note that, although fluting may have facilitated hafting, there is no evidence that it was absolutely necessary, since many Folsom points, for example, were not fluted and yet were successfully used. They cite several other lines of evidence that suggest that the Folsom fluting process may have been guided by other than purely technological considerations. First, they argue, it was a wasteful process because of the high frequency of failure during the manufacturing process. Second, some fluted or partially fluted preforms were discarded during manufacture for no apparent technological reason, implying, perhaps, that they did not meet aesthetic or other nontechnological requirements. Finally, some points appear to have been fluted, but in fact were not, suggesting that the *appearance* alone may have served some purpose. These observations suggest to Frison and Stanford that the Folsom fluting process may have been in part an "art form" or may have had some "ritual" significance.

Although this suggestion is very provocative, the evidence is, unfortunately, largely ambiguous. For example, the fact that both poorly fluted and well-fluted preforms were occasionally not worked further into finished points could be explained, as Frison and Stanford suggest, because they failed to meet aesthetic or other nonfunctional requirements. Alternatively, however, these artifacts may simply have been lost, and it could be misleading to make an inference about how an artifact came to be deposited solely on the basis of how it *may* have been perceived by a prehistoric knapper.

The possible significance of points which were not actually fluted but which *appear* to have been fluted is similarly difficult to interpret. At first glance these artifacts might suggest that, since the "pseudo flutes" add nothing to the physical properties of the point, the mere *appearance* of fluting may have served some purpose. However, this interpretation is open to question because it presupposes how the artifact may have been thought of by the person who made and used it..

The interpretation that the fluting process was wasteful and was therefore conducted for non-technological reasons is based on three assumptions: first, that Folsom peoples had notions similar to ours about what constitutes wastefulness; second, that like us, they would discard a technology that was too expensive *unless* there were strong nontechnological reasons for continuing it; and third, that we have an accurate measure of the failure rate during the prehistoric fluting process.

Concerning the assumption about prehistoric concepts of wastefulness, the archaeological record does in fact indicate something about Folsom standards with respect to efficiency and conservation of resources in situations where raw material supply was not a limiting factor. Flenniken (1978) and others (Frison and Bradley 1980; Tunnell 1977) have shown that Folsom peoples attempted to reduce the time and effort invested in the manufacturing process prior to fluting in order to reduce loss in the event of unrecoverable failure. Folsom peoples also appear to have developed techniques for "recovering" and finishing preforms that were broken during the fluting process.

Having established, first, that fluting was not a functional necessity and, second, that Folsom peoples did, in fact, have concerns about the economical use of time and raw material, the pivotal question is whether the fluting process was wasteful enough to cause Folsom peoples to override their concerns for economy because of some underlying belief in the symbolic significance of fluting or the artifact itself.

Unfortunately, it may not be possible to determine just how efficient Folsom peoples were in fluted-point manufacture. As Crabtree (1966) and others have noted, the total number of points that were actually finished cannot be determined from the debris of point manufacture or from the total number of broken point bases that were carried back to the site for replacement. The success rates achieved by modern knappers are also difficult to interpret. First, modern-day success rates are highly variable, ranging from approximately 60 to 90 per-cent (Akerman and Fagan 1986; Flenniken 1978; Fox 1986; Sollberger 1985, 1986). Second, these tools are produced by highly skilled people who are focusing their efforts in a way that may rarely have been possible by Folsom knappers, and who are using techniques that cannot be demonstrated to be the same of those used by prehistoric knappers.

The fact remains, then, that we do not know how efficient Folsom and related peoples were in manufacturing fluted points. Without this information, it does not seem possible to determine whether the technical and material requirements of fluting were consistent with prehistoric standards of efficiency, or, alternatively, whether these requirements exceeded those standards and were reconciled by other values.

Approaching the problem from another perspective, there is evidence that the concept of fluting or the role of the fluted point in the society did, in fact, have cultural significance beyond the purely technological. This evidence is provided by the so-called "miniature point" (Figures 2b and 3). Miniature points were made from channel flakes or other flake types and shaped by unifacial or bifacial edge retouch that often left the center of the flake unmodified. The points were most often left unfluted but were occasionally unifacially fluted. On non-fluted artifacts produced by edge retouch, the unmodified center of the point often resembles a flute scar; for this reason these artifacts are often referred to as "pseudo fluted" points. In western North America miniature points have been reported from the Clovis component at Blackwater Draw Locality No. 1 in New Mexico (Haynes 1964), as well as from three Folsom complex sites: Adair-Steadman in Texas (Tunnell 1977), Elida in New Mexico (Hester 1962), and Lindenmeier in Colorado (Wilmsen and Roberts 1978). They are also present at eight sites in the East: the Fisher (Figures 2 and 3), Thedford II, and Parkhill sites in Ontario (Deller 1988; Deller and Ellis 1982; Roosa 1977; Storck et al. n.d.); Debert in Nova Scotia (MacDonald 1968); Vail in Maine (Gramly 1982); Templeton (6LF21) in Connecticut (Moeller 1980); Bull Brook in Massachusetts (Grimes 1979; Jordon 1960); and Williamson in Virginia (McCary 1951, 1975). Miniature points are also apparently

Figure 2. A) Full-size Barnes-type point, and **B)** miniature point from the Fisher site, Ontario.

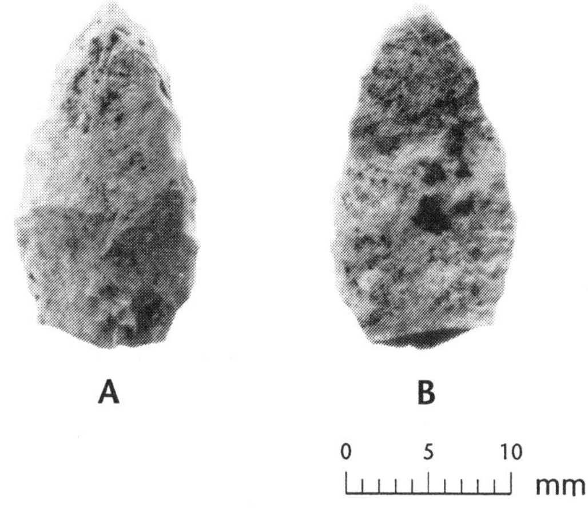

Figure 3. A) Obverse, and **B)** reverse faces of miniature point illustrated in Figure 2.

present in Alaska at Dry Creek II (Morlan and Cinq-Mars 1982) and in an assemblage from the Koyukuk River (Donald Clark, personal communication 1988). Despite these numerous occurrences, this potentially important artifact type has not received much attention; consequently, it is almost certainly even more widespread than the literature suggests.

Miniature points are quite different in most technological aspects from full-sized points. Because of this, most archaeologists assume that they were not functional and interpret them as toys, curiosities, facetious methods of demonstrating flint-knapping skill, practice pieces, and even as inclusions in medicine bundles (see, for example, Hester 1962; Moeller 1980). Regarding their possible ceremonial use, it is interesting to note the context of a miniature Hell Gap point that was excavated at the Jones-Miller bison-kill/processing site in eastern Colorado (Stanford 1978, 1979). The point was found near a 22-cm-diameter post mold located near the center of the bison butchering area. Other objects associated with the post mold include fragments of what is believed to be a bone flute and butchered canid remains. Stanford believes that the post mold may have supported a post analogous to the "medicine posts" of Historic period bison pounds and that the miniature point and other objects were offerings similar to those made by Historic hunt chiefs. Since there is evidence of cultural continuity from Hell Gap through Agate Basin to Folsom (Frison and Stanford 1982), it is conceivable that the ceremonial use of miniature points by Hell Gap people had earlier antecedents and that miniature "fluted" points were also used by early Paleoindian peoples in ceremonial activities.

Unfortunately, given the lack of contextual data for miniature "fluted" points, these interpretations must remain somewhat speculative. At the present time it is perhaps more important to emphasize the fact that, for the people who made them, there was clearly a strong physical and perceptual link between the miniature point and the full-sized point. This link is manifest in both the shape and appearance of the miniature point (particularly on those specimens with pseudo or actual flute scars), and, perhaps more importantly, in the fact that the artifact was frequently made on a channel flake, a manufacturing by-product of the full-sized point that was being mimicked. This is persuasive evidence that the production, use, and/or appearance of the full-sized point had a significance that extended beyond the actual role of that artifact in subsistence.

Additional evidence that fluted points had ideational as well as technological significance is indicated by the provision of unusually well-made and "scaled-up" points as part of a burial offering at the Anzick site in Montana (Canby 1979; Lahren and Bonnichsen 1974; Young and Bonnichsen 1984). The ceremonial importance of this type of artifact is further supported by the discovery of caches of fluted points (possibly including knives) that may have originally accompanied burials or were used in other special activities at the Thedford II site in Ontario (Deller and Ellis 1982), the Lamb site in New York (Gramly 1988), and at a recently discovered site in the state of Washington (Mehringer 1988). These "scaled-up," "larger-than-life" versions of normal "work-a-day" points or knives must have had special significance for their makers. While today we can only guess at their significance, it is more important for the purposes of this discussion to note that the practice of making "scaled-up" versions of working tools, illustrated by these three examples, occurs over a considerable geographic distance and in at least two distinct "cultures": Clovis (in New York and Washington) and Parkhill (in Ontario), the latter presumably a later cultural development from a Clovis "base." The critical observation is that, regardless of the idea that was expressed and regardless of the maker—whether an average knapper or a specialist—it was expressed in the same way by overstating the characteristics of the average-size tool.

Both miniature points and the "scaled-up" versions provide strong evidence that the artifact after which they were modeled had ideational significance, possibly in several different, albeit interrelated, realms of cultural behavior. Furthermore, whatever the significance, it was expressed similarly by widely separated groups of people. This action clearly indicates the presence of shared patterns of behavior and implies that the motivation/idea for that behavior may have been shared as well. As a result, the hypothesis that the concept of the fluted biface may have spread by diffusion cross-culturally must also consider the possibility that other ideas or kinds of behavior would have spread as well. This is critically important if one accepts the notion that the likelihood of cross-cultural diffusion having occurred decreases with the number and complexity of the ideas and behavioral patterns that would had to have been transmitted.

CULTURAL STRATEGIES, PERCEPTIONS, AND VALUES UNDERLYING EARLY PALEOINDIAN TOOL KITS

As mentioned earlier, the notion that the concept of the fluted biface may have diffused cross-culturally must take into account not only the technological and cultural significance of the artifact, but the possible significance of other continuities in early Paleoindian tool kits as well. These continuities indicate that the concept of the fluted biface was linked with other tool forms and perceptions about the requirements of a tool kit generally, as well as with ideas concerning the maintenance and resupply of that tool kit. Consequently, an explanation for the distribution of one element (in this case the concept of a fluted biface) must also explain the others.

In another paper (Storck 1988a), I discussed similarities among fluted-point assemblages across North America in flint-knapping craftsmanship, raw material selection for tool manufacture, and tool kit contents. I argued that similarities in these areas of cultural behavior reflected the presence of common underlying cultural strategies, perceptions, values, and possibly beliefs. If this is correct, the suggestion that the concept of the fluted point may have diffused across the continent must also account for the similarities in other aspects of material culture and the underlying behavior that it reflects. I argued in the publication previously cited that diffusion on this scale, implying not only the acceptance of a complex set of new and interrelated ideas but also the reshaping and even discarding of indigenous patterns of behavior by recipient groups, is much too extensive to be conceivable on either practical or theoretical grounds. Although this is perhaps an overstatement and an underestimation of the efficacy of diffusion, the fact remains that the simplest, and therefore scientifically preferred, explanation for the distribution of the fluted point and other continuities in early Paleoindian tool kits is that it was the result of colonization by an expanding population—indeed, as the title of this paper indicates, by "stateless imperialists." I argued that continuities in early Paleoindian tool kits across North America are underlain by a set of beliefs that rationalized and perpetuated a specific cultural identity, which the colonizing population consciously sought to maintain. In fact, this colonizing event may be the first example in the North American archaeological record of the spread of a belief system that, although reflected to us in what we perceive to be largely secular ways, may have contained within it a powerful driving force for expansion (perhaps, in part, "religious" or at least nonsecular in nature) beyond what was required for subsistence purposes. Surely we need to be cautious in this interpretation, but at the same time, we should also be alert for any evidence of underlying abstract beliefs and emotions that, together with the demands of the physical world, also shaped the archaeological record.

In looking for evidence of cultural strategies, perceptions, and possibly even beliefs in the archaeological record, I may appear to be advocating a normative approach, the very thing that Bonnichsen and Young, and others before them have cautioned against. Discussion of the strengths and weaknesses of various theoretical approaches to the study of archaeological material is a complex subject in its own right and cannot be considered here. I might say, however, that different approaches need not be thought of as mutually exclusive (for an interesting discussion of this viewpoint see Hodder 1986). Furthermore, since there are strong reasons for believing that behavior, and therefore material culture, is determined partly by normative or ideational concepts, we should develop rigorous and testable approaches to the study of this aspect of behavior. One useful approach—sometimes termed "contextual"—is the search for links or interrelationships between various aspects of material culture. In this paper I have argued that the fluted projectile point had significance that extended beyond subsistence and into an ideational realm of cultural behavior. I have proposed that this ideational realm may be discovered by looking for evidence of conflicting standards of behavior (such as maintaining a demanding fluting technology in the face of high standards of efficiency and raw material conservation) that could only have been reconciled ideologically. This ideational realm may also be revealed by evidence of one type of behavior influencing another (such as in the case of the relationship between full-size fluted points and miniature points). In a paper previously cited (Storck 1988a), I discussed possible links between flint-knapping craftsmanship, raw material selection, subsistence strategies, and tool kit contents among fluted-point assemblages across North America in an attempt to determine the organizational structure of the behavior underlying these assemblages and the normative forces that may have shaped them. In my view, these cultural norms must be taken into account by any hypothesis advocating diffusion as a mechanism of cultural transmission in the spread of material culture.

The questions raised by Young and Bonnichsen regarding the merits of the "single migration hypothesis" versus the "diffusion hypothesis" for "explaining" the spread of the fluted biface cannot be summarily dismissed, as two reviewers have recently suggested (Magne 1985; Shafer 1986). Rather, the controversy illustrates anew the need to determine whether there ever was, for example, a Clovis or a Folsom "culture" or, more broadly speaking, an early Paleoindian "culture" that transcended the multitude of fluted-point complexes across North America. In order to do this, it is necessary to go beyond an examination of similarities and differences in the technology of fluted-point manufacture and in the contents of associated tool assemblages, and to explore the complex interplay of cultural and ecological forces that gave them significance and meaning.

ACKNOWLEDGMENTS

A slightly different version of this paper was presented at the XII Congress of INQUA in Ottawa in 1987. I would like to thank Rob Bonnichsen, the organizer of the symposium in which this paper was given, for inviting me to participate and, later, for giving me the opportunity to publish a modified version of it in this book. This courtesy is especially appreciated and noteworthy, since we interpret part of the early Paleoindian record differently. I would also like to thank Andrew Stewart, who critically read several drafts of the paper, and three anonymous reviewers, who, being less familiar with what I meant to say as opposed to what I actually did say, prompted me to re-evaluate and clarify some of my thinking; I hope, from the reader's point of view, successfully.

My Ontario field work, which provided some of the data for this paper, was supported by the Royal Ontario Museum, and by research grants from The Canada Council and The Social Sciences and Humanities Research Council of Canada.

REFERENCES CITED

Akerman, K., and J. L. Fagan
1986 Fluting the Lindenmeier Folsom: A Simple and Economical Solution to the Problem, and Its Implication for Other Fluted Point Technologies. *Lithic Technology* 15:1–6.

Bonnichsen, R., and D. Young
1980 Early Technological Repertoires: Bone to Stone. In *The Ice-Free Corridor and Peopling of the New World,* edited by N. W. Rutter and C. E. Schweger, pp. 123–128. *Canadian Journal of Anthropology* 1.

Canby, T. Y.
1979 The Search for the First Americans. *National Geographic* 156:330–363.

Crabtree, D. E.
1966 A Stoneworker's Approach to Analyzing and Replicating the Lindenmeier Folsom. *Tebiwa* 9:3–39.

Deller, D. B.
1982 Some Paleo-Indian Cultures and Their Suggested Evolution in Southern Ontario and Michigan. Ms. in possession of author.
1988 *The Paleo-Indian Occupation of Southwestern Ontario: Distribution, Technology, and Social Organization.* Unpublished Ph.D. dissertation, Department of Anthropology, McGill University, Montreal.

Deller, D. B., and C. J. Ellis
1982 Archaeological Investigations at Thedford II, Crowfield and Other Paleo-Indian sites in Southwestern Ontario, 1981. Ms. in possession of authors.
1984 Crowfield: A Preliminary Report on a Probable Paleo-Indian Cremation in Southwestern Ontario. *Archaeology of Eastern North America* 12:41–71.
1988 Early Paleo-Indian Complexes in Southwestern Ontario. In *Late Pleistocene and Early Holocene Paleoecology of the Eastern Great Lakes Region,* edited by R. S. Laub, N. G. Miller, and D. W Steadman, pp. 251–263. Bulletin of the Buffalo Society of Natural Sciences No. 33. Buffalo.

Ellis, C. J.
1984 *Paleo-Indian Lithic Technological Structure and Organization in the Lower Great Lakes Area: A First Approximation.* Unpublished Ph.D. dissertation, Department of Archaeology, Simon Fraser University, Burnaby.

Ellis, C. J., and D. B. Deller
1988 Some Distinctive Paleo-Indian Tool Types from the Lower Great Lakes Region. *Midcontinental Journal of Archaeology* 13:111–158.

Eschman, D. F., and P. F. Karrow
1985 Huron Basin Glacial Lakes: A Review. In *Quaternary Evolution of the Great Lakes,* edited by P. F. Karrow and R. E. Calkin, pp. 79–93. Geological Association of Canada Special Paper No. 30. Ottawa.

Flenniken, J. J.
1978 Reevaluation of the Lindenmeier Folsom: A Replication Experiment in Lithic Technology. *American Antiquity* 43:473–480.

Fox, D. E.
1986 Discussion of the Akerman and Fagan Paper. *Lithic Technology* 15:8.

Frison, G. C., and B. A. Bradley
1980 *Folsom Tools and Technology at the Hanson Site, Wyoming.* University of New Mexico Press, Albuquerque.

Frison, G. C., and D. J. Stanford
1982 *The Agate Basin Site: A Record of the Paleo-Indian Occupation of the Northwestern High Plains.* Academic Press, New York.

Gramly, R. M.
1982 *The Vail Site: A Palaeo-Indian Encampment in Maine.* Bulletin of the Buffalo Society of Natural Sciences No. 30. Buffalo.
1988 Palaeo-Indian Sites South of Lake Ontario, Western and Central New York State. In *Late Pleistocene and Early Holocene Paleoecology of the Eastern Great Lakes Region,* edited by R. S. Laub, N. G. Miller, and D. W. Steadman, pp. 265–280. Bulletin of the Buffalo Society of Natural Sciences No. 33. Buffalo.

Grimes, J. R.
1979 A New Look at Bull Brook. *Anthropology* 3:109–130.

Haynes, C. V., Jr.
1964 Fluted Projectile Points: Their Age and Dispersion. *Science* 145:1408–1413.

Hester, J. J.
1962 A Folsom Lithic Complex From the Elida Site, Roosevelt County, N.M. *El Palacio* 69:92–113.

Hodder, I.
1986 *Reading the Past: Current Approaches to Interpretation in Archaeology*. Cambridge University Press, London.

Jordon, D.
1960 *The Bull Brook Site in Relation to "Fluted Point" Manifestations in Eastern North America*. Unpublished Ph.D. dissertation, Department of Anthropology, Harvard University, Cambridge.

Karrow, P. F., T. W. Anderson, A. H. Clarke, L. D. Delorme, and M. R. Sreenivasa
1975 Stratigraphy, Paleontology, and Age of Lake Algonquin Sediments in Southwestern Ontario, Canada. *Quaternary Research* 5:49–87.

Lahren, L., and R. Bonnichsen
1974 Bone Foreshafts from a Clovis Burial in Southwestern Montana. *Science* 186:147–150.

MacDonald, G. F.
1968 *Debert: A Palaeo-Indian Site in Central Nova Scotia*. Anthropology Papers of the National Museum of Canada No. 16. Ottawa.

Magne, M.
1985 Review of *Understanding Stone Tools: A Cognitive Approach* by D. E. Young and R. Bonnichsen. *Canadian Journal of Archaeology* 9:187–191.

Martin, P. S.
1973 The discovery of America. *Science* 179:969–974.

McCary, B. C.
1951 A Workshop of Early Man in Dinwiddie County, Virginia. *American Antiquity* 17:9–17.
1975 The Williamson Paleo-Indian Site, Dinwiddie County, Virginia. *The Chesopiean* 13:47–131.

Mehringer, P.
1988 Clovis Cache Found: Weapons of Ancient Americans. *National Geographic* 174:500–503.

Moeller, R. W.
1980 *6LF21: A Paleo-Indian Site in Western Connecticut*. Occasional Paper No. 2. American Indian Archaeological Institute, Washington, CT.

Morlan, R. E.
1977 Fluted Point Makers and the Extinction of the Arctic-Steppe Biome in Eastern Beringia. *Canadian Journal of Archaeology* 1:95–108.

Morlan, R. E., and J. Cinq-Mars
1982 Ancient Beringians: Human Occupation in the Late Pleistocene of Alaska and the Yukon Territory. In *Paleoecology of Beringia*, edited by D. M. Hopkins, J. V. Matthews, Jr., C. E. Schweger, and S. B. Young, pp. 353–381. Academic Press, New York.

Mosimann, J. E., and P. S. Martin
1975 Simulating Overkill by Paleoindians. *American Scientist* 63:304–313.

Nolin, A.
1981 *Sédimentologie et Géomorphologie Associées au Lac Glaciaire Algonquin, Près du Site Paléo-Indien Fisher, Stayner, Ontario*. Unpublished master's thesis, Département de Géographie, Université de Sherbrooke, Sherbrooke.

Nolin, A., and Q. H. J. Gwyn
n.d. The Geological Setting of the Fisher Site. In The Fisher site: Archaeological, Geological, and Paleobotanical Studies at the Fisher Site in Southern Ontario, edited by P. L. Storck. Ms. in possession of authors.

Roosa, W. B.
1977 Great Lakes Paleoindian: the Parkhill Site, Ontario. *In Amerinds and Their Paleoenvironments in Northeastern North America*, edited by W. S. Newman and B. Salwen, pp. 349–354. Annals of the New York Academy of Sciences No. 288.

Shafer, H. J.
1986 Review of *Understanding Stone Tools: A Cognitive Approach* by D. E. Young and R. Bonnichsen. *Geoarchaeology* 1:213–215.

Simons, D. B., M. J. Shott, and H. T. Wright, Jr.
1983 The Gainey Site (1979–1982): Variability in a Great Lakes Paleo-Indian Assemblage. Paper presented at the 46th Annual Meeting of the Society for American Archaeology, Pittsburgh.
1984a The Gainey Site: Variability in a Great Lakes Paleo-Indian Assemblage. *Archaeology of Eastern North America* 12:266–270.
1984b Paleoindian Research in Michigan: the Gainey and Leavitt Sites. *Current Research* 1:21–22.

Sollberger, J. L.
1985 A Technique for Folsom Fluting. *Lithic Technology* 14:41–50.
1986 Discussion of the Akerman and Fagan Paper. *Lithic Technology* 15:7.

Spiess, A., and D. B. Wilson
1987 *The Michaud Site: A Paleo-Indian Site in the New England-Maritimes Region*. Occasional Publications in Maine Archaeology No. 6. The Maine Historical Commission and the Maine Archaeological Society, Inc. Augusta.

Stanford, D. J.
1978 The Jones-Miller Site: An Example of Hell Gap

Bison Procurement Strategy. In *Bison Procurement and Utilization: A Symposium,* edited by L. B. Davis and M. Wilson, pp. 90–97. Plains Anthropologist Memoir No. 14.

1979 Bison Kill by Ice Age Hunters. *National Geographic* 155:114–121.

Storck, P. L.

1979 *A Report on the Banting and Hussey Sites: Two Paleo-Indian Campsites in Simcoe County, Southern Ontario.* Archaeological Survey of Canada Paper No. 93. Mercury Series. National Museum of Man, Ottawa.

1982 Palaeo-Indian Settlement Patterns Associated with the Strandline of Glacial Lake Algonquin in Southcentral Ontario. *Canadian Journal of Archaeology* 6:1–31.

1983 The Fisher Site, Fluting Techniques, and Early Paleo-Indian Cultural Relationships. *Archaeology of Eastern North America* 11:80–97.

1988a The Early Paleo-Indian Occupation of Ontario: Colonization or Diffusion? In *Late Pleistocene and Early Holocene Paleoecology of the Eastern Great Lakes Region,* edited by R.S. Laub, N.G. Miller, and D.W. Steadman, pp. 243–250. Bulletin of the Buffalo Society of Natural Sciences No. 33. Buffalo.

1988b Recent Excavations at the Udora Site: A Gainey/Clovis Occupation Site in Southern Ontario. *Current Research in the Pleistocene* 5:23–24.

Storck, P.L. (editor), with contributions by B. E. Eley, Q. H. J. Gwyn, J. H. McAndrews, A. Nolin, A. Steward, J. Tomenchuk, and P. von Bitter

n.d. The Fisher Site: Archaeological, Geological, and Paleobotanical Studies at an Early Paleo-Indian Occupation Site in Southern Ontario. Ms. in possession of authors.

Tunnell, C.

1977 Fluted Projectile Point Production as Revealed by Lithic Specimens from the Adair-Steadman Site in Northwest Texas. *The Museum Journal* 17:140–168.

Wilmsen, E. N., and F. H. H. Roberts, Jr.

1978 *Lindenmeier, 1934–1974: Concluding Report on Investigations.* Smithsonian Contributions to Anthropology No. 24. Washington, D.C.

Wright, H. T., and R. B. Roosa

1966 The Barnes site: A Fluted Point Assemblage from the Great Lakes Region. *American Antiquity* 31:850–860.

Young, D., and R. Bonnichsen

1984 *Understanding Stone Tools: A Cognitive Approach.* Center for the Study of Early Man, University of Maine, Orono.

Paleoindian Occupations of the Maritimes Region of Canada

DAVID L. KEENLYSIDE
Archaeological Survey of Canada
Canadian Museum of Civilization
Ottawa, ON, Canada K1A 0M8

The presence of early humans in the Maritimes region of Canada has been well documented since the mid-1960s. An eastern variant of the Clovis tradition dated to an average of 10,600 yr B.P. is clearly established at the Debert site in central Nova Scotia. What are believed to be closely related Paleoindian fluted-point finds have also been identified in the region; however their provenance is confined to surface-collected specimens.

Recent archaeological investigations on Prince Edward Island have identified a previously unrecognized cultural manifestation, which has provisionally been assigned to a late Paleoindian horizon ca. 9000–10,000 yr B.P. This hypothesized temporal placement is supported by various lines of archaeological evidence. These include stylistic considerations, stratigraphic evidence from the Prince Edward Island Jones site, and comparisons with dated late Paleoindian or early Archaic finds from eastern Quebec and southern Labrador coastal regions.

It is postulated that these early occupations represent the first manifestations of a people descendent from initial Paleoindian occupations of the Northeast. It is also proposed that what developed in the Gulf of St. Lawrence and Maritimes region, as an extension of traditional Paleoindian big-game hunting strategies, was an adaptation to a significant reliance on marine resources, in particular herding sea mammals, such as seal and walrus. The success of this adaptation to a maritime lifestyle seems to be reflected in the subsequent long-term cultural sequence and apparent rapid spread of these people throughout much of the Gulf of St. Lawrence region.

INTRODUCTION

For almost four decades, finds of Clovis-like material have been recognized in the Maritimes region of Canada. Formal identification and chronological control for this cultural horizon began in the early 1960s with field research at the Debert Paleoindian site in central Nova Scotia. The results of this research (MacDonald 1968) firmly established, in time and space, a Clovis-related occupation in the Maritimes. Currently, Debert remains the only radiocarbon-dated Paleoindian occupation in the northeastern Atlantic Maritimes region. This paper reviews this evidence in light of most recent finds and also examines the question of, and possible evidence for, a longer-term Paleoindian adaptation with increased dependence on maritime resources in the region.

MARITIMES PALEOINDIAN—INITIAL OCCUPATION

The Debert Site

The reader should note that a distinction must now be made between the original Debert site (BhDe-1) reported by MacDonald, which is located on former military Camp Debert, and the recently identified Paleoindian components, referred to as Belmont I and II (Preston, personal communication 1989), which are also found near Debert. MacDonald has extensively documented the results of his multidisciplinary project at Debert (1968, 1971) and, therefore, only a brief summary is presented here.

The Debert site is situated in north-central Nova Scotia at an elevation of ca. 25 m above sea level and lies approximately 7 km from the nearest coastline (Cobequid Bay). MacDonald's excavations identified a series of loci or occupation areas over an area of 8–9 acres. Despite the absence of preserved faunal remains, MacDonald believes the site's strategic location, situated between two micro-environments, was primarily for "intercepting game moving between micro-environments," in particular, woodland caribou (MacDonald 1968:120). Although no archaeological faunal evidence exists for the presence of caribou, the early Holocene paleoenvironment of the region would certainly have supported this species. Also supporting this hypothesis is evidence from recent blood residue tests described by T. Loy (B. Preston, personal communication 1990). Samples of blood residue obtained from Debert assemblage scraping implements have been tentatively identified as caribou.

The Debert Assemblage

Approximately 4,500 lithic artifacts were recorded from the Debert site, more than 1,000 of which were excavated. The majority of the lithic materials at Debert originate from mineral-rich basaltic deposits found along the Parrsboro area shoreline on the Bay of Fundy, some 50 km distant. Multicolored chalcedonies and brecciated cherts appear to have been preferred raw materials.

A wide range of diagnostic Paleoindian tool types characterizes the Debert assemblage (see Figure 1). Included are fluted lanceolate projectile points and knives (minimum of 140 specimens) (MacDonald 1968:70), bifacial knives and various drill types, limaces or slug-shaped unifaces, spurred end scrapers and denticulates, gravers, spokeshaves, and *pièces esquillées.* The abundance of debitage, preforms, cores, and anvil stones reflects the extensive production and reworking of implements that occurred at the site. Knapping techniques include pressure flaking, and direct, indirect, and bipolar percussion flaking.

Chronology

A series of 13 radiocarbon dates, obtained from hearth features, place the age of the Debert site at approximately 10,600 yr B.P. MacDonald believes that bracketing these dates as a series of seasonal occupations "covering no more than half a century . . . would be in accord with the homogeneity of the lithic assemblage" (MacDonald 1968:23).

Bonnichsen (this volume) has expressed concern that many reported pit features at Paleoindian sites, such as Debert, may be related to tree falls, rather than cultural events. MacDonald's detailed descriptions of features at Debert carefully examine their relationship to artifact or charcoal occurrences, while keeping in mind the possibility of disturbance through natural agencies such as tree throws:

> Feature 7, which comprises some seven distinct pits, can be traced into the till, of which 7f was the largest, and produced the greatest amount of charcoal. The pits surrounding 7f were little more than basins in the till, containing charcoal and waste flakes (many of which were fire-spalled) and partially covered by cappings of till. At first, it appeared that the till caps originated in post-occupation tree-throw, but since no pits, other than those filled with charcoal, were found from which the capping material could have originated, it is more likely that the cap represents the pit fill used to cover the pit after it was filled with charcoal and chips [MacDonald 1968:38].

MacDonald also notes a number of instances where a hearth feature has been destroyed by a tree throw (e.g., MacDonald 1968:36).

An excellent new opportunity to explore the nature and impact of tree-throw phenomena in relation to local stratigraphy will be afforded at the nearby Belmont sites

Figure 1. Selected sample of the Debert assemblage. **A)** Biface preform; **B–F)** Projectile points; **G)** Hafted knife; **H)** End scraper; **I)** Limace; **J)** Hafted knife; **K)** Drill; **L)** Unifacial stone awl; **M)** 'Spurred' end scraper; **N)** Denticulate graver; **O)** *Pièce esquillée;* **P)** Side scraper.

and could be constructively integrated into the upcoming planned field research program at these locales.

Belmont I and II Sites, Debert, Nova Scotia

In the fall of 1989, several previously unidentified Paleoindian components were discovered in close vicinity to Camp Debert, as a result of Government forestry activities. Preliminary testing by the Nova Scotia Museum confirms at least two major buried components ca. 1.5 km northeast of the Debert site and perhaps several additional small loci nearby. The Belmont I site is the largest of these and occupies about 5 acres. The Belmont II site occupies about 1 acre. Excavations at both sites by S. Davis in the summer of 1990 produced sizeable assemblages of Debert-like Paleoindian material (S. Davis, personal communication 1990).

Other Evidence of Paleoindian Fluted Points

Other finds of Clovis material from the three Maritime provinces indicate that the Debert occupation was not an isolated event, but is representative of a more widespread Maritimes Paleoindian presence dating 10,600–11,000 years ago (Figure 2).

Much of this evidence is documented in the literature

(Davis and Christianson 1988; Keenlyside 1984, 1985b; MacDonald 1968; Turnbull 1974; Turnbull and Allen 1978). Despite considerable testing at most localities, these specimens are primarily isolated surface finds that are not associated with cultural deposits. Morphologically and technologically, these finds display varying degrees of similarity to the Debert material (Table 1). In each of these occurrences only 'fluted' specimens are considered for the purpose of this overview. Other implement types found that may also be Paleoindian in origin have not been included here, owing to lack of dating or context.

The preference for exotic cherts or chalcedonies also prevails in most of these other occurrences. In the illustrated examples, the Prince Edward Island specimen (Figure 3e) is manufactured of the same Bay of Fundy chalcedony as used at Debert. The Quaco Head, New Brunswick, find is made from a tentatively identified red jasper from Colchester, Vermont. The Kingsclear, New Brunswick, specimen is fashioned from Munsungun Lake, Maine, chert.

Table 1. Metric Attributes* of Selected Debert, Nova Scotia, and Isolated Find Projectile Points from Nova Scotia, New Brunswick, and Prince Edward Island.

SPECIMEN	LENGTH	WIDTH	THICKNESS	BASAL DEPTH
a. Debert (1178)	109	35	10	12
b. Debert (1883)	73	26	7.5	10
c. Debert (3226)	55	27	9	6.5
d. Quaco Head, NB	116	36	11.5	12
e. Kingsclear, NB	66	26	10	4.5
f. Tryon, PEI	63	30	9	9
g. Amherst Shore, NS	56	29	8	6
Mean	77	30	9.0	8.5

All measurements in millimeters.
*See Keenlyside (1985a) for definition of metric attributes.

Maritimes Access Routes

The location of Paleoindian finds offers some indication of the routes followed during the initial spread of human occupation into the Maritimes. The St. John and St. Croix river tributary systems would have served as major thoroughfares, initially and, once groups became established, on a seasonal basis. The Gulf of Maine/Bay of Fundy coastal zone also would have been a major avenue of access, both as a route for the initial movement of people into the region and as a seasonal, north/south coastal corridor in relation to resource use.

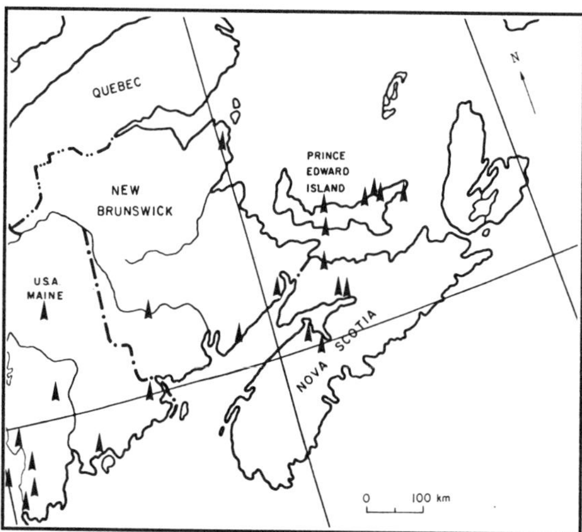

Figure 2. Distribution of Paleoindian finds in the Maritimes.

Along the Gaspé Peninsula of the St. Lawrence estuary, there is sound archaeological evidence for Plano-related occupations by ca. 7000–8000 yr B.P. (Benmouyal 1976). It is not clear however, if 10,000–11,000 years ago the St. Lawrence estuary actually served as a route of access for Paleoindian peoples or even was available, based on research of prevailing postglacial conditions. By the time subsistence patterns became more closely linked to marine resources, over the succeeding several millennia, it is evident that the St. Lawrence estuary served as a major corridor for the movement of people.

"Northumbria" Landbridge

Almost 30 years ago, Erskine (1961), applying botanical evidence, proposed the existence of an early Holocene land bridge connecting Prince Edward Island to the mainland. This was confirmed by geological research (Kranck 1972) that identified remnant postglacial beach strand lines in Northumberland Strait. This work has since been further refined (Scott et al. 1987). Earlier, I proposed that this land bridge, termed "Northumbria," had served as a thoroughfare to Prince Edward Island (Keenlyside 1983:Figure 6). Given its geographic expanse and natural setting, this would have been an area rich in natural resources for Paleoindian populations. A large inland lake, referred to by Kranck (1972) as Ancient Lake Tormentine, would have also been an attractive part of this paleolandscape.

Since the 'Northumbria' concept was first conceived, a fluted projectile point of the Debert type has been found near Tryon, at the Prince Edward Island end of

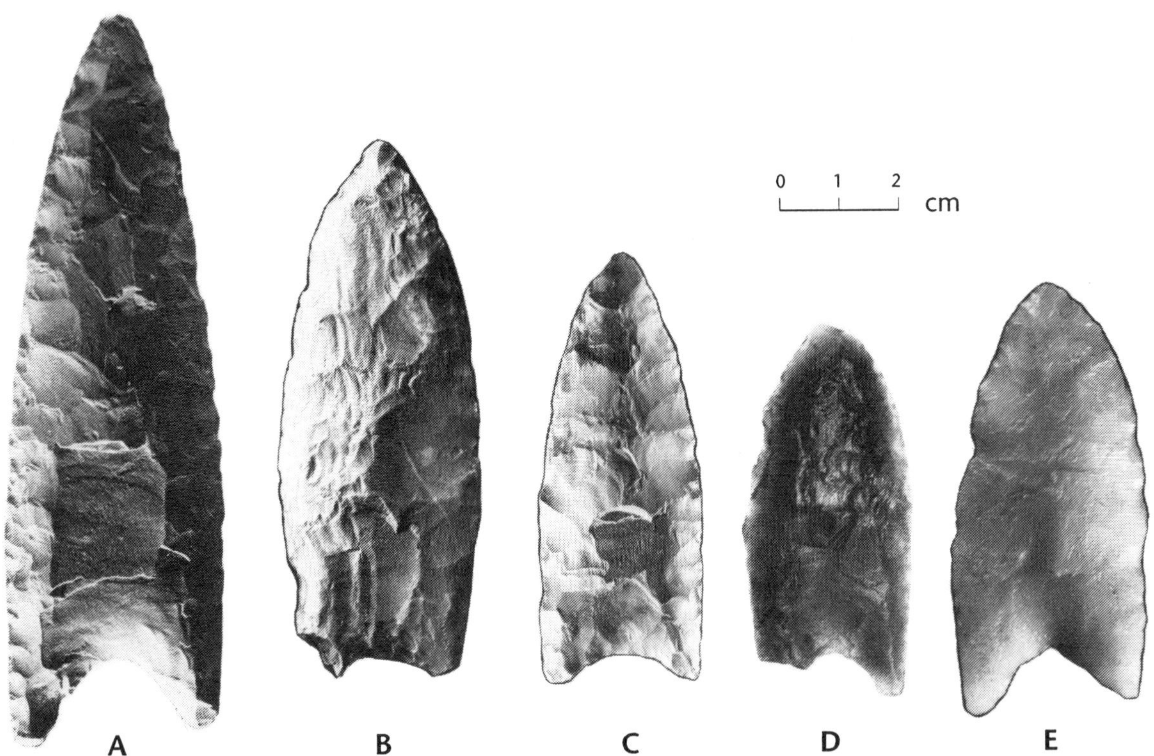

Figure 3. Maritimes early Paleoindian projectile points: **A)** Quaco Head, New Brunswick; **B)** New Horton Creek, New Brunswick; **C)** Kingsclear, New Brunswick; **D)** Amherst Shore, Nova Scotia; **E)** North Tryon, Prince Edward Island.

this land bridge. In April of 1987, another Debert-type fluted point was found at Amherst Shore, New Brunswick, at the mainland end of the land bridge. This latter specimen is also noteworthy as the first occurrence of a Paleoindian point find at sea level in the Maritimes region.

ARCHAEOLOGICAL EVIDENCE FOR LATE PALEOINDIAN OCCUPATION OF THE MARITIMES

Until recently, little archaeological data from the Northeast have been reported regarding the fate of these earliest Paleoindian populations or of sites and assemblages that relate to occupations by their descendents. Several significant recent studies that have shed some light on this question come from archaeological research on the southern Labrador coast (McGhee and Tuck 1975; Renouf 1977), adjacent coastal areas of eastern Quebec (Groison 1985), and also the central New England coast (Cavallo 1981). The significance of these studies will be discussed later in this paper.

Prince Edward Island is an area of the Maritimes that is showing considerable promise for establishing cultural continuity from an initial Clovis horizon into a late Paleoindian time period. Archaeological research by the author since 1981 on the north and east coasts of Prince Edward Island has identified a unique collection of stone projectile points from various site localities. These implements bear many of the attributes characteristic of Paleoindian projectile points, such as those identified at Debert, yet are distinctly different. This collection is the primary focus of this paper.

Contextual Data

This collection primarily comes from localities along Prince Edward Island's north and east shores. These are: 1) Basin Head/South Lake; 2) Little Harbour; 3) St. Peters Bay; 4) Savage Harbour; 5) New London Bay (Figure 2); and 6) the Tracadie River estuary of northeastern New Brunswick. Other isolated finds from along the north shore have been reported, and it is surmised that human populations exploited most of the Island's north coastal environs 9000–10,000 years ago.

Two of the site localities identified to date are not

found at shoreline elevation. The first is the Basin Head site (CcCm-6), initially reported by MacDonald (1968:124). This site is situated on a prominent headland 10–20 m a.s.l. and faces inland to a saltwater estuary. Testing of the site indicated that any primary contextual information had been lost, owing to extensive cultivation over many years. MacDonald describes the first point reported from this site (Figure 4a) as "thick and partially fluted but in outline and basal treatment is close to those from Debert." Three other specimens come from the site, one of which was collected during our 1981 field season (Figure 4c). The second locality (CcCm-18) is situated several kilometers south along the coast at Little Harbour and, like Basin Head, is found on an elevated headland facing inland to a saltwater estuary. In both these instances, the primary resource areas seem to have been the saltwater estuaries rather than the open coast. This pattern is also seen during later occupations of the region and may reflect seasonal preferences.

The other find localities at St. Peters Bay, Savage Harbour, and New London currently occur within a meter of sea level in tidal bays. Most of the specimens assigned to this early assemblage have been recovered

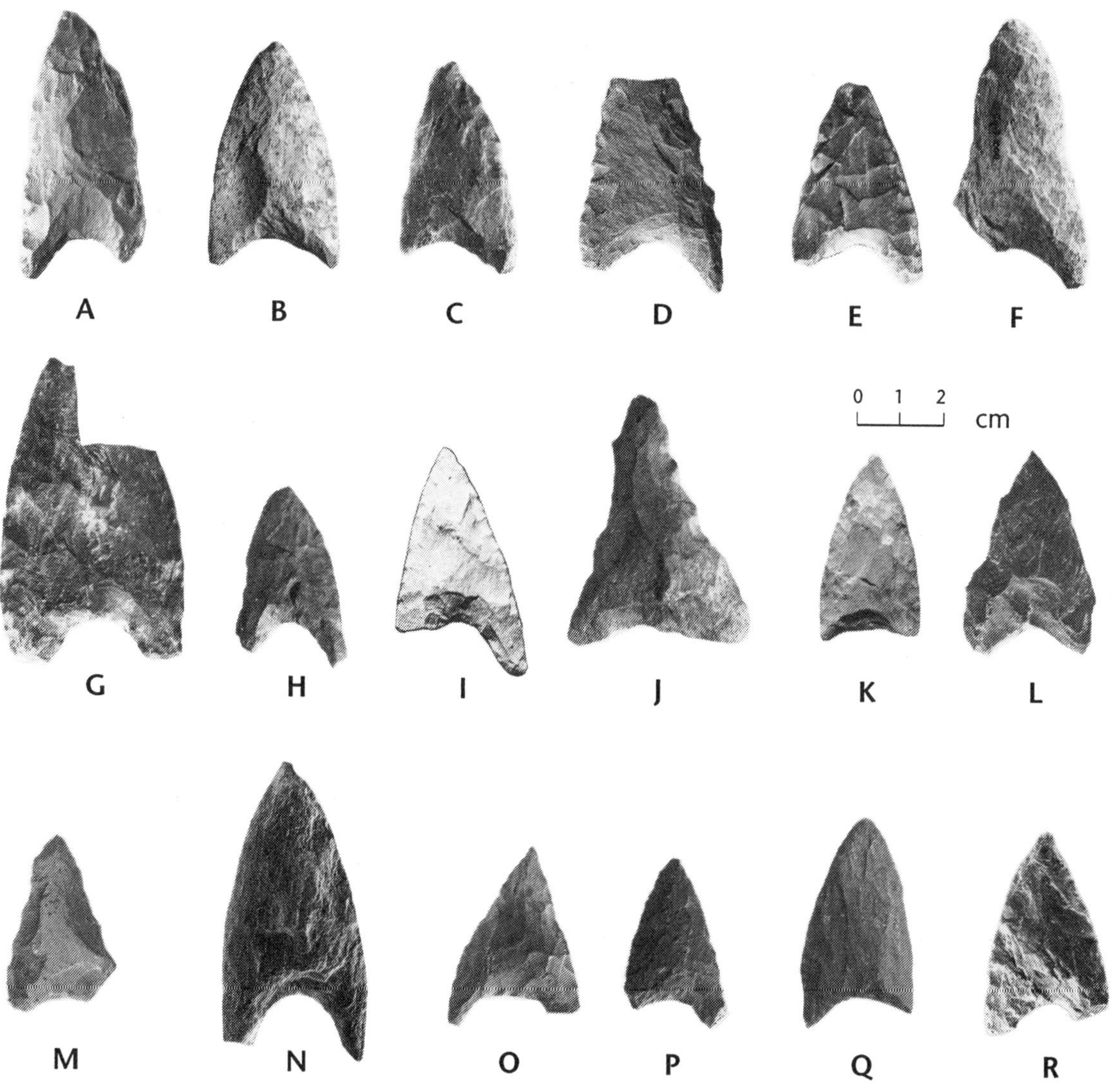

Figure 4. Maritimes late Paleoindian projectile points: **A–C)** Basin Head, Prince Edward Island; **D)** Little Harbour, Prince Edward Island; **E–M)** Jones Site, St. Peters Bay, Prince Edward Island; **N)** St. Peters Bay, Prince Edward Island; **O–P)** Savage Harbour, Prince Edward Island; **Q)** New London Bay, Prince Edward Island; **R)** Tracadie River estuary, New Brunswick.

from the beach intertidal zone. The absence of weathering on most specimens and their provenance near the erosional faces of sites suggest relatively recent exposure from a primary context as the result of generally rising sea-level conditions in the Maritimes (Grant 1977; Parent et al. 1985; Quinlan and Beaumont 1982).

The two specimens recorded from the Tracadie estuary of northeastern New Brunswick are also shoreline surface finds. One of the sites (CiDf-3) is situated at the estuary mouth and is partially submerged. The second site (CiDg-19) is located well up river, close to the head of tide.

Diagnostic Traits

Metric attributes for the Prince Edward Island sample are provided in Table 2. Diagnostic metric and nonmetric attributes include: triangular, often asymmetric outlines; predominantly slightly convex lateral edges; pronounced barbs with moderate to deeply indented basal edges; well-thinned blade bodies and basal edges, at times characterized by the removal of broad thinning flakes to aid hafting; an absence of basal or blade edge grinding; and considerable size variation, ranging from 29–86 mm in length.

Projectile-Point Lithology

With few exceptions, the sample of projectile points from Prince Edward Island appears to be associated with a single lithic source. The material is a fine-grained siliceous shale that is black, grey, or buff in color. Exposure to weathering results in marked changes to the color and texture of the rock surface. The primary source of this material is found on Ingonish Island, just off Cape Breton's northeast shore, a distance of ca. 120 km (72 miles) east of Prince Edward Island. A large quarry site for this material on Ingonish Island, reported by Nash (1978), seems to have been a preferred lithic source at various times in the Northumberland Strait region's prehistoric record. This preference probably stemmed from the fracturing characteristics of this raw material, which tend to follow the natural laminations. This would permit easy removal of large primary flakes during preform preparation and subsequent reduction stages in the knapping process. The natural striations in this material are very distinctive and usually take on the form of parallel, black linear inclusions. This gives the material an almost 'peppered' appearance. On most specimens the fracture line is oriented along the longitudinal axis or slightly obliquely angled and often coincides with the angle of flake removal. For the style of points in this sample, characterized by pronounced barbs, the longitudinal orientation would have provided greater strength. The emphasis on basal thinning and deep concavity of basal edges would almost have necessitated a longitudinal orientation.

Table 2. Metric Attributes of Selected PEI Late Paleoindian Projectile Points.

SPECIMEN	LENGTH	WIDTH	THICKNESS	BASAL DEPTH
1. CcCq-3:2493	86	46	9.5	10
2. CcCq-3:2475	46	30	7	9
3. CcCq-3:2494	49	33	5.5	8
4. CcCq-3:2503	44	36.5	6	3
5. CcCq-3:2505	40	24	5.5	4*
6. CcCq-3:1000	64	31	8	4
7. CcCq-3:2510	43	28	7	2
8. CcCq-3:2502	I	I	7	I
9. CcCq-3:2506	I	I	6	I
10. CcCq-3:2497	57	33	6.5	9*
11. CcCq-3:2501	I	30*	5	I
12. CcCq-3:2511	60	45	11	4
13. CcCq-3:2508	40	22	5.5	4
14. CcCq-3:2512	I	I	I	16*
15. CcCq-3:2500	44*	46	11	7
16. CcCq-3:2498	46	25	6.5	3
17. CcCq-3:2105	46*	25	7	3*
18. CcCp-7:1	73*	37	7	16
19. CcCm-18	70*	36	5	11.5
20. CcCr-1:49	41	25	7	5.5
21. CcCr-1:50	45	33	8	8*
22. VIII-C:179	63	30	9.5	8.5
23. CcCm-6:a	29	19	5	6
24. CcCm-6:b	55	33	6	7
25. CcCm-6:97	52	30	7	5
Range	29–86	19–46	3–11	2–16
Mean	52	31.5	7	7

All measurements in millimeters.
*Estimated.
I = Incomplete.

JONES SITE, ST. PETERS BAY

Site History

A large proportion of the Prince Edward Island material discussed in this paper, including the only specimen that has been recovered in a primary context, comes from the Jones site (CcCq-3) on St. Peters Bay. The Jones site, which was tested and excavated in 1983 and 1985, is a multicomponent stratified site situated just inside the entrance to St. Peters Bay on its north shore. This part of the bay is composed chiefly of alluvial sand sediments and wind-blown sand from nearby active dune areas. Seasonal high-tide flooding, ice rafting, and wave action have resulted in extensive erosion of the shoreline. The accelerated erosional processes of the submerging coastline cause new cultural material to be continually exposed on the beach adjacent to the site.

Cultural Stratigraphy

A minimum of six cultural components are defined; two are associated with late and early historic occupations, and at least four are prehistoric in age. A severe wind storm in the 1920s deposited sand across the site, in places in excess of 50 cm depth. This overburden has minimized the effect of modern agricultural disturbances. The basal stratum, which reaches a depth of 80 cm below surface, was largely undisturbed and yielded a small sample of cultural material tentatively assigned to a late Paleoindian horizon. Most of the components are interpreted as representing relatively brief time intervals. Excavations in 1985 at the site confirmed that this basal stratum was actively eroding at the beach surface and was the source of the described early projectile points from the site.

Absolute Dating

A single small sample of organic material associated with 'fire-reddened' features was excavated from the basal stratum of the site and submitted for dating. Although there was some evidence of root disturbance throughout the stratum, other disturbance was not apparent. The date obtained of 1255 ± 280 yr B.P. (S-2844) is considered unacceptable. Sufficiently earlier diagnostic material excavated from a number of the overlying levels clearly indicates some form of contamination or intrusion of more recent organic material into the basal stratum. A contributing factor may be annual flooding of the site, produced by high tides and storm activity. Diagnostic material from each of the six components seems to lie in the correct relative temporal sequence, further reinforcing the absence of major disturbance at the site.

Site Summary

The nature of the paleotopography and climate during the period of 8000–10,000 yr B.P. requires considerably more geological work in the immediate area of St. Peters Bay. Not until these factors are better understood can we relate the Jones site's current location and setting relative to the ancient shoreline position. Given the possibility that sea levels of 10,000 years ago may have been as much as 20–30 m lower than today (Grant 1977; Quinlan and Beaumont 1982), the site may have been situated on a river channel or saltwater estuary. The possibility also exists that St. Peters Bay was an inland lake or brackish pond. The large artifact assemblage from the Jones site certainly suggests a major focal point of human activity. Given conditions similar to that of today, fishing and/or marine-mammal hunting were probably key activities. The fact that this locale continued to be used in historic times by Micmac and Acadian peoples reflects the site's strategic location at the mouth of St. Peters Bay and its close proximity to the deep water channel.

Attempts to date the site's basal stratum, which is believed to be late Paleoindian in age, have not been successful. Nevertheless, the direct association of a fragmentary late Paleoindian point (Keenlyside 1985a:Figure 3:17) with the basal stratum is not in conflict with the proposed antiquity for this material. In addition, surface-collected specimens found at the beach-weathering contact zone of this horizon warrant assignment of the numerous other points from the site to this early horizon. The size of many of the specimens suggests that these implements tipped thrusting spears or darts thrown from atlatls. The barbed points are closely reminiscent of Northwest Coast sea-mammal hunting implements, such as those employed historically by the West Coast Makah people. In the East Coast context, these specimens would have been particularly well suited for use on marine mammals, such as seal or walrus (Keenlyside 1987).

EXTERNAL RELATIONSHIPS

An impression often created of the Paleoindian period is one of small roaming groups of people developing in relative isolation. Population numbers were probably small; however, we see represented a stone technological tradition that persisted over incredible distances within a relatively narrow time frame. This certainly attests to the mobility and adaptability of these people to various environments. Seasonal rounds must have brought various groups living along the Atlantic seaboard and major waterways into frequent contact with each other.

The Initial Paleoindian Occupation Period

Based on current evidence, fluted-point-associated assemblages and surface finds from Nova Scotia, New Brunswick, and Prince Edward Island represent the farthest northern spread of Paleoindian peoples in the Northeast. The stylistic and technological similarities between Debert and Maine site assemblages, such as Vail (Gramly 1982) and Michaud (Spiess and Wilson 1987), suggest a short time span was represented. The C-14 dating of these sites is not sufficiently precise to demonstrate a time gradient; however, it seems logical that the spread of Paleoindian people into the Maritimes took place rapidly as the result of a general northward movement. Although one can only speculate, it seems probable that the major avenue of entry would first have been along the coast, followed by a gradual spread up the major river systems into the interior lakes.

Stylistically, the Maritimes fluted points are strikingly similar. The Quaco Head and Amherst Shore finds, for example, are virtually indistinguishable from Debert points. The Kingsclear find, however, with its narrower form and shallow basal concavity, is perhaps closer to the Bull Brook form (cf. Figure 3c and Grimes [1979:Figure 9-2,3]). The fact that this point is made of Munsungun chert suggests trade or actual travel to the quarry site.

Late Paleoindian Occupation Period

Evidence for a northern spread of Paleoindian populations continues during this period. Specimens with cultural affinities to the Prince Edward Island assemblage appear along the Gulf of St. Lawrence north shore of eastern Quebec and southwest Labrador. McGhee and Tuck's archaeological research in the Strait of Belle Isle region in the early 1970s (McGhee and Tuck 1975) led to discovery of a series of multicomponent sites (including Pinware Hill and Cowpath) that produced a sequence of Early Archaic assemblages dating back to more than 8000 yr B.P. Following these investigations, a more extensive excavation at the Cowpath site by Renouf produced assemblages and corresponding early C-14 dates:

> Morphologically, these triangular points show a derivative relationship with the Paleo-Indian projectile points of the Northeast. Their concave bases with marked basal thinning executed by means of the removal of a few flakes from one or both faces, sometimes with one scar predominant, are reminiscent of the fluting of the distinctive Paleo-Indian point [Renouf 1977:37].

A comparison of these projectile points with the Prince Edward Island sample shows some similarities between the two groups, particularly in outline form and knapping technology. The size range tends to be smaller for the Labrador specimens and basal margins tend to be less concave, in contrast to many of the deeply concave-based Prince Edward Island projectile points; however, basal thinning techniques are distinctively similar.

The Cowpath site's earliest component yielded two C-14 dates of 8600 ± 315 yr B.P. (SI-2606) and 6850 ± 130 yr B.P. (I-8101) (McGhee and Tuck 1975:114a). Pinware Hill dates between ca. 9000 and 6000 yr B.P. (McGhee and Tuck 1975). Other elements of these assemblages include:

> small spurred and non-spurred end scrapers, the retouched flakes and flake knives, the pièces esquillées, and the various bifaces which typify the less complex eastern Paleo-Indian assemblages [Renouf 1977:37].

Similar, although perhaps slightly later material, is reported by Dominique Groison from eastern Quebec at two sites. Two C-14 dates associated with small triangular points place these occupations between 6000 and 7000 yr B.P. (Groison 1985).

Recent archaeological research on the Magdalen Islands has led to the discovery of several archaeological sites with triangular projectile points (McCaffrey 1986, personal communication 1989). Clearly, given the Islands' central Gulf location, well-developed boating skills and some marine navigation would have been necessary.

The existence of late Paleoindian materials in the southern Gulf of St. Lawrence fills a significant gap between the Labrador finds and earliest Maritime Paleoindian groups. I concur with McGhee and Tuck's observations that:

> if the vague similarities which we see between these assemblages (Labrador) and those of Debert and other eastern Palaeo-Indian sites are significant of cultural relationship, then the following picture of initial occupation is suggested. In the few millennia following deglaciation, we see the area to the south of the St. Lawrence River thinly occupied by small bands of Palaeo-Indians . . . some of these late Palaeo-Indian/ early Archaic groups moved northward along the north shore of the St. Lawrence River, maintaining a caribou hunting adaptation and perhaps supplementing this with seasonal coastal hunting or fishing [McGhee and Tuck 1975:104].

For broader regional comparisons, one must look a considerable distance outside the Gulf of St. Lawrence region to sites reported along the mid-Atlantic Coast. One site that has produced a similar projectile-point 'type' in a dated context is the multicomponent Turkey Swamp site, located in the northeastern portion of New Jersey's Coastal Plain (Cavallo 1981). Triangular-type projectile points with slightly concave bases predominate. Basal thinning is a common attribute and, in several instances, constitutes deliberate fluting scars. The lowest component at this site is dated between 7600 and 8700 yr B.P. Cavallo interprets this assemblage as:

> a direct outgrowth from an earlier regional Palaeo-Indian tradition, while maintaining certain elements of the earlier Palaeo-Indian tool kit, new techniques indicative of the Archaic period such as basal thinning, notching, and the addition of such elements as the chipped stone adze, suggest a technological shift within a cultural continuum [Cavallo 1981:16].

Another important site from New England is the

Whipple site in New Hampshire. Here, dates range from 8180 to 11,400 yr B.P. (Curran 1984:13). As one might expect from these early dates, the assemblage from Whipple bears a strong similarity to those from the Debert, Vail, and Bull Brook sites. Fluting techniques, other bifacial tools such as limaces, and specialized unifacial implements are present. Of note, however, is one of the projectile points from the site (cf. Curran 1984:34, Plate 1:1), which conforms closely to a number of the Prince Edward Island late Paleoindian finds. Although this specimen does differ somewhat from the other 'fluted' points in the assemblage, I believe that this is a good example of the degree of internal variability prevalent in most 'classic' Paleoindian assemblages. The tendency in the past has been to view the entire Paleoindian horizon with an archetypal fluted-point type in mind, rather than to look for transitional elements or evolving styles that may eventually have given rise to forms such as those seen in the Prince Edward Island sample.

DISCUSSION AND CONCLUSIONS

The unique early postglacial environment of the Canadian Maritimes provided an ideal setting for the evolution of a primarily land-based people to one with a greater reliance on coastal and marine resources. This expansion of the resource base necessitated the development of new technologies to exploit these new environments. The presence of a sophisticated sea-mammal hunting technology as early as 8000 years ago on the southern Labrador coast (McGhee and Tuck 1976) implies a considerably earlier developmental stage. I suspect that this may have taken place among the late Paleoindian peoples of the southern Gulf. Resource-rich bays, such as St. Peters, Basin Head, Savage Harbour, and others found along Prince Edward Island's north shore, appear to have been particularly attractive during this developmental period. Envisaged is a gradual increase in the reliance on marine resources, perhaps combined with improved water transportation and the development of a more sophisticated marine hunting technology.

The presence of a Paleoindian horizon nearly 11,000 years ago is well documented in each of the Maritime Provinces. The evidence presented, with particular reference to the Prince Edward Island assemblage, furnishes some of the 'missing pieces' in the chain of events for a gradual technological change and adaptive pattern over the 1000–2000 year period that followed initial human colonization. The rich cultural and sophisticated marine-adapted technology associated with the subsequent Maritime Archaic populations by 7000 years ago adds a convincing argument for a long-term occupation of maritime-adapted people in the region.

REFERENCES CITED

Benmouyal, J.
1976 *Archaeological Research in the Gaspé Peninsula, Preliminary Report.* Current Research Reports No. 3, pp. 7–18. Department of Archaeology, Simon Fraser University, Burnaby.

Cavallo, J.
1981 Turkey Swamp: A Late Paleo-Indian Site in New Jersey's Coastal Plain. *Archaeology of Eastern North America* 9:1–18.

Curran, M. L.
1984 The Whipple Site and Palaeo-Indian Tool Assemblage Variation: A Comparison of Intrasite Structuring. *Archaeology of Eastern North America* 12:5–40.

Davis, S. A., and D. Christianson
1988 Three Palaeo-Indian Specimens from Nova Scotia. *Canadian Journal of Archaeology* 12:190–196.

Erskine, D. S.
1961 *Plants of Prince Edward Island.* Canada Department of Agriculture, Publication 1088.

Gramly, R. M.
1982 *The Vail Site: A Palaeo-Indian Encampment in Maine.* Bulletin of the Buffalo Society of Natural Sciences 30. Buffalo.

Grant, D.
1977 Glacial Style and Ice Limits, The Quaternary Stratigraphic Record, and Changes of Land and Ocean Level in the Atlantic Provinces, Canada. *Géographie Physique et Quaternaire* 31:247–260.

Grimes, J. R.
1979 A New Look at Bull Brook. *Anthropology* 3:109–130.

Groison, D.
1985 Blanc-Sablon et le Paléo-Indian au Détroit du Belle-Isle. *Recherches Amérindiennes au Québec* XV:127–134.

Keenlyside, D. L.
1983 In Search of the Island's First People. *The Island Magazine* 13(Spring-Summer):3–7. Charlottetown.

1984 The Prehistory of the Maritimes. *Canada's Visual History,* Vol. 65. National Museum of Man, Ottawa.

1985a Late Palaeo-Indian Evidence from the Southern Gulf of St. Lawrence. *Archaeology of Eastern North America* 13:79–92.

1985b La Période Paleoindienne sur L'Ile du Prince Edouard. *Recherches Amérindiennes au Québec* XV:119–126.

1987 The First Maritimers. *Horizon Canada* 117:2192–2197. Montreal.

Kranck, K.
1972 Geomorphological development and Post-Pleistocene Sea Level Changes, Northumberland Strait, Maritime Provinces. *Canadian Journal of Earth Sciences* 9:835–844.

MacDonald, G. F.
1968 *Debert: A Palaeo-Indian Site in Central Nova Scotia.* Anthropology Papers of the National Museum of Canada No. 16. Ottawa.

1971 A Review of Research on Palaeo-Indian in Eastern North America. *Arctic Anthropology* 8:32–42.

McCaffrey, M. T.
1986 La préhistoire des Iles de la Madeleine: Bilan Préliminaire. In *Les Micmacs et la Mer,* pp. 98–102. Société Recherches Amérindiennes au Québec, Montréal.

McGhee, R., and J. Tuck
1975 *An Archaic Sequence from the Strait of Belle Isle, Labrador.* Archaeological Survey of Canada Paper No. 34. Mercury Series. National Museum of Man, Ottawa.

Nash, R.
1978 Prehistory and Cultural Ecology—Cape Breton Island, Nova Scotia. In *Papers from the Fourth Annual Congress, 1978,* edited by R. Preston, pp. 131–155. Canadian Ethnology Service Paper No. 40. Mercury Series. National Museum of Man, Ottawa.

Parent, M., J. M. Dubois, P. Bail, A. Larocque, et G. Larocque
1985 Paleogéographie du Québec Meridional Entre 12,500 et 8000 Ans BP. *Recherches Amérindiennes au Québec* XV:17–38.

Quinlan, G., and C. Beaumont
1982 The Deglaciation of Atlantic Canada as Reconstructed from the Post-Glacial Relative Sea-Level Record. *Canadian Journal of Earth Sciences* 19:2232–2246.

Renouf, P.
1977 A Late Palaeo-Indian and Early Archaic Sequence in Southern Labrador. *Man in the Northeast* 13:35–44.

Scott, D. B., F. S. Medioli, and A. Miller
1987 Holocene Sea Levels, Paleoceanography, and Late Glacial Ice Configurations near the Northumberland Strait, Maritime Provinces. *Canadian Journal of Earth Sciences* 24:668–675.

Spiess, A. E., and D. Wilson
1987 *The Michaud Site: A Paleoindian Site in the New England-Maritimes Region.* Occasional Publications in Maine Archaeology No. 6. The Maine Historical Society and the Maine Archaeological Society, Inc. Augusta.

Turnbull, C. J.
1974 The Second Fluted Point from New Brunswick. *Man in the Northeast* 7:109–110.

Turnbull, C. J., and P. Allen
1978 More Palaeo-Indian Points from New Brunswick. *Man in the Northeast* 15–16:147–149.

Late Pleistocene Human Occupation of the Eastern United States

BRADLEY T. LEPPER
The Ohio Historical Society
Newark Earthworks State Memorials
Newark, OH 43055

DAVID J. MELTZER
Department of Anthropology
Southern Methodist University
Dallas, TX 75275

Paleoindian groups in the eastern United States adapted to quite a different environmental setting (complex boreal/deciduous forests) than their better-known counterparts on the western Plains. As a consequence, the adaptations of eastern Paleoindians and the archaeological record they produced are quite distinct as well. These groups were likely generalized foragers, utilizing a wide range of resources with reduced residential mobility, all of which is reflected in a record composed largely of isolated fluted points and few sites. This general pattern is evident in the Paleoindian archaeology of the unglaciated Appalachian Plateau of east-central Ohio.

A HISTORICAL OVERTURE

So little is known of the late Pleistocene human occupation of the eastern United States, in comparison with certain other regions, that it becomes almost uncharitable to recall that archaeological research on the peopling of the Americas and the Pleistocene history of the first Americans actually began in the eastern United States nearly 150 years ago. It was in this region and at sites like Claymont (Delaware), Newcomerstown (Ohio), Little Falls (Minnesota), and especially Trenton (New Jersey) that our archaeological forebears first believed they had glimpsed the deep human past of the continent: the material remains of the first Americans, a purported Paleolithic race that ventured onto the continent during the frigid depths of the Ice Age. As Frederic

Ward Putnam triumphantly concluded at the close of the symposium on "Paleolithic man in eastern and central North America" (Putnam 1888), the research in this region surely demonstrated a Pleistocene human occupation. The only question that remained was just how far back into the Pleistocene that occupation went.

But today no one learns about Claymont, Newcomerstown, Little Falls, and Trenton, and for good reason. None of these sites provided unambiguous evidence of the Paleolithic affinities Putnam and others saw, and certainly none could be definitely assigned to even the latest Pleistocene age. How had researchers been led astray? For one thing, Paleolithic affinities were based on what proved to be shaky analogues with European forms. Similarity in form was taken to mean similarity in age; and the "ruder" or more primitive the tool, the greater its age, or so it appeared based on the European sequences. Equally important, most of these allegedly ancient American Paleolithic tools had "been found principally upon the surface or in the alluvium which is its equivalent" (Wilson 1889:373).

Tools that looked old that were found on undated surfaces certainly had the potential to be quite ancient. But as archaeologists and geologists for the BAE (Bureau of American Ethnology) and USGS (United States Geological Survey) showed, such evidence was equally interpretable as more recent archaeological debris. Drawing on analogues of historically known stone-tool production, the Federal scientists attributed the "rude" appearance of these stone tools to failures and rejects from the manufacturing process, an interpretation better suited to explain their position on the surface (Meltzer 1983).

The ensuing debate over the American Paleolithic failed to resolve the issue of the antiquity of the native Americans. Over the years archaeological attention began to focus on the one site circumstance that could, in the days before radiocarbon dating, provide unambiguous evidence of a Pleistocene human occupation: the kill site.

Why a kill site? Artifacts in apparent Pleistocene deposits or in the same stratigraphic unit as the remains of extinct fauna were questionable on multiple counts. (Were they artifacts? Had they been redeposited in older units? Were the deposits truly Pleistocene in age? How valid was the association of artifact and animal?) A kill site with artifacts discovered inset in the skeleton of an extinct animal was far less troubling: a point between the ribs could not be so readily dismissed as a natural occurrence, adventitious mixing, or fortuitous association.

Beginning in the late 1920s and continuing into the 1930s, a series of kill sites (many of which are now interpreted as the product of opportunistic scavenging) were discovered on the High Plains and in the Desert Southwest. Such sites demonstrated that the earliest Americans had been here during the Pleistocene, or at least witnessed its wane. More importantly, by virtue of the repeated association of artifacts with extinct fauna at a half-dozen sites on the Plains and in the Southwest, the Paleoindian horizon was posited to represent the widespread hunting of Pleistocene big game (Howard 1935; Roberts 1940).

THE FLUTED-POINT OCCUPATION OF EASTERN NORTH AMERICA

Once the Paleoindian occupation had been defined at Folsom and Clovis sites, and its characteristic fluted-point–bearing assemblage described, it began the inevitable migration to the other areas of the continent that contained these recognizable forms. Fluted points proved to be distributed over much of North America, including the eastern United States. What started as a local component soon stretched coast to coast, as the first (and perhaps only) truly continental archaeological horizon (Mason 1962:234; Shetrone 1936).

Throughout the 1950s fluted points were found as scattered surface finds across the eastern United States. By the early 1960s nearly 2,000 of these points had been recorded: over 80 were known from New York state (Ritchie 1957:Table 1), nearly 100 were recorded from the Delaware Valley (Mason 1959:5), over 100 were known for the state of Michigan (Mason 1958:3), over 500 were recorded for Ohio (Prufer and Baby 1963), and over 1,100 were tallied from the southeastern states (Williams and Stoltman 1965:675). There were, however, far fewer sites known: only Bull Brook (e.g., Byers 1954), Reagen (Ritchie 1953), Shoop (Witthoft 1952), and Williamson (McCary 1951). This disparity obviously presented some significant interpretive dilemmas, for the bulk of the eastern Paleoindian record lacked direct clues of its age, associated assemblages, subsistence patterns, and so on. Since the few known sites also lacked faunal associations or materials suitable for radiocarbon dating, the age and meaning of eastern Paleoindian materials had to be approached indirectly.

The "strong typological affinities" (Mason 1960:366) between Clovis and eastern fluted points (Mason 1959:2, 1960:375; Quimby 1958:247), and the extensive geochronological research in northern areas that linked fluted points with Pleistocene landscape features of reasonably well-known age (e.g., Mason 1958, 1960; Quimby 1958; cf. Ritchie 1957), together suggested that fluted-point occupations west and east were of "approximately the same order of antiquity" (Quimby 1958:247). Given that the age of the western Clovis materials was not known with precision, and the necessary constraints attached to dating archaeological materials using landscape features (Mason 1960:366–367; also Mason 1981:92), this conclusion was quite reasonable. Certainly, the inferred age of the eastern fluted points would later match well with acquired radiocarbon dates.

The inference that fluted points and their associated

tool kits were roughly contemporaneous east and west had clear implications for views of Paleoindian subsistence and settlement strategies. For one thing, the fact that the western Paleoindians seemed to rely on "big-game animals" suggested, admittedly without direct supporting evidence (Mason 1962:237), that it was "inconceivable that if such game was available [in the eastern United States] it would not have supplied an important source of food and clothing" (Mason 1959:15; also Quimby 1960:30; Williams and Stoltman 1965:674). That suggestion seemed corroborated by studies of the co-occurrence in the Great Lakes region (south of the "Mason-Quimby" line) (Martin 1967:100) of fluted points and Pleistocene fossils (Quimby 1960:31). Similar patterns were reported in the Southeast (Williams and Stoltman 1965:677).

A big-game hunting adaptation made sense in terms of the apparently rapid spread of fluted points across the continent (as evident in the strong similarities in points from widely separated areas), for such an adaptation to migratory animals would have "fastened" Paleoindian groups "to a vehicle for cultural specialization that cut across other ecological barriers" (Mason 1962:243) and would certainly explain the presence of exotic cherts in Paleoindian sites (Witthoft 1952:64). All of this was in keeping with a role for Paleoindians in the extinction of the Pleistocene megafauna (Martin 1967:100–101; Mason 1962:242–243).

Even so, it was quite apparent in the early 1960s that in order to determine whether all these quite reasonable inferences were correct, it was necessary to overcome the "frustrating" (Mason 1962:237; also Ritchie 1965:9) lack of kill sites in eastern North America. That would require intensive searching (Mason 1959:16), but it seemed "only a matter of time" before such discoveries were made (Williams and Stoltman 1965:674).

Throughout the 1960s and 1970s, over two dozen eastern fluted-point sites were discovered. Over that same period, many thousands of isolated fluted points were recovered from surface contexts, and by the early 1980s over 6,000 such isolates were known (Brennan 1982; Seeman and Prufer 1982; also Meltzer 1988:Table III). There were a number of observations that could be made of that larger body of data.

First, despite the accumulated evidence, there remained a scarcity of kill sites that might otherwise support a model of Paleoindian big-game hunting. That negative evidence should, perhaps, be tempered by the observation that very few of these Paleoindian sites preserved any organic remains, much less the bones of big-game species. Nonetheless, literally thousands of fossils of now-extinct Pleistocene megafauna, including mastodon, mammoth, and sloth, have been recovered from paleontological localities in this region (Meltzer 1986). The activity of searching areas that "would have been an excellent hunting ground for early man" (Shaler 1893:180) for the co-occurrence of human and megafaunal remains began as early as the mid-nineteenth century. Fossil localities such as Big Bone Lick (Kentucky), where natural salt resources would have regularly attracted (and did attract) "big-game" species, were often the very first places examined in the search for human remains:

> In 1869 I made extensive excavations at Big Bone Lick in Kentucky, partly with the hope of finding human remains mingled with the abundant bones of extinct mammalia which occur in the deposits of mud at that point. Here again I gathered only negative evidences which went to show that primitive man never hunted the elephant, the mastodon, the Ovibos and other large animals which frequented this region [Shaler 1893:180].

And yet, over the last century, nearly all these sites (and this especially includes Big Bone Lick) have failed to yield significant evidence for the association of Paleoindians and these "big-game animals" in a predator-prey relationship. (See the discussion in Meltzer 1988:23–24.)

Evidence for Paleoindian exploitation of Pleistocene megafauna as a specialized system of widespread, systematic, intense predation does not exist. Given the fossil record as it is now known, it seems unlikely that future discoveries will overturn this conclusion. The pattern that instead emerges from the evidence is that the now-extinct animal forms were occasionally hunted or scavenged as one subsistence activity and resource within a larger system (Meltzer 1988:24).

Second, the character of the Paleoindian archaeological record varied dramatically across eastern North America. Much of the Paleoindian archaeological record in the central and southern portions of eastern North America was composed of isolated fluted points. The sheer number and density of isolated points in this area far surpasses the number of isolates in the northern portion of eastern North America (Meltzer 1988:12).

In contrast, there are few sites in the southern and central forest region (MacDonald 1983:106). Those that occur tend to be restricted to certain activity classes: most are quarry or quarry-related sites. The proportion of isolates to sites is precisely the reverse of the pattern to the north in New England and Canada. There, sites (of all kinds) are relatively more abundant, and isolates less so (Meltzer 1988:12).

Differences in the age of the surficial deposits (much of the upland southeast region has not received any general sedimentation since the Tertiary, and thus the archaeological record is shallow and mixed [Dunnell 1988]), modern agricultural practices, and collecting activities may partly account for this pattern (Lepper 1983, 1985; Meltzer 1984). It becomes interesting to speculate, however, that this might also reflect differences in prehistoric land use and human adaptation.

In an attempt to account for these aspects of the

eastern Paleoindian archaeological record, Meltzer (1984; Meltzer and Smith 1986), among others (e.g., Dent 1985; Dincauze and Curran 1983; cf. Stoltman and Baerreis 1983), argued that Paleoindian adaptations could not be understood as a uniform strategy that extended across the region, but rather had to be explained in terms of the quite different environmental settings in which they were played out.

Adaptations to the complex boreal/deciduous forests that extended across much of the southern and central portion of eastern North America in the late Pleistocene, for example, would have been far different from adaptations that might have taken place in periglacial areas to the north. Certainly, the late Pleistocene forests of eastern North America would not have supported a specialized big-game hunting strategy. The ecological diversity and species richness of this region would have mitigated against high numbers of individuals per species (Meltzer 1988:8), and the Paleoindian groups who occupied the area would presumably have utilized a generalized subsistence strategy. Such a strategy likely included the exploitation of a variety of subsistence resources: seeds and nuts, small mammals, and, perhaps, an occasional large mammal.

The resources exploited by generalized foragers are extensive and dispersed; more importantly, activities like nut collecting leave little in the way of readily observable food remains or tools to mark their former location. As generalized foragers, these eastern Paleoindians would have rarely participated in the highly structured spatial behavior that produces sites (Binford 1980). Reuse of particular localities would have been less frequent, with the possibility of multiple occupations leading to a visible site record lessened. That adaptive behavior, it was argued, would produce an archaeological record dominated by scattered, isolated fluted points and a general scarcity of non-quarry sites.

The results of the attempt to apply that formulation to the entire record of eastern Paleoindians is given in detail in Meltzer and Smith (1986) and especially Meltzer (1984, 1988, 1989), and need not be repeated here. Because explanations of this magnitude use a necessarily broad brush in characterizing environments and regional adaptations, variation on the local level is frequently missed or misunderstood (Dincauze [1988] rightly identifies the problems in this regard with the arguments of Meltzer and Smith [1986]). Thus, it becomes useful here (and elsewhere—see Deller 1988; Lepper 1986; Shott 1986) to examine Paleoindian adaptations on a regional or local level to see how those adaptations conform to or vary from the more general expectations. Therefore, the remainder of the discussion turns to a much smaller spatial unit: the fluted-point occupation of Coshocton County, Ohio; an area especially rich in a fluted-point record. This portion of the paper will draw on recent research and publication by Lepper (1986, 1988, 1989).

A CLOSER LOOK AT THE FLUTED-POINT OCCUPATION: COSHOCTON COUNTY, OHIO

The matter of Paleoindian subsistence and settlement strategies and prehistoric land use can be examined more profitably by casting a sampling net over a much more confined area. In particular, it is useful to examine land use among Paleoindian groups as revealed through distributional studies of fluted-point materials in a relatively restricted area—in this case, Coshocton County, Ohio. This area includes the Walhonding and Tuscarawas rivers, which join, near the center of Coshocton County, to become the Muskingum River.

Prufer and Baby (1963:46), in the course of their statewide fluted-point survey, noted that this area had produced "ample evidence" of Paleoindian remains. Prufer (1971) followed this up with a survey which was concentrated on Coshocton County. He documented a high density of fluted points there, which was rather puzzling since this high frequency constituted an anomaly in the overall distributional pattern proposed for these artifacts in Ohio. The Appalachian Plateau was considered to have been a region that Paleoindians avoided (Prufer and Baby 1963:24).

Coshocton County's apparent contradiction of the general Paleoindian settlement pattern initially was interpreted as "a reflection of the raw material situation in this area" (Prufer 1971:310): notably, the presence of extensive outcrops of Upper Mercer chert. Seeman and Prufer (1982:158–159) later implied that this might not be the entire answer. Nevertheless, the presence of chert deposits must have been important for the fluted-point groups in the region (Prufer and Baby 1963:45), and the proximity of these quarries offered an important advantage for archaeological research here, increasing as it does the archaeological visibility of certain aspects of Paleoindian adaptive strategies.

Prufer's report concluded with the recommendation for "further research in this rich area" (Prufer 1971:310). Certainly, its high potential for producing the data necessary for an analysis of land-use patterns warrants such attention. As a result of these and other factors, Lepper initiated a research project in this area in 1982. A large number of public and private collections of prehistoric material were examined, and 410 fluted points, in varying stages of manufacture, were documented from 67 different localities (Lepper 1986, 1988).

Biases

Such a data set presents certain problems. How does one move from a large sample of surface-collected fluted points and their spatial coordinates as reported by avocational collectors to reliable inferences about general patterns of Paleoindian land use? There are two principle biases here: one attendant to the manner of fluted-point deposition, the other to their collection.

First, the localities where points were lost or discarded may not be where they were used. This means that point locations, settings, and environmental aspects may not inform directly on activities and, conversely, certain activities may not be represented in the distribution of points on the landscape. Nonetheless, as multipurpose tools employed in a variety of contexts, fluted points are no less (and probably more) representative of activities than other elements of the tool kit, and studies of their wear patterns and distribution should reflect something of the overall land-use system in which they operated.

Second, the manner in which these samples of fluted points were collected is neither systematic nor necessarily representative. The discovery of points depends on various natural and artificial agents of weathering and erosion that expose points on the surface (e.g., Lepper 1983, 1985). Once a specimen is exposed on the surface, it may or may not be observed and collected, depending on the frequency with which a particular area is frequented by observers. And, of course, such a specimen, if collected, may or may not be reported to an archaeologist, along with reliable information on its location.

As a result of these factors, this particular record must be seen as an "accidental sample" (Hopkins and Glass 1978:184) of the population of all the fluted points and localities ever used within Coshocton County: haphazard collections of observations for which no valid estimate of risks of error are obtainable (Hopkins and Glass 1978:184).

Such factors prohibit the valid application of techniques of statistical inference for developing generalizations about the distribution and morphology of the population of all of the fluted points that were ever deposited on the Coshocton landscape. They do not, however, preclude the use of such data in pattern exploration and the search of patterns for new insights (Tukey 1977:v).

But what of the fact that such patterns are based on surface data alone? Moeller (1983:27–28), for one, regards the context of surface finds as suspicious, if not spurious, and would relegate the use of distributional studies to the identification of "cultural patterning useful for locating undisturbed, buried sites" (Moeller 1983:27). Indeed, he claims that "surface finds are important only if they are associated with subsurface, in situ ones" (Moeller 1983:27). For Moeller, settlement pattern studies cannot begin until "large numbers of *real sites*, not just find spots of individual artifacts, are known in a region" (Moeller 1983:28, emphasis added).

Such a view would seem to hold that excavation of sites is the only means of reliable data acquisition. Yet there seems little justification for the *a priori* assumption that the archaeological record of late Pleistocene hunter-gatherers must be packaged in large, spatially discrete clusters of artifacts; or that certain questions about land use cannot be answered without recourse to excavation data. Indeed, as previously discussed, under certain conditions, we may expect the archaeological record of hunter-gatherers to be "scattered over the landscape rather than concentrated in recognizable 'sites'" (Binford 1980:9). As Foley (1981:163) argues, the archaeological record of hunter-gatherers must be viewed "not as a system of structured sites, but as a pattern of continuous artifact distribution and density" and that land-use patterns, in particular, can be identified best through "the study of non-discrete artifact distributions in specific zones" (Foley 1981:163; also Dunnell and Dancey 1983:269). Finally, it must be remembered that a buried site is just a buried surface collection.

The Data

The fluted-point archaeological record of Coshocton County, Ohio, consists largely of numerous isolated projectile points in various stages of manufacture from a variety of locations throughout the county. In order to interpret this record in terms of late Pleistocene hunter-gatherer land use, one must determine something about the variability between loci which have produced fluted points. This variability must be sought between the fluted points themselves and between the various combinations of different "kinds" of fluted points. A primary goal of Lepper's research has been to translate techno-functional variability between fluted points into "settlement" types, which can then be examined in their environmental context (Lepper 1986, 1988). The environmental context of these functionally diverse loci may be described and compared in terms of selected environmental attributes. The ultimate goal is to develop a model of Paleoindian land use for the central Muskingum River Basin, which can be compared with results obtained from similar studies in other regions.

An outline of the procedure for developing a settlement typology for fluted-point-yielding loci is presented in Lepper (1986, 1988). It involves a simple technological classification of fluted points, beginning with the distinction between broken and unbroken projectile points. Broken specimens were identified as points broken-in-use or points broken-in-manufacture, based on the presence or absence of lateral grinding. It is generally acknowledged that this edge grinding was the final step in fluted-point production and that its presence is a reliable index of finished points (Frison and Bradley 1980:51; Tunnell 1977:151; Young and Bonnichsen 1984:144–145).

Locations which yielded only points broken in the manufacturing process were classified as chert-processing loci. Locations which yielded only points broken-in-use, or points bearing evidence of having been used, were termed food-procurement/processing loci. If both manufacturing rejects and "used" points were documented from a single locality, then it was regarded as a workshop/occupation. Large workshop/occupations were differentiated arbitrarily from small workshop/ occupations by virtue of having more than 10 points reported for the particular locality. Finally, locations yielding only complete projectile points with no apparent indications of use were listed as undetermined activity loci. It is possible that these unbroken/unworn specimens reflect food-procurement/processing activities, since a likely context for the loss/abandonment of a fully functional, isolated point would be that of an unretrieved weapon tip. Alternatively, Gramly (1987) has presented the argument that some such finds might represent ceremonial offerings or grave goods.

This typology is not without certain problems. First and foremost among these is the problem of sampling adequacy. A food-procurement/processing loci consisting of two points broken-in-use would become a small workshop/occupation if, at a later date, someone were to find the base of a fluted point broken-in-manufacture at the same locality. The typology, potentially, may therefore reflect collecting intensity rather than important aspects of the Paleoindian settlement system.

A related problem concerns what Binford (1982:11) has referred to as the "tactical aspects of land use." It could be argued that the diversity of activities documented for workshop/occupations indicates that these functioned as residential base camps; however, it is also possible that at least some of these loci represent food-procurement/processing loci superimposed over former chert-processing loci or vice versa. Therefore, this simplified settlement classification assumes that sites were used as either multiple-activity base camps or single-activity special-purpose sites, but never both in succession. Clearly the prehistoric reality would have been more complex. Nevertheless, this typology attempts to maximize the information potential of surface-collected fluted points. It differentiates between localities where fluted-point production failures were discarded and localities where functioning fluted points ended their use-life. It is operationally simple and reliable, and the terminology explicitly eschews unwarranted ethnological connotations. The question remains, however: Can these units contribute to our understanding of late Pleistocene hunter-gatherer land use?

Large workshop/occupations were found to be oriented primarily towards providing the maximum access to economic resources. They are situated on broad, flat flood-plain terraces away from the main river, but immediately adjacent to a small stream. They occur at or near the flood plain-upland ecotone in close proximity to the outcrops of Upper Mercer chert as well as the diverse food resources of the flood plains, uplands, and interior hollows. Today they are exposed directly to the prevailing winds; their placement in low elevation situations would not have provided a strategic view for the site occupants.

Small workshop/occupations occur in a variety of locations. At least one is situated in an interior hollow sheltered from the elements, whereas another is located on a prominent ridge-top, directly exposed but providing a view for observation. In contrast to large workshop/occupations, the smaller sites are not situated at topographic ecotones, suggesting that they have more specialized functions.

Chert-processing loci tend to be located between chert outcrops and large workshop/occupations. They occur around the periphery of the uplands on upper flood-plain terraces or just inside interior hollows. None of these sites has been documented in overlook situations, and few seem to take shelter and protection from the elements into account in their positioning.

Food-procurement/processing loci are widely distributed throughout all of the topographic zones in the county, with the exception of ridge-top overlooks. However, fluted points appear to be used and broken-in-use most frequently on the major flood plains. Sampling bias is undoubtedly a contributing factor here. The fact that a large number of food-procurement/processing loci have been identified in both the uplands and interior hollows, in spite of the markedly reduced archaeological visibility in these areas, argues strongly for the importance of these landform zones in the Paleoindian subsistence system. A relatively high percentage of these sites occur in settings with a southern exposure, suggesting that incoming solar radiation was being maximized for either warmth or light.

Coshocton County Land Use

The essence of this analysis of Paleoindian land use is the distinction between "Multiple Activity Locations" and "Limited Activity Locations" (Wilmsen 1970:75), and the equation of these loci with residential base camps and specialized extraction stations, respectively. If these determinations are reasonably accurate, then the patterning in the geographic positioning of the various site types will reflect the general, long-term land-use strategies of Paleoindian hunter-gatherers in this region.

Chert-processing loci tend to be situated at favorable locations between outcrops of Upper Mercer chert and large workshop/occupations. Chert blanks were transported from the upland quarries to level, open areas out of the hills. Fluted points, preforms, and probably other tools were manufactured here, then transported to the large base camps where finishing touches were applied.

One might speculate that the large workshop/occupations represent base camps where relatively large segments of the population aggregated to exploit the chert outcrops and food resources. Small workshop/occupations are widely scattered throughout Coshocton

County. These sites may represent population dispersal. Whether such patterns coincide with seasonal food availability cannot be determined from the available data, but is certainly a possibility.

Food-procurement/processing loci most likely represent dispersed hunting camps and kill sites. The distribution of these loci and the lack of systematic and regular reuse of localities suggest that nonclustered or spatially variable resources were being exploited by small groups of foragers—a pattern noticeably different from that further north at sites like Debert (Nova Scotia) and Vail (Maine).

The land-use pattern described by this analysis for the Paleoindian occupation of the central Muskingum River Basin conforms fairly well to models of generalized hunter-gatherer settlement and subsistence (Binford 1980:6). It is quite possible, of course, that this view could be biased by the fact that this region may represent only part of a larger pattern, the remaining (potentially distinct) components of which are in other regions. Even so, the correspondence is noteworthy, given that the various "settlements" are limited to clustered and isolated fluted projectile points, and given that the Paleoindian settlement and subsistence system has long been regarded as somehow unique, especially in terms of high mobility and an extraordinary dependence on big-game (especially megafauna) hunting (Cleland 1976; Mason 1962, 1981).

A Look at a Comparable Case

There are indications that this pattern may characterize Paleoindian land use throughout the Appalachian Plateau (Lantz 1984; Lepper 1989) and perhaps other areas of eastern North America. Therefore, it is appropriate to discuss here the model developed by Gardner (1983), based on intensive research in the Shenandoah Valley of Virginia. This model has been used and elaborated by others, and points of similarity and difference with the discussion here should be noted.

Custer et al. (1983) present a general model, which predicts that regions like Flint Run, where lithic resources are densely concentrated in a few locations, will exhibit a cyclical settlement-lithic procurement pattern:

> According to this model, groups cycle their movements around specific quarry sources. The catchment area for any wandering range is determined by the state of the curated tool kit. Within this system, groups schedule their movements so that they can return to quarry sites to replenish their tool kits as they become depleted [Custer et al. 1983:269].

This model follows Gardner's (1983) notions of a "lithic determinism," which centers Paleoindian hunter-gatherers in a restricted catchment area around high-quality chert outcrops. There are questions that arise regarding the theoretical basis of the model. For example, is it possible, as the model implies, that stone sources were selected without consideration of the presence of other available resources, or were stone sources simply visited because their location happened to correspond to other useful resources? But there is a more basic issue here, and that is the evidence from which the model was derived.

The basis for the cyclical model, as distinct from a simple serial model (Custer et al. 1983:271), seems to be the dense concentration of sites around a particular chert source, the large size of some of the sites suggesting periodic reoccupations, and the apparent depletion of the tool kit with increasing distance from the quarry (Custer et al. 1983; Gardner 1977; Gardner and Verrey 1979).

In effect, the model is derived from the high archaeological visibility of these sites and related components. The question that must be asked, therefore, is whether the high visibility of these chert sources is a result of their importance in the settlement system, or a by-product of the activities that took place there (and the low visibility of activities away from the quarry).

In the Coshocton area there is a dense concentration of sites centered on discrete outcrops of Upper Mercer chert. A few of these sites are exceptionally large—suggesting periodic reoccupation (Prufer and Wright 1970:261). There is, however, no evidence for the depletion of the tool kit, i.e., a decrease in the size of fluted projectile points with increasing distance from Coshocton County (Lepper 1989:250–252). Importantly, such a relationship has not been quantitatively demonstrated for Flint Run either.

Alternatively, such "unusual" or "anomalous" patterns could be explained as a function of the higher archaeological visibility resulting from extreme redundancy in the Paleoindian land-use system in this region. This redundancy is a predictable consequence of the restricted availability of high-quality chert. It is not necessary to assume that Paleoindians restricted their mobility to relatively small territories centered on favorite chert quarries. The low site frequency and minimal artifact density throughout most of the Appalachian Plateau is the pattern that would be expected if Paleoindian populations were generalized foragers "mapping onto" food resources through residential mobility (Binford 1980).

In areas such as Coshocton County and Flint Run, biotic resources are not stable in space or time, and their distribution would change—perhaps not in a predictable manner. In contrast, chert outcrops remain fixed and predictable. A well-placed residential camp from which to exploit the outcrops of Upper Mercer chert would remain the same from year to year. A well-placed residential camp from which to hunt, say, white-tailed deer within a region could vary widely from year to year, or even month to month.

Redundancy of use would result in a relatively high archaeological visibility for the land-use system situated around the fixed, predictable chert source. The land-use system of the same groups foraging in the heterogeneous forested environments away from localized chert outcrops might leave only a diffuse and indistinct impression in the archaeological record.

It would seem, therefore, to determine whether groups truly cycled around specific lithic sources requires additional evidence other than the fact that there is a high density of sites and material around such sources. The density of archaeological material may not be the best indicator of its importance.

CONCLUSIONS

This brief review has touched on aspects of the adaptive strategies of Paleoindian groups living in the forested regions of eastern North America. While we have cited attempts to provide an overview of that occupation, the point to stress again in closing is the potential variability within that region—and the greater detail that is evident as one focuses on more restricted areas of space.

Gardner (1977:262) made the important observation, always worth repeating, that not all eastern fluted-point sites are alike. While the truth of that observation is incontestable, it is also true that differences among these sites are often subsumed under continental or pan-regional views of Paleoindian adaptive strategies. And it is equally true that those homogenized views are often derived by analogy from Paleoindian occupations that developed in quite distinct ecological settings.

Emphasis should be placed today and in the future on documenting and explaining the variability of Paleoindian assemblages within specific regions, environmental zones, and—where possible—temporal boundaries. Only then will it be possible to gauge the actual historical and evolutionary relationships among late Pleistocene human foragers in the Americas.

ACKNOWLEDGMENTS

DJM would like to thank Vance T. Holliday for presenting the earlier, single-authored version of this paper at the 1987 INQUA conference, when field work and the sagging price of West Texas crude prevented Meltzer's participation at the Ottawa meeting. BTL would like to express his gratitude to Karen Lepper, and DJM to Stephen and Florence Meltzer and Mike and Laurel Lovett, for their help in the preparation of this jointly authored paper. We would both like to thank our very helpful anonymous reviewers. A note on the division of labor: DJM is largely responsible for the first two sections, BTL for the larger third section. The final draft is a product of both our efforts.

REFERENCES CITED

Binford, L. R.
1980 Willow Smoke and Dog's Tails: Hunter-Gatherer Settlement Systems and Archaeological Site Formation. *American Antiquity* 45:4–20.
1982 The Archaeology of Place. *Journal of Anthropological Archaeology* 1:5–31.

Brennan, L.
1982 A Compilation of Fluted Points of Eastern North America by Count and Distribution: An AENA Project. *Archaeology of Eastern North America* 10:27–46.

Byers, D.
1954 Bull Brook—A Fluted Point Site in Ipswich, Massachusetts. *American Antiquity* 19:343–351.

Cleland, C. E.
1976 The Focal-Diffuse Model: An Evolutionary Perspective on the Prehistoric Cultural Adaptations of the Eastern United States. *Midcontinental Journal of Archaeology* 1:59–76.

Custer, J. F., J. A. Cavallo, and R. M. Stewart
1983 Lithic Procurement and Paleo-Indian Settlement Patterns on the Middle Atlantic Coastal Plain. *North American Archaeologist* 4:263–275.

Deller, D. B.
1988 *The Paleo-indian Occupation of Southwestern Ontario: Distribution, Technology and Social Organization.* Unpublished Ph.D. dissertation, Department of Anthropology, McGill University, Montreal.

Dent, R. J.
1985 Amerinds and Environment: Myth, Reality, and the Upper Delaware Valley. In *Shawnee-Minisink*, edited by C. W. McNett, Jr., pp. 123–163. Academic Press, New York.

Dincauze, D.
1988 Tundra and Enlightenment: Landscapes for Northeastern Paleoindians. *The Quarterly Review of Archaeology* 9:6–8.

Dincauze, D., and M. L. Curran
1983 Paleoindians as Generalists: An Ecological Perspective. Paper presented at the 48th Annual Meeting, Society for American Archaeology, Pittsburgh.

Dunnell, R. C.
1988 The Southeast in American Archaeology. Paper presented at the 50th Annual Meeting of the Southeastern Archaeological Conference, New Orleans.

Dunnell, R. C., and W. S. Dancey
1983 The Siteless Survey: A Regional Scale Data

Collection Strategy. In *Advances in Archaeological Method and Theory,* vol. 6, edited by M. B. Schiffer, pp. 267–287. Academic Press, New York.

Foley, R.
1981 Off-Site Archaeology: An Alternative Approach for the Short-Sited. In *Pattern of the Past,* edited by I. Hodder, G. Isaac, and N. Hammond, pp. 157–183. Cambridge University Press, Cambridge.

Frison, G. C., and B. A. Bradley
1980 *Folsom Tools and Technology at the Hanson Site, Wyoming.* University of New Mexico Press, Albuquerque.

Gardner, W. M.
1977 The Flint Run PaleoIndian Complex and Its Implications for Eastern North American Prehistory. In *Amerinds and Their Paleoenvironments in Northeastern North America,* edited by W. S. Newman and B. Salwen, pp. 257–263. Annals of the New York Academy of Sciences No. 288.

1983 Stop Me If You've Heard This One Before: The Flint Run Paleoindian Complex Revisited. *Archaeology of Eastern North America* 11:49–64.

Gardner, W. M., and R. Verrey
1979 Typology and Chronology of Fluted Points from the Flint Run Area. *Pennsylvania Archaeologist* 49:13–45.

Gramly, R. M.
1987 A Unique Fluted Point Site in Western New York. *Indian Artifact Magazine* 6:4–6, 54.

Hopkins, K. D., and G. V. Glass
1978 *Basic Statistics for the Behavioral Sciences.* Prentice-Hall, Englewood Cliffs, New Jersey.

Howard, E. B.
1935 Evidence of Early Man in North America. *The Museum Journal* 24:61–171.

Lantz, S.
1984 Distribution of Paleo-indian Projectile Points and Tools from Western Pennsylvania: Implications for Regional Differences. *Archaeology of Eastern North America* 12:210–230.

Lepper, B. T.
1983 Fluted Point Distributional Patterns in the Eastern United States: A Contemporary Phenomena. *Midcontinental Journal of Archaeology* 8:269–285.

1985 The Effects of Cultivation and Collecting on Ohio Fluted Points: A Reply to Seeman and Prufer. *Midcontinental Journal of Archaeology* 10:241–250.

1986 *Early Paleo-indian Land Use Patterns in the Central Muskingham River Basin, Coshocton County, Ohio.* Unpublished Ph.D. dissertation, Department of Anthropology, Ohio State University, Columbus.

1988 Early Paleo-indian Foragers of Midcontinental North America. *North American Archaeologist* 9:31–51.

1989 Lithic Resource Procurement and Early Paleoindian Land Use Patterns in the Appalachian Plateau of Hoio. In *Eastern Paleoindian Lithic Resource Use,* edited by C. J. Ellis and J. Lothrop, pp. 239–257. Westview Press, Boulder.

MacDonald, G. F.
1983 Eastern North America. In *Early Man in the New World,* edited by R. Shutler, pp. 97–108. Sage Publications, Beverly Hills.

Martin, P.
1967 Prehistoric Overkill. In *Pleistocene Extinctions: The Search for a Cause,* edited by P. S. Martin and H. E. Wright, Jr., pp. 75–120. Yale University Press, New Haven.

Mason, R. J.
1958 *Late Pleistocene Geochronology and the Paleo-indian Penetration into the Lower Michigan Peninsula.* Anthropological Papers No. 11. Museum of Anthropology, University of Michigan, Ann Arbor.

1959 Indications of Paleo-indian Occupation in the Delaware Valley. *Pennsylvania Archaeologist* 29:1–17.

1960 Early Man and the Age of the Champlain Sea. *Journal of Geology* 68:366–376.

1962 The Paleo-indian Tradition in Eastern North America. *Current Anthropology* 3:227–283.

1981 *Great Lakes Archaeology.* Academic Press, New York.

McCary, B. C.
1951 A Workshop Site of Early Man in Dinwiddie County, Virginia. *American Antiquity* 17:9–17.

Meltzer, D. J.
1983 The Antiquity of Man and the Development of American Archaeology. In *Advances in Archaeological Method and Theory,* vol. 6, edited by M. B. Schiffer, pp.1–51. Academic Press, New York.

1984 *Late Pleistocene Human Adaptations in Eastern North America.* Unpublished Ph.D. dissertation, Department of Anthropology, University of Washington, Seattle.

1986 Pleistocene Overkill and the Associational Critique. *Journal of Archaeological Science* 13:51–60.

1988 Late Pleistocene Human Adaptations in Eastern North America. *Journal of World Prehistory* 2:1–52.

1989 Was Stone Exchanged Among Eastern North American Paleoindians? In *Eastern Paleoindian*

Lithic Resource Use, edited by C. J. Ellis and J. Lothrop, pp. 11–39. Westview Press, Boulder.

Meltzer, D. J., and B. D. Smith
1986 Paleoindian and Early Archaic Subsistence Strategies in Eastern North America. In *Foraging, Collecting and Harvesting: Archaic Period Subsistence and Settlement in the Eastern Woodlands*, edited by S. Neusius, pp. 1–30. Occasional Paper No. 6. Center for Archaeological Investigations, Southern Illinois University, Carbondale.

Moeller, R. W.
1983 There Is a Fluted Baby in the Bath Water. *Archaeology of Eastern North America* 11:27–29.

Prufer, O. H.
1971 Survey of Palaeo-Indian Remains in Walhonding and Tuscarawas Valleys, Ohio. *Ohio Archaeologist* 21:309–310.

Prufer, O., and R. Baby
1963 *Palaeo-indians of Ohio.* Ohio Historical Society, Columbus.

Prufer, O., and N. Wright
1970 The Welling Site (33CO2): A Fluted Point Workshop in Coshocton County, Ohio. *Ohio Archaeologist* 20:259–268.

Putnam, F. W.
1888 Paleolithic Man in Eastern and Central North America. *Proceedings of the Boston Society of Natural History* 23:247–254.

Quimby, G.
1958 Fluted Points and Geochronology of the Lake Michigan Basin. *American Antiquity* 23:247–254.
1960 *Indian Life in the Upper Great Lakes, 11,000 B.C. to A.D. 1800.* University of Chicago Press, Chicago.

Ritchie, W. A.
1953 A Probable Paleo-indian Site in Vermont. *American Antiquity* 18:249–258.
1957 Traces of Early Man in the Northeast. *Bulletin of the New York State Museum and Science Service* 358.
1965 *The Archaeology of New York State.* Natural History Press, Garden City, NY.

Roberts, F. H. H.
1940 Developments in the Problem of the North American Paleo-indian. *Smithsonian Miscellaneous Collections* 100:51–116.

Seeman, M., and O. Prufer
1982 An Updated Distribution of Ohio Fluted Points. *Midcontinental Journal of Archaeology* 7:155–169.

Shaler, N.
1893 Antiquity of Man in Eastern North America. *The American Geologist* 11:180–184.

Shetrone, H.
1936 The Folsom Phenomena as Seen from Ohio. *Ohio State Archaeological and Historical Quarterly* 45:240–256.

Shott, M.
1986 *Settlement Mobility and Technological Organization among Great Lakes Paleo-indian Foragers.* Unpublished Ph.D. dissertation, Department of Anthropology, University of Michigan, Ann Arbor.

Stoltman, J. B., and D. Baerreis
1983 The Evolution of Human Ecosystems in the Eastern United States. In *The Holocene*, edited by H. E. Wright, Jr., pp. 252–268. Late Quaternary Environments of the United States, vol. 2, H. E. Wright, Jr., general editor. University of Minnesota Press, Minneapolis.

Tukey, J. W.
1977 *Exploratory Data Analysis.* Addison-Wesley, Reading, MA.

Tunnell, C.
1977 Fluted Projectile Point Production as Revealed by Lithic Specimens from the Adair-Steadman Site in Northwest Texas. *The Museum Journal* 17:140–168.

Williams, S., and J. B. Stoltman
1965 An Outline of Southeastern United States Prehistory With Particular Emphasis on the Paleo-indian Era. In *The Quaternary of the United States*, edited by H. E. Wright, Jr., and D. Frey, pp. 669–683. Princeton University Press, Princeton.

Wilmsen, E. N.
1970 *Lithic Analysis and Cultural Inference.* Anthropological Papers No. 16. University of Arizona, Tucson.

Wilson, T.
1889 The Paleolithic Period in the District of Columbia. *Proceedings of the United States National Museum* 12:371–376.

Witthoft, J.
1952 A Paleo-indian Site in Eastern Pennsylvania: An Early Hunting Culture. *Proceedings of the American Philosophical Society* 96:464–495.

Young, D. E., and R. Bonnichsen
1984 *Understanding Stone Tools: A Cognitive Approach.* Center for the Study of Early Man, University of Maine, Orono.

Resource Orientation of Clovis and Suwannee Age Paleoindian Sites in Florida

JAMES S. DUNBAR
Florida Bureau of Archaeological Research
Division of Historical Resources
Department of State
Tallahassee, FL 32399-0250

This is the latest in a series of Florida Paleoindian site distribution studies based on the state-wide occurrence of the diagnostic Clovis, Suwannee, and Simpson lithic projectile points and proboscidean ivory foreshafts. Evidence regarding late Pleistocene resources and environments is reviewed and related to site distribution patterns. A Florida landmass that was larger than today's but had a more arid climate is implicit in this compilation.

The majority of late Pleistocene Paleoindian sites occur in the two Florida Tertiary karst regions, where the Floridan Aquifer is the dominant water source and chert is abundant. Sites occur less frequently in areas marginal to and outside the Tertiary karst regions, where localized, climate-dependent ground-water systems are common and chert is scarce or absent. The analyses of site distribution patterns, and paleo-geohydraulic and environmental data indicate that lowered late Pleistocene ground-water levels increased the availability of lithic resources but decreased potable surface water, thereby affecting Paleoindian activity and settlement options.

INTRODUCTION

Like many regions in the eastern United States, certain regions in Florida have very large concentrations of Paleoindian artifacts, which have helped provide evidence of or at least support the argument that human occupation in the East was greater than in the West. Yet, as so many scholars have pointed out, there are few sites in the East that provide the ideal conditions found in western sites, such as Blackwater Draw and so many others. In part this is attributable to the generally poor preservation of bone and other organics, as well as the lack of stratigraphic depth and unquestioned site integrity. As a result, many investigations in the East have dealt with lithic studies either on a site-specific or regional basis. To a degree this paper carries on that tradition by looking at the distribution of Paleoindian diagnostic artifacts in Florida. However, the result of this distribution analysis, which includes a look at the paleoenvironmental implications, indicates that inundated Paleoindian sites in Florida appear to represent a setting in the eastern United States where stratigraphic integrity and organic remains are sometimes preserved.

In Florida three distinctly different geohydraulic regions are recognized (Bush 1982)—regions that would have supported different environments during times of lower sea level and more arid climate. Of the three geohydraulic regions, only one, the Tertiary karst region, has appreciable concentrations of Paleoindian sites, even though karst terrains tend to be arid because of poor soil-moisture holding capacity (Legrande 1973) and ground-water table fluctuation in response to sea-level change (Brooks 1973a and b). The large ground-water system that is held in the limestones of the Tertiary karst regions seems to have created a favorable setting for human occupation, and the chert within these limestones provided the material for lithic tool making. In the marginal and outlying areas, where other water sources are predominantly available and chert is absent, sites are far less frequent. Paleoenvironmental data suggest the reason for the apparent lack of sites is probably that of reduced water tables in the regions outside the Tertiary karst regions. Many Paleoindian sites located in former lowland terrestrial and wetland settings in the Tertiary karst regions are now inundated because of sea level rise and corresponding response by the inland Floridan aquifer.

HISTORICAL BACKGROUND

In 1875 Jeffries Wyman published an account of archaeological sites located along Florida's St. Johns River, including one location that produced a Clovis-like projectile point that he referred to as having a "peculiar form" (Wyman 1973). One of the first suggestions that extinct late Pleistocene animals and humans had coexisted in the southeastern United States came in 1915, when artifacts and human remains were discovered in a stratified fossil deposit at Vero, Florida (Sellards 1917). This and subsequent finds at the "Vero Man" and "Melbourne Man" sites were extensively reported by E. H. Sellards, the state geologist, and J. W. Gidley of the Smithsonian Institution (Gidley 1929). The Vero and Melbourne sites proved to be controversial, and accounts both supporting and discounting the association of early human populations with extinct Ice Age fauna appeared in the national literature (Sellards 1947).

In Florida during the 1930s and 1940s, mastodon remains and suspected early artifacts were recovered underwater from Wakulla and Ichetucknee Springs and on land at Bon Terra Farm (Connert 1932; Jenks and Simpson 1941; Neill 1953). Clarence Simpson, an assistant with the Florida Geological Survey, recorded several sites producing Clovis-like artifacts, including the Ichetucknee Springs locality, which contained carved proboscidean ivory foreshafts (Jenks and Simpson 1941; Simpson n.d.). Simpson (1948) was the first to propose a late Pleistocene age for the Clovis-like assemblage of Florida artifacts, although this hypothesis was not proven for another decade.

In 1950 John Goggin conducted test excavations at a site overlooking the confluence of the Santa Fe and Suwannee rivers, in an attempt to identify a component of the so-called "Santa Fe" complex of suspected Paleoindian lithic tools (Goggin 1950). Although the excavations produced no in situ remains, Goggin defined the Suwannee projectile point type (Figure 1c) as a new and distinct type in comparison to Clovis (Figure 1a,b) and other lanceolate forms.

In the early 1950s William Edwards (1952) recovered both lanceolate and notched projectile points below ceramic levels at the Lake Helen Blazes site near Melbourne, but little attention was given to the early component. Recognition that Suwannee and Clovis-like artifacts represented the Paleoindian tradition in Florida came in 1958 when Wilfred T. Neill uncovered a deep stratigraphic sequence containing Ceramic and Preceramic components in a sand hill overlooking Silver Springs run. The deepest cultural component produced Clovis and fluted and unfluted Suwannee projectile points at a depth of about 2.3 m below the surface and 30 cm below an Early Archaic level (Neill 1958). Ripley Bullen (1958) attained similar but less convincing results from excavations conducted at the Whitehurst site, which is located on a bluff overlooking Paynes Prairie near Gainesville.

In 1967 the Florida Geological Survey published the results of excavation work conducted by Clarence Simpson at Darby and Hornsby Springs. At Hornsby Springs, Suwannee points were generally recovered below Archaic artifacts. One test unit produced a mastodon tooth and a flint flake in a sealed deposit (Dolan and Allen 1961). Simpson's little-recognized Ichetucknee and Hornsby Springs sites had yielded late Pleistocene faunal remains in temporal association with artifacts and thus became acceptable as supportive evidence of a Paleoindian tradition in Florida.

The Simpson point (Figure 2a,b,c) was the third lanceolate projectile-point type to be recognized in Florida (Bullen 1968) and, along with the Clovis and Suwannee types, was identified as one of the early Paleoindian forms. By the mid-1960s there was no doubt that humans had occupied Florida during the late Pleistocene and had left behind an extensive assortment of Clovis, Suwannee, and Simpson projectile points and related stone and ivory artifacts.

By 1960 scuba diving became widely available and

Figure 1. Paleoindian projectile points from the Lower Aucilla River: **A)** Clovis fluted; **B)** Clovis fluted; **C)** Suwannee unfluted.

Figure 2. Simpson projectile points: **A)** Simpson unfluted, St. Marks River; **B)** Simpson fluted, Wakulla River; **C)** Simpson unfluted, Lower Aucilla River.

divers began discovering numerous underwater sites. Simpson led the way in the days of hard-hat diving and surface bobbing for artifacts using a glass-bottomed bucket and long-handled tongs, but scuba diving gave direct access to vast areas of unexplored submerged lands. Sites like Warm Mineral and Little Salt Springs were discovered by adventurous divers but were initially treated with a degree of skepticism by archaeologists (Goggin 1962). However, throughout the 1960s, too many diagnostic artifacts and fossils were discovered in submerged sinkholes, caves, and river bottoms for scientists to entirely ignore.

Paleontologists were the first to recognize the scientific potential of some of these underwater sites. Systematic surveys revealed a large number of underwater fossil sites spanning the Pleistocene epoch. Certain Florida river systems, primarily in karst terrain, were littered with Pleistocene fossil concentrations and yielded extensive skeletal remains of several individuals, most commonly horse and proboscideans (both mammoth and mastodon). Some Pleistocene fossil sites contained partially articulated skeletal remains indicative of primary deposition (Webb 1974, 1976). Other interesting finds, such as the discovery of a butcher-marked mammoth vertebra in the Santa Fe River (Bullen et al. 1970), and a Simpson point and other lithic artifacts and fossil bone from Silver Springs Cave, seemed to suggest that the materials may have been deposited under subaerial conditions (Neill 1964).

Ben Waller (1970) asserted that many river-channel Paleoindian artifact concentrations represented kill-butcher sites, based on the types of lithic tools and fossil bones present. He defined the typical kill-butcher site as occurring in karst river channels where rocky shallows (rapids) were adjacent to sinkholes or other deep sections of rivers. Waller hypothesized that these shallow areas were game trails utilized by large animals to cross rivers that would have been otherwise difficult to ford. He believed that game-trail crossings served as ambush points for Paleoindian hunters to immobilize their prey once the animals had been driven off the shallows into deeper water.

Wilfred Neill (1964) introduced a differing view, proposing the "Oasis Hypothesis." This hypothesis contended that some underwater Paleoindian artifact concentrations represented drowned terrestrial sites: sites that had either been utilized or occupied during a time of subaerial exposure and subsequently inundated by water level rise. Geologist Kelly Brooks (1973a, 1973b) further developed Neill's idea, proposing that the availability of surface water for drinking fluctuated so radically that it impacted prehistoric populations. Brooks recognized that potable water exists in Florida as climate-dependent perched systems (ponds, lakes and rivers) or as exposures of the drought-tolerant Tertiary limestone aquifer system—the Floridan Aquifer.

Based on paleontological evidence from Pleistocene fossil localities, S. David Webb (1974) proposed the eustatic-hydraulic cycle for the karstic terrains of Florida. During glacial phases of the Pleistocene, lowered sea level resulted in concomitant lowering of the surface of the Floridan Aquifer. During interglacial phases of the Pleistocene, sea level and aquifer level were higher. Landmass not only increased and decreased with sea level change on the continental margins but also in the interior, as ground-water systems fluctuated in response to climatic and/or sea-level change. Thus, cyclic draining and flooding of onshore (interior) lowland areas have occurred, with ground water responding to changes in climate and sea level, since the last glacial cycle (Dunbar 1981).

In the last two decades many additional terrestrial and underwater Clovis/Suwannee sites have been discovered (Allen 1967; Dunbar and Waller 1983; Waller 1970). One inundated human activity area of Clovis age that has been investigated is on a ledge 26 m below the water's surface at Little Salt Springs (Clausen et al. 1979). A terrestrial Paleoindian base-camp locality investigated at Harney Flats near Tampa has yielded assemblages of lithic tools discretely distributed around former activity areas (Daniel and Wisenbaker 1987). Most recently, investigations at the Page/Ladson site have revealed a possible Paleoindian level containing lanceolate points, two debitage flakes, a ground-stone implement believed to be a bola weight, and scattered elements of Pleistocene horse and proboscidean. This level occurs below a 10,000-year-old notched-point (Bolen) level and is separated from it by a sequence of dense clayey silts.

Although Clovis-age radiocarbon dates have been derived from artifact-bearing levels at the Little Salt Springs (Clausen et al. 1979) and Page/Ladson (Dunbar et al. 1988) sites, an in situ component containing early Paleoindian lanceolate points has yet to be dated in Florida, owing to the general absence of dateable material in terrestrial sites and in-place diagnostic artifacts underwater.

This paper will examine the relationship between Clovis/Simpson/Suwannee Paleoindian site distribution patterns and geologic and hydraulic factors that are believed to have existed in late Pleistocene Florida to determine if correlations exist.

GEOHYDRAULIC REGIONS OF FLORIDA

An understanding of how sea level, climate, and geology have interacted to control the extent of surface-water systems and how water-level fluctuations have affected available drinking water sources and usable terrestrial space is important to understanding Florida's prehistory. For example, lithic and potable water resources varied inversely with ground-water fluctuations through time. When water tables were low, the availability of lithic resources (chert) for tool production increased as outcrops emerged. Conversely, when water tables rose, the availability of potable surface water increased as did settlement options, but lithic resources decreased owing to inundation (Dunbar 1981).

There are three geohydraulic regions in Florida differing in lithology and permeability (adapted from Bush

1982:Figure 4) and therefore differing in their potential for yielding accessible lithic and potable water resources (Figure 3):

1. The *Tertiary karst regions* are located along the central Gulf Coast and in the north-central Florida Panhandle where chert-bearing limestones outcrop near or at the ground's surface (Figure 4). These formations range in age from mid-Eocene to early Miocene and are sometimes silicified or dolomitized. The Tertiary karst regions contain the major chert resources in Florida. Tertiary limestones, some containing chert, extend an unknown distance offshore along the Gulf Coast between Tampa and Apalachee bays.

   The limestone terrain is mature karst, including open (cavernous), well-developed, subsurface drainage that appears youthful because sea-level transgressions and regressions since the Miocene have resculptured fresh features on old rock exposures (Williams et al. 1977). The primary chert-bearing limestones include the Eocene Ocala Group, Crystal River Formation, Oligocene Suwannee Limestone Formation, and Miocene Tampa Stage, St. Marks Formation.

   The Floridan Aquifer is the dominant water source and is exposed in karst features such as sinkholes, springs, and river beds below the aquifer's surface. Areas of the earth's crust below the surface of the limestone aquifer either hold water as sinkhole ponds or discharge aquifer water from springs and karst river beds. Areas of the earth's crust above the top of the Floridan Aquifer do not hold water unless they are capable of perching precipitation. Along the Santa Fe River evidence of once-higher aquifer levels is recorded by the presence of now-extinct springs and river channels that were formed during the Talbot (12 m above present) and Pamlico (9 m above present) sea-level stages but are left dry by modern lower levels (Edwards 1948; Stubbs 1940). Although a few ground-water

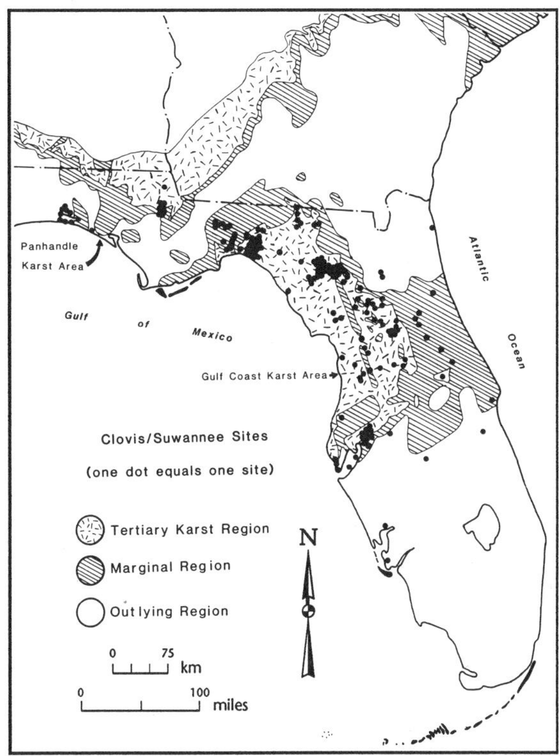

Figure 3. Map of Florida showing the distribution of Clovis/Suwannee sites in relation to the three geohydraulic regions of Florida.

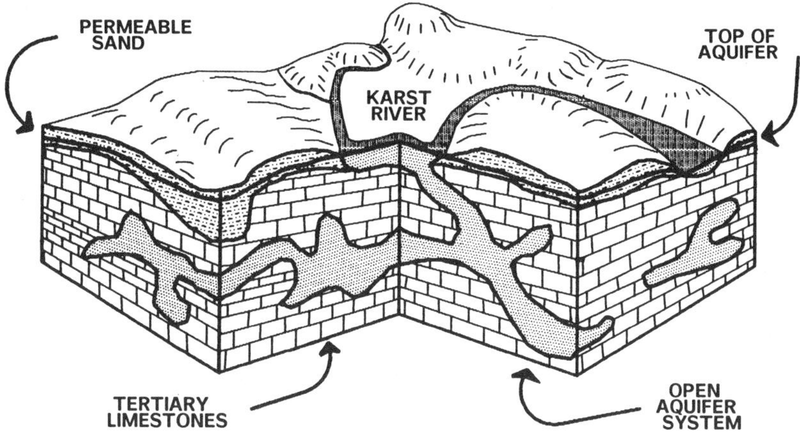

Figure 4. Geologic block diagram showing an idealized section through the Tertiary karst region. Note that the karst river represents an exposure of the otherwise underground Floridan Aquifer and that elevations above the aquifer's surface do not hold water.

systems are perched above the Floridan Aquifer in the Tertiary karst regions, a few "islands" of clay or other impermeable sediments block off the limestone's porous nature and allow wet-weather ponds to be perched above the impermeable strata. A typical upland karst landscape is not in close proximity to the aquifer's surface and tends to be drought-prone, supporting xeric habitats (Buono et al. 1979; LeGrande 1973; Williams et al. 1977). Therefore, as a generalization, surface water is uncommon in the Tertiary karst regions and is most abundant in lowland areas where the aquifer is near or above the ground's surface. Perched water systems above the aquifer are uncommon but where they occur they are very localized, generally intermittent, and dependent on local precipitation much more than other ground-water systems.

2. The *marginal region* surrounds and extends away from the Tertiary karst region (Figure 5). Here the Tertiary limestones are covered by up to 35 m of clastic sediments, except where sinkholes, spring caverns, or river channels expose the chert-bearing limestones. Lithic resources generally occur either as replacement cherts in the Tertiary limestones or as opaline cherts in the non-karst, Miocene Hawthorne Formation (Upchurch and Strom 1982). In the marginal region opaline cherts range from a fragile, almost vitreous lithology to a very fine-grained, tougher chert of better tool-making quality.

   Potable water sources occur where local, climate-dependent, perched ground-water systems are exposed as perched ponds or as occasional exposures of the Floridan Aquifer in sinks and river channels (Williams et al. 1977). In the marginal region the Floridan Aquifer usually underlies one or two perched systems. The near-surface ground-water system is generally referred to as the Superficial Aquifer. Perched ground-water systems below the superficial but above the Floridan Aquifer are known as secondary aquifers.

3. The *outlying region* (Figure 6) lies beyond the marginal region. Tertiary limestones are not accessible, since they are buried by more than 35 m of sediment overburden. Lithic resources are rare and are

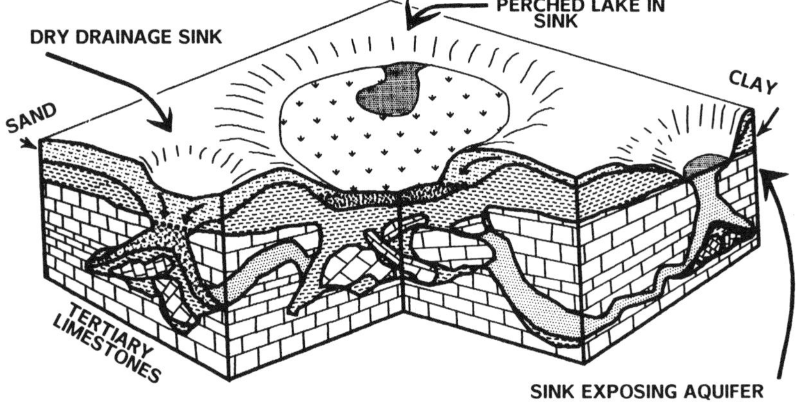

Figure 5. Geologic block diagram showing an idealized section through the marginal region. Note that some karst sinkholes, like the idealized drainage sink, do not hold water because the confining strata have been breached and backfilled with porous sand. Since the drainage sink is above the aquifer's surface, it does not hold water. The idealized perched lake is similar to the Harney Flats-type of karst feature. Harney Flats, like lakes or swamps, is mostly separated from the aquifer by a layer of confining sediments, but has an occasional sinkhole breaching the confining layer. Thus, many of the karst lowland basins perch water in some areas and expose the aquifer in others. The sinkhole exposing the aquifer is typical of the deep cenote type and exposes the aquifer because there was insufficient sediment to backfill the sink.

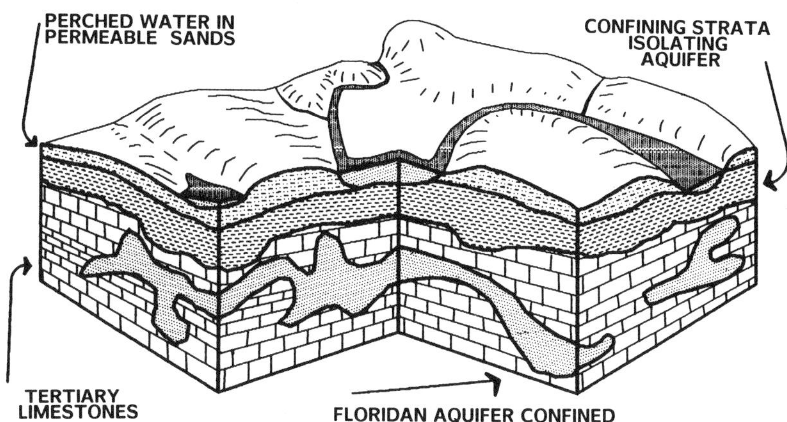

Figure 6. Geologic block diagram showing an idealized section through the outlying region. A superficial aquifer is held in the permeable sand and supported by the confining strata. The Floridan Aquifer is isolated by the confining strata except where rare sinkholes breach the sediments. Perched water-table ponds and lakes, as well as other surface-water exposures, are abundant during periods of near-modern precipitation amounts.

of inferior knapping quality, consisting of Quaternary lithographic limestones and opaline cherts from the Miocene Hawthorne Formation. Opaline cherts appear to be limited to the area between Tampa Bay and Sarasota eastward to the Peace River. Lithographic limestones (that flake like chert) outcrop along the Atlantic Coast from approximately Melbourne southward to Cutler Ridge in South Miami. This belt of lithographic limestone occurs along the coast and extends offshore.

Deep sinkholes and springs are uncommon in the outlying region, and the few that exist, like Little Salt and Warm Mineral Springs, have breached the Floridan Aquifer where the confining overburden is relatively thin (35 to 75 m). The Floridan Aquifer in the outlying region generally contains highly mineralized water. Potable water occurs in localized climate-dependent perched aquifer systems (Clark 1964).

Lithic Resource Potentials

The three geohydraulic regions differ in their potential for yielding lithic resources to prehistoric populations. The karst region has the greatest potential for yielding abundant, good knapping-quality material for lithic tool production. The marginal region has limited lithic resources, while the outlying region contains the least amount of lithic material and little that could be considered ideal for stone tool manufacture.

Potable Surface-water Potentials

Within the marginal and outlying regions perched or superficial ground-water systems are exposed at the surface in channels, swamps, lakes, and ponds. Superficial ground-water systems are separated from lower, more deeply buried systems by semi-confining or confining strata. The underlying stratum's ability or inability to transmit water downward determines if it has semi-confining or confining characteristics.

A confining sediment does not allow water to be transmitted through it; therefore a confining layer must be breached by a sinkhole or dissected by faulting before water can escape downward. Perched systems that are confined are totally climate-dependent and are independent of the draining effects that lowered sea levels had on the Floridan Aquifer during the Pleistocene.

Semi-confining strata support perched ground-water systems but allow some water to slowly migrate downward to a lower ground-water system. For example, precipitation in the marginal region north of the Santa Fe River replenishes a perched ground-water system, but, up to five months after a wet period, increased discharge in the Santa Fe River betrays the semi-confining nature of the perched system (Meyer 1962). Perched systems supported by semi-confining strata are less stable than confined systems because they are climate-dependent and lose water, although slowly, to deeper ground-water systems. Assuming that factors such as the size of the ground-water unit and evapotranspiration are the same, perched surface water supported by semi-confining strata are more likely to be intermittent than systems supported by confining strata.

At present surface water is more prevalent in the marginal and outlying regions than in the two Florida Tertiary karst regions. Precipitation is sufficient to keep perched systems replenished, in contrast to the karst regions, where precipitation seeps quickly through porous sand to the level of the Floridan Aquifer. For example, although perched ponds exist in depressions on hilltops outside the karst regions, they cannot be supported in the Tertiary karst regions because of the well-drained soils (for a similar example, see Figure 5 [Drainage sink compared with a perched lake]). It seems ironic that one of the nation's largest ground-water systems, the Floridan Aquifer, occurs near the surface where potable water is seemingly the most scarce, while much smaller local perched aquifers support myriads of swamps, rivers, lakes, and ponds.

PREVIOUS SITE DISTRIBUTION STUDIES

Clarence Simpson (1948) was the first to systematically compile a list of "Folsom-like" lanceolate point sites in Florida. Additional site distribution studies, based on the occurrence of Clovis and other lanceolate forms, were subsequently reported by AENA (1982); Allen (1967); Bullen (1958, 1962); Dunbar and Waller (1983); Neill (1964); Science Applications, Inc. (1979); Waller (1970); and Waller and Dunbar (1977). These compilations indicate that Florida contains one of eastern North America's largest Paleoindian site concentrations. Site clusters occur in two areas of the state where chert-bearing limestones of Tertiary age are at or near ground surface. The largest Tertiary karst region is located along the Ocala Ridge, from Florida's central peninsula westward to the Gulf of Mexico between Tampa and Tallahassee. The second region is located in the Florida Panhandle in Jackson and Holmes counties and extends into Alabama, Georgia, and South Carolina. Although little is known regarding the distribution of Clovis/Suwannee point sites in the Tertiary karst regions of southeastern Alabama and southwestern Georgia, Paleoindian sites have been recorded in the southeastern part of South Carolina and adjacent counties of Georgia (Goodyear and Charles 1984).

When compared with the geohydraulic regions of Florida, the site distribution studies indicate that Clovis, Suwannee, and Simpson sites are concentrated in the Tertiary karst regions and rapidly decrease in number with increased distance away from these areas. The present sample agrees with previous compilations and suggests that Paleoindian sites are disproportionately concentrated within the Tertiary karst regions.

Supporting the idea that the present sample and previous compilations accurately reflect site distribution patterns is the observation that the majority of Clovis/Suwannee Paleoindian sites have been recorded in rural areas where rapid development has not occurred. Most sites are located in rural west-central and northern Florida, where construction and earth-moving activities, other than farming, have been minimal. Conversely, in east-central and southern Florida, where rapid development and earth moving are widespread, few sites of Clovis/Suwannee age have been located, even though the potential for site discovery seems much greater. In the outlying region along the eastern seaboard and along the Gulf Coast in the Pensacola area, ground-disturbing development is occurring at an alarming pace, yet few Clovis/Suwannee sites have been encountered. Conversely, along the border of the Tertiary karst and marginal regions near Tampa, rapid development has led to the discovery of several Clovis/Suwannee sites, including the Harney Flats site (Hi507) (Daniel and Wisenbaker 1987) and one of the state's larger quarry clusters. The Tampa area has a large bay, karstified flat-bottomed prairies surrounded by uplands (including Harney Flats), and the karstic Hillsborough River. Therefore, the distribution of known Paleoindian sites is believed to accurately reflect geographic areas of preferred cultural activity and occupation.

THE SITES

The majority of Clovis/Suwannee-age Paleoindian sites have been located because recent human activities or natural erosion have exposed artifacts for easy discovery. Most terrestrial Paleoindian sites have been discovered as a result of ground-disturbing development or farming activities (Florida, now the fourth most-populated state, is growing by some 1,000 persons a day). Inundated sites are most frequently discovered when erosion exposes artifacts to divers (Waller 1969, 1970) or when industrial dredging displaces material to fill areas where it is later recovered (Goodyear and Warren 1972; Warren 1970, 1972).

This study considers an area a site if it has produced one or more diagnostic artifacts. Perhaps the most questionable "sites" in terms of knowing their precise locations are the dredge-barrow sites that Goodyear and Warren (1972) identified as the original source of artifacts recovered from dredge fill around Tampa Bay. Although the precise site locations may not have been known, the larger areas excavated for fill material were identified (Goodyear and Warren 1972).

Underwater sites, particularly those in river channels, that have been partially eroded by current action have sometimes been viewed as questionable because of the potential for downstream transport. For many years archaeologists in Florida were reluctant to investigate sites in flowing water because it was assumed that current action had destroyed archaeological information (Clauser 1973). This reluctance did little to stimulate funding and research. However, most karst rivers do not transport the particulate sediment loads normally associated with non-karst rivers like the Mississippi (Puri et al. 1967; Vernon 1951). Because karst rivers do not carry a silt-sized sediment load, it follows that the downstream transport of much larger artifacts and fossils also has not taken place. Redeposited artifacts from inundated sites on karst river bottoms are believed to have been displaced vertically downward, but evidence indicates they remain adjacent to their site of origin. It should be noted that, while vertical displacement of artifacts from shallower to deeper locations does occur, displacement up slope and over great distances does not.

For example, the Norden site (8Gi40) and the Fowler Bridge Mastodon site (8Hi393) are stratigraphically deflated where they occur in the river channel but adjacent stratified components extend out of the channel on land (Dunbar 1981). A stratigraphically deflated site located in Little River that was surface collected within a grid system revealed an artifact scatter still suggestive of activity areas (Willis 1988). The Page/Ladson site (8Je591) and others like it represent the most striking examples of karst river sites because they retain stratified components in the "erosive" area of the central channel. The Page/Ladson site, located in the Aucilla River in a sediment-filled sinkhole, contains in situ cultural components in uneroded deposits 3 to 7 m thick (Dunbar et al. 1988; Dunbar et al. 1989).

All the above-mentioned sites have stratigraphically deflated components in the river channel, with related components directly adjacent on land. The Page/Ladson site has in situ components both on land and underwater. There is no evidence that artifacts have been significantly washed downstream but good evidence to suggest that finds of redeposited materials may lead to discoveries of uneroded portions of terrestrial and/or underwater archaeological components. Therefore it is assumed that concentrations of diagnostic Paleoindian artifacts collected from Florida river systems represent true site locations even though most sites seem to lack stratigraphic integrity.

SITE DISTRIBUTION PATTERN

Diagnostic artifacts included in this study reside both in public and private collections. This sample is an update, with some additions, of the distribution sample presented by Dunbar and Waller in 1983 and, as such, represents the largest Florida site-by-site documentation thus far compiled.

A total of 564 diagnostic artifacts (543 lithic points and 21 ivory foreshafts) (see Figure 7) recovered from 172 sites (Figure 3) are documented in this sample. The study includes several recently discovered sites, most of which are located within the areas of previously known concentrations, primarily inside the Tertiary karst regions. The majority of sites (122 sites or 71% of the sample) occur within the Tertiary karst regions (Table 1). The marginal region (Table 2) is second, with 29 sites (17%), and the outlying region (Table 3) last, with 21 sites (12%). In terms of the number of diagnostic artifacts recovered from the sites, 445 diagnostic artifacts, or 79% of the total, were recovered from the Tertiary karst regions. The sites in the marginal region produced 88 diagnostic artifacts, or 16% of the sample; sites in the outlying region produced 31 diagnostic artifacts, or 5% of the total. (One site in the outlying region, Little Salt Springs, yielded Clovis-age radiocarbon dates, but produced no diagnostic artifacts). As might be expected, the number of lithic diagnostic artifacts decreases with increased distance away from the lithic resource base in the Tertiary karst regions.

All ivory artifacts, fragments from 21 ivory foreshafts, have been recovered from sites within the Tertiary karst regions. Sites that have yielded ivory foreshafts occur in karst rivers that have a below-average potential for erosion and favorable soil conditions for bone preservation. Other than the alkaline sediments in sinkholes, karst rivers, and lake basins, most of the Tertiary karst regions are blanketed by soil that is not conducive for preserving bone or ivory. In contrast, in the marginal and outlying regions along the Atlantic Coast from Brevard to Dade counties, soil conditions are alkaline over broad areas. Although many Pleistocene fossil localities have been found in the so-called "Melbourne Bed," no ivory foreshafts have been recovered, and, though present, Clovis/Suwannee lithic artifacts are rare. Overall, the recognized assemblage of diagnostic artifacts, including ivory foreshafts, is rare in

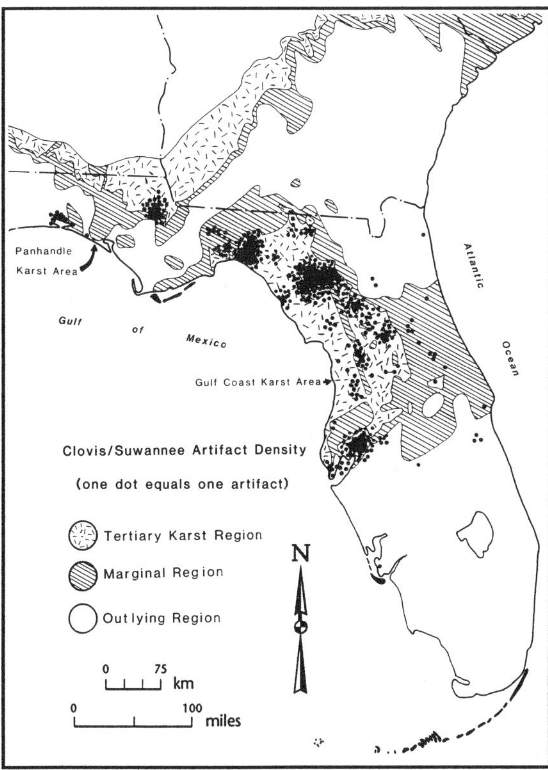

Figure 7. Map of Florida showing the distribution density of Clovis/Suwannee diagnostic artifacts in relation to the geohydraulic regions of Florida.

these regions, even though the conditions that would have insured their preservation are present. The scarcity of both ivory and lithic diagnostic artifacts, particularly in the outlying region, suggests that Florida Paleoindian populations were either extensively concentrated in the Tertiary karst regions or that Paleoindian peoples outside of the karst regions favored a tool kit that is largely unrecognized, rather than Clovis or Clovis-like artifacts.

Of the total number of sites, 81, or 47%, are inundated underwater locations, while 50, or 29%, are terrestrial locations. The other 41 sites (24%) are located in flood-prone areas (river flood plains) or have terrestrial and wetland components. Considered from a slightly different perspective, 122 sites (71%) are or have components located in wetland or inundated situations. Perhaps most striking, 155 sites, or 90% of the sample, are located in, adjacent to, or are less than a day's walk from karst features (sinkholes, caves, river channels, etc.). Clearly, many lowland areas now holding water were dry during the Paleoindian occupation of Florida and were utilized by the early inhabitants. The lowland areas most preferred were connected to the Floridan Aquifer by one or more karst features, suggesting that potable surface water in any of the geohydraulic regions of Florida was scarce during the late Pleistocene. Despite late Pleistocene low-water stands and because of its massive size, the Floridan Aquifer appears to have provided the most reliable source of drinking water.

Site Locations Within Physiographic Zones

Florida Clovis/Suwannee sites are typically located within five physiographic settings or "zones." Zone, as the term is applied here, refers to areas of much smaller geographic size than the geohydraulic regions that share similar physiographic features and contain sites. Collectively, these "zones" represent a small portion of the Florida landmass that otherwise appears to be devoid of late Pleistocene Paleoindian sites. Some zones occur in one of the three previously discussed geohydraulic regions, while others cross from one geohydraulic region into another.

Comparison of the distribution of Clovis/Suwannee sites with Florida's geohydraulic regions shows site concentrations indicative of resource orientation around scarce water but abundant chert supplies. The comparison of site distribution densities within physiographic zones allows for finer sorting and site predictive modeling. The five major physiographic zones are:

1. *Karst river valley zones*—The largest concentrations of Clovis/Suwannee sites, 104 sites or 60% of the sample, occur in the karst river valleys. Most karst river channels are located in the Tertiary karst regions, but some extend into the marginal region until the sediment above bedrock becomes too thick for the river to down cut through and expose the limestone. Karst river sites are located overlooking rivers, in the flood plains, or directly in the channel bottoms. The Butler site in the Santa Fe River and the Aucilla River Page/Ladson site are representative of this site type.
2. *Karst lowland basin zones*—The second largest concentration of sites occurs within the Tertiary karst and marginal regions, where large karstified lakes, prairies, and swamps are surrounded by high ground. These karst features are connected directly to the Floridan Aquifer by occasional sinks or springs. Twenty-five sites, or 15% of the sample, are located in or overlook these types of features. The Whitehurst site, which overlooks Paynes Prairie, and Harney Flats are typical examples of the sites located in or around lowland karst basins. It should be mentioned that three sites (2% of the sample) occur in similar but non-karst settings. They are located in or adjacent to lake bottoms in the outlying regions.
3. *Upland karst zones*—Upland karst sites occur along the Ocala Ridge in north-central Florida and in the Jackson and Holmes County cave district in the panhandle of Florida. Eleven sites (6% of the sample) have been discovered in upland karst areas. The upland karst areas are found within the Tertiary karst regions where well-developed dry-cave systems and numerous chert outcrops co-occur.

   The Withlacoochee State Forest, on the borders of Hernando and Citrus counties, contains four upland site localities and is a good example of an upland karst location. Parts of the Withlacoochee State Forest are topographically diverse and highly karstified, with elevations abruptly changing (at least for Florida) from 60 to 3 m above sea level. Sediment cover over the limestone also varies from hilltop to hilltop. Some limestone areas are covered with confining clay sediments, while other areas are covered by porous sand. Thus, areas of xeric well-drained karst habitats occur adjacent to areas of mixed hardwoods and perched ponds. The dry cave systems are located at an average elevation of 27 m above sea level, and most are accessible without climbing gear. Chert resources occur as silicified boulders of Crystal River Formation or Suwannee Limestone Formation.
4. *Isolated karst zones*—Isolated, generally cenote-type sinkholes occasionally have an associated Clovis/Suwannee site. Five sites, or 3% of the sample, are located around isolated sinkholes. Isolated karst zones occur in all geohydraulic regions of Florida but are most common in the Tertiary karst regions, less common in the marginal region,

and least common in the outlying region. Little Salt Springs, a site in the outlying region, has produced cultural remains dating to the Clovis period. Although the sites may not be Clovis/Suwannee in age, Devil's Den in the Tertiary karst region and Warm Mineral Spring in the outlying region (along with Little Salt Springs) represent some of the most well-known sites located in Florida cenotes.

5. *Coastal and St. Johns River lowlands zones*—Coastal lowlands include modern bays and broad lagoons adjacent to the coastline. Bays and lagoons are at or within a meter of present sea level. The St. Johns River is a broad interconnected series of lowland features apparently formed by higher sea-level stands. The coastal and St. Johns River lowland zones are located in the marginal and outlying regions of the state. Coastal lowland sites associated with Chactawhatchee and Tampa bays on the Gulf Coast are found in areas with karst connections to Tertiary limestones. Sites in and along the St. Johns River occur in this lowland valley from the very borders of the Tertiary karst region to areas in the outlying region like Lake Hellen Blazes. The valley of the St. Johns River is of interest, since it is the only lowland corridor leading from the Tertiary karst region to the Atlantic Coast. For example, the sites located along the St. Johns River lead from the Silver Springs area southward to the Melbourne and Vero "Man" site areas of the Atlantic Coast. There are 13 sites, or 8% of the distribution sample, that are located in karstified areas connected to the Tertiary limestones, as opposed to 11 sites, or 6% of the sample, that are associated with non-karst areas.

Within each geohydraulic region, but most noticeably in the Tertiary karst regions, site clustering, indicating patterned site placement, occurs in certain physiographic zones, primarily the lowlands. The great majority of sites are confined to three physiographic zones. The karst rivers, karst lowland basins, and upland karst zones contain 81% of the Paleoindian sites represented in this sample. All three zones share the characteristic of having open karst features (cenote sinkholes, caves, spring vents, etc.). The limestone rivers, with numerous sinkholes and caves, normally represent the most highly developed karst areas and contain 60% of the recorded sites in this sample. The lowland karst basins, which are less karstified, contain the next largest concentration of sites, with 15% of the sample. The upland karst zones are actually more karstified than the lowland basins, but contain only 6% of the sample.

The density of site locations within each physiographic zone appears to be directly proportional to the abundance of karst features that expose and deeply penetrate the acquifer's surface. The low frequency of sites in the upland karst zones suggests lowland locations were greatly favored, although karstification may have helped make the uplands attractive.

PALEO-GEOHYDROLOGY, CLIMATE, AND DISTRIBUTION

The Floridan Aquifer is estimated to hold several trillion gallons of water and represents one of the nation's largest ground-water systems (Cooper et al. 1953). Although factors such as precipitation, discharge, and earth tides cause fluctuations in the Floridan Aquifer (Meyer 1962), they are relatively minor because of the aquifer's large size. When sea level drops, however, the open (cavernous) nature of karst terrains allows the aquifer to deflate (although not necessarily on a 1:1 basis with the sea) and withdraw beneath the ground's surface (Brooks 1973a).

Well-drained karst terrain, sufficiently above the ground water it holds, has an effect on environment as great as climate and tends to promote xeric habitats (Legrande 1973). A tendency towards xeric habitats can be seen today in some areas of the Tertiary karst regions, a condition that would have been exacerbated during lower stands of the Floridan Aquifer. It seems unusual then, that many late Pleistocene fossil and Paleoindian sites are located in the Tertiary karst regions, where surface water was reduced by lower aquifer levels and drier habitats would have been promoted regardless of precipitation amounts.

If the Tertiary karst regions were "artificially" arid during the late Pleistocene, owing to the nature of karst, then it becomes important to understand where the best sources of potable water were likely to have occurred. In the marginal and outlying regions, confining and semi-confining sediments were certainly capable of supporting perched surface-water systems, assuming sufficient precipitation occurred. However, pollen and geologic core data indicate that the climate during the last Wisconsin glacial stage was more arid than at present and shallow lake basins in the marginal and outlying regions were dry (Watts 1983).

For example, Lake Okeechobee, located in the outlying region, today averages between 1,450 and 1,900 km^2 in size. During the late Pleistocene and early Holocene, however, Lake Okeechobee was dry except for one period of seasonal intermittence around 12,000 years ago, or about the time of the Two Creeks interstade (Brooks 1974; Gleason et al. 1974). A few lakes with modern depths greater than 18 m in the marginal and outlying regions held water by about 15,000 years ago in North Florida and by about 13,000 years ago in South Florida. Moderation of an arid Ice Age climate appears to have occurred about 15,000 to 12,000 years ago in the latitudes of the Tertiary karst regions. During this time broad-leafed mesic forest became established in the marginal region of Northeast Florida around Sheelar Lake (Watts 1980, 1983). The appearance of mesic forest 15,000 years ago is interpreted here as an indication that precipitation and perched ground-water systems supported the new vegetation assemblage, but the quantity of available ground water was such that only the very deep lake basins held water. Subsequent to 12,000 years ago a dryer climatic phase ensued, which seems to have peaked about 10,000 years ago. This phase lasted until shallow lake basins in the marginal and outlying regions began flooding around 8500 yr B.P. (Brooks 1973a, 1973b; Watts 1983).

The environment and local habitats in the marginal and outlying regions appear to have varied during the Clovis/Suwannee occupation of Florida. Climate in North Florida seems to have experienced the most pronounced moderation away from arid conditions about 12,000 years ago. In South Florida the climate remained drier than in the north; however, a peak in climatic moderation also occurred about 12,000 years ago. Changes in vegetation assemblages between 12,000 and 10,500 yr B.P. suggest the climate was again dry, although deep lakes were present.

From the standpoint of paleobotanical assemblages, environmental conditions in the Tertiary karst regions are just now beginning to be studied and are not yet well defined as of this writing. Perhaps the best environmental indicators come from paleontological lines of evidence.

The fossil record in the Tertiary karst regions shows that drought-tolerant animals like the peccary *(Platygonus)* occurred in upland areas where dry grassland and savanna habitats are believed to have existed. Another form of peccary *(Mylohyus)* is believed to have favored wetter habitats as a relatively solitary forest dweller and occupied karst river basins like the Ichetucknee River. Herbivores such as mastodon, horse, and camel appear to have ranged throughout the Tertiary karst regions, occupying uplands far away from the intermediate karst plains and lowlands. Other herbivores, including the mammoth, bison, tapir, and Jefferson sloth, seem to have remained closer to lowland habitats, since their fossil remains are not recorded from upland locations (Webb 1974).

In the Aucilla River the Page/Ladson and Black Hole Cave sites have components dating 18,000 and 20,500 years old that, so far, have yielded no large animal fossils. At the Page/Ladson site younger components, dating from about 15,000 to 10,500 yr B.P., contain fairly abundant large animal remains, including mastodon, horse, and camel. The apparent absence or scarcity of Pleistocene megafauna in the Aucilla River area prior to about 15,000 years ago suggests harsh environmental conditions. Even though the Black Hole Cave and Page/Ladson sites contained wetland species such as cypress 18,000 to 20,000 years ago, they represent rare occurrences in the bottoms of sediment-lined sinkholes that are now 10 to 13 m below sea level. Because the remains of large Pleistocene herbivores are abundant in the sediments that postdate 15,000 yr B.P., an environmental shift favoring an influx of megafauna is assumed (Dunbar 1987). The paleontological record from the Aucilla River appears to coincide with the timing of climatic moderation as seen in pollen core data from Sheelar Lake in the marginal region.

Lowland karst areas appear to have supported varied habitats during the last Wisconsin glacial stage, including a number of small wetland refugia located in the deepest karst depressions in karst lowland areas. These oases appear to have existed because of their proximity to the Floridan Aquifer. Areas that were adjacent to the marginal region, like the Santa Fe River, also had the potential for ground-water recharge from the more highly elevated Superficial Aquifer. Delayed action recharge in the Santa Fe River area may have occurred then as it does today; water lost from the Superficial Aquifer through semi-confining strata appears in the river basin about five months after a period of rain (Meyer 1962). Although it may never be proven, it is possible, even probable, that factors local to a particular area, such as delayed action recharge or the lack thereof, determined the abundance and seasonal persistence of potable surface water in a given lowland area.

It may have been in the intermediate elevations—the karst plains between the uplands and lowlands—that many of the grazing animals spent their time, but there is no doubt they frequented karst lowland areas and left their skeletal remains disproportionately concentrated around former oases locations. In the Tertiary karst regions, water resources were restricted during the late Pleistocene, but were present in lowlands that are now inundated.

CONCLUSIONS

Clovis/Suwannee sites located in and around clusters of sinkholes and other low-lying spots are believed to have been situated around former oases locations. As such, Neill's original Oasis Hypothesis has been revived with modifications. The great majority of lithic resource-oriented Clovis/Suwannee sites occur in the Tertiary karst regions of Florida. Secondary concentrations of Clovis/Suwannee sites occur outside of the Tertiary karst regions, where Tertiary cherts and aquifer water are generally buried and were either occasionally exposed in deep sinkholes or were not accessible as resources for exploitation.

The distribution of Florida Paleoindian sites is largely confined to three of five identifiable physiographic zones, where multiple karst features expose the Floridan Aquifer and chert was available for tool production. That 90% of the sites in this sample are located in karst features exposing the Tertiary limestones and Floridan Aquifer, or lie adjacent to or within a day's walk of such features, is conclusive evidence of the importance of these features to Clovis/Suwannee peoples. The preference for lowland site locations and the simple fact that the aquifer was exposed, even though sometimes deeply below the ground's surface, indicates potable water was of overriding importance some 10,000 to 12,000 years ago. Site occurrences are remarkably predictable and support the contention that the availability of potable water and, perhaps to a lesser extent, lithic resources were conscious concerns of the Clovis/Suwannee peoples who once inhabited this region.

Clearly the number and distinctive distribution of Florida sites containing diagnostic Clovis, Suwannee, and Simpson projectile points and proboscidean ivory foreshafts are impressive. Uneroded karst wetland and inundated sites are unique and rank among the most potentially significant archaeological sites, not only because of their size and frequency but because they offer good organic preservation that is so rare in the eastern United States. Expressed as a hypothesis, the Florida Clovis/Suwannee site concentration pattern can be summarized as follows.

Karst River Model of Natural Resource Hypothesis

The river basins in the (two) Tertiary karst regions of Florida have the greatest concentration of Clovis/ Suwannee Paleoindian sites because unique environmental conditions during the late Pleistocene created natural resource accumulations that complemented technology and subsistence behavior. Stable habitats in the karst regions supported grazing animals, but dry intervals concentrated game herds at oases locales. During droughts, oases in the karst river and lake bottoms offered water, food, and bone and lithic resources for Paleoindian exploitation. As a result, major site clusters in Florida became centered around rivers like the Santa Fe and Aucilla because multiple resources were available and repeated exploitation could be supported. During wet periods, when widespread intermittent water sources were available, game herds migrated away from oases locales and were followed by mobile bands of Paleoindian hunters and gatherers. A semi-sedentary Paleoindian lifeway may have existed in Florida, with prolonged occupations around karst rivers and karstified lowlands, and less frequent periods of high hunter-gatherer mobility. Supporting the idea that Paleoindian settlement may have been less mobile is a recent chert-source study conducted by Goodyear and Upchurch in the Tampa Bay region, who found no exotic imported rock. All chert from their sample is local (Goodyear, personal communication).

ACKNOWLEDGMENTS

Acknowledgments must be extended to the Florida Bureau of Archaeological Research, the Florida Museum of Natural History, and the Fort Walton Temple Mound Museum for making their collections and documented site information available for this study. Calvin Jones, Randy Daniel, and Mike Wisenbaker are to be thanked for sharing information on Harney Flats and other Paleoindian sites in that vicinity. Al Goodyear and Mark Brooks added much of the information regarding sites in and surrounding Tampa Bay, their childhood stomping grounds. Finally, special recognition must be extended to Ben Waller and Don Serbousek, avocational archaeologists who have long been interested in Paleoindian studies and have done much to promote the better understanding of this resource base. Both have promoted the interaction of professional and avocational interests, and have spearheaded as well the successful drive to prove that some Paleoindian sites in karst rivers have scientific importance.

Table 1. Tertiary Karst Region Clovis/Suwannee Sites.

COUNTY*	PHYSIOGRAPHIC SETTING (KARST TOPOGRAPHY)	LOCATION:SITE	DIAGNOSTICS	UNIFACE TOOLS
Alachua	River valley	Santa Fe River:Lilly Spring	Lithic: 1	?
	River valley	Santa Fe River:Running Lake	Lithic: 1	?
	River valley	Santa Fe River:Hornsby Springs	Lithic: 4	Abundant
	River valley	Sante Fe River:Darby Springs	Lithic: 6	Abundant
	Lake or prairie	Paynes Prairie:Bolen Bluff	Lithic: 17	Abundant
	Lake or prairie	Paynes Prairie:Mouth of Prairie Creek	Lithic: 1	?
	Lake or prairie	Lochloosa Lake:Brunt Island	Lithic: 1	?
	Lake or prairie	Levy Lake (prairie):East Side Canal	Lithic: 1	?
	Lake or prairie	Orange Lake:A-100	Lithic: 1	?
	Upland	N.W. end of County:No Name Site	Lithic: 1	?
	Upland	N.W. Uplands:Lowell Barrow Pit	Lithic: 1	?
	Upland	West Central Uplands:Power Line Site	Lithic: 1	?
	Upland	Southwest Uplands:Domino Hammock	Lithic: 2	?
Citrus	River valley	Crystal River:Crystal River	Lithic: 1	?
	Lake	Lake Tsala Apopka:Inverness	Lithic: 1	?
	Upland	Karst Area Withlacoochee State Forest: Simpson Site	Lithic: 4	Abundant
	Upland	Karst Area Withlacoochee State Forest: Forest Tower	Lithic: 1	Abundant
	Upland	Karst Area Withlacoochee State Forest: Spratt Site	Lithic: 1	?
Columbia	River valley	Santa Fe River:River Rise	Lithic: 7	?
	River valley	Santa Fe River:Halfway Site	Lithic: 1	?
	River valley	Santa Fe River:Lien Site	Lithic: 11	?
	River valley	Santa Fe River:Trestle Site	Lithic: 2	?
	River valley	Santa Fe River:Santa Fe 16 Power Line	Lithic: 1	?
	River valley	Santa Fe River:Wilder's Rise	Lithic: 1	Abundant
	River valley	Suwannee River:Waldron Landing	Lithic: 2	?
	River valley	Suwannee River:Rock Island Shoals	Lithic: 7	?
Dixie	River valley	Steinhatchee River:Fish-hook Hole & Falls	Lithic: 15	Present
Gilchrist	River valley	Suwannee River:Butler South	Lithic: 1	?
	River valley	Santa Fe River:Butler Site	Lithic: 46	Abundant

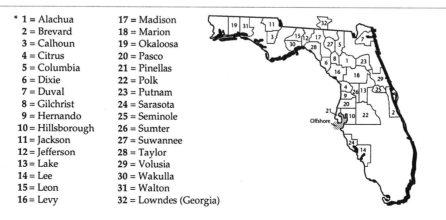

* 1 = Alachua
2 = Brevard
3 = Calhoun
4 = Citrus
5 = Columbia
6 = Dixie
7 = Duval
8 = Gilchrist
9 = Hernando
10 = Hillsborough
11 = Jackson
12 = Jefferson
13 = Lake
14 = Lee
15 = Leon
16 = Levy
17 = Madison
18 = Marion
19 = Okaloosa
20 = Pasco
21 = Pinellas
22 = Polk
23 = Putnam
24 = Sarasota
25 = Seminole
26 = Sumter
27 = Suwannee
28 = Taylor
29 = Volusia
30 = Wakulla
31 = Walton
32 = Lowndes (Georgia)

CONTEXT UNDERWATER	FLOOD-PRONE	TERRESTRIAL	PLEISTOCENE FAUNA REMAINS	BUTCHER-MARKED PLEISTOCENE BONE	INFORMATION SOURCE**; COMMENTS
X			?	–	FMNH—Simpson Collection.
X			?	–	FMNH—Simpson Collection.
X	X	X	Proboscidean	–	FMNH—Simpson Collection; see Dolan and Allen 1961.
X	X	X	Proboscidean	–	FMNH—Simpson Collection; see Dolan and Allen 1961.
	X	X	None	–	FMNH—Simpson and Burkhardt Collection; see Bullen 1958 and Goggin 1950.
	X		?	–	FMNH Collection.
X			None	–	Norden Collection.
		X	None	–	FMNH Collection.
		X	None	–	FMNH Collection.
		X	None	–	FMNH Collection.
		X	None	–	Waller Collection; see Bullen 1969.
		X	None	–	Allan Mizell Collection.
		X	None	–	FMNH—Burkhardt Collection.
		X	?	–	See Wilfred T. Neill 1964.
	X		?	–	Ben Waller Collection.
		X	None	–	FMNH—Simpson and Cason Collections; near Dames Cave and Lizzie Hart Sink
		X	None	–	S. Anderson Collection; near Forest Tower Cave.
		X	None	–	G. Spratt Collection; near unnamedcave.
X			?	–	Paul Lien Collection.
X			?	–	Paul Lien Collection.
X			?	–	Paul Lien and B. Royal Collections.
		X	None	–	FMNH—Simpson Collection.
X			?	–	Lou Hill Collection.
	X	X	Horse	–	Wilder Collection.
X			?	–	B. Jones, and D. Mangham Collections.
X			?	–	FMNH—Simpson, B. Jones, D. Mangham, and J. Moore Collections.
X			Proboscidean; Other	–	Waller and B. Page Collections.
X			?	–	Lou Hill Collection.
X	X	X	Horse	–	FMNH—Simpson, Waller, B. Page, and P. Lien Collections; see Dolan and Allan 1961, and Goggin 1950.

** **FMNH** = Florida Museum of Natural History
BAR = Bureau of Archaeological Research

Table 1. (continued) Tertiary Karst Region Clovis/Suwannee Sites.

COUNTY*	PHYSIOGRAPHIC SETTING (KARST TOPOGRAPHY)	LOCATION:SITE	DIAGNOSTICS	UNIFACE TOOLS
Gilchrist	River valley	Santa Fe River:Dorset Landing	Lithic: 10	?
	River valley	Santa Fe River:Scotts Bridge	Lithic: 1	?
	River valley	Santa Fe River:River Estates	Lithic: 11	Present
	River valley	Santa Fe River:Santa Fe Springs	Lithic: 5	Present
	River valley	Santa Fe River:Ben's Bridge	Lithic: 15	Abundant
	River valley	Santa Fe River:Boat Launch	Lithic: 2	Present
	River valley	Santa Fe River:Wilson Bend	Lithic: 1	?
	River valley	Santa Fe River:Wilson Springs	Lithic: 1	?
	River valley	Santa Fe River:Roberts Site	Lithic: 1	?
	River valley	Santa Fe River:Santa Fe IA	Lithic: 9	?
	River valley	Santa Fe River:Dunnagan's Old Mill	Lithic: 5	Present
	River valley	Santa Fe River:Waller Spring	Lithic: 1	?
	River valley	Santa Fe River:Norden Site	Lithic: 11	Abundant
	River valley	Santa Fe River:Hollingsworth Bluff	Lithic: 1	?
	River valley	Santa Fe River:SR 47 Bridge	Lithic: 1	?
	River valley	Santa Fe River:Near Norden Site	Lithic: 1	?
	River valley	Santa Fe River:Rum Island	Lithic: 3	?
Hernando	Upland	Near Withlacoochee State Forest: Rivenbark	Lithic: 4	Present
Hillsborough	River valley	Hillsborough River:Racetrack	Lithic: 9	?
	River valley	Hillsborough River:Flint Creek Landing	Lithic: 3	?
	River valley	Hillsborough River:Harney Gap	Lithic: 1	?
	River valley	Hillsborough River:Cow Creek	Lithic: 3	Abundant
	River valley	Hillsborough River:Fowler Bridge	Lithic: 1	Present
	Lake, prairie or swamp	Hillsborough River Swamp: Cypress Creek Swamp	Lithic: 1	?
Jackson	River valley	Chipola River:Blue Springs	Lithic: 1	?
	River valley	Chipola River:Peacock Bridge #1	Lithic: 10	?
	River valley	Chipola River:Peacock Bridge #2	Lithic: 2	?
	River valley	Chipola River:Chason Site	Lithic: 2	?
Jefferson	River valley	Wacissa River:Alexon Site Area	Lithic: 2	Present
	River valley	Wacissa River:Yeager Camp	Lithic: 1	Present
	River valley	Aucilla River:Black Hole Cave	Lithic: 1	Present
	River valley	Aucilla River:Gator Hole	Lithic: 2	Present
	River valley	Aucilla River:Page/Ladson	Lithic: 16 Ivory: 8	Abundant
	River valley	Aucilla River:Ladson Rise	Ivory: 2	Abundant
	River valley	Aucilla River:Simpson/Page Site	Lithic: 2	?
	River valley	Aucilla River:Bennett Bend	Lithic: 1	?
	River valley	Aucilla River:Blind Creek	Lithic: 2	?
	River valley	Aucilla River:Cut Off Sink	Lithic: 2	?
	River valley	Aucilla River:Ward Island #1	Lithic: 4 Ivory: 4	?
	River valley	Aucilla River:Ward Island #2	Lithic: 5	Present

CONTEXT			PLEISTOCENE	BUTCHER-MARKED	INFORMATION SOURCE**;
UNDERWATER	FLOOD-PRONE	TERRESTRIAL	FAUNA REMAINS	PLEISTOCENE BONE	COMMENTS
X		X	?	–	FMNH—Simpson and Waller Collections.
X			None	–	Dale Stone Collection.
X	X	X	Proboscidean; Horse	–	Waller and Burkhardt Collections; (many other artifacts reported in other collections).
X			Proboscidean; Horse; Tapir	–	Waller Collection, Mid River Springs.
X			Multiple	–	Waller and P. Lien Collections.
X			?	–	Waller Collection.
X			?	–	Waller Collection.
X			Tapir; Other	–	Waller Collection.
X			Proboscidean	–	Waller Collection.
X			Multiple	Mammoth	Waller Collection; see Bullen et al. 1970.
X	X	X	Proboscidean; Horse; Camel	–	FMNH—Simpson and Waller Collections.
X			?	–	J. Moore Collection.
X	X	X	Multiple	–	Norden and BAR Collections.
X			Proboscidean	–	Waller Collection.
X			?	–	J. Moore Collection.
X			?	–	J. Moore Collection.
X			?	–	J. Knight and P. Lien Collections.
		X	None	–	Rivenbark Collection.
	X	X	None	–	Anderson, Waller, Lein, and McDonald Collections.
	X	X	None	–	FMNH—Simpson, Lein, S. Anderson Collections; see Simpson 1948.
	X		Bison	–	S. Anderson Collection.
	X	X	Proboscidean	–	Guimares and Anderson Collections.
X		X	Proboscidean; Other	Marks on Geochelone may be from butchering	S. Anderson and BAR Collections; see Clayton 1981.
	X	X	?	–	S. Anderson Collection.
X			?	–	Lazarus Data Ft. Walton Museum.
X			?	–	Hub Chason Collection.
X			?	–	Hub Chason Collection.
X			?	–	Hub Chason Collection.
X			Bison; Horse; Other	Bison	K. Bennett, C. Willis, Lou Hill, FMNH—Alexon, and BAR Collections; see Webb et al. 1984.
X	X		Horse; Tapir	–	Gingery and BAR Collections.
X			Multiple	–	K. Bennett Collection.
X			Multiple	–	B. Proctor Collection.
X	X	X	Multiple	Mastodon left radius	B. Page, D. Ross, Waller, E. Moore, C. Willis, and K. Bennett Collections; see Dunbar et al. 1989.
X			Multiple	–	BAR Collection.
X			?	–	B. Page Collection.
X			?	–	K. Bennett Collection.
X			?	–	K. Bennett Collection.
X			Sloth	–	Ohmes Collection.
X			Multiple	–	Grissit Collection.
X			Proboscidean	–	C. Willis and L. Hill Collections.

Table 1. (continued) Tertiary Karst Region Clovis/Suwannee Sites.

COUNTY*	PHYSIOGRAPHIC SETTING (KARST TOPOGRAPHY)	LOCATION:SITE	DIAGNOSTICS	UNIFACE TOOLS
Jefferson	River valley	Aucilla River:Mandalay	Lithic: 6 Ivory: 1	Present
	River valley	Aucilla River:Twin Sinks	Lithic: 4	Present
	River valley	Aucilla River:Williams #2	Lithic: 1	?
	Coastal swamp	Sand hill overlooking Gum Swamp: Pinhook Sand Hills	Lithic: 1	?
	Coastal swamp	Sand hill (Cody Scarp) overlooking coastal swamp:Don Ohmes Site	Lithic: 1	?
Lake	Lake	Lake Griffin:Fruitland Park	Lithic: 1	?
	Lake	Lake Harris:West Bank	Lithic: 1	?
Leon	River valley	St. Marks River:Natural Bridge Sinks	Lithic: 6	Present
Levy	River valley	Wacassassa River:Midway Site	Lithic: 3	Present
	River valley	Wekiva River:Wekiva Springs	Lithic: 1	?
	River valley	Wekiva River:Wekiva Bend	Lithic: 2	?
Madison	River valley	Northern Withlacoochee River: Fish Weir Site	Lithic: 1	Present
Marion	River valley	Silver River:Silver Springs Cave	Lithic: 2	Present
	River valley	Silver River:Scrub Jay	Lithic: 1	?
	River valley	Silver River:Silver River #1	Lithic: 5	Present
	River valley	Silver River:Silver Bluff	Lithic: 9	Present
	River valley	Ocklawaha River:Delks Bend	Lithic: 1	?
	River valley	Ocklawaha River:Mound Site	Lithic: 1	?
	River valley	Ocklawaha River:Lake Eaton	Lithic: 1	?
	River valley	Southern Withlacoochee River: SR 200 Site	Lithic: 12	?
	River valley	Southern Withlacoochee River: Izard Landing	Lithic: 1	?
	River valley	Southern Withlacoochee River: Rainbow Springs Run #1	Lithic: 5	Present
	Lake	Johnson's Lake:Johnson's Lake Site	Lithic: 2	Present
	Upland	N.W. Karst Hill & Valley: Power line crossing	Lithic: 1	?
	Upland	N.W. Karst Hill & Valley: Meadowbrook Farm	Lithic: 1	?
	Upland	N.W. Karst Hill & Valley:Fairfield	Lithic: 3	Abundant
Sumter	Lake	Lake Panasoffkee:S.W. Shore	Lithic: 1	?
	Lake	Lake Deaton:Deaton	Lithic: 1	?
Suwannee	River valley	Ichtucknee River:Bison Landing	Ivory: 1	?
	River valley	Ichtucknee River:Jug Springs	Lithic: 1	?
	River valley	Ichtucknee River:Simpson's Camp	Ivory: 1	Present
	River valley	Ichtucknee River:Simpson's Flats	Lithic: 6 Ivory: 2	Present
	River valley	Ichtucknee River:Devil's Bend	Lithic: 1	Present
	River valley	Ichtucknee River:Area VII	Lithic: 1	?

CONTEXT UNDERWATER	FLOOD-PRONE	TERRESTRIAL	PLEISTOCENE FAUNA REMAINS	BUTCHER-MARKED PLEISTOCENE BONE	INFORMATION SOURCE**; COMMENTS
X			Proboscidean; Other	–	B. Page, R. Alexon, and D. Ross Collections.
X			Proboscidean	–	C. Willis and L. Hill Collections.
X			?	–	B. Page Collection.
	X	X	?	–	C. Willis informant.
	X	X	?	–	Ohmes Collection.
		X	None	–	S. Cumbaa informant.
		X	None	–	Waller Collection.
X	X	X	Proboscidean	–	FMNH—Simpson, D. Willis, J. Page, and B. Page Collections.
X			Multiple	Flaked horse tibia	Norden Collection.
X		X	?	–	See Neill 1964.
X	X		Proboscidean	–	Norden Collection; mastodon reported eroding out of river bank in 1974.
X		X	?	–	BAR Collection.
X			Proboscidean	–	See Neill 1964 and 1971.
		X	None	–	See Neill 1971; overlooks swampy drainage into Silver River.
X			Multiple	–	Waller and P. Lien Collections.
		X	None	–	See Neill 1958 and 1971; sand hills overlooking Silver River.
X			?	–	Waller Collection.
	X		?	–	Waller Collection.
	X		?	–	Waller Collection; part of drainage system into Ocklawaha River via Eaton Creek and swampland.
X			?	–	Waller, P. Lien, and C. Rasmussen Collections.
X			?	–	P. Lien Collection.
X			Proboscidean (tooth enamel)	–	N. Fallier, P. Lien, and R. McDonald Collections.
		X	None	–	Waller Collection and B. Purdy informant.
		X	None	–	Waller Collection.
		X	None	–	Waller Collection; see Waller 1972.
		X	None	–	Waller Collection.
	X		?	–	Waller Collection.
	X		?	–	Waller Collection.
X	X		Bison	–	FMNH—Roberts Collection.
X			Proboscidean	–	FMNH—Simpson Collection.
X	X		Proboscidean; Horse; Camel	–	FMNH Collection.
X	X		Proboscidean Other	Horse ilium	Waller, FMNH—Simpson, and F. Garcia Collections.
X	X		Proboscidean	–	C. Willis informant and BAR file report.
X			?	–	FMNH Collection.

Table 1. (continued) Tertiary Karst Region Clovis/Suwannee Sites.

COUNTY*	PHYSIOGRAPHIC SETTING (KARST TOPOGRAPHY)	LOCATION:SITE	DIAGNOSTICS	UNIFACE TOOLS
Suwannee	River valley	Ichtucknee River:DOT Landing	Lithic: 3 Ivory: 1	Present
	River valley	Suwannee River:Butler North	Lithic: 6	?
	River valley	Suwannee River:Little River	Lithic: 1	?
	River valley	Suwannee River:Moore Site	Lithic: 1	Abundant
	River valley	Suwannee River:Ellaville	Lithic: 3	?
	River valley	Suwannee River:Benson	Lithic: 1	?
Taylor	River valley	Aucilla River:SR 14 #1	Lithic: 1	?
	River valley	Aucilla River:SR 14 #2	Lithic: 1	?
	River valley	Aucilla River:Palm Tree Site	Lithic: 1	Present
	River valley	Aucilla River:River Sink	Lithic: 11	Abundant
	River valley	Aucilla River:Williams #1	Lithic: 3 Ivory: 1	Abundant
	River valley	Aucilla River:Willis Site	Lithic: 2	?
	River valley	Rocky Creek:Rocky Creek Site	Lithic: 6	Present
Wakulla	River valley	St. Marks River:Big Bend	Lithic: 1	?
	River valley	St. Marks River:Gluckman Dock	Lithic: 1	?
	River valley	St. Marks River:New Port	Lithic: 1	?
	River valley	St. Marks River:Sunken Spring	Lithic: 1	Present
	River valley	Wakulla River:Olin Site	Lithic: 1	?
Lowndes, Georgia	River valley	Upper Withlacoochee River:State Line	Lithic: 1	?

CONTEXT			PLEISTOCENE	BUTCHER-MARKED	INFORMATION SOURCE**;
UNDERWATER	FLOOD-PRONE	TERRESTRIAL	FAUNA REMAINS	PLEISTOCENE BONE	COMMENTS
X			Proboscidean	–	FMNH, Waller, and BAR Collections.
X			?	–	P. Lien and F. Tatum Collections.
X			?	–	See Simpson 1948.
X			?	–	J. Moore Collection; notes as many as 40 turtle-back scrapers recovered.
X			?	–	B. Page Collection.
X			?	–	B. Page Collection.
		X	None	–	Norden Collection.
X			?	–	K. Walker Collection.
X			Multiple	–	FMNH—Serbousek, BAR—Serbousek, and Serbousek Collections.
X			Multiple	–	Serbousek and Waller Collections.
X			Multiple	–	Fallier, Tall Timbers Research Station, Willis, and M. Hutto Collections.
	X		None	–	C. Willis Collection.
		X	?	–	Avant Collection.
X			?	–	B. Page Collection.
X			?	–	D. Gluckman Collection.
X			Multiple	–	D. Ross Collection.
X			Proboscidean	–	Fallier Collection.
X			Proboscidean	–	Avant Collection.
X			?	–	B. Jones Collection.

Table 2. Marginal Region Clovis/Suwannee Sites.

COUNTY*	PHYSIOGRAPHIC SETTING	LOCATION:SITE	DIAGNOSTICS	UNIFACE TOOLS
Alachua	Miocene clay upland	Blues Sink:IFAS Site***	Lithic: 1	Present
	Karst Lake	Lake Lochloosa:North Shore***	Lithic: 2	?
Brevard	Coastal lagoon	Banana River:Sykes Creek	Lithic: 1	?
Calhoun	Miocene clay upland; Karst River valley	Chipola River:274 Site #1***	Lithic: 1	?
	Miocene clay upland; Karst River valley	Chipola River:John Boy #1***	Lithic: 8	?
	Miocene clay upland; Karst River valley	Chipola River:John Boy #2***	Lithic: 2	?
	Miocene clay upland; Karst River valley	Chipola River:Johnson Shoal***	Lithic: 1	?
	Miocene clay upland; Karst River valley	Chipola River:272 Site #2***	Lithic: 1	?
Hillsborough	Karst Prairie	Harney Flats:Six Mile***	Lithic: 1	?
	Karst Prairie	Harney Flats:East Lake Mall Site***	Lithic: 1	?
	Karst Prairie	Harney Flats:Bartolotti Site***	Lithic: 8	?
	Karst Prairie	Harney Flats:Harney Flats Site***	Lithic: 31	Abundant
Lake	River valley with occasional Karst features	Middle St. Johns River:Astor	Lithic: 1	?
	River valley with occasional Karst features	Middle St. Johns River:Snyder Site	Lithic: 3	Present
Leon	Miocene clay upland; Karst Lake	Lake Lafayette:Lafayette #1***	Lithic: 1	?
	Miocene clay upland; Karst Lake	Lake Lafayette:Lafayette #2***	Lithic: 2	?
	Miocene clay upland; Karst Lake & Swamp	Lake Jackson:Lake bottom site***	Lithic: 3	?
	Miocene clay upland; Karst Lake & Swamp	Lake Jackson:North Shore***	Lithic: 1	?
	Miocene clay upland; Karst Lake & Swamp	San Louis Ridge:San Louis	Lithic: 1	None
	Miocene clay upland; Karst Lake & Swamp	Cody Scarp:Johnson Sand Pit	Lithic: 2	Abundant
Marion	River valley with occasional Karst features	Middle St. Johns River: Silver Glen Springs***	Lithic: 2	?
	River valley with occasional Karst features	Middle St. Johns River:Salt Springs***	Lithic: 1	?
Pasco	Karst River in marginal region	Pithlachascotee River:Anderson Site***	Lithic: 2	?

* 1 = Alachua
2 = Brevard
3 = Calhoun
4 = Citrus
5 = Columbia
6 = Dixie
7 = Duval
8 = Gilchrist
9 = Hernando
10 = Hillsborough
11 = Jackson
12 = Jefferson
13 = Lake
14 = Lee
15 = Leon
16 = Levy
17 = Madison
18 = Marion
19 = Okaloosa
20 = Pasco
21 = Pinellas
22 = Polk
23 = Putnam
24 = Sarasota
25 = Seminole
26 = Sumter
27 = Suwannee
28 = Taylor
29 = Volusia
30 = Wakulla
31 = Walton
32 = Lowndes (Georgia)

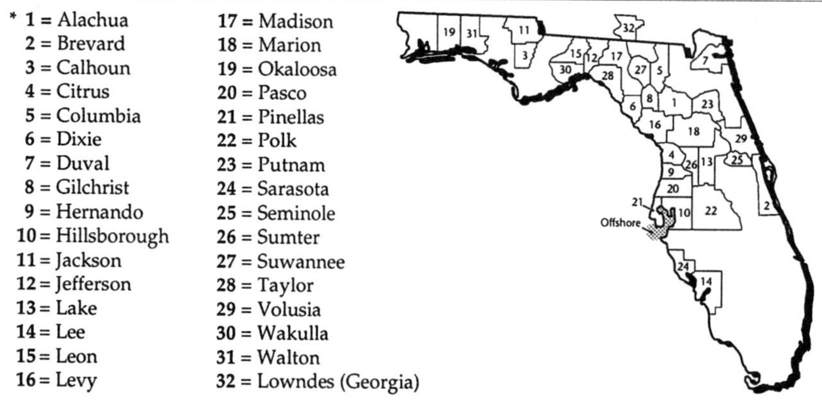

CONTEXT UNDERWATER	FLOOD-PRONE	TERRESTRIAL	PLEISTOCENE FAUNA REMAINS	BUTCHER-MARKED PLEISTOCENE BONE	INFORMATION SOURCE** COMMENTS
		X	None	–	Norden Collection.
		X	None	–	Waller and Curhman Collections.
		X	?	–	B. Knoder Collection.
X			?	–	Chason Collection.
X			?	–	Waller and Chason Collections.
X			?	–	Chason Collection.
X			?	–	Chason Collection.
X			?	–	Chason Collection.
		X	None	–	C. Jones informant.
		X	None	–	P. Lien Collection
		X	None	–	C. Jones informant
	X	X	?	–	BAR, M. Harold, Guimares, and S. Anderson Collections; see Daniel and Wisenbaker 1984
	X		?	–	Allen Doran informant.
		X	None	–	See Neill 1971.
		X	None	–	S. McNutt informant.
		X	None	–	C. Willis Collection.
X			None	–	Fallier Collier; collected when lake drained by sinkhole unplugging.
		X	None	–	
		X	None	–	BAR Collection.
		X	None	–	BAR Collection.
X		X	?	–	Dunbar Collection; see Neill 1964.
		X	?	–	See Neill 1964.
		X	None	–	S. Anderson Collection and informant.

** **FMNH** = Florida Museum of Natural History
BAR = Bureau of Archaeological Research

*** Located in or near open karst features (sinks, spring caves, etc.)

Table 2. (continued) Marginal Region Clovis/Suwannee Sites.

COUNTY*	PHYSIOGRAPHIC SETTING	LOCATION:SITE	DIAGNOSTICS	UNIFACE TOOLS
Pinellas	Dredge spoil from Gulf of Mexico	Mainland Beaches:Pinellas Point***	Lithic: 1	?
	Dredge spoil from Gulf of Mexico	Tampa Ciega:Boca Ciega***	Lithic: 4	?
Putnam	River valley with occasional Karst features	St. Johns River:Drayton Island***	Lithic: 1	?
	River valley with occasional Karst features	St. Johns River:Rollstown	Lithic: 1	?
Volusia	River valley with infrequent Karst features	Southern St. Johns River: Watson's Landing	Lithic: 1	?
Wakulla	Coastal lowlands with occasional Karst features	Wakulla Springs (Karst):Wakulla Springs***	Lithic: 3	Present

Table 3. Outlying Region Clovis/Suwannee Sites.

COUNTY*	PHYSIOGRAPHIC SETTING	LOCATION:SITE	DIAGNOSTICS	UNIFACE TOOLS
Alachua	Lake	Santa Fe Lake:Melrose	Lithic: 1	?
	Lake	Santa Fe Lake:Martin Island	Lithic: 1	?
Brevard	River valley	Southern St. Johns River:Hellen Blazes Site	Lithic: 3	?
Duval	Beach	Jacksonville Beach:Jacksonville Beach	Lithic: 1	?
Lee	Coastal lagoon; Bay	Charlotte Harbor:Main Land Site	Lithic: 1	?
Okaloosa	Bay	Chactawhatchee Bay:Chactawhatchee #1***	Lithic: 1	?
	Bay	Chactawhatchee Bay:Chactawhatchee #2***	Lithic: 1	?
	Bay	Chactawhatchee Bay:Chactawhatchee #3***	Lithic: 3	?
	Bay	Chactawhatchee Bay:Chactawhatchee #4***	Lithic: 1	?
	Bay	Chactawhatchee Bay:Chactawhatchee #5***	Lithic: 1	?
	Bay	Chactawhatchee Bay:Chactawhatchee #6***	Lithic: 1	?
	Bay	Chactawhatchee Bay:Chactawhatchee #7***	Lithic: 1	?
Pinellas	Bay	Tampa Bay:Maximo Park***	Lithic: 1	?
Polk	Lake	Weohyokapka Lake:Nalcrest Site	Lithic: 5	Abundant
	Lake	Lakeland:Lakeland	Lithic: 1	?
Seminole	Lake	Lake Jessup:Spring Hammock	Lithic: 1	?

* 1 = Alachua
2 = Brevard
3 = Calhoun
4 = Citrus
5 = Columbia
6 = Dixie
7 = Duval
8 = Gilchrist
9 = Hernando
10 = Hillsborough
11 = Jackson
12 = Jefferson
13 = Lake
14 = Lee
15 = Leon
16 = Levy
17 = Madison
18 = Marion
19 = Okaloosa
20 = Pasco
21 = Pinellas
22 = Polk
23 = Putnam
24 = Sarasota
25 = Seminole
26 = Sumter
27 = Suwannee
28 = Taylor
29 = Volusia
30 = Wakulla
31 = Walton
32 = Lowndes (Georgia)

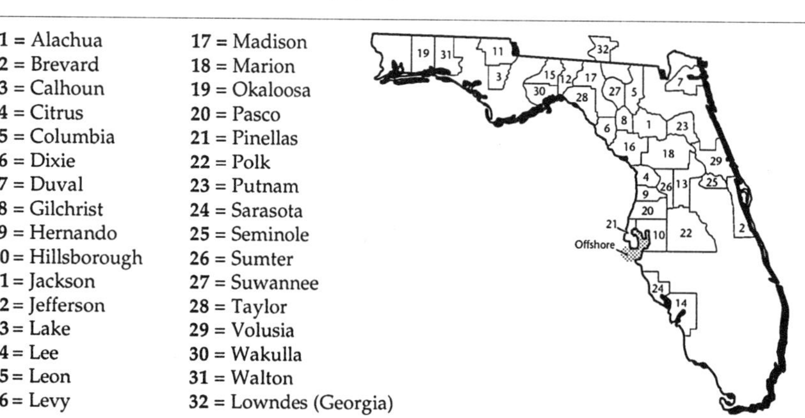

CONTEXT UNDERWATER	FLOOD-PRONE	TERRESTRIAL	PLEISTOCENE FAUNA REMAINS	BUTCHER-MARKED PLEISTOCENE BONE	INFORMATION SOURCE**; COMMENTS
X			?	–	M. Brooks informant.
X			?	–	M. Brooks informant; see Warren 1970.
	X		?	–	Waller Collection.
X			?	–	M. Stallings informant.
		X	None	–	See Wyman 1973.
X			Multiple	–	See Neill 1964.

CONTEXT UNDERWATER	FLOOD-PRONE	TERRESTRIAL	PLEISTOCENE FAUNA REMAINS	BUTCHER-MARKED PLEISTOCENE BONE	INFORMATION SOURCE** COMMENTS
		X	None	–	FMNH Collection.
	X		None	–	FMNH—Simpson Collection.
		X	None	–	See Bullen 1958.
	X		?	–	FMNH Collection.
		X	?	–	See Bullen 1962.
		X	None	–	William Lazarus data from FWTM.
		X	None	–	W. Lazarus/FWTM data.
		X	None	–	W. Lazarus/FWTM data.
		X	None	–	W. Lazarus/FWTM data.
		X	None	–	W. Lazarus/FWTM data.
		X	None	–	W. Lazarus/FWTM data.
		X	None	–	W. Lazarus/FWTM data.
		X	?	–	M. Brooks informant.
X			None	–	See Bullen and Beilman 1973, and Waller 1983.
X			None	–	See Simpson 1948.
	X		None	–	W. Hauser Collection.

** **FMNH** = Florida Museum of Natural History
BAR = Bureau of Archaeological Research

*** Located in or near open karst features (sinks, spring caves, etc.)

Table 3. (continued) Outlying Region Clovis/Suwannee Sites.

COUNTY*	PHYSIOGRAPHIC SETTING	LOCATION:SITE	DIAGNOSTICS	UNIFACE TOOLS
Sarasota	Sinkhole	Little Salt Springs:Little Salt Springs***		?
Walton	Bay	Chactawhatchee Bay:Chactawhatchee #8***	Lithic: 1	?
	Gulf coast	Sunnyside Beach:Sunnyside Beach	Lithic: 1	?
Offshore	Bay	Tampa Bay:Site 1, Big Bend Site 2, Mangrove Pt.	Lithic: 5	Present

Table 4. Clovis/Suwannee Site Combined Data.

REGION	NUMBER OF SITES	DIAGNOSTICS		PLEISTOCENE FAUNA REMAINS	BUTCHER-MARKED PLEISTOCENE BONE
		LITHIC	IVORY		
Tertiary Karst	122 / 71%	424 / 78%	21 / 100%	45	6
Marginal	29 / 17%	88 / 16%	0	1	0
Outlying	21 / 12%	31 / 6%	0	1	1
Statewide Totals	172	543	21	47	7

NOTE: Of the litchic diagnostic artifacts, 439 (81%) were classified in the heterogeneous group Suwannee, 78 (14%) were Clovis, and 26 (5%) were Simpson types. Of the 172 sites, 122 (71% of the sample) have wetland or underwater components. Only wetland and underwater sites have bone preservation. Of the 122 wet sites, 47 (38.5% of wet sites) have Pleistocene fauna remains. A total of 52 sites (30% of the total sample) are known to have uniface tool kits present. A total of 155 sites (90% of the sites) are located in or near open karst features.

REFERENCES CITED

Allen, R. R.
1967 Studies on the Paleo Indian Era in Florida. Undergraduate Paper, University of Florida, Department of Anthropology, Gainesville.

Archaeology of Eastern North America
1982 A Compilation of Fluted Points of Eastern North American by Count and Distribution: An AENA Project. *Archaeology of Eastern North America* 10:27–45.

Brooks, H. K.
1973a Late Pleistocene and Holocene Climatic Change in Peninsular Florida. Ms. on file, Department of Geology, University of Florida, Gainesville.

1973b Holocene Climatic Changes in Peninsular Florida. *Geological Society of America Annual Meeting Abstracts* 5:558–559.

1974 Lake Okeechobee. In *Environments of South Florida: Present and Past,* edited by P. J. Gleason. Memoir No. 2. Miami Geological Society, Miami.

Bullen, R. P.
1958 *The Bolen Bluff Site on Paynes Prairie, Florida.* Social Sciences Paper No. 4. Contributions of the Florida State Museum, University of Florida Press, Gainesville.

1962 Suwannee Points in the Simpson Collection. *Florida Anthropologist* 15:83–88.

1968 *A Guide to the Identification of Florida Projectile Points.* Florida State Museum, Gainesville.

1969 A Clovis Fluted Point from the Santa Fe River. *Florida Anthropologist* 22:36–37.

Bullen, R. P., and L. E. Beilman
1973 The Nalcrest Site, Lake Weohyakapka, Florida. *Florida Anthropologist* 26:1–22.

Bullen, R. P., S. D. Webb, and B. I. Waller
1970 A Worked Mammoth Bone from Florida. *American Antiquity* 35:203–205.

Buono, A., R. M. Spechler, G. L. Barr, and R. M. Wolansky
1979 *Generalized Thickness of the Confining Bed Overlying the Floridan Aquifer, Southwest Florida*

CONTEXT UNDERWATER	FLOOD-PRONE	TERRESTRIAL	PLEISTOCENE FAUNA REMAINS	BUTCHER-MARKED PLEISTOCENE BONE	INFORMATION SOURCE** COMMENTS
X			Multiple	Geochelone wood stake driven through	See Clausen et al. 1979—based on C_{14} dates.
		X	None	–	W. Lazarus/FWTM data.
		X	None	–	W. Lazarus/FWTM data.
X			?	–	See Goodyear and Warren 1972.

UNIFACE TOOLS	RELATION TO WATER TABLE OR SEA LEVEL: UNDERWATER	FLOOD-PRONE	WETLAND/TERRESTRIAL	TERRESTRIAL
45	66	8	26	22
5	10	2	2	15
2	5	3	0	13
52	81 / 47%	13 / 8%	28 / 16%	50 / 29%

Management District. Map, U. S. Geological Survey, Reston, VA.

Bush, P. W.
1982 *Predevelopment Flow in the Tertiary Limestone Aquifer, Southeastern United States: A Regional Analysis from Digital Modeling*. U.S. Geological Survey Water Resource Investigations, 82-905.

Clark, W. E.
1964 *Possibility of Salt-Water Leakage from Proposed Intracoastal Water Way near Venice, Florida Well Field*. Report of Investigations No. 38. Florida Division of Geology, Tallahassee.

Clausen, C. J., A. D. Cohen, C. Emiliani, A. J. Holman, and J. J. Stipp
1979 Little Salt Springs, Florida: A Unique Underwater Site. *Science* 203:609–614.

Clauser, J. W.
1973 *Archaeological Excavations of Itchetucknee Springs, Suwannee County, Florida*. Miscellaneous Project Report Series No. 10. Division of Archives, History and Records Management, Tallahassee.

Clayton, D. H.
1981 Part III: Faunal Report for 8Hi393c/uw. In *Report on Phase II Underwater Archaeological Testing at the Fowler Bridge Mastodon Site (8Hi393c/uw) Hillsborough County, Florida*, pp. 107–135. Florida Division of Archives, History and Records Management, Tallahassee.

Connert, J. H.
1932 Recent Find of Mammoth Remains in the Quaternary of Florida, Together with Arrow-head. *Science* 75:516.

Cooper, H. H., W. E. Kenner, and E. Brown
1953 *Groundwater in Central and Northern Florida*. Report of Investigations No. 10. Florida Geological Survey, Tallahassee.

Daniel, R. I., and M. Wisenbaker
1984 *Salvage Excavations at Harney Flats: A Paleo-Indian Base Camp in Hillsborough County, Florida*. Federal Highway Administration Report of Archaeological Excavations. Florida Bureau of Archaeological Research, Division of Archives, History and Records Management, Tallahassee.

1987 *Harney Flats: A Florida Paleo-Indian Site.* Baywood Publishing Co., Farmingdale, NY.

Dolan, E. M., and G. T. Allen, Jr.
1961 *An Investigation of the Darby and Hornsby Springs Sites, Alachua County, Florida.* Special Publication No. 7. Florida Geological Survey, Tallahassee.

Dunbar, J. S.
1981 The Effect of Geohydrology and Natural Resource Availability on Site Utilization at the Fowler Bridge Mastodon Site (8Hi393c/uw) in Hillsborough County, Florida. In *Interstate 75 Highway Phase II Archaeological Report No. 5,* pp. 63–106. Florida Division of Archives, History and Records Management, Tallahassee.
1987 Page/Ladson Site (Je591) Fourth Field Season Report: Site Stratigraphy and Implications. Ms. on file, Bureau of Archaeological Research, Tallahassee.

Dunbar, J. S., and B. I. Waller
1983 A Distribution Analysis of the Clovis/Suwannee Paleo-Indian Sites of Florida—A Geographic Approach. *Florida Anthropologist* 36:18–30.

Dunbar, J. S., S. D. Webb, and M. K. Faught
1988 Page/Ladson (8Je591): An Underwater Paleo-Indian Site in Northeastern Florida. *Florida Anthropologist* 41:442–452.

Dunbar, J. S., S. D. Webb, and D. Cring
1989 Culturally and Naturally Modified Bones from a Paleoindian site in the Aucilla River, North Florida. In *Bone Modification,* edited by R. Bonnichsen and M. Sorg, pp. 473–497. Center for the Study of the First Americans, University of Maine, Orono.

Edwards, R. A.
1948 An Abandoned Valley near High Springs, Florida, *The Quarterly Journal of the Florida Academy of Sciences* 2:125–132.

Edwards, W. E.
1952 *The Helen Blazes Site of Central Florida.* Unpublished Ph.D. dissertation, Columbia University, New York.

Gidley, J. W.
1929 Further Study of the Problem of Early Man in Florida. In *Exploration and Field work of the Smithsonian Institution in 1928,* pp. 13–20. Washington, D.C.

Gleason, P. J., A. D. Cohen, W. G. Smith, H. K. Brooks, P. A. Stone, R. L. Goodreck, and W. Spackman, Jr.
1974 The Environmental Significance of Holocene Sediments from the Everglades and Saline Tidal Plain. In *Environments of South Florida: Present and Past,* edited by P. J. Gleason, pp. 287–341. Memoir No. 2. Miami Geological Society, Miami.

Goggin, J. M.
1950 An Early Lithic Complex from Central Florida. *American Antiquity* 16:46–49.
1962 Recent Developments in Underwater Archaeology. *Proceedings of the 16th Southeastern Archaeological Conference Newsletter* 8. Macon.

Goodyear, A. C., and T. Charles
1984 *An Archaeological Survey of Chert Quarries in Western Allendale County, South Carolina.* Research Manuscript Series No. 195. Institute of Archaeology and Anthropology, University of South Carolina, Columbia.

Goodyear, A. C., and L. O. Warren
1972 Further Observations on Submarine Oyster Shell Deposits of Tampa Bay. *Florida Anthropologist* 25:52–66.

Jenks, A. E., and H. H. Simpson, Sr.
1941 Beveled Artifacts in Florida of the Same Type as Artifacts Found Near Clovis, New Mexico. *American Antiquity* 6:314–319.

Legrande, H. E.
1973 Hydrological and Ecological Problems of Karst Regions. *Science* 179:859–864.

Meyer, F. W.
1962 *Reconnaissance of the Geology and Groundwater Resources of Columbia County, Florida.* Report of Investigations No. 30. Florida Geological Survey, Tallahassee.

Neill, W. T.
1953 Notes on the Supposed Association of Artifacts and Extinct Vertebrates in Flagler County, Florida. *American Antiquity* 19:170-171.
1958 A Stratified Early Site at Silver Springs, Florida. *Florida Anthropologist* 11:32–52.
1964 Points and Extinct Animals in Florida. *Florida Anthropologist* 17:17–32.
1971 A Florida Paleo-Indian Implement. *Florida Anthropologist* 24:61–71.

Puri, H. S., J. W. Yon, Jr., and W. R. Oglesby
1967 *Geology of Dixie and Gilchrist Counties, Florida.* Bulletin No. 49. Florida Geological Survey, Tallahassee.

Roberts, F. H. H., Jr.
1936 Additional Information on the Folsom Complex. *Smithsonian Miscellaneous Collections* 95(10). Washington, D.C.

Science Applications, Inc.
1979 A Cultural Resource survey of the Continental

Shelf from Cape Hatteras to Key West. In *Prehistoric Archaeology,* vol. 2. Bureau of Land Management, New Orleans, Louisiana.

Sellards, E. H.
1917 On the Association of Human Remains and Extinct Vertebrates at Vero, Florida. *The Journal of Geology* 25:4–24.
1947 Early Man In America; Index to Localities and Selected Bibliography, 1940–1945. *Bulletin of the Geological Society of America* 58:955–978.

Simpson, C. J.
1948 Folsom-Like Points from Florida. *Florida Anthropologist* 1:11–15.
n.d. Yuma Type Points from Florida, Field Notes to a Colleague. Ms. on file, Florida State Museum, Gainesville.

Stubbs, S. A.
1940 Solution A Dominant Factor in the Geomorphology of Peninsular Florida. *Proceedings of the Florida Academy of Sciences* 5:149–167.

Upchurch, S. B., and R. N. Strom
1982 *Trace Metal Characterization of Florida Chert.* Star Grant 80-072 Report. Department of Geology, University of South Florida, Tampa.

Vernon, R. O.
1951 *Geology of Citrus and Levy Counties, Florida.* Bulletin No. 33. Florida Geological Survey, Tallahassee.

Waller, B. I.
1969 Paleo-Indian and Other Artifacts from a Florida Stream Bed. *Florida Anthropologist* 22:37–39.
1970 Some Occurrences of Paleo-Indian Projectile Points in Florida Waters. *Florida Anthropologist* 23:129–134.
1972 Meadowbrook Farms No. 2 Site. *Florida Anthropologist* 25:128.
1983 Florida Anthropologist Interview with Ben Waller. *Florida Anthropologist* 36:31–39.

Waller, B. I., and J. Dunbar
1977 Distribution of Paleo-Indian Projectiles in Florida. *Florida Anthropologist* 30:79–80.

Warren, L. O.
1970 The Kellogg Fill from Boca Ciega Bay, Pinellas County, Florida. *Florida Anthropologist* 23:163–167.
1972 Commercial Oyster Shell of Tampa Bay: 1966 Progress Report. *Florida Anthropologist* 15:49–51.

Watts, W. A.
1980 Late Wisconsin Climate of Northern Florida and Origin of Species-Rich Deciduous Forest. *Science* 210:325–327.
1983 Vegetational History of the Eastern United States 25,000 to 10,000 Years Ago. In *The Late Pleistocene,* edited by S. C. Porter, pp. 294–310. Late Quaternary Environments of the United States, vol. 1, H. E. Wright, Jr., general editor. University of Minnesota Press, Minneapolis.

Webb, S. D.
1974 *Pleistocene Mammals of Florida.* University Presses of Florida, Gainesville.
1976 Underwater Paleontology of Florida's Rivers. *National Geographic Society Reports, 1968 Projects,* pp. 479–481. Washington, D.C.

Webb, S. D., J. T. Milanich, R. Alexon, and J. S. Dunbar
1984 A Bison Antiquus Kill Site, Wacissa River, Jefferson County, Florida. *American Antiquity* 49:384–392.

Williams, K. E., D. Nicol, and A. F. Randazzo
1977 *The Geology of the Western Part of Alachua County, Florida.* Report of Investigations No. 85. Florida Geological Society, Tallahassee.

Willis, C.
1988 Controlled Surface Collection of the Little River Rapids Site (8Je603). *Florida Anthropologist* 41:453–470.

Wyman, J.
1973 *Fresh-Water Shell Mounds of the St. Johns River, Florida.* A. M. S. Press, Inc., New York. Reprint of the 1875 edition.

Late Pleistocene Cultural Occupation on the Southern Plains

EILEEN JOHNSON
The Museum of Texas Tech University
Lubbock, TX 79409

Based on ethnographic hunter-gatherer theory and data, and paleoclimatic and ecosystemic data, an environmental-cultural construct is proposed for the southern Plains region at the end of the Pleistocene. The construct proposes that Clovis peoples were organized as foragers, i.e., generalists, in their approach to subsistence. Clovis peoples had a broad-spectrum, meat-related subsistence base organized around a foraging structure based on opportunistic behavior patterns that allowed for both hunting and scavenging of animals and the practice of exploitation of bone resources with use of a minimal lithic tool kit and general conservancy of lithic materials. The Clovis point was a focal point of the tool kit and a multipurpose tool (weaponry, butchery, and perhaps plant gathering). The evaluation of the fit of the construct with the data is hampered by the disparate field methodologies and research approaches that have led to variable quality and a biased nature of the data. The key anomalies are the lack of residential sites, and lack of data on plant-gathering activities and on the role of plants in the subsistence base. Strong points for a foraging organization structure are the equitable climate, availability of a variety of potential game-animal resources, and the broad-based animal-resource utilization demonstrated in the archaeological record.

INTRODUCTION

This review deals with human use and occupation of the southern Plains at the end of the Pleistocene and presents a construct for the human subsistence base and subsistence-related organization. This first-approximation construct is based on ethnographic hunter-gatherer data, paleoclimatic conditions, and lithic and bone data from archaeological sites. The time period under discussion is the late Wisconsinan (ca. 25,000–11,000 yr B.P.), and the construct focuses on the very latest segment known archaeologically as the Clovis period (ca. 11,500–11,000 yr B.P.). Clovis occupation of the region is well established, with several sites having some level of excavation (Hester 1972; Johnson and Holliday 1985; Leonhardy 1966; Sellards 1938). However, most known Clovis sites appear as isolated finds of Clovis points (cf. Meltzer 1986a, 1986b). The existence of Clovis precursors is a subject of debate (cf. Bryan 1978, 1986; Dincauze 1984), but a few localities in the region suggest the potential for pre-Clovis occupation. Although none of the localities are unequivocal, they cannot be discounted totally.

The accumulated data appear to indicate a particular economic behavioral pattern in response to and fostered by climatic conditions and abundant animal-food resources. The southern Plains at the end of the Pleistocene was a vast stretch of grasslands with an abundant water supply and a wide variety of potential game animals (Johnson 1986, 1987; Lundelius et al. 1983). The construct proposes that Clovis peoples in particular, and perhaps their precursors in general, had a broad-spectrum, meat-related subsistence base organized around a foraging structure based on opportunistic behavior patterns that allowed for both hunting and scavenging of animals and the practice of exploitation of bone resources with use of a minimal lithic tool kit and general conservancy of lithic material.

The basis for modeling the southern Plains late Pleistocene human subsistence and subsistence-related organization is a combination of modern theory, ethnographic analogy, and prehistoric "facts." The term "construct," as used here, is defined as an idea or perception formed by the orderly arrangement of data. A series of propositions are put forth based on the construct. These propositions are meant as statements of relationships from which testable hypotheses and operational definitions can be developed (cf. Binford 1977:2–3). A construct and its propositions, then, can be used as the building blocks to form a model composed of a series of related and integrated hypotheses. The prehistoric "facts" consist of interpretations of the data preserved in the fossil record that provide either direct or indirect evidence of a past condition, event, or behavior. The accuracy of these "facts" is only as good as the quality of the data on which they are based. This quality was evaluated on the basis of field recovery methodology and associational context. The quality of the data is variable. This variability and the biased nature of the data are the reasons why the lower construct level was chosen over the higher model level, and why the construct is considered to be a first approximation. Much more high-resolution data from high-quality field work is needed to test adequately the ideas. The major sections of the review are a discussion of the modern and fossil data that form the building blocks of the construct, a presentation of the construct, and then a comparison of the construct with the available archaeological data to evaluate the degree of fit.

PHYSIOGRAPHIC AND CLIMATIC BACKGROUND

The southern Plains is a general, informal term covering the southern portions (below the 37° Parallel) of the Great Plains and Central Lowland provinces (Figure 1) (Fenneman 1931; Hunt 1974). These provinces, covering most of Oklahoma and Texas and eastern New Mexico, include the Osage Plains and southern portion of the High Plains sections that are composed of a number of defined physiographic regions (Figure 1). The Great Plains and Central Lowland provinces are characterized as grasslands (albeit their natures differ). During the late Pleistocene, the southern Plains biome, in terms of grasslands and attendant herd herbivores, extended beyond the geographic boundaries of today. It may be more appropriate to speak of a general southern grasslands that extended to the Gulf Coastal Plain (cf. Lundelius et al. 1983) and into Mexico. Today the southern Plains has a strongly continental climate (a large temperature range that is not influenced by large bodies of water). Rainfall maxima occur in the spring and fall as a result of frontal lifting of warm moist air. Summer rains occur mainly through intense thunderstorms that depend on, among other factors, daytime heating and the absence of high pressure. Summer droughts are common in the southern Plains, due to high pressure that dominates the region during this time (Barry 1983; Haragan 1983:67). Precipitation gains through winter snowfall are minimal (Barry 1983). The climate of the eastern portion of the southern Plains also is dominated by a flow of moist maritime air originating over the Gulf of Mexico and, secondarily, the Atlantic Ocean (Friedman 1983; Imbrie et al. 1983).

THEORY

In dealing with the extinct systems of the Pleistocene, be it the ecosystems, climate, or culture, a basic assumption is that modern systems can provide the models for understanding and reconstructing past systems. Ethnographic data on hunter-gatherer groups are used to provide analogues for understanding extinct Pleistocene and Holocene hunter-gatherer groups (e.g., Binford 1980; Isaac 1978; Keene 1981; Winterhalder 1981a). However, it must be kept in mind that just as no place today duplicates the climatic and ecosystemic conditions that existed during the Pleistocene, the cultural responses to those conditions probably are not duplicated in the current ethnographic record. The search is for the best approximation, given the theoretical framework being used. Some general theories and concepts are emerging that are applicable to the archaeological record (e.g., Bettinger 1980; Winterhalder and Smith 1981). Hunter-gatherer groups exist today under a variety of conditions. Their responses provide some universals in which to interpret the archaeological record (e.g., Bettinger 1980; Binford 1980; Hayden 1981). Data on specific groups under specific conditions also prove helpful, given what is currently known about Pleistocene and Holocene conditions at a specific site or region.

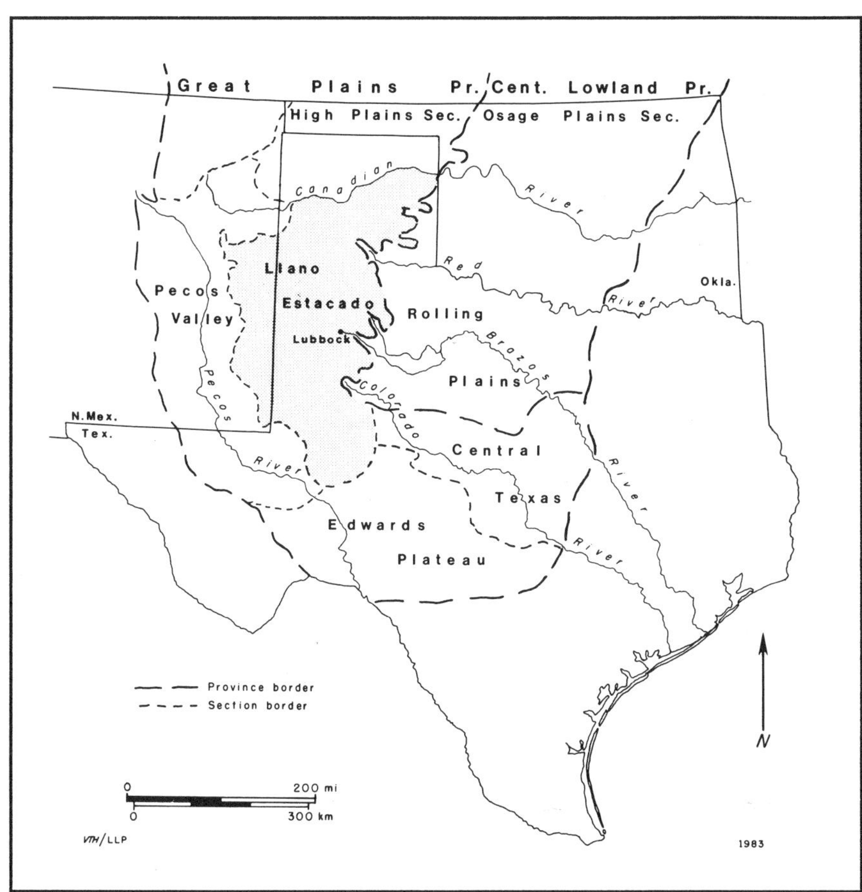

Figure 1. The southern Plains region.

The approach to human-land relationships is in the context of a technological-environmental explanation, given the concept that culture is an adaptation to the environment and that the subsistence system was closely linked to the environment (Binford 1968; Childe 1951; Clarke 1968; Durham 1976; Kirch 1980; Steward 1955; White 1959). The interaction, therefore, between culture and environment is facilitated by technology (Bettinger 1980; Hayden 1981; Steward 1938, 1955). Much theory in current hunter-gatherer studies is couched in terms of optimal foraging strategies (Bettinger 1980; Hayden 1981; Winterhalder and Smith 1981). Optimal foraging theory attempts to explain strategies for the most favorable resource procurement or adaptation with respect to specific criteria, and involves a set of methods in which to understand subsistence patterns in terms of a cost-benefit analysis in exploiting various resources (Durham 1981:218; Keene 1981:172; O'Connell and Hawkes 1981:99). The goal is to "account for subsistence behavior in terms of . . . simple principles that weigh the relative costs and payoffs of different economic choices as a basic for adaptive solutions" (Bettinger 1980:221). Hunter-gatherer seasonal movement is viewed as "a balancing mechanism for maintaining and conserving the resource base while exploiting it at an optimal level" (Hayden 1981:375).

A number of concepts applicable to the archaeological record follow from the above theoretical perspective. Environmental diversity looks at the "number and proportional representation of different species in a given environment" (Bettinger 1980:204), whereas climatic stability deals with the amount of temporal variation, both seasonal and long-term. A high-diversity environment contains numerous species in approximately equal proportion. High diversity, coupled with a stable climate (nonseasonal), produces a steady food supply and stable subsistence (Hayden 1981:349, 378). Patchiness (Bettinger 1980:207) and patch selectivity (Winterhalder 1981a:68) deal with the distribution of resources within the group's territory. Patchiness is concerned with the cost of resource procurement (amount of time and energy expended to obtain resources or defend subsistence territory) as the differential distribution of those resources changes. Patch selectivity is concerned with the number and types of habitats in which a forager chooses to obtain resources, and the relationship between patch quality, foraging time, and travel time. Diet breadth examines the selectivity (use) of those resources and is the set of prey species a hunter will pursue if encountered during a procurement venture (Winterhalder 1981a:68, 1981b:23).

Efficiency and effectiveness appear as hallmarks of hunter-gatherer strategies that can be viewed from the concept of risk management (another type of cost-benefit analysis). As Keene (1981:180) notes, there is "always a risk associated with any procurement strategy . . . but this risk can be ameliorated through cultural means." Risk management involves consideration of the personal well-being of individuals (safety), as well as the certainty of procuring the resource (success/failure rate). Highly stable resources are relatively secure, whereas low stability resources are less secure. This latter category may involve seasonal resources that experience periodic fluctuations or mass migration of herd animals. Within this scheme, plant resources are low risk/high yield, while animal resources are high risk/low yield. The economic choices made are a balancing act in that the most efficient strategies for hunting are not conducive to efficient gathering activities (Hayden 1981:361), therefore invoking scheduling considerations. Pooling of resources from individual hunting efforts (food sharing) ameliorates the risk to the group as a whole, both in terms of daily intake and efficient use of the meat before it can spoil (Hayden 1981:373).

The general terms "hunter-gatherer" and "forager" frequently are used in a generic sense to refer to this lifeway system as a whole. However, groups have organized themselves differently and approached the use and procurement of resources in different ways. Hunter-gatherer groups have been categorized in a more defined manner as generalists (forager) or specialists (collector), based on the relationship between subsistence mode, climatic regime, and social (structural) organization (Binford 1980). For purposes of this discussion, Table 1 (based on Binford 1980; Harako 1981; Hayden 1981; Silberbauer 1981) lists the more appropriate major characters of these categories applicable to the archaeological record.

Some resource and demographic universals from ethnographic hunter-gatherer groups are applicable to the archaeological record (Bettinger 1980; Hayden 1981; Rogers and Black 1976). Hunter-gatherers are organized into an egalitarian band society with a stable group size of about 25–50 people, although composition fluctuates. Smaller units of people from the group are formed for daily task and overnight subsistence activities. A seasonal round of activities is followed, thereby involving movement of both people and residential locations within that round of activities. The degree of movement is a function of group size, optimal procurement distances, and environment as related to the supply of food (Hayden 1981:378-379). This seasonal activity and movement produces two major site types, residential and procurement locations, in at least two modes: home base and satellite camps, and animal-kill and plant-gathering locales, respectively. In hunter-gatherer groups from temperate and tropical zones, hunting constitutes on the average about 35% of subsistence (varying from 10%– 60%). Plant gathering forms the main part of the subsistence base, on the average of 65% (varying from 90%–40%) (Hayden 1981:357). Two major hunting patterns are discernible, that of small-scale hunts and communal hunts. Small-scale hunts can occur as cooperative ventures or as a lone hunter or two-party joint venture. Hunter-gatherers have a home range that encompasses the territorial resources; and primary labor division is gender-oriented, males being the hunters and females being the gatherers. However, gender lines become blurred during the many attendant tasks associated with communal hunts or during times of scarcity when both sexes may be involved in gathering activities.

The Mbuti Pygmies (archer groups) of the Zaire Forest (Harako 1981) in equatorial Africa provide additional data concerning hunter-gatherer groups living under climatic conditions that lack seasonal extremes and have high-diversity environments. Although seasonality, comparatively, is negligible, seasonal differences do occur in terms of rainy and nonrainy seasons, and this climatic aspect governs their annual cycle (seasonal round). The Mbuti move into their hunting range during seasons of little or no rain, with a 2- to 3-month stay at each hunting (satellite) camp, and return to their home base camp during the rainy season for about a 4-month stay. Their base camp is repeatedly occupied, whereas the location of hunting (satellite) camps may change each year. The habitat in terms of available resources strongly influences the choice of hunting camp locations, and camps are moved when hunting or gathering activities are no longer easy within a 5-km radius (Harako 1981:535). Home ranges tend to be small; few species migrate seasonally, and hunting is a localized activity.

The Mbuti have a broad-spectrum subsistence base, both in terms of plants and animals used on a regular basis. Mammals, birds, and reptiles are hunted. Elephant is one of several large-game herd animals hunted. A high resource diversity exists with a low risk of failure for providing food on a daily basis. Generally, meat is consumed within a week, even that dried for storage (Harako 1981:533). In equatorial regions in general, little to no storage occurs due to the reduced risk of periodic fluctuation in resources and high probability of spoilage (Hayden 1981:380). Approximately 30% of the Mbuti diet is from hunting and 10% from fishing (Hayden 1981:355, Table 10.3).

Among the archer groups, two major hunting patterns are followed, one using the bow and arrow (done on a daily basis) and the other using the spear (done on an intermittent basis). Bow-and-arrow hunting is on an as-encountered basis, whether as a lone archer or in a collective hunt. Collective hunts are neither structured nor targeted because game is selected on an encounter basis and an individual archer shoots at what comes his way. Spear hunting generally is on an as-encountered basis focused on large game animals, although infrequently is on a targeted basis for elephants. Spear hunting is done in three modes: (1) most commonly by partners or a lone hunter; (2) by a small group of four to five specialists; and (3) by a large organized group, including children as lookouts. Spear hunting is a time-consuming and arduous task involving long distances travelled and is considered highly dangerous. The small-group spear hunters search for generic large game (mammals) other than elephant, although if they encounter elephants they may pursue them. The large organized group is structured, with a targeted prey (elephant) and highly variable membership. This type of hunt may involve more than one band, and multiband cooperative ventures are on an informal basis (individuals on friendly terms with the initiating band). Scavenging carcasses determined to be a day or two dead is an acceptable behavior and is termed a successful hunt (Harako 1981:532). Butchering begins after the kill, and as much meat and by-products as possible are transported back to the hunting camp that day. If the processing takes more than the day, the hunting group returns the next day from the hunting (satellite) camp instead of establishing an overnight field camp. When a very large animal (elephant, sometimes buffalo) is killed, the entire band may travel to the kill site for the day in order to process the animal(s).

Table 1. Major Characteristics of Hunter-Gatherers Applicable to the Archaeological Record.

NO.	GENERALISTS (FORAGERS)	SPECIALISTS (COLLECTORS)
1	seasonal residential moves among a series of resources	few residential moves; frequent field (hunting) camp moves
2	site types: a. residential home base satellite camps b. procurement kill (1 to several species) scavenge	site types: a. residential home base field camp b. procurement kill (1 species) small (few animals) large (many animals) c. other cache
3	repeated use of (yearly return to) home base	new home base occupied each year
4	smaller home range	larger home range
5	year-round food resources	seasonal fluctuation in food resources
6	food gathered daily; no storage	storage of food
7	size of foraging group variable and on whatever-available basis (nonsystematic)	small task group and for specific resources (systematic)
8	broad-spectrum subsistence base (at least in terms of game animals)	narrowly focused subsistence base (at least in terms of game animals)
9	lesser redundancy of land use for kill sites	greater redundancy of land use for kill sites
10	localized hunting forays	long-distance hunting forays
11	primary hunting method is encounter basis	primary hunting method is targeted resource
12	minor hunting method is a targeted resource	minor hunting method is encounter basis
13	site procurement locations represent limited quantity of resources processed during any one episode	site procurement locations represent larger quantity of resources processed during any one episode
14	overnight hunting camps rare	overnight hunting camps common
15	equatorial climates	temperate to cold climates

DATA BASE

Paleoclimate

Changes in the sea-surface temperatures of the Gulf of Mexico and the Atlantic Ocean presumedly influenced the paleoprecipitation patterns of the late Wisconsinan with a change in air mass trajectories that carried moisture from these bodies of water (Barry 1983; Friedman 1983; Imbrie et al. 1983). In general, the paleoclimate of the Southwest was wetter than today, particularly in the winter, while it was drier in the Southeast, particularly in the summer (Barry 1983; Imbrie et al. 1983). Throughout the Southwest, ground-water tables in general rose more than 10 m. This elevated ground-water table, in addition to increased precipitation, appears responsible for the pluvial lakes (Smith and Street-Perrott 1983). The unglaciated southern Plains appears to have been a transition zone from the wetter Southwest to the drier Southeast. Overall, the late Wisconsinan paleoclimate of the southern Plains was an equitable, humid, maritime one, greatly influenced by the Gulf of Mexico, cooler (3–8° C) than today, and with a reduced annual temperature range (Haragan 1983; Porter 1983). Grassland environments were prevalent, although wooded areas apparently existed at certain times in the eastern portion (Bryant and Holloway 1985). Although forested conditions during the late Wisconsinan were proposed for the western portion, particularly the southern High Plains (Bryant and Holloway 1985; Hafsten 1961; Oldfield and Schoenwetter 1975; Wendorf 1970), more recent data from other lines of evidence demonstrate that the region was a grasslands throughout the late Pleistocene (Holliday 1987).

The early part of the late Wisconsinan was an interglacial from about 25,000 to 20,000 yr B.P. Glacial maximum is set at about 18,000 yr B.P. (Porter 1983). Deglaciation (the stagnation and melting of the Laurentide ice sheet) began around 17,000 yr B.P. and reached a peak about 13,500 yr B.P. Massive discharge of glacial meltwaters down the Mississippi River into the Gulf of Mexico occurred between 15,000 and 11,000 yr B.P. (Baker 1983; Friedman 1983). Sea-level minimum occurred between 23,000 and 15,000 yr B.P., with a rapid rise from 15,000 to 10,000 yr B.P. During full-glacial times, the Gulf of Mexico waters were lowered at least 80 m, although winds, currents, and littoral drift apparently were the same along the Gulf Coast as now (Barry 1983). The time of 11,000 yr B.P. marks the biotic and ecosystemic end of Wisconsinan conditions on the southern Plains (Baker 1983; Johnson 1986, 1987; Lundelius et al. 1983).

During the late Wisconsinan on the southern Plains, pluvial lake levels in the western portion rose and fell (Smith and Street-Perrott 1983), while river valleys in the eastern portion underwent moderate incising and aggradation and experienced river metamorphosis, especially underfitness where today the stream is too small for the valley in which it flows (Baker 1983). Changes in precipitation, evaporation, temperature, humidity, wind, and cloud cover were responsible for the changes in the lake levels (Smith and Street-Perrott 1983), while immense changes in stream loads and discharges presumedly related to climatic changes (Baker 1983) affected the river valleys.

Around 29,000 yr B.P. pluvial lake levels in the western portion of the southern Plains were high, indicating a significant increase in precipitation and a reduction in the annual evaporation rate over today (Reeves 1965, 1966; Smith and Street-Perrott 1983). During full-glacial times, pluvial lake levels were intermediate. Climatically, a lowered annual temperature of 2.8–5.6° C, a lowered summer temperature of 4.4–5.6° C, increased annual precipitation of about 26 cm, and a 27% reduction in annual evaporation rate occurred (Reeves 1965, 1966; Smith and Street-Perrott 1983). The eastern portion experienced a 4° C annual temperature decrease, with summer temperature maximum around 21–22° C (about 5.5–5.6° C lower than today) (Bryant 1977; Bryant and Holloway 1985). Sea-surface temperatures along the Gulf Coast were slightly cooler (overall difference of about 2° C lower), with a February temperature of 20° C and an August one of 26° C (Imbrie et al. 1983). A more winter-like atmospheric circulation pattern is proposed (Barry 1983), having an augmented westerly jet stream over the southern Plains that would enhance winter precipitation and reduce summer precipitation.

During post-glacial times, the pluvial lake levels in the western portion of the southern Plains rose (a high lake level at 16,000 yr B.P.) and then returned to intermediate levels (Reeves 1965, 1966; Smith and Street-Perrott 1983). The Mississippi River was an immense proglacial drainage system (Baker 1983), and sea level in the Gulf of Mexico rose rapidly (Bloom 1983). An equitable, humid, maritime-like climate occurred over the southern Plains, with cool summers, mild winters, and abundant precipitation (Lundelius et al. 1983). Significant areas of open grassland environments existed on the southern Plains, including parklands and savannas (Bryant 1977; Lundelius et al. 1983). This scenario, then, was the climate and environment for the possible pre-Clovis period of the southern Plains.

By 12,500 yr B.P. pluvial lake levels were dropping and the lakes were becoming seasonal rather than permanent (Reeves 1973), owing to a lowering of the water table and reduction in ground water (Haynes 1975) coupled with a reduction in precipitation (Reeves 1973). Nevertheless, between 12,000 and 11,000 yr B.P., an equitable, humid, maritime-like paleoclimate continued that lacked seasonal extremes, with a lower mean annual temperature than today, cooler summers, and warmer winters that lacked extended freezing conditions. In the western portion (southern High Plains), mean annual temperature was about 10–13° C (Johnson 1987) compared with 15° C today (Haragan 1983). A lowered summer temperature of at least 5.6° C existed, with a winter temperature at or above 0° C (Johnson 1986, 1987). The mean annual temperature in the eastern portion (central Texas) was slightly warmer, probably about 13–15° C compared with 18–21° C today (Haragan 1983). Summers also were slightly warmer than on the southern High Plains (Johnson 1987). A winter rainfall pattern persisted, coupled with cool, dry summers. Greater precipitation, more effective moisture, lower evaporation rate, and greater humidity than today continued. Open grassland environments increased, with parklands along the draws of the southern High Plains (Johnson 1986, 1987) and savannas or scrub grasslands occurring on the rest of the southern Plains (Bryant 1977; Lundelius et al. 1983). This scenario, similar to the preceding one, then, was the climate and environment for the Clovis period on the southern Plains.

Archaeological Sites

Few human-related late Pleistocene sites are known on the southern Plains, although isolated surface finds of Clovis points are common (Meltzer 1986a, 1986b). Eight sites were selected for consideration because the collections had one or more of the following features: human-induced modifications to megafaunal remains; appropriate radiocarbon ages; Clovis points; and/or buried remains (i.e., not surface material). Accessible collections from these sites were reviewed by the author to determine if human-induced modifications to megafaunal remains were present; if so, what type (cf. Johnson 1989; Johnson and Shipman 1986). Description of individual specimens occur in Johnson (1985; 1987; 1989) and Johnson and Shipman (1986). Key specimens not in those publications are discussed briefly. Human-induced modifications were categorized as cut lines, fracture features, or tool use (Johnson 1985; Johnson and Shipman 1986). Other agency modifications also occurred, indicating complex life histories for many elements in the assemblages.

Table 2 summarizes the general data from the eight sites. Two of the sites have multiple late Pleistocene occupations that brought the sample size to 10. These 10 occupations are categorized as potential pre-Clovis, pre-Clovis or Clovis, and Clovis (Table 2), based on radiocarbon ages and/or presence of Clovis points. Mammoth age-structure categories follow those of Saunders (1980:95). Table 3 presents measurement data on the associated Clovis points. Measurement data on Clovis points from three sites were taken by the author, while additional data and sites come from Sellards (1938) and Hester (1972).

Seven U.S. localities within the late Pleistocene southern Plains grasslands biome occasionally cited as possible pre-Clovis sites are: Friesenhahn Cave (Alexander 1978; Irwin 1971; Jennings 1968; Stanford 1983); Levi Rockshelter (Alexander 1978; Stanford 1983); Cueva Quebrada (Lundelius 1984); Lewisville (Alexander 1978; Irwin 1971; Stanford 1983; West 1983; Wheat 1971); Waco Mammoth (Fox and Smith 1987); Congress Avenue (Briggs 1987); and Burnham (Wyckoff 1988). These localities were discounted and not included in this discussion. The lithic flakes recovered during the initial excavations of Friesenhahn Cave (Evans 1961) came from Holocene deposits (Graham 1976). The complex cave stratigraphy at Levi Rockshelter greatly adds to the confusion in interpreting site data. Clarification is needed in the stratigraphy, geochronology, point taxonomy, and relationship of faunal remains to lithics (cf. Alexander 1963; Stanford 1983) before a late Pleistocene occupation can be demonstrated. Marks put forth as cut lines (Lundelius 1984:461) on the femur of an extinct horse in the Cueva Quebrada assemblage were determined instead to be the result of carnivore scoring (Johnson and Shipman 1986:48). Recent testing at Lewisville (Stanford 1983) indicates that the radiocarbon ages probably are erroneous (not pre-Clovis in age) and that the site may represent a Clovis occupation. However, the relationship between the proposed hearths, the Clovis point, the megafaunal remains, and the recently recovered lithic resharpening flakes still is unclear. Therefore, Lewisville was not considered for discussion in either the pre-Clovis or Clovis categories.

The Waco Mammoth locality (Fox and Smith 1987) appears to represent a catastrophic death scene of at least 15 mammoth and has a radiocarbon date of ca. 28,000 yr B.P. The carcasses are articulated and appear to be of a female-and-young band in typical death position (Gary Haynes, personal communication 1985). Although human intervention has been put forward as the possible cause of death (Fox and Smith 1987), evidence in terms of human-modified bones or lithics is lacking. Flood waters in a crevasse appear the more probable death-related situation (Paul Heinrich, personal communication 1985). The reliability of the radiocarbon age is doubtful, due to its being an apatite date (Herbert Haas, personal communication 1986).

Possible human involvement in the Congress Avenue locality has focused on the partial remains of a mastodon. The locality is dated to the late Pleistocene, based on the geology and geomorphic position of the river terrace. However, evidence for human intervention is lacking in terms of human-modified bones or lithics.

At Burnham (Wyckoff 1988), two apparent tools have been found 1.5 m from extinct bison remains in the same deposit. Water-processed matrix concentrates from the deposit have yielded five apparent resharpening flakes. Snail shell from the same deposit has yielded a radiocarbon age of 31,150 yr B.P., a probably unreliable age that is far too old (Wyckoff 1988:1). Extinct bison were hunted by humans into the early Holocene, and clarification is needed in the geochronology and the relationship of the bison remains to the lithics before a

Table 2. Summary of General Site Data.

PERIOD	SITE	PROCURED ANIMALS* (MNI; age class; sex)	EVIDENCE OF HUMAN-INDUCED BONE MODIFICATION**
Potential Pre-Clovis	Cooperton	mammoth (1; Y; M?)	H
	Bonfire Shelter	mammoth (1; ?; ?) horse (1; A; ?)	H, K, C
Pre-Clovis/Clovis	Bonfire Shelter	mammoth (1; ?; ?) horse (3; S; ?) camel (1; A; ?) bison (1; ?; ?)	H
	Duewall-Newberry	mammoth (1; Y; M?)	H, K, D, C
	Lubbock Lake	mammoth (1; ?; ?) horse (1; A; ?) camel (1; A; ?) bison (1; A; ?)	H, D, C
Clovis	Lubbock Lake	mammoth (3; 1Y, 2J; 1F?, ?) horse (2; 1A, 1J; ?) camel (1; A; ?) bison (1; A; ?) giant bear (1; A; M) giant armadillo (1; A; ?)	H, D, C, U
	Blackwater Draw Locality No. 1	mammoth (5; 5MA; ?) horse (1; A; ?) camel (1; A; ?) bison (1; A; ?)	H, D, C, U
	Miami	mammoth (5; 1MA, 2J; 3F, ?)	hack marks?
	Domebo	mammoth (1; YA; F?)	
	McLean	mammoth (1; ?; ?)	

***A** = adult; **F** = female; **J** = juvenile; **M** = male; **MA** = mature adult; **S** = sub-adult; **Y** = young adult.

late Pleistocene occupation can be demonstrated. Therefore, this locality is not considered for discussion in either the pre-Clovis or Clovis categories.

A number of Mexican localities within the late Pleistocene southern Plains grasslands biome have been excavated. At several of these localities, bones of extinct megafauna and lithic tools were recovered. At Rancho La Amapola (El Cedral), San Luis Potosí, megafaunal remains were recovered in a well-stratified sequence from spring and lake deposits (Lorenzo and Mirambell 1986a). A broken horse tibia and two lithic tools were recovered from different strata radiocarbon dated between 15,000 and 34,000 yr B.P. A zone of charcoal surrounded by proboscidean foot elements dated to ca. 32,000 yr B.P. (Lorenzo and Mirambell 1986a:111). Extensive excavations at Cerro de Tlapacoya, in the Valley of Mexico, exposed well-stratified deposits in 18 localities that cross-cut a number of geomorphic settings and depositional environments (Lorenzo and Mirambell 1986a; Mirambell 1973). Several lithic flakes and tools were recovered from different deposits radiocarbon dated between 15,000 and 23,000 yr B.P., while remains of deer and black bear were found near proposed hearths that radiocarbon dated between 22,000 and 24,000 yr B.P. The hearths were in pebble to cobble-sized clasts of beach deposits and represented circular cleared areas that contained charcoal and ash.

The major problem with these localities is that, from

NO. CLOVIS POINTS	NO. & TYPE OF NONPOINT LITHIC TOOLS	RADIOCARBON AGES		MATERIAL DATED
0	3 hammerstones, 1 "anvil"	19,100 ± 800	GX-1214	tooth plate
		17,575 ± 550	GX-1215	long bone
		20,400 ± 450	GX-1216	rib
0	14 "anvils"	12,430 ± 490	AA-344	diffuse charcoal
0	9 "anvils"			
0	0			
0	0			
1	2 "anvils"	11,100 ± 100	SMU-548	wood
5	56 flaked lithics	11,630 ± 400	A491	carbonized plants
		11,170 ± 360	A481	carbonized plants
		11,040 ± 500	A490	carbonized plants
3	1 retouched flake			
3	1 retouched flake, 1 utilized flake	11,045 ± 647	SM-695	wood
		11,220 ± 500	SI-172	bone
		11,200 ± 600	SI-175	humic acids
1	0			

C = cut line; **D = dynamic loading points; **H** = helical fracture surfaces; **K** = cone flakes; **U** = use as tool.

the published reports, a direct association of bones and tools cannot be demonstrated and a detailed discussion of bone modification is not provided on which to make a judgment. The relationships between proposed hearths, lithic tools and flakes, and megafaunal remains still are unclear. The complex stratigraphy and multiple localities within a location add to the confusion in interpreting the data. Clarification is needed in the long-distance stratigraphy, geochronology, and relationships of faunal remains to lithics before a late Pleistocene human occupation can be demonstrated. The localities are not necessarily discounted as potential pre-Clovis, but are excluded from discussion because they do not meet the criteria established in this particular study.

At least 15 mammoth localities have been excavated in the Valley of México, with ages ranging from post-23,900 yr B.P. (radiocarbon assay on organics) to as late as 6200 yr B.P. (obsidian-hydration date) (Lorenzo and Mirambell 1986b:38, 105). Five of these localities had lithic flakes or tools associated with mammoth remains. Non–Clovis-type projectile points were recovered with mammoth at Santa Isabel Iztapan localities I and II (Lorenzo and Mirambell 1986b:42, 49). Flakes were recovered at Tepexpan-Arellano, Los Reyes Acozac, and Chimalhuacán-Atenco localities (Lorenzo and Mirambell 1986b:55, 77, 116). These localities indicate a probable late Pleistocene human occupation in the Valley of México. However, because of the presence of

Table 3. Data on Associated Clovis Points.

SITE	ACCESSION NO.	MEASUREMENT (MM) AND NUMERICAL DATA								
		1	2	3	4	5	6	7	8	9
Lubbock Lake	TMM892-74	46.5	24.1	1.5	4.0	4.4	3.1	1.5	2	15.5
BWD No. 1*	TMM937-72	13.0	6.0	2.0					2	5.0
	ENMU2-214	29.0	11.0	3.0			10.0		2	5.0
	ENMU2-221	60.0	15.0	2.0			6.0		2	6.0
	W-127 (Warnica)	4.0	8.0	2.0					2	
	W-135 (Warnica)	11.0	5.0	2.0			7.0			
	CO-5 (Collins)	12.0	16.0	2.0			10.0		1	
	EL-10	36.0	10.0	3.0			15.0		2	13.0
	EL-30	13.0	7.0	2.0			6.0		2	6.0
	EL-33	4.0	3.0	1.5						
	EL-47	15.0	7.0	2.0			5.0		2	
	EL-90	19.0	11.5	3.0					1	16.0
	TMM976-2	78.0	22.0						1	
Miami**	TMM976-3	113.0	30.0							
	Mead's Point (No. 45)	116.0	30.0						1	
Domebo	MGP64.8.1	40.9[a]			3.6					
	MGP64.8.2	78.1	25.0	2.5	1.3	7.5	37.3	2.0	2	33.5
	MGP64.8.3	67.8	19.6	1.4	2.3	5.4	24.5	2.2	2	23.0
McLean	TTU47.73.3	82.7	23.5	2.5	4.0	5.7	28.6	3.0	1	38.6

1 = length; **2** = basal width; **3** = basal thickness; **4** = proximal thickness; **5** = midpoint thickness at juncture of ground/unground edge; **6** = maximum length of edge grinding; **7** = depth of basal concavity; **8** = maximum number of flutes on one side; **9** = maximum length of flutes.

* From Hester (1972:182–217).

** From Sellards (1938:1007).

[a] Base missing; length of specimen.

projectile points different from the Clovis type and the lack of discussion on bone modification at these localities (in lieu of personal inspection of the collections), they were not considered further for discussion.

Potential Pre-Clovis Category

Based on radiocarbon ages, two sites appear as potential contenders for pre-Clovis status. Both sites lack human-modified lithics, although small boulders and cobbles may have been anvils and hammerstones. Human intervention is based on bone data (cf. Johnson 1985). The category is labeled as potential pre-Clovis because of possible problems with the radiocarbon ages. Cooperton (Anderson 1975), in southwestern Oklahoma on the Osage Plains (Figures 1 and 2), yielded the partial remains of a subadult male (?) mammoth (Mehl 1975:165). The hind legs were missing, apparently removed by erosion that exposed the site. The humeri and right scapula were broken, while the remaining skeletal elements apparently were intact. Anderson (1975:153) notes that the humeri were broken at the point of minimum diameter above the distal end (mid-diaphysis above the supracondyloid ridge) and that associated fragments could be reassembled, although some pieces were missing. One humeral diaphyseal segment was found next to a small granite boulder interpreted as an anvil. Materials testing analysis (Bonfield 1975:164) indicated that the breaks were "green" bone fractures. Anderson (1975:171) interpreted the site as a scavenging event to quarry bone for tool manufacture.

Bonfield's (1975) analysis, albeit brief, was a milestone in attempting to apply materials analysis and fracture mechanics to fossil bone. The initial review of the collection based on a limited sample indicates, however, that two fracture patterns are present. Helical fractures from tensile-shear failure in a wet bone state occur on some segments, such as MGP64.153 bone specimens 2C and 7A. Other segments exhibit rectilinear fractures

MATERIAL	REMARKS
E	reworked, new tip, new base
A	reworked
B	reworked, new tip, impact scar
A	snapped base
E	snapped base
A	reworked, new tip
A	snapped base
E	impact fracture
A	reworked, new base, new tip?
E	snapped base
A	reworked, new tip
E	impact fracture
C	reworked, new tip
C	snapped at base; impact scar
?	
G	impact fracture
G	impact fracture
G	reworked, new base
E	impact fracture

A = alibates
B = basalt
C = chert, unknown source
E = Edwards Formation chert
G = gray mottled chert, unknown source

from tensile failure in a dry bone state (cf. Johnson 1985). The relationship of the helical fractures and rectilinear fractures to Bonfield's (1975) "green breaks" is not yet known, and the assemblage warrants an in-depth analysis to determine the extent of the human role in the bone modification.

Because of the apparent human-induced bone modifications, the age of the Cooperton mammoth is crucial. The three radiocarbon ages (Table 2) are on bone apatite CO_2 from pieces of three elements from the one skeleton. Two of the ages overlap at two sigmas, but the third does not. However, the ages are reasonably close (within 1000 years) and give a general time well within the glacial period. Haynes' (1968) early work showed that bone apatite CO_2 ages were reliable if samples were pretreated with acetic acid; those procedures and techniques were followed in determining the Cooperton ages (Anderson 1975:156). More recent research, however, indicates that bone apatite is irreversibly contaminated by exchange with outside carbonate (Hassan et al. 1977), although more accurate ages may be obtained if sequential heating of bone is followed in deriving the apatite CO_2 (Haas and Banewicz 1980). Free carbonates occurred in the soil profile at Cooperton (Nichols 1975). Because of these problems associated with bone apatite CO_2 dating, the Cooperton ages are suspect.

Bonfire Shelter (Bement 1986; Dibble and Lorrain 1968), in the Trans-Pecos area of Texas on the Stockton Plateau (Figures 1 and 2), is a stratified, multicomponent rockshelter composed of late Pleistocene and Holocene culture-bearing deposits. Bone Bed 1 in the late Pleistocene sediments is composed of five bone-bearing strata, two of which contain bones that appear to be modified by humans. Carnivore-modified bones also occur. The lower of the two strata, Stratum H-1, contains the broken remains of mammoth and extinct horse around several small limestone blocks (Bement 1986:38).

Horse metatarsal TMM 40806-273/391 was opened through mid-diaphyseal impact loading, creating helical fracture surfaces, cone flakes, and other bone debris. A mark on the diaphysis of the distal end conforms to macrovisual criteria for a cut line but could not be confirmed through SEM analysis because of cortical surface erosion (Johnson and Shipman 1986). The age of the deposit is crucial. The one age determination (Table 2) is difficult to evaluate. Cretaceous carbonate that could contaminate the diffuse charcoal and yield an erroneously older date is abundant in the rockshelter. On the other hand, at two sigmas, the determination overlaps with the known range for the Clovis period (Haynes 1980). The material, therefore, may represent a Clovis-period occupation rather than a potential pre-Clovis one.

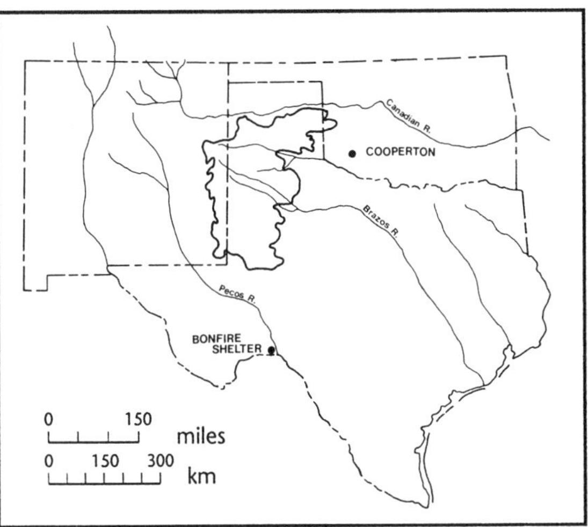

Figure 2. Potential pre-Clovis sites on the southern Plains.

Pre-Clovis or Clovis Category

Three sites fall into this uncertain category, based on the lack of both radiocarbon ages and Clovis points, although geological and faunal evidence indicate a late Pleistocene age. Human intervention is based on bone data.

Stratum E of Bone Bed 1 at Bonfire Shelter (Figure 3) contains the broken remains of mammoth, horse, camel, and bison around small limestone blocks (Bement 1986:33; Dibble and Lorrain 1968:28). The mammoth material exhibits helical fracture surfaces (Johnson 1989; Johnson and Shipman 1986). The stratum is bracketed by a lower age of 12,430 ± 490 yr B.P. (AA-344) (Bement 1986:8) and an upper age of 10,230 ± 160 yr B.P. (TX-153) (Dibble and Lorrain 1968:33), indicating a probable Clovis-period age (cf. Haynes 1980) for the activity.

Duewall-Newberry (Carlson et al. 1984; Steele and Carlson 1989), in southeastern Texas along the Brazos River (Figures 1 and 3), yielded the partial remains of a subadult male (?) mammoth. The humeri and right femur exhibit helical fractures, dynamic loading points, cone flakes, and flake scars. Cut lines occur on several ribs. Mid-diaphyseal loading was used to fracture the long bones. An age estimate of 10,000–12,000 yr B.P. based on geologic setting (Carlson et al. 1984; Steele and Carlson 1989) indicates a probable Clovis-period age for the activity.

Lubbock Lake (Holliday 1985; Johnson 1987), in western Texas on the southern High Plains (Figures 1 and 3), is a deeply stratified, multicomponent site composed of culture-bearing late Pleistocene and Holocene deposits. At least two late Pleistocene occupation levels occur, the older of which is undated. Geological evidence and the age of the upper cultural level indicate an age of 11,500 yr B.P. or older (Holliday and Johnson 1984; Johnson and Holliday 1985). The bone bed contains the remains of mammoth, horse, camel, and bison. Cut lines occur on various elements from these species, and those on the bison remains were confirmed by SEM analysis (Johnson 1989; Johnson and Shipman 1986).

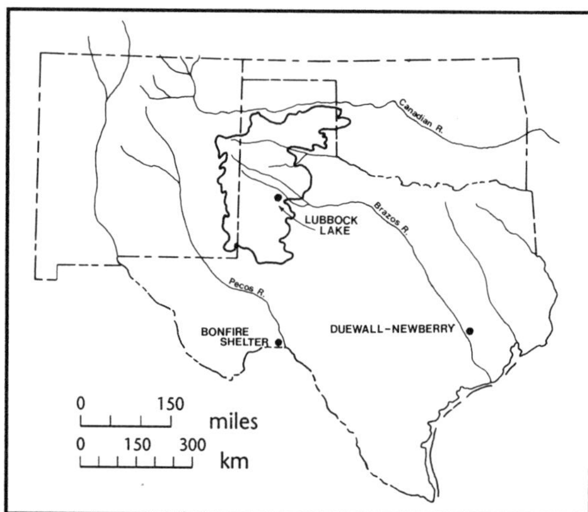

Figure 3. Pre-Clovis or Clovis sites on the southern Plains.

Clovis Category

Based on radiocarbon ages and/or presence of Clovis points, five sites are in this category. Human intervention is based on the occurrence of lithic tools and bone data.

The upper late Pleistocene occupation level at Lubbock Lake (Figure 4) dates to the Clovis period (Table 2). At least seven megafaunal species were processed, whose remains exhibit cut lines, helical fracture surfaces, dynamic loading points, and evidence of tool use (Johnson 1985, 1987, 1989; Johnson and Holliday 1985; Johnson and Shipman 1986). Fractured mammoth limb elements were recovered associated with two large caliche boulders. Mid-diaphyseal impact was used to fracture the humerus and produce radial diaphyseal segments (Johnson 1985). Modified lithic tools are absent, although a Clovis point was recovered from the bone bed during dredging operations that uncovered the site. The point (TMM 892-74) had been resharpened and used as a butchering tool (Johnson 1987).

Blackwater Draw Locality No. 1 (Hester 1972), in eastern New Mexico on the southern High Plains (Figures 1 and 4), is another well-stratified, multicomponent site composed of culture-bearing late Pleistocene and Holocene deposits. Several Clovis-age occupations are known, one of which yielded cylindrical bone shafts (Hester 1972:117), apparently made from mammoth cortical bone, that were used in hafting Clovis points (Johnson 1985; Lahren and Bonnichsen 1974). The most extensive occupation excavated involved at least five mammoth and other Rancholabrean fauna (Hester 1972; Hughes 1984; Lundelius 1972). The mammoth represent individual kill or scavenging events (Saunders 1980). Remains from Mammoth #2 exhibit cut lines. Remains from horse, camel, and bison recovered from "behind the North Bank" during excavations of the mammoth also exhibit cut lines, as well as dynamic impact features and evidence of tool use (Hughes 1984; Johnson 1989).

Eight Clovis points and a large number of other lithic tools were found in association with four of the mammoth (Hester 1972; Hughes 1984; Warnica 1966). At least four of the points had been reworked. A Clovis point, at least 15 lithic tools, and a hammerstone or grinding stone were found with Mammoth #2. The Clovis point (EL-10), found with the ribs (Warnica 1966:346), was not reworked but had an impact scar that removed the apex of the tip. Confusion exists, however, as to whether or not some or all of the tools associated with the four mammoth were redeposited by stream action (Hester

1972:85; Warnica 1966:355). Samples of carbonized plants associated with the mammoth excavations yielded ages from within the Clovis period (Table 2) (Haynes 1980; Haynes et al. 1966).

Miami (Sellards 1938), in western Texas on the southern High Plains (Figures 1 and 4), yielded the partial remains of five mammoth around and in a pluvial lake (playa). The mammoth represent a single kill event of a small family group (Saunders 1980:94). Marks on ribs that appear to be hack marks from butchering could not be confirmed through SEM analysis because of cortical surface erosion (Johnson and Shipman 1986). Long bones were not fractured. Three Clovis points and a flake tool were recovered with the remains. Two points were found within separate rib piles and one near a vertebra (Sellards 1938:1007). One (TMM 976-3) exhibits an impact scar that removed the apex of the tip, and another (TTM 976-2) has a refashioned tip and exhibits lateral edge damage, indicating its use as a butchering tool. Radiocarbon ages are not available.

Domebo (Leonhardy 1966), in southwestern Oklahoma on the Osage Plains (Figures 1 and 4), yielded the remains of a subadult female (?) mammoth (Mehl 1966:27). The disarticulated but associated elements were not fractured. The presence or absence of cut lines on the elements could not be determined because most elements are still encased in field jackets. Cut lines were not found on the few accessible elements. Three Clovis points and two flake tools were recovered with the mammoth. One point (MGP64.8.2), found near disarticulated ribs and vertebrae (Leonhardy 1966:18), has a refashioned tip with an impact scar. A second point (MGP64.8.3), found near two articulated vertebrae (Leonhardy 1966:19), appears to be the original tip-blade with a new base. The reworking seen on these tools appears as refitting, rather than modification for use as

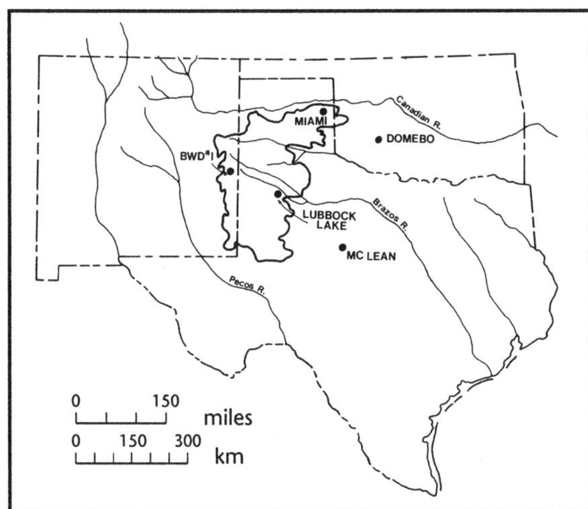

Figure 4. Clovis-age sites on the southern Plains.

butchering tools. The third point (MGP64.8.1), found near two vertebrae, is a midsection with an impact scar that removed the tip. Radiocarbon ages on various materials (Table 2) indicate an event well within the Clovis period (Haynes 1980; Leonhardy 1966).

McLean (Bryan and Ray 1938; Ray 1930, 1942), in central Texas on the Osage Plains (Figures 1 and 4), is an unexcavated multicomponent site composed of culture-bearing late Pleistocene and Holocene deposits. A Clovis point was found in association with a mammoth skeleton exposed in an arroyo cut through the site. The point (TTU 1947.73.3) exhibits an impact scar that removed the tip. The nature of the site is unknown, and radiocarbon ages are not available.

A total of 19 Clovis points were recovered from the excavations and sites discussed (Table 3). Several features are noticeable: (1) eight have impact scars on the tip, indicating use as weapons; (2) seven have the lateral edges and/or tip reworked, and at least two of these have additional damage that indicates use other than as a weapon; and (3) length and blade-tip morphology are variable. The first two features indicate that the Clovis point was at least a dual-function tool (weapon and butchering), if not a multifunctional tool. This observation is coupled with the very low number of non-points recovered from the discussed sites (except for Blackwater Draw Locality No. 1, whose tool-skeleton associations are unclear) to indicate strongly that the Clovis point was a focal point of the tool kit and a multipurpose tool. The Texas Clovis point survey results (Meltzer 1986a, 1986b) substantiate these observations and also indicate that the highest percentage of reworked points come from the southern High Plains. Length and blade-tip morphology are variable because of the resharpening and reuse occurring. Hester (1972:97) recognized this variability in the series of Clovis points (11) from Blackwater Draw Locality No. 1 and erected two types, albeit attributing the difference to stylistic modes.

Using other types of data, Hester and Grady (1977:92) estimated that the home range of southern High Plains Paleoindian bands in general had a radius of about 144–193 km. Good-quality chert outcrops on the southern High Plains are rare, but a home range of this size would include outcrops along the eastern (Holliday and Welty 1981) and western (Shelley 1984) escarpments. A general conservancy of lithic material overall for the Paleoindian period on the southern High Plains is indicated by the resharpening, reuse, and recycling of tools and by the use of locally available silicified caliche and quartzites (Johnson 1987; Johnson and Holliday 1981). This conservancy and scarcity of good lithic resources is underscored by the use of bone as a utilitarian tool resource (Johnson 1985, 1987). For the Clovis period on the southern High Plains, this conservancy trend is seen primarily in the resharpening and reuse of tools (particularly Clovis points) and is reflected in the employment of bone expediency tools for butchering tasks.

Saunder's (1980) model of Clovis hunting patterns for mammoth indicated two modes for procuring mammoth. Mammoth were hunted and cropped as a kin group, creating sites that reflect multiple individuals from a single event (catastrophic), with an appropriate age and sex structure. Mammoth also were hunted or scavenged as individuals, creating sites that reflect either lone individuals or multiple individuals from several events (accumulative), with an inappropriate age and sex structure. If indeed mammoth herd behavior was similar to that of modern African elephants, then the expectable age-sex pattern for mammoth hunted on an individual basis should be young-adult to adult males. Isolating healthy females or young from the herd would have been a very high-risk venture. The mixed age-sex pattern argues strongly for a scavenging mode of procuring individual mammoths as an alternative to the active hunting mode.

CONSTRUCT

Based on ethnographic hunter-gatherer theory and data and paleoclimatic and ecosystemic data, an environmental-cultural construct can be hypothesized for the southern Plains at the end of the Pleistocene. A major assumption is that climatic equability (nonseasonal, lacking temperature extremes) can be substituted for equatorial conditions. The series of propositions are drawn from the Mbuti Pygmies (archer groups) analogy (Harako 1981). This generic construct for a southern Plains paleohunter-gatherer group is compared in the Discussion section with the available data to examine how well the two concur.

For this construct, a mild, humid climate prevailed with a maritime pattern. Seasonality was expressed in terms of an annual rainy (winter) and nonrainy cycle. Abundant surface water available year-round ameliorated any adverse affects a nonrainy period may have produced. A mosaic vegetation pattern produced a high-patchiness, heterogeneous resource base that provided habitat for a wide variety of animals. This combination produced a high-diversity environment. Climatic stability, coupled with the high-diversity environment, indicated a steady food supply and stable subsistence that provided a low risk of failure and an opportunity for wide diet breadth. Clovis peoples practiced a foraging (generalist) subsistence strategy with a broad-based resource orientation and a procurement plan of encounter and targeted hunting.

From this general statement, several propositions follow. If Clovis peoples practiced a foraging strategy, then the expected social organization is that of an egalitarian band society. Given the climatic stability, an annual round governed by a rainy and nonrainy cycle is expectable. If an annual round was followed, governed by a rainy and nonrainy cycle, then both home base and satellite camps would be inhabited at different times of the year. If few residential moves were made, then home base sites could be recognized based on time of year occupied (winter), size of site (larger), quantity and variety of materials (greater), stratified remains, and distribution over the landscape (fewer). If few residential moves were made, then satellite camps could be recognized based on time of year occupied (nonwinter), size of site (smaller), quantity and variety of materials (lesser), and distribution over the landscape (more). If satellite camps were moved when subsistence efforts went beyond a certain radius, then a minimum home range could be identified based on the number of recognizable home bases and satellite camps.

If a broad-spectrum subsistence was practiced, then the major portion of the subsistence base would be from plants (carbohydrates) and a lesser portion of the base from meat (protein, fat). Plant remains and plant-associated tools would be expected to be common refuse at satellite camps. If relatively secure resources provided a low-risk, high-yield return, then both encounter and targeted hunting would occur, with encounter hunting being the primary method. If encounter hunting was the primary method, then a variety of game animals would be hunted; that variety of species would be reflected in the kill sites; and multiple-species kill sites would be the most common kills. If targeted hunting was a secondary method, then only one game animal would be hunted; that single species would be reflected in the kill sites; and single-species kill sites would be less common. If encounter hunting was practiced, then generic large game (mammals) would be hunted by small groups of male hunters, or generic game (mammals, birds, reptiles) would be hunted by partners or a lone hunter. If targeted hunting was practiced, then a single-species large game mammal would be hunted by a large organized group (adult males, females, children) on a structured basis as a communal hunt. If scavenging was an acceptable practice, then carcass treatment would be the same as for a kill and the event would appear as a single-species targeted hunt. If scavenging was an acceptable practice, a scavenging event could be distinguished from a targeted event by the number of animals represented and the species represented, if different from the single-species target identified as the normal prey.

If processing of the large game animals was accomplished at the kill, then meat and hides were brought back to the residential sites. If meat and hides were brought back to the residential sites, then kill sites could be identified on the basis of the representation of complete or nearly complete carcasses of the large game animals. If processing of small game animals was accomplished at the residential sites, then residential sites could be identified on the basis of the representation of complete or nearly complete carcasses of small game animals. If food was gathered on a daily basis, then overnight hunting camps would be rare. If food was gathered on a daily basis, then food storage would not be practiced on a routine basis. If the climate was equitable and food resources stable, then the need for food storage would not exist. If the climate was equitable, if food resources were stable, if food storage was unnecessary, and if food could be obtained on a daily basis, then the resources taken would be pooled and shared for the benefit of the group.

DISCUSSION

No pre-Clovis sites are clearly identified on the southern Plains. The possible settlement and subsistence patterns for pre-Clovis are therefore difficult to summarize, owing to the equivocal nature of the data and the small number of localities within a large time span (up to 8,000 years). However, if the potential pre-Clovis category and pre-Clovis or Clovis category are combined, the data from the five sites would appear to indicate a meat-related subsistence base oriented around large herd mammals and a fracture-based bone technology involving quarrying of mammoth limb elements. Given the climatic parameters, food storage would not be practical. Potential residential sites are unknown. Excavated sites appear to be either for animal procurement, bone quarrying, or a combination of both. Animal-procurement sites appear to occur in two modes, the major one being multiple-species procurement, the minor one single-species (mammoth) procurement. The mammoth at Duewall-Newberry (from the uncertain pre-Clovis or Clovis category) was processed for meat (cut lines on nonfractured elements), in addition to the limbs being quarried. At Cooperton (potential pre-Clovis category), apparently only quarry activities were conducted. Because the meat appears not to have been taken, Cooperton may represent a scavenging location for technological rather than subsistence purposes. Neither the time of year of any of these activities nor their frequency is known.

The evidence for utilization of plant resources undoubtedly is under-represented in the archaeological record. The problem is one of recognition that is governed by the threshold phenomenon. The threshold phenomenon deals with the minimal and reflects the lowest level of resolution needed to characterize an event in order to distinguish it from other similar events or to permit its earliest detection in the fossil record (e.g., Ascher and Ascher 1965; Mayr 1966). Systematic plant usage or the level of usage may not have been high enough to cross the archaeological threshold. What data are available to support a plant-related subsistence for Clovis peoples are the landscape distribution and the possible cause of the levered breakage pattern of Texas Clovis points (cf. Meltzer 1986a, 1986b). Clovis peoples did have a broad-spectrum meat-related subsistence, utilizing mammals, birds, and reptiles. Frozen caches (cf. Frison and Todd 1986) were not possible, and dried material would spoil under the humid conditions. Clovis points served a dual function as a weapon and hafted butchery tool and may have been multifunctional if also used in plant-gathering activities. The Clovis point appears to have been the focus of the lithic tool kit; what few other tools were used were primarily amorphous flake tools of an expedient nature. Fracture-based bone technology involved two traditions: quarrying mammoth limb elements for tool blanks; and fracturing ungulate and large carnivore (giant bear) limb elements for bone expediency tools. Residential sites are unknown. Excavated sites appear to be either animal-procurement or a combination of animal-procurement and bone-quarry sites. Animal-procurement sites occur in two modes, either as multiple-species procurement or as single-species (mammoth) procurement. In turn, mammoth-procurement sites occur in two modes, either as individuals or as single-event multiple groups. Neither the time of year of any of these activities nor their frequency is known.

In comparing the construct with the recovered Clovis period data, six items were examined in terms of a hunter-gatherer generalist foraging strategy: (1) basis for hunting; (2) type of major site; (3) specialized site; (4) size of home range; (5) lack of storage; and (6) climatic regime. Opportunistic hunting appears as a broad-spectrum meat-related subsistence base, utilizing a variety of animal food from a wide array of vertebrates both large and small (highly diverse environment). Diet breadth was wide, but not all available resources were used. In constructing the light-weight tool kit, the bulk of time would be invested in fashioning a multipurpose hafted spear point. The rest of the kit could be quickly assembled, either struck from a lithic core (amorphous flake tools) or fashioned at a kill (bone expediency tools) as needed. The light weight and expedient nature of the tool kit suggest that its design was for efficiency in traveling and performing a wide variety of tasks. Targeted hunting occurs only in terms of cropping small herds of mammoth.

The major site type is that of procurement. The different procurement-site modes can be identified with a forager hunting strategy. Multiple-species sites appear to represent the four to five professional hunters searching on an encounter basis, i.e., opportunistic hunting. Single-species group (mammoth herds) sites appear to represent the organized group of hunters and attendant helpers focused on a specific prey, i.e., targeted hunting. Single-species individuals (mammoth) appear to represent scavenging events. The excavated sites lack evidence of camping activities in connection with the processing of carcasses. Such transitory camping events may be below the threshold of archaeological recognition. However, this lack of overnight camping would be expectable if a foraging strategy was being invoked. The situation also implies that the major residential sites would be the home base and satellite camps.

Specialized tool-resource procurement sites occur in terms of quarrying mammoth limb elements for radial segments used in fashioning stylized implements, such as foreshafts. Foreshafts were an integral part of the hafting mechanism for Clovis points. Mammoth humeri in particular were the targeted elements and were fractured mid-diaphysis at the narrowest point using a single anvil mode. A number of radial segments could be produced for transport back to a residential site, where further reduction and modification produced a finished product. An assumption was made that a 32- to 193-km home range would be "small," but little empirical data for comparison are available on the size of hunter-gatherer home ranges or home territories beyond a subjective large or small designation. However, data from groups in the Australian Western Desert and the Kalahari (harsh environments and unstable climates) indicate a home-range size of 1,900 to 2,500 km^2 (Hayden 1981:382). Groups living in more stable and less harsh settings presumedly would have "smaller" home ranges. Using the available estimates, southern Plains Clovis peoples would have had a home range of about 3,217 to 117,000 km^2. Such figures appear unrealistic because they are larger than the home range estimates for hunter-gatherers under harsh environments.

The configuration of that home range is also an important aspect in that it could affect the actual size of the home territory and the types of resources within it. The vast majority of recorded Clovis sites (excavated and surface) on the southern High Plains are in the draws, although isolated points come from the uplands (Meltzer 1986b) and mammoth occasionally were killed around the playas (Sellards 1938). Quartzite gravels and silicified caliche outcrops are in the draws. The draws acted as highways for the Protohistoric and Historic Indians and early Spanish explorers (Holden 1962) and undoubtedly did so for the prehistoric groups. The draws and the resources that they contained are the dominant feature that would have influenced and shaped the home range. The home range configuration, therefore, probably was an oblong pattern (along the draws) with a lineally extended catchment basin.

With year-round food resources available, the risk of failure to provide was minimized so that adequate daily food provisions could be available, thereby obviating the need for a stored-food larder. More directly to the point, climatic conditions were not conducive to extended storage of food products. The paleoclimatic regime was mild, humid, lacked seasonal temperature extremes, and had rainy and nonrainy periods. The high-diversity environment was fostered by this stable climate.

The potential pre-Clovis sites provide a glimpse of the possible foundations of the Clovis economy that would suggest a great time depth to the forager strategy. The site data suggest a similar pattern, with some differences. The significance of the differences is difficult to judge because of the small number of sites involved. The most prominent difference is the lack of direct evidence for a lithic tool kit, although indirect evidence occurs in the form of cut lines on bones. The meat-related subsistence base is neither as broad a spectrum as for Clovis nor a narrow (focused) one. Four large game mammals (bison, horse, camel, mammoth) appear to form the base. Targeted hunting (cropping of mammoth herds) appears lacking. Scavenging activities during the Clovis period appear centered on meat acquisition, whereas data from the potential pre-Clovis indicate scavenging could also occur for technological purposes (mammoth bone quarrying) only. These potential pre-Clovis sites may all prove to date to the Clovis period, in which case the data would greatly strengthen the forager strategy construct for Clovis peoples on the southern Plains.

The major gaps in the Clovis record in terms of the construct are the lack of residential sites, lack of data on the seasonal timing and frequency of economic activities, and lack of data on plant-gathering activities and on the role of plants in the subsistence base. If indeed Clovis peoples practiced a forager strategy, then, based on the construct, assumptions could be made concerning these aspects. Those assumptions, however, do not validate the construct.

CONCLUDING REMARKS

The construct is a first-approximation attempt at depicting a late Pleistocene lifestyle for the southern Plains. Generalist hunter-gatherers had a broad-spectrum, meat-related subsistence based primarily on encounter-basis hunting. The tool kit was expedient in nature, including both lithic and bone tools, but focused on a multipurpose spear point. Tool resource sites for bone were tied to game animal carcasses and the butchering operation, and therefore could occur across the landscape wherever and whenever a large mammal was killed. Tool resource sites for good-quality lithic material were limited to rare outcrops in specific places along the escarpments. Camps were moved infrequently over an annual round, creating a provincial and limited nomadism governed by a rainy and nonrainy cycle rather than by seasonal changes in temperature and attendant conditions. This economic pattern was fostered by a nonseasonal, maritime climate and an extensive grasslands ecosystem that had an abundant surface water supply.

The key anomaly is the lack of residential sites. If home bases were reoccupied, only two-to-four satellite camps occupied per year, and the locations of satellite camps were different from year to year, then the main residential sites should be large, intensively used, and relatively numerous over the cultural time span. Although Hester (Wendorf and Hester 1975: Hester and Grady 1977) reported a number of Clovis campsites for the southern High Plains, none has been excavated; therefore their real nature and the activities represented are not known. Lewisville may represent a residential site if a contemporaneous relationship can be demonstrated for the various data classes recovered.

Home range and home territory probably are not synonymous in terms of range utilization and conservation of the resources. Modern hunter-gatherers have a much larger home territory than the home range utilized in any one yearly cycle. Although the Clovis home range may have been small (i.e., the area needed to search for food on a yearly basis), the home territory may have been approximately the same size or, more likely, was much larger. Despite the high-diversity environment, unless the same patch of ground was used year after year (which would not have been conducive to a practice of conservation of the resources), activities had to occur in different places within the home territory and home base presumedly would be moved occasionally (over the years). Clovis occupation sites are buried in the draws and stream valleys of the southern Plains, but to date these sites represent procurement locations along the valley axes. Residential locations may, therefore, be in a different topographic setting (e.g., on the uplands or in the draws and valleys on terraces above the axes).

Nutritional stress is an aspect not addressed by the construct because of the constant and stable food supply (both plant and animal). However, the availability of food resources does not imply the quality or nutritional value. Ethnographic hunter-gatherer groups generally avoid carnivores as a food resource (Hayden 1981:399) unless under nutritional stress (e.g., need for fat in the diet). An intake low in carbohydrates and high in lean meat constitutes a low-energy diet (a high-risk situation to the individual, immediately and in the long term, and to the group in the long term). The carnivores (bear, wolf) utilized by the Clovis peoples may represent scavenged carcasses (low-risk procurement). However, hunter-gatherer ethnographic data (Harako 1981; Hayden 1981) indicate that scavenged carcasses were of game animals normally hunted. If the utilization of carnivores signals nutritional stress, then carnivores would have to have been actively hunted at the time of need, since finding a scavenged carcass is a fortuitous event. The high risk of nutritional stress may have outweighed the high risk of hunting the carnivores.

The deteriorating climate at the end of the Pleistocene contributed to megafaunal extinctions, the beginning of the Holocene warming trend, and greater seasonality. These climatic changes set the stage both for the cultural change and for the continuity that occurred with the early Holocene hunter-gatherers. The most marked changes in the archaeological record are those of the meat-related subsistence base (focused on bison) and of the projectile-point type (Folsom point). Targeted resource (bison) appears the primary hunting mode, with a narrow-based meat-related subsistence. The late Pleistocene hunter-gatherer foragers appear to become early Holocene hunter-gatherer collectors. Cultural response as a combination of change and continuity indicates an evolution of the regional cultural group (i.e., Clovis into Folsom), rather than replacement (i.e., Clovis by Folsom) by an outside group.

ACKNOWLEDGMENTS

The friendly interaction of several colleagues and their constructive criticisms and skepticism are greatly appreciated. In particular, thanks are due to Herbert Haas (Southern Methodist University), Gary Haynes (University of Nevada, Reno), Paul Heinrich (Louisiana State University), Ernest L. Lundelius Jr. (University of Texas, Austin), David J. Meltzer (Southern Methodist University), Pat Shipman (John Hopkins School of Medicine), and Gentry Steele (Texas A & M University), for sharing information, ideas, and unpublished data. Access to the collections at Texas Memorial Museum (Austin) was through the courtesy of Drs. William G. Reeder (Director, TTM) and Ernest L. Lundelius, Jr. (Director, Vertebrate Paleontology Laboratory, TTM); and at the Museum of the Great Plains through the courtesy of Stephen Wilson (Director) and Dan Provo (Curator). I greatly appreciate their time and efforts on my behalf and the support of their staffs. However, interpretations and any errors are mine. Technical assistance was provided by the staff of the Museum of Texas Tech University. Nick Olson, Museum Photographer, did the drafting and photographic work. Linda Lamb typed the drafts and final copy. Their services are greatly appreciated. This manuscript is part of the ongoing regional research of the Lubbock Lake Project into cultural adaptations to ecological change on the Southern Plains. Bone technology research was funded specifically by National Science Foundation grant BNS78-11155. The data base for this research was generated through other Lubbock Lake supporting grants and agencies: National Science Foundation (SOC75-14857; BNS76-12006; BNS76-12006-A01), National Geographic Society, Texas Historical Commission (National Register Program), Moody Foundation (Galveston), Center for Field Research (EARTHWATCH), City and County of Lubbock, West Texas Museum Association, Institute of Museum Research, the Museum of Texas Tech University, and the Lubbock Lake Community Volunteers.

REFERENCES CITED

Alexander, H. L., Jr.
1963 The Levi Site: A Paleo-Indian Campsite in Central Texas. *American Antiquity* 28:510–528.
1978 The Legalistic Approach to Early Man Studies. In *Early Man in America from a Circum-Pacific Perspective,* edited by A. L. Bryan, pp. 20–22. Occasional Papers No. 1. Department of Anthropology, University of Alberta, Edmonton.

Anderson, A. D.
1975 The Cooperton Mammoth: An Early Man Bone Quarry. *Great Plains Journal* 14:130–164.

Ascher, R., and M. Ascher
1965 Recognizing the Emergence of Man. *Science* 147:243–250.

Baker, V. R.
1983 Late-Pleistocene Fluvial Systems. In *The Late Pleistocene,* edited by S. C. Porter, pp. 115–129. Late Quaternary Environments of the United States, vol. 1, H. E. Wright, Jr., general editor. University of Minnesota Press, Minneapolis.

Barry, R. G.
1983 Late-Pleistocene Climatology. In *The Late Pleistocene,* edited by S. C. Porter, pp. 390–407. Late Quaternary Environments of the United States, vol. 1, H. E. Wright, Jr., general editor. University of Minnesota Press, Minneapolis.

Bement, L. C.
1986 *Excavation of the Late Pleistocene Deposits of Bonfire Shelter Val Verde County, Texas.* Archeology Series Paper No. 1. Texas Archeological Survey, University of Texas at Austin.

Bettinger, R. L.
1980 Explanatory/Predictive Models of Hunter-Gatherer Adaptation. In *Advances in Archaeological Method and Theory,* vol. 3, edited by M. B. Schiffer, pp.189–255. Academic Press, New York.

Binford, L. R.
1968 Post-Pleistocene Adaptations. In *New Perspectives in Archaeology,* edited by S. R. Binford and L. R. Binford, pp. 313–341. Aldine, Chicago.
1977 *For Theory Building in Archaeology.* Academic Press, New York.
1980 Willow Smoke and Dogs' Tails: Hunter-Gatherer Settlement Systems and Archaeological Site Formation. *American Antiquity* 45:4–20.

Bloom, A. L.
1983 Sea Level and Coastal Morphology of the United States through the Late Wisconsin Glacial Maximum. In *The Late Pleistocene,* edited by S. C. Porter, pp. 215–229. Late Quaternary Environments of the United States, vol. 1, H. E. Wright, Jr., general editor. University of Minnesota Press, Minneapolis.

Bonfield, W.
1975 Deformation and Fracture Characteristics of the Cooperton Mammoth Bones. *Great Plains Journal* 14:158–164.

Briggs, A.
1987 Mammoths and Mastodons at the Congress Avenue Site, Austin. Paper presented at the "Mammoths, Mastodons, and Human Interaction" symposium, Waco, Texas.

Bryan, A. L. (editor)
1978 *Early Man in America from a Circum-Pacific Perspective.* Occasional Papers No. 1. Department of Anthropology, University of Alberta, Edmonton.
1986 *New Evidence for the Pleistocene Peopling of the Americas.* Center for the Study of Early Man, University of Maine, Orono.

Bryan, K., and C. N. Ray
1938 Long Channelled Point Found in Alluvium Beside Bones of Elephas Columbi. *Bulletin of the Texas Archeological and Paleontological Society* 10:263–268.

Bryant, V. M., Jr.
1977 A 16,000 Year Pollen Record of Vegetational Change in Central Texas. *Palynology* 1:143–156.

Bryant, V. M., Jr., and R. G. Holloway
1985 A Late-Quaternary Paleoenvironmental Record of Texas: An Overview of the Pollen Evidence. In *Pollen Records of Late-Quaternary North American Sediments,* edited by V. M. Bryant, Jr. and R. G. Holloway, pp. 39–70. American Association of Stratigraphic Palynologists Foundation, Dallas.

Carlson, D. L., D. G. Steele, and A. G. Comuzzie
1984 Mammoth Excavations at the Duewall-Newberry Site on the Brazos River in Texas, 1983. *Current Research in the Pleistocene* 1:63–64.

Childe, V. G.
1951 *Social Evolution.* Henry Schuman, New York.

Clarke, D. L.
1968 *Analytical Archaeology.* Methuen, London.

Dibble, D. S., and D. Lorrain
1968 *Bonfire Shelter: A Stratified Bison Kill Site, Val Verde County, Texas.* Miscellaneous Papers No. 1. Texas Memorial Museum, Austin.

Dincauze, D. F.
1984 An Archaeo-Logical Evaluation of the Case for

Pre-Clovis Occupations. In *Advances in World Archaeology*, vol. 3, edited by F. Wendorf and A. Clause, pp. 275–323. Academic Press, New York.

Durham, W. H.
1976 The Adaptive Significance of Cultural Behavior. *Human Ecology* 4:89–121.
1981 Overview: Optimal Foraging Analysis in Human Ecology. In *Hunter-Gatherer Foraging Strategies*, edited by B. Winterhalder and E. A. Smith, pp. 218–231. University of Chicago Press, Chicago.

Evans, G. L.
1961 The Friesenhahn Cave. *Bulletin of the Texas Memorial Museum* 2:1–22.

Fenneman, N. M.
1931 *Physiography of Western United States*. McGraw-Hill, New York.

Fox, J. W., and C. B. Smith
1987 Herd Bunching of *Mammuthus columbi* at the Waco Mammoth Site. Paper presented at the "Mammoths, Mastodons, and Human Interaction" symposium, Waco, Texas.

Friedman, I.
1983 Paleoclimatic Evidence from Stable Isotopes. In *The Late Pleistocene*, edited by S. C. Porter, pp. 385–389. Late Quaternary Environments of the United States, vol. 1, H. E. Wright, Jr., general editor. University of Minnesota Press, Minneapolis.

Frison, G. C., and L. C. Todd
1986 *The Colby Mammoth Site. Taphonomy and Archaeology of a Clovis Kill in Northern Wyoming*. University of New Mexico Press, Albuquerque.

Graham, R. W.
1976 *Pleistocene and Holocene Mammals, Taphonomy, and Paleoecology of the Friesenhahn Cave Local Fauna, Bexar County, Texas*. Unpublished Ph.D. dissertation, University of Texas, Austin.

Haas, H., and J. Banewicz
1980 Radiocarbon Dating of Bone Apatite Using Thermal Release of CO_2. *Radiocarbon* 22:537–544.

Hafsten, U.
1961 Pleistocene Development of Vegetation and Climate in the Southern High Plains as Evidenced by Pollen Analysis. In *Paleoecology of the Llano Estacado*, edited by F. Wendorf, pp. 59–91. Museum of New Mexico Press, Santa Fe.

Haragan, D. R.
1983 *Blue Northers to Sea Breezes: Texas Weather and Climate*. Hendrick-Long Publishing Co., Dallas.

Harako, R.
1981 The Cultural Ecology of Hunting Behavior among Mbuti Pygmies in the Ituri Forest, Zaire. In *Omnivorous Primates: Gathering and Hunting in Human Evolution*, edited by R. S. O. Harding and G. Teleki, pp. 499–555. Columbia University Press, New York.

Hassan, A. A., J. D. Termine, and C. V. Haynes, Jr.
1977 Mineralogical Studies on Bone Apatite and Their Implications for Radiocarbon Dating. *Radiocarbon* 19:364–374.

Hayden, B.
1981 Subsistence and Ecological Adaptations of Modern Hunter/Gatherers. In *Omnivorous Primates: Gathering and Hunting in Human Evolution*, edited by R. S. O. Harding and G. Teleki, pp. 344–421. Columbia University Press, New York.

Haynes, C. V., Jr.
1968 Radiocarbon Analysis of Inorganic Carbon Fossil Bone and Enamel. *Science* 161:687–688.
1975 Pleistocene and Recent Stratigraphy. In *Late Pleistocene Environments of the Southern High Plains*, edited by F. Wendorf and J. J. Hester, pp. 57–96. Fort Burgwin Research Center, Southern Methodist University, Dallas.
1980 The Clovis Culture. *Canadian Journal of Anthropology* 1:115–121.

Haynes, C. V., Jr., P. E. Damon, and D. C. Grey
1966 Arizona Radiocarbon Dates VI. *Radiocarbon* 8:1–21.

Hester, J. J.
1972 *Blackwater Locality No. 1. A Stratified, Early Man Site in Eastern New Mexico*. Fort Burgwin Research Center, Southern Methodist University, Dallas.

Hester, J. J., and J. Grady
1977 Paleoindian Social Patterns on the Llano Estacado. *The Museum Journal* 17:78–96.

Holden, W. C.
1962 Indians, Spaniards, and Anglos. In *A History of Lubbock*, edited by L. L. Graves, pp. 17–44. West Texas Museum Association, Lubbock.

Holliday, V. T.
1985 Archaeological Geology of the Lubbock Lake Site, Southern High Plains of Texas. *Geological Society of America Bulletin* 96:1483–1492.
1987 A Reexamination of Late-Pleistocene Boreal Forest Reconstructions for the Southern High Plains. *Quaternary Research* 28:238–244.

Holliday, V. T., and E. Johnson
1984 The Lubbock Lake 1983 Field Season. *Current Research in the Pleistocene* 1:11–13.

Holliday, V. T., and C. Welty
1981 Lithic Tool Resources of the Eastern Llano Estacado. *Bulletin of the Texas Archeological Society* 52:201–214.

Hughes, E.
1984 *Blackwater Draw Locality No. 1: A Case Study of Conservation, Collection Management, and Site Data Reconstruction Techniques.* Unpublished master's thesis, Texas Tech University, Lubbock.

Hunt, C. B.
1974 *Natural Regions of the United States and Canada.* W. H. Freeman and Company, San Francisco.

Imbrie, J., A. McIntyre, and T. C. Moore, Jr.
1983 The Ocean around North America at the Last Glacial Maximum. In *The Late Pleistocene,* edited by S. C. Porter, pp. 230–236. Late Quaternary Environments of the United States, vol. 1, H. E. Wright, Jr., general editor. University of Minnesota Press, Minneapolis.

Irwin, H. T.
1971 Developments in Early Man Studies in Western North America, 1960–1970. *Arctic Anthropology* 8:42–67.

Isaac, G.
1978 Food-Sharing and Human Evolution: Archeological Evidence from the Plio-Pleistocene. *Journal of Anthropological Research* 34:311–325.

Jennings, J. D.
1968 *Prehistory of North America.* McGraw-Hill Book Company, New York.

Johnson, E.
1985 Current Developments in Bone Technology. In *Advances in Archaeological Method and Theory,* vol. 8, edited by M. B. Schiffer, pp.157–235. Academic Press, New York.

1986 Late Pleistocene and Early Holocene Vertebrates and Paleoenvironments on the Southern High Plains, U.S.A. *Géographie Physique et Quaternaire* 40:249–261.

1987 *Lubbock Lake: Late Quaternary Studies on the Southern High Plains.* Texas A&M University Press, College Station.

1989 Human Modified Bones from Early Southern Plains Sites. In *Bone Modification,* edited by R. Bonnichsen and M. Sorg, pp. 431–472. Center for the Study of the First Americans, University of Maine, Orono.

Johnson, E., and V. T. Holliday
1981 Late Paleoindian Activity at the Lubbock Lake Site. *Plains Anthropologist* 26:173–193.

1985 A Clovis Age Megafaunal Processing Station at the Lubbock Lake Landmark. *Current Research in the Pleistocene* 2:17–19.

Johnson, E., and P. Shipman
1986 Scanning Electron Microscope Studies of Bone Modification. *Current Research in the Pleistocene* 3:47–48.

Keene, A. S.
1981 Optimal Foraging in a Nonmarginal Environment: A Model of Prehistoric Subsistence Strategies in Michigan. In *Hunter-Gatherer Foraging Strategies,* edited by B. Winterhalder and E. A. Smith, pp. 171–193. University of Chicago Press, Chicago.

Kirch, P. V.
1980 The Archaeological Study of Adaptation: Theoretical and Methodological Issues. In *Advances in Archaeological Method and Theory,* vol. 3, edited by M. B. Schiffer, pp. 101–156. Academic Press, New York.

Lahren, L., and R. Bonnichsen
1974 Bone Foreshafts from a Clovis Burial in Southwestern Montana. *Science* 186:147–150.

Leonhardy, F. C. (editor)
1966 *Domebo: A Paleo-Indian Mammoth Kill in the Prairie-Plains.* Contributions of the Museum of the Great Plains No. 1. Lawton.

Lorenzo, J. L., and L. Mirambell
1986a Tlapacoya: 35,000 Anos de Historia del Lago de Chalco. Instituto Nacional de Antropologia e Historia, *Coleccion Cientifica* 155:1–297.

1986b Mamutes Excavados en la Cuenca de Mexico (1952–1980). Instituto Nacional de Antropologia e Historia, *Cuaderno de Trabajo* 32:1–151.

Lundelius, E. L., Jr.
1972 Vertebrate Remains from the Gray Sand. In *Blackwater Locality No. 1. A Stratified Early Man Site in Eastern New Mexico,* edited by J. J. Hester, pp. 148–163. Fort Burgwin Research Center, Southern Methodist University, Dallas.

1984 A Late Pleistocene Mammalian Fauna from Cueva Quebrada, Val Verde County, Texas. In *Contributions in Quaternary Vertebrate Paleontology,* edited by H. H. Genoways and M. R. Dawson, pp. 456–481. Special Publication No. 8. Carnegie Museum of Natural History, Pittsburgh.

Lundelius, E. L., Jr., R. W. Graham, E. Anderson, J. Guilday, J. A. Holman, D. W. Steadman, and S. D. Webb
1983 Terrestrial Vertebrate Faunas. In *The Late Pleistocene*, edited by S. C. Porter, pp. 311–353. Late Quaternary Environments of the United States, vol. 1, H. E. Wright, Jr., general editor. University of Minnesota Press, Minneapolis.

Mayr, E.
1966 *Animal Species and Evolution*. Belknap Press of Harvard University Press, Cambridge.

Mehl, M. G.
1966 The Domebo Mammoth: Vertebrate Paleomorphology. In *Domebo: A Paleo-Indian Mammoth Kill in the Prairie-Plains*, edited by F. C. Leonhardy, pp. 27–30. Contributions of the Museum of the Great Plains No. 1. Lawton.
1975 Vertebrate Paleomorphology of the Cooperton Site. *Great Plains Journal* 14:165–168.

Meltzer, D. J.
1986a A Study of Texas Clovis Points. *Current Research in the Pleistocene* 3:33–36.
1986b The Clovis Paleo-indian Occupation of Texas: Results from the TAS Survey. *Bulletin of the Texas Archeological Society* 57:27–68.

Mirambell, L.
1973 Excavaciones en Sitios Pleistocénico y Postpleistocénicos en Tlapacoya, Estado de México. *Boletín de Instituto de Antropologia y Historia* 4.

Nichols, J. D.
1975 Soil at the Cooperton Site. *Great Plains Journal* 14:139–143.

O'Connell, J. F., and K. Hawkes
1981 Alyawara Plant Use and Optimal Foraging Theory. In *Hunter-Gatherer Foraging Strategies*, edited by B. Winterhalder and E. A. Smith, pp. 99–115. University of Chicago Press, Chicago.

Oldfield, F., and J. Schoenwetter
1975 Discussion of the Pollen-Analytical Evidence. In *Late Pleistocene Environments of the Southern High Plains*, edited by F. Wendorf and J. J. Hester, pp. 149–179. Fort Burgwin Research Center, Southern Methodist University, Dallas.

Porter, S. C. (editor)
1983 *The Late Pleistocene*. Late Quaternary Environments of the United States, vol. 1, H. E. Wright, Jr., general editor. University of Minnesota Press, Minneapolis.

Ray, C. N.
1930 Report on Some Recent Archaeological Researches in the Abilene Section. *Bulletin of the Texas Archaeological and Paleontological Society* 2:45–58.
1942 Ancient Artifacts and Mammoth Teeth of the McLean Site. *Bulletin of the Texas Archeological and Paleontological Society* 14:137–138.

Reeves, C. C., Jr.
1965 Pleistocene Climate of the Llano Estacado. *Journal of Geology* 73:181–188.
1966 Pleistocene Climate of the Llano Estacado II. *Journal of Geology* 74:642–647.
1973 The Full-Glacial Climate of the Southern High Plains, West Texas. *Journal of Geology* 81:693–704.

Rogers, E. S., and M. B. Black
1976 Subsistence Strategy in the Fish and Hare Period, Northern Ontario: The Weagamow Ojibwa, 1880–1920. *Journal of Anthropological Research* 32:1–43.

Saunders, J. J.
1980 A Model for Man-Mammoth Relationships in Late Pleistocene North America. *Canadian Journal of Anthropology* 1:87–98.

Sellards, E. H.
1938 Artifacts Associated with Fossil Elephant. *Bulletin of the Geological Society of America* 49:999–1010.

Shelley, P. H.
1984 Paleoindian Movement on the Southern High Plains: A Re-evaluation of Inferences Based on Lithic Evidence from Blackwater Draw. *Current Research in the Pleistocene* 1:35–36.

Silberbauer, G.
1981 Hunter/Gatherers of the Central Kalahari. In *Omnivorous Primates: Gathering and Hunting in Human Evolution*, edited by R. S. O. Harding and G. Teleki, pp. 455–498. Columbia University Press, New York.

Smith, G. I., and F. A. Street-Perrott
1983 Pluvial Lakes of the Western United States. In *The Late Pleistocene*, edited by S. C. Porter, pp. 190–212. Late Quaternary Environments of the United States, vol. 1, H. E. Wright, Jr., general editor. University of Minnesota Press, Minneapolis.

Stanford, D.
1983 Pre-Clovis Occupation South of the Ice Sheets. In *Early Man in the New World*, edited by R. Shutler, Jr., pp. 65–72. Sage Publications, Beverly Hills.

Steele, D. G., and D. L. Carlson
1989 Excavation and Taphonomy of Mammoth

Remains from the Duewall-Newberry Site, Brazos County, Texas. In *Bone Modification*, edited by R. Bonnichsen and M. Sorg, pp. 413–430. Center for the Study of the First Americans, University of Maine, Orono.

Steward, J. H.
1938 Basin-Plateau Aboriginal Socio-political Groups. *Bureau of American Ethnology Bulletin* 120.
1955 *Theory of Culture Change*. University of Illinois Press, Urbana.

Warnica, J. M.
1966 New Discoveries at the Clovis Sites. *American Antiquity* 31:345–357.

Wendorf, F.
1970 The Lubbock Subpluvial. In *Pleistocene and Recent Environments of the Central Great Plains*, edited by W. Dort, Jr. and J. K. Jones, Jr., pp. 23–36. University of Kansas Press, Lawrence.

Wendorf, F., and J. J. Hester (editors)
1975 *Late Pleistocene Environments of the Southern High Plains*. Fort Burgwin Research Center, South Methodist University, Dallas.

West, F. H.
1983 The Antiquity of Man in America. In *The Late Pleistocene*, edited by S. C. Porter, pp. 364–382. Late Quaternary Environments of the United States, vol. 1, H. E. Wright, Jr., general editor. University of Minnesota Press, Minneapolis.

Wheat, J. B.
1971 Lifeways of Early Man in North America. *Arctic Anthropology* 8:22–31.

White, L. A.
1959 *The Evolution of Culture*. McGraw-Hill, New York.

Winterhalder, B.
1981a Foraging Strategies in the Boreal Forest: An Analysis of Cree Hunting and Gathering. In *Hunter-Gatherer Foraging Strategies*, edited by B. Winterhalder and E. A. Smith, pp. 66–98. University of Chicago Press, Chicago.
1981b Optimal Foraging Strategies and Hunter-Gatherer Research in Anthropology: Theory and Models. In *Hunter-Gatherer Foraging Strategies*, edited by B. Winterhalder and E. A. Smith, pp. 13–35. University of Chicago Press, Chicago.

Winterhalder, B., and E. A. Smith (editors)
1981 *Hunter-Gatherer Foraging Strategies*. University of Chicago Press, Chicago.

Wyckoff, D.
1988 Back to Burnham: There Were Pre-Clovis People in Oklahoma! *Oklahoma Archeological Survey Newsletter* 8(2):1–3.

Paleoindian Occupation in the Central American Tropics

ANTHONY J. RANERE
Department of Anthropology
Temple University
Philadelphia, PA 19122

RICHARD G. COOKE
Smithsonian Tropical Research Institute
Apartado 2072
Balboa, República de Panamá

In this paper we review the evidence for Paleoindian occupation in Central America, paying particular attention to the paleogeographical and paleoecological settings of the remains. Fluted points have been recovered in sites and as isolated surface finds over a wide geographic area and in a variety of ecological settings in Central America. North American Clovis-like lanceolate and waisted points have been found as far south as Costa Rica and Panama. The technologically and typologically distinct fluted fishtail points, similar to ones described from South America, occur as far north as Belize and Chiapas, Mexico.

Pollen and phytolith sequences from four Central American localities indicate that the late Pleistocene was considerably cooler and somewhat drier than at present. Montane forest formations extended downslope 600 to 900 m lower than their present ranges. Forests along the Pacific Coast of the region were more open and interspersed with patches of savanna, while in the Petén, Guatemala, savannas were replaced by montane forests between 11,000 and 10,000 years ago. Large herbivores, including mammoth, the mastodont-like gomphotheres, giant ground sloths, and horse, were conspicuous components of the late Pleistocene Central American fauna. A consideration of the resources present in these primarily forested biomes, coupled with data on the size, distribution, and content of Paleoindian sites, suggests to us that Paleoindian populations in Central America were organized as small, highly mobile, and widely dispersed bands of hunters. Finally, similarities in settlement distributions and lithic technology between Paleoindian and Early Archaic periods suggest population continuity rather than replacement.

INTRODUCTION

In this paper we use the term Paleoindian in its now-classic sense to refer to the time period from the late Pleistocene to the early Holocene, approximately 11,500 to 9000 years ago, when populations usually characterized as specialized big-game hunters and identified by the presence of fluted points ranged throughout the Americas. We have, therefore, restricted our consideration of archaeological finds in Central America (here we include the territory between the Isthmus of Tehuántepec and the Atrato Trough at the Panama-Colombia border) to those which incorporate fluted points or those which fall chronologically within this 11,500- to 9000-year period on the basis of secure radiometric and/or stratigraphic dating.

IDENTIFYING A PALEOINDIAN PRESENCE IN CENTRAL AMERICA

The first fluted point ever described in print may well be a Guatemalan specimen described by Francisco Ximénez in 1722 (but only brought to the attention of the archaeological community 256 years later by Bray [1978]). Reports of other fluted-point finds from Central America have appeared in the literature since 1952 (Swauger and Mayer-Oakes 1952). To date, fluted points have been identified from southern Mexico (García-Bárcena 1979, 1982), Guatemala (Bray 1978; Brown 1980; Coe 1960; Gruhn and Bryan 1977), Belize (Hester et al. 1980; Hester et al. 1981; MacNeish et al. 1980), Costa Rica (Acuña 1983; Sheets, personal communication; Snarskis 1979; Swauger and Mayer-Oakes 1952), Panama (Bird and Cooke 1977, 1978; Cooke 1984; Sander 1959, 1964), extreme northwest Colombia (Correal 1983), and possibly Honduras (Bullen and Plowden 1963). Several of the reported points have been isolated surface finds, while others are from sites that have not been (and perhaps cannot be) excavated. Only two sites with dated Paleoindian components have been excavated, and both are in the northern portion of the Central American tropics (Los Tapiales, Guatemala [Gruhn and Bryan 1977] and Los Grifos, Chiapas, Mexico [García-Bárcena 1979; Santamaría 1981]).

Given the uneven nature of the data on the Paleoindian presence in Central America, the only two ways to approach the subject that permit incorporation of all Paleoindian finds are: (1) to focus on the technology and typology of the points themselves; and (2) to look at the environmental context of the localities involved.

CENTRAL AMERICAN FLUTED POINTS: TYPOLOGY AND TECHNOLOGY

Because many of the fluted points recovered from Central America are surface finds without good associations (in some cases the exact find spots are not even known) and because a number of the fluted-point sites with associations are incompletely published, the only way of comparing all the localities in terms of material remains is to focus on the points themselves. A number of attempts to characterize Central American fluted points have already been published (e.g., Bird and Cooke 1977, 1978; Bray 1978; García-Bárcena 1982; MacNeish 1983; Mayer-Oakes 1986; Snarskis 1979). These authors all distinguish lanceolate (Clovis-like) points from stemmed (fishtail) points and most identify a "waisted" (Clovis-like) variant as well. Some (e.g., Bray 1978; Mayer-Oakes 1986) would make even further distinctions, but for our purposes a three-variant scheme (Clovis lanceolate, Clovis waisted, and fishtail) will be sufficient. Fluted-point localities in the Central American tropics and the variant(s) found at each (cf. Bray 1978; García-Bárcena 1982; MacNeish 1983) are recorded on Figure 1.

We would like to emphasize here a distinction between Paleoindian point types which Junius Bird (1969) made long ago—that is, the South American fishtail forms are different from the North American lanceolate forms not only in shape, but also, and perhaps more importantly, in the lithic reduction sequence which produces them. The similarities in manufacturing technology between the Chilean, Ecuadorian, and other isolated South American points, which Bird described in his 1969 article, and the Panamanian fishtail points are quite clear (Bird and Cooke 1977, 1978). Although we have not seen the fishtail specimens from further north in Central America, published descriptions and illustrations do suggest that similar manufacturing techniques were used in their production and not the techniques associated with Clovis points (e.g., García-Bárcena 1982; MacNeish 1983).

The Central American Clovis points (both lanceolate and waisted varieties) appear to be made following the same lithic reduction sequence documented for North American fluted points (e.g., Crabtree 1966; Judge 1973; Rovner 1980; Wilmsen 1974; cf. Flenniken 1978). The sequence begins with a large flake blank, which is bifacially thinned to produce a preform biconvex in cross-section. A number of these bifacial preforms with and without basal flutes were recovered at Turrialba, Costa Rica (Figures 2 and 3) (see also, Snarskis 1979:Figures 4 and 5). In contrast, the fishtail points of Central and South America tend to be made on flake blanks that are not much thicker than the finished points (Bird 1969). Often, sections of the ventral surface of the original flake blank can be seen on the finished product (Figure 4) (see also illustrations in Bird 1969; Mayer-Oakes 1986). Thinning flakes removed from the fishtail preforms tend to broaden at their distal end and overlap each other in the center of the point (Figure 5) to such an extent that in some specimens thickness at the center is less than at areas midway between the center and edges (Bird and Cooke 1978).

Clovis and fishtail points share certain manufacturing characteristics as well, fluting being the most obvious one. Final retouch in both Clovis variants and in fishtail points was accomplished through the removal of short pressure flakes. In addition, the lower portions of all these Paleoindian point types (sides and bases) have ground edges.

The almost complete overlap of the distribution of Paleoindian point forms in the region between Chiapas and eastern Panama should not obscure the fact that Central America represents the southernmost limit of the Clovis-like fluted points and the northern limit of the fishtail points (Figure 6). One could interpret this pattern by positing a stylistic change in point form as Paleoindian populations migrated through Central America (cf. Bray 1978; Ranere 1980; Schobinger 1973; Willey 1966). Snarskis (1979:137) has suggested that such a change to waisted and finally stemmed forms in Central America (and a similar change in eastern North America) may have occurred "as part of a different ecological adaptation required of Early Man in forested areas."

An alternative interpretation of the evidence sees the development of fishtail points as a southern South American innovation that subsequently spread northward (Rouse 1976). Mayer-Oakes (1986) has even suggested an independent origin for fluting in the Ecuadorian highlands, where several different point styles (including fishtail) from El Inga exhibit various sorts of fluting and basal thinning. A more likely scenario recognizes the North American origin of fluting, which spread through Central America and into South America either by migration or diffusion at the same time that the fishtail point style was moving northward (Bryan 1983; Gruhn and Bryan 1977). Choosing between alternatives is made difficult by the scarcity of dated fluted-point sites (not to mention the reliability of the dates) in Central and South America.

CHRONOLOGY

Central American fluted points occur in dated stratigraphic contexts at only two sites: Los Tapiales in highland Guatemala (Gruhn and Bryan 1977), and Los Grifos Rockshelter in Chiapas, Mexico (García-Bárcena 1979,

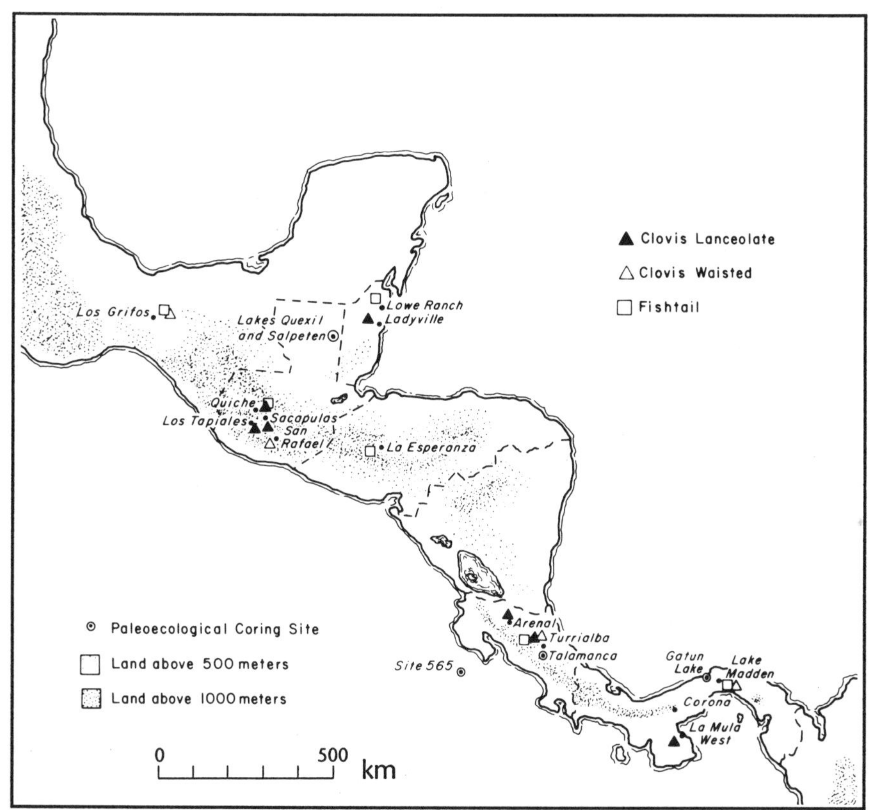

Figure 1. Paleoindian localities and paleoecological coring sites in Central America.

1982; Santamaría 1981). A single fluted-point base and a channel flake with an attached "ear" were among 100 artifacts (and nearly 1,500 flakes) recovered from an excavated area of nearly 250 m^2 at Los Tapiales. Bifaces, uniface points, burins, gravers, end scrapers (several with lateral spurs), blades, and retouched flakes made up the rest of the assemblage. Gruhn and Bryan (1977) described the fluted point as similar to western Clovis points (in spite of the hint of a shoulder on one edge) and noted that the assemblage from Los Tapiales shares several specific tool types with western North American fluted-point assemblages. The age of the occupation is bracketed by C-14 dates of 8810 ± 110 yr B.P. (Tx-1630) and 11,170 ± 200 yr B.P. (GaK-4889). The authors viewed the occupation as short term and felt that the 10,710 ± 170 yr B.P. (Tx-1631) date provided the best estimate of the age of that occupation. A second date of 9860 ± 185 yr B.P. (GaK-4890) was also accepted by the excavators as being associated with the densest occupational levels. Moreover, three dates on hearth charcoal ranging from 4730 to 7820 yr B.P. had to be rejected as inconsistent with dates of other fluted-point occupations. The case for an eleventh millennium B.P. occupation at Los Tapiales is strengthened by C-14 dates from the site of La Piedra del Coyote, 2 km distant from Los Tapiales. These dates are 10,650 ± 1350 yr B.P. (Tx-1632), 5320 ± 90 yr B.P. (Tx-1633), 10,020 ± 260 yr B.P. (Tx-1634), and 9430 ± 120 yr B.P. (Tx-1635). Artifacts recovered from a test excavation at the site yielded only retouched flakes and a scraper fragment (Gruhn and Bryan 1977:254). On the strength of the evidence from both Los Tapiales and La Piedra del Coyote, we are probably safe in assigning the Paleoindian occupation of this highland Guatemalan region to the eleventh millennium B.P.

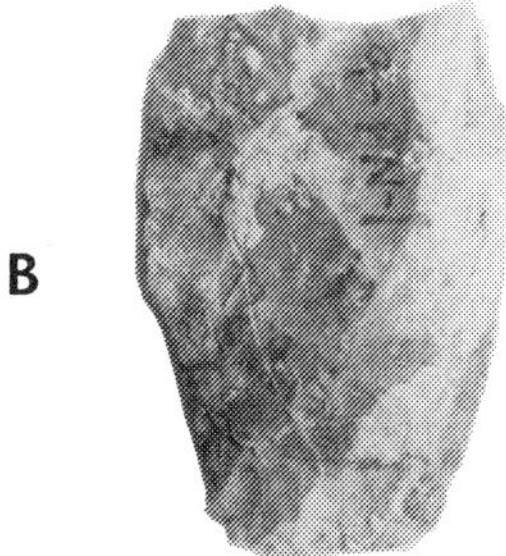

Figure 2. Two basal portions of fluted preforms from the Turrialba site, Costa Rica (length of specimen A is 10.3 cm).

The only other site in the Central American tropics where fluted points have been dated is Los Grifos Rockshelter in Ocozocoautla, Chiapas, Mexico (García-Bárcena 1979, 1982; Santamaría 1981; Santamaría and García-Bárcena 1984a, 1984b). A single waisted Clovis point and two fishtail points were found in association in a layer with bracketing radiocarbon dates of 8930 ± 150 yr B.P. (I-10760) and 9460 ± 150 yr B.P. (I-10761). A third radiocarbon date of 9540 ± 150 yr B.P. (I-10762) dates an older occupational layer, as does a single obsidian-hydration determination of 9300 years. The preceramic assemblages from Los Grifos are dominated by simple edge-retouched cutting and scraping tools (Santamaría and García-Bárcena 1984a, 1984b) and lack artifact types (e.g., bifaces, end scrapers with lateral spurs, blades from prepared cores) found in North American fluted-point assemblages. Los Grifos is the only locality in Central America where faunal remains occur in association with Paleoindian artifacts. These remains are reported to be of modern taxa only (including freshwater and terrestrial mollusks), which is congruent with the dates derived from the site (García-Bárcena 1982).

There is a second site in Ocozocoautla, the Santa Marta Rockshelter, which is only 300 m from Los Grifos and has cultural deposits contemporary with the Paleoindian layers in Los Grifos (García-Bárcena and Santamaría 1982; MacNeish and Peterson 1962). Radiocarbon dates of 9280 ± 290 yr B.P. (I-9259) and 9330 ± 290 yr B.P. (I-9260) date this earliest phase of occupation (García-Bárcena and Santamaría 1982). A third date from this phase, 6310 ± 130 yr B.P. (I-8620), was rejected by García-Bárcena because it was obtained on a sample that was too small to be treated for the removal of organic contaminants (García-Bárcena and Santamaría 1982). No fluted points were recovered from the Santa Marta Rockshelter. Recovered instead were small crude leaf-shaped points, which formed part of an assemblage of simple chipped-stone tools that included choppers, scraper-planes, scrapers, denticulates, perforators, knives, and burins (García-Bárcena 1982). A

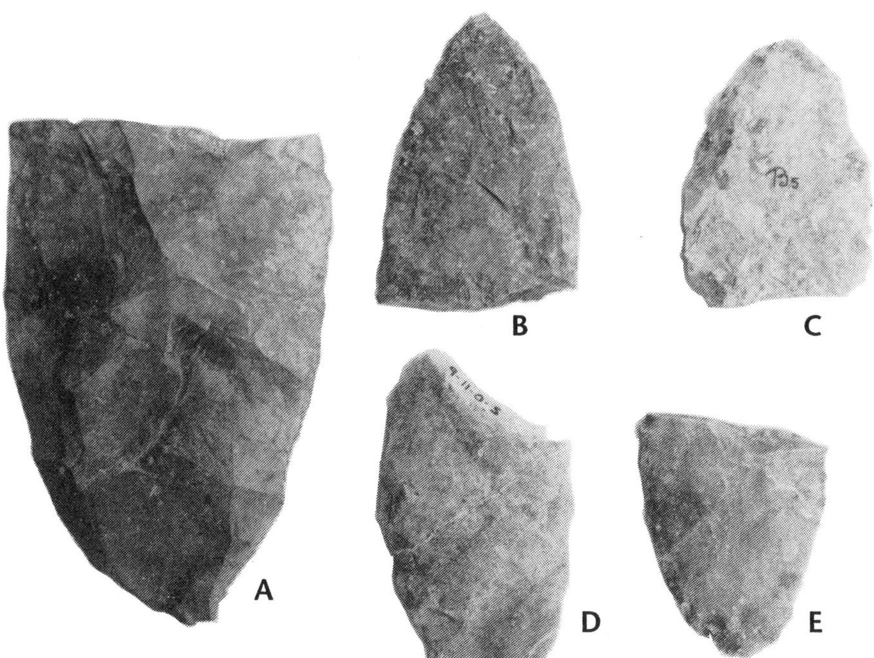

Figure 3. Broken preforms recovered from the Turrialba site, Costa Rica (length of specimen A is 11.6 cm).

number of bone tools, including lanceolate points, also occurred in the 9300 yr B.P. occupation.

Associated with these lithic and bone artifacts was a completely modern fauna, consisting primarily of rabbit *(Sylvilagus)*, armadillo *(Dasypus)*, deer *(Odocoileus)*, turtle *(Kinosternon)*, iguana, freshwater shellfish *(Pachychylus)*, and crab. The most common plant remains were *Celtis*, but the presence of grinding-stone bases and handstones suggests the use of other plant foods as well (García-Bárcena 1982). The presumably contemporary assemblage from neighboring Los Grifos Rockshelter does not contain ground-stone tools (Santamaría and García-Bárcena 1984a). We must agree with García-Bárcena (1982) that further research is needed to clarify the relationships between these two late-tenth millennium B.P. occupations. Nonetheless, the sites do seem to reflect the initial adjustments made by Central American populations to an essentially modern environment, i.e., one without large herbivores.

Additional information on the relative ages of Clovis and fishtail points in Central America can perhaps be gleaned from the Turrialba (Finca Guardiria) site in Costa Rica (Castillo et al. 1987; Snarskis 1977, 1979). All the Clovis-like points from the site were collected from the uppermost of three terraces along the Reventazón River. The single fishtail point was recovered on the lowest terrace, suggesting that it belonged to a different—and later—occupation. Cultural remains from the three terraces at Turrialba include not only Clovis and fishtail components but later Archaic and early Ceramic components as well (Snarskis 1979). Recently, however, systematic collections from the higher terrace that produced most of the Clovis points and preforms has permitted the identification of artifact types associated with the Clovis occupation to be made with some confidence (Castillo et al. 1987). In general terms, the distributional study confirms Snarskis's (1979, 1984) initial interpretation that a number of tools with counterparts in the Clovis tradition of North America are, in fact, found in Costa Rica as well. These tools include bifacial knives, keeled scraper-planes, end scrapers with lateral spurs, side scrapers, large blades, and burins. The Turrialba Clovis assemblage is, therefore, more similar to the one from Los Tapiales than to Los Grifos and presumably dates from the eleventh millennium B.P. or earlier.

What does the Central American evidence reveal about the relationships between Clovis and fishtail fluted points? First, the radiocarbon dates for Los Tapiales and Los Grifos are consistent with the proposition that lanceolate fluted points are earlier than waisted and fishtail forms. Second, the horizontal stratification at Turrialba hints at the possibility that both lanceolate and waisted Clovis variants appear earlier in Central America than fishtail forms. Third, the evidence from Los Grifos indicates that waisted and fishtail variants co-occurred for at least part of the sequence. Fourth, the dates for Los Grifos are surprisingly late for fluted points (but so are the radiocarbon dates for El Inga, 9030 ± 144 yr B.P. [R-1070/2] being the earliest determination [Mayer-Oakes 1986]). Finally, the dating of fluted points at Los Tapiales and Los Grifos provides support for the independent origin of the fishtail-point tradition in southern South America.

CENTRAL AMERICAN PALEOECOLOGY: 11,500–9000 YR B.P.

In a previous paper, Ranere (1980) argued that Paleoindians penetrated Central America initially by moving south through highland forests that were floristically similar to North American temperate forests. The reasoning behind the argument was that groups would expand to the limits of an environment with which they were familiar before moving into a different environment. The paleoecological evidence then available indicated that much of Central America was forested during the time period involved (ca. 11,500 to 9000 yr B.P.), leading to the conclusion that Paleoindian populations must, therefore, have moved through and become adapted to tropical forests in Central America before expanding into the South American continent. Given recent demonstrations of late Pleistocene aridity in several parts of the lowland American tropics (e.g., Leyden 1984, 1985; Salgado-Labouriau 1980; Schubert 1988) and the growing recognition that late Pleistocene/early

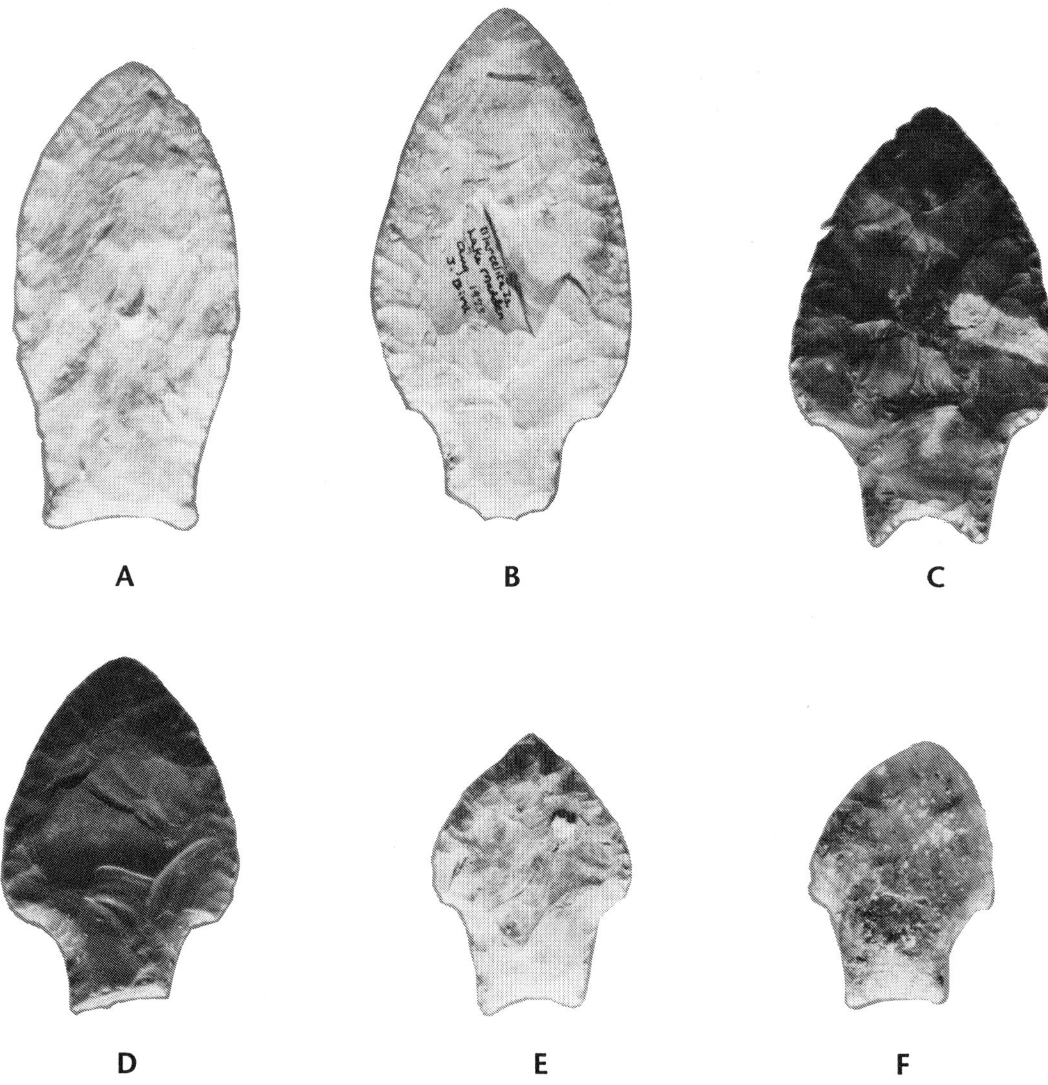

Figure 4. Fluted points from Madden Lake, Panama (length of specimen A is 7.6 cm). A portion of the ventral surface of the original flake blank is visible in specimen D. Both specimens E and F have been resharpened.

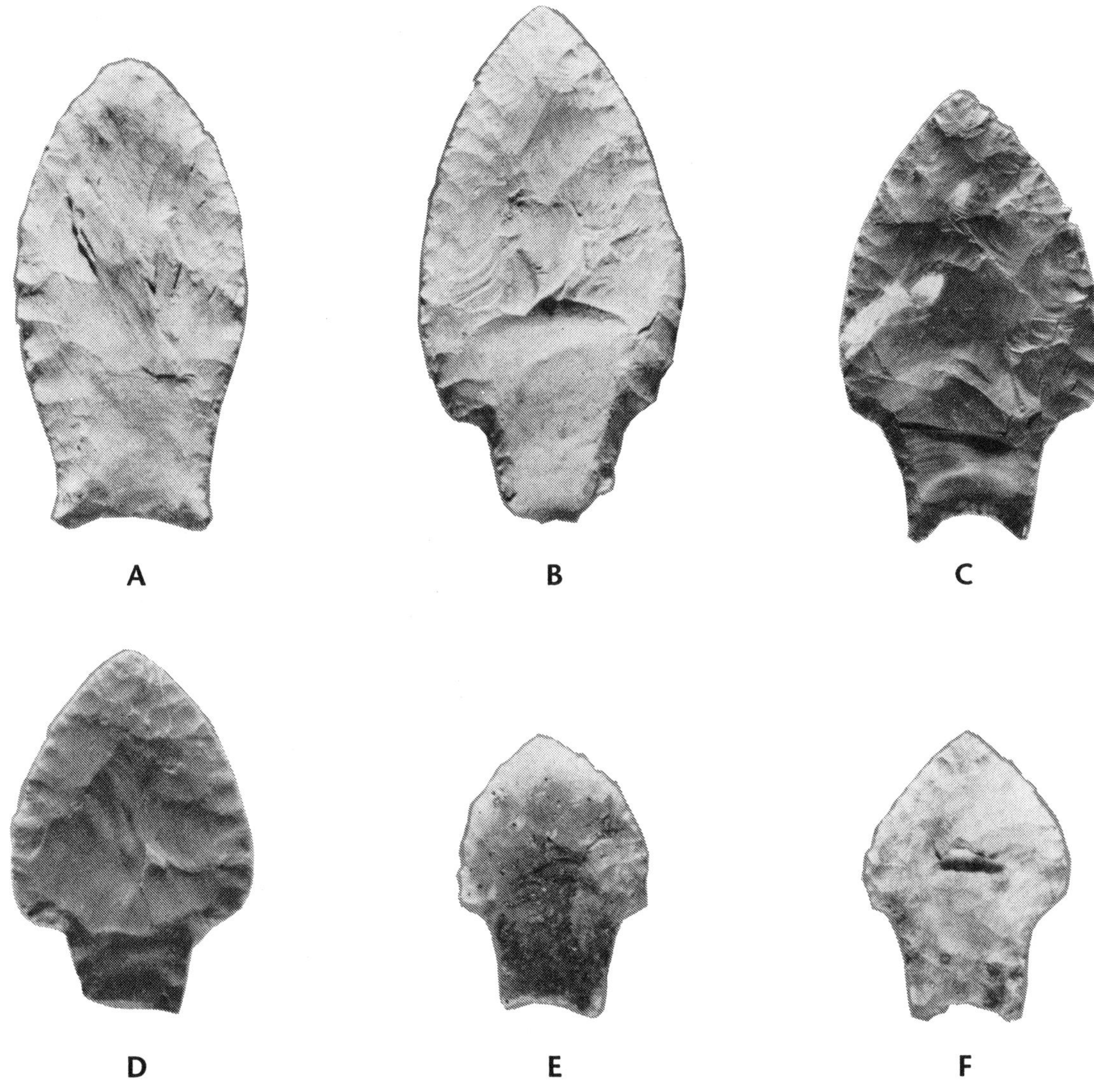

Figure 5. The opposite faces of the Madden Lake fluted points shown in Figure 4 (length of specimen A is 7.6 cm). Flake scars from the large expanding thinning flakes, which are characteristic of fishtail points, are visible on specimens B, C, and D. Basal tangs are missing from both B and D.

Holocene vegetation formations have no modern analogues, it seems prudent to re-examine the paleoecological record for Central America.

A series of cores taken near sea level in the Chagres River Basin, Panama, have provided a continuous pollen and phytolith record for the last 11,300 years (Bartlett and Barghoorn 1973; Piperno 1985). The river was dammed below the coring sites, forming Gatún Lake in the construction of the Panama Canal. The area today receives approximately 2,500 mm of rain annually, seasonally distributed, and has a semi-evergreen forest cover. Bartlett and Barghoorn divided the pollen sequence into four periods, the earliest of which dates between 11,300 and 9000 yr B.P. The pollen record during this time period is dominated by tropical forest tree genera, including members of the Bombacaceae, *Phytelephas, Dialyanthera, Virola, Copaifera, Swartzia, Bursera,* and *Lafoensia.* The phytolith record fully corroborates the pollen evidence for the presence of a tropical rain forest in the region between 11,300 and 9000 yr B.P. Piperno (1985:14–15) notes that the abundance of Palmae, Marantaceae (herb understory), and Palmae/Bromeliaceae (epiphytes) phytoliths, coupled with the rare occurrence of grass and the absence of sedge (Cyperaceae), represents "a pattern one would expect from a mature forest situation."

Pollen of *Iriartea*, Ericaceae, and *Symplocos*, which today normally grow at elevations of 1,200, 1,000, and 500 m above the coring locations, were also present during this time period. Elevations near the coring localities reach only 300 m above sea level, suggesting cooler temperatures and the presence of montane forests ca. 900 m lower than their modern range 11,300–9000 years ago (Ranere 1980:43). Piperno (1989) notes that the canopy appears to have been somewhat more open during this time period than later, perhaps reflecting a somewhat drier as well as cooler climate. The Madden Lake locality, which has yielded eight examples of fluted points (seven fishtail and one waisted) (Bird and Cooke 1977, 1978; Cooke 1984), is only 30 km upstream from the coring sites. The conclusion that Paleoindian populations were living in tropical forests, at least in the Panama Canal area, seems inescapable.

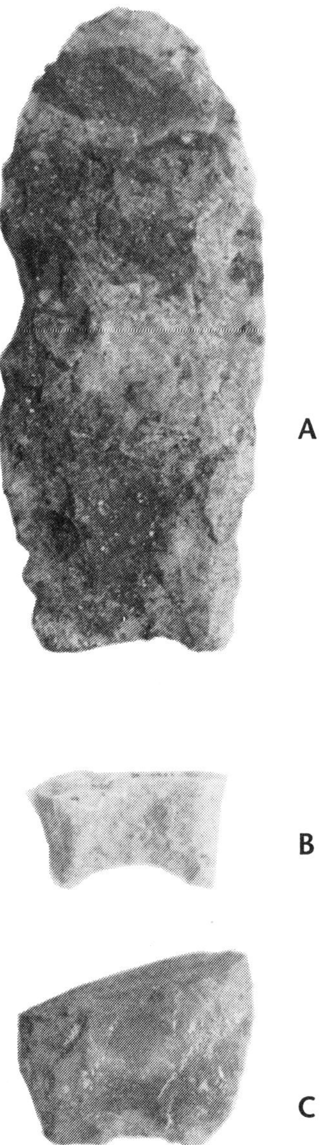

Figure 6. Fluted points from the Turrialba site, Costa Rica. The complete Clovis lanceolate point (7.4 cm in length) has been damaged by the plow along the left margin. Basal fragment B may be the stem of a fishtail point; fragment C appears to be a Clovis lanceolate base.

Moving northward, a 13-m core from a bog-filled lake in the Cordillera de Talamanca of Costa Rica produced a pollen sequence that extended back through the Holocene well into the late Pleistocene (Martin 1964). During the late glacial maximum, *páramo* vegetation, found today at elevations 600–650 m above the core site (whose elevation is 2,400 m), contributed the bulk of the pollen at the site. Beginning around 11,000 yr B.P., montane forest genera, including *Quercus*, *Alnus*, and *Podocarpus*, began appearing in the pollen record. The montane rain forest, which characterizes the area surrounding the core site today, became established between 9000 and 8000 years ago. Thus, vegetation formations in the Costa Rican highlands were depressed approximately 600 m around 11,000 yr B.P., a time when Paleoindian populations would, presumably, have been entering the region.

The Turrialba quarry/workshop (elevation 700 m), the largest Paleoindian site yet discovered in Central America, is located about 50 km from the Talamancan core site on the eastern slopes of the Cordillera Central (Snarskis 1979). The area now receives 4,000 mm of rain annually and, in the absence of agricultural activities, would be covered by tropical rain forest. It is reasonable to deduce, on the basis of the altitudinal depression recorded in the Cordillera de Talamanca core, that the area supported a montane forest of some kind for most of the 11,500–9000 yr B.P. time period. Hence, the Paleoindian groups who were manufacturing Clovis-like and fishtail fluted points at Turrialba and probably at the site of Florencia-1, 2 km distant (Acuña 1983), were operating in a montane forest context. The Arenal-Tilarán region of northwestern Costa Rica, where an isolated Clovis point was recently recovered (Sheets, personal communication) near the continental divide (elevation 500 m), presents a similar situation. The region today receives between 2,000 and 4,000 mm of rain annually (Sheets 1984) and, like the Turrialba Valley, was probably also under montane forest.

A third pollen record of interest was recovered from marine sediments of Deep Sea Drilling Project Site 565, located 67 km west of the Nicoya Peninsula, Costa Rica (Horn 1985). Horn places the Pleistocene/Holocene boundary at the beginning of Zone 1, which is characterized by a sharp decline in pine pollen and an increase in Urticales and *Piper* pollen. This suggests to her an expansion of tropical forests at the expense of the pines. Thus, the offshore pollen data confirm the results of the highland Costa Rican and lowland Panamanian pollen data in indicating a major depression of montane vegetation zones in Central America during the late Pleistocene. More significantly, there is no evidence in the pollen record for a widespread replacement of tropical forests by savannas in western Costa Rica during the late Pleistocene, although a peak in *Gramineae* pollen in the middle of Zone 2 does suggest to Horn more open vegetation on a local scale. In Horn's words:

> Past variations in temperature and moisture availability in the Pacific lowlands of Costa Rica more likely resulted in changes in the composition of lowland forests, with wet-habitat trees and shrubs dominating during periods of greater effective moisture, and more drought-tolerant species expanding their ranges during drier phases [Horn 1985:538].

If the Pacific lowlands of northwestern Costa Rica, the driest part of the country, were not grasslands in the late Pleistocene, it is unlikely that open biomes prevailed in any part of that country—or in lower Central America, for that matter. A reduction in precipitation or an increase in seasonality would have simply expanded xeric formations at the expense of mesic ones (Cooke and Ranere 1989). The fluted Clovis point from the Hartman collection (Swauger and Mayer-Oakes 1952) is presumed to have come from the lowlands opposite the coring site.

A final pollen sequence to be considered was recovered from lake sediments in the Petén, Guatemala (Leyden 1984). Both Lake Quexil and Lake Salpetén were shallow and moderately saline before 10,750 yr B.P. The dominance of herbs and aquatics led Leyden to infer the presence of savannas prior to 10,750 yr B.P., although pollen of *Byrsonima*, the most characteristic savanna tree, was absent. The presence of *Juniperus*-type pollen, most likely *Juniperus comitana*, at Salpetén from 10,750 to perhaps 8500 yr B.P. suggests to Leyden that the low hills of the surrounding region (maximum elevation 400 m) were covered by a *Juniperus comitana* scrub. Since this species now occurs only above 1,200 m (and 200 km distant), a depression of elevational ranges in excess of 800 m would have been required for *Juniperus comitana* to occupy the uplands near the coring area. Moreover, pollen from temperate or tropical montane tree species like *Ulmus*-type, *Quercus*, and *Pinus* dominates the early Holocene record, indicating that elevational ranges and temperatures remained low well into the Holocene (Leyden 1984).

Rainfall in the Petén (900–2,500 mm annually) is lower than for most areas of Central America, but higher than that of Lake Valencia (Leyden 1985; Salgado-Labouriau 1980), the Galápagos (Colinvaux and Schofield 1976), southern Amazonia (Absy and Van der Hammen 1976), and the northern South American savannas (Van der Hammen 1974), where late Pleistocene aridity has been documented and open landscapes inferred. A modest reduction in rainfall at the end of the late Pleistocene would, indeed, have changed the nature of the vegetation in the Petén, particularly in light of the karstic topography and excessive drainage for much of the area. Only additional research will show whether or not the late Pleistocene vegetation of the Petén was savanna, as Leyden (1984) has inferred, or some form of dry tropical forest, perhaps thorn scrub.

Significantly lower late Pleistocene and early Holocene temperatures and downward displacements of montane plant species 600 to 900 m (in comparison with modern ranges) are recurring conclusions in the Central American paleovegetational studies summarized above. The degree of magnitude is similar to that experienced during this time period in the more intensely studied cordilleras of both North and South America (e.g., Baker 1983; Heusser 1983; Van der Hammen 1974). There is also some evidence for greater dryness (i.e., longer periods of seasonal drought) during the late Pleistocene in the Central American data, although there is no indication whatsoever—at least for lower Central America—that the region was arid. Tropical forests are reconstructed at the end of the Pleistocene for all three regions in Panama and Costa Rica where late Pleistocene pollen and phytolith records have been published (Bartlett and Barghoorn 1973; Horn 1985; Martin 1964; Piperno 1985). We suspect that forest formations of one description or another covered most of Nicaragua, Honduras, El Salvador, and much of Guatemala and Chiapas in the late Pleistocene as well.

If we are to reconstruct accurately the history of the Central American vegetation, we must increase the number of coring sites. There must always have been some patches of edaphic savannas and open woodlands in the drier sections of Central America throughout the late Pleistocene that expanded and shrank in response to climatic changes. However, these patches are no more likely to have coalesced into a savanna corridor along the entire length of the Central American Pacific Coast (Lynch 1978) than they were to have disappeared altogether in the early Holocene, leaving Central America completely covered by a closed-canopy forest (Cooke and Ranere 1989).

THE LATE PLEISTOCENE FAUNAS OF CENTRAL AMERICA

Even though no firm association between Paleoindian remains and late Pleistocene faunas has yet been documented in Central America, we could hardly avoid a consideration of these faunas in a discussion of Paleoindians. Not only should we be aware of the resources available to the late Pleistocene occupants of

Central America, particularly in view of their alleged partiality to the taking of large game, but the faunas provide information on vegetation, which we can use to amplify and perhaps correct the picture presented by four scattered localities with reported late Pleistocene/early Holocene botanical records. We must also consider the probability that the structure and composition of late Pleistocene vegetation in Central America were in part determined by the feeding habits and movements of the now-extinct megafaunal taxa that once populated the area.

Surprisingly little has been written on the impact that megaherbivores would have had on tropical vegetation (but see Janzen and Martin 1982; Owen-Smith 1987); or, better put, the impact that the sudden disappearance of megaherbivores would have had on the vegetation. Even paleontologists normally view the changes in the structure and composition of vegetation formations that occurred between the late Pleistocene and early Holocene as being climatically driven (e.g., Graham and Lundelius 1984; Guthrie 1984; Slaughter 1967). However, Owen-Smith (1987) has recently stood an old argument "on its head" by suggesting that the early Holocene vegetation patterns were a *result* of the disappearance of the megaherbivores, not a cause of the disappearance. He describes the impact of extant megaherbivores (i.e., elephant, rhinoceros, and hippopotamus) on various African habitats to support his position.

Owen-Smith (1987) argues that late Pleistocene megaherbivores (body mass in excess of 1,000 kg), like their modern African counterparts, would have been little affected by short-term climatic fluctuations (e.g., droughts, excessive rainfall) and, as adults, would have been nearly invulnerable to nonhuman predators. Their populations would tend, therefore, to reach saturation levels as they do in Africa (at which point dietary deficiencies limit further growth). In both Africa and Asia, the browsing and trampling of elephants in forest habitats favor the growth of gap-colonizing plant species at the expense of the slower-growing shade-tolerant trees. In Africa the feeding habits and trampling of elephants have transformed mature woodlands into shrub coppice and open-tree coppice grassland.

Janzen and Martin (1982:Table 1) list more than 15 genera of Central American large herbivores that became extinct in the late Pleistocene or early Holocene. Among these genera are a number of animals that Owen-Smith (1987) has called megaherbivores (animals exceeding 1,000 kg): giant ground sloths *(Eremotherium, Megatherium,* the Mylodontidae), the mastodont-like gomphotheres *(Cuvieronius* and *Haplomastodon),* mammoth *(Mammuthus), Toxodon,* and the camel-sized *Macrauchenia.* Other now-extinct genera were nearly as large: another ground sloth *(Megalonychidae),* giant armadillos *(Pampatherium* and *Chlamytherium),* glyptodonts *(Glyptodontidae),* and the bear *(Arctodus).* Only a single modern Central American species, the tapir *(Tapirus bairdii,* 260 kg), rivals in size the "smallest" of the extinct late Pleistocene herbivores listed by Janzen and Martin: horse *(Equus,* 450 kg), llama *(Paleolama,* 300 kg), giant capybara *(Neochoerus,* 130 kg), and the flat-headed peccary *(Platygonus,* 130 kg). The late Pleistocene megafauna of Central America included browsers, grazers, and omnivores adapted to a range of forest, edge, and savanna environments (Janzen and Martin 1982:Table 1).

In a recent review of human impact on native faunas (Cooke and Ranere 1990), we reviewed the late Pleistocene fossil vertebrates reported by Gazin (1957) near Ocú (El Hatillo) and Pesé (La Coca) on the Azuero Peninsula, Panama. Unlike the Chagres River Basin, which drains into the Atlantic, these neighboring localities are on a peninsula that juts out into the Pacific Ocean. Hence, environmental reconstructions of them would be more germane to the question of the existence of a late Pleistocene grassland corridor along the Pacific coastal plain of Central America. The collections are justly famous for the large number of ground sloths *(Eremotherium mirabile)* encountered, particularly at El Hatillo (we restrict our discussion here to the El Hatillo locality which Gazin [1957] judged to be the more recent of the two). However, a number of other taxa were represented, including two mylodont sloths (cf. *Glossotherium tropicorum* Hoffstetter and *Scelidotherium* sp.) and two glyptodonts *(Glyptotherium* and *Lomaphorus*). Other extinct taxa at El Hatillo include a mastodont-like proboscidean (the gomphothere *Cuvieronius hyodon),* a horse *(Amerhippus* sp.), and the giant capybara *(Neochoerus,* cf. *robustus).* Deer *(Odocoileus),* peccary *(Tayassu* sp.), a turtle *(Pseudemys* sp.), and the muscovy duck *(Cairina moschata)* complete the list of recovered taxa. Given the varied habitat preferences of the extant taxa and the inferred feeding patterns of the extinct taxa (see Cooke and Ranere 1990:Figure 2), the late Pleistocene environment around El Hatillo is best reconstructed as a seasonal swamp formation at the fossil locality itself and open woodlands adjacent to the locale (Cooke and Ranere 1990). This is, of course, exactly the sort of vegetation that is created and maintained by megaherbivores in modern African and Asian forests (Owen-Smith 1987:355–356).

PALEOINDIANS AND TROPICAL FORESTS

The paleontological evidence for grazers found in localities scattered from Mexico to Panama (e.g., Alvarado 1986; Alvarez 1984; Gazin 1957) makes it clear that Central America was not an unbroken forest during the late Pleistocene. Nevertheless, the paleobotanical data from the Isthmus suggest to us that, at the end of the Pleistocene (10,000–11,500 yr B.P.), savannas occupied discontinuous patches in a predominantly forested landscape.

We concede that this is an extrapolation on our part, but feel it is more compatible with the admittedly meager paleobotanical evidence than the reconstruction of a grassland corridor through the Isthmus.

We are on firmer ground in claiming that Paleoindians were exploiting tropical forest biomes in Central America, since fluted points have been recovered in both the Chagres watershed of Panama (Bird and Cooke 1978) and the Costa Rican highlands (Snarskis 1979), areas where good paleobotanical records document the presence of late Pleistocene forests (Bartlett and Barghoorn 1973; Martin 1964; Piperno 1985). Of course, the scarcity of bona fide Paleoindian localities enables one to argue that groups only entered tropical forests on a temporary basis, i.e., to pursue game or search for economically important resources, such as lithic raw materials. These groups would presumably return to the patches of savanna and open woodland in the driest regions of Central America after such forays. While one *can* explain the recovery of Paleoindian remains in tropical forest contexts in this fashion, it is not the most parsimonious of choices, given the consistent association of Paleoindian artifacts with late Pleistocene/early Holocene forests (and the scarcity of such remains in areas where savannas are likely to have been most prominent). A more straightforward explanation of the evidence is that Paleoindian populations were adapted to living in Central American tropical forest biomes.

There exist, however, some very real doubts, both logical and substantive, about the ability of human populations to live in tropical forests by hunting and gathering alone. In fact, the view that tropical forests would have provided an impenetrable barrier to the southward expansion of Paleoindians seems to be as important in postulating the existence of a grassland corridor through Central America as any paleoecological considerations (e.g., Lothrop 1961; Sauer 1944). In his review of the evidence for Paleoindians in Central and South America, Lynch (1978:475) expressed it this way: "I have a subjective feeling that 'openness' ranked high on the Paleoindian list of desirable habitat characteristics." A recent review of the evidence for prehistoric hunter-gatherers in Brazil did not even consider Amazonia, even though it constitutes more than 50 percent of the country, because "data on hunter-gatherers are too sparse and imprecise to warrant discussion" (Schmitz 1987:56). This is not a situation limited to the Neotropics; archaeological sites in Africa's Ituri forest with preagricultural deposits appear to be occupied only during those climatic intervals when the forest was replaced by open savanna vegetation (Van Noten 1977).

Skepticism about the ability of tropical forests to sustain hunter-gatherers has also surfaced in the literature on contemporary human ecology. Hart and Hart (1986) point out that the Ituri pygmies rely on agricultural products as their source of carbohydrates. They further provide a very bleak assessment of the plant-food availability for sustained human occupation of the Ituri forest. Other studies of potential plant-food resources for humans in tropical forests, both in the Americas and Africa, point out just how limited these resources are in comparison with most other biomes (e.g., Hladik et al. 1984; Milton 1984; Piperno 1989; Vincent 1984). In contrast, animal densities in tropical forests, while by no means high, are sufficient to provide substantial amounts of meat to forest-dwelling populations in both the Old and New Worlds (e.g., Chagnon and Hames 1979; Eisenberg and Thorington 1973; Hart and Hart 1986). Contemporary forest dwellers either grow much of their food or trade for it, allowing them to maintain much more stable settlements and higher population densities than would be possible by hunting and gathering alone. In the absence of agriculture, the key elements to a successful adaptation to tropical forest resources would appear to be low population densities, high mobility, and a focus on hunting combined with opportunistic gathering.

Perhaps if we recognize that late Pleistocene biotic communities were different from modern ones, we can see our way out of the dilemma of insisting that a grassland corridor must have been present in order for Paleoindians to make their way through Central America (e.g., Lynch 1978) or, finding no convincing evidence for the existence of that corridor, insisting that Paleoindians were forest-adapted groups (e.g., Ranere 1980). It is becoming increasingly clear that the modern communities of plants and animals do not predate 9000–10,000 years ago (e.g., Davis 1983; Guthrie 1984; Leyden 1984) and that late Pleistocene climates and/or plant-animal interactions (cf. Janzen and Martin 1982; Owen-Smith 1987) promoted a very different sort of biotic landscape than that of today—the number and diversity of now-extinct large herbivores being the most obvious.

Since the Paleoindians were accomplished hunters, it may well have been that the presence of adequate big-game populations, more than the particular structure of the vegetation, determined whether or not they could survive in any given area. This would, perhaps, account for the recovery of Paleoindian remains in almost every environmental context reconstructed for late Pleistocene/early Holocene Central America: (1) lowland closed-canopy semi-evergreen forests in interior (Chagres River) and coastal (Pacific terminus of the Canal) Panama; (2) montane rain forests and semi-evergreen forests in the Costa Rican highlands; (3) deciduous forests with interspersed savanna patches in the Pacific lowlands of northwestern Costa Rica; (4) montane forests in the Guatemalan and Chiapas highlands, perhaps pine in the Quiché Basin and pine-oak in the valley of Guatemala and Ocozocoautla (and perhaps at La Esperanza, Honduras as well); (5) alpine meadows at Los Tapiales, 3,150 m above sea level in Guatemala; and (6) savanna/open woodland in Belize.

In spite of this diversity of habitats and the wide geographic dispersal of the Central America Paleoindian remains, the absolute number of localities is not high. This is, in part, a reflection of the limited amount of archaeological research carried out in Central America on the Paleoindian period. However, several projects in the region which involved large-scale intensive surveying have yielded Paleoindian remains ranging from modest numbers to few (e.g., Brown 1980; Cooke and Ranere 1984; MacNeish et al. 1980; Sheets 1984) to none at all (e.g., Lange and Norr 1986). Site size tends to be small as well, suggesting that the Paleoindian population in Central America consisted of small highly mobile and widely spaced bands (Brown 1980; MacNeish and Nelken-Terner 1983; Zeitlin 1984).

There are many more Early Archaic (ca. 9000 to 7000 yr B.P.) sites known for Central America than Paleoindian sites (e.g., Brown 1980; MacNeish and Nelken Terner 1983; Weiland 1984, 1990). Both the lithic assemblages and the settlement distributions suggest a Paleoindian ancestry for this early tropical forest Archaic pattern (Ranere 1980). The continuity is particularly clear in Panama, where seven sites with components assigned to this 9000–7000 yr B.P. period have been documented in a survey of the Santa María River watershed in central Pacific Panama (Cooke and Ranere 1984; Ranere 1990; Weiland 1990). An additional 13 sites with bifacial thinning flakes are probably assignable to this period as well, although a Paleoindian age for some of them remains a possibility. Radiocarbon dates for four of these components range from 8560 ± 160 yr B.P. (Beta-5101) to 7100 ± 230 yr B.P. (Beta-9576). A series of notched and stemmed points made by well-controlled bifacial flaking characterizes the lithic industry. Sometime after 8000 yr B.P., the first cobble tools suitable for processing plant foods appear in the archaeological record (Valerio 1987). The sites are all small, contain limited amounts of occupational debris, and are distributed from the coast to near the continental divide. These data suggest only modest changes in the sort of adaptations—widely dispersed and highly mobile small bands of hunter-gatherers—that appear to characterize the Paleoindian occupation of the tropics.

This adaptive pattern stands in marked contrast to the one that succeeded it in central Panama. The same Santa María Basin survey identified over 200 sites dating between 7000 and 3000 yr B.P. (Weiland 1984, 1990). Besides being more numerous by a factor of 10, many of these sites are larger than the Early Archaic sites and are occupied on a more continuous (if not permanent) basis. The disappearance of bifacial flaking (and stone points) and the presence of large numbers of plant-processing tools (edge-ground cobbles and boulder milling stones) reflect a fundamental reorientation of the subsistence economy. The earliest evidence for intensive use of coastal resources (fish, mollusks, and crustaceans) and of agriculture appear in Panama at 7000 yr B.P. (Cooke and Ranere 1984; Piperno et al. 1985).

SUMMARY

At the end of the late Pleistocene, central Panama was a cooler and, perhaps, drier place than it is today. The most significant vegetational difference is that montane forests grew at elevations of at least 600 and, perhaps, 1,000 m below their current positions, greatly increasing their areal extent. The region also held at least 17 genera of large herbivores, in sharp contrast to the five (*Odocoileus, Mazama, Tayassu, Tapirus,* and *Hydrochoerus*) remaining today. Because so few sites have been excavated and dated, the best evidence for assessing the nature of the Paleoindian adaptation in Central America is provided by comparing the distribution of sites and isolated fluted-point finds with the paleoecology of their settings. While the largest number of Paleoindian localities have been reported from highlands where montane forest formations of various sorts have been reconstructed for the late Pleistocene, they also occur in settings from lowland forests and savannas to highland alpine meadows. The predominance of highland settings may simply reflect the fact that Paleoindian populations entered Central America using a highland route and resided there longer than they did in the lowlands.

Studies on the availability of food resources in tropical forests and on the hunting and gathering activities of contemporary tropical forest peoples point to a subsistence economy that emphasizes hunting by widely spaced, small mobile bands as the most viable alternative for Paleoindian populations. The distribution of Central American Paleoindian sites and the tools recovered from them are consistent with this interpretation. Continuity between Paleoindian and Early Archaic populations in Central America is indicated both by the nature of the lithic assemblages and by the settlement pattern. The emphasis on hunting may well have been the critical factor that allowed human populations to move rapidly into the forests, savannas, and alpine meadows of Central America at the end of the late Pleistocene and to survive successfully there for the next four thousand years.

Postscript

Since this paper was originally written, three Paleoindian sites have been investigated by the authors in Panama. The Westend site, a workshop for the manufacture of bifaces, was located on the eroded slopes of an island in Madden Lake (Lago Alajuela) very near the localities that earlier produced seven fishtail and one waisted Clovis point. Workshop debris included large numbers of thinning flakes with heavily ground striking platforms. Also recovered was a preform fragment apparently broken in the final thinning process. Unfortunately, no finished bifaces were collected from the site, so we cannot determine if fishtail and/or waisted Clovis points were the end product of the reduction sequence. Identification of other Paleoindian tools on the site is complicated by the presence of Ceramic period lithic materials on the same eroded surface.

A Clovis workshop/campsite (La Mula West) has also been identified near the Parita Bay coastline in central Pacific Panama within 50 km of the late Pleistocene fossil localities of Ocú and Pesé. This Paleoindian locality actually falls within the boundaries of the large third millennium B.P. agricultural settlement of La Mula-Sarigua. The initial reconnaissance of La Mula-Sarigua identified the presence of bifacial thinning flakes on the eroded surface at the west end of the site but no diagnostic artifacts (Hansell 1988). Our re-examination of the location led to the recovery of over 30 biface fragments, 6 of which are fluted. Clovis lanceolate is the predominant and perhaps only point form represented at La Mula West (some of the fragments may have come from Clovis waisted forms as well). A 1 m^2 test pit dug into the face of the eroding bank at the site yielded over 100 specimens stratified below the third millennium B.P. occupation layer and lying just above bedrock. Biface fragments, a probable channel flake, blades, and utilized flakes were recovered in situ. Unfortunately, very little charcoal was present in the Paleoindian layer and dates on total organic content of the soils were several thousand years too young.

The Corona Rockshelter, located in the foothills of central Panama (elevation 270 m), is the third Paleoindian site recently examined by us. It was initially recorded and tested in 1983 as part of the Santa María basin survey (Valerio 1985), but its antiquity was not recognized at the time because no diagnostic materials were recovered from the 1 m^2 test pit. Radiocarbon dates of 10,440 ± 650 yr B.P. (Beta-19105) near the base of the deposits and 7440 ± 280 yr B.P. (Beta-19411) midway through the deposits prompted us to excavate a 1 x 4 m trench in this small shelter. Unfortunately, the earliest deposits were restricted to an area of less than 1 m^2 of the excavated trench, owing to the bedrock configuration of the shelter floor. Only flakes, including several bifacial thinning flakes with ground platforms, were associated with the Paleoindian occupation of the site. Corona appears to have been used as a temporary campsite throughout its history but with rather more intensive occupation during the Early Archaic and Late Preceramic (ca. 9000–4500 yr B.P.) than either earlier or later periods.

Taken together, these three sites suggest that Paleoindian sites in Central America may be more common than implied earlier in the main body of this paper. Otherwise, their location, size, and material remains are consistent with our characterization of the Paleoindian occupation in the region.

ACKNOWLEDGMENTS

We wish to thank Julieta de Arango, Directora Nacional de Patrimonio Histórico, Panamá, for permission to photograph the fluted points from the Chagres basin. We also thank Michael Snarskis and the Museo Nacional de Costa Rica for providing access to the Turrialba collections and for permission to photograph them. Figure 1 was produced by Muriel Kirkpatrick, Temple University, and Figures 2 through 6 by Carl C. Hansen, Smithsonian Tropical Research Institute, Panama.

REFERENCES CITED

Absy, M. L., and T. Van der Hammen
1976 Some Paleoecological Data from Rondonia, Southern Part of the Amazonian Basin. *Acta Amazonica* 6:293–299.

Acuña, V.
1983 Florencia-1, un Sitio Precerámico en la Vertiente Atlántica de Costa Rica. *Vínculos* 9(1–2):1–14.

Alvarado, G. E.
1986 Hallazgos de Megamamíferos Fósiles en Costa Rica. *Revista Geológica de América Central* 4:1–46.

Alvarez, T.
1984 Restos de Mamíferos Recientes y Pleistocénicos Procedentes de las Grutas de Loltún, Yucatán, Mexico. In *Restos de Moluscos y Mamíferos Cuaternarios Procedentes de Loltún, Yucatán*, edited by T. Alvarez and O. J. Polaco, pp. 7–35. Cuaderno de Trabajo 26, Departamento de Prehistoria, INAH, México.

Baker, R. G.
1983 Holocene Vegetational History of the Western United States. In *The Holocene*, edited by H. E. Wright, Jr., pp. 109–127. Late Quaternary Environments of the United States, vol. 2, H. E. Wright, Jr., general editor. University of Minnesota Press, Minneapolis.

Bartlett, A. S., and E. S. Barghoorn
1973 Phytogeographic History of the Isthmus of Panama during the Past 12,000 Years (a History of Vegetation, Climate and Sea Level Change). In *Vegetation and Vegetational History of Northern Latin America*, edited by A. Graham, pp. 203–299. Elsevier Scientific Publishing Company, New York.

Bird, J. B.
1969 A Comparison of South Chilean and Ecuadorian "Fishtail" Projectile Points. *The Kroeber Anthropological Society Papers* 40:52–71.

Bird, J. B., and R. G. Cooke

1977 Los Artefactos Más Antiguos de Panamá. *Revista Nacional de Cultura* 6:7–31.

1978 The Occurrence in Panama of Two Types of Paleo-Indian Projectile Points. In *Early Man in America from a Circum-Pacific Perspective,* edited by A. L. Bryan, pp. 263–272. Occasional Papers No. 1. Department of Anthropology, University of Alberta, Edmonton.

Bray, W.

1978 An Eighteenth Century Reference to a Fluted Point from Guatemala. *American Antiquity* 43:457–460.

Brown, K. L.

1980 A Brief Report on Paleoindian-Archaic Occupation in the Quiche Basin, Guatemala. *American Antiquity* 45:313–324.

Bryan, A. L.

1983 South America. In *Early Man in the New World,* edited by R. Shutler, Jr., pp. 137–146. Sage Publications, Beverly Hills.

Bullen, R. P., and W. W. Plowden, Jr.

1963 Preceramic Archaic Sites in the Highlands of Honduras. *American Antiquity* 28:382–385.

Castillo C., D., E. Castillo O., M. Rojas G., and C. Valldeperas A.

1987 *Análisis de la Lítica Lasqueada del Sitio 9-FG-T en Turrialba.* "Tesis de Grado," Escuela de Antropología y Sociología, Universidad de Costa Rica, San José.

Chagnon, N., and R. Hames

1979 Protein Deficiency and Tribal Warfare in Amazonia: New Data. *Science* 20:910–913.

Coe, M. D.

1960 A Fluted Point from Highland Guatemala. *American Antiquity* 25:412–413.

Colinvaux, P. A., and E. K. Schofield

1976 Historical Ecology in the Galapagos Islands, I. A Holocene Pollen Record from El Junco Lake, Isle San Cristobal. *Journal of Ecology* 64:989–1012.

Cooke, R. G.

1984 Archaeological Research in Central and Eastern Panama: A Review of Some Problems. In *The Archaeology of Lower Central America,* edited by F. W. Lange and D. Z. Stone, pp. 263–302. University of New Mexico Press, Albuquerque.

Cooke, R. G., and A. J. Ranere

1984 The "Proyecto Santa María": A Multidisciplinary Analysis of Prehistoric Adaptations to a Tropical Watershed in Panama. In *Recent Developments in Isthmian Archaeology: Advances in the Prehistory of Lower Central America,* edited by F. W. Lange., pp. 31–53. BAR International Series 212, Oxford.

1990 Precolumbian Influences on the Zoogeography of Panama: An Update Based on Archaeological and Documentary Evidence. In *Proceedings of the Symposium on the Zoogeography of Middle America.* Tulane, New Orleans, in press.

Correal Urrego, G.

1983 Evidencia de Cazadores Especializados en el Sitio de la Gloria, Golfo de Urabá. *Revista de la Academia de Colombiana de Ciencias Exactas, Físicas y Naturales* XV:77–82.

Crabtree, D. E.

1966 A Stoneworker's Approach to Analyzing and Replicating the Lindenmeier Folsom. *Tebiwa* 9:3–39.

Davis, M. B.

1983 Holocene Vegetational History of the Eastern United States. In *The Holocene,* edited by H. E. Wright, Jr., pp. 166–181. Late Quaternary Environments of the United States, vol. 2, H. E. Wright, Jr., general editor. University of Minnesota Press, Minneapolis.

Eisenberg, J. F., and R. W. Thorington, Jr.

1973 A Preliminary Analysis of a Neotropical Mammal Fauna. *Biotropica* 5:150–161.

Flenniken, J. J.

1978 Reevaluation of the Lindenmeier Folsom: A Replication Experiment in Lithic Technology. *American Antiquity* 43:473–480.

García-Bárcena, J.

1979 *Una Punta Acanalada de la Cueva Los Grifos, Ocozocoautla, Chiapas.* Cuaderno de Trabajo 17, Departamento de Prehistoria, INAH, Mexico.

1982 *El Precerámico de Aguacatenango, Chiapas, México.* Colección Científica 110, INAH, Mexico.

García-Bárcena, J., and D. Santamaría

1982 *La Cueva de Santa Marta Ocozocoautla, Chiapas.* Colección Científica 111, INAH, Mexico.

Gazin, C. L.

1957 Exploration for the Remains of Giant Ground Sloth in Panama. *Smithsonian Institution Annual Report for 1956* 4272:341–354.

Graham, R. W., and E. L. Lundelius, Jr.

1984 Coevolutionary Disequilibrium and Pleistocene Extinctions. In *Quaternary Extinctions: A Prehistoric Revolution,* edited by P. S. Martin and R. G. Klein, pp. 223–249. University of Arizona Press, Tucson.

Gruhn, R., and A. L. Bryan
1977 Los Tapiales: A Paleo-Indian Campsite in the Guatemalan Highlands. *Proceedings of the American Philosophical Society* 121:235–273.

Guthrie, R. D.
1984 Mosaics, Allelochemics, and Nutrients: an Ecological Theory of Late Pleistocene Megafaunal Extinctions. In *Quaternary Extinctions: A Prehistoric Revolution*, edited by P. S. Martin and R. G. Klein, pp. 259–298. University of Arizona Press, Tucson.

Hansell, P. K.
1988 *The Rise and Fall of an Early Formative Community: La Mula-Sarigua, Central Pacific Panama.* Unpublished Ph.D. dissertation, Department of Anthropology, Temple University, Philadelphia.

Hart, T. B., and J. A. Hart
1986 The Ecological Basis of Hunter-gatherer Subsistence in African Rain Forests: The Mbuti of Eastern Zaire. *Human Ecology* 14:29–55.

Hester, T. R., T. C. Kelley, and G. Ligabue
1981 *A Fluted Paleo-Indian Projectile Point from Belize, Central America.* Working Papers No. 1. Center for Archaeological Research, University of Texas, San Antonio.

Hester, T. R., H. J. Shafer, and T. C. Kelley
1980 Lithics from a Preceramic Site in Belize. *Lithic Technology* 9:9–10.

Heusser, C. J.
1983 Quaternary Palynology of Chile. In *Quaternary of South America and Antarctic Peninsula*, vol. 1, edited by J. Rabassa, pp. 5–22. A. A. Balkema, Rotterdam.

Hladik, A., S. Bahuchet, C. Ducatillion, and C. M. Hladik
1984 Les Plantes à Tubercule de la Forêt Dense d'Afrique Centrale. *Revue d'écologie (Terre & Vie)* 39:249–290.

Horn, S. P.
1985 Preliminary Pollen Analysis of Quaternary Sediments from Deep Sea Drilling Project Site 565, Western Costa Rica. In *Initial Reports of the Deep Sea Drilling Project*, by R. von Huen, J. Aubouin, et al. LXXXIV:533–547.

Janzen, D. H., and P. S. Martin
1982 Neotropical Anachronisms: The Fruits the Gomphotheres Ate. *Science* 215:19–27.

Judge, W. J.
1973 *Paleo-Indian Occupation of the Central Rio Grande Valley in New Mexico.* University of New Mexico Press, Albuquerque.

Lange, F. W., and L. Norr (editors)
1986 *Prehistoric Settlement Patterns in Costa Rica.* Journal of the Steward Anthropological Society 14 (1 and 2).

Leyden, B.
1984 Guatemalan Forest Synthesis after Pleistocene Aridity. *Proceedings of the National Academy of Sciences (USA)* 81:4856–4859.

1985 Late Quaternary Aridity and Holocene Moisture Fluctuations in the Lake Valencia Basin, Venezuela. *Ecology* 66:1279–1295.

Lothrop, S. K.
1961 Early Migrations to Central and South America, an Anthropological Problem in Light of Other Sciences. *Journal of the Royal Anthropological Institute* 91:97–123.

Lynch, T. F.
1978 The South American Paleo-Indians. In *Ancient Native Americans*, edited by J. D. Jennings, pp. 455–489. W. H. Freeman and Company, San Francisco.

MacNeish, R. S.
1983 Mesoamerica. In *Early Man in the New World*, edited by R. Shutler, Jr., pp. 125–135. Sage Publications, Beverly Hills.

MacNeish, R. S., and A. Nelken-Terner
1983 *Final Annual Report of the Belize Archaic Archaeological Reconnaissance.* Center for Archaeological Studies, Boston University, Boston.

MacNeish, R. S., and F. A. Peterson
1962 *The Santa Marta Rock Shelter, Ocozocoautla, Chiapas, Mexico.* Papers of the New World Archaeological Foundation No. 14. Brigham Young University, Provo, Utah.

MacNeish, R. S., S. J. K. Wilkerson, and A. Nelken-Terner
1980 *First Annual Report of the Belize Archaic Archaeological Reconnaissance.* Papers of the R. S. Peabody Foundation for Archaeology. Philips Academy, Andover.

Martin, P. S.
1964 Paleoclimatology and a Tropical Pollen Profile. *Report of the VIth International Congress on Quaternary (Warsaw 1961), vol. II: Palaeo-climatological Section*, pp. 319–323. Lodz.

Mayer-Oakes, W. J.
1986 Early Man Projectile and Lithic Technology in the Ecuadorian Sierra. In *New Evidence for the Pleistocene Peopling of the Americas*, edited by A. L. Bryan, pp. 133–156. Center for the Study of Early Man, University of Maine, Orono.

Milton, K.
1984 Protein and Carbohydrate Resources of the Maku Indians of Northwestern Amazonia. *American Anthropologist* 86:7–27.

Owen-Smith, N.
1987 Pleistocene Extinctions: the Pivotal Role of Megaherbivores. *Paleobiology* 13:351–362.

Piperno, D.
1985 Phytolithic Analysis of Geological Sediments from Panama. *Antiquity* 59:13–19.

1989 Non-affluent Foragers: Resource Availability, Seasonal Shortages, and the Emergence of Agriculture in Panamanian Tropical Forests. In *From Foragers to Farmers: The Evolution of Plant Domestication,* edited by D. Harris and G. Hillman, pp. 538–554. Allen and Unwin, London.

Piperno, D., K. H. Clary, R. G. Cooke, A. J. Ranere, and D. Weiland
1985 Preceramic maize from Panama. *American Anthropologist* 87:871–878.

Ranere, A. J.
1980 Human Movement into Tropical America at the End of the Pleistocene. In *Anthropological Papers in Memory of Earl H. Swanson, Jr.*, edited by L. Harten, C. Warren, and D. Tuohy, pp. 41–47. Special Publication of the Idaho Stare Museum of Natural History, Pocatello.

1990 The Manufacture and Use of Stone Tools During the Preceramic in the Santa Maria River Basin of Central Panama. In *Cazadores y Recolectores en América: Cultura y Medio Ambiente Durante el Pleistoceno y Holoceno,* edited by G. Correal U. and R. G. Cooke. BAR International Series, Oxford, in press.

Rouse, I.
1976 Peopling of the Americas. *Quaternary Research* 6:567–612.

Rovner, I.
1980 Comment on Bray's "An Eighteenth Century Reference to a Fluted Point from Guatemala." *American Antiquity* 45:165–167.

Salgado-Labouriau, M. L.
1980 A Pollen Diagram of the Pleistocene-Holocene Boundary of Lake Valencia, Venezuela. *Review of Paleobotany and Palynology* 30:297–312.

Sander, D.
1959 Fluted Points from Madden Lake. *Panama Archaeologist* 2:39–51.

1964 Lithic Material from Panama: Fluted Points from Madden Lake. *Actas del XXXV Congreso de Americanistas* 1:183–192.

Santamaría, D.
1981 Preceramic Occupations at Los Grifos Rock Shelter, Ocozocoautla, Chiapas, Mexico. *X Congreso de la Unión Internacional de Ciencias Prehistóricas y Protohistóricas, Miscelánea* IV:63–83, México.

Santamaría, D., and J. García-Bárcena
1984a *Raspadores Verticales de la Cueva de Los Grifos.* Cuaderno de Trabajo 22, Departmento de Prehistoria, INAH, México.

1984b *Raederas y Raspadores de Los Grifos.* Cuaderno de Trabajo, Departamento de Prehistoria, INAH, México.

Sauer, C. O.
1944 A Geographic Sketch of Early Man in America. *Geographic Review* 34:529–573.

Schmitz, P. I.
1987 Prehistoric Hunters and Gatherers of Brazil. *Journal of World Prehistory* 1:53–126.

Schobinger, J.
1973 Nuevos Hallazgos de Puntas "Colas de Pescado" y Consideraciones en Torno al Origen y Dispersión de la Cultura de Cazadores Superiores Toldense (Fell I) en Sudamérica. *Atti del 40 Congresso Internazionale degli Americanisti* 1:33–50. Genoa.

Schubert, C.
1988 Climatic Changes During the Last Glacial Maximum in Northern South America and the Caribbean: a Review. *Interciencia* 13(3):128–137.

Sheets, P. (editor)
1984 Investigaciones del Proyecto Prehistórico Arenal 1984. *Vínculos* 10(1–2). Museo Nacional de Costa Rica, San José.

Slaughter, B. H.
1967 Animal Ranges as a Clue to Late-Pleistocene Extinction. In *Pleistocene Extinctions: The Search for a Cause,* edited by P. S. Martin and H. E. Wright, Jr., pp. 155–168. Yale University Press, New Haven.

Snarskis, M. J.
1977 Turrialba (9-FG-T), un Sitio Paleoindio en el Este de Costa Rica. *Vínculos* 3(1-2):13–25.

1979 Turrialba: A Paleo-Indian Quarry and Workshop Site in Eastern Costa Rica. *American Antiquity* 44:125–138.

1984 Central America: The Lower Caribbean. In *The Archaeology of Lower Central America,* edited by F. W. Lange and D. Z. Stone, pp. 195–232. University of New Mexico Press, Albuquerque.

Swauger, J. L., and W. J. Mayer-Oakes
1952 A Fluted Point from Costa Rica. *American Antiquity* 17:264–265.

Valerio L., W.
1985 Investigaciones Preliminares en Dos Abrigos Rocosos en la Región Central de Panamá. *Vínculos* 11(1–2):17–29.
1987 *Análisis Funcional y Estratigráfico de Sf-9 (Carabalí), un Abrigo Rocoso en la Región Central de Panamá.* "Tesis de Grado," Escuela de Antropología y Sociología, University of Costa Rica, San José.

Van der Hammen, T.
1974 The Pleistocene Changes of Vegetation and Climate in Tropical South America. *Journal of Biogeography* 1:3–26.

Van Noten, F.
1977 Excavation at Matupi Cave. *Antiquity* 51:35–40.

Vincent, A. S.
1984 Plant Foods in Savanna Environments: a Preliminary Report of Tubers Eaten by the Hadza of Northern Tanzania. *World Archaeology* 17:131–148.

Weiland, D.
1984 Prehistoric Settlement Patterns in the Santa María Drainage of Central Pacific Panama: A Preliminary Analysis. In *Recent Developments in Isthmian Archaeology: Advances in the Prehistory of Lower Central America,* edited by F. W. Lange, pp. 31–53. BAR International Series 212, Oxford.
1990 Preceramic Settlement Patterns in the Santa Maria Basin, Central Pacific Panama. In *Cazadores y Recolectores en América: Cultura y Medio Ambiente durante el Pleistoceno y Holoceno,* edited by G. Correal U. and R. G. Cooke. BAR International Series, Oxford, in press.

Willey, G. R.
1966 *An Introduction to American Archaeology, vol. 1: North and Middle America.* Prentice-Hall, Englewood Cliffs, NJ.

Wilmsen, E. N.
1974 *Lindenmeier; A Pleistocene Hunting Society.* Harper and Row, New York.

Zeitlin, R. N.
1984 A Summary Report on Three Seasons of Field Investigations into the Archaic Period Prehistory of Lowland Belize. *American Anthropologist* 86:358–369.

Paleoindians in South America: A Discrete and Identifiable Cultural Stage?

THOMAS F. LYNCH
Department of Anthropology
McGraw Hall
Cornell University
Ithaca, NY 14853

The definition of Paleoindians has become increasingly difficult, but also more interesting, as emphasis has shifted from typology to chronology and then to adaptation and environmental context. Despite the lack of complete and consistent flaked-stone industries in South America, such as characterize Paleoindians in North and even Central America, the link is still most easily established through fluted points, edge grinding, snub-nosed end scrapers, thumbnail scrapers, knife-scrapers, perforators, and blade technology. Lack of a discrete chronological horizon, comparable to the Clovis period in North America, relates to the continuing dispute over cultural associations for earlier South American dates, the possibility of an earlier Archaic adaptation, and the question of the locus of Paleoindian origins.

While the Paleoindian adaptation of North America may have been somewhat arbitrarily segregated from other adaptations (those not typified by a reliance on extinct, large-game species), patterns of South American discoveries, as well as the diverse environments and resources of the Andes, have not led to a similarly convenient simplification. At the same time, the South American Paleoindian adaptation is less easily distinguished from the following, and partly contemporary, Archaic pattern. Common to both adaptations are features such as the use of small and solitary animals as well as herding animals, seasonally scheduled movements between resource zones, and the likely attention to plants and maritime products. Archaic adaptations here may be distinguished from Paleoindian ones by broader-spectrum economies, with concomitant changes in settlement patterns and densities, altered frequencies of major classes of artifacts, and increasing prominence of decorative arts, ritual, burial, exotic trade goods, narcotics, and cultigens.

Students of earliest South America have been preoccupied with the practical problems and polemic surrounding proofs of a putatively pre-Paleoindian human presence. The arguments are likely to remain unsettled for many years, given the controversial nature of the sites, artifacts, and claimed associations of cultural activities with dated materials and/or extinct animals. A possibly more fruitful task is to try to define the Paleoindian culture that virtually all of us admit to be real, whether we derive it from North America, evolve it independently in South America, or even if we like to use the term Paleoindian.

The definition of Paleoindian culture has become increasingly difficult, but also more interesting, as emphasis has shifted away from typology to chronology, and then to adaptation and environmental context. Of course, we are still concerned with technological definition and chronological boundaries, as witness the recent studies by Bryan (1986), Mayer-Oakes (1986), and Uceda (1986) that concentrate mostly on those issues. Throughout South America we lack complete and consistent flaked-stone industries—based on living, hunting, and workshop aspects—such as can be used to define the Clovis and Folsom cultures of the North. Nevertheless, the link between the continents is still most easily shown by fluted and wide-stemmed points, edge grinding on lanceolate points, snub-nosed and spurred end scrapers, thumbnail scrapers, knife-scrapers, perforators, and blade technology. Today we are perhaps less interested in the tool types per se than in their suggestions of hunting, butchering, and hide preparation.

In South America, even if we restrict the discussion to the Andean West, the Paleoindian adaptation lacks a clear-cut chronological horizon comparable to the North American Clovis period (Lynch 1983). This relates not so much to a dearth of radiocarbon dates, which have begun to pattern nicely as they accumulate in considerable number (see Rick [1987] for Peru), as to the very unsolved problems that I must now leave aside. These include the disputed cultural associations for dates before 12,000 years ago, the possibility (to me very faint) of an earlier Archaic-like adaptation much like the generally later Archaic stage, and the question of the locus of Paleoindian origins (a limiting factor if in North America). Bryan (1983) and Mayer-Oakes (1986) postulate that a stemmed-point hunting tradition evolved independently in South America, while Guidon (1984) claims that two of more than 200 similar sites in the district of São Raimundo Nonato, Brazil, date before, rather than after, the last glacial stage (but see also Lynch [1990a]). Ranere (1980) argues the likelihood that Paleoindians adapted to a forest-dwelling strategy and then back again, rather than coming through lower Central America and Colombia when conditions were briefly both colder and drier during the Paleoindian florescence. Finally, the South American Paleoindian stage is hard to fix in time because it is poorly defined as a culture or adaptation. This is the problem I take up here, concentrating on Paleoindian relationships with the environment.

While the Paleoindian adaptation of North America may have been somewhat arbitrarily segregated from other adaptations (that is, those not typified by a reliance on extinct large-game species), patterns of South American discoveries, as well as the diverse environments and resources of the Andes, have not led to a similarly convenient simplification. In North America there are only three nations, and there is a remarkably consistent approach to method and interpretation. In South America there are many nations, many approaches to archaeology, and few tendencies toward methodological or terminological consistency. South American archaeology has not been characterized by a passion for analytic convenience or neatly defined concepts, such as would promote a simple, continent-wide separation of Paleoindians from contemporary or later peoples less narrowly adapted to large-game species. Also, the open *pampas, punas, paramos* [1], thorn forests, and savannas were good habitats in which to hunt these animals, but they were generally smaller, disjunctive, and less well stocked than the North American equivalents (Guilday 1967). (The extensive Argentine *pampas* are a possible exception.) In South America there were no mammoths, bison, or camelops, although the late Pleistocene fauna included other camelids (*Palaeolama, Protauchenia,* etc.), mastodons, horses of three genera, very large edentates of the Megatheriidae and Mylodontidae (*Scelidotherium, Mylodon*), as well as various glyptodons, toxodons, and the giant capybara (*Neochoerus*). All are extinct, and all but the last have been claimed, at one site or another, to be in association with human beings. This is a diverse list of game animals, to which can be added, at several well-documented sites throughout the Andean zone, many extant and usually smaller mammals, birds, and edible plants (Lynch 1983). This notion of "diversity from the beginning" does not fit comfortably with an older classical definition of North American Paleoindians, but surely it will not surprise anyone old enough to remember history teachers who portrayed seventeenth- and eighteenth-century America as if it were populated only by yeoman farmers and tomahawk-waving Indians. Our archaeological caricature of the Paleoindian hunter may die equally slowly.

I am quite willing to admit that the Paleoindians (or whatever Ranere [this volume] wishes to call them as they came through lower Central America) may have been broadening their adaptation, becoming less classically Paleoindian, and hunting fewer large animals when they arrived in South America. In my opinion, however, Paleoindian peoples arrived in South America perhaps as little as 500 years after humans were present in North America (Lynch 1990a). The spread of Paleoindians down the Andean valleys, flanks, and high plains appears as rapid as the migration westward in

North America of beaver trappers and lumbermen during the recent European period of domination. Similarly, the exploitation of resources by South American Paleoindians was so thorough and ill-adapted to the natural ecology that there was a devastating effect on the species that were sought. It has been argued that, even allowing for excessive taxonomic splitting (especially among the glyptodons), South America lost more major mammals during the late Pleistocene than any other continent (Martin 1984:374).

If it is impossible to pin the South American Paleoindians down to a discrete chronological horizon comparable to that of the North American Clovis period, we can still bracket them roughly between 12,000 and 10,000 (or possibly as late as 9000) years ago. The end date will prove most difficult because the Paleoindian tradition merges into, or evolves into, the later Archaic tradition, as the descendants of the first South Americans multiplied, diversified, broadened their subsistence strategies, and moved into new environments. As Meltzer (Meltzer and Lepper, this volume) argues, in the case of the central and southern United States, viewing the Paleoindians as generalized forest foragers provides a tidy answer to the question of their fate. Rather than considering them to be our first *desaprecidos,* he evolves them with little significant change into the subsequent Archaic peoples. While this is a healthy reaction to the classical economic and cultural segregations, it misses an interesting and most likely significant trend and counter-trend: The Paleoindians were highly specialized in the beginning, surely, as they entered the Americas; from specialized hunting, they turned, during the Archaic tradition, to more generalized hunting and gathering; and finally, with agriculture, Americans again specialized intensively on selected, efficiently exploited herd animals and plant concentrations. The broad-spectrum Archaic economies, so well and nondestructively adapted to the natural ecology, may prove to be distinctive in important ways from the narrowly specialized Paleoindian and agricultural adaptations that preceded and followed them.

It seems that the Archaic broad-spectrum economies flourished in a number of habitats apart from the open habitats suitable for Paleoindian communal hunting. Possibly this diversification was partly a result of human demographic pressure, and probably it had something to do with over-exploitation and extinction of several species of prey, most notably the gregarious horse. Nevertheless, judging by the work of Rick (1980), among others, the Paleoindian open-ground hunting specialization must have continued, for perhaps thousands of years, parallel to the Archaic tradition. We can follow this epi-Paleoindian way of life—based now on deer, camelids, smaller rodents, and birds—at least on the high *punas* of Peru and northern Chile.

There is a strong parallel in the south-central Andes with the Great Basin and California, surveyed by Willig (this volume). Work by Ochsenius (1986), Núñez (1983), Santoro (1987), Santoro and Núñez (1987), and myself (Lynch 1986), in the Puna de Atacama, shows a similar concentration of sites around late Pleistocene lakes, salt marshes, meadows, springs, and water courses where animal and plant resources were concentrated, in response to temporarily high surface and phreatic water levels that were fed by melting glaciers and snow fields. Likewise, associations with extinct animals have not yet been confirmed in this region (cf. Lynch 1990b).

There are two major environments in western South America that might well have been used by Paleoindians, but about which we know very little. These are the lowland forest, or selva, which may have been fairly open in late Pleistocene times (Campbell and Frailey 1984) or perhaps the scene of the initial adaptations, following Ranere (1980); and the ocean shore, most of which is now submerged (Richardson 1981). Sites are not preserved well in the lowland forest, and as archaeologists have taken more pleasure in surveying invigorating open landscapes than closed wet forest, the case for that zone is totally moot. However, on parts of the Pacific Coast, where oceanic plate subduction has caused uplift throughout postglacial time, seaside sites would have been well preserved through the Paleoindian period. Here we see the use of maritime resources (sea mammals, fish, and shellfish) beginning only after about 10,000 years ago, as at the north Chilean Las Conchas site (9680 ± 160 yr B.P. [Llagostera 1979]) and the south Peruvian Ring site (7415 ± 65 yr B.P. on charcoal, 10,575 ± 105 yr B.P. on shell carbonate [Sandweiss et al. 1988:Table 2]), after the Paleoindian adaptation is already in decline. This situation parallels Sanger's (1987) findings on the Maritimes zone of northeastern North America. For generations the first object of reconnaissance in South American archaeology has been to find sites, especially sites with dry and well-preserved deposits. Still, it is remarkable and surely significant that virtually all early sites in western South America are found in environmental zones that would have been tundra, *puna, páramo,* steppe, savanna, or perhaps open thorn-forest landscapes. In addition, the early Andean sites are characteristically found near water, not only in the dry south-central Andes and at lower elevations, but also where fresh water is readily available. This distribution is, I believe, related to the habits of the game animals and the hunting methods employed. It is reasonable to presume collective hunting, drives, and surrounds for herding and semi-gregarious animals.

There are no great indications of Paleoindian hunting procedures in South America, except possibly fire drives. Nevertheless, if we can extrapolate anything from the culture of the north Eurasian antecedents of the Paleoindians, communal hunting was a distinctive attribute, and quite possibly an innovation, of the Upper Paleolithic. In the end, our most useful indication of hunting strategy is probably the location of sites near and overlooking fresh water. Inasmuch as these hunters lacked long-range weapons, large game must have been driven, stalked at watering places, or perhaps hunted from stands situated along paths to and from water.

Our simplifications of culture types and periods have been convenient, but, finally, how will we distinguish, in a more meaningful way, our Paleoindians from their partly contemporary Archaic descendents? Perhaps the Paleoindians were somewhat more mobile and had more specialized ideas of what they would accept for dinner, but I think we have to accept some very important continuities and commonalities in both stages. These include the use of small and solitary animals as well as herding animals, seasonally scheduled movements between resource zones, and the likely attention to plants and maritime products.

The distinctions between Paleoindian and Archaic lifeways are sometimes subtle, mostly quantitative, but important cumulatively. The transition itself, from an emphasis on hunting efficiently captured large game to a broader-spectrum economy, must have been gradual. Many of the "new" tools, resources, and patterns of use must have had their origins before the Archaic proper, even though archaeologists rarely find them. As the two ways of life, like the epi-Paleolithic and Mesolithic of Europe, must have been partly contemporary, any definition based mainly on chronology, or even on the presence and absence of classes of artifacts, is bound to fail. Participating groups may even have switched back and forth as the emphases of their procurement strategies changed to fit temporary conditions. In a longer treatment of this subject, I would surely go beyond the issues of the Paleoindian environment and the degree of specialization to it. It would be important to extend the definition to distinctions based on changing settlement patterns, population density, and altered frequencies of major classes of artifacts such as grinding stones, which were used for grinding cosmetics and narcotics, as well as food. Other noted characteristics of the South American Archaic cultures, which serve to distinguish them in a quantitative way from Paleoindian culture, are the increasing prominence of decorative arts, ritual, burial, and exotic trade goods.

Footnote

1. Briefly, the *pampas* are relatively low-elevation grasslands, of low relief, characterized by numerous grass species and variable rainfall. *Punas* are very high (above 3,000 m), moderately well watered to very dry and saline, with tough bunch grasses, dwarf shrubs, and cushion and rosette-shaped plants. The *páramo* is similarly high, flat to rolling, quite wet, and covered with dense, tall grasses.

ACKNOWLEDGMENTS

I thank Richard Morlan for reading a version of this paper, in my absence, at the XIIth Congress of the International Union for Quaternary Research, Ottawa, 1987. Also, I am grateful to an anonymous reviewer for helpful criticism and to Bev. Phillips for preparation of the manuscript.

REFERENCES CITED

Bryan, A. L.
1983 South America. *In Early Man in the New World,* edited by R. Shutler, Jr., pp. 137–146. Sage Publications, Beverly Hills.
1986 Paleoamerican Prehistory as Seen from South America. In *New Evidence for the Pleistocene Peopling of the Americas,* edited by A. L. Bryan, pp. 1–14. Center for the Study of Early Man, University of Maine, Orono.

Campbell, K. E., and D. Frailey
1984 Holocene Flooding and Species Diversity in Southwestern Amazonia. *Quaternary Research* 21:369–375.

Guidon, N. (editor)
1984 *L'Aire Archéologique du Sud-est du Piauí (Brésil). Vol. 1: Le Milieu et les Sites.* Éditions Recherche sur les Civilisations, Synthèse No. 16. Paris.

Guilday, J. E.
1967 Differential Extinction during Late-Pleistocene and Recent Times. In *Pleistocene Extinctions: The Search for a Cause,* edited by P. S. Martin and H. E. Wright, Jr., pp. 121–140. Yale University Press, New Haven.

Llagostera Martinez, A.
1979 9,700 Years of Maritime Subsistence on the Pacific. *American Antiquity* 44:309–324.

Lynch, T. F.
1983 The Paleo-Indians. In *Ancient South Americans,* edited by J. D. Jennings, pp. 87–137. W. H. Freeman and Company, San Francisco.
1986 Climate Change and Human Settlement around the Late-Glacial Laguna de Punta Negra, Northern Chile: The Preliminary Results. *Geoarchaeology* 1:145–161.
1990a Glacial-Age Man in South America? A Critical Review. *American Antiquity* 55:12–36.
1990b Quaternary Climate, Environment, and the Human Occupation of the South-Central Andes. *Geoarchaeology* 5:199–228.

Martin, P. S.
1984 Prehistoric Overkill: The Global Model. In

Quaternary Extinctions: A Prehistoric Revolution, edited by P. S. Martin and R. G. Klein, pp. 354–403. University of Arizona Press, Tucson.

Mayer-Oakes, W.
1986 El Inga: A Paleo-Indian Site in the Sierra of Northern Ecuador. *Transactions of the American Philosophical Society* 76:1–235.

Núñez Atencio, L.
1983 Paleoindian and Archaic Cultural Periods in the Arid and Semi-Arid Regions of Northern Chile. In *Advances in World Archaeology*, vol. 2, edited by F. Wendorf and A. E. Close, pp. 161–203. Academic Press, New York.

Ochsenius, C.
1986 La Glaciación Puna Durante el Wisconsin, Desglaciación y Máximo Lacustre en la Transición Wisconsin-Holoceno y Refugios de Megafauna Postglaciales en la Puna y Desierto Atacama. *Revista de Geografía a Norte Grande* 13:29–58.

Ranere, A. J.
1980 Human Movement into Tropical America at the End of the Pleistocene. In *Anthropological Papers in Memory of E. H. Swanson, Jr.*, edited by L. B. Harten, C. N. Warren, and D. R. Tuohy, pp. 41–47. Special Publication of the Idaho State Museum of Natural History, Pocatello.

Richardson, J. B., III
1981 Modeling the Development of Sedentary Maritime Economies on the Coast of Peru: A Preliminary Statement. *Annals of the Carnegie Museum* 50:139–150.

Rick, J. W.
1980 *Prehistoric Hunters of the High Andes.* Academic Press, New York.
1987 Dates as Data: An Examination of the Peruvian Preceramic Radiocarbon Record. *American Antiquity* 52:55–73.

Sandweiss, D. H., J. B. Richardson, E. J. Reitz, J. T. Hsu, and R. A. Feldman
1988 Early Maritime Adaptations in the Andes: Preliminary Studies at the Ring Site, Peru. In *Ecology, Settlement and History of the Osmore Drainage, Southern Peru*, edited by D. Rice and C. Stanish. B.A.R. International Series, Oxford.

Sanger, D.
1987 Surveying and Testing along the Maine Coast. Paper presented at "The Human Story" Conference, Center for the Study of Early Man, University of Maine, Orono.

Santoro Vargas, C. M.
1987 *Settlement Patterns of Holocene Hunting and Gathering Societies in the South Central Andes.* Unpublished master's thesis, Cornell University, Ithaca, New York.

Santoro Vargas, C. M., and L. Núñez Atencio
1987 Hunters of the Dry Puna and Salt Puna in Northern Chile. *Andean Past* 1:57–109.

Uceda Castillo, S. E.
1986 *Le Paijanien de la Région de Casma (Perou): Industrie Lithique et Relations avec les Autres Industries Précéramiques.* Unpublished Ph.D. dissertation, Institute of Quaternary Studies, University of Bordeaux I.

The Peopling of Northern South America

GERARDO I. ARDILA CALDERÓN
Universidad Nacional de Colombia
Bogotá, Colombia

Fluted points in northern South America are very rare. They have occasionally been found, but always on eroded surfaces and lacking lithic associations. For these reasons, the points cannot be related to known lithic complexes, much less dated with any precision. Two fluted-point specimens are known from Colombia: The first is a fishtail point of unknown provenience; the second (lacking a basal section) is a specimen similar to the El Inga and Madden Lake fluted points, which have been found on the surface of the Gulf of Uraba on the frontier with Panama. In the stratified sites of the Bogotá highlands (2,600 m above sea level) where there are remains of extinct fauna (mastodon and horse in Tibitó), no projectile points have been found. In Venezuela, fluted points and fragments have been found at the El Cayude site (unpublished) on the Paraguana Peninsula north of the known sites of the Pedregal River. These artifacts are similar to the El Inga and Madden Lake fluted points.

These South American fluted points are not Clovis in type, and some authors hypothesize an independent origin for them. Their distribution in the lowlands and their probable relationship with the early bifacial artifacts excavated in the Colombian highlands may indicate they are of Pleistocene age. In the Colombian highlands, marginal retouch, pressure flaking, and bifaces in general disappear at the beginning of the Holocene. Only an edge-trimmed tool tradition continues, which persists through the European conquest.

INTRODUCTION

The question of the early peopling of South America and its importance for establishing the earliest date of human entry in the Americas has aroused the ever-growing interest of a good number of colleagues; and not a few controversies among them every time a new corpus of data is interpreted. The attention of specialists has been polarized between the northern and southern extremes of the New World, a division that has given rise to the search for extreme links (with frequently unhappy results). The central region of the Americas—Central America and northern South America—was completely unattended to until very recent times.

In northern South America investigations of early human occupations have been few and concentrated in very specific areas (Figure 1). We have only the work of Cruxent in Venezuela and Correal in Colombia, the pioneer researchers who eventually received the assistance and cooperation of other workers.

Evaluation of the archaeological evidence in northern South America is difficult because of the large areas in which the archaeological record is completely unknown. Even investigated areas have, within themselves, large voids and important questions that remain to be answered. At the same time, isolated or occasional finds, lacking archaeological context or collected from surface sites, tend to appear more important than they really are, owing to the feeling that "so very few times cultural remains belonging to the Paleoindian stage have been found that any find, every bit of evidence deserves consideration" (Bird and Cooke 1979:7). We run the risk of overestimating the evidence by attempting to go beyond it and generalizing to conclusions that, while possibly valid for a specific site at a given moment of its history, may lose their significance completely when translated to a different space or time. However, it is also dangerous not to try to go beyond description, not to try to construct hypotheses to guide the process of research and to define important questions.

In this paper I intend to stand aside from the grand discussions. It is my intention to inform the reader about what we know, as well as something about the most important things that we do not know, concerning early humans and the peopling of the north of South America. It is impossible in our case to use the word "Clovis" seriously; nothing allows us such liberty.

GEOGRAPHIC BACKGROUND

Far from being a homogeneous region, characterized by abundant forest, high humidity, and limited faunal species, as it has been sometimes been defined (see Borrero 1983:9), northern South America possesses a great variety of environments, climates, and resources that would have offered thousands of different possibilities to early human colonizers (Figure 3a). Temperature and floral and faunal assemblages change with elevation, forming well-defined biotic belts (see Figure 3). At the same time, the varied distribution of rains and solar radiation over the Andean slopes and lowlands form more or less humid or dry areas. Together these factors combine to produce a mosaic emphasized by geological and soil characteristics.

After entering Colombia the Andes divide into three different branches, forming the Sierra Occidental, Sierra Central, and Sierra Oriental ranges, the latter reaching the central coast of Venezuela. To the north rise the Sierra Nevada de Santa Marta (with an elevation exceeding 5,000 m) and other lower-elevation ranges like the Serranias de San Jacinto, San Jerónimo, and San Luis (in Venezuela); to the south lie the Sierra de la Macarena. In the lowland areas, mountains, hills, and high mesas interrupt the plains (see Figures 1 and 2). Between the Sierra Occidental and Sierra Central ranges lie the broad valley of the Magdalena River and the valley of the Cauca River, a tributary of the Magdalena. The Rivers Cauca and Magdalena receive all the water from the interior slopes of the Andes, while to the north in Venezuela, Lake Maracaibo is the receptor of many rivers flowing from the Mérida Range, the Pamplona Massif, and the Perija Range (Figures 1 and 2). East of the Andes lie the vast savannas of the Orinoco and the jungles of the Amazon (Figure 3a). North of the Andes are the Caribbean lowlands, which are in general warm and dry; to the west, a narrow and very humid belt of low coastal lands extends to the Pacific Ocean from the foothills of the Sierra Occidental of Colombia.

The coastal lowlands of the Atlantic Ocean and the inter-Andean valleys are relatively dry, with yearly rainfall averages between 1,000 and 2,000 mm, although large areas within this zone receive less than 1,000 mm of precipitation per year. This region is generally covered with succulent grassland. In contrast, the foothills and exterior slopes of the Andes reach yearly precipitation values of over 3,000 mm. The northern part of Chocó, west of the Andes, and the jungles of the Amazon Basin to the east are among the rainiest places in the world (see Monasterio 1980; Ochsenius 1980a; Oster 1979).

Although northern South America has a wide range of environments, the greatest differences are found between the lowlands (from sea level to 1,000 m elevation, with a mean temperature of 25° C) and the highlands (over 2,000 m elevation, and mean temperatures between 16° and 0° C). In this paper, I will refer to the highlands and lowlands as the major geographical divisions.

PLEISTOCENE ECOLOGY IN NORTHERN SOUTH AMERICA

There have been several paleoecological studies conducted in northern South America; the majority of these have followed an ordered plan of research lasting over 30 years. The main body of research has been carried out by Thomas Van der Hammen and his co-workers, but important work by other researchers has contributed to complete and broaden the panorama (Absy 1979a, 1979b; Monasterio 1980; Ochsenius 1980a; Salgado-Labouriau 1980; Schubert 1980, among others). This research has changed the concept of a supposed Pleistocene "stability of the tropics," demonstrating instead the great variety of changes that occurred during Pleistocene glacial phases. These changes modeled the geomorphology of the region and determined floral and faunal assemblages in the high mountains and tropical lowlands (Salgado-Labouriau 1980:159–169). In the tropical Andean area, the vegetation belts are well defined and their elements are very sensitive to small

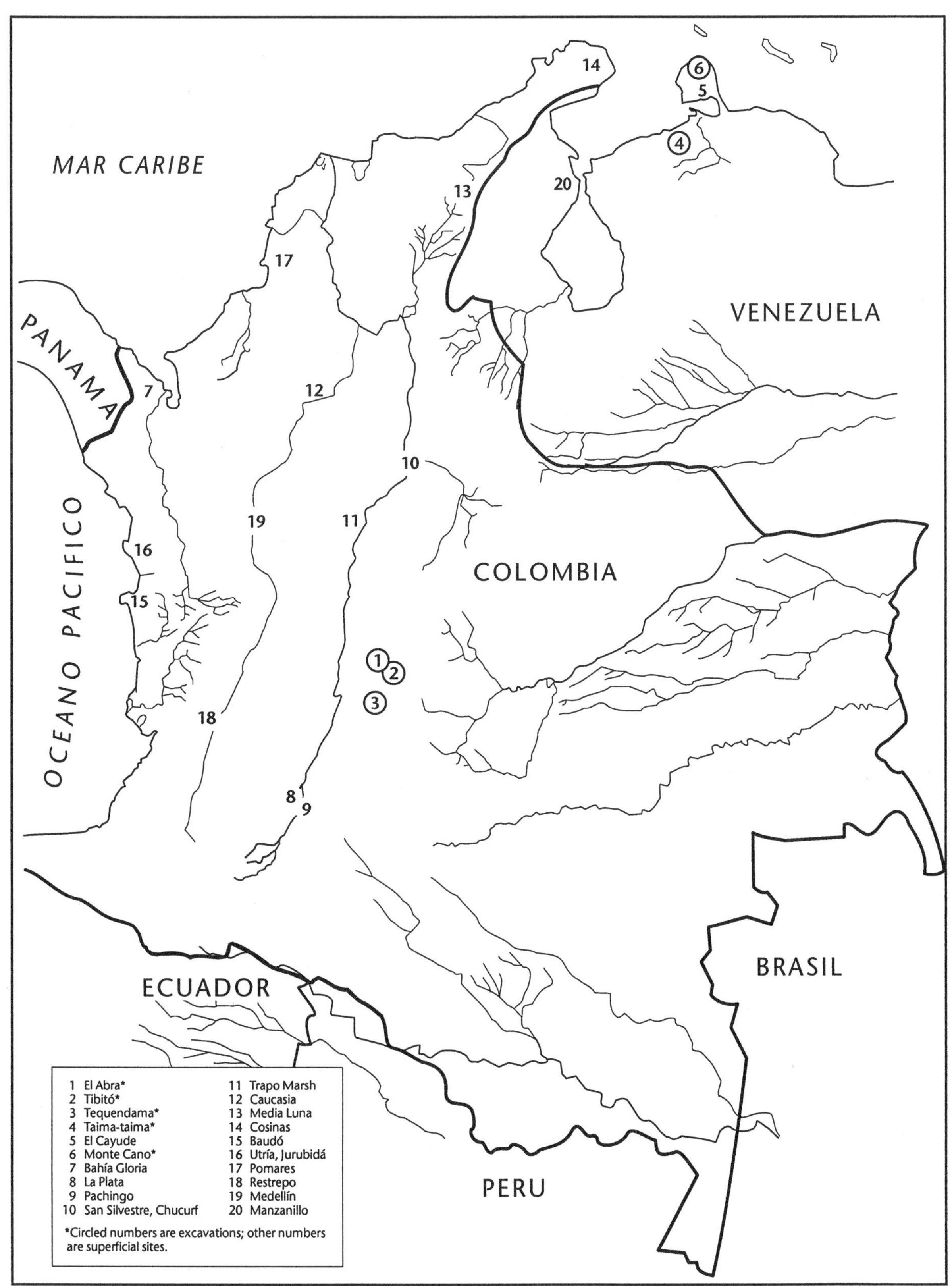

Figure 1. Early human sites in northern South America.

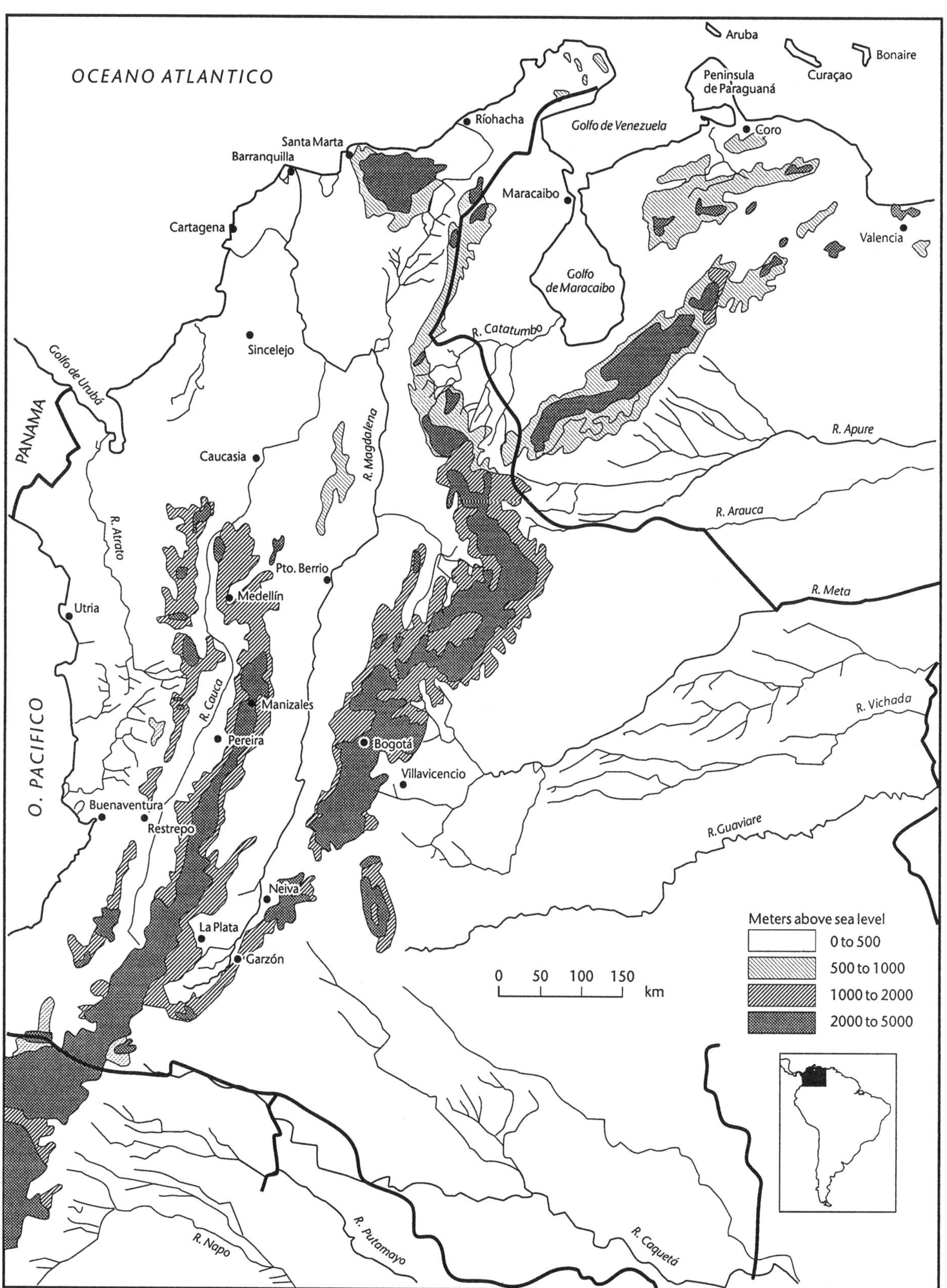

Figure 2. Region of the northern part of South America that is discussed in this paper.

changes in temperature and humidity. During the Pleistocene the phenomena of transformation were not simple; in the words of Van der Hammen:

> The changes in vegetation in the Andes caused by climatic oscillation were not simply vertical movements of zones or altitudinal belts but rather frequent rearrangements of species and types of vegetation, all of which might have conducted to reordering and different zone location than those known today for this area [Van der Hammen 1986c:261].

In addition to the complexity of these changes, there are some areas that have not been well investigated. Obviously, generalizations are not always possible. Thus, it is convenient to present separately the available data for the major regions.

Caribbean Coastal Lowlands

In addition to climatic variation, the ecological characteristics of the coastal zone were subject to a number of other phenomena. These factors included oscillations in sea level, the rise and fall in the flow of the rivers coming from the Andes, the effect of wind dynamics between land and sea, and the tectonic movements of the coast itself (see Ortiz-Troncoso 1985).

There are many studies available concerning the paleoecology of the Caribbean Coast. Especially important are those of Van der Hammen and Wijmstra for Guyana, Surinam, and French Guiana (Van der Hammen 1986b:44–46). Another type of research using taxonomic, biogeographic, and paleoclimatic analysis is presented by Ochsenius (1980a:8–20) for the arid zone of extreme northern South America. Finally, for the flood plain of the lower Magdalena-Cauca-San Jorge system, Van der Hammen and co-workers have studied peat sequences (Van der Hammen 1986a, 1986b:48–50).

A 30-m profile in the littoral zone near Georgetown, Guyana, allowed the construction of a pollen diagram that reflects something of the history of the area during the last interglacial period, the last glaciation, and part of the Holocene. The deepest part of the profile shows that 45,000 years ago the area was a mangrove swamp *(Avicennia-Rhizophora)*, which subsequently retreated before freshwater swamp forest. During the period of the last glaciation (Würm), the swamp forest was greatly reduced and the area covered with open Graminae vegetation. At that time the area was above modern sea level. This situation remained more or less stable until the beginning of the Holocene, when the sea gradually invaded the site. About 8500 yr B.P. mangrove swamp elements appeared again. At the same time, microforaminifera were deposited in the profile, thus indicating that the shoreline was located farther inland than today. Subsequent marine regression resulted in a return to swamp forest and open marshes. Van der Hammen (1986b:45) calls attention to the fact that this profile not only reflects the glacial-interglacial eustatic fluctuation of the sea level, but also shows that grassland-savanna dominated the area during at least a part of the last glacial period.

The recorded profile of events near Georgetown confirms records from a large part of the neighboring coastal area. Deep sections taken from Surinam and other parts of Guyana correspond to the Georgetown section, which probably reflects sequences of eustatic sea-level movements caused by glacial and interglacial episodes during the Quaternary. In summary, climatic change and sea-level variation in the regions of Guyana and Surinam during the Pleistocene led to a replacement of mangrove and forest swamps by grass savannas and open forest (Van der Hammen 1986b:45–47).

Several studies of Quaternary tectonics have been made on the Venezuelan coast. Ochsenius (1980a:12–13) describes a probable set of processes that occurred in this zone, indicating an accelerated elevation of the area during the last 20,000 years that may have reached an average of a little less than 1 m per 1000 years. With conclusions based principally on geomorphological analysis and the presence of Pleistocene herbivores *(Cuvieronius hyodon* and *Megatherium)* on some offshore islands, Ochsenius argues for the existence of a land connection between the coast of Coro and the Paraguana Peninsula, and land bridges between peninsular and insular territories. He suggests that the Paraguana Peninsula was linked with the island of Aruba, and the Paria Peninsula with Trinidad. Ochsenius believes that the Gulf of Venezuela and a great part of the eastern Venezuelan platform emerged during the last glacial maximum (18,000–14,000 yr B.P.), isolating the Lake Maracaibo Basin and producing dry extended plains that connected the Guajira Peninsula, the Paraguana Peninsula, and even the island of Aruba (Ochsenius 1981:368).

In contrast to the existence of humid climates and dense forest proposed by several authors, Ochsenius has attempted to demonstrate that the region dominated by the Arid Pericaribbean Belt was extremely dry during a great part of the Pleistocene. The primary evidence for his proposal, in addition to the presence of neoendemisms in typical elements of the current flora, is the presence of animal taxa of greatly diverse ecotones at a single site dated around 14,000 yr B.P.:

> The concentration of fossil fauna in rich areas of waterholes that yet function along the coast, such as Muaco, Taima-taima, La Guadalupe, or Cucuruchu, confirms that the 'kill sites' corresponded to the last sources of superficial waters; and these sites were often visited by both beast and man. Their geographical setting does not differ in the least from other locations in the tropics and subtropics, demonstrating a similarity to northeast

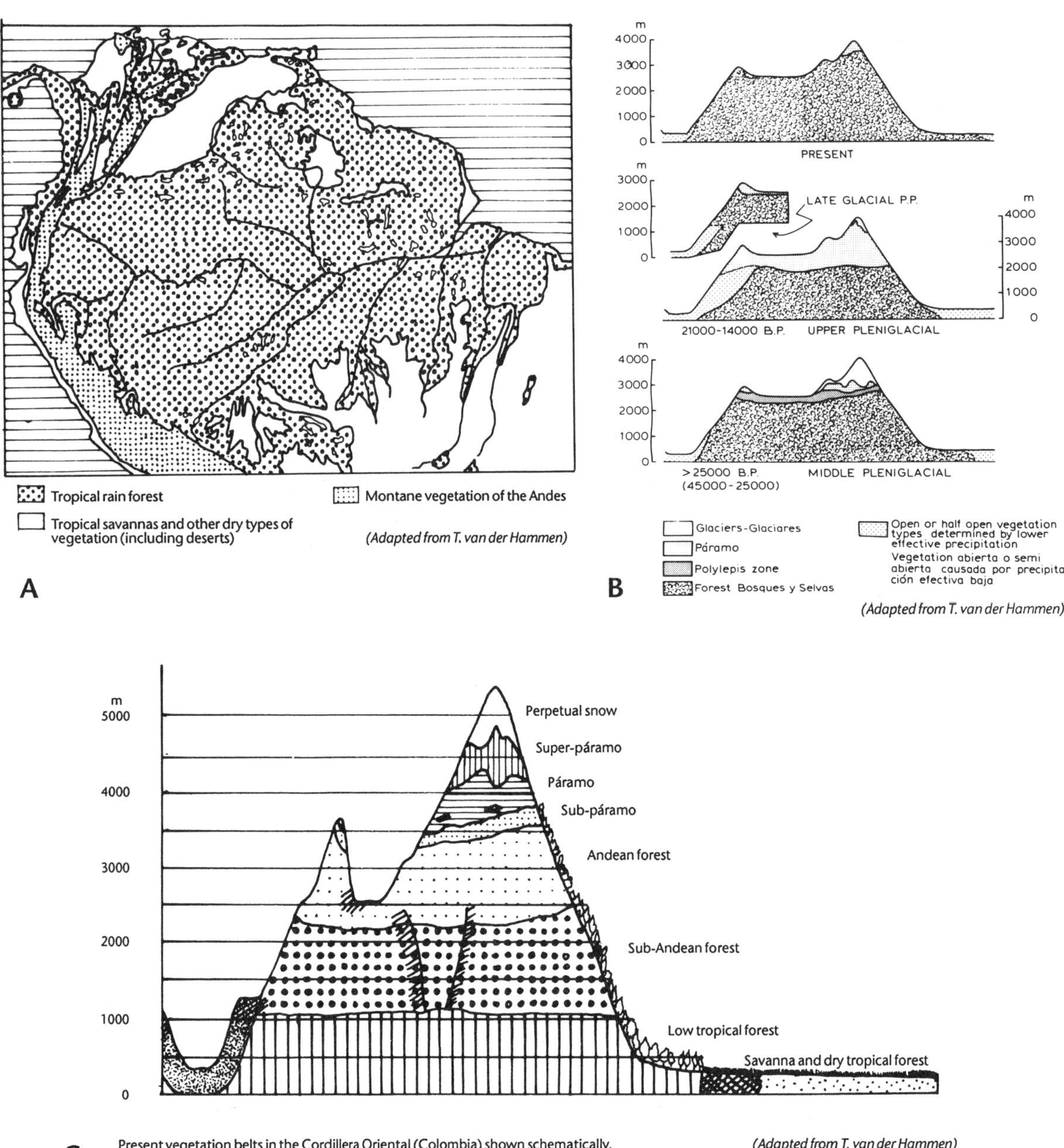

Figure 3. **A)** Distribution of main vegetational formations in northern South America. **B)** Scheme of movements of altitudinal limits of forest and open bridges between lowlands and highlands from the Middle Pleniglacial until the present. **C)** Present vegetational belts in the Sierra Oriental (Colombian portion).

Brazil, a region in which extreme dryness and a xeromorphic tapestry of the *caatinga* type have predominated yesterday and today; there, as in the Arid Pericaribbean Belt, multiple remains of fossil Vertebrae have been recovered at fossil waterholes [Ochsenius 1981:368].

The flood plain of the lower Magdalena-Cauca-San Jorge system forms a type of "inner delta" that is one of the greatest fluvial flood zones in the world. It is permanently covered by water about eight months each year. Deep corings made in the area by Van der Hammen and his colleagues yielded an alternating sequence of peat bogs and gray clays that indicate fluctuations in the amount of sediment brought by flood waters, changes in flood levels, and the extension of swampy bogs (Van der Hammen 1986a:12). Currently, the level of the swampy flood-plain surface is 20 m above sea level, but:

> during the last glaciation, sea level descended about 80 meters with respect to today's level; and by then the present day flood plain was cut by erosion to more than 15 meters below the current sea level. . . . In the Holocene, the swampy valley floor was gradually filled with fluvial sediment, simultaneously experiencing a differential subsidence in the central part as well as the compacting of the sediments [Van der Hammen 1986a:12].

The levels of peat signify periods of low floods, and the layers of gray clay periods of high floods. During the driest periods, savanna vegetation and open forest covered the former swamp, and gallery forest vegetation occupied the river borders and *caños*. Fluctuation of floods depended on the increase or decrease of the effective precipitation in the Andes, the catchment basin of the Cauca-Magdalena system.

In comparing the dry periods of this area with data from other regions in the Amazon tropical forest—the Orinoco savannas, the high Andean areas, and sectors of low inter-Andean valleys—a concordance of dry and humid periods is found in the northern part of South America. This concordance acted in a modified way upon the different ecosystems of the area. With respect to the lowland marshes of the Magdalena River, Van der Hammen emphasized:

> Summing up the evidence from the lower Magdalena area, we must conclude that this is a very dynamic and complex geosystem, subject to constant change, and that its dynamics reflect processes and events occurring elsewhere in the Andean geosystem [Van der Hammen 1986b:50].

Correal cites H. Duque, who stated that:

> during the Pleistocene period, the Caribbean Sea should have covered the western parts of the departments of Cordoba, Sucre, and Bolivar and the northwestern sector of the department of Antioquia, as far as the line extending from Ovejas to the Sierra de San Jeronimo. Sea waters also covered sectors of the departments of Bolivar, Atlántico, and Magdalena, reaching an extended arch between Ovejas and the Santa Marta Bay, with only sectors of the Sierra de San Jacinto emerging [Correal 1977:36].

This situation may have occurred during one of the Pleistocene marine-transgression phases, but could not have existed during the regressing phases, when sea level descended about 80 m (see Van der Hammen 1986b) and the coastline retreated several kilometers north, similar to what occurred in the other Caribbean sectors.

Finally, Van der Hammen draws our attention to the importance of the effect of sea-level changes on river mouths in the coastal zone. During low sea-level phases, marine influence may have extended beyond present estuaries, thus affecting the relationship between brackish, saltwater, and freshwater boundaries. These changing relationships would have modified zonal boundaries of estuary ecology (Van der Hammen 1986a:17).

It can be concluded that if the lowlands of the Caribbean Coast experienced dry and humid stages related to major changes in temperature, effective precipitation, and sea level, these phases differed in intensity and had a varied affect on flora and fauna in different regions. Nonetheless, we must point out the significant expansion of open and semi-open vegetational zones, especially grass savannas, during the colder stages of the Pleistocene, zones that were covered by dense forest in warmer periods.

Tropical Rain Forest and Savanna

The lowland tropical forest is very important to the appearance of early humans in northern South America (see Figure 3a). The apparent homogeneity of the environment contradicts the estimated high number of taxa. The most satisfying explanation of this:

> postulates the fragmentation of the forest in various cycles long and intense enough during dry periods to allow the differentiation between previously homogeneous groups, the development and extension of forest refugia, and other important details [Meggers n.d.:9].

This fragmentation must have occurred during dry stages that forced the formation of isolated relict forests occasionally connected by gallery forest. "Pollen data from cores of sediments from this area have shown that the tropical forest was temporarily replaced by grass savanna, presumably during a certain interval of the Pleistocene age" (Absy 1979a:73).

In Rondonia, in the southern part of the Amazon Basin, studies were made of two profiles consisting of fluvial deposits. These profiles offer information on the end of the glacial period. Information from more recent studies focuses on the Holocene (see Absy 1979a, 1979b; Meggers 1976; Ochsenius 1980b).

In reference to these sites, Van der Hammen states:

> In the upper section of recent river valley sediments, elements of the humid tropical forest completely dominate. In the lower portion again savanna elements appear to have been much more abundant. The Holocene age of the uppermost recent sediments seems to be well-established;

> their pollen content is entirely in agreement with the present situation. The lower part of these river valley sediments might still be of Holocene or Late Glacial age. Although we do not know the exact age of the other sections, it is clear that they represent Quaternary sediments from an earlier phase. We cannot as yet be certain that they represent, e.g., the Last Glacial period; but the data presented here show, without reasonable doubt, that there were periods during the Pleistocene when savannas partly replaced forest in certain areas. As indicated below, there are good reasons to suppose that those periods coincided with the phase of maximum glaciation in the northern hemisphere and in the Andes [Van der Hammen 1986b:52–53].

It is thus necessary to carry out further studies in the Amazon forest. The little data presently available support the theory of refugia, demonstrating that there were periods in which savannas replaced dense forest during the Pleistocene.

Wijmstra and Van der Hammen (1966) also studied pollen diagrams from lakes located in the savannas of the eastern *llanos* of Colombia and the Rupununi Savanna in Guyana. In Lake Agua Sucia near the Ariari River in the area of San Martín in Colombia, profiles with intercalated peat bogs provide information on the alternation of open-savanna vegetation and *Byrsonima* forest related to high and low water levels during the Holocene. The Rupununi Savanna pollen profile is taken from Lake Moreiru. In the zone above the sediments pertaining to the final stage of the glacial period, evidence of more or less equal proportions of savanna and open forest species is found. Van der Hammen explains his conclusions:

> If the calculated date of c. 13,000 B.P. is correct, this implies that the extreme grass-savanna period immediately preceding it, which was associated with very low lake levels, would be of Upper Pleniglacial age (the last very cold part of the last glacial period in the northern temperate areas); and also that the effective precipitation was low, probably lower than today, especially when we take into account that the mean annual temperature was also probably lower. The previous period must have been wetter, and the whole sequence of the lower part of the diagram is apparently in phase with that from Lake Fuquene in the Andes (see below). There is no doubt that we urgently need more sections and more ^{14}C datings. However, the available data already prove an alternation of drier and wetter phases in the Holocene and in the Late Pleistocene, and they are highly suggestive of the former incidence of a very dry period in the Upper Pleniglacial and of a wet period in the Late Glacial [Van der Hammen 1986b:48].

Highlands and Inter-Andean Valleys

So far, paleoecological studies of the inter-Andean valleys have not been published. Knowledge of some sectors of the interior Andean slopes proceeds mainly from comprehensive research of high Andean zones. The highlands and especially the Sierra Oriental of Colombia have been extensively studied, and the history of this area's climate and vegetation during the last million years is well known. Another advantageous feature of the highlands research is the association of paleoecological investigations with archaeological excavations (see Ardila 1985, 1986; Correal et al. 1977; Van der Hammen 1985, 1986b, 1986d; Van der Hammen and Correal 1978). As the description of paleoenvironmental conditions is relevant here only as it relates to early human occupation of the highlands, I will limit the discussion to those events that seem to be relevant from this perspective.

Many of these studies have been made in the *altiplano*, or high basin, of Bogotá (elevation 2,600 m), an area that was a lake throughout most of the Pleistocene. The history of lake level changes is principally related to changes in effective precipitation, evaporation, and temperature. The change in environmental conditions can be related to altitudinal displacement of vegetation belts (see Figure 3b,c).

During the period between 30,000 and 21,000 yr B.P., the high basin of Bogotá was sprinkled with ponds and marshes resulting from high annual precipitation. By this time the great lake that had covered the basin had already dried up and only a few small lakes remained, such as Lake Fuquene. During the Middle Pleniglacial climatic phase (approximately 45,000–25,000 yr B.P.) and the beginnings of the Upper Pleniglacial (around 21,000 yr B.P.), high lake and pond levels occurred, along with a moderately cold climate and high-Andean forest vegetation. This situation was possible because of very low temperatures and effective precipitation much higher than that of today (Van der Hammen 1986c).

The driest phase of the Pleniglacial was between 21,000 and 14,000 yr B.P., at which time Lake Fuquene also dried up:

> Such a dry period corresponds closely to a very cold period, when glaciers in the northern hemisphere reached their greatest extension and sea level was very low. In the Sierra Oriental, the flatlands were covered by swampy vegetation and the tree line descended locally to an altitude of 2000 meters. It is probable that dry semi-open vegetation of the southern part of the Magdalena Valley advanced until making contact with the flatland marshes at an altitude of 2000 meters approximately (Figure 3B). In the period around 20,000 B.P., glaciers had already retreated considerably if compared with the period of great extension; that is, during the Middle Pleniglacial and the first part of the Upper Pleniglacial between

60,000 and 23,000 B.P. approximately [Van der Hammen 1986c:250] (see Figures 1 and 2).

The cold and dry conditions of the Upper Pleniglacial period resulted in an immense zone of grasses and low scrub vegetation. Large herbivore populations, such as mastodon, horse, and deer (*Odocoileus, Mazama*), flourished, together with many rodent species.

The area covered by low vegetation is defined by Van der Hammen:

> We must then conclude that in the period between 21,000 and 14/13,000 B.P. there were open extensive areas of low vegetation in the Sierra Oriental, including part of the Magdalena river valley, part of the Sierra Occidental slope, the *altiplano* zone, and the hills and mountains surrounding the *altiplanos*. The eastern slopes may have been covered up to an altitude of 2000 meters by jungles, but probably there was contact between the tropical savanna zone of the eastern *llanos* and the *páramo* zones in some valleys or dry transversal zones [Van der Hammen 1985:7].

From 14,000 to approximately 12,000 yr B.P., increased humidity and warmer temperatures occurred, reaching an "optimum" between 12,000 and 11,000 yr B.P. This period constituted the Guantiva interstadial (Van der Hammen 1985). The El Abra stadial followed, a very cold period between 11,000 and 10,000 yr B.P., after which the Holocene began, with a climate similar to that of the present.

The change from a Pleistocene to a Holocene climate signified an ascent in tree-line elevation and the elimination of open vegetational "bridges" between highlands and lowlands. At the same time, great open vegetal zones were reduced to small isolated areas. Some of these areas are located by Van der Hammen in the upper and middle Magdalena Valley and in the western and northern part of the Bogotá Savanna and other high basins, inter-Andean valleys, and high marshes. Since open vegetation zones constitute the ecotone of large herbivores, the reduction of these zones played an important role in the extinction of large populations of megafauna, though it is probable that a few individuals may have persisted until the early Holocene in dry sectors of the Magdalena Valley (see Van der Hammen 1981, 1986d). Radiocarbon dates on a few mastodon bones (Van der Hammen 1981, 1985, 1986d) fall within the period between 21,000 and 10,000 yr B.P., a range that coincides very well with the beginning of open vegetation "bridges" and the extension of this zone.

At the beginning of the Holocene, dense Andean forest predominated in the highlands and sub-Andean forest occupied the lower parts of the *altiplano*. As the environment changed, many smaller animals replaced the large Pleistocene herbivores; deer (*Odocoileus* and *Mazama*) were very important to the early Holocene human inhabitants of the *altiplanos*.

ARCHAEOLOGICAL EVIDENCE

Projectile Points

Various types of projectile points that can be assigned to a Pleistocene or early Holocene age are known from northern South America. The first group corresponds to the well-known El Jobo lanceolate points, described by Cruxent for the sites along the Pedregal River and in the area surrounding the city of Coro in Venezuela (see Cruxent 1979b:77–89; Krieger 1974:96). Associated artifacts have not been well described since a great number of these point finds are from surface collections. At the kill site of Taima-taima, however, a point midsection was found in the pelvic cavity of a young mastodon. Dates on the horizon range from 14,000 to 12,000 yr B.P. The discovery of another fragmentary El Jobo point at Taima-taima, also in the pelvic cavity of a mastodon, was reported previously by Cruxent.

A second group of points are similar to the Madden Lake fluted points of Panama (Figure 6) (Bird 1969; Bird and Cooke 1978, 1979). All points of this type found in northern South America have been recovered from eroded surfaces and have no associations of any kind. The first example (Figures 4:1 and 6:14) was discovered by Correal on the western margin of the Gulf of Uraba, in the area of Gloria Bay (Figure 1:7). Unfortunately, as this point lacks a basal section, a more detailed analysis is difficult (see Correal 1983). Several complete points and fragments have recently been found in northern Venezuela by Oliver (personal communication). Sketches of these surface finds (Figure 6:1–13) were prepared using Xerox copies of illustrations given to me by Oliver. Most of these points were recovered from the El Cayude site south of the Paraguana Peninsula, although one specimen (Figure 6:4) comes from the Pedregal River Valley. Judging from the estimated dates for similar points from the El Inga site, these specimens may date a little later than the El Jobo points. Another point (Figure 6:15) that could be included in this group was initially described by Robledo (1955:217–230). The artifact is quartzite and of unknown origin, although Robledo acquired it in Manizalez. According to Bird (1969), this specimen can be described as a "fishtail" point.

The third group of points (Figure 4:2–4) is characterized by intentionally fluted, stemmed chert points with marked shoulders and slightly convex edges exhibiting secondary pressure retouch (Table 1). The first specimen belongs to a collection in the Museo del Oro (Figure 4:4) and is registered as coming from the municipality of Restrepo in the Department of Valle, Colombia (see Reichel-Dolmatoff 1986:Figures 1 and 2). The second

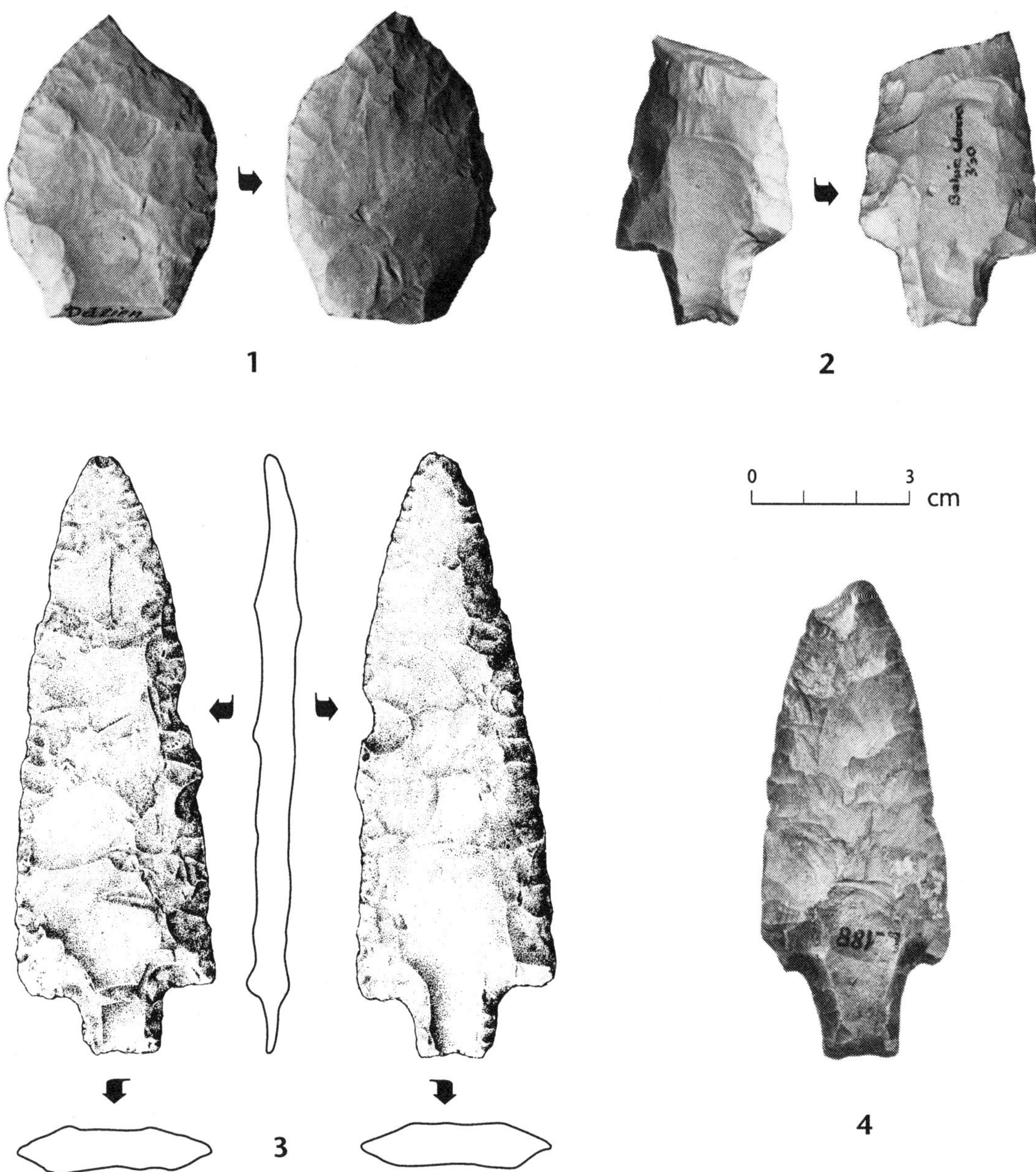

Figure 4. Projectile points: **1)** Gloria Bay, Uraba Gulf (Madden Lake Type); **2)** Murcielaqos Cave, Gloria Bay, Uraba Gulf (Restrepo Type); **3)** Medellin City. Antioquia University collection (Restrepo Type); **4)** Restrepo Town. Gold Museum collection (Restrepo Type).

example (Figure 4:3) is curated in the collection of the Universidad de Antioquia and was found in 1955 in the suburbs of Medellin (Ardila 1985). The third specimen (Figure 4:2) was excavated by Correal at Murcielagos Cave, Gloria Bay, from a yellow clay stratum between a depth of 0.55 and 0.70 m . Unfortunately, this stratum is undated (Correal 1983:80). Another point of this type was recently recovered near the mouth of La Miel River in the middle Magdalena Valley.

Bray (1984:309) sees similarity in form between these Restrepo-type points and a point from Belize. He also compares the Restrepo points to a series of Paijan points from the north coast of Peru and the Ecuadorian Andes that have been dated to around 10,000 yr B.P. I, however, find too many differences between the specimens from Colombia and those from Belize, Peru, and Ecuador to suggest relationships between them. A formal nexus may be better established between the Paijan-Cubilan

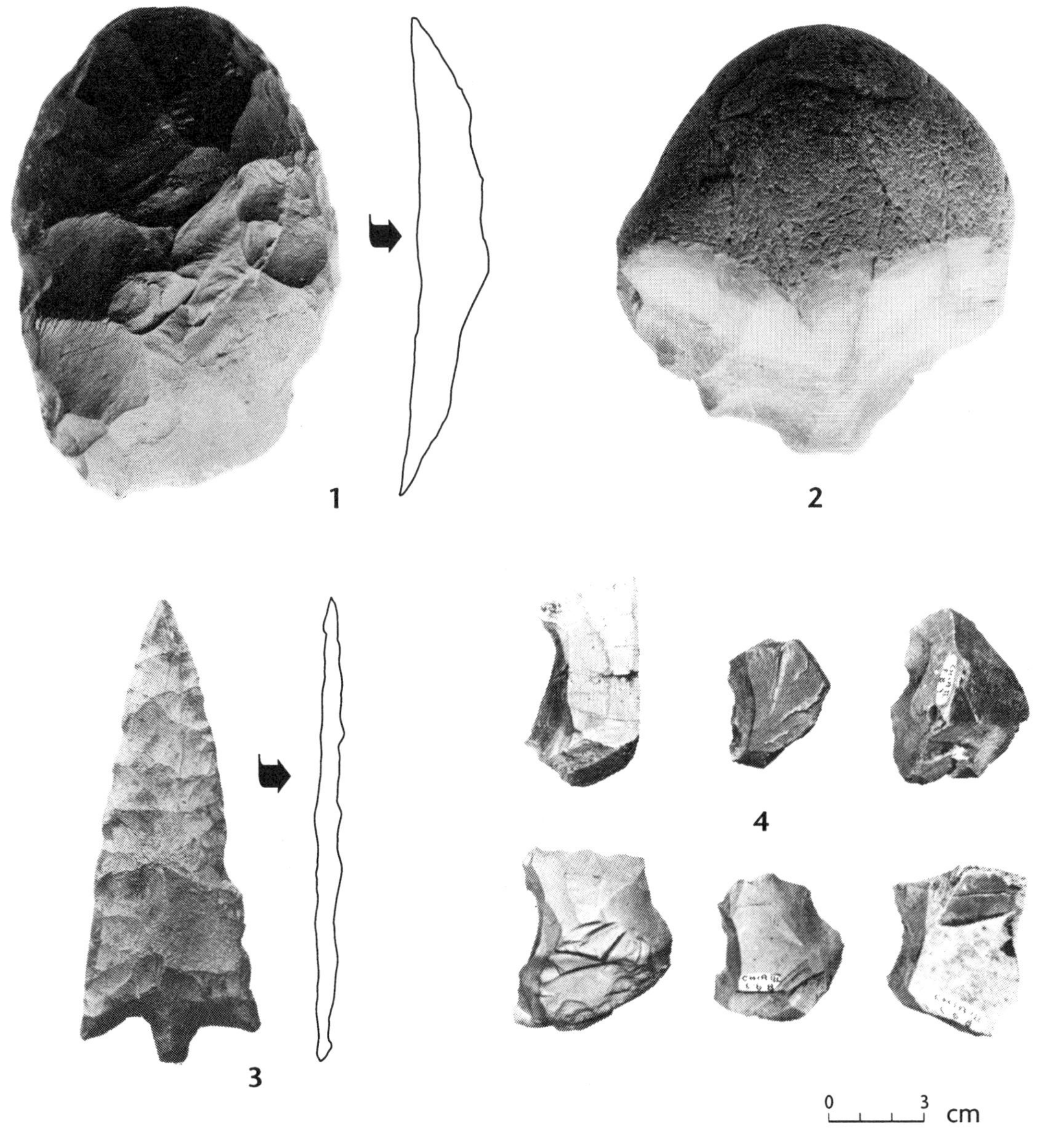

Figure 5. Artifacts from northern South America: **1)** Convex-plane scraper. Puerto Berrio, Magdalena River; **2)** Chopper. Puerto Berrio, Magdalena River; **3)** Projectile point (Paijan-Cubilan?). Puerto Berrio; **4)** Abriense-class tools. Altiplano of Bogotá.

points and a point (Figure 5:3) associated with plano-convex (keeled) scrapers and choppers (Figure 5:1,2) found on an extensive surface site in Puerto Berrío in the middle Magdalena Valley (Ardila 1985). The probable nexus between these artifacts was suggested by L.F. Bate (personal communication).

Six interesting specimens found out of dated context in the valley of Popayán in the upper Cauca Valley between 1,500 and 2,000 m in elevation have recently been reported (Illera and Gnecco 1986). The constancy of basal thinning and the general morphology of at least three of these points suggest a relationship to types defined by Mayer-Oakes (1986) in Ecuador (El Inga Broad Stemmed and El Inga Shouldered Lanceolate). Previous studies of collections of obsidian microlithic artifacts from the region of Popayán (Gnecco 1982) have also emphasized a technological relationship between these industries and El Inga. However, the association of

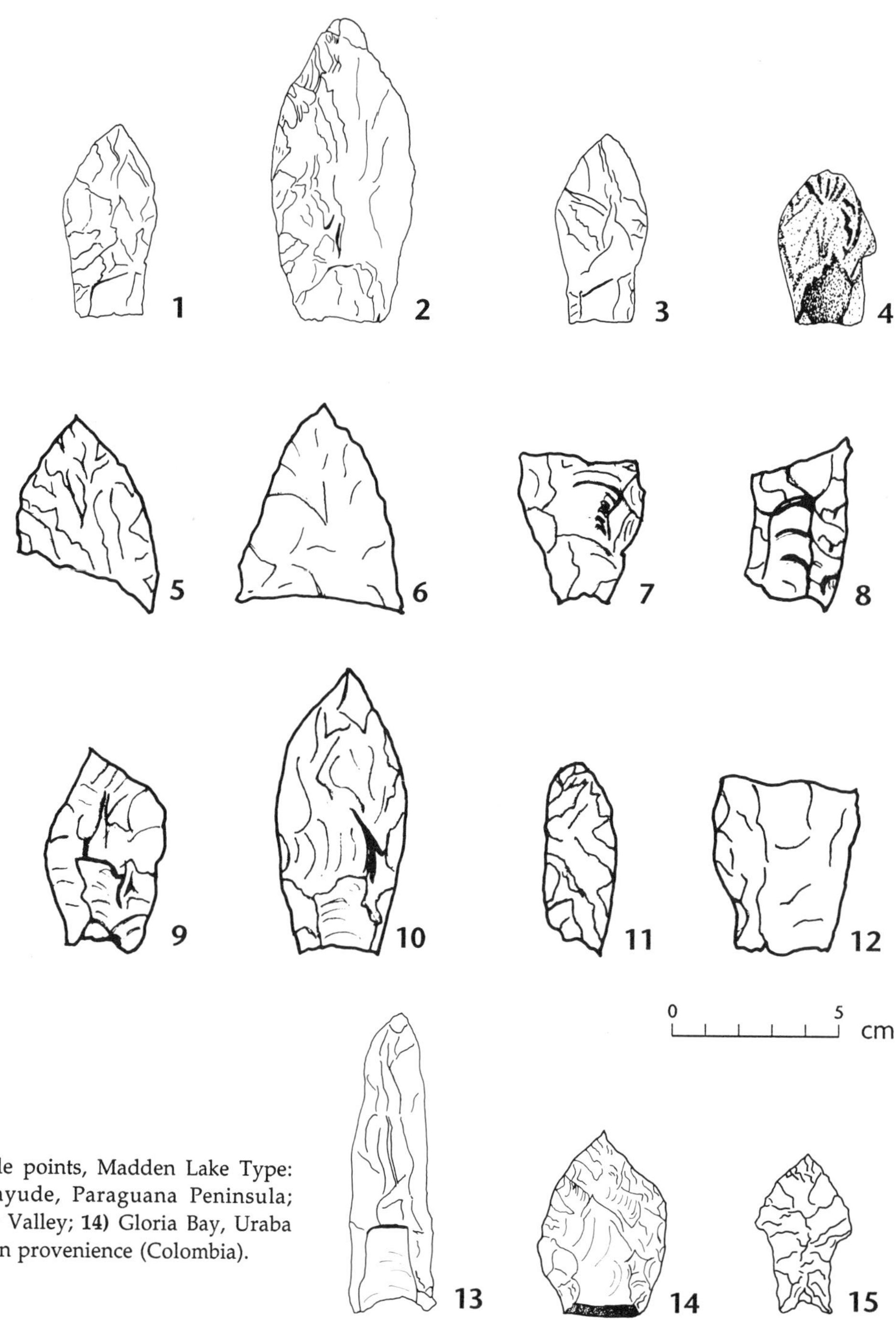

Figure 6. Projectile points, Madden Lake Type: **1–3, 5–13)** El Cayude, Paraguana Peninsula; **4)** Pedregal River Valley; **14)** Gloria Bay, Uraba Gulf; **15)** Unknown provenience (Colombia).

abundant ceramic fragments with these lithic assemblages compels a great deal of caution when considering their age.

In addition to these projectile points, other specimens of varied provenience have been reported. These points have generally been casual finds that could be assigned only with difficulty to a cultural epoch or specified chronological period. Because of their characteristics, it is probable that they may have been fabricated and utilized in later periods.

No projectile points have been found in the *altiplano* of Bogotá, which contains all the known stratified preceramic sites in Colombia. This includes even Tibitó, which has been described as a mastodon- and horse-kill site. The only exception to this observation may be a bifacial fragment recovered from a deep level of the Tequendama rockshelter site. This

Table 1. Dimensions of the Artifacts Illustrated.

FIGURE	NO.	MAX. LENGTH	MAX. WIDTH	STEM LENGTH	STEM WIDTH MIN.	STEM WIDTH MAX.	MAX. WIDTH	WEIGHT	TOOL TYPE[b]
4	1[a]	58	40	—	—	—	3.5	—	PF
4	2[a]	51	35	13	14	18	7	—	PF
4	3	113	36	11	13	18	7	—	P
4	4	91	36	18	15	20	6.5	28	P
5	3	139	56	12	7	15	8	—	P
5	1	97	68				18	—	S
5	2	88	83				40	—	C

[a]See Correal 1983:79–80.
[b]**P** = projectile point; **PF** = projectile point fragment; **S** = scraper; **C** = chopper.
All linear measurements in millimeters; all weights in grams.

specimen is interpreted by its discoverers as a projectile point fragment that was reworked into a scraper after it was broken (see Correal and Van der Hammen 1977:68). The small size of the fragment does not allow inference concerning its morphological or technological characteristics.

An Archaeological Review of the Lowlands

All archaeological investigations in the lowlands of northern South America have been exploratory in character, with the exception of work by Cruxent near Coro, which I will discuss later. The presence of surface lithic sites in the Colombian lowlands was first reported in 1965 by Reichel-Dolmatoff, who located various zones with abundant lithic artifacts scattered on the surface (see Reichel-Dolmatoff 1986:47). North along the Pacific Coast, in the area of the Alto Baudo, Jurubida, and Chori rivers and Utria Bay (Figures 1 and 2), large crude percussion-flaked core tools made of quartzite were found. These artifacts obliged Krieger to include Chocó in the localities belonging to his pre-projectile-point stage (Krieger 1974:84). Along the Caribbean Coast at the site of San Nicolas, an eroded hill in the lower Sinú River Valley, and at the site of Pomare, located above the Dique Canal in the Department of Bolivar, Reichel-Dolmatoff discovered hundreds of lithic artifacts. Knives, scrapers, and stones modified by percussion constituted the tool assemblages.

Years later, Correal carried out an extensive two-year exploratory project, searching for early preceramic sites in the Magdalena River Valley and along the Atlantic Coast. Correal (1977) reported about 25 localities with artifacts, although no stratified sites were detected, with the probable exception of the El Espejo site on the Minas River in the Department of Cesar. All the other sites are surface sites on old eroded terraces near the swamps and confluences of the rivers. This pattern of site distribution is explained if we consider that Holocene sedimentation in the low river valleys generally exceeds 30 m in depth. Thus far, the only detected archaeological sites are those located on high terraces. To date extensive investigations have not yet been undertaken in these river valleys.

The sites discovered by Correal are primarily concentrated in the upper or middle-upper valley of the Magdalena River. The assemblages consist of crude percussion-flaked implements, and large heavy choppers and chopping tools (Figure 5:2). These tools are almost always accompanied by plano-convex scrapers, made on large flakes with prepared percussion platforms, which occasionally exhibit retouch by pressure flaking (Figure 5:1). Site locations published by Correal include Boulder, El Hotel, and La Argentina in the upper Magdalena Valley near Neiva and Villa Vieja, and the San Silvestre and Chucuri marshes in the middle Magdalena Valley (Figures 1 and 2). Projectile points associated with these assemblages have been reported only from a site located on the border of the Trapo marsh, along the Caño Negro near Puerto Berrío (Figure 5:3) (Ardila 1985).

Correal also explored a part of the upper Cauca River Valley between Ansermanueva and Cali, and the alluvial terraces near the mouth of the La Vieja River. He found surface lithic artifacts and some fragmentary isolated *Stegomastodon* remains, but was unable to establish any association between the fossil bones and the stone tools.

In the Orinoco *llanos* and Amazon jungle, investigations of early periods have not been undertaken, although some authors have tacitly accepted the presence of a large human population in the Amazon territory 10,000 years ago (Meggers 1976:18–19, 1979:255). Meggers, following several authors, estimates that the first diversification of major language stocks (Macro-Chibchan, Ge-Pano-Cariban, and Andean-Equatorial) occurred during a stage of forest contraction and refugia formation a little less than 10,000 years ago (see Meggers 1976:Figure 6). At present, however, there is no archaeological evidence of any kind regarding the early settlers of these extensive regions.

As is evident from this brief description of archaeological investigations that have been carried out in the lowlands of northern South America, only in the area surrounding the city of Coro, Venezuela, have attempts been made to develop a regular program of research. In 1966 Cruxent reported over 45 sites and more than 20,000 artifacts from an area of 1,000 km^2 in the Pedregal River Valley (Rouse and Cruxent 1966:35). The region in which the main sites are found is known as El Jobo.

In 1959–1960 Cruxent excavated the site of Muaco, east of Coro, that was discovered in 1952 by Royo y Gómez (1960:154–157). There the first radiocarbon date for the El Jobo complex was obtained from *Glyptodon* scutes, which gave an age of 16,375 ± 400 yr B.P. (Rouse and Cruxent 1966:191; Royo y Gómez 1960:157). In 1962 Cruxent discovered the Taima-taima site, located about 2 km east of Muaco. Both sites are permanent water holes, and Taima-taima was initially baptized as Los Pozos de Royo y Gómez. The first excavations at Taima-taima were carried out between 1962 and 1967 by Cruxent, with further work in 1970. A total area of about 150 m^2 was excavated. In 1969 Cruxent located a nearby new site, Cucuruchu, which was free of possible water-hole modification. An area of 100 m^2 was excavated.

Based on the finds near Coro and those west of Lake Maracaibo (at Manzanillo and Rancho Peludo), Cruxent proposed the existence of a Joboid series, which consists of the succeeding artifact complexes of Camare, Las Lagunas, El Jobo, and Las Casitas. The Camare and Las Lagunas complexes lacked projectile points, which appeared with the El Jobo complex. These lanceolate specimens are characterized by lenticular cross-sections, rounded bases, roughly trimmed edges, and are made of quartzite (Rouse and Cruxent 1966:37). In the later Las Casitas complex, El Jobo points are found in association with "another type of point that has a triangular blade and a stem at its base, by which it remains fixed to the haft" (Rouse and Cruxent 1966:38).

Unfortunately, Cruxent's proposal that different artifact complexes correspond to the various terraces of the Pedregal River (unacceptable from any point of view without geomorphological analysis of the sites) has generated a great distrust on the part of many specialists as regards all finds from this region (Lynch 1983). This position ignores very important data obtained by Cruxent and other investigators. Today we rely on new information offered by excavations and surface finds (Ochsenius and Gruhn 1979; Oliver, personal communication; Rodriguez 1985).

The recent publication of the final report on the 1976 Taima-taima excavations frees me from adding to the accumulation of critical literature on the chronology of the Joboid series—its deficient definition and other problems of analysis—and allows me to concentrate upon the Taima-taima kill site. The report (Ochsenius and Gruhn 1979) discusses topics that contribute to clarifying and solving earlier arguments about the site, as in the case of site chronology.

The discussions on stratigraphy (Bryan 1979) and radiocarbon dates (Bryan and Gruhn 1979) are concrete and clear and, in my judgment, leave no doubt concerning the interpretation of the chronology of the site. In general terms, the stratigraphy of the site is synthesized by Bryan:

> The Late Pleistocene and Holocene sediments at Taima-taima can readily be divided into four units which accumulated on and above a basal cobble pavement. Unit I, the saturated grey sand above the cobble pavement, contains the only undeniable cultural evidence at the site [Bryan 1979:41].

Of the total of 27 available radiocarbon dates, only three appear to be statistically discordant. Although these three dates do not significantly alter the results, the authors (Bryan and Gruhn 1979) reserve the anomalous dates so as not to put at risk the consistency of the chronology. For the focus of this paper, only Unit I, which has been dated between approximately 12,600 and 13,400 yr B.P., is of interest, "the time which the young mastodon was slain and butchered, about 13,000 B.P." (Bryan and Gruhn 1979:56-57).

Although mastodon remains *(Stegomastodon* and *Haplomastodon)* of older individuals appear in the basal layers, the authors consider the remains of the juvenile to be the only irrefutable evidence that mastodon in Unit I were killed by humans. Nonetheless, some adult mastodon bones were used as anvils by the human occupants of this site. Stratigraphic analysis indicates that when the juvenile was killed, a thin layer of sand covered the basal cobble pavement. Therefore, there was no possibility that the animal was mired in slime, nor were its movements impaired, as has been traditionally believed.

The lack of projectile points at some kill sites and the discovery of an El Jobo point fragment in the pelvic cavity of the juvenile mastodon have led the authors to offer diverse explanations. Gruhn (1979) speculates that the hunters may have wounded the victim in a place away from the spring and later chased it until it collapsed at the water hole, often visited by these animals. Ochsenius (1979:93) disagrees with Gruhn's reconstruction of the mastodon's death and does not believe that the animal was forced to the water hole by the hunters. He instead suggests that both humans and animals sought water there, although humans may have been guided by a second intention. Cruxent (1979a) draws our attention to the existence of both young and adult mastodons at Taima-taima, animals that may have been converted to food for hunters. Cruxent suggests that, considering the large size of the prey, a projectile point would have been insufficient and used only as an auxiliary weapon to wound the animal in its vulnerable parts. Cruxent conjectures that the projectile points used for this purpose may have been poisoned by applying Eurphorbiaceae juice (locally called *quaritoto)* over them. After being wounded and poisoned, the animal was finally killed by other means, such as wooden spears, clubs, and stones.

Bones of *Equus, Pararctotherium, Glossotherium, Glyptodon,* and other taxa were contained in the same stratigraphic unit as the mastodon; however, there is no clear evidence that humans were hunting these animals. It is interesting that at the base of the red sand layer immediately above Unit I, on the Unit I/II disconformity, there are no mastodon remains, although remains of *Equus, Macrauchenia, Glyptodon,* and some unidentified bone fragments were found. The absence of mastodon in this horizon, which probably dates to around 11,000 yr B.P., leads Bryan (1979:49) to propose their extinction at this time. Bryan suggests the occurrence of two biophases, distinguished by the absence of mastodon in the second phase, which may be associated with a decrease in humidity. Ochsenius (1979) believes that mastodons migrated during this period to more humid regions, although he advocates climatic continuity in the region of Taima-taima.

The erosive action of the springs makes it difficult to study the tools. Moreover, El Jobo stone and bone tools are not abundant and cannot be easily put into formal categories. In this respect Cruxent declares:

> I am completely convinced that the majority of instruments that are encountered in a Paleoindian kill site are fundamentally circumstantial and 'atypical.' We cannot expect that the lithic or bone artifacts of the hunter must be the same typologically at the kill site as those used in his habitation or living area. There are various reasons for these distinctions between kill sites and campsites: different raw materials utilized, specialized activities at the kill site which are rarely carried out at the base camp, and the simplicity due to improvisation at the kill site [Cruxent 1979b:85].

Lithic tools described by Cruxent are grouped into categories of projectile points, flake tools, and "tools of expediency." Only two of the projectile-point fragments discussed came from the Taima-taima site. Both of these tools were found in the pelvic cavities of mastodons, a provenience that may suggest a particular method of killing these animals. Cruxent analyzed these points, reconstructing the missing parts based on his knowledge of similar specimens. He classifies them as nonstemmed El Jobo lanceolate points, which have been worked by bifacial pressure retouch. A midsection of this type of point can be recognized by the characteristic form of the cross-section. Nonetheless, the reconstruction of an artifact when distal thirds are missing is very risky, since the interpreter may give way to his expectations and construct a model different from the original form. Additionally, some of these artifacts may be knives or multipurpose tools, differentiated from a projectile point by marked retouching on one edge. It is also important to consider that El Jobo points present a certain diversity within the same type category (Cruxent 1979b:79).

Along with two flake tools associated with megafauna bones in Unit I are 14 "tools of expediency." This group is divided into six categories that include a scraper, an anvil, and four other tools groups peculiarly classified according to the characteristics of the handle, or grip. We understand that these are amorphous tools, classified primarily by function rather than form. Finally, the Taima-taima assemblage includes six bone pieces, one of which was used as an anvil; and six flakes, used to separate meat from bones or to skin prey, according to Cruxent's interpretation.

An Archaeological Review of the Highlands

Archaeological investigations of early humans in the highlands area of northern South America have been concentrated in the region of Bogotá, in the enormous *altiplano* of the Sierra Oriental. Although the work accomplished by Correal and Van der Hammen is extensive, I will review here only the data pertaining to the sites of El Abra, Tequendama, and Tibitó. In contrast with the situation in other regions, excavations at these sites have been carried out rigorously and carefully. Data are clear, abundant, and wholly trustworthy, and the description and classification of tools precise and well documented.

Tequendama

In 1970, three years after the initiation of the first research on early humans in Colombia and the conclusion of excavations at the El Abra site, Correal and Van der Hammen located rockshelter sites in Madrid, Ubate, Bojaca, and Soacha. They selected a complex of sandstone rocks located at 2,570 m above sea level in the southwestern part of the *altiplano* of Bogotá, on the outer perimeter of the *altiplano* (Figure 1). This locale would have been a natural route between the Magdalena Valley and the highlands of Bogotá. The site of Tequendama contained an important stratigraphic sequence several meters thick and yielded over 16 radiocarbon dates (Correal and Van der Hammen 1977:39). An abundance of lithic and bone material at the site indicated a series of preceramic occupations, separated by short periods of abandonment. These archaeological levels were called "Occupation Zones." Zone I is correlated with the Guantiva interstadial and the El Abra stadial of the late glacial period, and is thus dated between 12,500 and 10,100 yr B.P. Zone II, dated between 9500 and 8500 yr B.P., corresponds to the beginning of the Holocene period. Zone III, dated between 7000 yr B.P. and 6000 yr B.P., relates to the beginning of the climatic optimum. We will deal here with the first two zones.

It was possible to clearly identify two different tool classes in the site. The first, called the "Tequendamiense Class" by the excavators, is limited to Zone I; that is, it dates to the late Pleistocene. This class is characterized by carefully worked tools, with pressure flaking used to apply delicate marginal retouching on the working edges. "Lidite," the raw material generally used, is fine grained with excellent conchoidal fracture qualities, although quartzite, diorite, or basalt were also used. Many artifacts are made of these foreign materials, which were probably brought from the Magdalena Valley. Plano-convex (keeled) scrapers are typical of this class. Bifaces are also present, although not in large percentages. Examples of these tools include a thin bifacial quartzite blade, a strangulated bifacial implement with bilateral notching, and a bifacial piece that seems to be a reworked projectile-point fragment.

The second tool class, "Abriense," ranges in time from the late Pleistocene to the sixteenth century, the time of the European conquest. Pressure-flaking techniques were never used on these tools; rather, they were made by direct percussion with no platform preparation. No bifacial artifacts have been found and, to be precise, neither have any unifacial tools, since the complete tool face of these artifacts is not worked (Figure 7). Rather, only a few flakes have been removed to achieve the desired edge. This tool class has been defined at the El Abra site as belonging to the "Edge-trimmed Tool Tradition," characterized as follows:

> Diagnostic of the tools of the Edge-trimmed Tool Tradition are simple scrapers, knives, and spokeshaves which have their working edges retouched by percussion flaking. Both cores and flakes are used in the manufacture of these tools. Such tools also have been classified as "simple stonework" by Stothert, who defines the category as shaving artifacts made by the removal of primary flakes from relatively unprepared cores [Hurt et al. 1976:14].

During the deposition of Zone 1, the shelter was located within the open *páramo*. Two fire pits surrounded by mammal bones and two limited areas of tool concentration that were interpreted as workshops were found at the base of the shelter. The animal bones indicate a preference for deer *(Odocoileus* and *Mazama)* (40%) and small mouse *(Sigmodon)* and guinea pig *(Cavia)* (30%). The remaining 30% of the fauna consisted of rabbit *(Sylvilagus)*, armadillo *(Dasypus)*, and kinkajou *(Potos)*. Lithic tools belong to the "Tequendamiense" and "Abriense" classes, although the latter are more frequent. The "Abriense" tools were fabricated at the site using local raw material (chert), whereas the "Tequendamiense" tools were transported, probably from the Magdalena River Valley. Correal and Van der Hammen estimate that:

> the percentage of cutting instruments was more than 50%, scrapers 30%, and perforators 7%. The frequency of concave scrapers is low. Keeled scrapers and laminated knives are found only in this zone and the following. Bone tools are not altogether missing, though few were found, in the high part of the zone [Correal and Van der Hammen 1977:168, see also 107–108].

During the deposition of Zone II, various environmental changes occurred. The beginning of the Holocene had brought the site into the expanding Andes forest zone (Figure 3b,c). The precipitation was much greater than in the preceding period and formed marshy areas on the *altiplano*, although conditions were drier in the immediate area of the site. Several fire pits surrounded by a great number of mammal bones were found within the shelter. In the middle of the shelter, workshops can be clearly observed at the sides of the hearths. Only one object is made of basalt; local chert was used for other tools. This chert is of lesser quality and hardness than the raw material used in Zone I. Faunal remains demonstrate a change in food preference: The relative frequency of deer reaches only around 15%, while rodent remains constitute 75%. These consist of small mouse, guinea pig, and mountain paca *(Stictomys)*. Rabbit, armadillo, shrew *(Cryptotis)*, opossum *(Didelphis)*, long-tailed weasel *(Mustela)*, and puma *(Felis)* are also present. "Tequendamiense" tools with retouched edges disappear from the archaeological record and only "Abriense" tools are found. There is an increase in end scrapers and concave scrapers that may be related to a major dedication to woodworking. Among the refuse around the hearths were snail remains *(Drymaeus* and *Plekocheilus)*, which may have been collected in the neighboring forest.

El Abra

The continuous archaeological sequence and abundant information offered by the Tequendama site clarified results from the previously excavated El Abra site. This

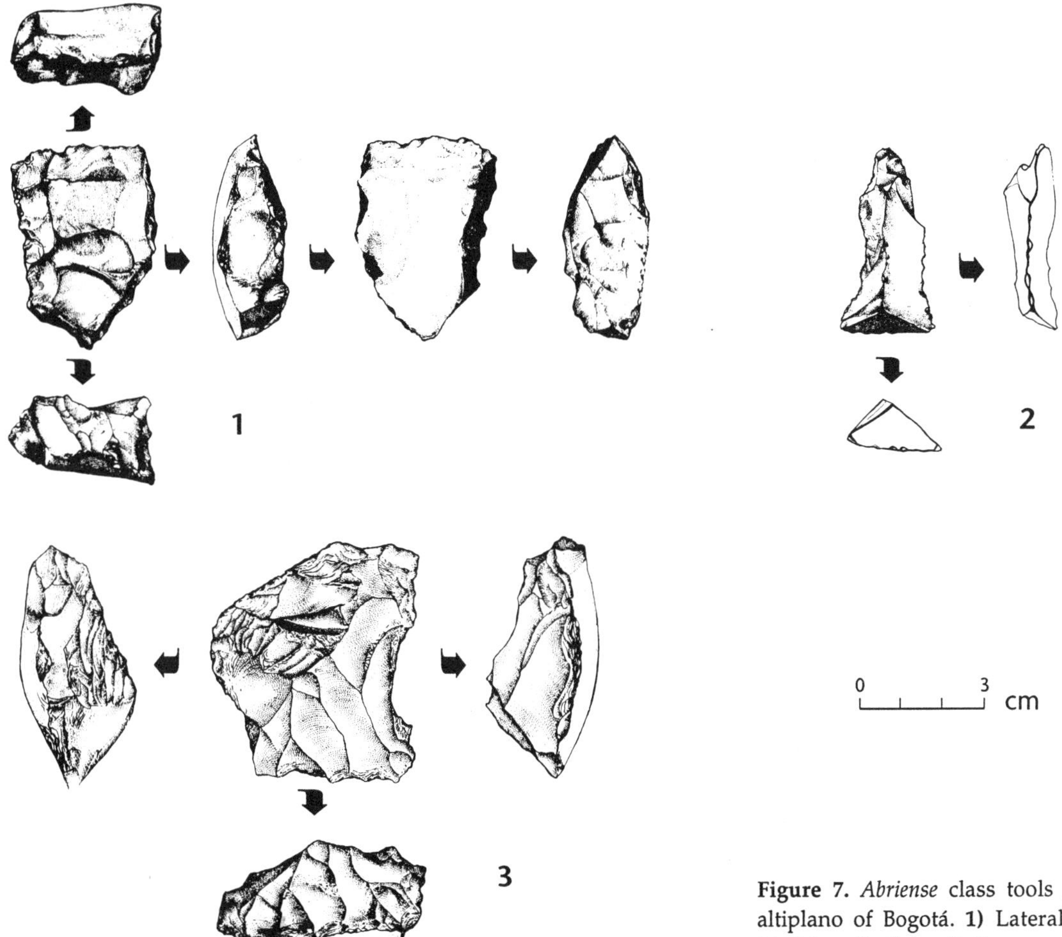

Figure 7. *Abriense* class tools from the altiplano of Bogotá. **1)** Lateral scraper; **2)** Prismatic flake; **3)** Concave scraper.

site is located near the town of Zipaquira in the west-central part of the *altiplano,* a little above the level of the Pleistocene lake of Bogotá. El Abra was the first stratified site in the Colombian or Venezuelan highlands to be studied. From 1967 to 1969 partial excavations were carried out in three shelters on the western side of a narrow corridor with parallel rock walls leading into the high basin of Bogotá.

Five major stratigraphic units extending from the Middle Pleniglacial to the Holocene were defined at this site. Fifteen reliable radiocarbon dates indicate the chronological limits of each sedimentary layer. The archaeological remains proceed from Units C3, C4, D1, D2, and D3, with limiting dates between 12,500 ± 160 and 7250 ± 100 yr B.P. These dates correspond to the late glacial (Guantiva interstadial and El Abra stadial) and early Holocene periods. However, the investigators have doubts about the actual antiquity of human occupation of the shelter:

> The period of the first human occupation of the El Abra rockshelters remains unclear. Before the excavations in 1969, test cuts were placed in critical areas of rockshelters 2 and 3 by Van der Hammen and Correal; later, treasure searchers seriously disturbed the earth fill of shelter 3. In the latter site, 29 small chert flakes were found in a seemingly undisturbed layer at the two-meter deep base of the test quadrant made in 1967. The associated layer apparently corresponded to those belonging to the C2 sediment unit. Judging by carbon 14 dates taken from the overlying C3 level (ca. 13,000–10,000 years B.P.), these tools, if actually found in undisturbed layers, would be older than 12,500 years [Correal et al. 1977:90].

In another publication in reference to the same topic, Van der Hammen and Correal declare:

> A few flakes and artifacts (amongst them two choppers) were found in the El Abra rockshelters in layers corresponding with the Upper Pleniglacial. However, as long as no more abundant and directly dated material is found, not much can

be said about the presence of man in the area of the Sabana de Bogotá. Extremely interesting finds including large choppers and chopping tools on terraces in the Magdalena valley might represent an early tradition, but nothing definite can be said about their age and they might represent local adaptations or survivals of a culture of Late Glacial or Holocene age. However, the prospects of finding satisfactorily datable artifacts of Late Pleniglacial age in Colombia seem to be favorable [Van der Hammen and Correal 1978:183].

More recently, Van der Hammen is more categorical when he affirms:

> the first indications of the presence of man come from the C1/2 level of the El Abra rockshelters: two 'choppers' and some flakes. This layer (calcareous loess material) corresponds mainly to the Fuquene Stadial (approximately 21,000–13/14,000 B.P.) [Van der Hammen 1985:12].

Another problem posed by El Abra is the characteristics of the occupations. Everything seems to indicate that these occupations were of brief duration by a few individuals who only occasionally fabricated their tools in the shelter.

El Abra tools belong to the "Abriense" class or Edge-trimmed Tool tradition. The only artifacts related to the "Tequendamiense" class, or formal retouched tools, are the two aforementioned choppers and a plano-convex (keeled) scraper made of black lidite (and therefore transported from outside of the *altiplano).* The fauna corresponds to the previously described fauna of Tequendama, although we may mention that in situ domestication of the guinea pig occurred a little before the Christian era at this site.

Tibitó

In 1980 Correal excavated Tibitó, a site north of Bogotá in which evidence of human intervention in the form of various zones of burned bones of extinct fauna is incontrovertible. Very close to the site are terraces where lithic artifacts had been surface collected, although neither megafauna remains or projectile points had been found. Knowing that Van der Hammen had previously collected a fragment of mastodon molar in the vicinity, Correal explored the area until locating a concentration of fragmented mastodon *(Cuveronius hyodon, Haplomastodon)* and horse *(Equus)* bones. A few tools, deer bones, and charcoal closely associated with the megafauna remains were recovered from an unaltered stratum sealed by recent sediments. This stratum produced a date of 11,740 ± 110 yr B.P. (Correal 1981); that is, within the Guantiva interstadial and corresponding to Zone I of Tequendama and more clearly defined occupations at El Abra.

The associated bones belong to several individuals of differing species, a fact which leads Correal to interpret Tibitó as a kill and butchering site. Correal emphasizes that the:

> selective disposition of remains in zones 1-2-3 [three distinct horizontal zones of concentration of artifacts, bone fragments, and charcoal] . . . zones in which associations of molar teeth (principally) are evident and some remains of postcranial skeletons (horse and mastodon) . . . this new situation, as well as the total absence of mastodon limb bones, obliges us to consider the character of zones 1-2-3 within a cultural context much broader than that which transcends from the simple act of killing and carving up the remains of game animals [Correal 1981:129–130].

Associated tools include scrapers made on cores, cutting flakes, and a few bone perforators. All these artifacts can be included in the "Abriense" class, with the exception of a carefully worked plano-convex (keeled) scraper ("Tequendamiense"), similar to those from Tequendama, El Abra, the lowlands of the Magdalena, and some tools in the Joboid series. It seems that some deer and mastodon bones were also used as tools. Again, projectile points are absent.

OVERVIEW AND CONCLUSIONS

Early human sites in northern South America exhibit a wide technological diversity. If it is true that many things are known from the highlands and some sectors of the lowlands, there remain enormous territories completely unknown or erroneously outlined, so that any attempt to generalize or to explain is difficult.

Working from the best-known data, we may propose a hypothetical model of the first peopling of this region. During the Upper Pleniglacial (21,000–14,000 yr B.P.), cold climatic conditions prevailed in the highlands and dry conditions in the lowlands. These conditions led to the descent of the tree line to 2,000 m in elevation and to the establishment of open contact areas between sectors of the Magdalena Valley and the *altiplano* west of the Sierra Oriental, and between the Orinoco *llanos* and the *altiplano* to the east (Figure 3b). These conditions resulted in movement of fauna (particularly mastodons) between the open lowlands and the extensive non-forested regions of the *altiplano.* Surely, at the end of the Upper Pleniglacial, human groups ascended to the *altiplano* during part of the year, carrying with them tools ("Tequendamiense"), which they had fabricated in the Magdalena Valley. These tools included end scrapers, laminated knives, plano-convex scrapers, and heavy choppers. On the *altiplano,* they made more extensive use of flakes or fragments of local chert and limited edge retouch ("Abriense"). These people were hunters of mastodon, horse, and deer (at Tibitó) and, in lesser proportion, of minor rodent species (at Tequendama), although we do not yet know their hunting methods. All factors seem to indicate that these hunters probably returned to the Magdalena Valley, where they dwelt for most of the year (see Van der Hammen 1981:86, 1985). It is probable that the hunting groups that visited the *altiplano* prior to the Guantiva interstadial brought lithic projectile points with them that have not been found. However, from the moment of their establishment in the highlands, they would have replaced stone with other material (wood, bone, antler) when unable to find appropriate stone for the fabrication of projectiles.

In the late glacial (14,000–10,000 yr B.P.), especially during the Guantiva interstadial (12,500–11,000 yr B.P.), precipitation increased noticeably and the tree line began to ascend, reaching an altitude of 3,000 m. Open areas decreased in size and forest vegetation covered a great part of the *altiplano*. In the lowlands the increase in humidity led to the enlargement of the forest zone. At this time the "open bridges" between lowlands and *altiplano* closed, isolating human and animal populations (Van der Hammen 1981, 1986d).

We have proof that by the end of the Upper Pleniglacial (± 14,000 yr B.P.), human groups were present in several areas of northern South America, including the *altiplano* of Bogotá and Taima-taima. This implies that humans must have been present in northern South America from at least the beginning of the Upper Pleniglacial (± 21,000 yr B.P.). If we consider that the first occupants of shelters in the Bogotá area transported their tools from the neighboring Magdalena Valley, we may assume that at the end of the Upper Pleniglacial there were groups that fabricated and used bifacial tools in the Magdalena Valley. Large and heavy choppers are found in that area, though their association is not conclusive. (See El Abra and the archaeological review of the lowlands). In the lowlands, the Upper Pleniglacial was a dry period that allowed the expansion of open or semi-open vegetational zones. This situation, however, did not equally affect all lowland regions, but influenced climatic conditions in a manner directly proportional to present conditions (naturally with small exceptions caused by current anthropogenic alterations), making today's dry zones drier and amplifying their extent, and decreasing humidity in zones that are humid today. In the same way, open vegetational "bridges" were established between lowlands and highlands. Likewise, "bridges" connecting dry and open areas occurred along the Magdalena River and on the Caribbean Coast. A similar situation led to the formation of extensive savannas and restricted forest environments in the Orinoco *llanos*.

Accepting in general terms the model of settlement proposed by Ranere (1980) for Central America, we must consider that the first settlers of northern South America had adapted to the characteristics of the dry tropical lowlands during their crossing through Central America. Large prey (mastodon, horse, deer) lived in dry environments with open or semi-open vegetation (see Correal 1981; De Porta 1961; Hoffstetter 1975; Ochsenius 1979, 1980a; Van der Hammen 1981, 1985, 1986d). Judging by the location of the main concentrations of lithic tools (especially choppers and keeled scrapers) in the Magdalena Valley and on the Atlantic Coast, it appears that these peoples preferred to settle in the ecotone zones between open and forested territories, which offered the advantage of resources available from various environments.

The presence of choppers and keeled scrapers in all these localities can be explained by a relatively quick colonization of the Caribbean lowlands and some of the inter-Andean valleys (especially the Magdalena Valley). This colonization would have been possible because of equitable climatic conditions and the presence of human inhabitants in neighboring territories (see Borrero 1983; Bryan 1978; Lynch 1983). The Guantiva interstadial (12,500–11,000 yr B.P.) is manifested in the lowlands by an increase in precipitation and by the expansion of dense forest from its original area that would have impeded contacts between open areas. This expansion noticeably decreased and isolated human and animal groups, with the result that the former diversified culturally and the latter, the megafauna, became extinct. Thus, at the end of the Pleistocene, we would find that a great cultural diversification had commenced in northern South America, which relates to an independent origin of some features such as fluting of projectile points. The date of ca. 13,000 yr B.P. suggested for the El Jobo point type coincides with the Guantiva interstadial, which may explain the very localized distribution of El Jobo. The problem arises when attempting to explain the association of El Jobo points with other elements (choppers and keeled scrapers) that exhibit broad dispersal patterns.

During the El Abra stadial (dated between 11,000 and 10,000 yr B.P.), projectile points probably corresponded to the Madden Lake type that has been reported for the Caribbean area (Figure 6). As the type name indicates, the fabricators of these points (as well as their descendants) may have had a close relationship with fabricators of similar artifacts described in Panama (Bird and Cooke 1978, 1979), although I do not believe such a nexus extended farther south (see Bird 1969; Borrero 1983; Lynch 1983; Schobinger 1972). The points recently described from Popayán (Illere and Gnecco 1986) may belong to the same period and be related to the El Inga assemblages, but they are not related to the points from the Caribbean. The presence of stems, traditionally considered a late feature, and the occurrence of fluting or basal thinning, typically considered early traits, suggest that Restrepo points pertain to the early Holocene period.

As other authors have pointed out (Bray 1984:308), northern South America was characterized by both great cultural diversity and stability during the late glacial and early Holocene periods. The human adaptive patterns (where known in the *altiplano)* exhibit an extraordinary permanence, with each phase lasting a thousand years and displaying only slight changes in tool-type frequencies.

In any case, nothing can be concluded beyond the working hypotheses until more extensive programs are undertaken in the lowlands of northern South America, research programs that will allow us to locate and excavate datable stratified sites. The extensive Caribbean lowlands of Colombia and Venezuela, the long inter-Andean valleys (especially the Magdalena Valley), the enormous Orinoco savanna regions, and the eastern foothills of the Andes possess the keys for understanding the settlement of South America. I would be satisfied if my paper stimulated field research in those regions.

ACKNOWLEDGMENTS

I am grateful to Gonzalo Correal, Thomas Lynch, J.R. Oliver, Gerardo Reichel-Dolmatoff, and Thomas Van der Hammen for their counsel, suggestions, and discussion; and for permission to use personal communications or materials not yet published. I would like to thank Robson Bonnichsen and Thomas Lynch for the invitation to participate in the INQUA symposium. I am also grateful to Roberto Lleras for his collaboration in the preparation of an English text, to Ruth Gruhn for her painstaking work in correcting the manuscript, and especially to Monica Lucia Espinosa for her sustained assistance.

REFERENCES CITED

Absy, M. L.
1979a *A Palynological Study of Holocene Sediments in the Amazon Basin.* Master's thesis, University of Amsterdam, the Netherlands.
1979b Quaternary Palynological Studies in the Amazon Basin. *Abstracts of the Fifth Symposium of International Association for Tropical Biology.* La Guaira, Venezuela.

Ardila, G.
1985 El Hombre Temprano en Colombia. Ms. in possession of author.
1986 Fechados y Bibliografía Sobre la Etapa Lítica en Colombia. *Maguaré* 3(3):63–74. Revista del Departamento de Antropología de la Universidad Nacional de Colombia, Bogotá.

Bird, J.
1969 A Comparison of South Chilean and Ecuadorian "Fishtail" Projectile Points. *The Kroeber Anthropological Society Papers* 40:52–71.

Bird, J., and R. Cooke
1977 Los Artefactos más Antiguos de Panamá. *Revista Nacional de Cultura* 6:7–31. Panamá.
1978 The Occurrence in Panama of Two Types of Paleo-Indian Projectile Points. In *Early Man in America from a Circum-Pacific Perspective,* edited by A. L. Bryan, pp. 263–272. Occasional Papers No. 1. Department of Anthropology, University of Alberta, Edmonton.

Borrero, L. A.
1983 Distribuciones Discontinuas de Puntas de Proyectil en Sudamérica. Paper presented at the 11th International Congress of Anthropological and Ethnological Sciences, Vancouver.

Bray, W.
1984 Across the Darien Gap: A Colombian View of Isthmian Archaeology. In *The Archaeology of Lower Central America,* edited by F. W. Lange and D. Stone, pp. 305–338. University of New Mexico Press, Albuquerque.

Bryan, A. L. (editor)
1978 *Early Man in America from a Circum-Pacific Perspective.* Occasional Papers No. 1. Department of Anthropology, University of Alberta, Edmonton.

Bryan, A. L.
1979 The Stratigraphy of Taima-taima. In *Taima-taima: A Late Pleistocene Paleo-Indian Kill Site in Northernmost South America. Final Report on the 1976 Excavations,* edited by C. Ochsenius and R. Gruhn, pp. 41–52. Programa CIPICS, Monografias Cientifica, Universidad Francisco de Miranda, Coro, Venezuela.

Bryan, A. L., and R. Gruhn
1979 The Radiocarbon Dates of Taima-taima. In *Taima-taima: A Late Pleistocene Paleo-Indian Kill Site in Northernmost South America. Final Report on the 1976 Excavations,* edited by C. Ochsenius and R. Gruhn, pp. 53–58. Programa CIPICS, Monografias Cientifica, Universidad Francisco de Miranda, Coro, Venezuela.

Correal Urrego, G.
1977 Exploraciones Arqueológicas en la Costa Atlántica y Valle del Magdalena. Sitios Precerámicos y Tipologías Líticas. *Caldasia* 11(55):33–129. Bogotá.
1981 *Evidencias Culturales y Megafauna Pleistocénica en Colombia.* Fundación de Investigaciones Arqueológicas Nacionales, Banco de la República. Bogotá.

1983 Evidencia de Cazadores Especializados en el Sitio de La Gloria, Golfo de Urabá. *Revista de la Academia Colombiana de Ciencias Exactas, Físicas y Naturales* 15:77–82.

Correal Urrego, G., and T. Van der Hammen
1977 *Investigaciones Arqueológicas en los Abrigos Rocosos del Tequendama.* Biblioteca del Banco Popular, Premios de Arqueología No.1. Bogotá.

Correal Urrego, G., T. Van der Hammen, and W. Hurt
1977 La Ecología y Tecnología de los Abrigos Rocosos en El Abra. *Revista de la Universidad Nacional* 15:77–99.

Cruxent, J.
1979a Observations Concerning Mastodon Procurement at Taima-taima. In *Taima-taima: A Late Pleistocene Paleo-Indian Kill Site in Northernmost South America. Final Report on the 1976 Excavations,* edited by C. Ochsenius and R. Gruhn, pp. 105–108. Programa CIPICS, Monografias Cientifica, Universidad Francisco de Miranda, Coro, Venezuela.

1979b Stone and Bone Artifacts from Taima-taima. In *Taima-taima: A Late Pleistocene Paleo-Indian Kill Site in Northernmost South America. Final Report on the 1976 Excavations,* edited by C. Ochsenius and R. Gruhn, pp. 77–89. Programa CIPICS, Monografias Cientifica, Universidad Francisco de Miranda, Coro, Venezuela.

De Porta, J.
1961 La Posición Estratigráfica de la Fauna de Mamíferos del Pleistoceno de la Sabana de Bogotá. *Boletín de Geología* 7:37–104. Universidad Industrial de Santander, Bucaramanga.

Gnecco, C.
1982 *Excavaciones Arqueológicas en Los Arboles. Cajbío, Cauca.* Informe manuscrito presentado a la Fundación de Investigaciones Arqueológicas Nacionales. Banco de la Republica, Bogotá.

Gruhn, R.
1979 Synthesis: A Reconstruction. In *Taima-taima: A Late Pleistocene Paleo-Indian Kill Site in Northernmost South America. Final Report on the 1976 Excavations,* edited by C. Ochsenius and R. Gruhn, pp. 109–110. Programa CIPICS, Monografias Cientifica, Universidad Francisco de Miranda, Coro, Venezuela.

Hoffstetter, R.
1971 Los Vertebrados Cenozoicos de Colombia: Yacimientos, Faunas, Problemas Planteados. *Geología Colombiana* 8:37–62. Universidad Nacional de Colombia, Bogotá.

Hurt, W. R., T. Van der Hammen, and G. Correal Urrego
1976 *The El Abra Rockshelters, Sabana de Bogotá, Colombia, South America.* Indiana University Museum Occasional Papers and Monographs, No. 2. Bloomington.

Illera, C. H., and C. Gnecco
1986 Puntas de Proyectil en el Valle de Popayán. *Boletín Museo del Oro* 17:44–57. Bogotá.

Krieger, A.
1974 *El Hombre Primitivo en América.* Ediciones Nueva Visión, Buenos Aires.

Lynch, T.
1983 The Paleo-Indians. In *Ancient South Americans,* edited by Jesse Jennings, pp. 87–137. W. H. Freeman and Company, San Francisco.

Mayer-Oakes, W. J.
1986 El Inga: A Paleo-Indian Site in the Sierra of Northern Ecuador. *Transactions of the American Philosophical Society* 76(4). Philadelphia.

Meggers, B.
1976 Fluctuación Vegetacional y Adaptación Cultural Prehistórica en Amazonia: Algunas Correlaciones Tentativas. *Relaciones de la Sociedad Argentina de Antropología* 10:11–26.

1979 Climatic Oscillation as a Factor in the Prehistory of Amazonia. *American Antiquity* 44:252–266.

n.d. Aplicación del Modelo Biológico de Diversificación a las Distribuciones Culturales en las Tierras Tropicales Bajas de Sudamérica. *Amazonia Peruana* 4(8):7–38. Lima.

Monasterio, M.
1980 Los Paramos Andinos como Región Natural. Características Biogeográficas Generales y Afinidades con otras Regiones Andinas. In *Estudios Ecológicos en los Páramos Andinos,* edited by M. Monasterio, pp. 15–27. Universidad de los Andes, Mérida, Venezuela.

Ochsenius, C.
1979 Paleoecology of Taima-taima and Its Surroundings. In *Taima-taima: A Late Pleistocene Paleo-Indian Kill Site in Northernmost South America. Final Report on the 1976 Excavations,* edited by C. Ochsenius and R. Gruhn, pp. 91–103. Programa CIPICS, Monografias Cientifica, Universidad Francisco de Miranda, Coro, Venezuela.

1980a *Cuaternario en Venezuela. Introducción a ia Paleoecología en el Norte de Sudamérica.* Cuadernos Falconianos. Ediciones UNEFM, Coro, Venezuela.

1980b *Palinología en Sudamérica. Breve Reseña sobre las*

Floras del Cuaternario Superior. Cuadernos Falconianos. Ediciones UNEFM, Coro, Venezuela.

1981 Ecología del Pleistoceneo Tardío en el Cinturón Arido Pericaribeño. *Revista CIAF* 6(1–3):365–372. Bogotá.

Ochsenius, C., and R. Gruhn (editors)
1979 *Taima-taima: A Late Pleistocene Paleo-Indian Kill Site in Northernmost South America. Final Report on the 1976 Excavations*. Programa CIPICS, Monografias Cientifica, Universidad Francisco de Miranda, Coro, Venezuela.

Ortiz-Troncoso, O. R.
1985 Poblamiento Temprano del Litoral de Sudamérica. Paper presented at the 45 Congreso Internacional de Americanistas, Bogotá.

Oster, R.
1979 Las Precipitaciones en Colombia. *Colombia Geográfica* 6(2). Instituto Geográfico Agustín Codazzi, Bogotá.

Ranere, A.
1980 Human movement into Tropical America at the End of the Pleistocene. In *Anthropological Papers in Memory of Earl H. Swanson, Jr.*, edited by L. Harten, C. Warren, and D. Tuohy, pp. 41–47. Special Publication of the Idaho State Museum of Natural History, Pocatello.

Reichel-Dolmatoff, G.
1986 *Arqueología de Colombia: Un Texto Introductorio.* Fundación Segunda Expedición Botánica, Bogotá.

Robledo, E.
1955 Migraciones Oceánicas en el Poblamiento de Colombia. *Boletín Instituto de Antropología* 1(3):215–234. Medellín.

Rodríguez, M. H.
1985 Grupos Precerámicos del Noroccidente de Venezuela y su Relación con la Cuenca del Lago de Maracaibo. *Gens* 1(2):38–53. Caracas.

Rouse, I., and J. Cruxent
1966 *Arqueología Venezolana.* Ediciones Vega, Caracas.

Royo y Gómez, J.
1960 El Yacimiento de Vertebrados Prehistóricos de Muaco, Edo. Falcón, Venezuela, con Industria Lítica Asociada. *International Geological Congress, Reports of 21st Session* 4:154–157. Copenhagen.

Salgado-Labouriau, M. L.
1980 Paleocología de Los Páramos Venezolanos. In *Estudios Ecológicos en los Páramos Andinos,* edited by M. Monasterio, pp. 158–169. Universidad de los Andes, Mérida, Venezuela.

Schobinger, J.
1972 Nuevos Hallazgos de Puntas "Colas de Pescado," y Consideraciones en Torno al Origen y Dispersión de la Cultura de Cazadores Superiores Toldense (Fell I) en Sudamérica. *Atti del 40 Congresso Internazionale de gli Americanisti* 1:33–50. Genoa.

Schubert, C.
1980 Aspectos Geológicos de Los Andes Venezolanos: Historia, Breve Síntesis, el Cuaternario y Bibliografía. In *Estudios Ecológicos en los Páramos Andinos*, edited by M. Monasterio, pp. 29–45. Universidad de los Andes, Mérida, Venezuela.

Van der Hammen, T.
1981 Environmental Changes in the Northern Andes and the Extinction of Mastodon. *Geologie en Mijnbouw* 60:369–372. Amsterdam.

1985 Paleoecología y Estratigrafía de Yacimientos Precerámicos de Colombia. Paper presented at the 45 Congreso Internacional de Americanistas, Bogotá.

1986a Fluctuaciones Holocénicas del Nivel Inundaciones en la Cuenca del Bajo Magdalena—Cauca—San Jorge (Colombia). *Geología Norandina* 10:11–18. Bogotá.

1986b *The Paleoecology of Tropical South America.* Netherlands Foundation for the Advancement of Tropical Research (Wotro), Report for the Year 1982, pp. 35–91. The Hague.

1986c La Sabana de Bogotá y Su Lago en el Pleniglacial Medio. *Caldasia* 15:249–262.

1986d Cambios Medioambientales y la Extinción del Mastodonte en el Norte de los Andes. *Revista de Antropología* 2(1–2). Universidad de los Andes, Bogotá.

Van der Hammen, T., and G. Correal Urrego
1978 Prehistoric Man on the Sabana de Bogotá: Data for an Ecological Prehistory. *Palaeogeography, Palaeoclimatology, and Palaeoecology* 25:179–190.

Wijmstra, T. A., and T. Van der Hammen
1966 Palynological Data on the History of Tropical Savannas in Northern South America. *Leidse Geologische Mededelingen* 38:71–90. Leiden.

Stratified Radiocarbon-dated Archaeological Sites of Clovis Age and Older in Brazil

RUTH GRUHN
Department of Anthropology
University of Alberta
Edmonton, AB, Canada T6G 2H4

Six stratified occupation sites in Brazil have yielded radiocarbon dates of 11,000 yr B.P. or older. The oldest site, Toca do Boqueirão da Pedra Furada in Piauí, is a large rockshelter with a continuous series of occupation levels extending back to more than 32,000 yr B.P. A flake and pebble tool industry occurs with hearths in the occupation levels dated between 32,000 and 17,000 yr B.P.; and there is evidence for rock art at this time. An occupation level at a nearby rockshelter, Toca do Sitio do Meio, has a radiocarbon date of 14,300 yr B.P. In Minas Gerais three rockshelters, Lapa Vermelha IV, Abrigo de Santana do Riacho, and Lapa do Boquete, have radiocarbon-dated evidence of occupation before 11,000 yr B.P. (back to 15,300 yr B.P. and more at Lapa Vermelha). Utilized quartz or chert flakes and cores are featured in the early assemblages. The stratified open site of Alice Boër, in the state of São Paulo, yielded a stemmed projectile point and uniface chert tools from a level radiocarbon dated to 14,200 yr B.P., and there are uniface chert artifacts in stratigraphically lower levels. These late Pleistocene Brazilian assemblages do not in any way resemble Clovis technology. They indicate that eastern South America was settled by populations with unspecialized lithic industries well before the appearance of the Clovis complex in North America.

This contribution to the symposium is meant to serve as a reminder that the earliest radiocarbon-dated archaeological materials in a large part of the Western Hemisphere bear no conceivable relationship to Clovis; and are dated so early that they flatly contradict the notion that the Clovis complex represents the initial peopling of the New World. For the vast scrub-forest upland area of eastern Brazil, there are now known a half-dozen well-stratified and radiocarbon-dated occupation sites (Figure 1) that are over 11,000 years old, with unspecialized lithic industries that are nothing like Clovis. Reports have been published on all of these sites; and a fine

Figure 1. Map of Brazil indicating location of sites mentioned in text: **1)** Alice Boër; **2)** Lapa Vermelha IV; **3)** Abrigo de Santana do Riacho; **4)** Lapa do Boquete; **5)** Toca do Boqueirão da Pedra Furada; **6)** Toca do Sitio do Meio.

summary, well illustrated with stratigraphic profiles, has recently been provided by Prous (1986a). However, North American archaeologists have not yet familiarized themselves with this literature. I will review each site very briefly, with the expectation that readers of this paper will go on to examine the original detailed reports cited.

Starting in the south, the Alice Boër site is located near the city of Rio Claro in the state of São Paulo, on a tributary of the Paraná River. Excavations at the site were initiated in the early 1970s by Maria Beltrão (Beltrão 1974; Bryan and Beltrão 1978; Hurt 1986); and further work is proposed for the locality. The site is situated on the flood-plain terrace, and the deposits consist of alluvial sands and gravels. The main cultural zone is a 2-m-thick stratum of clayey sand, Bed III, with fine bedding unfortunately much disturbed by ants; but the zone contains artifacts and flakes of chert throughout. Thermoluminescence dates on suitable burned chert flakes from the upper part of Bed III range in a stratigraphic series from approximately 2200 to 11,000 yr B.P. (Beltrão et al. 1986). Below this section, a small charcoal sample from the midpart of Bed III yielded a radiocarbon date of 14,200 yr B.P., with a very large range of statistical error. Associated with this horizon was the earliest example of a contracting-stemmed bifacial projectile point, a type that continued throughout the upper part of Bed III. Although such an early date for a bifacially flaked projectile point must be verified by further work in the locality, the fact remains that the thermoluminescence and radiocarbon dates are stratigraphically consistent, and that artifacts were recovered from even lower strata. A few unifacially retouched flakes and burins were found in the lower part of Bed III below the level of the radiocarbon sample. Below a sterile riverine sand deposit (Bed IV) was an alluvial gravel stratum, Bed V. A unifacial core scraper, a unifacial end/side scraper, and several chert flakes were found on the surface of Bed V.

Farther north, in Minas Gerais State, the area of Lagoa Santa, an extensive limestone zone with many fossiliferous caves just north of the city of Belo Horizonte, has attracted the interest of researchers concerned with the question of early humans since the nineteenth century. In the 1970s intensive scientific excavations in the area were carried out by Annette Laming-Emperaire and her associates, who concentrated upon a large rockshelter known as Lapa Vermelha IV (Laming-Emperaire 1979; Laming-Emperaire et al. 1975; Prous 1986a, 1986b).

Lapa Vermelha IV is located at the top of a steep slope, above a small basin. The rockshelter proved to be the mouth of a solution cavern. Sediments below 9 m depth were restricted to the mouth of a solution tube only 2 m wide. Scattered bones of a single individual *Glossotherium* were found in red clay sediments at a depth of 11.4 to 11.9 m, below a date of 9520 yr B.P. Below this level, a consistent stratigraphic series of four radiocarbon dates on charcoal in the sediments filling a very narrow crevice next to the cave wall ranged from 10,200 ± 200 yr B.P. to 15,300 ± 400 yr B.P. Human skeletal remains, including a cranium, mandible, pelvic fragments, and long bones, were found here in the zone dated between 10,200 and 11,600 yr B.P., along with a few flakes and cores of quartz (an exotic material), and scattered fragments of charcoal. The very oldest sedimentary zone, earlier than the crevice fill and therefore older than 15,000 yr B.P., yielded charcoal fragments, a few quartz flakes and cores, and a unifacially retouched side scraper of metamorphosed limestone. Radiocarbon dates of 22,410 yr B.P. and >25,000 yr B.P. were obtained from this oldest sedimentary zone.

Farther north of Belo Horizonte, excavations have been carried out in the Abrigo de Santana do Riacho, a very large rockshelter in the Serra do Cipó, a quartzite formation about 60 km north of Lagoa Santa, by André Prous and his associates (Prous 1981, 1986a, 1986b). A number of human burials were exposed in levels radiocarbon dated between 7900 and 9460 yr B.P. Only a very restricted area of a lower zone, Level 8, was exposed; but a large hearth, several flakes of quartz crystal, and fragments of red ocher were found in this lower zone. A radiocarbon date of 11,960 ± 250 yr B.P. was obtained on charcoal from the hearth. Bedrock was not reached in the excavation.

Much farther north in Minas Gerais, about 30 km northwest of the town of Januária, is another extensive limestone zone with many caves and rockshelters, located during a survey by Alan Bryan and myself in 1976. Test excavations have been initiated by André Prous and associates in a large rockshelter known as the Lapa do Boquete (Prous 1986a, 1986b). A test excavation proceeded through stratified silt deposits with abundant evidence of human occupation to a stalagmitic deposit. The occupation level just above the stalagmitic deposit featured thick plano-convex end scrapers and scrapers made on flakes. A radiocarbon date of 11,000 ± 1100 yr B.P. was obtained on a charcoal sample from this occupation level. Within the stalagmitic deposit was possible evidence of an earlier occupation, in the form of a dozen chert flakes and fragments which may have been utilized. The test excavation was forced to close before reaching the bedrock floor.

The longest essentially continuous occupation sequence in the New World, well stratified and radiocarbon dated, has been uncovered in several seasons of excavation at the large rockshelter known as the Toca do Boqueirão da Pedra Furada (Delibrias and Guidon 1986; Guidon 1984, 1986; Guidon and Delibrias 1986), in the state of Piauí in Northeast Brazil. By 1986 excavations in one-half of the rockshelter had reached a depth of about 4 m. The early deposits are of sand and sandstone clasts derived by weathering from the high sandstone overhang that forms the shelter. The radiocarbon dates, which occur in a consistent series, are on charcoal from hearths. Two dates of about 32,000 yr B.P. came from the lowest level excavated as of 1986; eight dates ranging from about 30,000 to 23,000 yr B.P. from the next higher early level; a date of about 21,000 yr B.P. from the third higher early level; and a date of about 17,000 yr B.P. for the fourth higher early level. Evidence for rock art, in the form of wall spalls bearing red paint, occurred directly associated with the dated hearths in the levels dated at ca. 32,000 years ago, between 30,000 and 23,000 years ago, and 17,000 years ago. It has recently been announced that further excavations in 1987 have revealed even lower occupation levels and produced radiocarbon dates greater than 39,000 yr B.P. (Guidon and Parenti n.d.).

Guidon has designated the lithic assemblages from the early levels (as of 1986, totaling over 2,000 artifacts) the Pedra Furada phase; divided into four stages on the basis of shifts in frequency of artifact types. The artifacts are made on pebbles and flakes of quartz or quartzite by unifacial direct percussion or bipolar percussion. Tool types include pebble choppers, pointed pebbles, a variety of flake scrapers, denticulated flakes, and hammerstones; and there are many cores and unretouched flakes.

The long sequence at the Toca do Boqueirão da Pedra Furada is not unique in the area. A few kilometers away is the large rockshelter known as the Toca do Sitio do Meio (Guidon 1984, 1986). At this site, stratigraphy was less clear owing to very large boulders incorporated in the fill, making it difficult to trace the lower strata continuously across the area of excavation. However, four radiocarbon dates ranging from 12,000 yr B.P. to 14,300 yr B.P. were obtained on samples of charcoal from hearths in the lowest levels reached by excavation. Numerous artifacts of quartz or quartzite, including pebble choppers, retouched flakes, and hammerstones, were recovered from the lower levels. In future projected work at this site, Guidon hopes to be able to move the boulders and proceed much deeper to bedrock. She fully expects material as early as the Pedra Furada phase.

These late Pleistocene occupation sites in eastern Brazil feature unspecialized lithic industries, consisting in most cases of amorphous flakes and cores of chert or quartz with limited retouch or simply utilized working edges. Such industries are well known from Upper Pleistocene contexts in northern China (Qiu 1985; Jia and Huang 1985) and in Southeast Asia (Anderson 1987). It is likely that these simple tools, comprising distinctive lithic traditions that continued throughout the prehistoric sequences in eastern Brazil, were used to shape a variety of wooden weapons and utensils; such items made up 99% of the material culture of interior Brazilian tribes in the ethnographic present. Unfortunately, due to poor preservation of food refuse, very little direct information pertaining to the subsistence economy of the late Pleistocene peoples of eastern Brazil is available at this time.

In sum, these six well-stratified and radiocarbon-dated occupation sites indicate the presence of human populations with unspecialized lithic industries in eastern Brazil in the late Pleistocene, millennia before the appearance of the Clovis complex in North America. The notion of the Clovis hunters as the initial population of the New World is rendered untenable by the South American data. The Clovis complex was only a regional North American phenomenon, and a comparatively late one at that. To understand the circumstances of the initial peopling of the New World, it is imperative to maintain a broad hemisphere-wide perspective and to consider other models of human migration and adaptation (e.g., Fladmark 1978,1979; Gruhn 1988).

REFERENCES CITED

Anderson, D. D.
1987 A Pleistocene-Early Holocene Rock Shelter in Peninsular Thailand. *National Geographic Research* 3:184–198.

Beltrão, M. M. C.
1974 Datacões Arqueológicas Mais Antigas do Brasil. *Anais da Academia Brasileira de Ciencias* 46:211–251.

Beltrão, M. M. C., C. R. Enriquez, J. Danon, E. Zuleta, and G. Poupeau
1986 Thermoluminescence Dating of Burnt Cherts from the Alice Boër Site, Brazil. In *New Evidence*

for the Pleistocene Peopling of the Americas, edited by A. L. Bryan, pp. 203–213. Center for the Study of Early Man, University of Maine, Orono.

Bryan, A. L., and M. M. C. Beltrão
1978 An Early Stratified Sequence near Rio Claro, East-central São Paulo State, Brazil. In *Early Man in America from a Circum-Pacific Perspective*, edited by A. L. Bryan, pp. 303–305. Occasional Papers No. 1. Department of Anthropology, University of Alberta, Edmonton.

Delibras, G., and N. Guidon
1986 The Rock Shelter Toca do Boqueirão do Sitio da Pedra Furada. *L'Anthropologie* 90:307–316.

Fladmark, K. R.
1978 The Feasibility of the Northwest Coast as a Migration Route for Early Man. In *Early Man in America from a Circum-Pacific Perspective*, edited by A. L. Bryan, pp. 119–128. Occasional Papers No. 1. Department of Anthropology, University of Alberta, Edmonton.
1979 Routes: Alternate Migration Corridors for Early Man in North America. *American Antiquity* 44:55–69.

Gruhn, R.
1988 Linguistic Evidence in Support of the Coastal Route of Earliest Entry into the New World. *Man* 23:77–100.

Guidon, N.
1984 Les Premières Occupations Humaines de l'Aire Archéologique de São Raimundo Nonato—Piauí—Brésil. *L'Anthropologie* 88:263–271.
1986 Las Unidades Culturales de São Raimundo Nonato Sudeste del Estado de Piauí—Brasil. In *New Evidence for the Pleistocene Peopling of the Americas*, edited by A. L. Bryan, pp. 157–171. Center for the Study of Early Man, University of Maine, Orono.

Guidon, N., and G. Delibrias
1986 Carbon-14 Dates Point to Man in the Americas 32,000 Years Ago. *Nature* 321:769–771.

Guidon, N., and F. Parenti
n.d. Toca do Boqueirão do Sitio da Pedra Furada: Escavações 1987. Ms. in possession of authors.

Hurt, W. R.
1986 The Cultural Relationships of the Alice Boër Site, State of São Paulo, Brazil. In *New Evidence for the Pleistocene Peopling of the Americas*, edited by A. L. Bryan, pp. 215–220. Center for the Study of Early Man, University of Maine, Orono.

Jia Lanpo, and Huang Weiwen
1985 The Late Palaeolithic of China. In *Palaeoanthropology and Palaeolithic Archaeology in the People's Republic of China*, edited by Wu Rukang and J. W. Olson, pp. 211–223. Academic Press, New York.

Laming-Emperaire, A.
1979 Missions Archéologiques Franco-bresiliennes de Lagoa Santa, Minas Gerais, Brésil—le Gran Abri de Lapa Vermelha (P.L.). *Revista de Pré-Historia* I(1):53–89. São Paulo.

Laming-Emperaire, A., A. Prous, A. Moraes, and M. M. C. Beltrão
1975 *Grottes et Abris de la Región de Lagoa Santa, Minas Gerais, Brésil.* Cahiers d'Archéologie d'Amerique du Sud. Paris.

Prous, A.
1981 Fouilles du Gran Abri de Santana do Riacho (MG), Brésil. *Journal de la Societé des Americanistes* 67:163–183.
1986a L'archéologie au Brésil: 300 Siècles d'Occupation Humaine. *L'Anthropologie* 90:257–306.
1986b Os Mais Antigos Vestigios Arqueológicos no Brasil Central (Estados de Minas Gerais, Goias, e Bahia). In *New Evidence for the Pleistocene Peopling of the Americas*, edited by A. L. Bryan, pp. 173–182. Center for the Study of Early Man, University of Maine, Orono.

Qiu Zhonglang
1985 The Middle Palaeolithic of China. In *Palaeoanthropology and Palaeolithic Archaeology in the People's Republic of China*, edited by Wu Rukang and J. W. Olson, pp. 187–210. Academic Press, New York.

Fishtail Projectile Points in the Southern Cone of South America: An Overview

GUSTAVO G. POLITIS
División Arqueología
Facultad de Ciencias Naturales y Museo de La Plata
Paseo del Bosque
1900 La Plata, Argentina

Fishtail projectile points (FTPPs) have been widely considered to be favored indicators of the early peopling of South America since their discovery by J. Bird in Fell's and Palli Aiki caves. In this paper, extant data and models related to the origins of fishtail projectile points from the Southern Cone of South America are summarized. The degree of similarity between specimens from different regions is analyzed using numerical techniques. The relationship between North American fluted points and South American fishtail projectile points is also discussed on the basis of technological and morphological characteristics, as well as contextual association.

At present, only two areas in the Southern Cone of South America have produced clearly defined fishtail projectile points: the southern tip of Patagonia; and the eastern *Pampas,* Uruguay, and the southern plains of Brazil. In both regions, radiocarbon dates place the early human occupation between ca. 9500 and 11,000 yr. B.P. Though an independent origin of the South American fishtail projectile points cannot be proven, the technological characteristics and contextual data suggest that beyond some general bifacial traits, there is no clear evidence supporting a North American FTPP origin.

INTRODUCTION

Fishtail projectile points (FTPPs) are widely considered to be favorable and sometimes diagnostic indicators of the early peopling of South America. Their great value as such was initially recognized as the result of Junius Bird's research at Fell's and Palli Aike caves, Magallanes Province, Chile, during the 1930s (Bird 1938). At these locations, Bird discovered a wealth of fishtail projectile points associated with extinct megamammals within levels subsequently dated between 11,000 and 10,000 yr B.P. Following Bird's discoveries, archaeologists dealing with early humans in South America began to search for this particular type of projectile point. Nevertheless, for many years after these early finds in the southern tip of Patagonia, few fishtail projectile points were obtained in stratigraphic position with a clearly associated cultural context. Recently, however, several discoveries made through systematic excavations and surface collections at the Cueva del Medio site in Chile and the Cerro La China and Cerro El Sombrero sites in Argentina have afforded new information concerning the characteristics, chronology, and significance of fishtail projectile points. A fishtail projectile point as considered in this paper follows Bird's classic definition of:

> a barbless, stemmed form with and without fluting, with rounded shoulders, the stem tapering towards a concave base, the stem side generally but not always terminating in slightly expanded, rather sharp prongs or corners. Where these were present the stem sides tend to be concave in profile and minimum stem width occurs forward of or above the base [Bird 1969:56–57].

FTPPs have also received the less popular names of "Fell's Cave Stemmed" (Mayer-Oakes 1986), "Pisciforme" or "Caudopisciforme" (Schobinger 1971), and "Ictiomorfa" (Bate 1982) points.

An important issue concerning the FTPPs is their relationship to early North American fluted points. This relationship has primarily been claimed on the basis of well-elaborated bifacial retouch, rounded shoulders, and the presence of a fluted channel. Lynch (1983) argues that bifacial stone projectile points could not have originated independently in both North and South America within a period of a few years.

The aim of this paper is threefold: first, to summarize the extant data and models related to the FTPPs in the Southern Cone; second, to evaluate the degree and kind of similarities of FTPPs from different regions of the Southern Cone using numerical analytical techniques; and third, to discuss the relationship between the North American fluted points and the South American FTPPs.

NATURAL ENVIRONMENT OF THE SOUTHERN CONE OF SOUTH AMERICA

The Southern Cone of South America includes the present territories of Argentina, Uruguay, Paraguay, Chile, and southeastern Brazil. The rugged Andes dominate the western portion of this region along the Pacific Coast. In the far south, the mountains plunge abruptly into the Pacific Ocean and result in a series of drowned embayments or fjords. Towards the north, two long parallel mountain ranges extend the length of Chile, forming a narrow intermontane valley.

Near the tropics in northern Chile and Argentina, the Andes become wider (over 600 km), forming a high intermontane plateau or *Puna.* Andean highland climates, as well as soil and vegetation, are strongly influenced by altitude and are accordingly cool to cold in the higher elevations, even in the latitude of the tropics (Willey 1971). Moving southwards, high-altitude climates become colder and drier in Chile, Bolivia, and northwestern Argentina. Although trees grow in the southern section of the Andes, much of the region is unforested and consists of grassland, bushland, or desert. The narrow coastal shelf on the Pacific side of the Andes in northern Chile has an extremely dry desert climate, but the heat is moderated by the winds of the Humboldt ocean current. The central valley of Chile has a Mediterranean climate; the soils are rich and the rains abundant. The long southern archipelago of Chile, a continuation of the coastal mountain range, is cold, wet, and covered by a rain forest.

East of the southern Andes lies the high semi-desert Patagonian Plateau, where cold winds blow constantly. The soil is shallow and not very fertile, trees are scarce, and most of the area is a grassland. North of Patagonia are the *Pampas,* extended grasslands of Argentina and Uruguay, with rich soil, low elevation, and temperate climate.

The transitional zone from temperate to tropical lowlands is a large area known as the Gran Chaco, which includes part of Argentina, Paraguay, and Bolivia. This arid to semiarid flat plain is characterized by a concentrated rainy season resulting in a varied vegetational cover that includes sections of grassland, parkland, bushland, and, along the main rivers, tropical forest (Bennett and Bird 1960).

The southern section of the eastern Brazilian highlands is also included in the Southern Cone. Grasslands and scattered trees are typical, and the variety of plant life is great. The climate is subtropical, with abundant rainfall and little variation in temperature throughout the year.

THE INITIAL DATA: FROM THE 1930S TO THE 1970S

In 1937 Junius Bird found 15 whole and fragmentary FTPPs at Fell's Cave and a single point stem in Palli Aike Cave (Bird 1938) (Figure 1). Later, Emperaire (1963) reported four more specimens from Fell's Cave, and John Fell (the owner of the land where the site is located) recovered other items, now exhibited at the Punta Arenas Museum in Chile (Bird 1969). The archaeological context of the layer where the Fell's Cave FTPPs were found, which contained other lithic tools such as two discoidal stones, large scrapers in a variety of forms, and bone implements, characterizes Period I, also called Magallanes I. Associated faunal remains included the bones of American horse *(Parahipparion saldiasi),* giant ground sloth *(Mylodon listai),* and guanaco *(Lama*

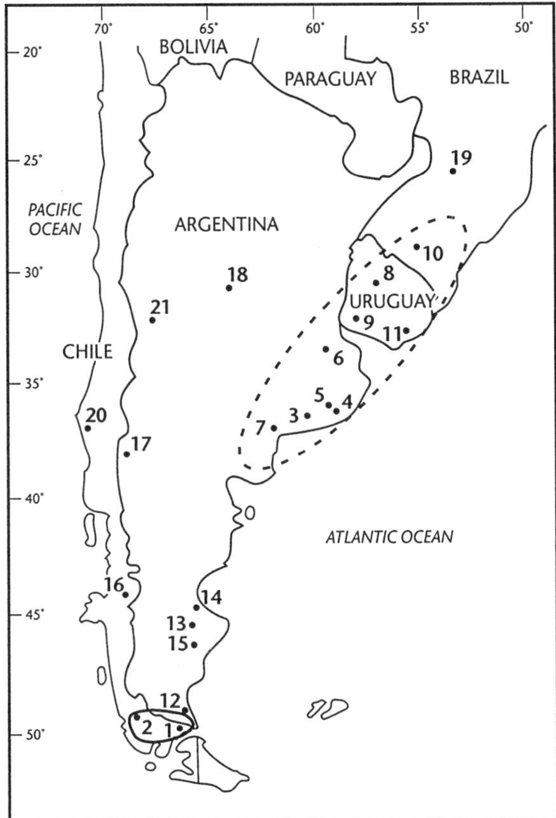

Figure 1. Map showing the major distribution areas of typical fishtail projectile points, some of which have well-documented contexts. Unbroken line = southern tip of Patagonia; dashed line = southern Brazil, Uruguay, and the eastern Argentine Pampas. **1)** Fell's and Palli Aike caves; **2)** Cueva del Medio; **3)** Arroyo Pinto (Flores); **4)** Cerro La China; **5)** Cerro El Sombrero; **6)** Tacuarembo and Cerro Largo; **7)** Rio Sauce Chico; **8)** Lobos; **9)** San Cayeta-no; **10)** Rio Grande do Sul; **11)** Cabo Polonio, Valizas, and Santa Teresa (Department of Rocha). Atypical or reported (not illustrated) FTPP point finds are: **12)** Abrigo de los Pescadores; **13)** Los Toldos; **14)** Caleta Olivia; **15)** El Ceibo; **16)** Aysen; **17)** Rio Limay; **18)** Rio Tercero; **19)** Itapiranga; **20)** Temuco; **21)** La Crucecita.

guanicoe). Several radiocarbon dates (Table 1) locate this occupational episode between 11,000 and 10,000 yr B.P.

In 1952 Menghin published the results of his excavations at Cave 3 of Los Toldos, a site located on the Patagonian Plateau of Argentina. Menghin (1952) reported the presence of two probable FTPP fragments within the "Toldenese level," correlating this level with Fell's Cave Period 1. In the early 1970s Cardich re-excavated Cave 3, refining the definition of "Toldenese." An FTPP broken stem, found within the "Toldenese level," was dated between 10,000 and 8750 yr B.P. (Cardich 1978; Cardich et al. 1973). The level also included subtriangular projectile points, well-shaped side and end scrapers, bifacial knives, and an unevenly smoothed discoidal tool. Faunal associations consisted basically of guanaco, although a few American horse *(Parahipparion)* and bird remains were also found. Bird, who analyzed the broken stem, thought it a "poor example," but included it as an FTPP, primarily on the basis of association, stratigraphic position, and the type of artifacts found in the overlying strata (Bird 1969). The three possible FTPP specimens from Los Toldos were later analyzed by Aguerre (1979), who concluded that none of them could be positively assigned to the FTPP type. The body fragment does not conform to the typical outline of the group and therefore could also be interpreted as a knife with a retouched base (see Aguerre 1979:42). The two broken stems are also not necessarily assignable to the FTPP type, since neither has concave sides and the bases are straight.

Until the end of the 1960s the only well-known record of FTPPs in the Southern Cone was restricted to the Magallanes Province in Chile. In 1972 Madrazo reported 14 specimens (mainly broken stems and a few complete points) recovered from the Cerro El Sombrero hill site in the low Tandilia Mountain Range (Buenos Aires Province, Argentina). The archaeological material was scattered on the surface of the hilltop of a quartzite outcrop and was represented by the above-mentioned points and unifacial and bifacial debris (Madrazo 1972). No excavations were done by Madrazo at the site.

In 1972 Schobinger reported an FTPP-like specimen found on the surface at the La Crucesita site (Mendoza Province, Argentina). He concluded that the point was an FTPP, although the dimensions of the body were atypical. Schobinger later reported a large number of other FTPPs from the Southern Cone, a few of them quite deviant from the original Fell's Cave type, contributing to the knowledge of the geographical distribution of FTPPs in this area (Schobinger 1973). Schobinger lists the following complete and broken specimens: three from southern Brazil (Itapiranga and Rio Grande do Sul state); twenty from Uruguay; and about five from Argentina (two from the Buenos Aires province, in addition to the ones recorded by Madrazo; one from Mendoza; one from Neuquen; and one from Cordoba). These examples were primarily discovered in out-of-context surface collections or in museum collections with little specific provenience information. One of the main problems, however, is that not all the specimens reported by Schobinger appear to fall within Bird's definition of an FTPP. Although most of these points are similar to those found at Fell's Cave (i.e., those from Rio Grande do Sul, Brazil; and Cerro Largo, Rincón Bonete, Fortaleza Santa Teresa, and Valizas, Uruguay), some specimens are so different that they can hardly be considered FTPPs. In other instances, the available morphological information is ambiguous (i.e., the specimen from the Treinta y Tres State, Uruguay, or the one

Table 1. Radiocarbon Dates Associated with Fishtail Projectile Points.

SITE NAME	RADIOCARBON DATE YR B.P.	LAB. SAMPLE NUMBER	LAYER	REFERENCE
Fell's Cave	11,000 ± 170	I-3988	First Occup.	Bird 1969
Fell's Cave	10,720 ± 300	W-915	19	Bird 1969
Fell's Cave	10,080 ± 160	I-5146	18	Saxon 1976
Cerro La China 1	10,790 ± 120	AA-1327	Lower Level	Flegenheimer 1987
Cerro La China 1	10,730 ± 150	I-12741	Lower Level	Flegenheimer 1987
Cerro La China 3*	10,610 ± 180	AA-1328	Unit b	Flegenheimer 1987
Cueva del Medio	9,595 ± 115	PITT-0344	Fell I	Nami 1989
Cueva del Medio	10,310 ± 70	GR-N-14912	Fell I	Nami 1989
Cueva del Medio	10,550 ± 120	GR-N-14911	Fell I	Nami 1989
Cueva del Medio	12,390 ± 180	PITT-0343	Fell 1	Nami 1989

*Not directly associated.

reported by Lehmann-Nitsche in 1907). Nevertheless, Schobinger gathered an abundant amount of data on specimens spread over regions where, as in the case of Uruguay, published references on FTPPs were scarce.

Molina (1972) reported the stratigraphic recovery of an FTPP from the Alero de los Pescadores site (Province of Santa Cruz, Argentina), 80 km north of Fell's and Palli Aike caves. Observing the drawing published by Molina, this projectile point does not seem to be similar to those found in Fell's and Palli Aike caves, but instead looks like a lanceolate point with a concave base and no stem. A few scattered and atypical specimens from western Patagonia, Aysen in Chile and Gobernador Moyano in Santa Cruz, were reported by Bate (1982). Another purported FTPP was found by J. Bird and A. Gordon near Temuco, on the coast of south-central Chile (T. Dillehay, personal communication).

Thirty-three complete and broken specimens from various Uruguayan surface sites were reported in 1974 by Bosch et al. (1980). Most of these artifacts show strong resemblances to the classic Fell's type, though, unfortunately, no information about their cultural context or site setting was available. This, however, was the first Uruguayan publication on FTPPs, and it included examples not only from museums but from amateur collections.

Meneghini (1977) reported two other Uruguayan sites at the Cerro de los Burros locality (Department of Maldonado). This locality produced a broken point and an FTPP stem. Cerro de los Burros is a low hill (170 m above sea level), where bifacial and thin and thick unifacial artifacts were found on the hilltop and slopes in a surface context. An excavation by Meneghini on the uneven surface of the hill yielded a variety of materials in a single compact cultural level. No associated fauna were recovered, and there are no chronological estimates for these sites. The data obtained suggest that the Cerro de los Burros sites are multicomponent quarry sites.

THE NEW DATA: THE LAST 10 YEARS

Recent investigations carried out in the *Pampas* and Patagonia have produced relevant information concerning the chronology and geographic distribution of FTPPs. Silveira (1978) reported a basalt FTPP found in a surface collection at the Rio Sauce Chico site, Buenos Aires Province. The specimen was recovered from a deflated area in a surface association with simple and double side scrapers, end scrapers, and a variety of side-retouched flakes, suggesting several different chronological occupations. Because of the nature of the find, it is extremely difficult to assess the associational context of this point. Another specimen curated at the Museo Etnográfico of Buenos Aires, probably from Lobos (Buenos Aires Province) but lacking specific contextual data, was reported by Eugenio (1983). A third FTPP was registered at the San Cayetano (Buenos Aires Province) local museum by the author. This specimen was found in a surface assemblage collected by the landowner, Mr. Menna, along with typical artifacts of the Interserrana tradition (see Politis 1984). The point, whose measurements are displayed in Table 2, is small, made of reddish chalcedony, and exhibits evidence of extensive resharpening on the mid and distal sections, producing a rounded tip (Figure 2c). It has no fluted channel.

Cardich (1979) mentions a surface find near the El Ceibo site (Santa Cruz Province, Argentina), but no measurements, illustrations, or morphological information are provided. Nevertheless, Cardich

Table 2. Measurements of Selected South American Fishtail Projectile Points.

SPECIMEN	MAX. LENGTH	MAX. WIDTH	MAX. THICKNESS	MIN. STEM WIDTH	MAX. BASE WIDTH	KEY[a]
Fell's Cave						
41.1 1979a	68	34.5	5.5	17.5	18	1
41.1 1979b	57	30	7.3	16	17.5	2
41.1 1979c	54	24	5	12	13	3
41.1 1979d	47	26	4.5	14	15	4
41.1 1979e	42	30	5.3	17	17	5
41.1 1979f	36	20.5	5.3	12.5	14.5	6
41.2 8303	50	31	8	17.3	19	7
Cueva del Medio						
1	40.4	17.5	8	11	13	8
2	48	27	6	19	20.5	9
Cerro La China						
88	41	22	6	13	15	10
455	42	23	6	13	14	11
San Cayetano	38.5	23	6	16	18	12
Lobos	51.5	28	5	13	16.5	13
Sauce Chico	48	27	7	17.5	19	14
Uruguay*	—	38.5	7.6	18.5	19.5	15
Uruguay**						
1	71.5	42	5.5	23.5	26	16
4	55	22	5	14	14.5	17
8	53.5	30	6.5	19	21	18
16	62	31	6	17	21	19
17	63	27	5.5	17	—	20
19	68	24	7	15	20	21
Uruguay, Alegre col.						
1	46	25	4	13	14	
2	35	21	5	14	17	
Rio Grande do Sul,AAP Nro.37	46	22	7	12.5	15	22

All measurements in millimeters.
*Cast measured at Junius Bird's Laboratory, AMNH, New York.
**Measurements taken from Bosch et al. (1980).
[a]Key for the fennogram displayed in Figure 3.

(personal communication) is confident that the point closely resembles the FTPPs of Fell's and Palli Aike caves.

During a recent visit to Uruguay, Lic. Roberto Bracco and I examined the Alegre collection, which consists of materials from the northeastern Department of Rocha, primarily surface sites on the beaches of Laguna Negra. This collection contains a wide variety of stemmed projectile points, among them a few that fall within the FTPP type. One specimen was made of limestone, has extremely rounded edges, and lacks a fluted channel. A second example was made from flint or a highly silicified limestone, and has a slightly concave base and a fluted channel on one side (see measurements of both specimens in Table 2). Four more points have some morphological characteristics, such as very rounded shoulders and stems with slightly expanded bases, which are similar to the FTPP type. These points are not included in the present analysis, however, because: (1) they are thicker than the classic FTPPs, displaying a kind of rhomboidal cross-section that suggests another kind of reduction process; and (2) the proportions between the body and stem also differ from the classic FTPP type, showing a maximum body width that is close to the maximum base width. These examples are on the edge of the range of variation of the abundant stemmed projectile points so common in the surface sites of Uruguay.

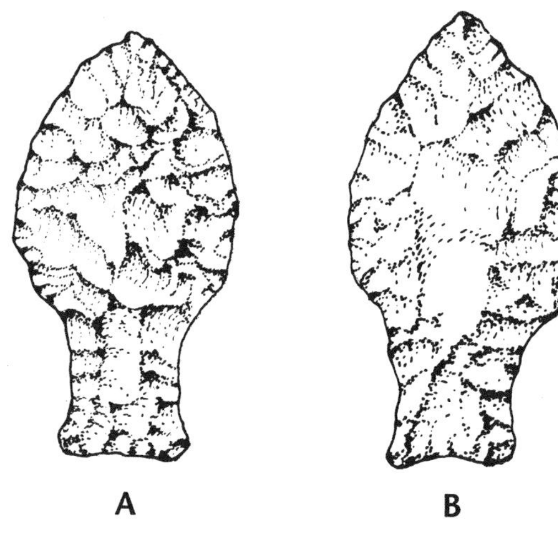

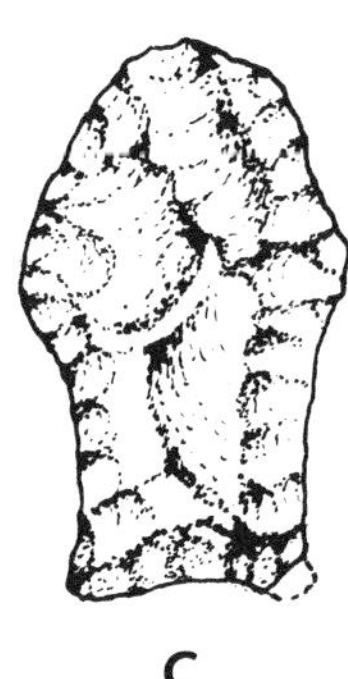

Figure 2. (Actual size) **A)** FTPP from Lobos, Buenos Aires Province (after Eugenio 1983). **B)** "Classic" FTPP from Fell's Cave (after Emperaire et al. 1963). **C)** FTPP from San Cayetano (Buenos Aires Province) displaying extensive body resharpening.

Two major contributions to FTPP studies in the Southern Cone were made by Nora Flegenheimer (1986, 1987) and Hugo Nami (1985–1986, 1987, 1989). Flegenheimer carried out research at the Cerro La China and Cerro El Sombrero sites in the southeastern Argentine *Pampas*. Nami excavated at the Cueva del Medio site in southern Chilean Patagonia.

Cerro La China is a very low hill (227 m above sea level) surrounded by a plain (Flegenheimer 1987), where three sites were excavated. At Site 1, a rockshelter, two FTPP preforms, a complete specimen, and the fragment of a second point were recovered from Layer 2, along with several additional lithic artifacts and one *Eutatus seguini* scute. Layer 2 has been radiocarbon dated at 10,720 ± 300 yr B.P. and 10,790 ± 120 yr B.P. (Flegenheimer 1987) (see also Table 1). Site 2 is an open-air site located approximately 85 m from Site 1. Artifacts recovered from Site 2, Unit b, equivalent to Site 1, Layer 2, included two complete FTPPs and several chipped-stone tools. The scarcity and fragmentary condition of the remains (with the exception of the points) suggest that this was not a true camp (see discussion in Flegenheimer 1986). Site 3, an open-air site, presents a similar stratigraphic profile. Unit b, dated at 10,610 ± 180 yr B.P., produced a high artifactual density. Although some of the debitage indicates that bifacial reduction took place at the site, no bifacial projectile points or other bifacial instruments were recovered. Flegenheimer concludes, based on the dates, the stratigraphic situation of the remains, and the characteristics of the raw material used, that the earliest occupations of the three sites are closely correlated

Following publication of Madrazo's report (Madrazo 1972), a large number of complete and broken FTPPs and other artifacts were added to the original Cerro El Sombrero site collection, most of them found by the Lobería museum's team and by Flegenheimer (Flegenheimer 1986). The new collections produced 29 FTPP fragments: 4 nearly complete specimens, 3 medial sections, and 22 stems. Four atypical points that resemble resharpened FTPPs, several fragments that may represent different bifacial reduction stages, and a few nearly complete bifacial preforms were also collected from the site. Several stems and broken FTPPs, together with two complete specimens, were also recovered. The unusually high density of artifacts and the different manufacturing steps represented at the site suggest that point manufacturing and point replacement activities were carried out at El Sombrero (Flegenheimer 1987).

The Cueva del Medio site is a cave located in the Ultima Esperanza Province (Chile), 1 km east of Mylodon Cave and 135 km northwest of Fell's and Palli Aike caves (Nami 1985–1986). In the Fell I component at Cueva del Medio, two complete FTPPs (see Table 2) were found in a hearth in close association with the bones of American horse *(Hippidium sp.)*, guanaco, and probably an extinct feline *(Felis listai)* (Nami 1985–1986). The lithic material recovered in this component includes not only the FTPPs, but a variety of artifacts made of tuff, chalcedony, and vulcanite: end scrapers, side scrapers, and knives (Nami 1987, 1989). The faunal association also included ground sloth *(Mylodon listai)*, canid *(Dusicyon culpaeus)*, and cervid remains. Bones of American horse are the most abundant faunal remains, suggesting that this mammal was the primary prey species. Four radiocarbon samples from hearth charcoal produced dates of: 9595 ± 115 yr B.P.; 10,310 ± 70 yr B.P.; 10,550 ± 120 yr B.P.; and 12,390 ± 180 yr B.P. (see Table 1). These dates agree with the estimated chronology of the faunal association. It should be noted that the last two dates come from the same hearth. In this sense, as the date of 12,390 yr B.P. is a little older than the rest, the younger date of 10,550 yr B.P. may be considered the more probable of the two until new samples are processed. The nature of this undisturbed association, based on initial reports of the site, offers new and relevant data for discussing the archaeology of Ultima Esperanza, as well as its relationship to the Fell's and Palli Aike caves' area.

THE PROPOSED MODELS

Several models have been proposed to explain the significance of FTPPs as regards the early peopling of South America. A relationship between the South American FTPPs and the North American fluted points has been widely hypothesized, based on chronology and the presence of one or two fluted faces in both groups of points. Most of these discussions include very asymmetrical qualitative and quantitative information, since, as was stated above, scant data have been available from the southern part of South America.

Two alternative hypotheses discussed by Willey (1971) that account for the origin of the early South American projectile points are: (1) these points correspond to a local development from Chivateros; or (2) they are derived from the early fluted points of the North American Plains. A connection between the Fell's Cave and El Inga points was early postulated by Mayer-Oakes (1963, 1986), followed by several authors. Bird (1969) compared the Fell's Cave and El Inga (Ecuador) points, analyzing the similarities between seven different attributes: blank preparation, occurrence of fluting or long basal flake scars, marginal grinding of the stem edge, form, pattern of breakage, measurements, and nature of the site. Bird concluded that the sum of the similarities makes a reasonable case for a close connection and identity between the two point groups. Schobinger (1969, 1971) went further with FTPP origin and diffusion theory, suggesting that the FTPP type derived from the fluted points of the North American Plains. He includes El Inga in this tradition. Schobinger also postulates a dispersal along the eastern flank of the Andes and adjacent lowlands prior to the development of the dense postglacial Amazon forest. Although Lynch (1978, 1983) agrees with Schobinger's first hypothesis, he sees the Andean highlands of western South America as favoring a swift north-to-south displacement along the continent. Moreover, Lynch postulates two larger and complementary traditions: the Clovis-derived FTPPs; and El Jobo, which he sees as strongly resembling the Lerma projectile-point type of Texas.

Alternative models to a Clovis or Folsom origin of the South American FTPPs have been proposed by Bryan (1975), Rouse (personal communication to Snarskis 1979), and Borrero (1983), among others. Bryan argues that the thick lanceolate South American projectile points (i.e., the El Jobo series) are made on the basis of a different "mental template" than the FTPPs and therefore must belong to a different tradition (Bryan 1975). Based on the chronology of the Taima-taima site, Bryan postulates that the El Jobo type is older than the North American fluted points and that bifacial projectile points were invented in South America. Irving Rouse has also proposed that the FTPP type originated in South America and diffused northwards (see Snarskis 1979).

The present controversy surrounding the origin and significance of FTPPs was recently analyzed by Borrero (1983), who recognizes four FTPP-producing "centers": southeastern Panama, the highlands of Ilaló (Ecuador), the lowlands of Uruguay and the Argentine *Pampas*, and southern Patagonia. Borrero rejects the idea that diffusion resulted in the appearance of FTPPs in four separate regions of South America and criticizes the characterization of an archaeological culture and/or industry based solely on a single trait. He instead advocates the comparison of adaptive systems. Borrero argues that most previous studies have searched for chronological similarities on too general a level to obtain significant results, concluding:

> Mas probablemente, sobre la base de la evidencia disponible, puede edificarse un argumento que favorezca la aparición de puntas de proyectil de modelo Fell por variación azarosa alrededor de los extremos límites del concepto de punta de proyectil penetrante [Borrero 1983:10].
>
> (But probably, based on the foundation of available evidence, one could construct an argument which favors the appearance of Fell-model projectile points as [simply] a result of random variation within the extreme limits of the concept of a penetrating projectile point [Editor's translation].)

The above opinions suggest that the question of FTPP origins revolves around two basic concepts: independent invention; and diffusion. These concepts are linked with two primary aspects of the peopling of the Americas' issue: the displacement of migratory hunting bands; and the dynamics of cultural systems in relation to ecological change.

NUMERICAL ANALYSES

Multivariate analysis may prove helpful in our effort to understand the early peopling of the Americas. Numerical analyses were used to measure the type and degree of similarity of the Southern Cone FTPPs. This approach, although not conclusive, widens our perspective in the study of cultural traits when taken in conjunction with morphological observations and technological inferences. In the case of the FTPPs, the measurements considered relevant for the analyses were: maximum length, maximum width, maximum thickness, maximum base width, and minimum stem width. Although the length of the stem would have been a very useful measurement for comparing body and stem correlations, it was not taken into account because an objective determination of where the stem begins is made difficult by the rounded shoulder of the FTPP type.

Gathering this information was difficult because of the scarcity of published data and the impossibility of examining every reported FTPP. The Fell's Cave series and the cast of a Uruguayan specimen were measured by the author at the American Museum of Natural History, New York, while the data from the Cerro La China and Cueva del Medio sites were kindly given to me by N. Flegenheimer and H. Nami, respectively. I also measured the San Cayetano specimen. Maximum lengths, widths, and thicknesses of the specimens from Lobos, Rio Grande do Sul, Sauce Chico, and Uruguay were obtained from published papers (Bosch et al. 1980; Eugenio 1983; Schobinger 1973; Silveira 1978). The minimum stem width and the maximum base width of the Rio Grande do Sul and Uruguayan specimens were obtained from scale drawings provided by Schobinger (1973) and Bosch et al. (1980).

The basic data matrix was formed by 22 FTPPs and 5 characters. Only typical specimens, those that fall within Bird's definition of an FTPP and exhibit slightly biconvex to almost plain cross-sections, were included in the study. With the exception of the cast from Uruguay, only complete specimens were considered.

The "Taxonomic Distance Coefficient" (Sokal 1961) and the "Pearson Product-Moment Coefficient" (Michener and Sokal 1957) were calculated (Figure 3). The UPGMA (Unweighted Pair of Group Method Using Arithmetic Averages) (Sokal and Michener 1958) was applied for the cluster analysis. Finally, a "Principal Component Analysis" (Sneath and Sokal 1973) was also performed (Figure 4). These calculations were run using the NT-SYS program (Rohlf et al. 1971).

Although some activities, such as edge resharpening, would affect the numerical relationships between the projectile points, thus introducing disturbing data in the matrix, some general trends can be observed. Preliminary results indicate that the clusters observed do not correlate with the geographical distribution of FTPPs. Specimens from Patagonia, the *Pampas*, Uruguay, and southern Brazil appear in close association within the same clusters. It is important to note that only five points (22%) fall outside of the internal range of variation of the Fell's Cave series. In other words, the specimens from the different Southern Cone areas are not

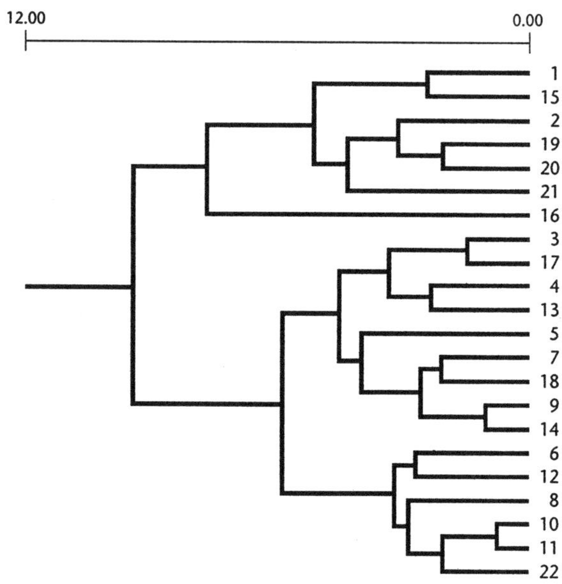

Figure 3. Fennogram grouping 22 fishtail projectile points, based on data displayed in Table 2. Identification numbers are shown in the rightmost column of Table 2.

segregated morphologically as they are geographically. This observation supports the hypothesis that in addition to having the same morphological and technological characteristics, the specimens included in the data matrix share strong stylistic features reflected in their mutual metrical relationships.

The chart displayed in Figure 3 shows three main clusters, which can be interpreted in different ways. The cluster formed by Examples 1, 2, 15, 16, 19, 20, and 21 groups the larger-sized FTPPs used in the data matrix, while the cluster formed by Examples 3, 4, 5, 7, 9, 13, 14, 17, and 18 includes medium-sized FTPPs. The third cluster, formed by Examples 6, 8, 10, 11, 12 and 22, represents the smaller points. It is important to note that all three clusters contain FTPPs from the Fell's Cave series. These groups could be interpreted as represent-

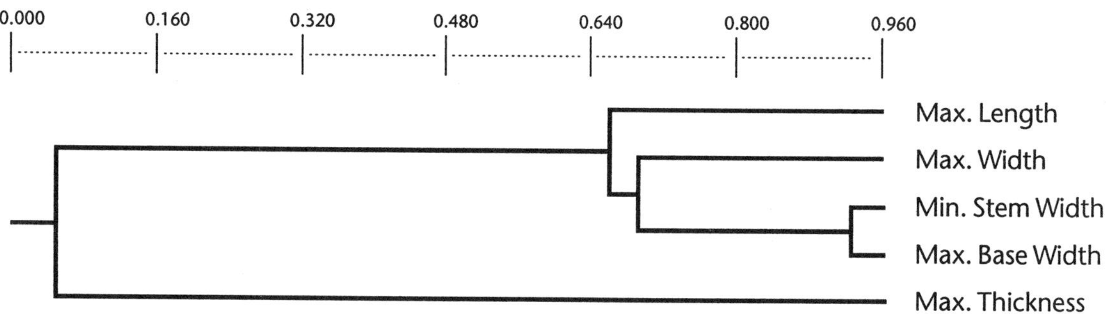

Figure 4. Fennogram displaying "Principal Component Analyses."

ing three basic alternatives: (a) functional differences; (b) stylistic variations, including the final size of the instrument; or (c) different stages in the process of reduction and resharpening during the projectile point's life cycle. Because at the present stage of lithic studies we do not know how ethnicity and activity, style and function are reflected at the level of the assemblage, it is difficult to determine which of the three alternatives is correct (Sackett 1982). Additionally, the available data are insufficient for an in-depth discussion regarding these alternatives, owing largely to the scarcity of contextual information. A few observations on the technology and morphology of the FTPPs included in this study are:

1. The rounded tips of several FTPPs (i.e., Examples 41.1 1979b; 41.1 1979c; and 41.1 1979d from the Fell's Cave series) suggest that these points were resharpened for a function other than use as a projectile point. Coincidentally, the straight lateral edge of Fell's Cave Example 41.1 1979g (see Bird 1969:Figure 5) results in an asymmetrical instrument, more efficient for cutting or scraping than for penetration purposes.
2. Table 2 shows that variation in thickness is somewhat independent from maximum width and length. Results of the "Principal Component Analysis" (Figure 4) exhibit the same trend, indicating that point thickness is not as strongly affected by resharpening as maximum width and length.
3. Although the FTPP bodies show clear size variability between clusters, the stems remain more stable. This situation would be expected when the projectile point was resharpened after breakage or wear. Thus, Examples 41.1 1979e and 41.1 1979f from the Fell's Cave series (see Bird 1969:Figures 5j,k) indicate extensive body resharpening, resulting in a distortion between the proportion of body and stem. Other smaller FTPPs, such as the San Cayetano and Cueva del Medio specimens, also suggest body resharpening.

These observations lead us to favor the third alternative of differing reduction and resharpening stages. In this sense, the first cluster groups FTPPs showing no or very light resharpening, while the second cluster represents FTPPs with moderate resharpening. The third cluster consists of extensively resharpened FTPPs. In other words, beyond some stylistic features, the three clusters represent three different stages in the reduction sequence. Of course, this hypothesis does not exclude the existence of small FTPPs, which could be grouped with the extensively resharpened examples. In fact, the third FTPP cluster may include some of these small points.

Other FTPP-like specimens reported by Schobinger but not considered in this data matrix may be atypical examples or, conversely, could represent examples marginal to the morphological variation produced by the reduction sequence. The La Crucesita specimen would therefore be a point in the very first stage of use with no reactivation, while the Rio Tercero point would represent a final step in the resharpening cycle. More data must be obtained in order to discuss both hypotheses, since these isolated finds do not give us enough information about their position in the reduction process.

DISCUSSION

Two main topics will be discussed in this section. First, are all the Southern Cone FTPPs the same type, and, if so, what is their significance in terms of cultural history? Second, are the North American early fluted points the predecessors of the South American FTPPs?

Taking into account the preceding analyses, there are only two regions within the Southern Cone where FTPPS clearly occur. One is a very restricted area in the southern tip of Patagonia, which includes the Magallanes and Ultima Esperanza provinces in Chile. The other includes the eastern *Pampas* of Argentina and Uruguay, and the southern plains of Brazil. Other areas of the Southern Cone have been surveyed with similar intensity but have produced no evidence of FTPPs, eliminating, in great measure, sampling biases or uneven coverage. These areas include Patagonia, west-central Argentina, *Puna*, and central and southern Chile. Uneven coverage would apply to Paraguay, the Chaco and Mesopotamia of Argentina, and possibly southeastern Brazil.

Although there are many isolated FTPP surface finds, in the few places where FTPPs have been radiocarbon dated, most of the dates place them between 11,000 and 10,000 yr B.P. (Fell's Cave, Cueva del Medio, and Cerro La China). This roughly concurs with Lynch's statement that "all archaeologists seem to agree that the fishtail points—as found in Fell's Cave, Toldenese I and El Inga contexts—are Paleo-Indian in date" (1983:108).

No FTPPs have yet been recorded in later contexts (early Holocene times) from *Pampean* and Patagonian sites. The two *Pampean* Paleoindian sites where the faunal association includes extinct megamammals (Arroyo Seco 2 and La Moderna) did not produce projectile points, even though significant areas of the sites were excavated. In Patagonia a number of sites dated to shortly after 10,000 yr B.P. have been investigated, among them Arroyo Feo (Gradin et al. 1979), Traful 1 Cave (Curzio et al. 1982), Cuyín Manzano (Ceballos 1982), Cueva de las Manos (Gradin et al. 1976), La Martita (Aguerre 1982), and others. None, however, have yielded FTPPs.

The technological characteristics of FTPPs from both regions in which they occur are similar. Regarding the specimens from southern Patagonia, Bird states:

> Instead of preparing an initial, bifacially shaped blank to be thinned and finally formed by second-

> ary chipping the preference was to start with a large flake of approximately the same thickness as the finished product [Bird 1969:55].

This same procedure seems to have been similarly used to prepare the Pampean examples. Low frequencies of fluting, varying numbers of basal-thinning flake scars, and marginal grinding of the stem edges characterize both sets of points. The pattern of breakage of the El Sombrero and Fell's Cave points are comparable (see Flegenheimer 1986), with the most common fracture being across the stem, towards the narrowest portion.

The numerical analysis produced similar results, demonstrating that *within a given shape and technology*, specimens from both regions cannot be differentiated. Although we know little of the adaptive strategies related to these points, especially those from the Pampean sites, the data suggest that from a morphological and technological viewpoint, the FTPPs from Patagonia, *Pampas*-Uruguay, and possibly southern Brazil are the same model.

However, another question then arises: What does this disjunct distribution mean? We can assume that the Southern Cone FTPPs are chronologically restricted and geographically discontinuous, but we do not know how they operated within the cultural system. I strongly agree with Borrero's statement:

> Creo que lo esencial para señalar es qué *no sabemos* que es lo que miden las distribuciones de puntas de proyectil [Borrero 1983:2].
>
> (I think that essentially we *do not* yet know what the spatial distribution of the Fell's Cave projectile-point type means [Author's translation].)

Because of the scarcity of contextual information, it is difficult to ascertain whether the function and position of FTPPs within the technological and subsistence systems were the same in both regions. What I want to emphasize is that *the hunter-gatherers who lived in both regions shared similar morphological and technological concepts during Paleoindian times*. It does not mean that they were the same "people," or that they shared other cultural traits. I am referring exclusively to the technological and morphological concepts involved in the production of this particular projectile-point type.

Nevertheless, the reason for this discontinuous geographic distribution remains unsolved. As I will not discuss the Los Toldos specimens, owing to Aguerre's doubts (Aguerre 1979), the northernmost Patagonian FTPP finds come from the central and northern part of Santa Cruz Province, assuming that the Caleta Alluvia and El Ceibo points are classic examples[1]. The southernmost Pampean FTPP comes from the Rio Sauce Chico site. There is approximately 1,200 km between these sites. On the other hand, if we consider only the typical and well-reported Patagonian specimens, the distance from the southern tip of Patagonia to the Rio Sauce Chico site is 1,600 km. The lack of well-documented finds in the intervening area may correspond either to an actual absence of FTPPs in the central and northern Patagonian Plateau or, conversely, may be merely because of little exploration. Surveys and excavations carried out in various areas of Patagonia support the first hypothesis, although it should be noted that levels older than 10,000 yr B.P. were reached in very few sites. It remains to be seen whether more intensive research in this large area will help fill the gap in our record.

The second topic considered here is that of the origin of the Southern Cone FTPPs and their relationship to the North American fluted points. When scholars who believe in a North American origin of FTPPs (including the El Inga types) expound their models, an explicit or implicit idea of fluted-point–manufacturing migratory bands, moving quickly from north to south, becomes evident. Most of these scholars adopt the Haynes-Martin model of a rapid, wavelike expansion of a specialized hunting culture out of the American Arctic (cf. Lynch 1983). An extreme example of the hypothesis of a genetic linkage between early South American projectile points and North American fluted points is represented by Lynch's statement:

> Technological continuity between the stone tool industries of the North American Paleo-Indians and those of their South American descendant is evident beyond any reasonable doubt. It is unlikely that would have been independently invented, by chance within a period of a few hundred years in both continents [Lynch 1983:103].

Given the present state of knowledge concerning the early cultures of South America, testing this model is extremely difficult. A major problem is attempting to explain the broad distribution of the FTPPs in terms of diffusionist models without a clear idea of human migration and adaptation patterns during the late Pleistocene. Moreover, without hypothetically or empirically linked criteria, or integrated models of migration and adaptive strategies, these studies do not reliably explain pre-Clovis or Clovis migration (Dillehay 1988a). Nevertheless, some general observations may be made, based on the present evidence.

Chronologically, the time spans of Clovis–Folsom points and FTPPs exhibit slight differences. The Clovis culture is considered to be the first fluted-point complex in North America (Jennings 1978), and most researchers concur on a range of 12,000 to 11,000 yr B.P. The Folsom complex, which is almost restricted to the North American Plains, is usually dated between 11,000 and 10,000 yr B.P. (Carlson 1983). Other early points, termed Plainview and described as an "Unfluted Folsom," are roughly contemporaneous with Folsom (Jennings 1978). Within the Southern Cone, the few radiocarbon dates associated with FTPPs (excepting the older date from Cueva del Medio because of the discrepancy among samples) have yielded dates of 11,000 to 9500 yr. B.P., a range only slightly younger than the North American fluted points. It is important to note, however, that the 12,000 yr B.P. age estimated for the more ancient Clovis fluted points was obtained from hundreds of radiocarbon dates from dozens of Paleoindian sites, while the 11,000 yr B.P. maximum age for the South American FTPPs was estimated based on a few radiocarbon dates from three sites. Thus, it is possible that the overlap between Clovis and FTPP ages would increase with more radiocarbon dates from early South American sites.

Although some characteristics are shared by the Clovis–Folsom projectile points and the FTPP groups, several technological and morphological differences should be stressed. The fluted channel is the main characteristic of the early North American points. In contrast, the shape of the stem and rounded shoulders is considered the outstanding trait of the FTPPs, while fluting is not very common. Of all the Fell's and Palli Aike cave examples, only one point has fluting on both sides, two have fluting on one side, and fifteen have a varying number of basal-thinning flake scars up to 19 mm in length (Bird 1969). At the Cerro La China sites, two preforms (a fluted stem and a complete specimen) are fluted on one side; while of the twenty-nine FTPP fragments from the El Sombrero site, four are fluted on both faces and six on one (Flegenheimer 1987). Neither of the Cueva del Medio FTPPs has a channel. Of the thirty-three FTPP specimens reported from Uruguay (Bosch et al. 1980), five have fluting on both faces and six on one. Most of the FTPPs display only varying amounts of basal-thinning flake scars. Sometimes, a facet of an original blank assumes the role of a channel flake (called "pseudo-fluted") (see Mayer-Oakes 1986). Only for the Cerro La China and Cerro el Sombrero series are fluted channel flakes reported (Flegenheimer, personal communication). Flegenheimer believes that the fluting was done in the final shaping stage. Moreover, when a flute scar is present on an FTPP, it differs from the fluted channel of the North American points, never reaching the depth of the Clovis-Folsom types.

Some preliminary technological observations suggest that the manufacturing steps involved in the FTPP production process differ from those followed during the reduction of a Clovis or Folsom preform[2]. Bird (1969) observed that on several FTPPs, secondary chipping had produced good edges and shape, while proportionally large sections of the original flake surface remained intact. On the other hand, the deep parallel flake scars, which transversely cross the fluted and unfluted early North American projectile points, are absent on the FTPPs. These morphological traits indicate clear-cut differences between the production of a North American fluted point and an FTPP.

Some new discoveries in South America of bifacially worked tools that date prior to 11,000 yr B.P. lead us to consider the alternative hypothesis that FTPPs derived from local antecedents. Two willow leaf-like bifacially retouched specimens with rhomboidal cross-sections recovered from Monte Verde, southern Chile (Dillehay 1988b), and dated at ca. 13,000 yr B.P. are relevant to this discussion. Other examples are two types of bifacially flaked projectile points (one with a contracting stem and the other a leaf-shaped form) from southern Brazil that have been dated at about 14,000 yr B.P. (Bryan 1986; Hurt 1986). Although these specimens are probably not related to the FTPP model, they do provide evidence that the concept of bifaciality was present in South America prior to the spread of fluted points on the North American Plains.

These observations indicate that the postulated relationship between North American fluted points and FTPPs is more apparent than real. Aside from a few shared general traits, no in-depth technological and morphological similarity can be assumed. In addition, although the contextual associations suggest broadly similar traits, such as a hunter-gatherer way of life adapted to the exploitation of big game, strong dissimilarities should be stressed. North American Paleoindians had an economy clearly based on now-extinct megamammals (mammoth and long-horn bison) and a mass-kill hunting technique. This resulted in kill sites typically located at the edges of ponds or channels, or in the bottom of deep gullies ("jump sites"). These sites yielded Clovis, Folsom, and other related fluted points, as well as prismatic knives, flat flake knives, and bone and antler projectile points (Carlson 1983; Frison 1983; Jennings 1978). In Patagonia the faunal remains associated with FTPPs indicate that guanaco was the primary faunal resource, with extinct American horse and mylodon playing secondary roles in Paleoindian game-hunting preferences (Mengoni Goñalons 1986). Nevertheless, recent discoveries at Cueva del Medio and current faunal analysis by Mengoni Goñalons suggest that American horse may have competed with guanaco as a primary food resource at some sites. Most FTPPs have come from camp sites located in caves and shelters, such as Fell's Cave, Palli Aike, Cueva del Medio, and Cerro La China. With the exception of Cerro El Sombrero, open-air sites have yielded only isolated finds lacking clear contextual associations. No true early mass-kill sites have been found in Patagonia, the *Pampas*, or Uruguay.

One of the primary arguments of those who believe in a Clovis-derived FTPP origin is the presence of a few Central American and northern South American sites containing projectile points that are morphologically related to one or both types[3]. Although sites such as Turrialba in Costa Rica (Snarskis 1979), Lake Madden in Panama (Bird and Cooke 1978), and El Inga in Ecuador (Bell 1960; Mayer-Oakes 1963, 1986) are considered evidence of a "fluted point horizon," some caution must be used.

Turrialba produced several types of projectile points,

some of them within the range of classic Clovis and "fishtail" models. The site has not yet been excavated and all finds are from surface collections, thus making it extremely difficult to identify context and to understand the association between the various point types. This has led me not to consider Turrialba as irrefutable proof of the north-to-south diffusion of fluting, at least until the chronology and context of the site are better known. Similar precautions should be taken with the Lake Madden projectile points.

In the case of El Inga, or more broadly, the Ilaló region, the "Fell's Cave Stemmed" form represents 17% of all points obtained by excavation and 18% of those found on the surface (Mayer-Oakes 1986). Among them, Mayer-Oakes recognizes four main varieties of point bases: normal, pseudo-fluted, fluted, and basally thinned. He concludes that:

> El Inga evidence is interpreted to support the idea that development of the fluting concept was at an early to intermediate stage, attaining the level of Clovis fluting technology [Mayer-Oakes 1986:153].

Although systematic excavations have been carried out in the Ilaló region, problems of chronology have not yet been resolved. The oldest radiocarbon date obtained from El Inga soil samples (9030 yr B.P.) was associated with two "Fell's Cave" stemmed points (Mayer-Oakes 1981), while thirteen obsidian-hydration dates ranged from 9301 to 11,248 yr B.P. (Mayer-Oakes 1986). In brief, although Turrialba, El Inga, and Lake Madden produced projectile points morphologically related to the FTPP type, and, at El Inga, associated with early dates, further research is needed to better understand these discoveries. It must also be considered that morphologically similar specimens may have played different roles when incorporated into different adaptive systems (Borrero 1983). The Clovis model proposes that fluted, bifacially chipped projectile points are the diagnostic artifact assemblage of the earliest peopling of the New World. Although this model might suffice for considering the possible link between a specific type of technological and economic adaptation, it does not explain the social and demographic peopling of the Americas by migratory or colonizing groups adapted to different environments (Dillehay 1988a). Finally, until a well-documented record is compiled and a comprehensive knowledge of early human technology developed, I prefer not to consider El Inga, Lake Madden, and Turrialba as "proof" of the proposed north-to-south Clovis migration.

FINAL REMARKS

In this paper, I have attempted to summarize the data relevant to FTPPs from the Southern Cone of South America, while discussing their technological and morphological characteristics and their contextual association. I then dealt with the possible Clovis ancestry of the South American FTPPs. The extant evidence is scarce, and studies on this subject are largely incomplete; thus no final conclusion can be arrived at.

Although the above observations do not *prove* an independent origin of the South American FTPPs, they also do not support a genetic affiliation with the North American fluted points. If North American fluted points were the predecessors of the South American FTPPs we should expect to see, among other things: older dates for the North American fluted points; a significant group of shared traits, at least at a more specific level of analysis; clearly intermediate finds linking two widely separated areas; and an absence of bifacial predecessors in South America. None of these expectations has been confirmed. As a consequence, I cannot agree with Lynch, Schobinger, or other proponents of a long-range Clovis-FTPP genetic affiliation. The chronological data of the FTPPs show them to be only slightly younger than Clovis points. Consequently, a very rapid migration, as the Martin model proposes, must be accepted to support a Clovis FTPP ancestry. Rather, I would prefer to consider a model showing early human bands slowly adapting to new environments, from Alaska to Tierra del Fuego, during a period of several millennia instead of a few hundred years. Technological characteristics suggest that beyond some general bifacial traits, there is no clear evidence to strongly support the hypothesis that FTPPs derived from North American fluted points. Additionally, there is no clear-cut spatial distribution of a fluted point horizon in South America. Overall, the concept of regional development seems a more worthy model for explaining the origins and development of the First Americans' cultures.

Footnotes

1. Although both specimens were reported several times (Bate 1982; Cardich 1979), there were no available illustrations, and I had no opportunity to observe these specimens. Nevertheless, these points are cited as FTPP examples owing to the absence of any comments suggesting atypical characteristics.
2. I discussed this hypothesis with Hugo Nami, who has studied in-depth the technological procedures involved in the southern Patagonian FTPPs. Nami has also observed several differences between both technologies.
3. I will not deal here more extensively with the northern South American early projectile points, since they are discussed in this volume by Thomas Lynch and Gerardo Ardila Calderón.

ACKNOWLEDGMENTS

I wish to express my deepest thanks to Nora Flegenheimer and Hugo Nami for permission to use their unpublished data, as well as for their comments; to Jose M. Prado for his help with the numerical analysis; to Bernard Dougherty, Maria Jose Figuerero Torres, Guillermo Mengoni Goñalons, and Tom Dillehay for their helpful comments; and to Patricia Madrid and Carlos Tremoullies, who made the drawings. I am also in debt to my colleges from Uruguay, Jorge Femenias and Roberto Bracco, who showed me collections from their country and kindly discussed with me their ideas about fishtail projectile points. Finally, I wish to acknowledge Dr. John Hyslop for his cooperation while I was studying the collection from Fell's and Palli Aike caves and the American Museum of Natural History for allowing me access to the collections. The research was funded by CONICET of Argentina.

REFERENCES CITED

Aguerre, A. M.
1979 Observaciones sobre la Industria Toldense. *Sapiens* 3:35–54.
1982 Informe Preliminar de las Excavaciones en la Cueva 4 de La Martita—Departamento Magallanes—Provincia de Santa Cruz. Paper presented at the 7th Congreso Nacional de Arqueología Argentina, San Luis.

Bate, L. F.
1982 *Origenes de la Comunidad Primitiva en Patagonia.* Serie Monograficas 1. Cuicuilco, Mexico.

Bell, R. E.
1960 Evidence of a Fluted Point Tradition in Ecuador. *American Antiquity* 26:102–106.

Bennett, W. C., and J. B. Bird
1960 *Andean Culture History.* American Museum of Natural History Handbook Series No. 15. New York.

Bird, J. B.
1938 Antiquity and Migrations of the Early Inhabitants of Patagonia. *The Geographical Review* 28:250–275.
1969 A Comparison of South Chilean and Ecuadorean "Fishtail" Projectile Points. *The Kroeber Anthropological Society Papers* 40:52–71.

Bird, J. B., and R. Cooke
1978 The Occurence in Panama of Two Types of Paleo Indian Projectile Points. In *Early Man in America from a Circum-Pacific Perspective,* edited by A. L. Bryan, pp. 263–272. Occasional Papers No. 1. Department of Anthropology, University of Alberta, Edmonton.

Borrero, L. A.
1983 Distribuciones Discontinuas de Puntas de Proyectil en Sudamerica. Paper presented at the 11th International Congress of Anthropological and Ethnological Sciences. Vancouver, Canada.

Bosch, A., J. Femenías, and A. Olivera
1980 Dispersión de las Puntas de Proyectil Líticas Pisciformes en el Uruguay. *III Congreso Nacional de Arqueología del Uruguay.* Montevideo.

Bryan, A. L.
1975 Paleoenvironments and Cultural Diversity in Late Pleistocene South America: A Rejoinder to Vance Haynes and a Reply to Thomas Lynch. *Quaternary Research* 5:151–159.
1986 Paleoamerican Prehistory as seen from South America. In *New Evidence for the Pleistocene Peopling of the Americas,* edited by A. L. Bryan, pp. 1–14. Center for the Study of Early Man, University of Maine, Orono.

Cardich, A. J.
1978 Recent Excavations at Lauricocha (Central Andes) and Los Toldos (Patagonia). In *Early Man in America from a Circum-Pacific Perspective,* edited by A. L. Bryan, pp. 296–300. Occasional Papers No. 1. Department of Anthropology, University of Alberta, Edmonton.
1979 Un Motivo Sobresaliente de las Pinturas Rupestres de "El Ceibo" (Santa Cruz). *Relaciones de las Sociedad Argentina de Antropología* XIII:163–182.

Cardich, A. J., L. A. Cardich, and A. Hajduk
1973 Secuencia Arqueológica y Cronología Radiocarbónica de la Cueva 3 de Los Toldos (Santa Cruz). *Relaciones de la Sociedad Argentina de Antropología* VII:85–123. Buenos Aires.

Carlson, R.
1983 The Far West. In *Early Man in the New World,* edited by R. Shutler, Jr., pp. 73–96. Sage Publications, San Francisco.

Ceballos, R.
1982 El Sitio Cuyín Manzano. *Centro de Investigaciones Cientifícas de Río Negro, Serie Estudios y Documentos* 9:1–66.

Curzio, D., E. A. Crivelli, and M. J. Silveira
1982 La Cueva Traful I (Provincia de Neuquén, Republica Argentina): Informe Preliminar. *Actas del VII Congreso Nacional de Arqueología (Colonia del Sacramento, Uruguay),* pp. 36–49. Montevideo, Uruguay.

Dillehay, T. D.
1988a How New is the New World? *Antiquity* 62:94–97.
1988b The Palaeoindian Debate. *Nature* 332:150–152.

Emperaire, J., A. Laming-Emperaire, and H. Reichlen
1963 La Grotte Fell et Autres Sites de la Region Volcanique de la Patagonie Chiliene. *Journal de la Societé des Americanistes* 52:169–254.

Eugenio, E.
1983 Una Punta "Cola de Pescado" de Lobos, Provincia de Buenos Aires. *ADEHA* 2:20–31.

Flegenheimer, N.
1986 Evidence of Paleoindian Occupation in the Argentine Pampas. Paper presented at The World Archaeological Congress, Southampton, England.
1987 Recent Research at Localities Cerro La China and Cerro El Sombrero, Argentina. *Current Research in the Pleistocene* 4:148–149.

Frison, G.
1983 The Western Plains and Mountain Region. *Early Man in the New World,* edited by R. Shutler, Jr., pp. 19–124. Sage Publications, San Francisco.

Gradin, C. J., C. A. Aschero, and A. M. Aguerre
1976 Investigaciones Arqueológicas en la Cueva de Las Manos, Alto Río Pinturas, Santa Cruz. *Relaciones de la Sociedad Argentina de Antropología* X:201–270. Buenos Aires.
1979 Arqueología del Área Río Pinturas, Provincia de Santa Cruz. *Relaciones de la Sociedad Argentina de Antropología* XIII:183–227. Buenos Aires.

Hurt, W.
1986 The Cultural Relationships of the Alice Boer Site, State of Sao Paulo, Brazil. In *New Evidence for the Pleistocene Peopling of the Americas,* edited by A. L. Bryan, pp. 215–219. Center for the Study of Early Man, University of Maine, Orono.

Jennings, J. D.
1978 Origins. In *Ancient Native Americans,* edited by J. D. Jennings, pp. 1–42. W. H. Freeman and Company, San Francisco.

Lynch, T. F.
1978 The South American Paleo-Indians. In *Ancient Native Americans,* edited by J. D. Jennings, pp. 455–490. W. H. Freeman and Company, San Francisco.
1983 The South American Paleo-Indians. In *Ancient Native Americans,* edited by J. D. Jennings, pp. 87–137. 2nd. edition. W. H. Freeman and Company. San Francisco.

Madrazo, G. B.
1972 Arqueología de Lobería y Salliquelo (Provincia de Buenos Aires). *Etnía* 15:1–18.

Mayer-Oakes, W. J.
1963 Early Man in the Andes. *Scientific American* 208:116–128.
1981 A Typology for Early Man Projectile Points in South America. Paper presented at the 9th Annual Midwest Conference of Andean and Amazonian Archaeology and Etnohistory, Columbia.
1986 Early Man Projectile Points and Lithic Technology in the Ecuadorian Sierra. In *New Evidence for the Pleistocene Peopling of the Americas,* edited by A. L. Bryan, pp. 133–156. Center for the Study of Early Man, University of Maine, Orono.

Meneghini, U.
1977 *Nuevas Investigaciones en los Yacimientos del "Cerro de los Burros."* Author edition, Montevideo, Uruguay.

Menghin, O. F. A.
1952 Fundamentos Cronológicos de la Prehistoria de Patagonia. *RUNA* V:23–43.

Mengoni Goñalons, G. L.
1986 Patagonian Prehistory: Early Exploitation of Faunal Resources (13,500–8500 B.P.). In *New Evidence for the Pleistocene Peopling of the Americas,* edited by A. L. Bryan, pp. 271–279. Center for the Study of Early Man, University of Maine, Orono.

Michener, C. D., and R. R. Sokal
1957 A Quantitative Approach to a Problem in Classification. *Evolution* 11.

Molina, M.
1972 "El Abrigo de los Pescadores" (Provincia de Santa Cruz). *Anales de Arqueología y Etnología* XXIV–XXV:239–250. Mendoza.

Nami, H. G.
1985–1986 Excavación Arqueológica y Hallazgo de una Punta de Proyectil "Fell I" en la Cueva del Medio, Seno de Ultima Esperanza, Chile. *Anales del Instituto de la Patagonia* 16:103–110.
1987 Informe sobre la Segunda y Tercera Expedición a la Cueva del Medio: Perspectivas Arqueológicas para la Patagonia Austral. *Anales del Instituto de la Patagonia* 17:73–106.
1989 New Dates for the Paleoindian Societies of South America. *Current Research in the Pleistocene* 6:18–19.

Politis, G. G.
1984 Investigaciones Arqueológicas en el Área Interserrana Bonaerense. *Etnía* 32:7–52.

Rohlf, F. J., J. Kishpaugh, and D. Kirk
1971 *NT-SYS Numerical Taxonomy System of Multi-*

variate Statistical Programs. Technical Reports, State University of New York at Stony Brook.

Sackett, J. R.
1982 Approaches to Style in Lithic Archaeology. *Journal of Anthropological Archaeology* 1:59–112.

Saxon, E. C.
1976 La Prehistoria de Fuego-Patagonia: Colonización de un Habitat Marginal. *Anales del Instituto de la Patagonia* 7:63–73.

Schobinger, J.
1969 *Prehistoria de Sudamérica.* Nueva Colección Editoeise Labor. Barcelona.
1971 Una Punta de Tipo "Cola de Pescado" de La Crucesita (Mendoza). *Anales de Arqueología y Etnología* XXVI:89–97.
1973 Nuevos Hallazgos de Puntas "Cola de Pescado" y Consideraciones en Torno al Origen y Dipersión de la Cultura de Cazadores Superiores Toldense (Fell I) en Sudamérica. *Atti del XL Congresso Internazionale degli Americanisti* 1:33–50. Roma-Genova.

Silveira, M. J.
1978 Hallazgo de una Punta "Cola de Pescado" en la Provincia de Buenos Aires. Paper presented at the V Congreso Nacional de Arqueología Argentina. San Juan, Argentina.

Snarskis, M. J.
1979 Turrialba: A Paleo-Indian Quarry and Workshop Site in Eastern Costa Rica. *American Antiquity* 44:125–138.

Sneath, P. H., and R. R. Sokal
1973 *Numerical Taxonomy.* W. H. Freeman and Company, San Francisco.

Sokal, R. R.
1961 Distance as a Measure of Taxonomic Similarity. *Systematic Zoology* 10:70.

Sokal, R. R., and C. D. Michener
1958 A Statistical Method for Evaluating Systematic Relationships. *University of Kansas Science Bulletin* 38:1409–1438.

Willey, G. R.
1971 *An Introduction to American Archaeology, Volume II: South America.* Prentice-Hall, Englewood Cliffs, New Jersey.

Peopling of the New World: A Discussion

RICHARD E. MORLAN
Archaeological Survey of Canada
Canadian Museum of Civilization
Hull, PQ, Canada J8X 4H2

This brief discussion focusses on three topics that emerge from a consideration of all the papers in this volume: (1) alternative interpretations of the scanty Beringian data base; (2) disparate inferences concerning Paleoindian subsistence that are often ill supported by data; and (3) the need to examine more thoroughly and systematically the structure of the fluted-point record across the Americas.

The past ten years have witnessed the publication of an unprecedented number of collected paper volumes, important site reports, and stand-alone reviews devoted to the peopling of the Americas. Systematic surveys, large-scale multidisciplinary projects, major excavations, and symposia too numerous to remember, much less to mention, have also made the past decade an exciting one in this field. One might expect that such a flurry of activity would have created a commensurate increase in our understanding of the subject, but I find no consensus as to the time and circumstances of the peopling of the Western Hemisphere. There is a wide range of opinion as to the technology and subsistence economy that might be expected in the New World sites. Yet the problem remains important, because it represents one of the most remarkable geographic and adaptive expansions of our species.

My comments do not represent a balanced treatment of each symposium paper, but they highlight several themes that various authors have touched upon. First, I want to mention the scanty Beringian data base reviewed by Clark (this volume) and Goebel et al. (this volume). That nearly all of the sites have come to light during the past 15 years suggests that more remain to be found. Clark presents three alternative hypotheses regarding the relationship between Beringian fluted points and those in the South: (1) northern origin of fluted points in a pre-microblade context; (2) southern origin and northward spread by either migration or diffusion; and (3) independent invention. He says that we cannot yet choose among these three alternatives. I suggest that there are other alternatives. All of Clark's hypotheses are predicated on the assumption that fluted points and microblades represent separate cultural traditions in Alaska and the Yukon. This view matches reconstructions by Dumond (1982), Goebel et al. (this volume), Hamilton (1989), and Haynes (1982). It is a view that seems well supported by both cumulative frequency distributions and cluster analysis showing marked differences between the Nenana complex and the Denali complex, the former possibly related to Clovis and the latter appearing to represent the arrival of microblade technology a half millennium later (Goebel et al., this volume).

To assign Nenana and Denali to separate cultural traditions is only one of several possible interpretations. The differences between them might be due to other factors such as functional or seasonal variables specific to each component. There are two reasons for considering that fluted points and microblades might have been made by the same people: (1) the assemblage from the Putu site; and (2) the composition of the Dyuktai tradition in Siberia.

The Putu site is somewhat difficult to interpret with confidence, because it is a relatively shallow site extensively disturbed by ground squirrels and possibly by cryoturbation (Alexander 1987). Haynes (1987:86) either overlooked it or ignored it when he stated that fluted points "have not been found in situ in Alaska." Goebel et al. (this volume) state that fluted points in Alaska "have yet to be found in clear late Pleistocene stratified contexts and appear to be younger than the Nenana and Clovis assemblages." Likewise, Hamilton (1989) notes discrepancies among the four radiocarbon dates from Zone II where the fluted points were found, and he concludes that fluted points "may have diffused into eastern Beringia from a center of origin farther south." In my opinion, the four radiocarbon dates from Putu Zone II were not created equal. The youngest, 5700 ± 190 yr B.P. (GaK-4939) is on charcoal "from combined samples" (Alexander 1987:36) or, more precisely, "a combined charcoal sample of small flecks discovered throughout the zone" (Alexander 1987:43). A date of 6090 ± 430 yr B.P. (GaK-4939) was obtained on soil from the "upper half of the zone" (Alexander 1987:43 [ascription to "lower half of the zone" on page 36 is apparently an error]). Soil from the lower half of the zone yielded a date of 8454 ± 130 yr B.P. (WSU-1318 [Alexander 1987:36, 42]). The oldest date, 11,470 ± 500 yr B.P. (SI-2382), is on charcoal from a hearth designated Feature 9, "the largest concentration of charcoal found at the site" (Alexander 1987:11, 36, 42). If any of these dates is related to the fluted-point assemblage, it is most likely the last mentioned, in view of the nature of the sample (charcoal) and its provenience (a hearth). If this date is correct, then the Putu fluted points are contemporaneous with the Nenana complex and may even be members of the complex, but at Putu they are associated with four lanceolate points, a triangular point that "fits within the range of variation of the Chindadn type from Healy Lake" (Alexander 1987:20), and 140 microblades. Alexander (1987:38) believes that as many as 200 microblade midsections may have been removed from the Putu site after being used to arm slotted antler points. Thus we are confronted with a difficult decision: (1) we can dismiss the Putu site as technologically mixed and discordantly dated owing to compressed stratigraphy and diagenetic disturbance; or (2) we can accept the concept that fluted points and microblades belong together in a single complex tool kit that is contemporaneous with more specialized manifestations known from the Nenana Valley.

The nearest possible ancestor in time and space for any of these Alaskan assemblages is the Dyuktai tradition of northeastern Siberia (Mochanov 1977, 1978). The technology of the Dyuktai tradition includes both well-made bifaces and microblades detached from a variety of core forms. Some of the cores are made on bifacial blanks, as seen in the well-known Yubetsu technique of preceramic Japan (see Morlan 1987). Experimental flint knapping suggests that the detachment of a long parallel-sided flake from the face of a knapped blank is one of the most difficult tasks of lithic craftsmanship. It is easy to detach such a flake wherever a prepared ridge is available to guide the fracture, and ridge flaking is a fundamental property of blade and burin technology. Microblade production also depends upon this principle, and the active area of the microcore must be maintained as a convex arc, requiring progressive invasion of adjacent knapped faces that lack the guiding ridges. Where better to expect the invention of fluting techniques than among people whose technology required them to confront such problems? I see the microblade technology of the Dyuktai tradition as a logical precursor of fluted points (Morlan 1987).

One must ask why microblades did not accompany fluted points south of the ice. Borrowing heavily from ideas put forth by Dale Guthrie (1983), I have argued: (1) that microblades were used to arm slotted antler points; (2) that such points were alternate weapons in a tool kit that also included fluted points; (3) that caribou antler is superior to all other materials for making armed osseous points; and (4) that such weaponry was too costly to maintain south of the range of caribou, where there are many high-quality chert sources that outcrop at the surface (Morlan 1987). Alan Bryan (personal communication) has raised a logical question: Why do we not find microblades in the Northeast where Paleoindians are believed to have hunted caribou?

I will return to this question after discussing a second theme—instant food—that runs through the papers in this volume. Inferences about instant food of Paleoindian vintage are made by referring to ethnographic data on hunters and gatherers, considering species diversity in broad environmental zones, noting opportunities in special landscape settings, and inferring generalized or specialized economies in the utter absence of archaeological data. Examples in this volume include: (1) David Keenlyside's suggestion that seaside locations point toward reliance on marine resources; (2) Ruth Gruhn's statement that a generalized foraging economy may be inferred from the unspecialized nature of the lithic assemblages in Brazil; and (3) parts of Eileen Johnson's construct that predicts undiscovered large campsites, a paradox she notes in her paper. Johnson, Tom Lynch, and Bradley Lepper and David Meltzer have carefully elaborated such arguments, and they are quite reasonable even if poorly supported by existing data. Jim Dunbar and Judith Willig have framed settlement pattern and subsistence reconstructions with reference to potable water supplies and chert resources; if these seem better supported it is because they appeal directly to specific data on the distributions of particular substances essential to human life.

In a few cases, however, the instant food arguments are so elaborated they border on mythology. An example is the purported Paleoindian reliance on caribou in the Northeast, based largely on discussions of site location, size, and layout, with reference to ethnographic data on caribou hunters and paleobotanical reconstructions of tundra vegetation. David Meltzer and Peter Storck have described this pattern in this symposium. Real data are scarce, including, for example, doubtful associations at Dutchess Quarry Caves Nos. 1 and 8, a toe bone at Holcombe, only 3 of 300 highly fragmented bone bits at Whipple, and unspecified data at Bull Brook, where beaver is also reported. Given the generally poor state of bone preservation in the northeastern sites, how can we hope to find data in support of reliance on caribou? Blood residues on stone tools might be one method. I have seen such residues on a fluted point from the Debert site in Tom Loy's former lab, and Loy and Erle Nelson have shown that the residues can provide radiocarbon dates as well as species identifications (Loy 1983; Nelson et al. 1986).

Meanwhile we finally have an association of fluted points with mastodon at Kimmswick (Graham and Kay 1988), but this is not the only eastern or midwestern association of humans with mastodon. Daniel Fisher's studies of mastodon sites in Michigan represent an important body of work (Fisher 1987) that was not included in this symposium, perhaps because no fluted points were found. Nonetheless, at least the Pleasant Lake mastodon is contemporaneous with the fluted-point complexes and bears important implications for arguments concerning Paleoindian subsistence in the Northeast. For now, the case for specialized caribou exploitation is too weak to make me wonder why microblades that could arm osseous points are absent in eastern fluted-point sites. There may not have been reliable access to caribou antler. Alternatively, perhaps microblade-like tools are not entirely absent but instead are less well made and harder to recognize, as suggested by a reanalysis of Shoop (Cox 1986) and some of the flakes from Meadowcroft Rockshelter (Adovasio et al. 1988).

Why was Meadowcroft Rockshelter not even mentioned in this symposium? Arguments about the radiocarbon dates may scare some people away, but the fact remains that a long record is stratigraphically below assemblages referred to the Archaic (Adovasio et al. 1988). Perhaps some would call them all Archaic, but if they are Paleoindian they provide direct evidence for the generalized foraging proposed here by Bradley Lepper and David Meltzer, and they deserve mention.

A third theme concerns the structure of the fluted-point record. One aspect of that structure is technological and stylistic variability among fluted points. As Judith Willig (this volume) notes, "No one set of eyes has yet looked upon all known western fluted points." I remember when James Griffin was reputed to have conducted his thumbnail test for hardness on the back of every prehistoric potsherd in North America. Because we have long since passed the time when any one person could cast his eyes on every fluted point in North America, we must find other ways of assembling a coherent data set on Paleoindian artifacts. A formal commission is needed to work on a uniform terminology, typology, and technology of fluted points on a continent-wide basis. Only such a survey could provide a secure framework for explaining variability, for assessing the roles of diffusion and migration, and for gauging whether the structure of the Paleoindian data bespeak greater time depth than we can now confirm for many regions of the Western Hemisphere.

Such a commission might also seek to improve our knowledge of a second aspect of the fluted-point record, viz., lithic procurement. Many authors in this and other symposia have noted the Paleoindian predilection for high-quality cherts and other cryptocrystalline stones. Paleoindians either camped near suitable sources, or they traded or carried good stone over great distances, often 200 km or more. Some writers have commented that Paleoindians must have been good geologists to satisfy their requirements for raw material of the quantity and quality found in their sites. In an earlier paper, Meltzer (1984–1985) noted the importance of distinguishing between primary outcrop and secondary glacio-fluvial sources, but the focus of his analysis was on mobility in different paleoenvironmental zones. We should additionally consider the amount of time needed to discover all these sources and to schedule seasonal activities or trading networks to replenish supplies. Whenever they got here, the Paleoindians did not come equipped with bedrock maps of the Western Hemisphere. They may have made the first ones, and we Quaternarists well know that it takes time to do so.

This brings me to my final point. We still do not know when humans arrived in the Americas, but we can approach the problem from two vantage points in the archaeological record: (1) the putative evidence for pre-Clovis occupation; and (2) the structure of the fluted-point record itself. Having said that, it is incumbent upon a discussant to point out which sites hang in the balance as putative evidence for pre-Clovis (or pre-

12,000 yr B.P.) occupation. The debate concerning the Meadowcroft Rockshelter radiocarbon dates is unresolved, but it is an important debate to be settled, perhaps by accelerator dating of the identified nut shells (Adovasio et al. 1988; Morlan 1988). Elsewhere in North America south of the Laurentide limit, we have the Shriver site in Missouri (Rowlet 1981), Burnham in Oklahoma (Tratebas 1989), the Dutton, Selby, and Lamb Springs sites in Colorado (Stanford and Graham 1985; Stanford et al. 1981), False Cougar Cave in Montana (Bonnichsen et al. 1986), and Wilson Butte Cave in Idaho (Gruhn 1965). This may not be an extensive list, but any of these sites might have been occupied by people who took earliest advantage of a habitable ice-free corridor in late glacial time.

Sites farther south, especially those in South America, may require an earlier entry of humans into the Americas. The earliest worth mentioning is Toca do Boquierao da Pedra Furada in Brazil, purportedly providing evidence as early as 45,000 years ago (Guidon 1986; Guidon et al. 1989). In addition, there are Lapa Vermelha, Santana do Riacho, Los Toldos, Tagua Tagua, Monte Verde, the Ayacucho phase at Pikimachay, Taima-taima (all in South America), some of the sites in Pueblo, Mexico, and possibly a few others that suggest substantial time depth for the colonization of the Americas (see Morlan 1988 for a critical summary).

These sites deserve further study while at the same time we intensify and systematize our study of the fluted-point data base. Such work will finally enable us to suggest useful calibrations for the convergent data on divergence of language, dental morphology, and serological traits (Greenberg et al. 1986)—but that's another story!

REFERENCES CITED

Adovasio, J. M., A. T. Boldurian, and R. C. Carlisle
1988 Who Are Those Guys?: Some Biased Thoughts on the Initial Peopling of the New World. In *Americans Before Columbus: Ice-Age Origins,* edited by R. C. Carlisle, pp. 45–61. Ethnology Monographs No. 12. Department of Anthropology, University of Pittsburgh, Pittsburgh.

Alexander, H. E.
1987 *Putu: A Fluted Point site in Alaska.* Simon Fraser University Publication No. 17. Archaeology Press, Simon Fraser University, Burnaby.

Bonnichsen, R., R. W. Graham, T. Geppert, J. S. Oliver, S. G. Oliver, D. Schnurrenberger, R. Stuckenrath, A. Tratebas, and D. E. Young
1986 False Cougar and Shield Trap Caves, Pryor Mountains, Montana. *National Geographic Research* 2:276–290.

Cox, S. L.
1986 A Re-analysis of the Shoop Site. *Archaeology of Eastern North America* 14:101–170.

Dumond, D. E.
1982 Colonization of the American Arctic and the Peopling of America. *American Antiquity* 47:885–895.

Fisher, D. C.
1987 Mastodont Procurement by Paleoindians of the Great Lakes Region: Hunting or Scavenging? In *The Evolution of Human Hunting,* edited by M. H. Nitecki and D. V. Nitecki, pp. 309–421. Plenum Press, New York.

Graham, R. W., and M. Kay
1988 Taphonomic Comparisons of Cultural and Noncultural Faunal Deposits at the Kimmswick and Barnhardt Sites, Jefferson County, Missouri. In *Late Pleistocene and Early Holocene Paleoecology and Archaeology of the Eastern Great Lakes Region,* edited by R. S. Laub, N. G. Miller, and D. W. Steadman, pp. 227–240. Bulletin of the Buffalo Society of Natural Sciences No. 33. Buffalo.

Greenberg, J. H., C. G. Turner II, and S. L. Zegura
1986 The Settlement of the Americas: A Comparison of the Linguistic, Dental and Genetic Evidence. *Current Anthropology* 27:477–497.

Gruhn, R.
1965 Two Early Radiocarbon Dates from the Lower Levels of Wilson Butte Cave, South-central Idaho. *Tebiwa* 8:57.

Guidon, N.
1986 Las Unidades Culturales de Sao Raimundo Nonato—Sudeste del Estado de Piaui—Brazil. In *New Evidence for the Pleistocene Peopling of the Americas,* edited by A. L. Bryan, pp. 157–171. Center for the Study of Early Man, University of Maine, Orono.

Guidon, N., F. Parenti, and J. Pellerin
1989 Deep in South American Past: Pedra Furada and Brazilian Prehistory. Paper presented at the First World Summit Conference on the Peopling of the Americas, Center for the Study of the First Americans, University of Maine, Orono.

Guthrie, R. D.
1983 Osseous Projectile Points: Biological Considerations Affecting Raw Material Selection and Design Among Paleolithic and Paleoindian Peoples. In *Animals and Archaeology: Hunters and Their Prey,* edited by J. Clutton-Brock and C. Grigson, pp. 273–294. BAR International Series 163, Oxford.

Hamilton, T. D.
1989 Late Pleistocene Environments and Peopling of Eastern Beringia. Paper presented at the First World Summit Conference on the Peopling of the Americas, Center for the Study of the First Americans, University of Maine, Orono.

Haynes, C. V., Jr.
1982 Were Clovis Progenitors in Beringia? In *Paleoecology of Beringia,* edited by D. M. Hopkins, J. V. Matthews, Jr., C. E. Schweger, and S. B. Young, pp. 383–398. Academic Press, New York.
1987 Clovis Origin Update. *Kiva* 52:83–93.

Loy, T. H.
1983 Prehistoric Blood Residues: Detection on Tool Surfaces and Identification of Species of Origin. *Science* 220:1269–1271.

Meltzer, D. J.
1984–1985 On Stone Procurement and Settlement Mobility in Eastern Fluted Point Groups. *North American Archaeologist* 6:1–24.

Mochanov, Y. A.
1977 *Drevneishie Etapy Zaseleniia Chelovekom Severo-Vostochnoi Azii (Most Ancient Stages of Human Settlement in Northeast Asia).* Nauka, Novosibirsk.
1978 Stratigraphy and Absolute Chronology of the Paleolithic of Northeast Asia. In *Early Man in America from a Circum-Pacific Perspective,* edited by A. L. Bryan, pp. 54–66. Occasional Papers No. 1. Department of Anthropology, University of Alberta, Edmonton.

Morlan, R. E.
1987 The Pleistocene Archaeology of Beringia. In *The Evolution of Human Hunting,* edited by M. H. Nitecki and D. V. Nitecki, pp. 267–307. Plenum Press, New York.
1988 Pre-Clovis People: Early Discoveries of America? In *Americans Before Columbus: Ice-Age Origins,* edited by R. C. Carlisle, pp. 31–43. Ethnology Monographs No. 12. Department of Anthropology, University of Pittsburgh, Pittsburgh.

Nelson, D. E., T. H. Loy, J. S. Vogel, and J. R. Southon
1986 Radiocarbon Dating Blood Residues on Prehistoric Stone Tools. *Radiocarbon* 28:170–174.

Rowlett, R. M.
1981 A Lithic Assemblage Stratified Beneath a Fluted Point Horizon in Northwest Missouri. *Missouri Archaeologist* 42:7–16.

Stanford, D., and R. W. Graham
1985 Archeological Investigations of the Selby and Dutton Mammoth Kill Sites, Yuma, Colorado. *National Geographic Society Research Reports* 19:519–541.

Stanford, D., W. R. Wedel, and G. R. Scott
1981 Archaeological Investigations of the Lamb Spring Site. *Southwestern Lore* 47:14–27.

Tratebas, A.
1989 The Burnham Site: Possible Pre-Clovis Evidence from Oklahoma. *Mammoth Trumpet* 5(1).

Clovis Origins

ROBSON BONNICHSEN
Center for the Study of the First Americans
University of Maine
Orono, ME 04473

Popular writers characterize the peopling of the Americas as a controversy between advocates of the Clovis and pre-Clovis occupations. Supporters of the late-entry model propose that the first Americans arrived about 11,500 years ago, whereas pre-Clovis advocates believe the Americas were populated well before 11,500 years ago. This characterization of the peopling of the Americas as a simple debate between Clovis and pre-Clovis antagonists oversimplifies a much more interesting situation. Regional syntheses presented in this volume either implicitly or explicitly support one of three intercontinental scale models: the late-entry migration model; the early-entry migration model; or the environmental-response model. An overview of regional models suggests there is a tremendous amount of variability in what is being called Clovis and that the definition and meaning attached to Clovis are ambiguous. Some authors favor a single migration, others suggest a diffusion pattern, while still others believe that Clovis originated at several independent centers in the New World.

The perspective that Clovis is the first basal culture in the New World is being challenged. Radiocarbon dates from a series of archaeological complexes, which include North and South American bifacially flaked projectile points, support the view that several cultural complexes are as early as Clovis. These include the Nenana complex, Alaska; the Goshen complex, northern Plains; the Western Stemmed point complex, Great Basin; the El Jobo point complex from northern South America; and the fishtail point complex from southern South America. The emergence of multiple projectile-point styles between 13,000 and 11,000 years ago during a period of rapid environmental change is seen as evidence that supports the environmental-response model.

The case for pre-Clovis occupation is based on research by an increasing number of investigators using the multidisciplinary approach, who integrate a variety of different lines of evidence. Evidence for pre-Clovis occupation occurs at: Bluefish Cave, Yukon Territory; Meadowcroft Rockshelter, Pennsylvania; Taima-taima, Venezuela; Pedra Furada, Brazil; and Monte Verde, Chile (Marshall 1990).

Authors of this volume document that artifacts assigned to the Clovis complex exhibit a great deal of variability from region to region. At present there is not a consensus for either documenting or interpreting variability of Clovis fluted-point assemblages.

To move our understanding of Clovis and its relationship to other cultural complexes forward, we must move away from our reliance on the normative approach, which does not accommodate the study of cultural change. To understand the causal factors responsible for the rise and demise of Clovis and other late Pleistocene flaked-stone assemblages, there is a need for developing systematic, empirical approaches that will allow us to discriminate between migration, diffusion, and in situ development. Such a framework is needed for assessing the meaning of inter- and intra-assemblage variability. In addition to traditional studies of the formal parameters of artifacts, a focus on stone-tool production procedures is seen as a meaningful approach for assessing inter- and intra-assemblage variability.

INTRODUCTION

Problem Orientation

Our goal in convening the 1987 INQUA symposium at Ottawa was to focus scientific attention on what is known about Clovis. The Clovis cultural complex is often cited by New World archaeologists as providing the first noncontroversial evidence important to understanding the peopling of the Americas. As the preceding papers demonstrate, there is not, however, a unified consensus regarding the meaning of the Clovis complex by specialists.

Clovis or Clovis-like points occur in North America and fishtail points occur in South America. Because of the widespread nature of this archaeological complex, all Clovis complex data are not readily accessible to all specialists. Our objective in convening the 1987 INQUA symposium was to bring regional specialists together to develop syntheses of knowledge on Clovis origins and adaptations. Our hope was that collectively these individual studies would provide an up-to-date interhemispheric overview of information relevant to the interpretation of the Clovis complex. What has resulted is a series of regional syntheses organized around what are often implicit models.

My objective in this concluding chapter is to examine scientific procedures used by various investigators seeking to explain Clovis origins. Several authors acknowledge the diversity of Clovis adaptations, but my emphasis will be on elucidating the models used to explain the rise and demise of Clovis. My examination involves a two-step process. First, I provide an overview of regional developmental models, which seek to explain the origin of the Clovis complex. These include the late-entry migration model; the early-entry, parallel-evolutionary migration model; and the environmental-response model. I then assess the assumptions on which these models are based and consider how well Clovis data from different regional sequences meet expectations of the three alternative models. The presentation is concluded with suggestions of what needs to be done to resolve unanswered questions regarding the Clovis complex.

REGIONAL MODELS

North America

Arctic: The Nenana Complex

Goebel et al. (this volume) propose that the Nenana complex of central Alaska has affinities with the Clovis complex of the Southwest. The Nenana complex assemblages, dated to approximately 11,300 yr B.P., are compared with assemblages from the Blackwater Draw and Murray Springs sites using cumulative frequencies and cluster diagrams. On the basis of similarities in the structure of artifact classes found in these assemblages, Goebel and colleagues conclude that the Nenana complex is more closely related to the Clovis complex of the continental United States than to the succeeding Alaskan Paleoarctic tradition.

They argue that, with the exception of the absence of fluted points, the Nenana and Clovis assemblages are identical. Neither Nenana nor Clovis display wedge-shaped cores, microblades, or transverse burins, *fossiles directeurs* of the central Alaskan Denali complex.

Goebel et al. (this volume) propose two possible models to explain the origin of Clovis. Model 1 calls for a common ancestral population that gave rise to the Clovis and Nenana complexes, which are characterized by the use of a biface and blade technology (Figure 1). They suggest that at about 12,000 yr B.P., the rapidly receding continental ice sheet in North America permitted rapid movement of northern groups through the Ice-Free Corridor (cf. Greenberg et al. 1986; Turner 1985). The Siberian antecedents of these groups are unknown. Asian assemblages, such as the lower level at Ushki I, Kamchataka Peninsula, which includes bifacially flaked projectile points and end scrapers but no wedge-shaped cores or microblades, are indications of a plausible source for the ancestral population. The Nenana complex is seen as an earlier phase of this complex and Clovis as a later phase (Figure 2).

The second model calls for a pre-Wisconsinan arrival of populations into North America who used blades and bifaces. Goebel et al. (this volume) propose that Clovis and Nenana are the remnants of a much earlier peopling event—one that occurred after 35,000 yr B.P.—that was characterized by retouched blades, bifacially flaked points and knives, end scrapers, side scrapers, perforators, and wedges. The absence of microblade technology in these industries indicates that the founding migration into the Americas took place prior to the miniaturization of north Asian lithic industries. Early Upper Paleolithic microlithic industries are known from Ust-Kova in the northern Angara region of central Siberia. This site has produced microblade technology with wedge-shaped cores, microblades, and transverse burins; and is radiocarbon dated at 23,920 yr B.P. Goebel and his co-workers conclude that American Paleoindians migrated from Siberia into the Western Hemisphere prior to the spread of the Late Upper Paleolithic microblade industries.

Conclusive pre-Clovis evidence for biface and blade technologies, which are proposed in both the early- and late-entry models, has yet to be discovered in Alaska, Canada, or the continental United States. An additional problem with the first model, which envisions Clovis as evolving from the Beringian Point Industry through an earlier Nenana-complex phase, is that Nenana complex radiocarbon dates overlap those of the Clovis complex (Haynes 1987) and are not demonstrably earlier than Clovis as required by this model.

Although Goebel and his co-workers should be complimented for performing detailed quantitative analyses comparing Clovis and Nenana assemblages, their comparisons are based on general morphological similarities. Detailed technological information is not presented that would confirm that artifact technology is identical in the Arctic and American Southwest, as claimed.

Clark (this volume) and Morlan (this volume) indicate that fluted points occur in eastern Beringia and down through the area of the Ice-Free Corridor (Carlson, this volume). Although some authors suggest there is a distinct Arctic-style variant of fluted points, Clark is careful to note that such a distinction is premature on the basis of a few superficial comparisons of projectile points. Arctic fluted points tend to have multiple flutes and are smaller than most fluted points from the Plains and Southwest. Clark further observes that a Clovis culture can hardly be said to exist in the Arctic, as kill and settlement sites comparable to those found in the continental Unites States have yet to be located in Alaska or the Yukon Territory.

Clark suggests three working hypotheses that can be used to explain the origin of the Arctic fluted-point pattern. These are known as: (1) the northern-origins hypothesis (Figure 3); (2) the southern-origins hypothesis (Figure 4); and (3) an independent-development hypothesis (Figure 5).

The northern-origins hypothesis proposes that fluted points developed from a non-microblade tradition and were taken south about 11,500 years ago. Clark concludes this hypothesis is plausible but is very weak for lack of supporting dates.

The southern-origins proposal envisions that the fluted-point pattern originated in the continental United States and moved northward through the Ice-Free Corridor. Two possible mechanisms may have been involved: actual migration of northward moving populations, or diffusion. The diffusion and migration hypotheses call for archaeological evidence of intermediate populations in the Ice-Free Corridor area. Evidence for such populations and dated remains is lacking at this time.

Independent development is the third possibility. Clark (this volume) proposes that Arctic fluted points may have developed on lanceolate points that date to the Archaic period. Given the lanceolate form, prevalence of basal thinning scars, and the presence of grinding on the lower and basal edges of these points, it would have been easy for fluting to have developed on lanceolate forms. Fluting may have diffused north from the South sometime between 8000 and 6000 years ago. If this did occur, it could account for the presence of fluted points

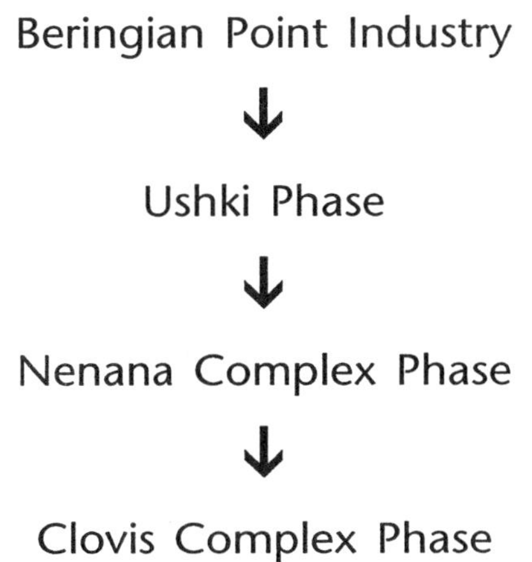

Figure 1. Late-entry developmental model (after Goebel et al., this volume).

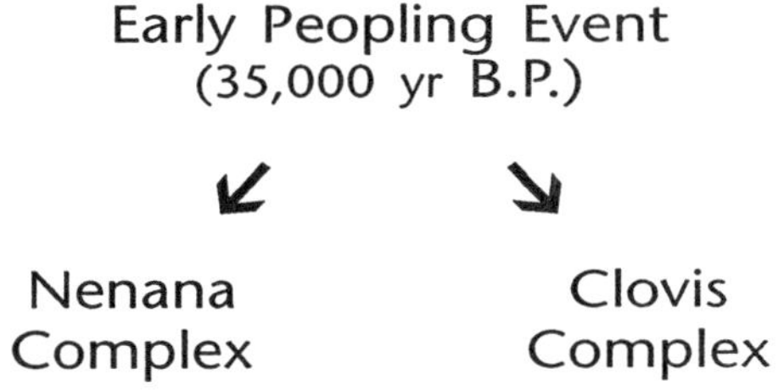

Figure 2. Early-entry developmental model (after Goebel et al., this volume).

Arctic Fluted Points

Clovis Complex in the United States

Figure 3. Northern-origins hypothesis (after Clark, this volume).

Arctic Fluted Points

Clovis in Continental U.S.A.

Figure 4. Southern-origins hypothesis (after Clark, this volume).

Arctic Fluted Points

United States Fluted Points

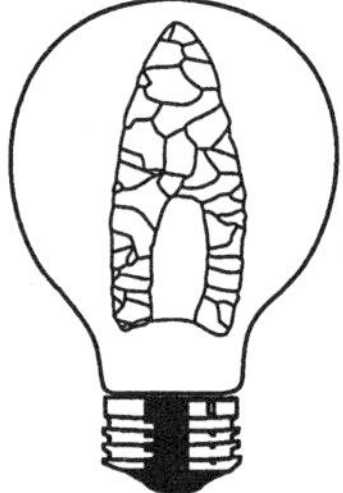

Figure 5. Independent-origins hypothesis (after Clark, this volume).

in the northern Archaic tradition. Clark concludes that the question of northern fluted-point origins should remain open, as there is not conclusive evidence to support any of the above hypotheses.

In his discussant comments, Morlan (this volume) adds yet another hypothesis to the northern-origins mix (Figure 6). He proposes that Arctic fluted points occur in the Paleoarctic tradition, which has its origin in the Dyuktai microblade tradition. Morlan suggests that Arctic fluted points served as end blades in slotted points made from antler that also held microblades in side slots. Morlan cites the Putu point from Alaska, which has been dated to 11,470 ± 500 yr B.P., as evidence of the association between fluted points and the Paleoarctic tradition. Morlan suggests that on the basis of this date, the Putu specimen, and thus Arctic fluted points, may be contemporaneous with the Nenana complex. Given the large correction factor on the Putu date, the Putu point may as old as the Nenana complex or it could be younger. Clark (this volume) notes that a fluted point was found in Level 2 of the Denali component at Dry Creek, which is a second association between fluted points and the Paleoarctic tradition. Carlson (this volume) cites Flenniken, who notes that the Putu point has flutes made by a pressure technique. I concur with Flenniken's observation and further suggest that these flutes were detached by the same type of tool used to detach microblades. Morlan's scenario suggests that Arctic fluted points, which were part of the Paleoarctic tradition, may have given rise to fluted points of the South. However, as Morlan notes, no evidence has been found south of the Laurentide ice sheet for an association between microblades and fluted points that would support his proposed model.

The Ice-Free Corridor

In his coverage of the Ice-Free Corridor region, an area that would have connected Beringia with the continental United States, Carlson (this volume) reviews what is known about the distribution of fluted points from this critical region. There are about 40 occurrences of fluted points. With the exception of Charlie Lake Cave, northern British Columbia, which produced a fluted point and associated radiocarbon dates ranging from 10,770 to 10,100 yr B.P., fluted points have not been found in acceptable dated contexts.

Carlson suggests that proto-Clovis may have originated from a biface-blade technology (cf. Goebel et al., this volume) (Figure 2) or from the Paleoarctic tradition (cf. Morlan, this volume) (Figure 6). He proposes that proto-Clovis populations moved south through the corridor about 14,000 years ago (Figure 7). No physical evidence has yet been found in the Corridor region to support this proposed migration route. Carlson suggests that fluted points from the Corridor are non-Clovis variants and mark the decline of fluting as a hafting technique. Specialized regional variants, such as the Peace River fluted, should be considered late.

Several investigators in this volume propose that reduction of point size is a function of chronology and is the end stage of a developmental sequence. This hypothesis assumes that after the extinction of large game animals at the end of the Pleistocene, smaller fluted points were used in the pursuit of smaller game. No one has presented strong evidence to support this proposition. There is considerable variation in point size at most fluted-point sites (see Fagan's [1988] study of fluted points from the Dietz site in southeast Oregon). Many points exhibit resharpening, which suggests that the size of individual points varied during their use-life. Without radiocarbon dates, there is no way to know if the Peace River variant and other fluted points from the Corridor are earlier than, the same age as, or later than dated Plains and Southwest Clovis sites.

Dyuktai

Arctic Fluted /Paleoarctic

Clovis

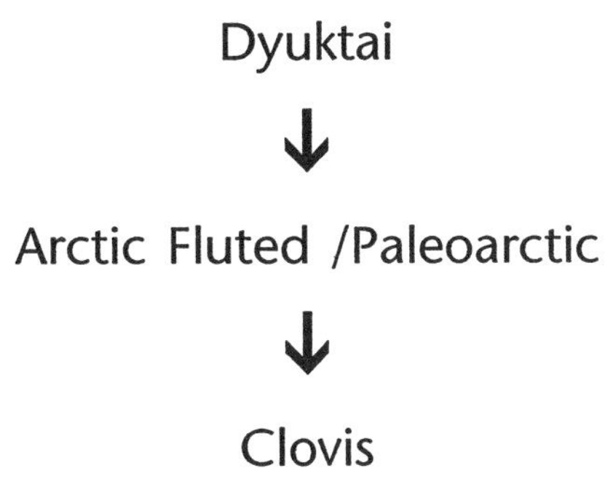

Figure 6. Dyuktai late-entry developmental model (after Morlan, this volume).

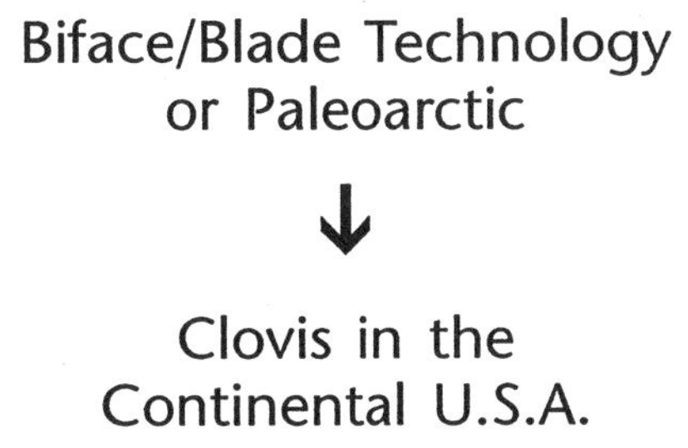

Western United States

Willig (this volume) proposes a western variant of Clovis. The geographical distribution of fluted complexes in the Far West includes western Washington and the Puget Lowlands, southern British Columbia, the entire Columbia-Snake River drainage system in the north, as well as California and the entire Basin-Range province of western North America. Titmus and Woods (this volume) document the distribution and variation of fluted points from Idaho that Willig would include in her western Clovis variant. There are no absolute dates on sites assigned to the western variant. Willig notes that there is nothing unique in the morphology or technology of the western variant of Clovis in form, size, presence of edge and basal grinding, channel scratching, and/or pressure flaking (cf. Haynes 1987) to distinguish these points from forms available from "classic" Clovis sites.

Willig believes that western Clovis developed from a pan-continental Clovis pattern and that regionalization occurred very early in the Far West. Willig further proposes that the Western Stemmed point pattern is derived from western Clovis and survives later in time than Clovis (Figure 8).

Pivotal to Willig's model is the concept of a western Clovis variant. She uses the term "variant" in a geographical, rather than a morphological, sense, in contrast to other investigators in this volume. Consequently, neither formal nor technological characteristics are offered in support for linking developmental phases in her regional phylogenetic model. It is not clear how basal Clovis is to be distinguished from the western Clovis variant. Furthermore, the connection between Clovis and Western Stemmed points is not clear-cut. Some authors (Bryan 1980, 1988, this volume) suggest that Western Stemmed points represent an independent cultural development that is contemporaneous with Clovis and persists longer in time. Additionally, the

Biface/Blade Technology
or Paleoarctic

Clovis in the
Continental U.S.A.

Figure 7. Late-entry developmental model (after Carlson, this volume).

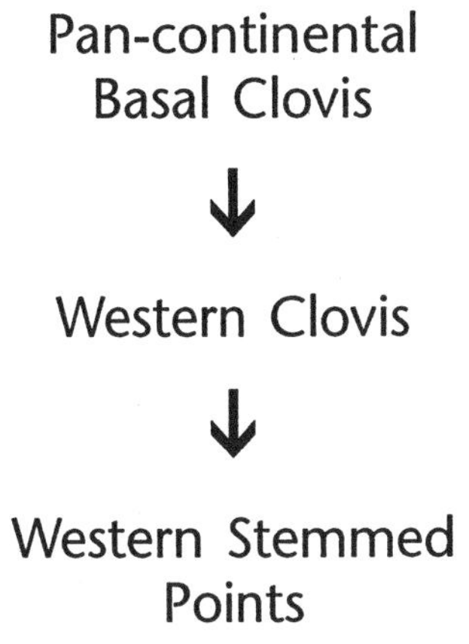

Pan-continental
Basal Clovis

Western Clovis

Western Stemmed
Points

Figure 8. Late-entry, basal-Clovis developmental model (after Willig, this volume).

tool-making procedures used to make Western Stemmed points are significantly different than those used to make Clovis points. (See discussion under environmental-response model).

Great Plains

Frison (this volume) defines the Goshen complex, first recognized at the Hell Gap site, Wyoming, in the early 1960s by the late Henry Irwin (1968). It was not until the discovery of the Mill Iron site in southeastern Montana, which contained in situ evidence of diagnostic projectile points, that this concept received support. Goshen points have been found at the Hell Gap, Carter/Kerr-McGee, Powars II (a Paleoindian red pigment mine), and Bentzen-Kaufman Cave sites. These occurrences suggest that Goshen is more than a local development.

The Mill Iron site is the most carefully excavated of the Goshen complex sites. The Goshen cultural level is a bison bone bed in which a camp and processing level occurs. Goshen site deposits occur 1.4–2.0 m below a flat-topped butte ca. 20 m high in the Humbolt Creek drainage. Nine accelerator dates on charcoal from the site form two groups: one clusters around 11,300 yr B.P. and the other is about 10,800 yr B.P. Characteristic artifacts from the Mill Iron assemblage include Goshen points, end scrapers, a transverse scraper, a single-prong graver, a three-pronged graver, a backed blade, a backed flake, *pièces esquillés*, a hammer or anvil, and bifaces.

The data on Goshen are not sufficient to determine which of two alternative models most aptly places Goshen in regional cultural developments. Frison reports that Henry Irwin (1968) originally suggested that Goshen is a Clovis variant (Figure 9). This comment is difficult to interpret. Goshen points are as old as "classic" Clovis points from the Plains and the Southwest, are not fluted, and have a thinning style discretely different than most Clovis points. Thus, thinning was achieved without fluting. Without this trait, it is difficult to see how Goshen can be interpreted as a Clovis variant.

Frison, on the other hand, proposes that Goshen is a cultural development that follows Clovis and occurs before Folsom (Figure 10). The early radiocarbon dates from the Mill Iron site are as old as the earliest Clovis

Figure 9. Basal-Clovis developmental model (after Irwin 1960).

Figure 10. Northern Plains Clovis developmental model (after Frison, this volume).

dates (Haynes 1987:Table 1) and therefore do not support a developmental model arising from a basal Clovis pattern. The technological traits of platform faceting, platform isolation, and grinding are offered as characteristics shared in common by Goshen and Folsom point-production technology. Frison does not outline his perception of Clovis and Goshen ties. Many of the same production procedures reported for Goshen and Folsom also occur in Clovis production technologies. An additional developmental model, not mentioned by Frison, is that Goshen could be a unique cultural development of Clovis age. (See discussion under environmental-response model.)

Johnson's primary objective (this volume) is to consider subsistence patterns of late Pleistocene peoples in the southern Plains, rather than phylogenetic or cultural-evolution questions. Nonetheless, she does propose a threefold evolutionary sequence: pre-Clovis, Clovis, and Folsom. Although Johnson notes that none of the pre-Clovis sites are unequivocal, the Cooperton site, Oklahoma, and Bonfire Shelter, Texas, remain contenders for the pre-Clovis category. Other sites or levels that may be either pre-Clovis or Clovis include Stratum E of Bone Bed 1 at Bonfire Shelter; Duewall-Newberry, Texas; and the pre-Clovis level at the Lubbock Lake site, Texas. Evidence for the presence of humans is inferred from the altered remains of megamammals. In the southern Plains, Clovis is know from the excavated sites of Lubbock Lake, Blackwater Draw Locality No. 1, Miami, Domebo, and McLean (unexcavated). All these sites have produced Clovis projectile points.

According to Johnson (this volume), climate change, increased seasonality, and expansion of grasslands at the end of the Pleistocene led to an adaptation of the Clovis pattern by local pre-Clovis populations. Clovis peoples practiced a generalist foraging subsistence strategy with a broad-based resource orientation similar to their forebears. With continued climatic deterioration at the end of the Pleistocene, accompanied by megafaunal extinctions, Holocene warming, and greater seasonality, the stage was set for changes in human adaptive practices. The late Pleistocene hunter-gatherer foragers appear to have given rise to Folsom hunters who targeted specific resources, e.g., bison, and became Holocene hunter-gatherer collectors (Figure 11).

Johnson adopts an environmental-response model to explain the transition from pre-Clovis to Clovis to Folsom by in situ populations. She does not, however, provide arguments in support of her continuity model. It is not clear why other possibilities, such as migration, have been excluded from consideration. Nor is it evident what leads her to suggest that material remains from pre-Clovis assemblages can be linked to Clovis patterns.

Eastern North America

Paleoindian groups in eastern North America adapted to a number of different environmental settings, including tundra and boreal and deciduous forests in rather different ways (Lepper and Meltzer, this volume; Meltzer 1988; Meltzer and Smith 1986). Considerable variation exists in both the shape and technology of fluted points, as well as other aspects of fluted-point assemblages from this region.

In the Great Lakes region, Storck (this volume) reviews fluted-point complexes. Following Deller and Ellis (1988), he reports three distinct fluted-point complexes from southern Ontario: the Gainey, Parkhill, and Crowfield complexes. Storck proposes that these complexes represent a developmental sequence out of Clovis. The Gainey complex, named after a site in Michigan, is characterized by points with parallel sides, shallow bases, and single flute scars that are often quite short. Storck suggests that these points are similar to Clovis in the West and those from the Bull Brook site in Massachusetts.

The Parkhill complex, named after the Parkhill site in southern Ontario, is characterized by the Barnes point type. This point type has a medium- to small-sized leaf shape with a pronounced "waist," and single and occasionally multiple flutes removed from a central prepared platform. The Parkhill complex is represented by 11 and possibly as many as 20 sites. The Fisher site, a Parkhill complex site, occurs on a shoreline of glacial Lake Algonquin that dates between 11,500 and 10,400 yr B.P.

Fluted points from the Crowfield complex, named after a site in southwestern Ontario, are wide, thin, and exhibit multiple flute scars. Storck infers this is the youngest in the Great Lakes fluted-point sequence, as the Crowfield points most closely resemble the Holcombe point type, which is thought to postdate 10,400 yr B.P. (Figure 12). Because these assemblages are not dated, other interpretations are possible. For example, all the assemblages could be approximately the same age and represent different groups of people moving into recently deglaciated terrain

Fluted points from the northeastern United States and adjacent areas of Canada deviate from styles of fluted points represented in the Desert Southwest and Great Plains. Bonnichsen et al. (1990) provide an overview of fluted-point styles from Maine and the Maritime provinces. One of the most diagnostic regional variants are Debert points. They are typified by deep basal notches, long ears, and flutes that usually do not extend beyond the mid-length of the point. They share affinities with points from the Vail site (Gramly 1982).

Another variant, found in northern Maine, is Moosehorn points (Bonnichsen et al. 1983), which are similar to fluted points from the Windy City site (Payne 1987). Moosehorn specimens are longer and more lanceolate

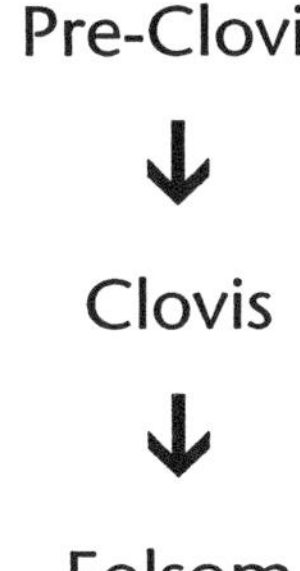

Figure 11. Southern Plains pre-Clovis developmental model (after Johnson, this volume).

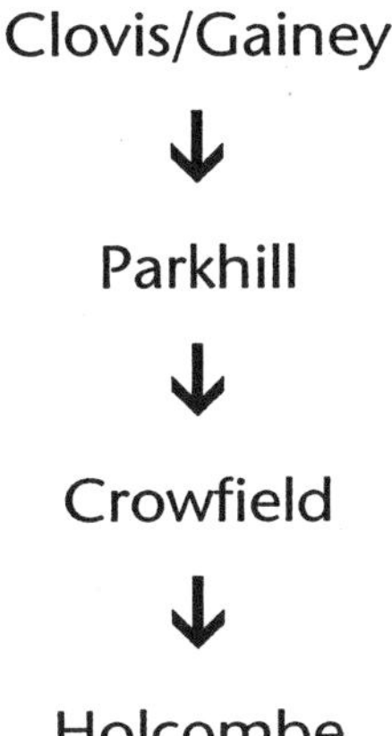

Figure 12. Great Lakes basal-Clovis developmental model (after Storck, this volume).

than most fluted points, and have flutes that extend the full length of their faces. These contrast with small lanceolate forms that vary from specimens with basal thinning at the Jones site, Prince Edward Island (Bonnichsen et al. 1990; Keenlyside, this volume), to specimens with short flutes at the Turkey Swamp site, New Jersey (Cavallo 1981).

Some investigators believe that fluted points in northeastern North America are younger than Clovis and represent developments from a basal Clovis horizon (Haynes et al. 1984). When radiocarbon dates are averaged, it can be shown that Debert, Vail, and Whipple date to about 10,500 years ago. I have argued that the radiocarbon dates from these sites may be the product of forest fires and tree throws rather than of human origin, and that eastern fluted points may be as old as their western counterparts (Bonnichsen 1990). Indirect evidence that supports this argument is the occurrence of fluted-point sites on kame terraces along the margins of glacial spillway channels at Munsungun and Chase lakes, northern Maine. These data imply that humans were residing along the margins of meltwater streams produced by waning ice sheets.

Some authors (Cavallo 1981; Keenlyside, this volume) suggest that fluted points underwent a developmental sequence in northeastern North America. The small fluted points from the Turkey Swamp and Jones sites may postdate Clovis and represent a development out of Clovis (Figure 13). Unfortunately, no stratified dated sites containing multiple levels of fluted points have been found that would demonstrate this proposed evolutionary sequence.

Dunbar (this volume, personal communication 1990) provides an overview of the distribution of fluted-point sites and related point forms in Florida. Important styles include fluted points that resemble western Clovis, fluted and unfluted Suwanee points, and Simpson points. All these point types are concentrated in Tertiary karst regions, in which the Floridan Aquifer is the dominant water source and chert is abundant. Presumably, late Pleistocene water holes were a focal point of human settlement and subsistence. Although a radiocarbon chronology is absent from the known Florida Paleoindian record, most prehistorians have adopted the view that Clovis is earliest, and that Suwanee and Simpson developed from a basal Clovis pattern (Figure 14); however Dunbar, at least, recognizes that all of the styles of Florida fluted points could be contemporaneous.

In summary, an accurate chronology has yet to be developed for eastern Paleoindian fluted-point sites (Bonnichsen 1990). The lack of faunal and organic remains throughout most of this region mitigates against reliable reconstructions of how fluted-point users adapted to one or more past environments. Consequently, it is not yet possible to determine if eastern fluted points are as old as those from western fluted-point sites. Nor is it possible to determine if there is a regional developmental sequence of fluted-point styles, whether different point styles are contemporaneous, whether widely dispersed point-distribution patterns represent one or more adaptive patterns or a long-standing generalized foraging pattern, or whether stylistic differences are indicative of different adaptive patterns. More field work and reliable dating are needed to gauge actual historical and evolutionary relationships among late Pleistocene human groups in eastern North America.

Central America

Ranere and Cook (this volume) discuss the Paleoindian period (11,500–9000 yr B.P.) in Central America. Fluted-point finds are known from southern Mexico, Guatemala, Honduras, Costa Rica, and Panama. Only two sites with dated Paleoindian components—Los Tapiales, Guatemala, and Los Grifos, Chiapas, Mexico—have been excavated. Both are in the northern portion of the Central American tropics. Most other Central American Paleoindian points are surface finds without good associations. The points themselves usually occur in three varieties: Clovis lanceolate, Clovis waisted, and fishtail. Fishtails differ not only in terms of shape, but, perhaps more importantly, in terms of technology.

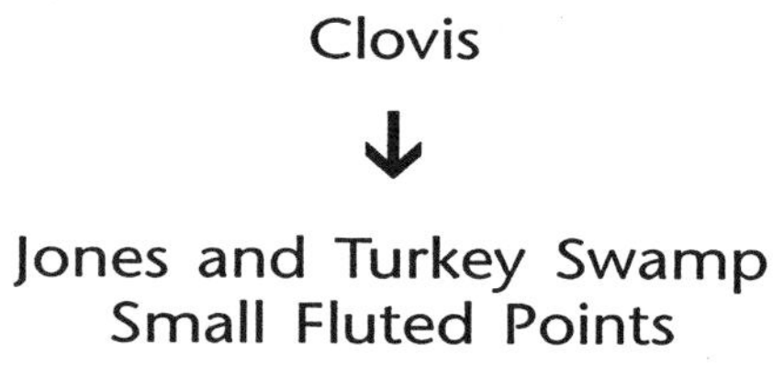

Figure 13. Northeastern Clovis developmental model (after Keenlyside, this volume).

Clovis

↓

Suwanee

↓

Simpson

Figure 14. Florida Clovis developmental model (after Dunbar, this volume).

The Central American fluted points (both lanceolate and waisted varieties) have clear affinities with North American Clovis points. The lithic reduction sequence begins with a large flake blank, which is bifacially flaked so that it has a biconvex cross-section. A number of these forms, with and without basal flutes, were recovered at Turrialba, Costa Rica. In contrast, fishtail points of Central and South America are generally made on flake blanks that are slightly thicker than the finished product. Thinning flakes tend to broaden at their distal end and overlap each other in the center of the point. Clovis and some fishtail points share fluting, final pressure retouch, and basal and lateral edge grinding. In terms of distribution, Central America represents the southernmost limit of the Clovis-like fluted points and the northern limit of the fishtail points.

One can interpret the overlap of the Clovis-like fluted points and fishtail points in several different ways. One model posits a change in point form as Paleoindian populations migrated through Central America. Snarskis (1979:137) has suggested a transition from Clovis-like fluted, to waisted, and finally to stemmed forms in Central America (Figure 15). An alternative model proposes an independent development of fishtail points in southern South America, which then spread northward (Rouse 1976) (Figure 16). A third model, set forth by Mayer-Oakes (1986), suggests an independent origin for fluting in the Ecuadorian highlands (Figure 17). Here, several different point styles occur, including fishtail and El Inga points, which exhibit various styles of fluting and thinning patterns. A fourth model proposes that fluting originated in North America, which then spread southward through Central and South America, either by migration or diffusion, at the same time the fishtail was moving northward (Bryan 1973) (Figure 18). The dearth of dated fluted-point sites and lack of detailed analysis of artifact assemblages makes the choice between these alternative models a difficult one.

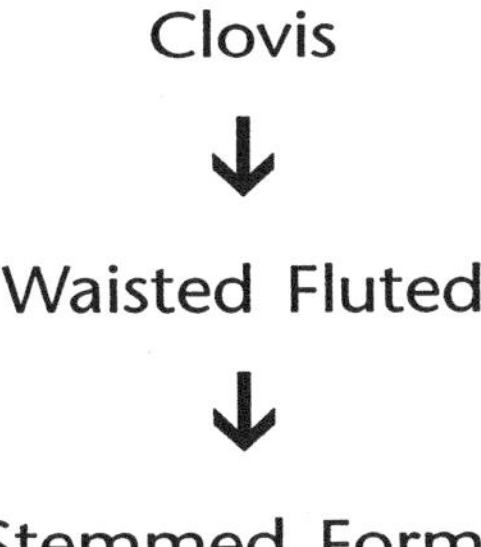

Figure 15. Central American Clovis developmental model (after Snarskis 1979).

Fishtail Points
South American Origins

Fishtail Points
in Central America

Figure 16. South American origin of fishtail points (after Rouse 1976).

South America

Northern South America

Lynch (this volume) proposes that the link between Paleoindian complexes in North and South America can most readily be shown through the distribution of fluted and wide-stemmed points, edge grinding on lanceolate points, snub-nosed scrapers, thumbnail scrapers, knife-scrapers, and blade technology—an inventory normally associated with Clovis. He notes, however, that Paleoindian adaptation in South America lacks the clear-cut chronological horizon, culture, and adaptive patterns characteristic of the Clovis period in North America. Lynch suggests that Clovis descendants arrived in South America perhaps as little as 500 years after human entry into North America (cf. Bryan 1977; Mosimann and Martin 1975).

Ardila (this volume) indicates that points similar to the Madden Lake points (fishtail points) of Panama are known from northern South America. Most of these points come from eroded surfaces and lack associations with other archaeological materials. Occurrences are noted from the Gulf of Uraba in the area of Gloria Bay, Colombia. Additional fragments have been found in northern Venezuela: these surface specimens are from the El Cayude site south of the Paraguana Peninsula and the Pedregal River Valley. Ardila believes that these points postdate El Jobo points.

Another group of points that appears to be related to the fluted-point tradition is characterized by intentionally fluted stems, pronounced shoulders, and convex blade edges with secondary pressure retouch. These points are reported from the municipality of Restrepo in the Departement of Valle, Colombia. Other samples are from the suburbs of Medellin, and from Murcielagos Cave in Gloria Bay.

Other specimens found out of dated context are from the valley of Popayan in the upper Cauca Valley at 1,500-2,000 m above sea level. Basal thinning and the general morphology of three of these points are similar to Mayer-Oakes' (1986) fluted forms from Ecuador (El Inga Broad Stemmed and El Inga Shouldered Lanceolate).

Independent Origins of multiple styles of Fluted Points in Ecuadorian Highlands

Figure 17. South American independent-origins model for many styles of fluted points (after Mayer-Oakes 1986).

Clovis

Independent Origins in Continental U.S.A.

Fishtail

Independent Origins in South America

Figure 18. Independent-origins model for North American Clovis and South American fluted points (after Bryan 1983 and Gruhn et. al. 1977).

Ardila proposes that fishtail fluted points (cf. Madden Lake type) from the Caribbean coastal zone of Colombia may have close relationships with those reported from Panama. He does not believe that this connection should be extended to include points found farther south. Stemmed forms, which are usually considered a late feature, may date to the early Holocene. Ardila does not see a connection between the fluted points found in northern South America and those from the southern part of the continent.

Southern South America

Politis (this volume) indicates that fishtail projectile points have been recorded from several areas of the Southern Cone of South America. They are known from the southern tip of Patagonia; and the eastern *Pampas* of Argentina, Uruguay, and the southern plains of Brazil. Radiocarbon dates from these regions place human occupation between 11,000 and 9500 yr B.P. Fishtail projectile points were first documented by Bird (1938) at Fell's and Palli-Aike caves, Magallanes Province, Chile. These early finds are complemented by recent research at the Cueva del Medio site in Chile, and the Cerro La China and Cerro El Sombero sites in Argentina.

Fishtail projectile points, as defined by Bird (1969:56-57), have rounded shoulders, concave-sided stems that frequently terminate with slightly expanding sharp-pronged corners, and may or may not be fluted.

Two alternative hypotheses have been proposed to explain the occurrence of fishtail projectile points: (1) they are related to fluted points in North America; or (2) they have an independent origin in South America. With respect to the first hypothesis, Lynch (1983) argues, on the basis of bifacially flaked retouch, rounded shoulders, and the presence of fluting, that fishtail points did not have an independent origin in South America, but rather derived from North American antecedents. Luis Borrero (see Politis, this volume) proposes an independent invention of fishtail points in southeastern Panama, the highlands of Ecuador, the lowlands of Uruguay, the Argentine *Pampas*, and southern Patagonia (Figure 19).

Going one step beyond earlier investigations, Politis (this volume) performed cluster analyses on technological and morphological traits of southern South American fishtail projectile-point assemblages. The technological procedures for manufacturing fluted and unfluted points from southern Patagonia and the *Pampas* appear to be the same. Rather than beginning with prepared bifacially flaked blanks, artisans of both regions started with large flakes of approximately the same thickness as the finished product. Points from both regions exhibit a low frequency of fluting and varying numbers of basal-thinning flake scars. Numerical analysis based on five different measurements did not allow points from the two regions of Argentina to be segregated into discrete populations. These data suggest that the fishtail points from the *Pampas*, Patagonia, Uruguay, and possibly southern Brazil are based on the same model.

The chronological record from fishtail-point sites does not resolve the basic question of whether the emergence of this style of point represents actual migration, diffusion, or independent invention. Yet, some important trends are beginning to emerge. First, new data indicate that the radiocarbon ages of fishtail points, which date to 11,000 years ago (Politis, this volume: Table 1), temporally overlap the age of fluted-point sites in the American Southwest and Plains. Second, there is not a strict morphological and technological continuity between North American fluted points and South American fishtail points. Not only are there differences in shape but there are also differences in reduction strategies. Third, the occurrence of bifacially worked tools in pre-11,000-year-old contexts in South America, e.g., Monte Verde, suggests to Politis that the development of the fishtail-point style may have local antecedents.

Figure 19. South and Central American independent-origins model (after Borrero [Politis, this volume]).

MODELS

In constructing models to explain the rise and demise of the Clovis complex, authors must make decisions about four dimensions of human society: (1) operational dynamics of how past societies functioned, as inferred from artifactual and environmental signatures; (2) temporal placement; (3) spatial distribution in the landscape; and (4) how cultural change occurred through time. In the following discussion, I outline the major models used to explain Clovis origins and discuss some of the assumptions on which these models are based.

Late-Entry Migration Models

Paul S. Martin and co-workers (Diamond 1987; Martin 1967, 1973, 1984, 1987; Mosimann and Martin 1975) propose that a small band of human hunters entered the Americas from Siberia via the Bering Land Bridge about 12,000 years ago. These spear-wielding big-game hunters were channeled southward through the Ice-Free Corridor between the receding margins of the Cordilleran and Laurentide ice sheets. Known archaeologically by their lanceolate fluted points, the hunters moved rapidly southward along the eastern flanks of the Canadian Rockies.

Martin and others envision that this epic migration into an unsettled continent from the Old World was made possible by population growth, coupled with territorial expansion and an effective killing technology. In one of several alternative simulation scenarios, Mosimann and Martin (1975) propose that human populations doubled every 20 years. After 17 generations or 340 years, at a population increase of 1.4% per year, they were able to saturate the previously uncolonized landscape. This expanding bow-shaped wave of human hunters decimated 33 genera in North America, or about 70% of the big-game animals. From the time of initial arrival in North America to their arrival in Terra del Fuego, South America, at 10,600 yr B.P., only 800 years passed before this rapidly expanding population had totally colonized the Americas.

The Martin Blitzkrieg model is foreshadowed in the work of Haynes (1964). Haynes' position has evolved, and he no longer supports the viewpoint that the Clovis culture came directly from Asia. He now believes that the Clovis pattern had its origin in the Americas. Nonetheless, he proposes that the Clovis culture has its antecedents in the Upper Paleolithic of eastern Europe and central Asia. Haynes (1987:88, 1990) sees the Clovis pattern, with the exception of fluted points, as sharing nine traits in common with eastern European and Asian sites (e.g., Dolni Vestonice Pavlov, Czechoslovakia, and Mezhirich, the Ukraine). These traits include blades, end scrapers, burins, shaft wrenches, cylindrical bone points, knapped bone, unifacial flake tools, red ocher, and circumferentially chopped tusks. He notes that the Clovis tool kit is remarkably similar to the 18,000-year-old Mal'ta burial from near Lake Baikal, U.S.S.R., where two children were buried with bevel-based cylindrical bone points and red ocher. The dentition of the Baikal children has Caucasoid rather than Mongoloid affinities, thus raising a fundamental problem, as Turner (1985) has demonstrated that the dentition of Amerindians is related to the Asian sinodont pattern. Haynes proposes that Caucasoid bands from Central Asia, bearing an eastern European Upper Paleolithic hunter's tool kit, intermixed with sinodont peoples. During late glacial times, the ancestors of Clovis migrants modified their stone and bone tool kit, and sinodonty became a dominant genetic pattern.

The overkill model has several predictive implications that can be partially tested against the archaeological record. The most important of these predictions are:

1. Fluted-point sites should be older in northernmost North America and younger by as much as 800 years in southern South America. (In contrast, the Haynes' model predicts that the manufacture of fluted points is a continental North American innovation. Thus, fluted points in continental North America should be older than in Alaska and South America.)
2. The overkill model predicts an unprecedented human population growth that is linked to the use of a new and efficient killing technology that rapidly spread throughout the Americas. Therefore, the Clovis tool kit should occur as an archaeological horizon throughout North and South America.
3. The Clovis cultural complex represents a single human culture with a shared value system. This construct predicts that tool assemblages, artifact forms, and manufacturing techniques should be homogenous and exhibit little variability from site to site and region to region.

Discussion of Late-Entry Models

Because it has often been stated that Clovis is the earliest New World cultural complex, the sudden and widespread appearance of Clovis requires an explanation. The Clovis culture model uses the normative approach. The normative approach views culture as an integrated system in which all of the parts are functionally related in such a way that some sort of equilibrium is maintained (Young and Bonnichsen 1984:3-5). Units in the system are subsystems, e.g., settlement, subsistence, lithic procurement, etc. While such connections do exist, focusing on functional integration tends to obscure the enormous range of variation found in any society.

In the case of Clovis, the normative approach is used to define the diagnostic artifact types that characterize the Clovis culture. Types are based on intuitive averaging techniques to derive central tendencies. Specimens that do not conform to these types are referred to as "variants." Investigators who adopt the normative approach appear to make the following assumptions: (1) a few carefully selected specimens represent an assemblage or a type; (2) assemblages and types have relatively discrete boundaries; and (3) it is the basic organizing (structural) principles, rather than diversity apparent at the empirical level, which are most appropriate and best describe the character of the group. The theory and method for isolating these principles are often unspecified. All the above assumptions are derived from a single underlying paradigmatic postulate: the basic unit of analysis is the group. Groups have discoverable, predictable patterns and structures.

Haynes' (1980) Clovis culture concept posits a list of types that presumably formed a tool kit that can be used to characterize the Clovis culture. When the list of Clovis artifacts is examined, it will be noted that no single site has produced all the artifact types included in the list. This approach appears to be based on the premise that sites that have yielded fluted Clovis points must belong to the Clovis culture. Given the small sample size of artifacts from most Clovis sites, one can understand why Haynes lumped remains from a number of sites together to try to come to a broader understanding of the Clovis pattern. From a methodological perspective, the Clovis culture concept is weak, as we are not told what sites produced the diagnostic artifacts.

An additional problem of the Clovis culture concept has to do with the concept of culture change. The normative approach assumes that each generation replicates the patterns of previous generations. Thus, the normative approach does not provide a mechanism for explaining culture change and variation in the archaeological record. In considering the differences between western and eastern fluted points, Haynes (1964:1408) indicates that sites reveal variations within individual collections that are as great as variations between collections. He concludes that variation is unimportant and that fluted points are indicative of a single founding population that spread from coast to coast.

Since the original formulation of the Clovis culture model more than thirty years ago, much subsequent work suggests that the concept of variation of fluted points and fluted-point assemblages needs to be rethought. Some of the most prominent fluted-point variants that have been recognized by regional workers as deviations from "classic" Clovis as found in the Southwest and Plains include: (1) an Arctic style represented by the Putu variant; (2) the small Peace River variant from the Ice-Free Corridor region; (3) the Gainey, Parkhill, and Crowfield variants from the Great Lakes region; (4) the Debert variant from Nova Scotia; (5) small basally thinned points from the Jones site, Prince Edward Island, and the Turkey Swamp site, New Jersey; (6) Moosehorn and Windy City points from Maine, which have full-length flutes; (7) Cumberland points, with long flutes and constricted stems, that come from a number of locations in eastern North America; (8) fishtail points from Panama and northern and southern South America; and (9) the El Inga series from highland Ecuador that includes stemmed fluted points.

To summarize, the Clovis model, as originally conceptualized, was based on the normative assumption that prehistoric human cultures can be identified on the basis of diagnostic artifacts that form a tool kit. Recent work has shown that there are many variants of fluted points that differ from the "classic" Clovis points of the Plains and Southwest in both outline form and technology.

Advocates of the various late-entry migration models differ with respect to how they address the variability documented within Clovis. Four types of models have been advanced to explain Clovis origins and regional variants. These include: (1) a migration model; (2) migration developmental models; (3) in situ developmental models; and (4) diffusion models. The Mosimann and Martin scenario (1975) is an example of a migration model. To demonstrate migration in an archaeological context, identical artifactual remains and similar dates are required to posit a migratory relationship between two or more assemblages.

The Mosimann and Martin model does not address the question of variability in fluted-point assemblages. It assumes that all fluted points were produced by a genetically linked human population, which shared a common cultural heritage, even though points from different regions have different forms, and were thinned and fluted using different techniques.

Several individuals propose migration developmental models to account for Clovis origins and regional variation in the archaeological record (see Clark, Frison, Morlan, Storck, all this volume). Migratory developmental models posit relationships between geographically separated assemblages and propose that cultural development has occurred between the time that archaeological assemblages were deposited at point A and point B. The regional models proposed by Goebel et al. (this volume) and Carlson (this volume) are further examples of this variety of model.

Carlson (this volume) suggests that fluting was spread by an original founding population moving from the Arctic to Tierra del Fuego (excluding the Northwest Coast). In the course of population expansion and geographic spread, continuous segmentation of the original population into numerous separate bands would have led to groups with their own knappers and transmission of technical knowledge from generation to generation. This development would have produced variation in fluting. Although this random-drift hypothesis is interesting, no data are presented in its support.

Migration developmental models emphasize similarities in tool classes or select technological traits, while ignoring differences in artifact forms and artifact-production patterns. Justification for selecting migration as an explanation rather than other explanations of variation is absent in most discussions of regional-migration developmental models. Other than Carlson's random-drift thesis, mechanisms responsible for change are not given serious consideration.

In situ developmental models constitute the third group of models used to explain Clovis, Clovis variants, and patterns that descended from Clovis. Carlson (this volume), Irwin (1968), Lynch (this volume), and Willig (this volume) assume that a basic ancestral Clovis population rapidly spread across what is now the United States. The descendants of this founding population adapted to local conditions. As this process occurred, a number of regional fluted-point variants developed.

A fundamental problem of positing an ancestral Clovis founding population to explain regional in situ development is the question of how to define basal Clovis occupations in archaeological contexts. For example, Willig (this volume) postulates a basal Clovis population in the Great Basin, but then observes that Great Basin fluted points cannot be distinguished from those in classic Clovis sites.

In a similar vein, Storck (this volume) proposes that the undated Gainey, Parkhill, and Crowfield points represent a developmental sequence; Frison (this volume) suggests the Goshen complex developed out of Clovis; Keenlyside (this volume) proposes that Prince Edward Island and Turkey Swamp points developed from Clovis; and Dunbar (this volume) reports that regional investigators believe that Suwanee and Simpson points evolved from Clovis. Carlson (this volume) indicates that the small Peace River variants must be late in time and implies that they developed from an earlier Clovis pattern.

All the proposed in situ developmental models lack empirical verification. Posited point sequences have not been found in stratigraphic context, nor have proposed developmental phases been independently dated. Without a firm radiocarbon chronology, we are unable to assess which of several competing hypotheses most adequately explains the eastern, northern, and southern fluted-point variants. Last, but not least, detailed studies documenting differences in the proposed developmental sequences and the mechanics responsible for these changes would be instructive.

In summary, strong support is not found for a late-entry migration into the Americas. The late-entry Clovis migration model of Mosimann and Martin (1975) and Martin (1984) predicts that fluted points should be older in northernmost North America and younger in South America. The current radiocarbon record from North and South American fluted-point sites does not support this prediction. There are no well-dated fluted-point sites of appropriate age (ca. 12,000 yr B.P.) from eastern Beringia (Clark, this volume) or the Ice-Free Corridor region (Carlson, this volume). Politis (this volume:Table 1) documents that dates of 11,000 ± 170 and 10,720 ± 300 yr B.P. associated with fishtail points (fluted and unfluted) from Fell's Cave, southern Chile, and at Cerro La China 1, Argentina, of 10,790 ± 120 and 10,730 ± 150 yr B.P. indicate that the emergence of fishtail points at the southern tip of the Southern Hemisphere overlaps the appearance of fluted points in North America. These ages suggest that fluted points from southern South America occur at approximately the same time as fluted points in North America.

The Early-Entry Migration Model

In seeking to explain the peopling of the Americas, Bryan (1969, 1973, 1977, 1978, 1980, 1986, 1987, 1988, 1990, this volume) and Gruhn (1988, 1990, this volume) propose an early migration of Amerindians from Northeast Asia in pre-Wisconsinan or Wisconsinan time. As suggested earlier by Fladmark (1979), the earliest colonists are envisioned as boat-using peoples who moved along the rich coastal ecotones of the Pacific Rim in western North America and into South America.

Bryan and Gruhn suggest an initial population of modern humans may have arrived in the Americas 50,000 years ago and perhaps earlier. These people adapted to a variety of environmental circumstances, with a simple core-flake tool technology. As population growth and geographical spread of the original group occurred, diversification took place, with adaptations to new environments giving rise to numerous social groups, economic adaptive patterns, and linguistic groups, thus setting the stage for parallel cultural development in North and South America.

Evidence for the original ancestral population in coastal regions has been drowned by rising sea levels in most places. Indirect evidence in support of this model is suggested by a number of language isolates and major subdivisions of language phyla along the Pacific Northwest Coast, in California, on the northern Gulf of Mexico Coast, and in Central America and South America. Following a conventional principle of historical linguistics, it is assumed that the development of language diversification is proportional to the time depth of human occupation of an area (Gruhn 1988).

The principal predictive implications of the early-migration, parallel-evolutionary model are:

1. Peoples who predate Clovis produced core and flake tool assemblages in North and South America.
2. Cultural, linguistic, and biological diversity of American Indian groups is a function of great time depth.
3. The earliest evidence of First Americans would occur along the coastal fringes of the Americas.

Bryan (this volume) and Gruhn (this volume) present several lines of evidence to counter the proposition that Clovis represents a specialized big-game hunting adaptation and is the oldest and first cultural complex in North America. They argue: (1) new data indicate that Clovis hunters and gatherers were generalists and therefore can not narrowly be categorized as only big-game hunters; (2) flake-tool traditions exist in South America that are earlier than and contemporaneous with Clovis; (3) several bifacially flaked projectile-point types developed in the Americas that are both earlier than and contemporaneous with Clovis.

The early-entry parallel-evolutionary model predicts that multiple cultural developments occurred in the Americas prior to the appearance of the Clovis pattern. Sites of pre-Clovis age include Bluefish Cave (24,000 yr B.P.), Yukon Territory (Morlan and Cinq-Mars 1989); Meadowcroft Rockshelter (14,000–14,500 yr B.P.), Pennsylvania (Adovasio et al. 1988:45); and several sites in Brazil, e.g., Toca Do Boqueirão da Pedra Furada (more than 45,000 yr B.P.) (Guidon 1989, personal communication), and Toca do Sitio do Meio (14,300 yr B.P.) in Piaui State. Sites in Minas Gerais, Brazil, dated to 15,300 yr B.P. at Lapa Vermelha IV, Abrigo de Santana do Riacho, and Lapa do Boquete have unspecialized lithic industries well before the appearance of Clovis in North America (Gruhn, this volume). Although space will not allow a detailed discussion of other early South American flake/pebble tool sites, important pre-Clovis assemblages are known from Taima-taima (13,000 yr B.P.), Venezuela (Gruhn and Bryan 1990); Tibitó (11,740 yr B.P.), Colombia (Correal 1986); Alice Boer (14,200 yr B.P.), south-central Brazil (Gruhn and Bryan 1990); and Monte Verde (ca. 33,000 yr B.P.), southern Chile (Dillehay and Collins 1991). See Morlan (1988), Lynch (1990), Gruhn and Bryan (1991), and Dillehay and Collins (1991) for discussions of the current debate surrounding these sites.

The early-migration model, the purpose of which is to explain the peopling of the Americas, does not fully explain Clovis origins. Not surprisingly, this model presents Clovis as originating in the Americas (Bryan, this volume), a position that Haynes (1987) has recently come to embrace. Nonetheless, an explanation is needed to account for the sudden appearance of multiple projectile-point styles in the Americas in late Pleistocene times. Although the early-migration parallel-evolution model provides one possible explanation for the occurrence of multiple projectile-point styles in the Americas in late Pleistocene times, it does not explain why there are no clear-cut developmental antecedents of the various projectile-point types or why these points suddenly appeared across the Americas between 13,000 and 11,000 years ago.

Critique of the Late-Entry and Early-Entry Models

The late-entry migration model, with its focus on chronology, does not answer two types of fundamental process questions important to understanding the peopling of the Americas. It does not inform us as to whether strictly historical processes or an interplay of environmental and historical factors led to one or more colonization events. Because it relies on the use of a normative typological approach for characterizing artifacts, which emphasizes form and occasional isolated technological traits, it does not provide a fine-grained theoretical framework for assessing inter- and intra-assemblage variability of artifact assemblages.

In contrast to the late-entry model, the early-entry model stresses: (1) an initial founding populating with a simple core and flake tool kit colonized the Americas; (2) the descendants of these early populations adapted to a variety of different environments; (3) parallel evolution occurred in a number of different environments, giving rise to cultural diversity by the end of the Pleistocene; and (4) rapid environmental change at the end of the Pleistocene acted as a catalyst leading to a number of independent projectile-point traditions, although simple core and flake tools continued to persist in some areas.

Bryan's simple core and flake tool kit is a hypothesis about the level of the earliest technology. This concept needs to be tested against the archaeological record from early sites. We need detailed reports that document how cores were preformed, how platforms were set up, what kind of flakes were detached from cores, and what kind of tools were used to manufacture cores and to alter flakes into serviceable implements. These detailed studies should allow us to assess whether a single population or several populations using flake and core tools immigrated to the Americas from Northeast Asia.

Environmental-Response Model

The environmental-response model proposes a more detailed formulation between environment and culture than previous models. It posits that the development of hunter and gatherer societies is intimately linked to the evolution of the earth's environmental systems. It is based on the general systems-theory assumption that the earth's orbital, atmospheric, oceanographic, climatic, geologic, pedologic, biologic, and cultural systems are systemically linked.

Of considerable importance is the Milankovitch hypothesis, which proposes that the earth is pulled out of precise equilibrium by the gravitational force of other planets, affecting precession of the equinoxes, orbital eccentricity, and obliquity of the rotational axis (Kutzbach 1983, 1984). Cyclic changes in orbit parameters are currently seen as potent forces that produce changes in linked atmospheric, climatic, geologic, glacial, biotic, and human-adaptive systems.

Broeker and Denton (1990) propose that variation in solar insolation is not the only factor determining climatic change. They believe that massive reorganizations of the ocean-atmosphere system are key events that link cyclic changes in the advance and retreat of Northern and Southern Hemisphere ice sheets. They propose that the sea and land evidence together point to a simultaneous change in the ocean and atmosphere 14,000 years ago. These reorganization events suggest a jump from a glacial to an interglacial mode. These abrupt jumps may underlie glacial-cycle jumps in general. More specifically, they are important for understanding the events associated with the termination of the last great Ice Age: the collapse of ice sheets, changes in positions of storm tracks, rising sea levels, increasing rates of vegetation change, the extinction of about 70% of terrestrial mammals in North America, and the sudden emergence of new human adaptive systems in North and South America (Bonnichsen et al. 1987).

The environmental-response model is supported by an increasing amount of data that indicates human populations were already in North America prior to the end of the last Ice Age. It proposes that global environmental change led to a disequilibrium between subsistence practices and the natural environment. The relationship that people had traditionally held with their environment was disrupted by the reorganization of plant and animal communities, which in turn affected human demographic patterns. Humans enhanced their survival success by responding to these rapidly changing conditions using generalist adaptive strategies, including big-game hunting. The primary means by which people responded to rapid climatic change at the end of the last Ice Age were technological innovation; acceptance of new traits; and restructuring of their social, economic, and technological organizations to accommodate changing environmental and cultural conditions.

The appearance of the Clovis archaeological pattern is coincident with other threshold events of the Earth's environmental systems during the late Pleistocene (Bonnichsen et. al. 1987). Yet these correlations do not answer the question: Where did the Clovis pattern originate? Many of the elements included in the Clovis pattern were likely derived from communal hunting patterns of Northeast Asia. By 25,000 yr B.P., human populations in central and eastern Siberia, northeastern and central China, and the Ukraine were armed with the knowledge for making lanceolate projectile points, bifacially flaked stone knives, triangular end scrapers; and procedures for flaking large mammal bones, constructing bone points and foreshafts, mining raw materials, and the skills needed for communal hunting.

During late Pleistocene time (ca. 14,000 yr B.P.), rapid changes in climate in Asia may have led one or more northeastern Asian populations to migrate to new habitats that ultimately led to the Americas (Greenberg et al. 1986). These people brought with them a sophisticated technical knowledge for hunting large game animals. Once in the Americas, they met indigenous populations who had traditionally produced wood, bone, and flaked-stone artifacts—items with low visibility in the archaeological record. About 11,500 years ago, under conditions of environmental stress and declining animal populations, innovation and diffusion of these new ideas would have been readily accepted to offset deteriorating subsistence opportunities. Through a process of stimulus diffusion, this new "techno-complex" rapidly spread from group to group, each interpreting the ideas of their neighbors in terms of their own traditions for making tools and ways of organizing human behavior, and in terms of the local context in which they found themselves. The acceptance and use of these innovations may have contributed to human population growth—a virtual explosion—at the very time when extensive mammalian extinctions were taking place.

The environmental-response model predicts:

1. Archaeological remains that predate the Clovis pattern should be found in the Americas.
2. The emergence and diffusion of new cultural patterns should be coincident with periods of greatest environmental change.
3. Many different human groups existed in the Americas during Clovis times who adopted the manufacture of projectile points and associated big-game hunting patterns at approximately the same time; each responded in light of their own traditions, and several projectile patterns emerged at approximately the same time.
4. The fluted-point pattern represents a widespread diffusion pattern, not a single human culture, and considerable variation should be found in the tool forms and manufacturing procedures from region to region.

The environmental-response model includes the assumption that the Americas were colonized many times. Colonization events may correlate with major environmental changes, such as the transition between interstadials and interglacials or between glacial and interglacial periods. In respect to late glacial time, it proposes that a techno-ideological complex may have been carried to the Americas by colonists; and that this complex spread across existing populations during a period of rapid environmental change, giving rise to several different bifacially flaked projectile-point patterns. The most important of these include the lanceolate points of the Nenana complex (11,300 yr B.P.) in central Alaska (Goebel et. al., this volume); the Goshen complex of the northwestern Plains (with dates clustering at 11,300 and 10,800 yr B.P.) (Frison, this volume); the Western Stemmed point tradition (12,000–10,000 yr B.P.) of the Great Basin (Bryan 1990:53); the El Jobo point tradition (13,000 yr B.P.) in northern Venezuela (Gruhn and Bryan 1984); and the Magellanic "fishtail" point tradition (11,000–10,000 yr B.P.) in southern South American (Bird 1938; Bryan 1973; Politis, this volume; Rouse 1976).

Young and Bonnichsen (1984, 1985), and Young et al. (1991) advocate the use of the cognitive approach as a complement to traditional approaches of artifact analysis that focus exclusively on artifact form. The cognitive approach can be used to characterize artifact production strategies and changes in production strategies through time. By examining both shape and production-strategy information, the analyst is in a much stronger position to assess the meaning of variation and guidelines for discriminating between migration, diffusion, and in situ development, than by using only shape data alone. Preliminary technological analyses of Clovis assemblages using the cognitive approach are providing tantalizing insights into the variability of the Clovis complex. Bonnichsen et al. (1983) and Young and Bonnichsen (1984), in a comparative analysis of the Moosehorn fluted points from Maine and the Anzick fluted points from Montana, illustrate that different fluting, beveling, and thinning procedures were used to make the Maine and Montana points. Consequently, it was concluded that these production strategies were weakly related and could best be explained as a function of diffusion.

Studies by Warren and Phagan (1988) in the Lake Mohave region and by Fagan (1988) at the Dietz site in the Great Basin indicate that production procedures and material choices, as well as artifact forms, of Mohave and Western Stemmed points are quite distinctive from those used for Clovis points. These observations support an interpretation of unique cultural traditions rather than a continuity model as suggested by Willig (this volume). Although Willig argues that there may be a gradation from fluted to stemmed forms, Bryan (1980, 1988) reports that stemmed and fluted points require very different kinds of hafting technologies: fluted points require a split haft; stemmed points of the Mohave and Western Stemmed point variety require socket hafts. Bryan (1988) also argues that stemmed points designed for insertion into sockets were innovated earlier and persisted longer than fluted points west of the Rocky Mountains.

Storck (this volume) argues that the fluted-point complex is an integrated ideational, functional, and technological complex, and would not have diffused—rather, migration by colonists must be responsible for the spread of this pattern. However, examples of the diffusion of integrated ideational, functional, and technological complexes can be found in the ethnographic literature. Wissler's (1926:82–90) study of the diffusion of the Sundance complex among different groups of Plains Indian bison hunters is an excellent example of cross-cultural transmission.

To summarize, the environmental-response model is seen as a promising model for explaining the timing and emergence of American projectile points, as well as the widespread reorganization that occurred in adaptive systems in North and South America during an unprecedented period of rapid environmental change. These dramatic shifts do not have modern analogues and occurred during the transition from a glacial to an interglacial period. It should be noted, however, that this model does not explain why El Jobo points from South America occur earlier than North American projectile-point styles.

CONCLUDING COMMENTS

In assessing where we are at in the overall question of understanding Clovis origins, it is useful to consider the basic questions that we are trying to answer and how well existing models answer these questions. We want to determine: (1) When and how did the Clovis pattern originate? (2) What settlement, subsistence, and lithic-procurement patterns are characteristic of the Clovis complex? (3) Where did these patterns develop? (4) How did the various regional manifestations of the Clovis complex spread? (5) And how did the Clovis complex evolve through time in different regions?

Investigators interested in Clovis origins have used three alternative models to investigate the problem: these are the late-migration, the early-migration, and the environmental-response models. Each has different predictive implications and addresses different questions. Contrary to popular literature, which often depicts the peopling of the Americas as a debate between advocates of the pre-Clovis early-entry model and the late-entry model, I have attempted to show in the preceding discussion that the early-entry and late-entry models are addressing different but complementary questions. Neither of these models addresses all the basic questions we are seeking to answer about Clovis origins, nor, for that matter, basic process questions about the peopling of the Americas.

The proposition that Clovis is the first and founding population to settle the Americas appears to be incorrect in light of current research. Work at Bluefish Cave, Yukon Territory; Meadowcroft Rockshelter, Pennsylvania; Taima-taima, Venezuela; Pedra Furada, northeastern Brazil (as well as other Brazilian sites); and Monte Verde, southern Chile, indicates that all these sites are of pre-Clovis age. Furthermore, the appearance of bifacially flaked projectile points that are earlier than or contemporaneous with Clovis-aged sites, e.g., the Nenana complex, the Goshen complex, the Western Stemmed point tradition, and El Jobo points, support the view that Clovis is not the first and founding population in the Americas.

A considerable diversity of opinion exists regarding the antecedents and place of origin of the Clovis complex. Goebel et al. (this volume) suggest that Clovis point technology developed in complete isolation from the Eurasian Upper Paleolithic. They propose that Ushki, Kamchatka, may be an earlier phase of the Nenana complex that gave rise to Clovis. Alternatively, they see possible ties with Ust'-Kova, central Siberia, which has bifaces and blades—classes of artifacts characteristic of Clovis assemblages. By contrast, Clark (this volume) suggests: (1) Clovis originated in the western Arctic from a microblade tradition; (2) Clovis originated in the continental United States and moved north; or (3) fluted points developed from lanceolate points and had an independent origin in the Arctic during the early Holocene. He concludes current data are not sufficient to discriminate between these alternatives. Morlan (this volume) proposes that Clovis had its origins in the Dyuktai tradition of Siberia. Haynes (1987) suggests that Clovis originated in the continental United States from a northeast Asian founding population. Bryan (this volume) indicates that Clovis probably originated in the southeastern United States. In respect to Central and South America, Lynch (this volume) suggests a migration from an original founding Clovis population. By contrast, Mayer-Oakes (1986) proposes an independent center of innovation in the Ecuador highlands at El Inga. Borrero (see Politis, this volume) proposes additional centers of innovation in the lowlands of Uruguay, the Argentine *Pampas,* and southern Patagonia. Obviously, all these hypotheses cannot be correct.

Radiocarbon dates from the Nenana complex are as old as dates from "classic" Clovis sites (Haynes 1987:Table 1). Therefore, the Nenana complex cannot be considered the antecedent of Clovis. Although Goebel et al. (this volume) have demonstrated there is an overlap in tool classes between Blackwater Draw and Murray Springs, differences in tool forms and reduction strategies are not considered in their formulation. The existing radiocarbon record does not support an American Arctic or Dyuktai origin for Clovis, nor for that matter, does it refute it. Fluted points from the Arctic tend to be smaller than those from Clovis sites in western North America. The lack of Clovis-age sites with associated fauna in Alaska and the Yukon Territory suggests that fluted points in the Arctic probably diffused northward from the continental United States, as has been suggested by Carlson (this volume).

Suggestions for an independent origin of fluted points in Central and South America lack supporting evidence. Why at approximately the same time period in widely separated geographic areas would independent groups of people, who were not in contact with one another, develop complex hunting systems using the same style of thinning the bases of projectile points? What could explain the emergence of several different projectile-point manufacturing systems at approximately the same time? Numerous decisions are involved in lithic production, tool hafting, and tool use. In short, a complex system of production and game-procurement knowledge underlies the use of bifacially flaked projectile points. Neither independent invention nor migration provides the answer for the sudden appearance of several different projectile-point traditions between 13,000 and 11,000 years ago.

Stimulus diffusion among existing populations appears to most parsimoniously explain the emergence of several independent traditions of bifacially worked projectile points in the Americas between 13,000 and 11,000 years ago. Stratigraphic evidence has yet to be located in North or South America that provides clear antecedents for Clovis, Western Stemmed, Goshen, Nenana, El Jobo, or Magellanic fishtail points.

As proposed by the environmental response model, it is probable that an ideo-technological complex from Northeast Asia, possibly carried by a handful of immigrants, arrived in the Americas at the end of the last Ice Age and diffused across small populations of indigenous peoples. As environmental stress occurred, the stage was set for these new and productive techniques to be accepted by numerous cultural groups. These new tool-production and game-procurement ideas caught on and spread like wildfire throughout the Americas. But these innovations were interpreted differently on a regional basis and gave rise to a number of different regional traditions.

In summary, we have much yet to learn about the causes that led to the rise and demise of Clovis and other late Pleistocene cultural patterns. To develop more adequate and defensible models, emphasis must be placed on how to discriminate between competing interpretive hypotheses. We have no lack of competing hypotheses that seek to explain Clovis. Now what we need are specialists who are willing to investigate competing hypotheses and develop empirical criteria that can be used to explain variation in Clovis patterns. Clearly, more detailed lithic technological studies such as those advocated by Fagan (1988), Warren and Phagan (1988), and Young and Bonnichsen (1984, 1985; Young et al. 1991) will add clarity to the present fuzzy picture produced by normative typology. In short, detailed studies of artifact forms, production technology, use-wear studies, and contextual information, in conjunction with well-documented environmental records, are needed to move our understanding of Clovis and other equally early cultural complexes forward.

ACKNOWLEDGMENTS

I wish to thank Alan Bryan, Ruth Gruhn, Bradley Lepper, Dennis Stanford, and Karen Turnmire, whose editorial assistance and critical evaluation of earlier drafts of this manuscript led to important improvements. Steve Bicknell of the Department of Anthropology, University of Maine, assisted with the graphics. I alone am responsible for omissions, errors, and interpretations.

REFERENCES CITED

Adovasio, J. M., A. T. Boldurian, and R. C. Carlisle
1988 Who Are These Guys? Some Biased Thoughts on the Initial Peopling of the New World. In *Americans Before Columbus: Ice Age Origins*, edited by R. C. Carlisle, pp. 45–61. Ethnology Monographs No. 12. Department of Anthropology, University of Pittsburgh, Pittsburgh.

Bird, J. B.
1938 Antiquity and Migrations of the Early Inhabitants of Patagonia. *The Geographical Journal* 28:250–275.

1969 A Comparison of South Chilean and Ecuadorean "Fishtail" Projectile Points. *The Kroeber Anthropological Society Papers* 40:52–7.

Bonnichsen, R.
1989 Construction of Taphonomic Models: Theory, Assumptions, and Procedures. In *Bone Modification*, edited by R. Bonnichsen and M. H. Sorg, pp. 515–526. Center for the Study of the First Americans, University of Maine, Orono.

1990 Radiocarbon Chronology of Northeastern Paleoindian Sites: Human Hearths or Forest Fires and Tree Throws? Submitted to *American Antiquity*.

Bonnichsen, R., B. Bourque, and D. E. Young
1983 The Moosehorn Fluted Point Discovery, Northern Maine. *Archaeology of Eastern North America* 11:36–48.

Bonnichsen, R., D. Keenlyside, and K. Turnmire
1990 Paleoindian Patterns in Maine and the Maritimes: An Overview. In *Archaeology in the Maritime Provinces: Past and Present Research*, edited by M. Deal. Council of Maritime Premiers, Fredericton. In press.

Bonnichsen, R., D. Stanford, and J. L. Fastook
1987 Environmental Change and Developmental History of Human Adaptive Patterns; the Paleoindian Case. In *North America and Adjacent Oceans During the Last Deglaciation: The Geology of North America, vol. K-3*, edited by W. F. Ruddiman and H. E. Wright, Jr., pp. 403–424. Geological Society of America, Boulder.

Broeker, W. S., and G. H. Denton
1990 What Drives Glacial Cycles? *Scientific American* 262(1):49–56.

Bryan, A. L.
1969 Early Man in America and the Late Pleistocene Chronology of Western Canada and Alaska. *Current Anthropology* 10:339–365.

1973 Paleoenvironments and Cultural Diversity in Late Pleistocene South America. *Quaternary Research* 3:237–256.

1977 Developmental Stages and Technological Traditions. In *Amerinds and Their Paleoenvironments in Northeastern North America*, edited by W. S. Newman and B. Salwen, pp. 355–368. Annals of the New York Academy of Sciences 288.

1978 An Overview of Paleo-American Prehistory from a Circum-Pacific Perspective. In *Early Man in America from a Circum-Pacific Perspective*, edited by A. L. Bryan, pp. 306–327. Occasional Papers No. 1. Department of Anthropology, University of Alberta, Edmonton.

1980 The Stemmed Point Tradition: An Early Technological Tradition in Western North America. In *Anthropological Papers in Memory of Earl H. Swanson, Jr.*, edited by L. B. Harten, C. N. Warren, and D. R. Tuohy, pp. 77–107. Special Publication of the Idaho Museum of Natural History, Pocatello

1986 Paleoamerican Prehistory as seen from South America. In *New Evidence for the Pleistocene Peopling of the Americas,* edited by A. L. Bryan, pp. 1–14. Center for the Study of Early Man, University of Maine, Orono.

1987 The First Americans: Points of Order. *Natural History* 6/87:6–11.

1988 The Relationship of the Stemmed Point and Fluted Point Traditions in the Great Basin. In *Early Human Occupation in Far Western North America: The Clovis-Archaic Interface,* edited by J. A. Willig, C. M. Aikens, and J. L. Fagan, pp. 53–74. Nevada State Museum Anthropological Papers No. 21. Carson City.

1990 The Pattern of Late Pleistocene Cultural Diversity in Asia and the Americas. In *Chronostratigraphy of the Paleolithic in North, Central, East Asia and America,* pp. 3–18. Institute of History, Philology and Philosophy, USSR Academy of Sciences, Siberian Branch, Novosibirsk.

Cavallo, J.

1981 Turkey Swamp: A Late Paleo-Indian Site in New Jersey's Coastal Plain. *Archaeology of Eastern North America* 9:1–18.

Correal Urrego, G.

1986 Apuntes Sobre el Medio Ambiente Pleistocenico y el Hombre Prehistorico en Colombia. In *New Evidence for the Pleistocene Peopling of the Americas,* edited by A. L. Bryan, pp. 115–131. Center for the Study of Early Man, University of Maine, Orono.

Deller, D. B., and C. J. Ellis

1988 Early Paleo-Indian Complexes in Southwestern Ontario. In *Late Pleistocene and Early Holocene Paleoecology of the Eastern Great Lakes Region,* edited by R. S. Laub, N. G. Miller, and D. W. Steadman, pp. 251–263. Bulletin of the Buffalo Society of Natural Sciences No. 33. Buffalo.

Diamond, J.

1987 The American Blitzkrieg: A Mammoth Undertaking. *Discover* June:82–88.

Dillehay, T. D., and M. B. Collins

1991 Confusion, Creativity, and Criticism: A Reply to Lynch's "Glacial Man." *American Antiquity.* In Press.

Fagan, J. L.

1988 Clovis and Western Pluvial Lakes Tradition Lithic Technologies at the Dietz Site in South-central Oregon. In *Early Human Occupation in Far Western North America: The Clovis-Archaic Interface,* edited by J. A. Willig, C. M. Aikens, and J. L. Fagan, pp. 389–416. Nevada State Museum Anthropological Papers No. 21. Carson City.

Fladmark, K. R.

1979 Routes: Alternative Corridors for Early Man in North America. *American Antiquity* 44:55–69.

Gramly, R. M.

1982 *The Vail Site: A Paleoindian Encampment in Maine.* Bulletin of the Buffalo Society of Natural Sciences No. 30. Buffalo.

Greenberg, J. H., C. R. Turner II, and S. L. Zegura

1986 The Settlement of the Americas: A Comparison of the Linguistic, Dental, and Genetic Evidence. *Current Anthropology* 27:477–497.

Gruhn, R.

1988 Linguistic Evidence in Support of the Coastal Route of Earliest Entry Into the New World. *Man* 23:77–100.

1990 Initial Settlement of the New World: The Coastal Model. In *Chronostratigraphy of the Paleolithic in North, Central, East Asia and America,* pp. 20–24. Institute of History, Philology and Philosophy, USSR Academy of Sciences, Siberian Branch, Novosibirsk.

Gruhn, R., and A. L. Bryan

1977 Los Topiales: A Paleo-Indian Campsite in the Guatemalan Highlands. *Proceedings of the American Philosophical Society* 121:235–273.

1984 The Record of Pleistocene Meagafauna at Taimia-taima, Venezuela. In *Quaternary Extinctions: A Prehistoric Revolution,* edited by P. S. Martin and R. G. Klein, pp. 128–137. University of Arizona Press, Tucson.

1991 A Review of Lynch's Descriptions of South American Pleistocene Sites. *American Antiquity.* In press.

Haynes, C. V., Jr.

1964 Fluted Projectile Points: Their Age and Dispersion. *Science* 145:1408–1413.

1980 The Clovis Culture. *Canadian Journal of Anthropology* 1:115–121.

1987 Clovis Origin Update. *Kiva* 52:83–93.

Haynes, C. V., Jr., D. J. Donahue, A. J. T. Jull, and T. H. Zabel

1984 Application of Accelerator Dating to Fluted

Point Paleoindian sites. *Archaeology of Eastern North America* 12:184–191.

Irwin, H. T.
1968 *The Itama: Late Pleistocene Inhabitants of the Plains of the United States and Canada and the American Southwest.* Unpublished Ph.D. dissertation, Harvard University, Cambridge.

Kutzbach, J. E.
1983 Modeling of Holocene climates. In *The Holocene,* edited by H. E. Wright, Jr., pp. 271–277. Late Quaternary Environments of the United States, vol. 2, H. E. Wright, Jr., general editor. University of Minnesota Press, Minneapolis
1984 The Seasonal Nature of climatic Forcing and Responses on Quaternary Time Scales—With Emphasis on the Period Since the Last Glacial Maximum. In *American Quaternary Association Eighth Biennial Meeting Program and Abstracts,* pp. 70–71. Boulder.

Lynch, T. F.
1978 The South American Paleo-Indians. In *Ancient Native Americans,* edited by J. Jennings, pp. 455–490. W. H. Freeman and Company, New York.
1983 The South American Paleo-Indians. In *Ancient Native Americans,* edited by J. Jennings, pp. 87–137. 2nd edition. W. H. Freeman and Company, San Francisco.
1990 Glacial-Age Man in South America? A Critical Review. *American Antiquity* 55:12–36.

Marshall, E.
1990 Clovis Counterrevolution. *Science* 249:738–742.

Martin, P. S.
1967 Prehistoric Overkill. In *Pleistocene Extinctions: The Search for A Cause,* edited by P. S. Martin and H. E. Wright, Jr., pp. 75–80. Yale University Press, New Haven.
1973 The Discovery of America. *Science* 179:969–974.
1984 Prehistoric Overkill: The Global Model. In *Quaternary Extinctions: A Prehistoric Revolution,* edited by P. S. Martin and R. G. Klein, pp. 354–403. University of Arizona Press, Tucson.
1987 Clovisia the Beautiful! *Natural History* 10:10–13.

Mayer-Oakes, W. J.
1986 Early Man Projectile and Lithic Technology in the Ecuadorian Sierra. In *New Evidence for the Pleistocene Peopling of the Americas,* edited by A. L. Bryan, pp. 133–156. Center for the Study of Early Man, University of Maine, Orono.

Meltzer, D. J.
1988 Late Pleistocene Human Adapations in Eastern North America. *Journal of World Prehistory* 2:1–52.

Meltzer, D. J., and B. D. Smith
1986 Paleo-indian and Early Archaic Subsistence Strategies in Eastern North America. In *Foraging, Collecting and Harvesting: Archaic Period Subsistence and Settlement in the Eastern Woodlands,* edited by S. Neusius, pp. 1–30. Center for Archaeological Investigations, Southern Illinois University, Carbondale.

Morlan, R. E.
1988 Pre-Clovis People: Early Discoveries of America? In *Americans Before Columbus: Ice-Age Origins,* edited by R. C. Carlisle, pp. 31–44. Ethnology Monographs No. 12. Department of Anthropology, University of Pittsburgh, Pittsburgh.

Morlan, R. E., and J. Cinq-Mars
1989 *Abstracts: The First World Summit Conference on the Peopling of the Americas,* edited by J. Tomenchuk and R. Bonnichsen, pp. 11–12. Center for the Study of the First Americans, University of Maine, Orono.

Mosimann, J. E., and P. S. Martin
1975 Simulating Overkill by Paleo-indians. *American Scientist* 63:304–313.

Payne, J.
1987 *Windy City (154-16): A Paleoindian Lithic Workshop in Northern Maine.* Unpublished master's thesis, Institute for Quaternary Studies, University of Maine, Orono.

Rouse, I.
1976 Peopling of the Americas. *Quaternary Research* 6:567–612.

Snarskis, M. J.
1979 Turrialba: A Paleo-Indian Quarry and Workshop Site in Eastern Costa Rica. *American Antiquity* 44:125–128.

Turner, C. G., II
1985 The Dental Search for Native American Origins. In *Out of Asia: Peopling of the Americas and the Pacific,* edited by R. Kirk and E. Szathmary, pp. 31–78. The Journal of Pacific History, Canberra.

Warren, C. N., and C. Phagan
1988 Fluted Points in the Mojave Desert: Their Technological and Cultural Context. In *Early Human Occupation in Far Western North America: The Clovis-Archaic Interface,* edited by J. A. Willig, C. M. Aikens, and J. L. Fagan, pp. 121–130. Nevada State Museum Anthropological Papers No. 21. Carson City.

Wissler, C.
1926 *The Relation of Nature to Man in Aboriginal America.* Oxford University Press, London.

Young, D. E., and R. Bonnichsen
1984 *Understanding Stone Tools: A Cognitive Approach.* Center for the Study of Early Man, University of Maine, Orono.

1985 Cognition, Behavior, and Material Culture. In *Stone Tool Analysis: Essays in Honor of Donald E. Crabtree,* edited by M. G. Plew, J. C. Woods, and M. G. Pavesic, pp. 91–133. University of New Mexico Press, Albuquerque.

Young D. E., R. Bonnichsen, D. Douglas, J. McMahon, and L. Swartz
1991 Exploring the Cognitive Approach: Low-Range Theory and Lithic Technology. In *Method and Theory for Investigating the Peopling of the Americas,* edited by R. Bonnichsen and G. Steele. Center for the Study of the First Americans, University of Maine, Orono. Volume in preparation.

General Index

Site Index

NORTH AMERICA

United States

Canada

Mexico

CENTRAL AMERICA

Costa Rica

Guatemala

Panama

SOUTH AMERICA

Argentina

Brazil

Chile

Colombia

Ecuador

Peru

Uruguay

Venezuela

EURASIA

Soviet Union